COMPETITION LAW AND ECONOMIC INEQUALITY

The gap between the rich and poor is widening across the globe. This book explores whether this major societal challenge of our time can be addressed by the means of competition law.

The primary goal of today's competition law is to ensure that market power does not lead to an inefficient production of goods and services. Nevertheless, even such efficiency-oriented curbing of market power may arguably contribute to the reduction of differences in how much people own and earn. Furthermore, many competition law regimes do take into account distributive considerations too.

The chapters investigate the relationship between competition law and economic (in)equality from philosophical, historical, and economic perspectives. Their inquiries concern the conceptual foundations of competition law and doctrinal frameworks of individual jurisdictions, as well as specific problems and markets. As such, the book provides a novel and comprehensive overview of whether and how competition law can contribute to more equality in both developed and developing countries.

The book is a must-read for researchers, public officials, judges, and practitioners within the competition law community. It will also appeal to anyone more broadly interested in issues of inequality and economic policy.

Volume 29 in the series Hart Studies in Competition Law

Hart Studies in Competition Law

Anti-Cartel Enforcement in a Contemporary Age: Leniency Religion
Edited by Caron Beaton-Wells and Christopher Tran

Public Procurement and the EU Competition Rules
Albert Sánchez Graells

The Concept of Abuse in EU Competition Law: Law and Economic Approaches
Pınar Akman

The Competitive Effects of Minority Shareholdings: Legal and Economic Issues
Panagiotis Fotis and Nikolaos Zevgolis

The More Economic Approach to EU Antitrust Law
Anne C Witt

Private Power, Online Information Flows and EU Law
Angela Daly

The Role of Competitors in the Enforcement of State Aid Law
Fernando Pastor-Merchante

The Legality of Bailouts and Buy Nationals: International Trade Law in a Crisis
Kamala Dawar

A Critical Account of Article 106(2) TFEU: Government Failure in Public Service Provision
Jarleth Burke

Dawn Raids Under Challenge
Helene Andersson

A Framework for European Competition Law: Co-ordinated Diversity
Christopher Townley

Evidence Standards in EU Competition Enforcement: The EU Approach
Andriani Kalintiri

The Metaphysics of Market Power: The Zero-sum Competition and Market Manipulation Model
George Raitt

Competition Law's Innovation Factor: The Relevant Market in Dynamic Contexts in the EU and US
Viktoria HSE Robertson

Competition, Effects and Predictability: Rule of Law and the Economic Approach to Competition
Bruce Wardhaugh

Fighting Cross-Border Cartels: The Perspective of the Young and Small Competition Authorities
Pierre Horna

Conceptualising Procedural Fairness in EU Competition Law
Haukur Logi Karlsson

Experimentalist Competition Law and the Regulation of Markets
Yane Svetiev

Access and Cartel Cases: Ensuring Effective Competition Law Enforcement
Helene Andersson

Competition Law and Economic Inequality
Edited by Jan Broulík and Katalin Cseres

Competition Law and Economic Inequality

Edited by
Jan Broulík
and
Katalin Cseres

•HART•
OXFORD • LONDON • NEW YORK • NEW DELHI • SYDNEY

HART PUBLISHING

Bloomsbury Publishing Plc

Kemp House, Chawley Park, Cumnor Hill, Oxford, OX2 9PH, UK

1385 Broadway, New York, NY 10018, USA

29 Earlsfort Terrace, Dublin 2, Ireland

HART PUBLISHING, the Hart/Stag logo, BLOOMSBURY and the Diana logo are trademarks of Bloomsbury Publishing Plc

First published in Great Britain 2022

A catalogue record for this book is available from the British Library.

A catalogue record for this book is available from the Library of Congress.

Library of Congress Control Number: 2022943447

ISBN: HB: 978-1-50995-923-5
ePDF: 978-1-50995-925-9
ePub: 978-1-50995-924-2

Typeset by Compuscript Ltd, Shannon

CONTENTS

PART II
ECONOMIC INEQUALITY IN DOCTRINES OF INDIVIDUAL JURISDICTIONS

PART III
SPECIFIC PROBLEMS AND MARKETS

LIST OF CONTRIBUTORS

Philipp Baschenhof received his LLM degree in Competition, Innovation and Information Law from New York University School of Law in 2021.

Alexander Beyleveld is a Senior Researcher at the Mandela Institute, University of the Witwatersrand School of Law.

Jan Broulík is an Assistant Professor in European Law and a member of the Amsterdam Centre for European Law and Governance and the Amsterdam Center for Law and Economics at the University of Amsterdam.

Firoz Cachalia is an Adjunct Professor of Law and Director of the Mandela Institute, University of the Witwatersrand School of Law.

Carola Casti is an Advisor at the Norwegian Agency for Development Cooperation.

Katalin Cseres is an Associate Professor of Law at the Amsterdam Centre for European Law and Governance and a Research Fellow at the Amsterdam Center for Law and Economics at the University of Amsterdam.

Christopher Decker is a Research Fellow at the Centre for Socio-Legal Studies, University of Oxford.

Elias Deutscher is a Lecturer in Competition Law and Intellectual Property Law and a member of the Centre for Competition Policy at the University of East Anglia.

Barbara Dufková is a PhD candidate at the Faculty of Law, Charles University and a Predoctoral Research Fellow at Peace Research Center Prague.

Ariel Ezrachi is the Slaughter and May Professor of Competition Law and the Director of the Centre for Competition Law and Policy at the University of Oxford.

Eleanor M Fox is Walter J Derenberg Professor of Trade Regulation at New York University School of Law.

Mary Guy is a Lecturer in Law at Lancaster University.

Mitja Kovac is a Professor of Civil and Commercial Law at the School of Economics and Business, University of Ljubljana.

Pascal McDougall is an Assistant Professor of Law at the University of Ottawa.

Juliane Mendelsohn is Junior-Professor of Law and Economics of Digitisation at the Ilmenau University of Technology.

Konstantinos V Sidiropoulos is an Associate at Zepos & Yannopoulos, Athens and a Lecturer in Law at the European Law and Governance School, Athens.

Elisabeth Wielinger is an Associate at Schima Mayer Starlinger attorneys-at-law, Vienna.

Amit Zac is a Post-Doctoral Fellow at the Centre for Law & Economics, ETH Zurich and a Research Fellow at the Centre for Competition Law and Policy, University of Oxford.

Introduction: Economic Inequality, Competition and Law

JAN BROULÍK AND KATALIN CSERES*

I. Setting the Scene

Extreme economic inequality presents a defining societal challenge of our time. At the same time, levels of competition intensity have been alarmingly low. As suspicion is growing that the inequality may be codetermined by the weak competitive pressure on businesses, a serious debate needs to be had as to the role of competition law in making the world more equal.

A. Economic Inequality and Competition

Figures on distribution of income and wealth reveal that inequality remains steep all around the world. In Europe, as one of the most equal regions, 36% of all income goes to only ten per cent of people.[1] Fifty per cent of the population at the other end of the income spectrum, in contrast, jointly earn mere 19% of the total.[2] In the US, the top tenth makes 46% while the bottom half just 13% of total income.[3] Developing and emerging economies may see even more pronounced inequalities. For instance, in the Middle East and North Africa, the share of the top ten per cent of earners in total income is 58% whereas the least earning fifty per cent must do with only 9%.[4] A look at the distribution of wealth reveals a grimmer picture still: in Europe, the US, and the Middle East and North Africa, the richest tenth of the population owns, respectively, 59%,[5] 71%,[6] and 77%[7]

* This book is an outcome of the Sustainable Global Economic Law project at the University of Amsterdam, https://sgel.uva.nl/.

[1] L Chancel et al, 'World Inequality Report 2022' (World Inequality Lab, 2022) wir2022.wid.world/www-site/uploads/2022/03/0098-21_WIL_RIM_RAPPORT_A4.pdf, 30.

[2] ibid 30.

[3] ibid 229.

[4] ibid 30.

[5] ibid 38.

[6] ibid 229.

[7] ibid 38.

of total net household wealth. In contrast, the poorest half holds only 4%,[8] 2%,[9] and 1%.[10]

These disparities are disturbing not only in themselves, ie from a moral point of view. They also cause significant concern among scholars and policy makers due to the adverse effects that they create. To be sure, some inequality may be inevitable and even provide the necessary incentives for the economy to work properly.[11] Yet, the current differences in how much people earn and own are so dramatic that they are liable to cause serious societal problems. From an economic perspective, inequality has been perceived as slowing down economic growth by preventing the less well-off part of society from contributing to it.[12] But there are also many other detrimental effects, such as reduced life expectancy, higher infant mortality or poor educational attainment.[13]

A specific and major concern is the social-political repercussions of economic inequality. Namely, a large income and wealth gap has been found to obstruct social mobility,[14] threaten social cohesion,[15] and undermine the very legitimacy of the market-based social order.[16] Part of the problem is that the gap tends to be self-perpetuating. This is because wealth provides its owners with political influence, which may be – and arguably often is – used to sway public policy in favour of the rich.[17] That is to say that economic inequality in addition jeopardises democracy itself.

Next to inequality, the world has been struggling also with soaring corporate concentration and power. In advanced economies, since 1980, industry concentration has increased by more than 30%, markups by more than 35%, and profitability by more than 140%.[18] In the US, the average industry concentration rose by 8 percentage points between 2000 and 2014.[19] In Europe, the increase in

[8] ibid 38.

[9] ibid 229.

[10] ibid 38.

[11] V Cerra, R Lama and N Loayza, 'Links Between Growth, Inequality, and Poverty: A Survey' (2021) IMF Working Paper 21/68, www.elibrary.imf.org/view/journals/001/2021/068/article-A001-en.xml.

[12] ibid; OECD, *In It Together: Why Less Inequality Benefits All* (Paris, OECD, 2015).

[13] K Pickett and R Wilkinson, *The Spirit Level: Why Equality is Better for Everyone* (London, Penguin, 2009).

[14] The Equality Trust, 'Social Mobility and Education', equalitytrust.org.uk/social-mobility-and-education.

[15] United Nations Development Programme, 'Humanity Divided: Confronting Inequality in Developing Countries' (2013) 3 www.undp.org/sites/g/files/zskgke326/files/publications/HumanityDivided_Full-Report.pdf.

[16] JB Baker and SC Salop, 'Antitrust, Competition Policy, and Inequality' (2015) 114 *Georgetown Law Journal Online* 1, 6.

[17] Eg, ibid 6–8; L Khan and S Vaheesan 'Market Power and Inequality: The Antitrust Counterrevolution and Its Discontents' (2017) 11 *Harvard Law and Policy Review* 235, 265–268.

[18] U Akcigit et al, 'Rising Corporate Market Power: Emerging Policy Issues' (2021) IMF Staff Discussion Note No 2021/001, www.imf.org/en/Publications/Staff-Discussion-Notes/Issues/2021/03/10/Rising-Corporate-Market-Power-Emerging-Policy-Issues-48619.

[19] M Bajgar et al, 'Industry Concentration in Europe and North America' (2021) OECD Productivity Working Paper No 18, www.oecd-ilibrary.org/economics/industry-concentration-in-europe-and-north-america_2ff98246-en.

average industry concentration between 2000 and 2014 was 4 percentage points,[20] the average post-merger HHI for mergers scrutinised by the European Commission went up from about 2,500 in 1995 to over 3,000 in 2014,[21] and the share of industries in which the four largest firms account for at least a half of industry turnover grew by more than 60% between 1998 and 2019.[22] While developing and emerging economies have often not seen such recent increases in market concentration and power, they have been displaying signs of limited competition already for a long while.[23]

The relationship between market power and inequality is not a straightforward one. As distributional effects of market power happen to be circumstantially contingent, its exercise against buyers may in some situations lead to less inequality.[24] It is hence not possible to generalise that market power is *always* distributively undesirable. On the other hand, there is growing econometric evidence showing that – *in the aggregate* – lacking competition between sellers and between employers does contribute to regressive economic distribution by transferring resources from (poor) consumers and workers to (rich) shareholders. For instance, a study into a sample of OECD countries has found that, on average, market power in product markets increases the wealth of the richest tenth of the population by 12–21% while reducing the income of the poorest fifth by 11% or more.[25] The effect may be even greater in developing and emerging economies, where businesses extracting rents from consumers are less likely to share these rents with the poor through wages and dividends.[26] Hence, inequality may not stem from capitalism in general, as famously argued by Piketty,[27] but only from those markets that lack sufficient rivalry.[28]

[20] ibid.

[21] P Affeldt et al, 'Market Concentration in Europe: Evidence from Antitrust Markets' (2021) DIW Berlin Discussion Paper No 1930, ssrn.com/abstract=3775524.

[22] G Koltay, L Szabolcs and TM Valletti, 'Concentration and Competition: Evidence from Europe and Implications for Policy' (2022) CESifo Working Paper No 9640, www.cesifo.org/en/publikationen/2022/working-paper/concentration-and-competition-evidence-europe-and-implications.

[23] FJ Díez, D Leigh and S Tambunlertchai, 'Global Market Power and its Macroeconomic Implications' (2018) IMF Working Paper 18/137, www.imf.org/en/Publications/WP/Issues/2018/06/15/Global-Market-Power-and-its-Macroeconomic-Implications-45975, 25.

[24] DA Crane, 'Antitrust and Wealth Inequality' (2016) 101 *Cornell Law Review* 1171, 1177–1208; TJ Brennan, 'Should Antitrust Go Beyond "Antitrust"?' (2018) 63 *The Antitrust Bulletin* 49, 56; HJ Hovenkamp, 'Antitrust Policy and Inequality of Wealth' [2017] *Competition Policy International Antitrust Chronicle* 1, 1; EA Posner and CR Sunstein, 'Antitrust and Inequality' (2022) ssrn.com/abstract=4023365, 9.

[25] SF Ennis, P Gonzaga and C Pike, 'Inequality: A Hidden Cost of Market Power' (2019) 35 *Oxford Review of Economic Policy* 518.

[26] I Lianos, 'Competition Law as a Form of Social Regulation' (2020) 65 *The Antitrust Bulletin* 3, 54.

[27] T Piketty, *Capital in the Twenty-First Century* (A Goldhammer tr, Cambridge, MA, Harvard University Press, 2014).

[28] E Elhauge, 'Horizontal Shareholding' (2016) 129 *Harvard Law Review* 1267, 1291–1301.

B. Economic Inequality and Competition Law

As a result, an increasing number of commentators are arguing in favour of promoting economic equality through laws protecting market competition. One route that has been advanced is based on the notion that usual enforcement against exploitation of market power prevents welfare transfers from consumers and workers to shareholders and, hence, that more of such enforcement will decrease inequality.[29] One possibility is then to enforce more actively within the existing legal framework, without any changes to it.[30] Alternatively, enforcement could be boosted by removing procedural hurdles, eg as regards collective private enforcement,[31] or by expanding the scope of substantive rules,[32] eg towards tacit collusion.[33]

A more daring approach is to take distributive considerations into account explicitly, whereas three possible areas of such direct incorporation may be identified. First, in so far as enforcers have administrative discretion, they have been advised to prioritise investigations and interventions in markets that are important for poorer people.[34] These would include markets for products in agriculture or healthcare and markets for labour of low-income people.[35] Second, equality may feature as a relevant factor in substantive competition analysis itself.[36] Competition law would in that case directly trade some efficiency for equality. While to the competition-policy audience this might sound unorthodox, many jurisdictions are in fact already engaging in such a trade-off by applying the consumer – rather than total – surplus standard, ie by assigning greater value to the welfare of consumers than to that of producers.[37] The proposal is to simply take this logic further and value the welfare of (ie say a euro paid by) the poor more than the welfare of (ie a euro paid by) a wealthy person.[38] Promotion of equality may then serve both as a 'shield', ie to render an otherwise unlawful conduct lawful,[39] and as a 'sword', ie vice versa.[40] This is possible not only on the level of analysis in a particular case but also on the level of rule design. For instance, a general exemption for workers' collective bargaining about wages from the scope of competition

[29] Eg Khan and Vaheesan (n 17).
[30] Baker and Salop (n 16) 18.
[31] Posner and Sunstein (n 24) 10.
[32] Baker and Salop (n 16) 21–24.
[33] Posner and Sunstein (n 24) 10.
[34] Crane (n 24) 1225; A Leigh and A Triggs, 'Markets, Monopolies and Moguls: The Relationship between Inequality and Competition' (2016) 49 *Australian Economic Review* 389, 401; MS Gal, 'The Social Contract at the Basis of Competition Law: Should We Recalibrate Competition Law to Limit Inequality?' in D Gerard and I Lianos (eds), *Reconciling Efficiency and Equity: A Global Challenge for Competition Policy* (Cambridge, Cambridge University Press, 2019) 106.
[35] Posner and Sunstein (n 24) 9; Baker and Salop (n 16) 18–20.
[36] Baker and Salop (n 16) 24–26; DI Waked, 'Antitrust as Public Interest Law: Redistribution, Equity, and Social Justice' (2020) 65 *The Antitrust Bulletin* 87, 90–92.
[37] Gal (n 34) 103.
[38] Posner and Sunstein (n 24) 11.
[39] Gal (n 34) 107; Crane (n 24) 1226–1228.
[40] Posner and Sunstein (n 24) 15; Baker and Salop (n 16) 24–26.

law may be seen as an example of a rule shielding, for distributive reasons, an activity restricting competition.[41] Third, distributive considerations may inform the design of remedies,[42] even if these considerations had played no role in the preceding assessment of lawfulness. For example, conduct that harms low-income consumers might be penalised more harshly.[43]

However, it needs to be recognised that there is also some scepticism towards competition law being employed to distributive purposes. To start with, certain commentators challenge the notion that violations of competition law systematically redirect resources from the poor to the rich and, hence, that an undifferentiated increase in enforcement will benefit the poor.[44] Further, it has been asserted that greater economic equality does not fall within the goals to be pursued by competition law and that it thus should not be traded for competition law's 'true' goals such as efficiency or, at most, consumer welfare. In other words, competition law is supposed to care only about the size of the (consumers') pie, not about how the pie is divided. A related argument is that determining how all relevant stakeholder constituencies – including those on eventual downstream markets[45] – are distributively affected by a given market conduct or merger would often prove enormously complex and, hence, costly or outright impossible.[46] It has also been suggested that there are many other sources of economic inequality that are entirely unrelated to competition issues, which is why competition law would merely be able to address a small portion of inequality.[47] These reasons bring the sceptics to conclude that efforts to reduce inequality should be left to other policies that can achieve the objective at a lower social cost, especially to tax-and-transfer policies.[48]

The debate about the possible role that competition law could play in tackling economic inequality is, in fact, part of the renewed 'battle for the soul of antitrust'.[49] A look at the history of competition laws on both sides of the Atlantic reveals that they were initially established with the core idea of competitive markets where economic power is dispersed and broadly defined economic opportunities are guaranteed.[50] Responding to broad concerns about the political and economic power of industrial elites and the harm posed to fair competition, the US Sherman Act was adopted in order to safeguard equality of opportunity for all businessmen and their ability to compete.[51] At the same time, European legal orders originally

[41] O Odudu, 'The Distributional Consequences of Antitrust' in P Marsden (ed), *Handbook of Research in Trans-Atlantic Antitrust* (Cheltenham, Edward Elgar, 2006) 607–608.

[42] Baker and Salop (n 16) 20–21; Leigh and Triggs (n 34) 401; Waked (n 36) 99–100.

[43] Baker and Salop (n 16) 20–21; Leigh and Triggs (n 34) 401.

[44] Crane (n 24).

[45] Baker and Salop (n 16) 25.

[46] Crane (n 24) 1223.

[47] Brennan (n 24) 56.

[48] Crane (n 24) 1225; Brennan (n 24) 56.

[49] EM Fox, 'The Battle for the Soul of Antitrust' (1987) 75 *California Law Review* 3.

[50] See chs 1 and 4 in this volume.

[51] DW Barnes, 'Antitrust, the Rule of Reason, and Democracy: A Letter from Justice William O. Douglas' (1999) 14 *Review of Industrial Organization* 2; RH Lande, 'Chicago's False Foundation: Wealth Transfers (Not Just Efficiency) Should Guide Antitrust' (1989) 58 *Antitrust Law Journal* 2.

followed the Ordoliberal tradition which has understood concentration of market power as a serious risk to the competitive process and as restraining the procedural guarantees of equal participation in the economic marketplace as well as in the political game.[52] However, the subsequent practice of competition law – beginning in the late 1970s in the US and in the late 1990s in the EU – has under the influence of the Chicago School tilted toward the pursuit of market efficiency, focusing much less on fairness or, more specifically, equality. In 1978, Bork in his seminal book *The Antitrust Paradox* argued that '[a]ntitrust … has a built in preference for material prosperity, but it has nothing to say about the way prosperity is distributed or used'.[53] Analysis of market power was accordingly supposed to focus on economic efficiency, and enforcement against monopolies had thus to be driven by the goal of correcting inefficiency rather than preventing wealth transfers from consumer to producers.[54] These views have since been influential around the globe.

As regards developing and emerging economies, the relationship between competition law and economic inequality may differ slightly. Most of these countries show high levels of both economic and political inequality and have few resources to support even the most promising public policies.[55] In addition, ownership is often held by groups that are directly opposed to the idea of market economy.[56] Still, in their quest for integration into the global economy, many of these countries have adopted policies to promote economic growth and development, including competition law.[57] In developing such policies, it has been realised that competition law based solely on efficiency considerations can potentially exacerbate the negative impact of rapid economic growth on equality. Hence, the countries have been advised to bear in mind the distributional effects of competition law,[58] and many of them have indeed framed their competition policy in ways that include broad and specific public-interest considerations.[59]

[52] E Deutscher and S Makris, 'Exploring the Ordoliberal Paradigm: The Competition-Democracy Nexus' [2016] *Competition Law Review* 187.

[53] RH Bork, *The Antitrust Paradox at War with Itself* (New York, Basic Books, 1978).

[54] I Lianos, 'The Poverty of Competition Law: The Short Story' in D Gerard and I Lianos (eds), *Reconciling Efficiency and Equity: A Global Challenge for Competition Policy* (Cambridge, Cambridge University Press, 2019) 76.

[55] U Aydin and T Büthe, 'Competition Law & Policy in Developing Countries: Explaining Variations in Outcomes; Exploring Possibilities and Limits' (2016) 79 *Law and Contemporary Problems* 1, 2.

[56] ibid 2.

[57] EM Fox, 'Competition, Development and Regional Integration: In Search of a Competition Law Fit for Developing Countries' in J Drexl et al (eds), *Competition Policy and Regional Integration in Developing Countries* (Cheltenham, Edward Elgar Publishing, 2012) 285.

[58] DD Sokol, TK Cheng and I Lianos (eds), *Competition Law and Development* (Stanford, Stanford University Press, 2013); J Drexl et al (eds), *Competition Policy and Regional Integration in Developing Countries* (Cheltenham, Edward Elgar Publishing, 2012); MS Gal et al (eds), *The Economic Characteristics of Developing Jurisdictions: Their Implications for Competition Law* (Cheltenham, Edward Elgar Publishing, 2015).

[59] EM Fox and M Bakhoum, *Making Markets Work for Africa: Markets, Development, and Competition Law in Sub-Saharan Africa* (Oxford, Oxford University Press, 2019); MS Gal, *Competition Policy for Small Market Economies* (Cambridge, MA, Harvard University Press, 2003).

II. About this Book

The aim of this book is to explore whether economic inequality can be addressed by the means of competition law. The book brings together legal scholars whose contributions to answering this question are informed by philosophical, historical as well as economic perspectives. The contributions discuss foundational aspects of the relationship between economic inequality and competition law (part I), the place of inequality considerations in competition law doctrines of selected legal systems (part II), and manifestations of inequality concerns in the context of specific problems and markets subjected to competition law (part III). This interdisciplinary and multidimensional approach allows the book to provide a novel and comprehensive overview of whether and how competition law can take part in making societies in both developed and developing parts of the world more equal.

A. First Part of the Book

The first part of the book investigates the very foundations of the relationship between economic inequality and competition law. Chapter one by Deutscher in particular traces how intellectual thinking about competition's impact on equality has developed over time. The chapter shows that early liberal economic and political thinkers such as Thomas More or Adam Smith understood competitive markets as conducive towards greater economic, social and political equality. This understanding of how competition relates to equality was rooted in a notion of economic liberty as non-domination and independence, and played an important role in the genesis of competition laws in the US and Europe. It was only with the advent of the Chicago School, Deutscher argues, that economic liberty started to be understood as an absence of interference with one's sphere of autonomy and that considerations about equality have been banned from the realm of competition policy. As shown by a growing body of research, nevertheless, the Chicago laissez faire approach has impacted distribution quite negatively. It may thus be time to return to an approach aspiring for markets that are at the same time competitive and egalitarian.

Mendelsohn's chapter two also reflects on the intellectual discourse on competition and (in)equality. Mendelsohn's lens is a social theory of 'reflexive modernisation' about how modernist thinking has coped with the fact that modernity's original liberal ideas of formal equality have never fully translated into material equality. This theory postulates that modernity has been questioning its assumptions while, nevertheless, remaining committed to a programme based on them. Mendelsohn draws parallels between material justice and neo-structuralist approaches to competition law on the one hand and between formal justice and welfarist approaches on the other; the welfarist turn of the last decades may then in her view be understood as clinging to flawed original ideas of modernity driven by an intellectual uncertainty and self-questioning. In its last section, the chapter observes that it is in line with the theory of reflexive modernisation to see contemporary digital giants as, at the same time, sinister amalgamators of power and efficient innovators benefiting consumers. Yet, to avoid further material inequality and poverty, the rise of digital bigness should not be left unchecked.

Chapter three by Zac, Casti, Decker and Ezrachi carries out an empirical investigation into how competition law affects economic inequality. The authors first introduce the theorised causal mechanism behind the investigated effects: inequality results from the exercise of market power in product as well as labour markets, and competition law curbs the exercise. Subsequently, relying on a dataset tracking how several indicators of competition law and economic inequality have developed over a number of years in a wide range of countries, they use a model to estimate the association between the indicators. The results mostly show more competition law being associated with some decrease in inequality, but they are not conclusive. The authors argue that this may be due to the high level of aggregation of their input data, significant heterogeneity in other factors determining inequality across countries and over time, and imperfections concerning the construction of the used competition law indices. More refined analyses may hence be necessary to reach less unambiguous answers about the effects of competition law on economic inequality.

B. Second Part of the Book

The second part of this book contains contributions that analyse the place of distributive considerations within competition laws of various jurisdictions, including developed as well as developing economies. Chapter four by Fox and Baschenhof discusses how the receptivity of four major jurisdictions towards equality/inequality has developed over time. The jurisdictions are the US, Germany, the EU (as a supranational legal system) and South Africa. Fox and Baschenhof assess each of them in terms of six questions: First, is an equality value embedded in the law? Second, is it a source of wisdom available to enforcers and jurists to decide priorities or reach outcomes in particular cases? Third, are consent decrees or clearances used as an occasion for imposing conditions that can help the less-well-off? Fourth, is more equality a separate mandate that can warrant an exemption or trump? Fifth, does the jurisdiction's competition law alleviate inequality? Sixth, would equality-leaning changes in competition law be feasible and likely to help close the inequality gap? The four jurisdiction studies are to illustrate the full range of approaches from antagonism towards equality serving as a relevant factor in competition law all the way to equality as a raison d'être of competition law. The conclusion of the chapter is that incorporation of equality values can be done with relative clarity and predictability and that it is a value choice to be made by each society.

In chapter five, Sidiropoulos takes an in-depth inquiry into the EU's constitutional peculiarities on the relevance of inequality considerations in the interpretation of Article 102 TFEU. He identifies the potential relevance of economic inequality for the interpretation and application of this article in light of the EU Treaties, so as to subsequently assess whether the current state of the law, as developed by the case law of the EU courts, includes economic inequality as a relevant concern. The constitutionally mandated holistic approach entails that inequality-related concerns and (re)distributive policy considerations may affect both the general interpretation and enforcement of Article 102 and its ad hoc application. In this regard, Sidiropoulos argues that the application of the provision must at least avoid contradicting redistributive policy considerations and other (in)equality-related concerns that are aimed at establishing an internal market committed to a highly competitive social market. His discussion of the relevant case law documents that the designed legal tests successfully reconcile the market-oriented objectives of Article 102 with equality-related concerns and redistributive policies, thereby allowing the provision to operate according to the constitutional role imposed on it by the Treaties.

Chapter six by Cachalia and Beyleveld focuses on South Africa. It argues that competition law has the potential of being utilised as one among many imperfect tools that, when deployed in a carefully coordinated way, could contribute to the reduction of economic inequality in South Africa. Such an application of competition law may in turn improve the functioning of South Africa's constitutional democracy as well as render South Africa a more economically just and fair country with improved levels of economic growth. At the same time, however, Beyleveld and Cachalia's inquiry into the South African Competition Act's goal 'to ensure that small and medium-sized enterprises have an equitable opportunity to participate in the economy; … [and] to promote a greater spread of ownership, in particular to increase the ownership stakes of historically disadvantaged persons'[60] exemplifies the difficulties a competition authority may face in addressing the competition-inequality nexus beyond the mere scope of its mandate in the area of actual enforcement.

Dufková's chapter seven explores whether and how competition law, as a primary regulatory tool to remedy market failures, should reflect concerns of economic inequality in Vietnam. Dufková argues that the experience of developing countries that have recently introduced competition laws can be instructive for the more developed part of the world because they have already faced the need to make their competition laws more responsive to issues connected to economic inequality. The purpose of her chapter is to elucidate how developing countries have attuned their competition laws to the economic inequality that characterises their economies and the model that emerges to see whether this model offers useful

[60] Section 2 of the South African Competition Act as amended by Act 18 of 2018.

lessons for developed countries. To this end, Vietnam's competition law system is used as an example, primarily because of its developing country status, rapid economic growth in recent years and fairly long history of competition regulation.

C. Third Part of the Book

In its third part, the book studies economic inequality in the context of specific problems and markets addressed by competition law. Chapter eight by Kovac and Wielinger in this vein considers the problem of network externalities. It proceeds from the starting point that the traditional legal-economic argument according to which redistribution is to be done primarily ex post through taxes does not apply to rents, ie profits that would not have been earned in a perfectly competitive economy. Focusing on network externalities, Kovac and Wielinger argue that competition law interventions against rent extraction that they enable may reduce inequality. No alteration to existing EU competition law is, according to the authors, necessary for that purpose; it will be sufficient if the law is enforced more vigorously.

Guy's chapter nine explores the links between tackling economic inequality in healthcare and competition law. Guy argues that while few such links have been drawn explicitly, these may nevertheless be inferred from competition reforms being used as a mechanism to address ongoing issues regarding the sustainability of healthcare systems in the face of rising healthcare costs. Her analysis is structured around the questions *whether* and *how* competition law *can* and *should* address economic inequalities in the healthcare context. She examines the EU competition law framework and the recourse to the exception under the rules of services of general economic interest in light of the wider *how* and *whether* questions, particularly when juxtaposed with the temporary relaxation of the antitrust and state aid rules to respond to COVID-19. Furthermore, by considering the competition framework of the Health and Social Care Act in England she offers important insights on the *how* and *whether* questions in view of the limited scope for competition within a taxation-funded system (the NHS) and in light of current developments.

Chapter ten by McDougall deals with bargaining by labour unions. It proposes that application of competition law to this phenomenon be governed by distributive justice operationalised through economic analysis. The perspective of static efficiency traditionally underlying competition analyses is presented as inappropriate because collective bargaining may in principle lead to no employment and output reduction and because other factors are anyway determining the level of output much more significantly. McDougall is, however, also challenging the blanket exemption granted to collective agreements between employers and employees by EU competition law. What needs to be done, he argues, is to evaluate with the help of economics whether the given instance of collective bargaining harms some of the people that it is intended to help. Finally, the chapter presents several policy tools to minimise such eventual distributive drawbacks of unionism.

The ten chapters of this book show how rich and multi-faceted the relationship between competition law and economic inequality is. If a single general lesson is to be drawn from the wealth of provided insights, competition law, at the very least, seems to have the potential to make the world more equal. The debate is, however, hardly at its end.

PART I

Conceptual and Empirical Foundations

1

Competition and Equality: A Republican Account

ELIAS DEUTSCHER*

Refrenate coemptiones istas diuitum,
ac uelut monopolii exercendi licentiam.
Suffer not thies ryche men to bye vp all, to ingrosse and forstalle,
and with theyr monopolye to kepe the market alone as please them.[1]

I. Introduction

Recent studies have thrust the trend towards growing industry concentration and corporate power into the limelight of contemporary competition policy debates. Some of these studies suggest that industry concentration and mark-ups are on the rise both in the US and, albeit to a lesser extent, in Europe.[2] Soaring levels of

* The author is immensely grateful to Kati Cseres and Jan Broulík, as well as the participants of the 'Should Wealth and Income Inequality Be a Competition Law Concern?' Amsterdam Conference for their insightful comments on various versions of this chapter.

[1] T More, *The Utopia: In Latin From the Edition of March 1518, and In English From The First Edition of Ralph Robynson's Translation in 1551 with Additional Translations, Introduction and Notes by JH Lupton* (first published 1516, Oxford, Clarendon Press, 1895) 57–58.

[2] See, for instance, J De Loecker, J Eeckhout and G Unger, 'The Rise of Market Power and the Macroeconomic Implications' (2020) 135 *The Quarterly Journal of Economics* 561; D Autor et al, 'The Fall of the Labor Share and the Rise of Superstar Firms' (2020) 135 *The Quarterly Journal of Economics* 645; M Bajgar et al, 'Industry Concentration in Europe and North America' (2019) OECD Productivity Working Paper No 18, doi.org/10.1787/2ff98246-en; MC Cavalleri et al, 'Concentration, Market Power and Dynamism in the Euro Area' (2019) ECB Discussion Paper No 2253, op.europa.eu/en/publication-detail/-/publication/259867c0-a679-11ea-bb7a-01aa75ed71a1; U Akcigit et al, 'Rising Corporate Market Power: Emerging Policy Issues' (2021) IMF Staff Discussion Note 2021/001, www.imf.org/en/Publications/Staff-Discussion-Notes/Issues/2021/03/10/Rising-Corporate-Market-Power-Emerging-Policy-Issues-48619; JP Weche and A Wambach, 'The Fall and Rise of Market Power in Europe' (2021) 241 *Jahrbücher für Nationalökonomie und Statistik* 555; T Philippon, *The Great Reversal: How America Gave up on Free Markets* (Cambridge, MA, Harvard University Press, 2019); G Gutiérrez and T Philippon, 'Declining Competition and Investment in the U.S.' (2017) NBER Working Paper 23583 www.nber.org/papers/w23583; G Koltay, S Lorincz and T Valletti, 'Concentration and Competition: Evidence from Europe and Implications for Policy' (2022) CESifo Working Paper No 9640, www.cesifo.org/en/publikationen/2022/working-paper/concentration-and-competition-evidence-europe-and-implications.

industry concentration and profitability are not only considered as signs of waning productivity, dynamism, and lack of competitiveness but they are also increasingly viewed to be a major cause of growing economic inequalities within our societies.[3] This perceived link between rising industry concentration and inequality, hence, poses anew a question that has been for a long time banished[4] from the antitrust policy discourse in the US and in Europe: what is the relationship between competitive markets and equality? Should competition law be used to bring about greater socio-economic equality? And if so, which form of equality should it promote?

This chapter purports to contribute to and enrich the growing literature on competition, competition law, and (in)equality[5] by shedding light on the conceptual foundations of the relationship between competitive markets and equality. The chapter proposes an intellectual history of the relationship between equality and competition from early liberal economic and political thought about competitive markets to the Chicago School. It shows that claims about the distributional regressivity of concentrated economic power ('monopoly regressivity thesis')[6] and the conduciveness of competitive markets towards greater socio-economic and political equality ('competition equality thesis') can be traced back to early modern political and economic thought, for instance in the writings of Thomas More, the English Levellers, Montesquieu, James Steuart, and Adam Smith. This egalitarian understanding of competitive markets, the chapter argues, was deeply rooted in a specific republican[7] notion of economic liberty as non-domination and

[3] See, for instance, Council of Economic Advisers to the US President, 'Benefits of Competition and Indicators' (2016) obamawhitehouse.archives.gov/sites/default/files/page/files/20160414_cea_competition_issue_brief.pdf; J Furman and P Orszag, 'A Firm-Level Perspective on the Role of Rents in the Rise in Inequality' in M Guzman (ed), *Toward a Just Society: Joseph Stiglitz and Twenty-First Century Economics* (New York, Columbia University Press, 2018) 19; J Stiglitz, 'Inequality, Stagnation, and Market Power' (2017) www.rooseveltinstitute.org/inequality-stagnation-market-power/; Philippon (n 2); S Ennis and Y Kim, 'Market Power and Wealth Distribution' in M Martinez Licetti et al (eds), *A Step Ahead: Competition Policy for Shared Prosperity and Inclusive Growth* (Washington, World Bank Publications, 2017); SF Ennis, P Gonzaga and C Pike, 'Inequality: A Hidden Cost of Market Power' (2019) 35 *Oxford Review of Economic Policy* 518; R Decker et al, 'Declining Business Dynamism: What We Know and the Way Forward' (2016) 106 *American Economic Review* 203. See, however, the 'superstar firm' thesis suggesting that increases in concentration can be explained by superior productivity of a minority of large-scale firms. Autor et al (n 2). See also for a more detailed discussion of this literature ch 3 in this volume.

[4] RA Posner, *Antitrust Law*, 2nd edn (Chicago, University of Chicago Press, 2001) 23–24; RH Bork, *The Antitrust Paradox: A Policy at War with Itself*, 2nd edn (New York, Maxwell Macmillan, 1993) 110–113.

[5] For some recent examples, DA Crane, 'Antitrust and Wealth Inequality' (2015) 101 *Cornell Law Review* 1171; JB Baker and SC Salop, 'Antitrust, Competition Policy, and Inequality' (2015) 104 *Georgetown Law Journal Online* 1; HJ Hovenkamp, 'Antitrust Policy and Inequality of Wealth' [2017] *Competition Policy International Antitrust Chronicle* 1; I Lianos, 'The Poverty of Competition Law: The Long Story' (2018) CLES Research Paper Series 2/2018, www.ucl.ac.uk/cles/sites/cles/files/cles_2-2018.pdf; D Gerard and I Lianos (eds), *Reconciling Efficiency and Equity: A Global Challenge for Competition Law?* (Cambridge, Cambridge University Press, 2019).

[6] Daniel Crane calls this the 'monopoly regressivity claim'. Crane (n 5) 1184.

[7] I use the term 'republican' in relation to 'republicanism' as a tradition of political thought which has its historical origins in the ancient Roman Republic, and not in reference to the Republican party

equal status which also left an important imprint on the formative era of US antitrust and the Ordoliberal foundations of EU competition law. With the rise of the Chicago School and the consumer welfare standard, this republican conception of economic liberty has been superseded by a narrow negative understanding of economic liberty that only perceives welfare-decreasing interference as undue restriction of liberty and is, hence, largely indifferent towards inequalities of economic opportunities, power, and wealth.

The chapter is organised as follows. Section II unearths the intellectual origins of the monopoly regressivity and competition equality theses in early modern liberal political and economic thought. Section III traces how the egalitarian ideal of republican liberty found its way into the normative foundations of early US and European competition law. Section IV describes how the Chicago and post-Chicago antitrust consensus purged antitrust law from considerations about equality and replaced the republican notion of economic liberty with a purely negative understanding of entrepreneurial liberty that is agnostic about imbalances of economic power and wealth. Section V concludes.

II. The Republican Tradition: Competitive Markets as Catalysts of Greater Equality

Capitalism and free competitive markets are nowadays often seen as a major source of socio-economic and wealth inequalities.[8] It, therefore, should not come as a surprise that competitive markets and equality are in contemporary debates often primarily framed as antonyms. What passes, however, often unnoticed is that this has not always been the case – all to the contrary. In early economic and political thought, monopoly and oligopoly have been associated with inequality of opportunity and wealth, while the advent of competitive markets was perceived as a catalyst of greater economic, social, and political equality. For a long time, as the philosopher Elisabeth Anderson puts it, 'the ideal of a free-market society used to be a cause of the left'.[9]

in the US. Q Skinner, *Liberty before Liberalism* (Cambridge, Cambridge University Press, 1998); Q Skinner, 'A Third Concept of Liberty: Isaiah Berlin Lecture' in The British Academy (ed), *Proceedings of the British Academy: 2001 Lectures*, vol 117 (Oxford, Oxford University Press, 2002); P Pettit, *Republicanism: A Theory of Freedom and Government* (Oxford, Oxford University Press, 1997). While some of its members still claim to stand in the tradition of republican thinkers, such as Thomas Jefferson, Thomas Paine or James Madison, the Republican party and republicanism have nowadays only little, if anything, in common.

[8] T Piketty, *Capital in the Twenty-First Century* (Cambridge, MA, Harvard University Press, 2017). This position is also articulated in ch 2 in this volume.

[9] E Anderson, 'Liberty, Equality and Private Government' in M Matheson (ed), *The Tanner Lectures on Human Values*, vol 35 (Cambridge, Cambridge University Press, 2016) 63.

A. A Synopsis of the 'Monopoly Regressivity' and 'Competition Equality' Theses in Early Liberal Economic and Political Thought

Claims suggesting that monopoly power is a source of socio-economic inequality, while competition is conducive to greater equality, are frequently greeted with a healthy dose of scepticism by the contemporary antitrust debate.[10] Modern welfare economics, indeed, lends little support to the monopoly regressivity thesis, as it eschews any interpersonal comparisons of utility and welfare.[11] Put simply, modern welfare economics is interested in how various market structures perform in bringing about a bigger cake, not how the cake is distributed. Mainstream antitrust scholars, therefore, object that economic models of competition allow us to make intelligible propositions about the distributive incidence of monopoly power and competitive markets only once we adopt a number of strong – and in their eyes often implausible – additional assumptions about the identity of consumers and producers, their relative wealth, and the extent they benefit from and bear monopoly rents.[12]

i. The Monopoly Regressivity Thesis

Important though it is, this critique of the monopoly regressivity thesis is oblivious to the fact that the terms 'monopoly', 'oligopoly', and 'competition' have not only an economic, but also an inherently political dimension and pedigree. Arguably, claims about the relationship between monopoly, competition, and equality become only intelligible once we trace them back to their origins in early modern political and economic thought. A good starting point to make sense of the monopoly regressivity thesis and its corollary, the competition equality thesis, is Thomas More's seminal and radically egalitarian narrative *Utopia*. First published in Latin in 1516 and in English in 1551, *Utopia* provides us with one of the – if not *the* – earliest definitions and critiques of 'monopoly' and 'oligopoly'.[13]

[10] Posner (n 4) 23–24; Crane (n 5); Hovenkamp (n 5).

[11] A Sen, *On Ethics and Economics* (Oxford, B. Blackwell, 1987) 29–31. For a detailed discussion I Lianos (n 5) 23–33.

[12] Posner (n 4) 23–24. For a detailed discussion Crane (n 5) 1177–1206.

[13] 'Quod si maxime increscat ouium numerus, precio nihil decrescit tamen; quod earum, si *monopolium* appellari non potest, quod non unus uendit, certe *oligopolium* est. Reciderunt enim fere in manus paucorum, eorundemque diuitum, quos nulla necessitas urget ante uendendi quam libet, nec ante libet quam liceat quanti libet.' More (n 1) 54–55 (emphasis added). Barker-Smith translated this passage as follows: 'And yet, even if the numbers of sheep should rise dramatically, the price won't fall; for although one can't speak about a monopoly as it isn't controlled by a single man, yet the wool trade is most certainly an oligopoly. It's in the hands of a small group of rich men who are under no necessity to sell before it suits them, and it only suits them when they can get their price.' T More, *Utopia: Translated, Edited and Introduced by Dominic Baker-Smith* (first published 1516, London, Penguin Classics, 2012) 34. See also JW Park, 'The Utopian Economics of Sir Thomas More' (1971) 30 *The American Journal of Economics and Sociology* 275, 277.

Book I of *Utopia* starts with a critical portrait of the social and economic conditions that prevailed in sixteenth-century England. It notably describes how the emergence of property rights and commodification of arable land through enclosures[14] contributed to the decline of husbandry.[15] What is striking about this account is that More formulated his critique of the accumulation of private property in the hands of a few landowners by drawing a direct link between enclosures and the emergence of monopolies and oligopolies.[16] Most importantly for our inquiry, More coined here for the first time the monopoly regressivity thesis by identifying concentrated economic power as a major source of wealth inequalities and poverty. More, indeed, used the terms 'monopoly' and 'oligopoly' as synonyms of the control that a small group of wealthy men ('*divitum*') hold over prices and trade.[17] What is more, he also claimed that the adverse effects of monopolistic and oligopolistic market structures hit particularly hard the poorest members of society who have to bear higher food and input prices.[18] The regressivity of economic power, in More's account, is further exacerbated by the fact that the arbitrary control monopolists and oligopolists exert over their industries keeps large parts of the population in unemployment and idleness, and thus annihilates any form of equality of economic opportunity.[19]

Thomas More is not the only early political thinker who decried the adverse distributive effects of monopolies and oligopolies. The social and political English Levellers movement active in the run-up to and during the English Civil War (1642–1651) also opposed economic privileges, monopolies, and other restraints of trade as manifestations of arbitrary and unaccountable power.[20] Similarly, Adam Smith criticised the negative impact of public and private restraints on trade as an obstacle to individuals' equal opportunity to engage in economic activity.[21] Smith stressed that these restraints prevented above all the poorest

[14] The term 'enclosure' describes the 'division or consolidation of communal fields, meadows, pastures, and other arable lands' into 'individually owned and managed farm plots of modern times'. Britannica, 'Enclosure' www.britannica.com/topic/enclosure.

[15] More (n 1) 51–58.

[16] ibid 54–55, 57–58.

[17] ibid 55, 57.

[18] ibid 54–55.

[19] ibid 54–55, 57–58. See, notably, 'Refrenate coemptiones istas diuitum, ac uelut monopolii exercendi licentiam.' This has been translated as follows: 'Suffer not thies ryche men to bye vp all, to ingrosse and forstalle, and with theyr monopolye to kepe the market alone as please them.' ibid 57–58.

[20] Anderson (n 9) 68, 72–73; W Walwyn, 'Gold Tried in the Fire. 4 June 1647' in A Sharp (ed), *The English Levellers* (Cambridge, Cambridge University Press, 2004) 76, 78–79; R Overton and W Walwyn, 'A Remonstrance of Many Thousand Citizens. 7 July 1646' in A Sharp (ed), *The English Levellers* (Cambridge, Cambridge University Press, 2004) 46; R Overton, 'An Arrow Against all Tyrants 12 October 1646' in A Sharp (ed), *The English Levellers* (Cambridge, Cambridge University Press, 2004) 62; J Lilburne et al, 'The Petition of 11 September 1648' in A Sharp (ed), *The English Levellers* (Cambridge, Cambridge University Press, 2004) 136–137; J Lilburne, 'England's New Chains Discovered. 26 February 1649' in A Sharp (ed), *The English Levellers* (Cambridge, Cambridge University Press, 2004) 144.

[21] See Book I, Chapter X entitled 'Inequalities Occasioned by the Policy of Europe' in A Smith, *An Inquiry into the Nature and Causes of the Wealth of Nations* (first published 1776, Oxford,

members of society from empowering themselves by becoming economically active and independent.[22] Just as the Levellers, Smith criticised exclusive rights and other forms of privileges as undue state favouritism being at odds with the principles of the rule of law and 'evidently contrary to that justice and equality of treatment which the sovereign owes to all the different orders of his subjects'.[23]

ii. The Competition Equality Thesis

Not only did early political and economic thinkers oppose concentrated forms of economic power, such as monopoly and oligopoly, for their adverse effects on equality of opportunity and adverse distributive effects, but they were also the first to coin the proposition that competitive markets promote equality. The belief that competition enhances equality has, for instance, been a central tenet of the pamphlets and speeches of the English Levellers. Early liberal political philosophers and economists, such as Montesquieu, James Steuart, or Adam Smith, also associated the emergence of competitive markets with greater socio-economic equality. All these protagonists had in common that they valued competitive markets for their levelling and equalising economic, social, and political impact. They witnessed the emergence of competitive markets against the backdrop of the preceding societal order of feudalism, which was characterised by economic subordination of lower classes to a feudal elite.[24] In eroding this inherently hierarchical order, the rise of competitive markets had a deeply transformative economic and societal impact.

The radical nature of this transformation becomes most palpable in Adam Smith's *Wealth of Nations* (1776), which celebrates the advent of competitive markets first and foremost as a 'great revolution'[25] that dismantled the social order of feudalism. Smith and other early political economists described how the emergence of markets brought about more equalised forms of bargains and exchanges that fundamentally differed from the hierarchical organisation of economic interactions between feudal seigniors and lower productive classes. By transforming relationships of economic subordination into more equalised forms of economic exchanges, the proliferation of competitive markets gradually diminished the

Oxford University Press, 1976) I, x, c; see in particular §§ 1–18, 135–139. On the egalitarian aspects of Smith's understanding of competitive markets, E Rothschild, 'Adam Smith and Conservative Economics' (1992) 45 *The Economic History Review* 74, 92–93; S Fleischacker, 'Adam Smith on Equality' in CJ Berry, MP Paganelli and C Smith (eds), *The Oxford Handbook of Adam Smith* (Oxford, Oxford University Press, 2013) 486–489; D Boucoyannis, 'The Equalizing Hand: Why Adam Smith Thought the Market Should Produce Wealth Without Steep Inequality' (2013) 11 *Perspectives on Politics* 1051.

[22] Smith (n 21) I, xi, c, § 1 and § 12, 135 and 138, § 31, § 32, 146, I, x, c, § 41 ff, 151 ff. For a similar critique, Montesquieu, Charles-Louis de Secondat, *De l'esprit des lois* (first published 1748, Paris, Garnier-Flammarion, 1979) Book XX, Chapter XXIII.

[23] ibid IV, viii, § 30, 654.

[24] J Steuart, *An Inquiry into the Principles of Political Oeconomy: Being An Essay on the Science of Domestic Policy in Free Nations* (London, A. Millar and T. Cadell, 1768) Book II, Chapter XIII, 240, 245; Smith (n 21) III, iii–iv, § 4–12, 412–420.

[25] Smith (n 21) III, iv, § 17, 422.

economic dependence of the lower productive classes on the feudal seigniors.[26] Incrementally, the ascent of competitive markets thus eroded the patterns of economic dependence, social subordination, and domination that characterised the feudal economic and social order.[27]

Early political and economic thinkers were adamant that this transformation triggered by the rise and expansion of competitive markets was not confined to the economic or social spheres but paved the way towards greater political emancipation, freedom, and equality. They emphasised how competitive markets not only dissipated existing economic relationships of subordination and domination but also generated a more equalised distribution of wealth and political power.[28] Adam Smith colourfully described how, with the ushering in of competitive markets, the feudal seigniors started to lose their 'whole power and authority' over the people by trading with more productive classes.[29] With the rise of 'independent' tradesmen, the 'great proprietors were no longer capable of interrupting the regular execution of justice, or disturbing the peace of the country'.[30] As a consequence, '[a] regular government was established in the country as well as in the city, nobody having sufficient power to disturb its operations in the one, any more than in the other'.[31] In a similar vein, Montesquieu and John Steuart observed how the dissemination of competitive markets incrementally diffused wealth and political power and set in motion a gradual transformation of the feudal system into a republican or democratic political order and society.[32] With the levelling and equalisation of economic relationships induced by the arrival of competitive markets, the feudal order, based on the subordination of the many to the domination of a few, gave way to a new form of society characterised by the equal subordination of all members of society to general laws of the republic ensuring equal freedom.[33] At the same time, these early liberal thinkers also coined the notion that a republican society and polity could not be sustained in the presence of privileges and excessive inequalities in status and wealth.[34]

The seventeenth- and eighteenth-century accounts of the nascent market society were hence also amongst the first to forge a link between the equalising tendency of competitive markets and the emergence of a more equal, republican political order. Adam Smith, for instance, viewed this equalising social and

[26] ibid III, iv, § 11–12, 419–420. See for a similar argument Steuart (n 24) Book II, Chapter XIII, 238–240.

[27] P Rosanvallon, *Le libéralisme économique: Histoire de l'Idée de marché* (Paris, Seuil, 1989) 48.

[28] Steuart (n 24) Book II, Chapter XIII, 245.

[29] Smith (n 21) III, iv, § 10, 418–419.

[30] ibid III, iv, § 15, 421.

[31] ibid III.

[32] Steuart (n 24) Book II, Chapter XIII, 238–239; Rosanvallon (n 27) 48–49. See also Montesquieu, (n 22) Book XX, Chapters IV to XXII.

[33] Steuart (n 24) Book II, Chapter XIII, 237, 242; for the view that there is a 'natural relation' between commerce and republican or democratic forms of government, see Montesquieu (n 22) Book V, Chapter VI; Book XX, Chapters IV, XIX–XXI.

[34] Montesquieu (n 22) Book V, Chapter VI. See also J-J Rousseau, *Du contrat social* (first published 1767, Paris, Flammarion 2001) I, ix, 64 and III, iv, 106.

political transformation as the most consequential and valuable implication of the rise of competitive markets. He underscored the importance of these broader political and societal repercussions observing that

> commerce and manufactures gradually introduced order and good government, and with them, the liberty and security of individuals, among the inhabitants of the country, who had before lived almost in a continual state of war with their neighbours, and of servile dependency upon their superiors. This, though it has been the least observed, is by far the most important of all their effects.[35]

It is against the backdrop of this inherently political understanding of the equality- and liberty-enhancing features of competitive markets that instances of concentrated and unaccountable private economic power were condemned as a source of 'oppression'[36] or a manifestation of what Anderson calls 'private government', incompatible with a society of free and equals.[37] Restraints to competition and economic privileges were indeed viewed as obstacles to the freedom and equal status of citizens. For, by restricting economic freedom, they deprived individuals of the opportunity to become economically 'self-employed, independent, masterless men'.[38]

In early political and economic thought, greater economic equality and economic liberty were hence tightly intertwined. The early proponents of competitive markets cast the independent and small proprietor, yeoman, or tradesman as the epitome of the republican independent 'freeman'.[39] The advent of competitive markets was heralded for freeing up access to property and professions, and for expanding the opportunity for individuals to become smallholders and independent traders. Early political economists, thus, assumed that – by dispersing economic power and bringing about equality of opportunity – competition would allow individuals to emancipate themselves by becoming independent economic agents.[40] A competitive economic order promoting broad-based incentives, participation, and economic opportunity was, in turn, believed to also generate an equal distribution of wealth and property.[41] In short, polycentric[42] competitive markets were viewed as 'institutional components of a free society of equals'.[43]

[35] Smith (n 21) III, iv, § 4, 412.

[36] Overton and Walwyn (n 20) 46. See also, for the criticism of the 'oppressive monopoly' as 'great abridgement of the liberties of the people', Walwyn (n 20) 79; Lilburne et al (n 20) 136; Lilburne (n 20) 144.

[37] Anderson (n 9) 66–68.

[38] Lilburne (n 20) 144; Anderson (n 9) 72.

[39] Smith (n 21) III, iii, § 19, 423–424.

[40] Anderson (n 9) 76–77.

[41] For the notion of 'broad-based economic opportunity' and a recent account of the link between economic liberty, broad-based opportunity and growth, see D Acemoglu and JA Robinson, *The Narrow Corridor* (London, Viking-Penguin, 2019) 194–200.

[42] For the notion of 'polycentricity', see M Polanyi, *The Logic of Liberty* (London, Routledge, 1951) 170–184.

[43] Anderson (n 9) 67–68, 72.

B. The Common Threads of a Republican Understanding of Competition and Economic Liberty

This synopsis of the historical origins of the monopoly regressivity and competition equality theses in early modern liberal economic and political thought yields several important insights. The most important one is that competitive markets were initially not associated with inequality. On the contrary, early political economists celebrated competitive markets for their tendency to promote economic liberty *and* equality, while decrying concentrated economic power as a source of unfreedom and inequality. This perceived positive relationship between competition and equality and the assumption of the regressivity of monopoly power have several common features.

i. *Two Dimensions of Equality*

A first common thread cutting across the early political and economic accounts is that they portray competition as the harbinger of two dimensions of equality. Comprehending equality primarily as equality of opportunity and equality of conditions, the early proponents of competition endorsed a procedural notion of equality which does not necessarily presuppose an equal distribution of wealth.[44] In their account, competition, by dispersing economic power, bringing down socio-economic hierarchies and, hence, levelling the playing field, promotes in the first place some procedural form of economic equality as equality of status, opportunity, and fairness – not equality of outcomes. This, however, does not mean that the idea of material equality and distributive justice is completely alien to their arguments in favour of competitive markets.[45] Rather, they assumed that competitive markets, by eroding instances of concentrated economic power, ensuring broad-based economic opportunities and a fair participative process, also indirectly promote distributive equality of income and wealth, as they simultaneously constrain the exercise of market power and bring about a more equal and merit-based distribution of wealth and political power.[46]

By contrast, monopoly and oligopoly power, as well as restraints of trade were thought to undermine the fairness of the competitive process and to impair both procedural and substantive equality. Early political and economic thinkers indeed identified two channels of the regressivity[47] of monopolistic or oligopolistic

[44] ibid 67.

[45] Fleischacker (n 21) 498.

[46] Steuart (n 24) Book II, Chapter XIII, 245.

[47] The 'monopoly regressivity' thesis cultivated by these early proponents of competitive markets differs from how it is understood by the contemporary literature, eg Crane (n 5). Along with the adverse distributive impact of monopoly power on 'substantive' equality it also accounts for the adverse effect of monopoly power on a procedural notion of equality as opportunity of market participants, which in turn may also have adverse distributive effects.

market concentration. On the one hand, concentrated economic power of monopolists or oligopolists reduces consumer surplus[48] by leading to price increases and shortages that disproportionately harm the poorest members of society while benefitting the rich.[49] On the other hand, monopoly and oligopoly power, by crowding out other players from the market or driving up input prices, prevents individuals from becoming economically active, keeping them in unemployment, idleness, and poverty.[50] This dual relationship between equal economic opportunities and equality of wealth also lies at the origins of competition law. In the 1602 *Darcy v Allein* case – the first competition law case of modern history – the Queen's Bench highlighted the adverse impact of monopoly on economic opportunities and its distributive knock-on effects to support its finding that monopolies are against the common law. It held that monopoly 'leadeth to the impoverishing of divers Artificers and others, who before by labor of their hands in their Art or Trade had kept themselves and their families, who now of necessity shall be constrained to live in idlenesse and beggary'.[51]

The relationship between competitive markets and equality in early economic thought thus had always a procedural dimension, in the form of equality of opportunity or fairness, and a substantive or distributive (socio-economic) dimension, in the form of equal distribution of income and wealth. Indeed, procedural equality in terms of equality of opportunity and equal freedom to take part in the competitive process was assumed to condition distributive equality and fairness. Competitive markets were thus considered as an institutional setting that secures a fair process of economic interactions and transactions amongst equals, the outcomes of which will be most of the time fair and not exhibit extreme inequalities of distribution.[52] Competition itself thus became synonymous with procedural and substantive equality, as it embodied a principle of equality of opportunity and fairness. This crystallises in the work of Adam Smith, who reverted to the concept of competition to illustrate his notion of procedural fairness that he associated with the allegory of the 'impartial spectator'.[53] In the *Theory of Moral Sentiments*, Smith wrote the following:

> In the race for wealth, and honours, and preferments, he may run as hard as he can, and strain every nerve and every muscle, in order to outstrip all his competitors. But if he should jostle, or throw down any of them, the indulgence of the spectators is entirely at an end. It is a violation of fair play, which they cannot admit.[54]

[48] See, for instance, Smith's description of the wealth transfer from consumers to monopolists as unfair 'taxation'. Smith (n 21) V, i, e, § 30, 754–755.

[49] More (n 1) 51–58; Smith (n 21) I, vii, § 26–27, 78–79.

[50] More (n 1) 54–55, 57–58; Smith (n 21) I, vii, § 28, 79; I, x, c, § 5 and 12, 135–138; V, I, e, § 30, 754–755.

[51] *Darcy v Allein ('The Case of Monopolies')* [1602] Trinity Term, 44 Elizabeth I In the Court of King's Bench. Reports, vol 11, 84b, 86a–87a.

[52] Boucoyannis (n 21) 1053.

[53] Fleischacker (n 21) 487.

[54] A Smith, *The Theory of Moral Sentiments* (first published 1759, New York, Penguin, 2009) II, ii, 101.

With this allegory, Smith was amongst the first to coin a distinction between what we would call today 'competition on the merits' and 'unfair competition'. It describes competition as a process governed by a certain set of rules that ensure a level playing field and equal opportunities for all participants. So long as the players compete within the perimeters set by these rules, both the process and the outcome of the game can be accepted as fair. In the absence of any distortions of the process by power imbalances or unfair conduct, and as long as the rules of the competitive process are not consistently favouring a specific group, the fairness of these outcomes can also be expected to be relatively equal. If the procedural impartiality of the competitive process is intact and equality of opportunity is ensured, any resulting inequalities of outcomes can be explained by differences in the competitive performance of the players.

ii. The Consonance between Equality of Opportunity of Competitors and Greater Distributive Equality in the Interest of Consumers

A second point that bears noting is that early proponents of competitive markets did not perceive any tension between greater equality of opportunity between competitors and consumer welfare. On the contrary, they assumed that greater equality between competitors would ensure an economic system that would put the consumer at the centre of economic activity and generate a roughly even distribution of wealth in the interest of consumers. Unlike the mercantilist system, which benefited in the first place the guilded professions and monopolists, competitive markets were considered to promote and be responsive to consumers' interests.[55] In other words, early economic thinkers asserted that competitive markets would secure an economic system that serves the interests of the many, not the few.

Central to the opposition of early political economists against monopolies, restraints of trade, and other forms of collusion was the perception that they unduly sacrifice the interests of consumers to that of producers.[56] By contrast, competitive markets characterised by broad-based economic opportunities, participation, and rivalrous interaction of many players were thought to prevent producers from colluding with each other and exploiting consumers. Adam Smith, for instance, highlighted that deconcentrated market structures ensure that economic agents are 'dispersed in distant places [and] cannot easily combine together'[57] and impose their interest upon their fellow citizens.[58] Accordingly, greater economic equality of opportunity and the de-concentration of economic power amongst many players also enhance greater distributive equality in the interest of consumers because they prevent producers from combining and abusing their economic power.

[55] Smith (n 21) IV, viii, § 49, 660. See also for the proposition that competition sets the 'just price' for merchandises Montesquieu (n 22), Book XX, Chapter IX.

[56] ibid IV, vii, § 50, 661.

[57] ibid I, x, c, § 23, 143; see also II, v, § 7, 361–362.

[58] ibid IV, viii, § 34, 654–655.

Conversely, greater concentration of economic power and less equality of opportunity among producers were believed to lead to greater distributive inequalities to the detriment of consumer interests.

iii. An Egalitarian Understanding of Economic Liberty

A third important insight of our synopsis of the origins of the monopoly regressivity and competition equality theses is that early proponents of competitive markets did not sense any tension between equality and economic liberty. Rather, they perceived equality and emancipation from economic subordination as the central feature and component of economic liberty. Their notion of economic liberty hence fundamentally differs from our contemporary negative notion of economic liberty as the absence of coercion or interference. Liberty in the negative sense suggests that we are free when nobody else is interfering and obstructing our otherwise unrestricted choices or actions. Economic liberty hence means the absence of state and private interference with the sphere of autonomy and choices of (other) market participants.[59]

This contemporary notion of liberty is of little help in explaining why early proponents of competitive markets perceived concentrated economic power in the form of combinations (ie guilds or cartels) or monopolies in themselves as an abrogation of economic liberty. Indeed, from the perspective of negative liberty the mere concentration of economic power within the hands of a single or few firms does not amount to an obstruction of negative liberty of other market participants, so long as this power is not abused in a way that the monopolist or cartel interferes or is likely to interfere with the sphere of autonomy of other market participants. Economic liberty in the negative sense is hence largely indifferent to the concentration and imbalances of economic power and ensuing inequalities in terms of opportunities or wealth.[60]

The egalitarian understanding of economic freedom cultivated by the early proponents of competitive markets thus sits uneasily with our contemporary negative conception of economic liberty as non-interference. Rather, it is reminiscent of a much older, republican notion of liberty which describes liberty as non-domination, that is to say the absence of domination or dependence upon somebody else's will.[61] This republican concept of liberty traces back to the political thought in the ancient Roman Republic, which defined liberty in opposition

[59] B Constant, *Political Writings* (Cambridge, Cambridge University Press, 1988) 307–328; I Berlin, 'Two Concepts of Liberty' in H Hardy (ed), *Liberty: Incorporating Four Essays on Liberty* (Oxford, Oxford University Press, 2002) 171–174; FA Hayek, *The Constitution of Liberty* (Chicago, University of Chicago Press 2011) 57, 60–61. For a detailed discussion of negative and republican conceptions of economic liberty in competition law E Deutscher, 'The Competition-Democracy Nexus Unpacked – Competition Law, Republican Liberty, and Democracy' (2022) *Yearbook of European Law* [forthcoming].

[60] P Pettit, *On The People's Terms: A Republican Theory and Model of Democracy* (Cambridge, Cambridge University Press 2012) 11.

[61] P Pettit, 'Freedom as Antipower' (1996) 106(3) *Ethics* 576, 576; Skinner (2002) (n 7) 255.

to servitude. Being free in ancient republican thought was synonymous with not being a slave but being a citizen capable of acting in one's own right.[62] From the perspective of republican liberty, we are free because (and as long as) we enjoy the status of free and independent citizens who are not subordinated to a master-slave-like relationship and not exposed to somebody else's capacity to interfere arbitrarily with our actions or choices.

It is this older, republican notion of liberty that lies at the heart of the close relationship between competitive markets, equality, economic liberty, and a republican form of government which was thrust into the limelight in the writings of early political economists. Instead of conceiving liberty in a purely negative sense as non-interference, the Levellers,[63] John Steuart,[64] and Adam Smith rather defined civil and economic liberty – in line with the republican tradition – in opposition to the 'subordination',[65] 'servitude',[66] or 'slavery'[67] prevailing under the feudal order. Consistent with the republican tradition, the notion of economic liberty celebrated by the early proponents of competitive markets thus had a strong egalitarian dimension. Economic liberty always meant equal liberty.[68] Whereas proponents of the modern notion of negative liberty do not object to imbalances of power,[69] the early advocates of competitive markets perceived concentrated economic power as a source of domination as it entrenched relationships of economic subordination and inhibited equality of opportunity as a precondition of the independent status of all citizens as free and equals. Consequently, not only the abuse of concentrated economic power leading to an undue interference with the sphere of autonomy of other market participants, but its mere existence were considered antithetical to the republican notion of economic liberty as non-domination.

It is also this egalitarian and republican notion of liberty as non-domination that builds the conceptual core of the claim advanced by the early political economists that the advent of competitive markets contributed to the emergence of a republican and democratic form of government. In their account, as competitive markets gradually eroded concentrated economic power, relationships of domination, and inequality, they promoted liberty as non-domination and thereby paved the way towards a republican society and policy of free and equals.[70]

[62] Pettit (n 7) 19–20; Skinner (1998) (n 7) 38–46. Cicero for instance defined liberty in clear opposition to servitude: MT Cicero, *On the Commonwealth and On the Laws* (Cambridge, Cambridge University Press 1999) I, § 47–49; II, § 42–48; III, § 37 b. For further discussion see Deutscher (n 59).

[63] J Lilburne, 'Postscript to The Freeman's Freedom Vindicated [1646]' in A Sharp (ed), *The English Levellers* (Cambridge, Cambridge University Press 2004) 31; Overton and Walwyn (n 20) 46; Lilburne et al (n 20) 136–137.

[64] Steuart (n 24) Book II, Chapter XIII, 240.

[65] ibid 238.

[66] Overton and Walwyn (n 20) 38.

[67] Smith (n 21) I, x, c, § 22, 142–143; III, iii, § 5, 400; III, iv, § 15, 421.

[68] This is a key feature of republican liberty. Cicero (n 62) I, 47; Pettit (n 60) 5.

[69] Pettit (n 60) 11.

[70] Steuart (n 24) Book II, Chapter XIII, 242–243; Montesquieu (n 22) Book V, Chapter VI; Book XX, Chapters IV, XII, XIX–XXI.

By virtue of their tendency to disperse concentrated economic power and minimise domination, competitive markets were thus perceived as a system of 'antipower'.[71] Conversely, the very existence (and not only the abuse) of concentrated economic power, monopoly, and privileges was condemned as an illegitimate form of private government and domination incompatible with liberty as non-domination and equality of the citizens within a republican society. Restrictions of competition had in these early accounts of competitive markets both an economic and a political dimension. They were not only criticised for their harmful impact on allocative efficiency but as 'a conspiracy against the publick'[72] – in short, as an assault on a republican society of free and equals.

III. The Egalitarian Tenets of the 'Republican Antitrust' Tradition in the US and in Europe

The egalitarian understanding of competitive markets as an institution of antipower, which levels economic hierarchies and opens up broad-based economic opportunities, has left a significant and lasting imprint on the ideological foundations of US and EU competition law. The republican idea that competitive markets act as a safeguard of a society of free and equals had an important bearing on the formative era of US antitrust law until the 1970s. It also influenced early European competition paradigms, such as the German Ordoliberal School. These 'republican antitrust' traditions, emerging on both continents towards the end of the nineteenth and during the early twentieth century, revolved around a few basic tenets that can be traced back to the republican ideas of the early political and economic thinkers canvassed in section II.

A. Competitive Markets as a Precondition of a Republican Society of Free and Equals

A first central tenet of the republican antitrust traditions on both sides of the Atlantic was that they perceived competitive markets in which economic power is dispersed polycentrically and evenly amongst a multitude of market players as a safeguard of republican liberty understood as non-domination and equality of status.

This idea lies at the roots of modern competition law. During the legislative debates of the Sherman Act, the proponents of the proposed antitrust statute

[71] Pettit (n 61) 588–591.
[72] Smith (n 21) I, x, c, § 27, 145; see also I, x, c, § 5, 135–136.

asserted that 'industrial liberty ... lies at the foundation of the equality of all rights and privileges'.[73] In a similar vein as the Levellers, John Steuart, or Adam Smith, early proponents of antitrust law understood economic liberty in the republican sense as equal liberty and status. They also perceived the concentration of economic power resulting from the emergence of powerful trusts and large-scale corporations as a remnant of the social hierarchies and relationships of subjugation that characterised the feudal and absolutist order of the past.[74] The adoption of the Sherman Act was informed by the republican belief that the concentration of economic power in the hands of a few large-scale corporations and the ensuing forms of dependence and subjugation are antithetical to the Jeffersonian ideal of an egalitarian society and polity, in which power and wealth are atomised amongst a multitude of independent and equal masterless men.[75]

Later, this Jeffersonian ideal of a society in which economic power is dispersed amongst many small and independent businessmen also lay at the core of the egalitarian critique of 'bigness' and the promise of a 'new freedom' spearheaded by Louis Brandeis and Woodrow Wilson. The progressive antitrust movement championed by Brandeis and Wilson faulted big business for its dominating impact on the rest of society. Industry concentration was perceived as an antonym to a republican society grounded in the equal and independent status of its citizens.[76]

On the other side of the Atlantic, too, the idea that competitive markets constitute a safeguard of republican liberty gained new ground in the first half of the twentieth century. The German Ordoliberal School advocated competitive markets as an epitome of a 'domination-free economic order' ('*herrschaftsfreie Wirtschaftsordnung*')[77] characterised by the decentralised, mutual self-adaptation of autonomous and independent market participants. Competition thus constituted for Ordoliberals the organising principle of an impersonal, 'domination-free' process of economic coordination that operates without any subordination or

[73] Senator Sherman 20 Cong Rec 2455 (1890) 2457.

[74] R Hofstadter, 'What Happened to the Antitrust Movement' in DA Crane and H Hovenkamp (eds), *The Making of Competition Policy: Legal and Economic Sources* (New York, Oxford University Press, 2013) 227; see also T Roosevelt, 'The Trusts, the People, and the Square Deal' in DA Crane and H Hovenkamp (eds), *The Making of Competition Policy: Legal and Economic Sources* (New York, Oxford University Press, 2013) 113.

[75] Hofstadter (n 74) 227; PH Brietzke, 'The Constitutionalization of Antitrust: Jefferson, Madison, Hamilton, and Thomas C. Arthur' (1987) 22 *Valparaiso University Law Review* 275, 276; R Pitofsky, 'The Political Content of Antitrust' (1979) 127 *University of Pennsylvania Law Review* 1051, 1058–1059.

[76] LD Brandeis, *Other People's Money: And How The Bankers Use It* (New York, Frederick A. Stokes Company, 1914) 152; W Wilson, *The New Freedom* (Leipzig, Tauchnitz, 1913) 23; W Wilson, 'The Tariff and the Trusts' in DA Crane and H Hovenkamp (eds), *The Making of Competition Policy: Legal and Economic Sources* (New York, Oxford University Press, 2013) 124.

[77] F Böhm (ed), Wettbewerb und Monopolkampf: Eine Untersuchung zur Frage des wirtschaftlichen Kampfrechts und zur Frage der rechtlichen Struktur der geltenden Wirtschaftsordnung (first published 1933, Baden-Baden, Nomos, 2010) 303. For a detailed discussion of the role of republican liberty in Ordoliberal thought see Deutscher (59).

hierarchical decision-making.[78] Concentration of economic power, by contrast, was in the eyes of Ordoliberal thinkers profoundly at odds with the ideal of a society of free and equals[79] because it introduces elements of hierarchy, subordination, and domination into economic exchanges and interactions.[80]

The Ordoliberals, therefore, warned that the excessive concentration of market power would entail a 're-feudalisation' ('*Refeudalisierung*') of economic and social relationships.[81] Instances of concentrated economic power were, in their view, inimical to the republican ideal of a domination-free society,[82] as they subject individuals to hierarchical forms of economic relationships and transactions that are characterised by domination rather than polycentric coordination of independent and autonomous economic plans.[83] In keeping with the republican tradition, Ordoliberals hence regarded the mere existence of concentrated economic power and not only its exercise as obstruction of liberty because it subjects market participants into relationships of dependency and subordination to the arbitrary will of more powerful economic players.[84]

The republican idea that competitive markets in which economic power is dispersed amongst many independent players constitute a safeguard against domination and a crucial pillar of a society of free and equals was hence a common feature of early antitrust movements on both sides of the Atlantic. Central to these republican antitrust paradigms was that they did not perceive a fundamental contradiction between equality and liberty. On the contrary, in a similar vein as the early proponents of competitive markets, they viewed equality of opportunity and status as an inherent element of liberty. They hence understood liberty not in a purely negative sense, as non-interference. Rather, in emphasising the importance of competitive markets in shielding the independent status of market participants against subordination and domination they adhered to a republican notion of liberty as non-domination. This republican notion of republican liberty as equal liberty also lay at the heart of the belief that competitive markets promote and economic concentration is detrimental to democracy.[85]

[78] ibid 64, 301, 305, 314. F Böhm, Freiheit und Ordnung in der Marktwirtschaft (first published 1971, Baden-Baden, Nomos, 1980) 36–37; W Eucken, Grundsätze der Wirtschaftspolitik (Tübingen, Mohr Siebeck, 2004) 22, 246.

[79] Böhm (n 78) 225.

[80] L Miksch, Wettbewerb als Aufgabe: Grundsätze einer Wettbewerbsordnung (Godersberg, Verlag Helmut Küpper, 1947) 15, 17, 27, 117, 119. Eucken (n 78) 51–52.

[81] F Böhm, 'Democracy and Economic Power in Cartel and Monopoly in Modern Law' in DA Crane and H Hovenkamp (eds), *The Making of Competition Policy: Legal and Economic Sources* (first published 1961, New York, Oxford University Press 2013) 273–279; Böhm (n 78) 258–259.

[82] Böhm (n 78) 225.

[83] Miksch (n 80) 15, 17, 27, 117, 119; Eucken (n 78) 22, 40, 51–52; Böhm (n 78) 221.

[84] Böhm (n 77) 237, 275–276; Eucken (n 78) 52, 174, 176–177, 246, 334.

[85] Senator Sherman 20 Cong Rec 2455 (1890) (n 73) 2457; Wilson (n 76) 191; Eucken (n 78) 16, 304–308; Böhm (n 78) 256–257; Böhm (n 81). For a detailed analysis, Deutscher (n 59); E Deutscher and S Makris, 'Exploring the Ordoliberal Paradigm: The Competition-Democracy Nexus' (2016) 11 *Competition Law Review* 181; E Deutscher, *Of Masters, Slaves, Behemoths and Bees: The Rise and Fall of the Link Between Competition, Competition Law and Democracy* (Florence, European University Institute, 2020).

B. Equality of Opportunity as the *Equalisandum* of Competition Law

A second central feature of the republican antitrust paradigms on both sides of the Atlantic was their adherence to the monopoly regressivity and competition equality theses. Republican antitrust paradigms in the US and Europe alike subscribed to the belief that competition law would contribute to a freer and more egalitarian society primarily by promoting equality of opportunity.

The republican antitrust tradition on both sides of the Atlantic indeed saw the preservation of the equality of opportunity among competitors as a central task of competition law. This becomes most apparent in Senator Sherman's warnings about the adverse impact of economic concentration on equality of opportunity, wealth inequality, and ultimately the integrity of the social order:

> Society is now disturbed by forces never felt before. The popular mind is agitated with problems that may disturb social order, and among them all none is more threatening than the inequality of condition, of wealth and opportunity that has grown within a single generation out of the concentration of capital into vast combinations to control production and trade and to break down competition.[86]

Consistent with this egalitarian concern about the concentration of economic power, the framers of the Sherman Act advocated the proposed antitrust statute as a safeguard of equality of opportunity for small, independent businessmen.[87] The enactment of the Sherman Act was in the first place a response to the widespread popular discontent over practices by big businesses that stifled smaller competitors' ability and opportunity to compete[88] and, thereby, 'crush[ed] out the little men and little enterprises'.[89] Abuses of economic power by large corporations and trusts were perceived as an assault on the 'right of every man to work, labor and produce in any lawful vocation and to transport his production on equal terms and conditions and under like circumstances'.[90]

Similar concerns about the adverse impact of concentrated power on equality of opportunity also informed Brandeis' and Wilson's call for tougher antitrust rules and intervention against big business. The progressive antitrust movement warned that the adverse impact of big business on equality of opportunity would fundamentally undermine the promise of the American free enterprise system and the American ideal of meritocracy anchored in the belief that 'the ambitious and gifted workingman makes his way up'.[91] To revitalise equality of economic

[86] 20 Cong Rec 2455 (1890) (n 73) 2460.
[87] Senator Sherman ibid 2457.
[88] Senator George 19 Cong Rec 8559 (1890) 8561; Senator Sherman 20 Cong Rec 2455 (1890) (n 73) 2457–2458.
[89] Senator George 19 Cong Rec 8559 (1890) (n 88) 8561.
[90] Senator Sherman 20 Cong Rec 2455 (1890) (n 73) 2457.
[91] Wilson (n 76) 24.

opportunity, Brandeis and Wilson called for antitrust laws which 'keep open the path of opportunity'[92] and 'look after the men who are on the make rather than the men who are already made'.[93] In line with the republican tradition, the progressive antitrust movement also underscored the fundamental relationship between equality of opportunity, republican liberty, and a republican form of government:

> The reason that America was set up was that she might be different of the world in this: that the strong could not put the weak to the wall, that the strong could not prevent the weak from entering the race. America stands for opportunity. America stands for a free field and no favor. America stands for a government responsive to the interests of all.[94]

The preservation of equality of opportunity was also a central feature of the Ordoliberal understanding of competition law. Ordoliberals indeed understood competition primarily as 'open markets'[95] and as an inclusive process that guarantees equal opportunities to carry out an economic activity.[96] This concern about equality of opportunity becomes particularly apparent in the distinction between legitimate methods of 'performance-based competition' ('*Leistungswettbewerb*') and illegitimate methods of 'hindrance competition' ('*Behinderungswettbewerb*') that lies at the heart of the Ordoliberal conception of competition law. To Ordoliberals, the central mandate of competition law consists of promoting and protecting performance-based competition which can be best approximated in English terminology as 'competition on the merits'.[97] This concept understands competition as a process in which all market participants enter into a rivalrous rule-based contest for consumer demand.[98] Performance-based competition is modelled on the basic principle of Adam Smith's 'impartial spectator' – discussed in section II – according to which every market participant 'may run as hard as he can, and strain every nerve and every muscle, in order to outstrip all his competitors', but may not 'jostle, or throw down any of them'.[99]

The Ordoliberals contrasted performance-based competition with hindrance competition. Whereas market players who engage in performance-based competition try to attract consumer demand only by improving their own economic performance, hindrance competition refers to any attempt to win the competitive

[92] LD Brandeis, 'Shall We Abandon the Policy of Competition?' in DA Crane and H Hovenkamp (eds), *The Making of Competition Policy: Legal and Economic Sources* (first published in 1934 in The Curse of Bigness, New York, Oxford University Press, 2013) 189.

[93] Wilson (n 76) 23–24.

[94] ibid 208–209.

[95] Eucken (n 78) 42, 264–269; Miksch (n 80) 38.

[96] Böhm (n 77) 272; F Böhm, 'Freiheit und Ordnung in der Marktwirtschaft' in N Goldschmidt (ed), *Grundtexte zur Freiburger Tradition der Ordnungsökonomik* (first published 1971, Tübingen, Mohr Siebeck, 2008) 306.

[97] Böhm (n 77) 206; Eucken (n 78) 42, 247–249; Miksch (n 80) 15, 54; P Behrens, 'The Ordoliberal Concept of "Abuse" of a Dominant Position and its Impact on Article 102 TFEU' (2015) Europa-Kolleg Hamburg, Institute for European Integration, Discussion Paper No 7/15, hdl.handle.net/10419/120873, 8, 11–12.

[98] Böhm (ed) (n 77) 207–209, 240, 257; Eucken (n 78) 244–249.

[99] Smith (n 54) II, ii, 101.

race by deteriorating or impairing rivals' ability to compete.[100] For Ordoliberals, distortions of competition resulting from hindrance competition do not only entail the misallocation of resources. More importantly, they undermine the equality of opportunity as the central benchmark of fairness of the competitive process and market system.[101] Any attempt by powerful firms to collectively or unilaterally hinder or exclude competitors from participating in the competitive process was therefore condemned by the Ordoliberals as an attempt to substitute private power relationships for the impersonal process of competition in determining the opportunities of individuals to participate and succeed in the market.[102]

The relationship between competition and equality in the republican understanding of competition law thus revolved primarily around the ideal of equality of opportunity. In other words, the *equalisandum* – that is to say, the state of affairs that antitrust law was supposed to equalise[103] – was primarily the equality of opportunity of all market participants. For republican antitrust paradigms on both sides of the Atlantic, the primary task of competition law was hence to prevent instances of excessively concentrated power and keep markets open for competitors. Greater economic opportunities and the erosion of economic concentration, in turn, would eventually level wealth inequalities.

C. Distributive Equality as a By-Product of Equality of Opportunity

This proposition that equality of opportunity amongst competitors would eventually promote greater distributive equality points towards a third assumption that underpinned the republican antitrust tradition on both sides of the Atlantic. The republican antitrust tradition, in fact, endorsed the belief – first articulated by early proponents of competitive markets – that keeping markets open and ensuring broad-based equality of opportunity would ultimately also enhance equality of wealth. This link between equality of opportunity and equality of wealth has two dimensions. On the one hand, it was premised on the idea that competition law, by preserving equality of opportunity and open markets, would actually enable individuals to become small, independent businessmen who will all get a fair share of the pie. On the other hand, it was also believed that greater equality of opportunity and the ensuing intensified competitive rivalry amongst multiple players would enhance a fairer and more equalised distribution of wealth in the interest of consumers. Promoting competitive opportunities for a multitude of small,

[100] Böhm (n 77) 38, 208–209, 219, 240–249, 257–265, 275–276; Eucken (n 78) 43, 247–249, 267, 296, 329.

[101] Eucken (n 78) 166, 183, 315; Böhm (n 78) 257.

[102] Böhm (n 77) 256, 271.

[103] Lianos (n 5) 10.

independent competitors would keep market power in check and thus prevent any unfair and regressive wealth transfers from consumers to large corporations.

Proponents of the Sherman Act, for instance, argued that greater competition would eventually ensure a fairer distribution of wealth for consumers.[104] The legislative debates of the Sherman Act bear abundant testimony to the fact that the distributive effects of monopoly power and the wealth transfer from both consumers and competitors to monopolies and cartels importantly informed the adoption of the Sherman Act.[105] The unfair distributive effects of cartels (trusts) and monopolies on consumers and, in particular, on the poorer classes also featured prominently in the criticism of big business by the progressive antitrust movement.[106]

The idea that competitive markets would enhance procedural fairness and at the same time ensure outcomes in the interest of consumers also found support in the structure-conduct-performance (S-C-P) paradigm of the Harvard School, which importantly shaped the economic analysis of antitrust law until the 1970s. Harvard scholars highlighted that the competitive process, by ensuring fair competitive opportunities and market access, could preserve a deconcentrated market structure that would maintain firms' incentives to compete and thereby hinder them from exercising market power (conduct) to the detriment of consumers (performance).[107]

Ordoliberals also assumed, albeit to a lesser extent than republican antitrust paradigms in the US, that competition law would contribute to a fairer[108] and often more equal distribution of wealth in the interest of consumers. The Ordoliberals emphasised that competition rules by guaranteeing the fairness of the competitive process would also secure the fairness and legitimacy of its outcomes.[109] In determining the opportunities of economic agents to participate in the competitive process and their responsiveness to the interests of consumers, the rules of the competitive game have a major bearing on the outcomes of the competitive

[104] Senator Sherman 19th Cong Rec 6041 (1888) 6041.

[105] See resolution submitted by Senator Sherman directing the Committee on Finance to inquire into and report on the trust problem, ibid. See also Senator Jones decrying how the Sugar trust extracts with its 'long fellonious fingers … the pennies from the pockets of the poor and the dollars from the pockets of the rich'. 20 Cong Rec 1457 (1890) 1457–1458. See also Senator Sherman 20 Cong Rec 2455 (1890) (n 73) 2458, 2460; RH Lande, 'Wealth Transfers as the Original and Primary Concern of Antitrust: The Efficiency Interpretation Challenged' (1982) 34 *Hastings Law Journal* 65; JB Kirkwood and RH Lande, 'The Chicago School's Foundation Is Flawed: Antitrust Protects Consumers, Not Efficiency' in R Pitofsky (ed), *How the Chicago School Overshot the Mark: The Effect of Conservative Economic Analysis on U.S. Antitrust* (Oxford, Oxford University Press, 2008).

[106] Brandeis (n 76) 151–152.

[107] C Kaysen and DF Turner, *Antitrust Policy: An Economic and Legal Analysis* (Cambridge, MA, Harvard University Press, 1959) 19, also 14–18, 44–45. Harvard scholars, however, were amongst the first to note that the distributive incidence of monopoly power is not always easy to establish. ibid 32.

[108] E-J Mestmäcker, *Wirtschaft und Verfassung in der Europäischen Union* (Baden-Baden, Nomos 2003) 36.

[109] The Ordoliberals acknowledged that competition tends to accentuate inequalities in the distribution of wealth, in so far as competitive success is heavily contingent upon consumers' idiosyncratic judgments and mere luck. Böhm (ed) (n 77) 230; Eucken (n 78) 300.

process in terms of distribution of wealth and income.[110] By guaranteeing a fair competitive process, competition law ensures that economic inequalities are the result of differences in the economic performance of the individual market participants rather than the outcome of arbitrary power.[111] The members of the Freiburg School thus recognised that the design of the institutional rules governing competition has important distributive consequences for competitors and consumers alike.[112]

The republican antitrust paradigms on both sides of the Atlantic thus acknowledged that the distribution and fairness of market outcomes largely depend on the design of the rules of the game that govern the competitive process. Competition law, by securing the equality of opportunity of competitors, also promotes as a by-product a more equal and fair distribution of wealth in the interest of consumers (see upper left-hand quadrant of Table 1.1 below). By the same token, the republican antitrust traditions warned that excessive economic concentration would not only frustrate equality of opportunity amongst competitors but also entail greater distributive inequalities to the detriment of consumers (see lower right-hand quadrant of Table 1.1 below). Just like the early political and economic thinkers, proponents of the republican antitrust paradigm adhered to the belief that the interests of small, independent competitors and consumers were largely in accord with each other.

Table 1.1 The relationship between equality of opportunity and distributive equality under the republican antitrust paradigm

	Positive distributive effects for consumers	Negative distributive effects for consumers
Equality of opportunity	Republican antitrust	
Inequality of opportunity		Republican antitrust

D. Competition, Republican Liberty, Equality, and the Judicial Interpretation of Antitrust Law

The ideal of an egalitarian, republican understanding of economic liberty and its realisation through competitive markets had a long-lasting impact on the formative era of competition law on both sides of the Atlantic. The interpretation of the antitrust law statutes by US courts until the early 1970s and EU competition law jurisprudence until the 1990s attributed an important weight to the preservation of equality of opportunity, notably of small competitors, against concentrated economic power.

[110] Böhm (ed) (n 77) 257, 300–301.
[111] ibid 257–262, 271–272; Miksch (n 80) 54; Eucken (n 78) 300.
[112] Böhm (n 77) 256.

i. Republican Antitrust and US Case Law

The formative case law of the US Supreme Court abounds with references to the antitrust laws as a safeguard of equality of opportunity which prevents single and collective instances of economic power from 'driving out of business the small dealers and worth men whose lives have been spent therein'.[113] Its early case law is anchored in the concern that combinations of economic power, by destroying the economic opportunities of an entire class of small entrepreneurs, would transform the 'independent business man … into a mere servant or agent of a corporation … bound to obey orders issued by others'[114] and subject to 'the sole power and … the sole will of one powerful combination of capital'.[115] On numerous occasions, the US Supreme Court highlighted the role of antitrust law in ensuring equality of opportunity, which allows 'every business, no matter how small' to take part in the competitive race.[116]

The US judiciary thus perceived the preservation of a polycentric market structure, in which economic power is dispersed amongst many players, as a safeguard of the economic livelihood and independent status of market participants, in particular of 'small, local enterprises'.[117] This egalitarian dimension of competition law was prominently articulated by Judge Learned Hand in *Alcoa*. Judge Hand asserted that the Sherman Act embodied a clear preference for 'a system of small producers, each dependent for his success upon his own skill and character, to one which the great mass of those engaged must accept the direction of a few'.[118] Accordingly, one of the central purposes of antitrust law 'was to perpetuate and preserve, for its own sake and in spite of possible cost, an organization of industry in small units which can effectively compete with each other'.[119]

The egalitarian objective of preserving broad-based economic opportunities and the independent status of small dealers importantly fashioned US antitrust case law. It, for instance, underpinned the strict treatment of vertical price restraints as *per se* violations of section 1 of the Sherman Act. In *Dr. Miles*, the Supreme Court cast vertical resale price maintenance restraints as an illegitimate form of subordination and domination, which subjugates retailers to the arbitrary will of manufacturers.[120] Similar considerations about the equality of opportunity

[113] *United States v Trans-Missouri Freight Asso.* 166 U.S. 290 (1897) 323. See also *United States v Swift & Co.* 286 U.S. 106 (1932) 118.

[114] *United States v Trans-Missouri Freight Asso.* (n 113) 324.

[115] ibid; *Fashion Originators' Guild, Inc. v FTC* 312 U.S. 457 (1941) 467.

[116] *United States v Topco Assocs. Inc.* 405 U.S. 596 (1972) 610. See for a similar concern about the opportunities and status of small, independent businesses *Klor's, Inc. v Broadway-Hale Stores, Inc.* 359 U.S. 207 (1959) 212–213; *Radiant Burners, Inc. v Peoples Gas Light & Coke Co.* 364 U.S. 656 (1960) 660.

[117] *United States v Columbia Steel Co.* 334 U.S. 495 (1948) Justice Douglas, Black, Murphy, Rutledge dissenting 538; *United States v Paramount Pictures* 334 U.S. 131 (1948) 159, 162, 164–165.

[118] *United States v Alcoa* 148 F.2d 416 (2d Cir. 1945) 427.

[119] ibid 429; *United States v United Shoe Machinery Corp.* 110 F. Supp. 295 (D. Mass. 1953) 342.

[120] *Dr. Miles Medical Co. v John D. Park & Sons Co.* 220 U.S. 373 (1911) 408. This hostile attitude towards vertical restraints is grounded in the ancient common law doctrine of 'restraints on alienation'. E Coke, *Institutes of the Laws of England* (1628).

of small, independent businessmen also manifested themselves in the application of antitrust law to unilateral conduct. During the tenure of Chief Justice Warren (the so-called Warren Court (1953–1969)), the Supreme Court's interpretation of section 2 of the Sherman Act and section 2(a) of the Robinson-Patman Act in predatory and geographic price discrimination cases – such as *Moore v Mead's Fine Bread* and *Utah Pie* – was also driven by concerns about the adverse impact of aggressive price cutting by large-scale corporations on the livelihood of smaller, local competitors.[121] The egalitarian ideal of republican liberty also had an important bearing on merger control during the Warren Court era and prompted the Court to prohibit even mergers with a combined market share of less than 10 per cent.[122] In *Brown Shoe*, the Supreme Court went as far as to suggest that, even though the Clayton Merger Act sought to protect 'competition, not competitors',[123] it could not

> fail to recognise Congress' desire to promote competition through the protection of viable, small, locally owned businesses. Congress appreciated that occasional higher costs and prices might result from the maintenance of fragmented industries and markets. It resolved these competing considerations in favor of decentralization.[124]

ii. Republican Antitrust and EU Case Law

The egalitarian impetus of the Ordoliberal understanding of economic liberty in its republican sense as non-domination also left an important imprint on the formative era of EU competition law.

The republican concern about the adverse impact of hierarchies and subordination on the status of independence of market participants, for instance, explains the restrictive approach of EU competition law toward vertical restraints. In a similar vein as the US Supreme Court's *Dr. Miles* ruling, the strict treatment of vertical restraints by the European Commission and the Court of Justice under Article 101 TFEU was grounded in the view that they tend to curtail the freedom and equal status of independent retailers.[125] This concern about preserving the independent status and equality of opportunity of traders carried particular weight in cases involving vertical restraints that hindered distributors from

[121] *Moore v Mead's Fine Bread Co.* 348 U.S. 115 (1954) 119; *Utah Pie Co. v Continental Baking Co.* 386 U.S. 685 (1967) 689.

[122] In *Brown Shoe* and *Pabst Brewing* the parties held a combined market share of less than 5%. *Brown Shoe Co. Inc. v United States* 370 U.S. 294 (1962) 328, 331–334, 343–344; *United States v Pabst Brewing Co.* 384 U.S. 546 (1966) 550–552. In *Von's Grocery* the combined market share of the merged entity was around 7.5%. *United States v Von's Grocery Co.* 384 U.S. 270 (1966) 272–273.

[123] *Brown Shoe Co. Inc. v United States* (n 122) 320, 344.

[124] ibid 344.

[125] See, for instance, the Case 56/64 *Consten and Grundig v Commission of the EEC* ECLI:EU:C:1966:41 at 342; Case 32/78 *BMW Belgium v Commission* ECLI:EU:C:1979:191 para 36; Case 86/82 *Hasselblad v Commission* ECLI:EU:C:1984:65 para 46.

engaging in parallel trade between EU Member States. Following *Consten and Grundig*, the Commission and the EU Courts consistently condemned vertical restraints, which entailed a de facto ban on parallel imports by independent distributors, as a restriction of competition by object.[126] This hostile approach against vertical restrictions of parallel trade reflects the fundamental role of small, independent traders as 'heroes'[127] and driving forces of European economic integration. The strict enforcement of Article 101 TFEU against vertical restraints is testament to the Commission's and judiciary's attempt to ensure that the gains of market integration are not exclusively reaped by large-scale companies. It was aimed at preserving the opportunities of small, independent traders to also engage in cross-border trade and benefit from the growing interpenetration of previously national markets. At the same time, protecting the economic opportunities of small, independent traders to engage in cross-border trade was perceived as being in the interest of consumers who would benefit from lower prices resulting from greater dealer competition.[128]

A second area of EU competition law where the influence of the egalitarian Ordoliberal understanding of economic liberty and competition had a long-standing and palpable impact is the abuse of dominance case law under Article 102 TFEU. The Ordoliberal distinction between performance-based and hindrance-based competition shaped the Court of Justice's interpretation of the prohibitive scope of Article 102 TFEU.[129] In *Hoffmann-La Roche* and subsequent cases, the Court defined the concept of abuse of a dominant position as unilateral conduct by a dominant firm that adversely affects the competitive market structure through methods other than 'normal competition'[130] or 'competition on the merits'[131] based on 'economic performance'.[132] By juxtaposing normal performance competition with methods having the 'effect of hindering'[133] competition, the Court reverted to the Ordoliberal distinction between performance-based and hindrance competition to define when dominant firm conduct unfairly undermines the competitive opportunities of smaller competitors.[134] Based on this distinction, the Court consistently condemned dominant firm conduct that tends to make it more difficult for smaller firms to compete at arm's length – such as tying, predatory pricing,

[126] Case 56/64 *Consten and Grundig v Commission of the EEC* (n 125) at 344; Case C-439/09 *Pierre Fabre Dermo-Cosmétique* ECLI:EU:C:2011:649 paras 47, 53–54.

[127] L Gyselen, 'Vertical Restraints in the Distribution Process: Strength and Weakness of the Free-Rider Rationale under EEC Competition Law' (1984) 21 *Common Market Law Review* 647.

[128] Case 56/64 *Consten and Grundig v Commission of the EEC* (n 125) at 343.

[129] H Schweitzer, 'Parallels and Differences in the Attitudes towards Single-Firm Conduct: What are the Reasons? The History, Interpretation and Underlying Principles of Sec. 2 Sherman Act and Art. 82 EC' (2007) EUI Law Working Paper 32/2007, ssrn.com/abstract=1093248. See also Deutscher (n 59).

[130] Case 85/76 *Hoffmann-La Roche v Commission* ECLI:EU:C:1979:36 para 90.

[131] Case T-228/97 *Irish Sugar v Commission* ECLI:EU:T:1999:246 para 111; Case C-202/07 P *France Télécom v Commission* ECLI:EU:C:2009:214 paras 44–45.

[132] Case 322/81 *Michelin v Commission* ECLI:EU:C:1983:313 para 70.

[133] Case 85/76 *Hoffmann-La Roche v Commission* (n 130) para 91.

[134] See, for instance J Kallaugher and B Sher, 'Rebates Revisited: Anti-Competitive Effects and Exclusionary Abuse Under Article 82' (2004) 25 *European Competition Law Review* 263, 268–272.

exclusive dealing, and rebates – as obstacles to economic opportunities of smaller, independent competitors.[135] The Court of Justice thereby attributed little weight to the assessment of the efficiency of the harmed competitors. On the contrary, the EU judiciary even found above-cost price cuts by dominant firms to be in breach of Article 102, although economists would suggest that they are unlikely to foreclose equally efficient competitors from the market.[136]

The egalitarian concern about power imbalances and their adverse effect on the economic opportunities of smaller rivals also underpins the principle that a dominant firm has a 'special responsibility not to allow its conduct to impair genuine undistorted competition on the common market'.[137] This principle prohibits dominant firms from engaging in conduct that risks further marginalising residual competition, cementing economic concentration, and increasing the dependence of market participants on the arbitrary will of the dominant firm.[138] The principle of special responsibility acknowledges the asymmetry in power and inequality of arms that exists between dominant firms and non-dominant rivals. It seeks to address the fact that certain business conduct by dominant firms may have an exclusionary effect on other market participants, while this is not the case if non-dominant firms adopt the same course of action.[139]

The principle of special responsibility thus recognises that certain conduct bestows dominant firms with a competitive advantage that non-dominant firms cannot possibly replicate. This inequality of arms is not necessarily caused by different degrees of efficiencies but might be the result of the mere difference in scale, scope, and financial resources between dominant firms and smaller competitors. In some abuse of dominance cases, the Court of Justice made this close link between the special responsibility of dominant firms and the equality of opportunity of smaller rivals even more explicit. The Court of Justice repeatedly stressed 'that a system of undistorted competition … can be guaranteed only if equality of opportunity is secured as between the various economic operators'.[140] The republican understanding of liberty as equal freedom of market participants is thus

[135] Case 40/73 *Suiker Unie and Others v Commission* ECLI:EU:C:1975:174 para 502; Case 85/76 *Hoffmann-La Roche v Commission* (n 130) paras 89–90; Case C-62/86 *AKZO v Commission* ECLI:EU:C:1991:286 para 149; Case T-83/91 *Tetra Pak v Commission (Tetra Pak II)* ECLI:EU:T:1994:246 paras 135, 137–140.

[136] Case T-30/89 *Hilti v Commission* ECLI:EU:T:1991:70 para 100; Case T-228/97 *Irish Sugar v Commission* (n 131) paras 117–124, 215–225; Case C-395/96 P *Compagnie Maritime Belge Transports and Others v Commission* ECLI:EU:C:2000:132 paras 115–119.

[137] Case 322/81 *Michelin v Commission* ECLI:EU:C:1983:313 para 57.

[138] Case 6/72 *Europemballage Corporation and Continental Can Company v Commission* ECLI:EU:C:1973:22 para 26; Case C-395/96 P *Compagnie Maritime Belge Transports and Others v Commission* (n 136) para 113.

[139] See, for instance, Case 27/76 *United Brands v Commission* ECLI:EU:C:1978:22 para 189; Case C-333/94 P *Tetra Pak v Commission* ECLI:EU:C:1996:436 para 37; Case C-202/07 P *France Télécom v Commission* (n 131) paras 105–106.

[140] See, for instance, Case C-18/88 *RTT v GB-Inno-BM* ECLI:EU:C:1991:474 para 25; Case C-49/07 *MOTOE* ECLI:EU:C:2008:376 para 51; Case C-280/08 P *Deutsche Telekom v Commission* ECLI:EU:C:2010:603 para 233.

deeply engraved in the normative fabric of Article 102 TFEU in particular and EU competition law more generally.

The egalitarian concern about the adverse impact of excessive industry concentration on the opportunities of smaller competitors also had important implications for EU merger policy. To be sure, competition law in Europe never displayed the same hostility towards merger-driven industry consolidation as US antitrust law during the Warren Court era. On the contrary, the European Commission and the Member States perceived international mergers as an important driving force of European market integration and a source of efficiencies and international competitiveness.[141] This, however, does not mean that concerns about industry concentration and its potentially detrimental impact on the survival of small businesses have been extraneous to EU merger control. Already in the 1960s, the Commission expressed the fear that excessive industry concentration through mergers would impair the competitive opportunities of small and medium-sized enterprises (SMEs).[142] The Commission thus viewed the creation of an effective merger control regime as an essential tool to ensure that merger-driven industry concentration would not thwart the equality of opportunity of independent SMEs,[143] which constitutes an important feature of economic freedom guaranteed under EU competition law.[144] At the same time, the Commission also stressed the adverse distributive consequences of excessive industry concentration for consumers[145] and workers.[146]

This objective of keeping industrial concentration in check also underpins the EC Merger Regulation 4064/89, as well as the revised EU Merger Regulation 139/2004. Both texts direct the Commission to assess mergers with respect to their 'effect on the structure of competition'[147] rather than their impact on consumer or total welfare. The egalitarian impetus of this structuralist goal of EU merger control also transpires from the early EU merger case law. In *Aerospatiale-Alenia/*

[141] European Commission, 'Le problème de la concentration dans le marché commun: The problem of concentration in the Common Market.' (1966). Information Memo P-1/66, www.aei.pitt.edu/40303/, 7–8. The following discussion draws on Deutscher (n 59).

[142] ibid 5, 9, 11, 26; IXth Report on Competition Policy (1979) 9–10; A Witt, *The More Economic Approach to EU Antitrust Law* (Oxford, Hart Publishing, 2016) 96.

[143] VIIth Report on Competition Policy (1977) 10–11; XIIth Report on Competition Policy (1982) 13; Commission Proposal Concerning the Control of Mergers – Information Memo P-37/73, July 1973 at 1.

[144] Commission Proposal Concerning the Control of Mergers – Information Memo P-37/73, July 1973 (n 143) 1.

[145] Proposal for a Regulation (EEC) of the Council on the Control of Concentrations between Undertakings 1973 COM (73) 1210 final 6.

[146] Commission Proposal Concerning the Control of Mergers – Information Memo P-37/73, July 1973 (n 143) 6.

[147] Council Regulation (EEC) No 4064/89 on the Control of Concentrations between Undertakings [1989] OJ L395/1 recitals 7, 9; Council Regulation (EC) No 139/2004 on the Control of Concentrations between Undertakings [2004] OJ L24/1 recitals 6, 8.

de Havilland the Commission, for instance, raised concerns about a merger between the two leading producers of regional aircraft inter alia because of its adverse effects on the competitive opportunities of smaller customers[148] and competitors[149] even though the latter were less efficient than the merged entity.

The Ordoliberal ideals of republican economic liberty and equality of opportunity thus fundamentally shaped the interpretation of all three substantive areas of EU competition law. The history of the Ordoliberal influence on EU competition law and the existing case law call into doubt misguided attempts to associate EU competition law with a 'big is good tradition'.[150] On the contrary, until the late 1990s, concerns about the negative impact of excessive economic concentration and imbalances of power on the equality of opportunity of small and independent competitors played a prominent role in EU competition law.

IV. The Decline of the Symbiotic Relationship between Competition and Equality

For centuries, the monopoly regressivity and competition equality theses shaped the economic and political thinking about competitive markets. The previous sections show that this republican understanding of competition as a catalyst and safeguard of economic liberty as non-domination and equal opportunities importantly influenced US antitrust until the 1970s and EU competition law until the late 1990s. Since then, the egalitarian understanding of competition cultivated by the republican antitrust paradigms in the US and in the EU has faded away. From the 1970s onwards, the Chicago and post-Chicago antitrust paradigms started to disparage concerns about equality of opportunity and distributive effects of economic concentration as 'antitrust populism'.[151] With the shift towards the so-called 'more economic approach' in the late 1990s and early 2000s,[152] the egalitarian impetus of competition law also started to dwindle in Europe. This section seeks to answer a simple question: How can we explain this decline of the monopoly regressivity and competition equality theses that underpinned the egalitarian thrust of the republican antitrust tradition on both sides of the Atlantic?

[148] Case No IV/M.053 Aerospatiale-Alenia/de Havilland [1991] OJ L334/42 paras 46, 70.

[149] ibid paras 30–33, 69.

[150] See for a recent version of this claim, N Petit, 'Competition Cases Involving Platforms – Lessons from Europe: Comment on Federal Trade Commission ("FTC") Hearing #3 on Competition and Consumer Protection in the 21st Century' (2018), www.ftc.gov/system/files/documents/public_comments/2018/10/ftc-2018-0088-d-0011-156146.pdf, 3.

[151] Posner (n 4) 23–28.

[152] Witt (n 142).

A. The Chicagoan Critique of the Republican Antitrust Tradition

The demise of the egalitarian dimension of competition is the combined effect of the failures of the republican antitrust approach and the rise of the Chicago and post-Chicago approaches to antitrust law. From the 1960s onwards, the Chicago scholars made the case that concerns about the protection of the economic liberty and opportunities of small businesses, in particular during the Warren Court era, had led antitrust policy astray. Cases such as *Utah Pie*[153] and *Brown Shoe*[154] served the Chicago School as emblematic examples of how concerns about equality of opportunity may lead to a situation where antitrust law, under the banner of economic liberty, accused larger businesses 'not of injuring competition but, quite simply, of competing'.[155] The Chicago Scholars pointed out that the republican antitrust approach had omitted to provide a principled framework that allowed competition authorities, courts, and businesses to distinguish between situations when the deterioration of competitors' equality of opportunity must be regarded as the result of legitimate competition, and when it must be sanctioned as an undue exercise of single or collective monopoly power.[156] Central to the Chicagoan critique was the argument that the failure of republican antitrust to formulate a clear limiting principle, which defines when the intervention of antitrust law is necessary and legitimate to preserve the economic liberty and equality of opportunity of small competitors, frustrated the negative economic liberty of efficient firms. The 'market egalitarianism'[157] of republican antitrust was hence increasingly perceived as a burdensome constraint on the entrepreneurial liberty notably of large-scale firms, as it seemed to justify or even compel continuous state interference with the commercial freedom of efficient businesses.

Against this backdrop, the Chicago School made three inter-related points that shook up the monopoly regressivity and competition equality theses underpinning the republican antitrust building. First, the Chicago School drove a wedge between the equality of opportunity of competitors and positive distributive outcomes for consumers that the republican tradition assumed to be largely aligned. The Chicago School contended that the egalitarian thrust of the republican antitrust approach not only stifled efficiencies and reduced consumer welfare but also had unfair distributive consequences. Chicagoans indeed asserted that republican antitrust was inherently unfair, as it abused competition law as a 'protectionist'[158] tool to guarantee the livelihood and privileges of a small, inefficient, relatively

[153] *Utah Pie Co. v Continental Baking Co.* (n 121).
[154] *Brown Shoe Co. Inc. v United States* (n 122).
[155] Bork (n 4) 387.
[156] A Director and EH Levi, 'Law and the Future: Trade Regulation' (1956) 51 *Northwestern University Law Review* 281.
[157] Bork (n 4) 216.
[158] RH Bork and WS Bowman Jr, 'The Crisis in Antitrust' (1965) 65 *Columbia Law Journal* 363, 364.

affluent, and predominantly white class of independent businesses at the expense of the great majority of consumers.[159] The Chicago School thus managed to portray republican antitrust and its concern about the equality of opportunity as an aberration, or even worse, the product of regulatory capture by a small – albeit influential – social group.[160] Second, by unpicking the methodological shortcomings of the Harvard School's S-C-P paradigm and highlighting the efficiency- and welfare-enhancing characteristics of firm size and industry concentration,[161] the Chicago School also debunked the assumption informing the monopoly regressivity thesis that greater industry concentration inevitably entails adverse distributive consequences for consumers.[162] Third, the Chicagoans cast doubt on the regressive distributive incidence of wealth transfers from consumers to producers to further weaken the monopoly regressivity thesis. Most notably, they pointed out that consumers tend to benefit from increases in producer surplus as they often own stocks, for instance through private wealth funds and pension schemes, and observed that producers are not necessarily always wealthier than consumers.[163]

Table 1.2 below depicts the fundamental transformation of thinking about competition and equality brought about by the Chicago School. On the one hand, the Chicago School cast doubt on the competition equality thesis which lay at the heart of the century-old idea that equality of opportunity between competitors is necessarily conducive to a more equal and fair distribution of resources in the interest of consumers. The Chicago scholarship showed, instead, that greater equality amongst competitors may have undesired distributive outcomes for society, as consumers will have to foot the bill for the preservation of an economy composed of many, yet inefficient, small and independent businesses (see upper right-hand quadrant in Table 1.2). On the other, they also sought to discredit the monopoly regressivity thesis, pointing out that concentration of market power and, hence, inequality of opportunities between competitors, may bring about distributive outcomes in the interest of consumers (see lower left-hand quadrant in Table 1.2).

Table 1.2 The relationship between equality of opportunity and distributive equality: the shift from republican to laissez-faire antitrust

	Positive distributive effects for consumers	Negative distributive effects for consumers
Equality of opportunity	Republican antitrust	Chicago School
Inequality of opportunity	Chicago School	Republican antitrust

[159] ibid 375–376.

[160] ibid 376.

[161] Director and Levi (n 156) 282, 285–286; Bork (n 4) 163–197. H Demsetz, 'Two Systems of Belief About Monopoly' in HJ Goldschmid, HM Mann, JF Weston (eds), *Industrial Concentration: The New Learning* (Boston, Little Brown, 1974) 166–174.

[162] Bork and Bowman (n 158) 368–369; Bork (n 4) 196–197; Posner (n 4) 113–116; Y Brozen, 'The Concentration-Collusion Doctrine' (1977) 46 *Yale Law Journal* 826, 827–831.

[163] Bork (n 4) 110–113; Posner (n 4) 21–24.

B. The Politics of the Consumer Welfare Standard: The Operationalisation of Negative Economic Liberty

The Chicago School also burst the close bond between liberty and equality that underpins the republican understanding of (economic) liberty as equal freedom and equality of status. Chicago Scholars defied the republican tradition which for centuries assumed that competitive markets would maximise liberty and equality as two dimensions of the very same concept of republican liberty. Instead, the Chicago School made the case that the pursuit of equality of opportunity through antitrust law would inextricably lead to excessive state interference with efficient business conduct and hence destroy negative entrepreneurial liberty. Unlike the republican tradition, which associated equality of opportunity with liberty and inequality of opportunity with unfreedom, the Chicago scholars posited that the promotion of equality of opportunity may destroy liberty, while inequality of opportunity may well be compatible with greater economic liberty (Table 1.3).

Table 1.3 The changing understanding of the relationship between liberty and equality

	Liberty	Unfreedom
Equality of opportunity	Republican antitrust	Chicago School
Inequality of opportunity	Chicago School	Republican antitrust

In short, Chicago scholars showed that what the republican antitrust tradition regarded as largely complementary or even synonymous goals of competition law were, in reality, often in stark conflict with each other. This tension between conflicting social and economic goals was, in the eyes of the Chicago scholars, the very reason for the 'crisis in antitrust'[164] as it would inevitably lead to inconsistent policy outcomes. To overcome this crisis, the Chicago School advocated a simple solution: namely, to purge antitrust law from ideological concerns about liberty, equality, and wealth distribution[165] and supersede them with the purportedly clear, precise, and unique goal of (consumer) welfare.[166] The adoption of welfare maximisation as the exclusive policy objective, Chicagoans argued, would ground antitrust law in the inherently coherent and logical axioms of neoclassical price theory, which would ensure the consistency of a workable and sound antitrust policy.[167]

Unlike what Chicago scholars and contemporary advocates of the consumer welfare standard tend to claim,[168] the Chicagoan welfare standard is anything but value-free and neutral in distributive terms. All to the contrary. The welfare standard served the Chicago School as a framework to replace the republican

[164] Bork and Bowman (n 158).

[165] Bork (n 4) 110–113; Posner (n 4) 23–29.

[166] RH Bork, 'The Goals of Antitrust Policy' (1967) 57 *The American Economic Review* 242, 244–246; Bork (n 4) 90–129.

[167] Bork (n 4) 5, 8, 91, 116–129.

[168] See, for instance, AD Melamed and N Petit, 'The Misguided Assault on the Consumer Welfare Standard in the Age of Platform Markets' (2019) 54 *Review of Industrial Organization* 741, 747.

conception of economic liberty as non-domination and equal status with a negative understanding of economic liberty that perceives any form of state intervention as coercion. Indeed, the welfare standard allowed the Chicago scholars to clearly and narrowly delineate those – in their view – rare instances in which businesses' unbridled exercise of negative economic liberty unduly interferes with the economic freedom of other market participants.[169] Using the welfare standard as the new normative benchmark, Chicagoans contended that this is only the case if business conduct interferes with the economic choices or opportunities of another market participant in such a way that it entails a deadweight loss due to a restriction of output (in the case of the total welfare standard, which was nevertheless mischaracterised by Bork as the consumer welfare standard)[170] or a reduction in consumer surplus (in the case of a genuine consumer welfare standard, also known as the consumer surplus standard). The welfare standard thus aligned the ideal of economic liberty protected by antitrust law with a very narrow concept of negative liberty, which perceives only welfare-reducing interference as a source of unfreedom. By contrast, domination flowing from the mere presence of concentrated economic power or from imbalances of power, opportunities, and wealth, which republican antitrust was concerned about, no longer qualified as obstacles to economic liberty that should alarm antitrust policy.

The Chicago School's paramount concern about preserving negative entrepreneurial liberty becomes most apparent in its approach towards error costs. The Chicago School coined the notion that the costs of over-enforcement (type 1 errors or false positives) always tend to exceed the costs resulting from underenforcement (type 2 errors or false negatives) of antitrust law.[171] The Chicago School warned that erroneous antitrust intervention has two forms of costs. On the one hand, the erroneous decision itself creates costs as it mistakenly prohibits efficient business conduct. On the other hand, false positives also create costs through deterrence, as other or future market players will also be dissuaded from engaging in efficient, welfare-enhancing conduct.[172] The costs of false positives, the Chicago School claimed, are in general high because even small gains in productive efficiencies are sufficient to outweigh substantial price increases.[173] This is because erroneously deterred efficient practices would reduce the costs of production for every unit across the whole range of industry output, while monopolistic practices only affect the fraction of industry output controlled by the alleged perpetrator firm(s).[174] At the same time, the Chicago School also cemented the view that the costs of false negatives tend to be low. This proposition was grounded

[169] See for a similar argument RJ Peritz, 'A Counter-History of Antitrust Law' (1990) 39 *Duke Law Journal* 263, 299–311; EM Fox, 'The Modernization of Antitrust: A New Equilibrium' (1980) 66 *Cornell Law Review* 1140, 1156–1157. For a more detailed exposition of this argument, see Deutscher (n 59).

[170] Bork (n 4) 110–113; Posner (n 4) 23–24.

[171] Bork (n 4) 143–144; FH Easterbrook, 'The Limits of Antitrust' (1984) 63 *Texas Law Review* 1, 15.

[172] Easterbrook (n 171) 15. See also for an insightful analysis of these two channels, J Broulík, 'Preventing Anticompetitive Conduct Directly and Indirectly: Accuracy Versus Predictability' (2019) 64 *The Antitrust Bulletin* 115, 120, 122.

[173] Easterbrook (n 171) 16.

[174] ibid 15–16.

in the assumption that markets would easily self-correct false negatives (ie erroneously acquitted anticompetitive, output-reducing behaviour), whereas judicial and legislative processes are unlikely to rectify judicial errors taking the form of false condemnations. While market entry will remedy undetected monopolistic practices, the potential efficiencies foregone by reason of mistaken inferences about the anticompetitive nature of a specific conduct will be forever lost.[175] The Chicago School thus entrenched the notion that the real problem of antitrust enforcement lies not in the risk that some instances of anticompetitive conduct go unchallenged but in the danger that efficient and aggressive competitive conduct is erroneously classified as anticompetitive.[176] In case of doubt, antitrust law should, therefore, err on the side of type 2 errors and the negative liberty of powerful firms.[177]

The assumption that state intervention tends in most cases to be more expensive than 'doing nothing'[178] and that type 2 errors are, therefore, preferable to type 1 errors, provided the Chicago School with a powerful economic argument in support of shielding the negative entrepreneurial liberty of alleged perpetrator firms against antitrust intervention. The Chicago School error-cost framework, indeed, puts some economic gloss on the assumption that in most cases the loss in commercial liberty suffered by powerful businesses as a consequence of antitrust intervention is not outweighed by any gains in the liberty and welfare of other market participants, in particular consumers, that would justify such state interference in the first place.[179] The Chicagoan welfare standard and error-cost framework thus encode a balance of rights, which is clearly geared towards preserving the negative liberty of businesses against state intervention. They thus provided the blueprint for a 'laissez-faire' antitrust approach whose ultimate aim is to insulate to the largest extent possible the entrepreneurial liberty of corporations against antitrust intervention. The Chicagoan endorsement of a laissez-faire approach also had important distributive implications as it slanted antitrust enforcement in a way that, in the case of doubt, condones the redistribution of wealth from consumers and competitors to corporate antitrust defendants.

C. The Chicago Laissez-Faire Antitrust Approach and the New Equilibrium

The impact of the Chicago School thought on US and EU competition law can hardly be overstated.[180] The precepts of the Chicagoan antitrust framework were

[175] ibid.
[176] Bork (n 4) 157.
[177] Easterbrook (n 171) 16.
[178] Coase, 'The Problem of Social Cost' (1960) 3 *Journal of Law and Economics* 1, 18.
[179] Bork (n 4) 134–135, 143–144, 157, 196.
[180] See also ch 2 in this volume for a similar account. See, however, A Bradford, AS Chilton and FM Lancieri, 'The Chicago School's Limited Influence on International Antitrust' (2020) 87 *The University of Chicago Law Review* 297.

wholeheartedly endorsed by the US Supreme Court.[181] The Chicago consensus on the welfare standard and error-cost framework also found growing support among practitioners and academics in Europe.[182] Albeit to a lesser extent than in the US, the Chicagoan laissez-faire antitrust framework had, with the rise of the so-called 'more economic approach', an important bearing on the thinking and case law of the EU Commission[183] and courts[184] during the late 2000s onwards.

How has this shift from a republican to a Chicago-inspired laissez-faire antitrust paradigm on both sides of the Atlantic affected markets and the distribution of wealth? To this date, existing studies only provide, at best, tentative answers to this question. What recent economic research, however, seems to suggest is that the Chicago School laissez-faire approach has definitely delivered on its promise of freeing big business from the strictures of antitrust (and other) regulation. A number of recent studies show that the industry concentration, price-cost margins, and corporate profits in numerous US and, at least to some extent, EU industries have soared over the last decades.[185] A growing number of economists and antitrust experts see this increase in industry concentration as a symptom of a decline in competition and a slow-down in business dynamism.[186] The relaxation of competition law enforcement under the auspices of the Chicago movement and its acolytes during the last decades, in particular in the US, is seen as an important cause of growing industry concentration.[187]

This rise in industry concentration and the ensuing accumulation of economic and political[188] power in the hand of a few powerful corporations are also

[181] See for the endorsement of the consumer welfare standard *Reiter v Sonotone Corp.* 442 U.S. 330 (1979) 343. See for the endorsement of the Chicagoan error-cost framework *Verizon Communications Inc. v Law Offices of Curtis Trinko* 540 U.S. 398 (2004) 407, 414.

[182] See for instance AJ Padilla and C Ahlborn, 'From Fairness to Welfare: Implications for the Assessment of Unilateral Conduct under EC Competition Law' in C-D Ehlermann and M Marquis (eds), *European Competition Law Annual 2007: A Reformed Approach to Article 82 EC* (Oxford, Hart Publishing, 2008); C Ahlborn, DS Evans and AJ Padilla, 'The Antitrust Economics of Tying: A Farewell to Per se Illegality' (2004) 49 *The Antitrust Bulletin* 287.

[183] See, for instance, Guidelines on the application of Art 81(3) of the Treaty [2004] OJ C101/97 para 24.

[184] See for recent endorsements of the consumer welfare standard Case C-67/13 P *Groupement des cartes bancaires v Commission* ECLI:EU:C:2014:2204 para 51; Case C-377/20 *Servizio Elettrico Nazionale and Others* ECLI:EU:C:2022:379 para 46. See, for instance, with respect to error costs opinion of Advocate General Wahl in Case C-177/16 *Biedrība 'Autortiesību un komunicēšanās konsultāciju aģentūra – Latvijas Autoru apvienība' Konkurences padome (AKKA)* ECLI:EU:C:2017:286 para 117.

[185] Bajgar et al (n 2); Autor et al (n 2); De Loecker, Eeckhout and Unger (n 2). See also the other studies cited in n 3.

[186] Council of Economic Advisers to the US President (n 3) 4–5; Decker et al (n 3); Philippon (n 2). See also the other studies cited in n 3.

[187] See, for instance, S Peltzman, 'Industrial Concentration under the Rule of Reason' (2014) 57 *The Journal of Law and Economics* 101; Council of Economic Advisers to the US President (n 3) 6–7, 9; O Ashenfelter, D Hosken and M Weinberg, 'Did Robert Bork Understate the Competitive Impact of Mergers? Evidence from Consummated Mergers' (2014) 57 *The Journal of Law and Economics* 67; JE Kwoka Jr, *Mergers, Merger Control, and Remedies: A Retrospective Analysis of U.S. Policy* (Cambridge, MA, MIT Press, 2015).

[188] JB Baker, 'Market Power in the U.S. Economy Today' (2017) www.equitablegrowth.org/market-power-in-the-u-s-economy-today/, 10; Stiglitz (n 3) 16; Z Teachout and LM Khan, 'Market Structure

increasingly perceived as a driver of growing economic inequalities.[189] Provided the studies are correct in finding a relationship between the relaxation of antitrust rules, rising corporate power and inequality levels, the implicit bias of laissez-faire antitrust in favour of the entrepreneurial liberty and interests of large-scale corporations appears to have had palpable distributive consequences. If this is the case, the adoption of the Chicagoan laissez-faire approach moved us toward a state of affairs against which the republican antitrust paradigm has always guarded: namely, a new equilibrium where markets neither promote equality of opportunity nor the distributive equality of wealth in the interest of consumers (depicted in the bottom right quadrant of Table 1.4 below). The rise of Chicago-style laissez-faire antitrust thus largely hollowed out the competition equality thesis that lay for centuries at the core of republican thought about competitive markets.

Table 1.4 The new equilibrium: less equality of opportunity and distributive equality in the interest of consumers

	Positive distributive effects for consumers	Negative distributive effects for consumers
Equality of opportunity	Republican antitrust	Chicago School
Inequality of opportunity	Chicago School	The new equilibrium (Republican antitrust)

Recent studies on rising corporate power and inequality not only suggest that the shift towards laissez-faire antitrust under the auspices of the Chicago School has driven a wedge between competitive markets and equality. Rather, they also provide new evidence in support of the monopoly regressivity and competition equality theses that Chicago scholarship claimed to have successfully debunked. Though the exact 'transmission mechanism'[190] between rising market power and inequality levels has yet to be conclusively determined, recent studies identify three complementary, albeit not always consistent, channels through which growing industry concentration and market power may contribute to greater inequality.

The first channel consists of the disparate distributive incidence of market power effects and the ensuing transfer of consumer surplus on different groups of consumers. A growing body of literature provides evidence that low-income households suffer greater welfare losses from market power effects, for instance in the form of higher prices, than high-income households. This is because

and Political Law: A Taxonomy of Power' (2016) 9 *Duke Journal of Constitutional Law and Public Policy* 37.

[189] Council of Economic Advisers to the US President (n 3) 2; Furman and Orszag (n 3); J Furman and P Orszag, 'Slower Productivity and Higher Inequality: Are They Related?' (2018) PIIE Working Paper 18-4, www.piie.com/publications/working-papers/slower-productivity-and-higher-inequality-are-they-related; Ennis, Gonzaga and Pike (n 3). See, however, Autor et al (n 2).

[190] A Zac et al, 'Competition Policy and the Decline of the Labour Share' (2021) ssrn.com/abstract=3824115, 4. See also for a review of the relevant literature ch 3 in this volume.

low-income households tend to have a smaller share in capital ownership and, therefore, benefit less from increased streams of profits or capital gains from market power than high-income households.[191] This disproportionate impact of market power on low-income households is even more pronounced when market power is exercised on essential, non-discretionary goods or services, such as groceries or fuel, on which low-income households tend to spend a much greater share of their disposable income than high-income households.[192] The growing literature on the regressive distributive incidence of market power on consumers thus casts doubt on the often-repeated Chicagoan claim that monopoly power does not have distributive effects because consumers indirectly benefit from gains in producer surplus through capital income, for instance as shareholders of firms through pension schemes.[193]

A second channel through which market power may drive or, at least, accentuate wealth inequalities is the decrease in the share of national income that goes to labour (the so-called 'labour share'), which is assumed to be more evenly distributed than capital income.[194] Several studies establish a direct link between the decline in the labour share and the steady rise in industry concentration and mark ups since the 1980s. They suggest that the decrease in the labour share is driven by the growing concentration of economic activity and mark ups in a few firms with a low labour share. The negative correlation between rising levels of mark ups and an industry-wide fall in labour share is explained by the firm's optimisation decision, which suggests that higher mark ups push firms to reduce their expenditure on inputs such as labour.[195] As increases in mark ups entail a reduction in aggregate output, they also lead to a reduction in demand for labour, notably for the low-skilled workforce.[196] The root causes of rising concentration levels and mark ups have, however, been explained in slightly divergent ways. Some studies suggest that rising concentration levels are the result of decreasing product market competition, notably due to a decline in antitrust enforcement following the Chicago School revolution since the 1980s.[197] Other studies, by contrast, attribute the rising concentration and mark up levels to intensified competitive pressure. In their account, globalisation, technological change and growing price sensitivity on the part of consumers have led to a 'winner takes most' competition and the rise

[191] WS Comanor and RH Smiley, 'Monopoly and the Distribution of Wealth' (1975) 89 *The Quarterly Journal of Economics* 177; Ennis and Kim (n 3); Ennis, Gonzaga and Pike (n 3); J Gans et al, 'Inequality and Market Concentration, When Shareholding is More Skewed than Consumption' (2019) 35 *Oxford Review of Economic Policy* 550.

[192] J Creedy and R Dixon, 'The Distributional Effects of Monopoly' (1999) 38 *Australian Economic Papers* 223.

[193] Posner (n 4) 23–24.

[194] Zac et al (n 190) 2.

[195] De Loecker, Eeckhout and Unger (n 2) 565–566.

[196] ibid 611.

[197] Gutiérrez and Philippon (n 2); G Gutiérrez and T Philippon, 'How EU Markets Became More Competitive Than US Markets: A Study of Institutional Drift' (2018) NBER Working Paper No 24700, www.nber.org/papers/w24700; Philippon (n 2).

of a few 'superstar firms' that benefit from greater scale and network effects.[198] Yet, even authors who ascribe the rise in industry concentration and market power to more rather than less competition do not exclude the possibility that the distributive effects of the rise of superstar firms might be further exacerbated by too lax an antitrust enforcement that fails to prevent successful superstar incumbents from erecting entry barriers.[199]

A third, slightly different, channel for the regressive impact of market power relates to the dispersion of labour income across firms. A number of studies show that income inequalities are driven to a lesser degree by the decrease in the aggregate labour share than by an increasingly unequal distribution of labour income between firms. That means employees performing the same job are remunerated differently depending on the firm they work for.[200] This unequal distribution of labour income coincides with an increasing concentration of economic activity and mark ups within the hands of a few firms that can at least in part be attributed to a relaxation of competition law enforcement.[201] An immediate consequence of growing industry concentration is an increasingly skewed distribution of revenues and profitability to the benefit of a few large firms. This, in turn, translates into disparate wages, as large firms are more likely to share some of their rents with their employees. These wage disparities may be further exacerbated when product market concentration also entails greater labour market concentration and strengthens the bargaining power of employers as workers have fewer opportunities to choose and move between jobs.[202] While the second and third channels appear at first sight to provide contradictory explanations for the adverse impact of industry concentration on the labour share, they might be complementary if they affect different groups of employees. That might be the case when the income of low-skilled workers or 'lower-level' employees declines with rising mark ups by virtue of firms' optimisation decision, while higher management will benefit from rent sharing.[203]

Recent studies on the channels through which industry concentration affects the labour share and entails labour income dispersion (ie the latter two channels above) also lend support to the republican belief that a competitive market structure enhances broad-based economic opportunity and, indirectly, secures a more even distribution of wealth. What has changed is that it is no longer only the individual economic opportunity of independent business(wo)men that is furthered by competitive markets, as it was believed by the idealised, pre-industrial account of competitive markets that shaped the republican thought about competitive

[198] Autor et al (n 2) 648–651.

[199] ibid 703–704.

[200] Furman and Orszag (n 189); J Song et al, 'Firming Up Inequality' (2019) 134 *The Quarterly Journal of Economics* 1; E Barth et al, 'It's Where You Work: Increases in the Dispersion of Earnings across Establishments and Individuals in the United States' (2016) 34 *Journal of Labor Economics* 67.

[201] Furman and Orszag (n 189) 10; Furman and Orszag (n 3) 35–38.

[202] Furman and Orszag (n 189) 11; Furman and Orszag (n 3) 38–42.

[203] I am indebted to Sean Ennis for this point.

markets and antitrust traditions. Rather, recent research suggests that a level competitive playing field and roughly equalised distribution of economic activity and profitability amongst firms affects through the transmission mechanism of labour remuneration the economic opportunities and distribution of wealth amongst employees and workers. Accordingly, a level playing field amongst firms may prevent abuses of market power that have regressive distributive effects on consumers and at the same time also enhance a more broad-based distribution of economic opportunities and wealth for independent businesses and workers.

The growing body of literature on the rise of corporate power and inequality also vindicate the crucial insight of the republican tradition that the procedural fairness and distributive outcomes of competitive markets are not just the 'godgiven' outcome of natural market forces, but are in part 'manmade' as they are shaped by the design of the legal framework in which markets operate.[204] This insight is even supported by studies that attribute rising consolidation and profitability levels to greater competitive pressure and the rise of superstar firms rather than a reduction in competition enabled by a decrease in antitrust enforcement. They point out that competition law enforcement may attenuate the distributive consequences of rising concentration levels by ensuring that superstar firms do not use their incumbency advantages to erect barriers to entry once they have won the 'winner takes more' race by virtue of their superior efficiency.[205] New research on the relationship between market power and inequality thus supports the republican view that growing concerns over yawning inequalities within our societies do not confront us with a stark choice between either greater equality *or* competitive markets. The real question is, instead, which type of competitive markets we want. In other words, whether we choose legal rules that skew market processes in favour of powerful incumbents or design rules that are conducive to greater equality of competitive opportunities and distributive equality. The history of republican thought about markets and its decline teaches us that these choices are above all political and, therefore, reversible. This raises the broader question of whether the revival of republican antitrust is possible to enhance a more egalitarian vision of competitive markets and, if so, whether it is desirable and what we are willing to sacrifice in the name of greater equality.

V. Conclusion

Recent studies suggesting a link between rising industry concentration, corporate power and inequality have fuelled a controversial academic and policy debate on the role of distributive equality for competition law. This debate largely turns around the question of whether and how market power undermines equality and

[204] For the 'manmade' versus 'natural' causes dichotomy used here, Furman and Orszag (n 189) 11; See also in this sense Smith (n 21) IV, ix, § 51, 687; Montesquieu (n 22), Book XX, Chapter XXII.

[205] Autor et al (n 2) 704.

whether and how competition law should address potential adverse implications of market power on inequality. This chapter goes beyond the current competition law and (in)equality debate by shedding new light on the conceptual foundations of the relationship between competitive markets and equality and their relevance for the design of competition law.

The belief that competitive markets enhance equality (competition equality thesis) and that monopoly power increases inequality (monopoly regressivity thesis) lies at the core of the contemporary competition law and equality debates. As shown by this chapter, both the competition equality and monopoly regressivity thesis can be traced back to the thought of early economic and political writers such as Thomas More, the English Levellers, Montesquieu, James Steuart, and Adam Smith. These thinkers celebrated the emergence of competitive markets because of their conduciveness towards greater socio-economic and political equality. Importantly, their egalitarian understanding of competitive markets was deeply rooted in a republican notion of economic liberty as non-domination and equal status. This republican understanding of competitive markets as institutional building blocks of a society of free and equals, the chapter shows, had an important influence on the formative era of US antitrust and the Ordoliberal foundations of EU competition law. The prominence of the competition equality and monopoly regressivity thesis started to wane with the rise of the Chicago School which replaced the egalitarian republican understanding of economic liberty with a narrow negative understanding of economic liberty that is largely agnostic about inequalities of economic opportunities, power, and wealth. The chapter dissects how the purportedly ideologically neutral welfare standard and the endorsement of a lopsided understanding of error costs coined by the Chicago School lay the groundwork for a 'laissez-faire antitrust' approach that is primarily concerned with protecting the negative entrepreneurial liberty of large firms from state interference. This laissez-faire approach has banned considerations about the equality of opportunity of competitors and the distributive incidence of economic concentration from the realm of modern antitrust policy.

The main takeaway of this chapter is that equality of opportunity and wealth played for centuries a central role in the liberal thought about competitive markets and the design of US and EU competition law. It also shows that the fact that this is no longer the case is, ultimately, an ideological choice which is all too often couched in the purportedly neutral concepts of welfare standards and error costs. By tracing the intellectual history of the competition equality and monopoly regressivity theses, the chapter highlights that this choice is not irreversible. Yet, though recent economic research seems to lend new support to the competition equality and monopoly regressivity theses, more research is needed to understand why and how rising concentration and corporate power drive inequality.[206]

[206] Autor et al (n 2); GJ Werden and LM Froeb, 'Don't Panic: A Guide to Claims of Increasing Concentration' (2018) 33 *Antitrust* 74.

While some studies indicate that the increase in concentration and inequality levels is the result of the relaxation of antitrust law following the Chicago School revolution in the 1980s and, therefore, 'manmade', others point towards 'natural' causes such as intensified 'winner takes most' competition and the rise of a few hyper-efficient superstar firms.[207] The insight that rising industry concentration and inequalities may be the result of a combination of 'manmade' and 'natural' causes poses intricate challenges for competition policy. Most fundamentally, it raises a number of far-reaching questions about the form and inclusiveness of innovation and growth we can expect competitive markets to generate. It also suggests that policymakers and judges will ultimately be confronted with the hard choice of deciding whether it is worthwhile to sacrifice some efficiency in the name of greater liberty, equality, and inclusiveness or vice versa. By exploring the history, implications and shortcomings of the contrasting views of republican and laissez-faire antitrust – namely, that competition law should promote liberty and equality vs competition law should enhance welfare – this chapter may offer some helpful normative considerations to decide in which direction the pendulum should swing.

[207] Furman and Orszag (n 189) 11.

2

Competition, Concentration, and Inequality through the Lens of the Theory of Reflexive Modernisation

JULIANE MENDELSOHN*

I. Introduction

The financial crisis of 2008 highlighted global inequality as one of the broader problems associated with our financial and economic systems and gave rise to powerful narratives such as the so-called 'one per cent'.[1] It is on these grounds that a new generation of economists, as well as social and legal theorists, have grown sceptical of the neoliberal models that form the foundation not only of financial market regulation, but also competition policy and other areas of economic governance.[2] Prominently, the work of Thomas Piketty shows persistent and growing levels of inequality in the historical evolution of income and wealth distribution.[3] Equally, Katharina Pistor's legal theory of finance shows how private law and its 'technologies' and institutions have operated over time to create power and 'privilege' attached to capital.[4] These findings and conclusions could seem to threaten an underlying assumption that legitimises competition as the primary process by which to allocate goods, namely that markets, over the short or long

* I would like to thank Jan Broulík and Katalin Cseres for the organisation of a thought-provoking conference on inequality in competition law and all its participants for insightful contributions. A special thank you goes to Jan Broulík for his guidance and invaluable comments on this chapter.

[1] See JE Stiglitz, 'Lessons from the Global Financial Crisis of 2008' (2010) 23 *Seoul Journal of Economics* 321.

[2] See the mission statement of the Institute for New Economic Thinking, New York, www.ineteconomics.org.

[3] See T Piketty, *Capital in the 21st Century* (Boston, Harvard University Press, 2014); T Piketty, *Capital and Ideology* (Boston, Harvard University Press, 2020).

[4] K Pistor, *The Code of Capital, How the Law Created Wealth and Inequality* (Princeton, Princeton University Press, 2019) 4; K Pistor, 'A Legal Theory of Finance' (2013) 41 *Journal of Comparative Economics* 315.

run, make societies better off and more equal. The perceived failure of markets to deliver these outcomes has nevertheless not led to a widely received critique or reformulation of competition law doctrine or a reconfiguration of competition law goals. Having regard to the prevalence of this critique in the overall discourse on the fairness and functioning of markets, this chapter attempts to articulate the precise way in which considerations of inequality challenge competition law, its goals, and functions.

While some competition law regimes explicitly formulate the alleviation of inequality as one of their goals – typically to meet other constitutional-economic goals that exist for specific structural or historic reasons, such as the agenda of black economic empowerment in South Africa,[5] the protection of competition and the furtherance of socio-economic goals are most commonly seen as being in tension with one another.[6] This chapter focuses mostly on the European Union where, despite the overarching treaty goal to 'promote … the wellbeing of its peoples' (Article 3(1) of the Treaty of the European Union (TEU)),[7] outright material or substantive equality goals are often said to be beyond the scope and outside of the rationality of competition law.[8] Since this points to a possible fundamental tension, this chapter investigates the paradox concerning the relationship between 'formal' or 'liberal' (allocative) and 'material' or 'substantive' (distributive) notions of justice, not only in law, but as a larger societal phenomenon.[9] In doing so it makes use of a theory of modernity known in sociology as 'reflexive modernisation' (see II). In addition, the theory of reflexive modernisation provides reason to believe that the exclusion of socio-economic or material goals (such as the alleviation of inequality) could threaten to undermine the very foundations and assumptions that legitimise free markets and competition in the first place.

To show this, this chapter is structured as follows: following this introduction, its second section looks at the phenomenon of inequality in modernity – in societies which postulated formal equality of all their persons. While the works of Piketty and Pistor deliver empirical and institutional evidence and explanations

[5] Act no 53 of 2003, The South African Broad-Based Black Economic Empowerment Act, Gazette No 25899, www.gov.za/sites/default/files/gcis_document/201409/a53-030.pdf; see also ch 6 in this volume; section IV.A of ch 4 in this volume; E Fox, 'South Africa, Competition Law and Equality: Restoring Equity by Antitrust in a Land Where Markets Were Brutally Skewed' (2019) *CPI Antitrust Chronicle*, www.competitionpolicyinternational.com/wp-content/uploads/2019/12/CPI-Fox.pdf.

[6] For a good wording, see R Whish and D Bailey, *Competition Law*, 10th edn (Oxford, Oxford University Press, 2021) ch 1.

[7] The CJEU expressly used the term 'consumer well-being' and not 'welfare' in its much-disputed *Österreichische Sparkasse* judgment. See Joined Cases T-213/01 and T-214/01 *Österreichische Postsparkasse AG and Bank für Arbeit und Wirtschaft AG v Commission of the European Communities* ECLI:EU:T:2006:151, [2006] ECR II-0160.

[8] Scepticism against social or distributive arguments in the private sphere was strongly expressed by Hayek: 'The whole idea behind distributive justice – that each individual ought to receive what he morally deserves – is meaningless … because the available product (its size, and even its existence) depends on what is in one sense a morally indifferent way of allocating its parts.' FA Hayek, *The Fatal Conceit*, vol 1 (WW Bartley ed, London, Routledge, 1988) 118. See also Whish and Bailey (n 6) 21.

[9] See Aristoteles, *Ethica Nikomachea* (I Bywater ed, Oxford, Oxford University Press, 1962) 1129a–1145a.

for rising inequality, this chapter addresses it through the lens of social theory and the philosophical foundations that underpin modern societies and capitalism. Here the so-called *discourse of modernity*[10] or *theory of reflexive modernisation*[11] postulates that the tension between (formal) freedom and (material) equality is the primary paradox of modernity. The theory of reflexive modernisation also goes beyond describing this paradox, to look at its effects. It suggests that neither position can ever truly trump the other and that instead modernity has become a highly reflexive process which constantly challenges its underlying assumptions (such as the belief in autonomy and equality of all persons). This process is not only reflexive and paradoxical, but also destructive. By not being able to abandon its liberal ideals but also becoming increasingly aware of their substantive shortcomings, modernity sets in motion a process which questions and undermines its own foundations (its promise of prosperity and equality). This is reflected in the suspicions of the 'demise of civil society' and 'creative destruction' already expressed in the works of Hegel and Schumpeter (see end of II, p 62).

The third section of this chapter turns to the debate on the goals of antitrust and competition law. It detects two opposed readings of the normative function of competition law. One that states that competition law only has the formal or liberal function of securing competition as a process and thus securing the market mechanism. The other argues that the original intent of competition law was to serve a distributive function and to serve material aims. The section uses the theory of reflexive modernisation to analyse the nature and causes of this highly polarised debate and suggests that there is value in accepting that there is an inherent and irresolvable paradox between the two positions.

The fourth section of this chapter then uses these theoretical findings to address one specific and recent manifestation of inequality: concentration of the digital economy. The 'per se' control of concentration was once central to competition law, but these structuralist foundations have eroded and given way to an analysis focussed on the overall efficiency effects and in turn, have grown ever less sceptical of concentration as such. With the rise of the tech giants, we are confronted with questions of concentration and 'bigness' anew. Since economic inequality refers to 'how economic variables are distributed – among individuals in a group, among groups in a population, or among countries',[12] the starting point for broader inequality considerations in competition law can be concentration and market power. While there is empirical evidence to suggest a correlation between overall industry concentration and inequality,[13] this chapter, again, turns to theoretical

[10] J Habermas, *The Philosophical Discourse of Modernity: Twelve Lectures* (F Lawrence tr, Jersey, Wiley, 1990).

[11] U Beck, A Giddens and S Lash (eds), *Reflexive Modernization: Politics, Tradition and Aesthetics in the Modern Social Order* (Cambridge, Polity Press, 1994).

[12] United Nations, 'Concept of Inequality' (2015) www.un.org/en/development/desa/policy/wess/wess_dev_issues/dsp_policy_01.pdf.

[13] SF Ennis, P Gonzaga and C Pike, 'Inequality: A Hidden Cost of Market Power' (2019) 35 *Oxford Review of Economic Policy* 518.

and philosophical arguments first put forward by Hegel and Schumpeter on the accumulation of wealth and resources in the hands of a few and the overall effects of this on the fibre that holds societies together. In line with the theory of reflexive modernisation, the section shows that the debate on concentration in the digital sphere is highly paradoxical and that it has become increasingly difficult to capture (quantify and legally identify) power and bigness at all. Lastly this chapter uses the ideas put forward by Hegel and Schumpeter to look at the possible dangers and equality effects of this elusive nature of digital concentration or digital bigness.

II. Reflexive Modernisation

While Piketty and Pistor deliver empirical and institutional evidence for growing inequality and postulate that the norms in place do not sufficiently close these gaps, this chapter turns to social theory (philosophy and sociology) to show why liberal doctrines and paradigms are at odds with – and oftentimes have almost a paradoxical relationship to – social goals and ideas of substantive or material justice. 'Modernity', as the term is used here, refers to the period in history since the Enlightenment.[14] The theory of reflexive modernisation relied upon here is used to explain larger structural changes in society in this period. It begins with a philosophical narrative of modernity (Hegel, Habermas) and feeds into later observations primarily put forward by sociologists who look at 'meta-changes, which are happening not within social structures but to them'.[15] In contrast to anthropology, sociology studies modern industrial rather than traditional societies: their systems of culture, economic realities and class structures and their relationship with language and nature. Sociology is thus an affirmation of the idea that modernity and the ideas of the Enlightenment – those of autonomy, individual or subjective rights, and the separation between public and private spheres – make modernity novel in ways that justify an isolated temporal field of study. In this chapter, a particular focus is placed on the invention, development and promise of the 'free market'.

While not mentioned or identified by all streams and types of sociology as such, to the extent that sociology looks at changes or meta-changes in society, it seems apt to differentiate between a first and second[16] or an early and a late modernity. The so-called *first modernity* begins with the normative force of the Enlightenment

[14] While this is a very broad use of the term, it is justified by the fact that the Enlightenment and the invention of autonomy and personhood fundamentally changed the structures of society and the social order.

[15] U Beck, W Bonß and C Lau, 'The Theory of Reflexive Modernization: Problematic, Hypotheses and Research Programme' (2003) 20 *Theory, Culture and Society* 1.

[16] Beck, Giddens and Lash (n 11); B Latour, *We Have Never Been Modern* (Boston, Harvard University Press, 1993); U Beck and W Bonß, *Die Modernisierung der Moderne* (Frankfurt am Main, Suhrkamp, 2001); M Auer, *Der privatrechtliche Diskurs der Moderne* (Tübingen, Mohr Siebeck, 2014); N Luhmann, *Die Gesellschaft der Gesellschaft*, vol 2 (Frankfurt am Main, Suhrkamp, 1998).

and belongs to the world of Immanuel Kant and Adam Smith, but also Thomas Hobbes and Hugo Grotius. As feudal social structures fell away, the individual and autonomous agent took centre stage. The first modernity is thus defined by the subjective rights of these individuals, who are by definition the agents of their own destiny, and by the formal assumption of equality of all persons.[17] It is the world in which civil society emerges as an entity that is wholly independent from the state; it creates and defines private institutions, and gives institutions such as the free market its normative force.[18] The first modernity and the ideas of Adam Smith are crucial for our thinking about competition: before Smith, free markets and economies did not exist in the way we know and speak of them today. From a legal perspective, this is the birthplace of subjective rights, the institutions of civil society (enterprise, the modern family), and the separation of public and private law.[19] The ideas of the first modernity are thus characterised by a high degree of individualisation and rationalisation.[20] These ideas gave rise to economies based on commercialisation, ever greater economic participation and the exploitation of natural resources.[21] While society at this time is still hierarchical and people are divided by classes and nation states, 'self-interest'[22] and an ever greater accumulation of wealth and resources gave rise to prosperity and trust in free markets, which remains largely unaltered today.

The course of modernity has not however been a linear projection of the ideas of the first modernity. In late modernity ever more cracks and insufficiencies start to show, and many begin to question whether liberal freedoms are attainable for large parts of society, and whether issues of material justice – equality and the reduction of poverty – are not too often left unquestioned in the name of liberal freedoms. One may look, for instance, at the atrocities committed in the name of the (western) nation state, ecological issues and the unsustainability of the economy, the presence of entrenched structures of economic power, and of entrenched and rising inequality. So looking, the limits and externalities of market and social

[17] Auer (n 16) 15.

[18] GWF Hegel, *Outlines of the Philosophy of Right* (first published 1821, TM Knox tr, S Houlgate ed, Oxford, Oxford University Press, 2008); in German: GWF Hegel, *Grundlinien der Natur des Rechts* (first published 1821, E Moldenhauer and KM Michel eds, Frankfurt am Main, Suhrkamp, 2004).

[19] Auer (n 16). For Beck this first modernity is the 'industrial society', a society largely coextensive with the nation-state, whose axial principle is the distribution of goods. See U Beck, *Risk Society: Towards a New Modernity* (M Ritter tr, New York, Sage, 1992).

[20] Max Weber understood rationalisation in four ways: practically, as an individual cost-benefit calculation; theoretically; bureaucratically, as a broader organisational principle for society; and metaphysically, as a disenchantment for broader society. See G Ritzer, *Classical Sociological Theory*, 8th edn (New York, McGraw-Hill, 2000) 2; Habermas (n 10) ch 1.

[21] Alexander writes: 'In early modernity, economic production focused on energy-based technology, and material goods; actors believed in the inevitability of progress; science was an object of blind faith; nature was perceived as inanimate matter to be mastered instrumentally – and the ugly realities of modernity began to show.' JC Alexander, 'Critical Reflection on 'Reflexive Modernization' (1996) 13 *Theory, Culture and Society* 133.

[22] Adam Smith famously wrote: 'It is not from the benevolence of the butcher, … but from their regard to their own self-interest.' A Smith, *An Inquiry Into the Nature and Causes of the Wealth of Nations*, vol 1 (first published 1776, WB Todd ed, Oxford, Oxford University Press, 1976).

orders that rest solely on liberal ideas then become apparent, and a pervasive sense of unfairness seeps into the overall discourse and reflection on the workings of our systems.[23] Indeed, looking at these deficits, one might argue that modernity has not fulfilled the promises once made to an – albeit different and more homogenous – society. The ideas belonging to *second modernity*[24] (or late modernity) are thus focussed on substantive and material justice; questioning and revoking the ideas and institutions of the first. In this light, fundamental assumptions about 'man' also change, and the individual is no longer seen as fully free and autonomous. Rather, she becomes *empirical*[25] – a product of socio-economic conditions and her place in global society.[26] Equally, the free market is seen as an institution that has led not only to wealth and progress but also to the destruction of the natural environment, ever greater externalities, large discrepancies of power and unsustainable inequality. Thus, this second modernity is, at its core, a critical assessment and a reckoning with the virtues and ideas of the first modernity and not a new design of modernity itself.[27]

How the second modernity affects the ideas of the first is a matter of contention. Rather than seeing this second phase of modernity as a deconstruction of the first (as done by theories of post-modernism),[28] the theory of *reflexive modernisation* focuses on the interplay and interdependence or the negative dialectic of the two. In doing so it does not deny the importance and continued importance of the ideas and principles of the first modernity – autonomy, individualism, and the free market – but observes how they interact with and become ever more contentious in light of the realisations of the second modernity. Here the world envisioned by Adam Smith falls under the critique of Karl Marx. Increasingly, it gets stuck between two truisms, making it paradoxical, and struggling to find its own bearings.[29]

Ulrich Beck, Anthony Giddens and Scott Lash coined the term *reflexive modernisation* to describe how, as Giddens puts it, 'simple modernization becomes reflexive modernization to the extent that it disenchants and then dissolves its own taken-for-granted premises'.[30] According to this theory, modernity becomes

[23] Anthony Giddens writes: 'Max Weber's steel cage in which he thought humanity was condemned to live for the foreseeable future, is a prison-house of technical knowledge; we are all, to alter the metaphor, to be small cogs in the gigantic machine of technical and bureaucratic reason.' A Giddens, 'Living in a Post-Traditional Society' in U Beck, A Giddens and S Lash (eds), *Reflexive Modernization: Politics, Tradition and Aesthetics in the Modern Social Order* (Cambridge, Polity Press, 1994) 58.

[24] A term primarily used by sociologist that differentiate their views late modernity from those proposed by post-modernist theory.

[25] See M Foucault, *The Order of Things: An Archaeology of the Human Sciences* (New York, Pantheon Books, 1970) 366.

[26] The latter applies both to modern day identity politics and critiques of the patriarchal society but also to early reflections on the plight of the working class and Marx's critique of the family.

[27] Auer (n 16) § 2.

[28] See Beck, Giddens and Lash (n 11) preface.

[29] Auer (n 16) § 2.

[30] Beck, Bonß and Lau (n 15) 3: 'Eventually this leads to the undermining of every aspect of the nation-state: the welfare state; the power of the legal system; the national economy; the corporatist systems that connected one with the other; and the parliamentary democracy that governed the whole'; Auer (n 16).

reflexive[31] (rather than reflective[32]) in the sense that it becomes self-monitoring and self-critical by directing its attention to the process of modernity itself. Modernity thus becomes its own theme. Within the reasoning of this theory modernity becomes reflexive in two ways:

First, it becomes *self-questioning* and self-referential, by growing ever more wary and critical of its own (original) assumptions. It does not and cannot deconstruct or rid itself of the ideals of the first modernity (autonomy, hierarchy, egalitarian equality, promises of growth and prosperity), but it equally cannot rise above the critique and realisation of the second modernity. Thus, modernity is said to have become discursive and deeply paradoxical.[33] It is stuck between two readings of itself, each of which carries significant normative and discursive weight, but neither of which fully negates the other: the modern person believes that she is autonomous and 'free' but also 'not-free'; she believes markets best allocate resources but also sees that that they do so unequally and lead to poverty and destruction. According to the theory put forward by Beck, Giddens and Lash, reflexivity means that this paradox between the first and the second modernity becomes ever-present and seems irresolvable.

Second, and in a more radical and practical way, modernity's reflexivity means that it does not only become self-questioning, but in time, *self-destructive*. In late modernity we acclimatise to the idea that modernity cannot fulfil its promises of (material) autonomy and prosperity to every individual. And yet, modernity cannot and does not change its liberal programme, but remains committed to individualism and its formal promises. In the face of ever greater externalities and negative feedbacks, the continued attempt of modernity to fulfil its original claims and ideas leads it on a path of intrinsic self-harm and impoverishment.[34]

[31] Beck clarifies the terminology as follows: 'The "reflexive" in "reflexive modernisation" is often misunderstood. It is not simply a redundant way of emphasizing the self-referential quality that is a constitutive part of modernity. Instead, what "reflexive modernisation" refers to is a distinct second phase: the modernization of modern society. When modernization reaches a certain stage, it radicalizes itself. It begins to transform, for a second time, not only the key institutions but also the very principles of society.' U Beck, 'The Reinvention of Politics: Towards a Theory of Reflexive Modernization' in U Beck, A Giddens and S Lash (eds), *Reflexive Modernization: Politics, Tradition and Aesthetics in the Modern Social Order* (Cambridge, Polity Press, 1994) 1.

[32] KS Chang writes: 'To reflect is to somehow subsume the object under the subject of knowledge. Reflection presumes apodictic knowledge and certainty … reflexive modernization is a form of social change driven by judgments and actions which are supposedly scientific or rational, but in practice comprised of reflexes (entangled with or contaminated by given knowledge, image, technology, wealth, power, desire, etc.), and therefore destined to engender a risk-ridden state of affairs in society.' KS Chang, 'Reflexive Modernization' in KS Chang, CF Epstein, P Kivisto and W Outhwaite (eds), *The Wiley-Blackwell Encyclopedia of Social Theory* (Hoboken, John Wiley and Sons, 2017).

[33] Habermas (n 10) ch 1; Auer (n 16).

[34] Auer (n 16) 74. Horkheimer and Adorno describe the Enlightenment in the following way: 'Enlightenment, understood in the widest sense as the advance of thought, has always aimed at liberating human beings from fear and installing them as masters. Yet the wholly enlightened earth is radiant with triumphant calamity. … That fate befell not only [Hegel's] philosophy, as the apotheosis of advancing thought, but Enlightenment itself, in the form of the sober matter-of-factness by which it purported to distinguish itself from Hegel and from metaphysics in general. For Enlightenment is totalitarian as only a system can be.' M Horkheimer and T Adorno, *Dialectic of Enlightenment* (first published 1944, E Jephcott tr, GS Noerr ed, Stanford, Stanford University Press, 2002) 1, 18.

This fundamental critique of modernity and of Smith's original ideas was first expressed by Hegel in his *Outlines of the Philosophy of the Right*.[35] According to this critique, a social and capitalist model that centres around individual demands and self-interest will necessarily lead to exponential increases in production and prosperity, but also, and inevitably, to the production of economic excesses and to poverty.[36] As Hegel puts it, despite the 'excess of wealth' that characterises modern capitalism, 'civil society is not rich enough, i.e. its own resources are insufficient to check excessive poverty and the creation of a penurious rabble'.[37] At the centre of this reading of modernity lies the economic argument that through the process of the ever-greater creation and accumulation of individual or private wealth, ever larger groups of society are excluded from market participation. By having no backstops, this process, according to Hegel, eventually undermines the very pillars and principles on which modern society and the free-market economy rests and the promises of equality and autonomy become meaningless, empty tropes. This is what Hegel called the 'tragedy of civil society'.[38] This suspicion can also be found at the heart of Schumpeter's idea of 'creative destruction'.[39] Schumpeter's theory of monopoly and oligopoly was an early illustration of the fact that markets do not lose their normative legitimacy in the face of market failure and by their creation of monopolies or oligopolies. Rather, according to Schumpeter (and his much-interpreted notion of 'creative destruction'), such phenomena can – and always will – be justified by efficiency gains such as the creation of overall welfare or high levels of innovation.[40] Modernity thus sets in motion a process by which ever greater inequalities can always be justified by the realisation of greater profits. Again, the resulting inequality, impoverishment, and entrapment of peoples in their socio-economic circumstances ultimately undermine the promises that justified the free market society in the first place.

III. The Paradoxical Goals of Competition Policy

Having described the theory of reflexive modernisation, this chapter uses this theory to examine the legitimacy of competition policy and its goals in light of growing inequality. Inequality is often cast aside as a problem that lies outside the scope of competition law. One that is to be tackled with distributive tools such as tax and social policies. Rising inequality, within – and perhaps even as a product

[35] Hegel (n 18).

[36] On Hegel's critique of civil society and concept of modernity, see Habermas (n 10) ch 2.

[37] Hegel (n 18) 222. See also B Ferro, 'Poverty and Recognition in Hegel's Philosophy of Right' in G Schweiger (ed), *Poverty, Inequality and the Critical Theory of Recognition* (Switzerland, Springer 2020) 59.

[38] 'Civil society' (terminology) was translated by Hegel from English into German as 'die bürgerliche Gesellschaft', which Marx later adapted into his notion of 'bourgeoise society'. See also Auer (n 16) 77.

[39] J Schumpeter, *Capitalism, Socialism and Democracy* (first published 1943, Routledge, Taylor & Francis e-Library, 2003) 81.

[40] ibid 87.

of – the competitive market system, may, however, call for a reassessment of this thinking. This is done by looking at the debate on the goals of competition law and policy more closely. The academic debate on the correct goals is not new and is very nuanced.[41] It is, however, possible to identify the two main opposing positions and schools of thought: early and neo-structuralists positions that support the distributive and material justice goals; and welfarist positions that narrow its role to the of securing formal freedoms.[42] This chapter does not develop a new theory or approach, nor does it definitively side with one of the existing approaches. Instead, it looks at the discursive relationship between formal and substantive theories of competition law.

The theory of reflexive modernisation can be used to explain tensions between formal freedom and material justice in competition law specifically and in private law more generally (as prominently shown in the work of Marietta Auer). According to this theory, these tensions are not only present, but prevalent and create an inescapable paradox. Fundamental private law institutions, such as freedom of contract, which is an embodiment of the ideas of the first modernity and without which modern private law is not thinkable, are blind to socio-economic discrepancies and are thus said to have an inherent problem with imbalances of power.[43] The existence of inequality and imbalances of power thus leads to a reflexive moment: freedom of contract is so fundamental to private law thinking that it necessitates our continued faith in the core ideas of liberalism and the self-governing free market economy. At the same time, we are also forced to accept and recognise the frequent existence of substantive or material shortcomings, in particular discrepancies of economic power between contract parties. These are growing so significant, in fact, that the freedom of contract is increasingly regarded merely as a formal principle.[44] This tension is also at the heart of the inequality debate in competition law, which centres around the question whether competition law should only protect the free-market process and mechanisms in place or should play the role of a distributive tool that secures fair material outcomes.[45]

The attempt to determine the correct interpretation of the goals of antitrust and competition policy often leads to search for its original goals. In a 1966 paper and later in *The Antitrust Paradox* Robert Bork argued that the Sherman Act intended courts to apply consumer welfare ('consumer want satisfaction') and moreover wealth maximisation standards as central parameters of antitrust analysis.[46]

[41] For a broader analysis, see ch 1 in this volume.

[42] See N Petit, *Big Tech and the Digital Economy* (Oxford, Oxford University Press, 2020) 20.

[43] See EJ Mestmäcker, 'The Role of Competition in a Liberal Society' in P Koslowski (ed), *The Social Market Economy, Theory and Ethics of the Economic Order* (Heidelberg, Springer, 1998) 329.

[44] Auer (n 16).

[45] Please note that even the consumer welfare standard is ultimately a distributive instrument, since it is not indifferent to outcomes, but distributes to consumers.

[46] R Bork, *The Antitrust Paradox*, 2nd edn (New York, The Free Press, 1993); R Bork, 'Legislative Intent and the Policy of the Sherman Act' (1966) 9 *The Journal of Law and Economics* 7; DA Crane, 'The Tempting of Antitrust: Robert Bork and the Goals of Antitrust Policy' (2014) 9 *Antitrust Law Journal* 835.

This set the tone for much of the further thought and writings of the Chicago School and their welfarist approaches. On the other side of the spectrum, structuralists (so-called Neo-Jeffersonians or Neo-Brandeisians) also argue based on original intent, using congressional records verbatim. While Bork's interpretation is often said to be agenda-driven, thereby convoluting original statements about structural measures and per se illegality with evidence of their effects on consumer welfare and overall efficiency goals to determine what congress actually intended,[47] (neo-)structuralists can rely *expressis verbis* on the statements made by the early framers of the antitrust laws. Relying on congressional records and statements, Lina Khan has recently argued that

> Congress enacted antitrust laws to rein in the power of industrial trusts, the large business organizations that had emerged in the late nineteenth century. Responding to a fear of concentrated power, antitrust sought to distribute it. … The law was '*for* diversity and access to markets; it was *against* high concentration and abuses of power.' … Senator Sherman, for example, described overcharges by monopolists as 'extortion which makes the people poor,' while Senator Richard Coke referred to them as 'robbery.'[48]

While original intent is less relevant in EU law, its ordoliberal traditions are keenly sought out when competition law is met with new or difficult challenges.[49] Many debates on competition and broader economic policy go a step further and argue along the lines of how economies ought to work by scrutinising original liberal ideas and the early design of the free market economy. After the financial crisis of 2008 several authors called for a return to the writings and principles of Adam Smith and an even more stringent application of formal liberal principles to avoid moral hazards.[50] On the other side of the spectrum, it is often pointed out that Smith's liberalism never included all sectors and branches of industry and did not envision capitalism at all costs or manifestations such as financialisation. In this volume, Deutscher, for instance, argues that original liberal assumptions (by thinkers such as Thomas More, the English Levellers, Montesquieu, James Steuart, and Adam Smith) always saw distributive equality as a by-product of competition or equality of opportunity.[51]

[47] See Bork, *The Antitrust Paradox* (n 46). Bork's views have been sharply criticised. See R Lande, 'A Traditional and Textualist Analysis of the Goals of Antitrust: Efficiency, Preventing Theft from Consumers, and Consumer Choice' (2013) 81 *Fordham Law Review.* 2349; R Lande, 'Wealth Transfers as the Original and Primary Concern of Antitrust: The Efficiency Interpretation Challenged' (1982) 34 *Hastings Law Journal* 65; EM Fox, 'The Modernization of Antitrust: A New Equilibrium' (1981) 66 *Cornell Law Review* 1140; ME Stucke, 'Reconsidering Antitrust's Goals' (2012) 53 *Boston College Law Review* 551.

[48] LM Khan, 'Amazon's Antitrust Paradox' (2017) 126 *Yale Law Review Journal* 564 with reference to Sen. Sherman and Sen. Coke.

[49] For an instructive overview, see J Cohen-Setton, 'Ordoliberalism and Germany's Approach to the Euro Crisis', (*Bruegel Blog*, 24 August 2014) www.bruegel.org/2014/08/blogs-review-ordoliberalism-and-germanys-approach-to-the-euro-crisis/.

[50] M Mussa, 'Adam Smith and the Political Economy of a Modern Financial Crisis' (2009) 44 *Business Economics* 3; D Bholat, 'How Would Adam Smith Fix the Financial Crisis?' (2009) 52 *Challenge* 60.

[51] Ch 1 in this volume with reference to said authors.

Such positions have great merit and help to address fundamental questions about the interpretation, purpose, and application of competition laws. If, however, as the theory of reflexive modernisation suggests, history has not been a linear projection of its original ideas and intentions, then perhaps such a line of historical analysis also has inherent limitations. The history of economic thought and competition policy has often been portrayed in a more fluid manner and as an almost cyclical development that oscillates between very liberal (neoclassical, welfarist, monetarist) and more social (structuralist Keynesian and macroeconomic) approaches.[52] The theory of reflexive modernisation suggests that this divide is even deeper and more fundamental. While none of the works of Beck, Giddens, Latour or Lash deal with the history of economic thought, they do propose that we read modernisation not as reflection, but also (in the words of Ulrich Beck) 'as confrontation'[53] and that this 'implies … a radicalization of modernity, which breaks up the premises and contours of industrial society and opens paths to another modernity'.[54] From the nature of the theory as well as the authors' several mentions of Marxism,[55] we must conclude that economically modernity's great paradox or dichotomy stems from our acceptance of both the ideas of classical economics (Smith, Ricardo) and also Marx's fundamental critique (undertaken only roughly a century later). This tension is immanent in the works of early sociologists but also in the work of theorists such as Schumpeter, who was writing in a time when the dichotomy between capitalism and socialism was still ever-present. When we apply the tension between Smith and Marx, almost 180 years later and in a world in which capitalism has very much survived (and socialism as an alternative has not), to competition law, tensions between the formal and the substantive are more subtle, yet (and this seems crucial) decisive.

As mentioned above, first antitrust and competition laws (the Sherman Act from 1890 but also the German Gesetz gegen Wettbewerbsbeschränkungen, GWB, from 1957) were focussed on structural deficits, in particular market power.[56] While these laws do not have a socialist or Marxist heritage, they were a reaction to some of the shortcomings (market failures) of the liberal ideal and unchecked market forces. Early antitrust laws were even considered a form of social regulation,[57]

[52] See J Cassidy, *How Markets Fail: The Logic of Economic Calamities* (New York, Farrar, Straus and Giraux, 2009); K Galbraith, *A History of Economics: The Past as the Present* (London, Penguin Books, 1991); J Mendelsohn, 'Thinking Macroprudentially' (2019) 38/3 *Banking and Financial Services Policy Report* 1.

[53] Beck (n 29) 59.

[54] ibid.

[55] See Beck, Giddens and Lash (n 11) 3, 110, 118, 199, 215. Giddens contrasts the ideas of the Enlightenment to those of Marx: 'The grand experiment of modernity, fraught with global hazards, is not all what the progenitors of Enlightenment had in mind when they spoke of the importance of contesting tradition. Nor is it close to what Marx envisaged – indeed, among many other endings today we may speak of the end of Prometheanism.' Giddens (n 23) 59.

[56] See F Böhm, 'Das Problem der Privaten Macht' (1928) 3 *Die Justiz* 324; CD Edwards, 'Conglomerate Bigness as a Source of Power' in GJ Stigler, *Business Concentration and Price Policy* (NBER, Princeton, Princeton University Press, 1955).

[57] I Lianos, 'The Poverty of Competition Law: The Long Story' CLES Research Paper Series 2/2018, www.ucl.ac.uk/cles/sites/cles/files/cles_2-2018.pdf, 13.

and ordoliberals saw market power as a problem as such.[58] Ordoliberal scholars such as Böhm saw competition laws as part of a larger economic constitution.[59] In contrast to welfarist positions that suggest competition policy only aids the market mechanism and serves procedural justice, this school of thought placed competition and labour policy on the outskirts of a larger private law legal order and saw both as corrective instruments that keep power imbalances in check and serve distributive goals.[60]

Over the past decade, political and larger structural or distributive considerations have, however, largely given way to a more monolithically welfare-based competition law analysis. In this sense, competition analysis has been refined over time to focus ever more closely on the intricacies of the competitive process in the relevant market(s) and the effects of competitive constraints on consumer welfare.[61] The 'welfare standard' originates from the Chicago revolution of antitrust law which sought to reform antitrust law into a more economically sound discipline and to (in the words of Robert Bork) rid it of its 'uncritical sentimentality'.[62] The so-called Chicago School of Antitrust placed the maximisation of efficiency and price theory at the heart of antitrust analysis and essentially neglected any intermediate effects on competitors or the structure of the market. Promoting a 'purist' reading of antitrust and one based solely on a welfarist analysis, the Chicago School quickly worked to refute the idea that size or concentration alone should be antitrust concerns, pointing to their potential welfare benefits in the form of productive efficiencies.[63]

In the less radical form in which it was later transported into EU competition law as part of the 'more economic approach', the consumer welfare standard (CWS) also aimed to refine the goals and the methodology of competition law: to make competition enforcement more objective, economic and evidence-based, and to give competition policy a more stringent and coherent objective.[64] The CJEU was reluctant to fully embrace the soft-law proclamation of the consumer

[58] For a detailed account, see ch 1 in this volume; Böhm (n 51). See also E Deutscher and S Makris, 'Exploring the Ordoliberal Paradigm: The Competition-Democracy Nexus' (2017) EUI Working Papers LAW 2017/03, ssrn.com/abstract=3166005.

[59] See F Böhm, 'Privatrechtsgesellschaft und Marktwirtschaft' (1966) 17 *Jahrbuch für die Ordnung von Wirtschaft und Gesellschaft* 75; in English: 'Rule of Law in a Market Economy' in A Peacock and H Willgerodt (eds), *Germany's Social Market Economy: Origins and Evolution* (London, MacMillan, 1989) 46; see also F Böhm, 'Freiheit und Ordnung in der Marktwirtschaft' (1971) 22 *Jahrbuch für die Ordnung von Wirtschaft und Gesellschaft* 11.

[60] Mestmäcker (n 41).

[61] According to Petit, the modern consumer welfare standard serves two functions: 'First, the CW standard makes it clear that the proscriptions enunciated in the antitrust rules are about conduct that reduces or is likely to reduce economic welfare and are not intended to prevent noneconomic harms such as harms to the political process or to serve other social objectives. Second, the CW standard provides a criterion to guide the formulation and case-by-case application of the specific rules that are used to identify prohibited, anticompetitive conduct.' Petit (n 40) 20.

[62] 'Uncritical sentimentality about the *little guy*'. Bork, *The Antitrust Paradox* (n 46).

[63] See RA Posner, *Antitrust Law*, 2nd edn (Chicago, University of Chicago Press, 2001).

[64] 'A standard based on economic science, the reasoning goes, would be objective and specific enough to keep competition law enforcement consistent throughout the EU, thus minimizing divergence and guarding against protectionism'. VI Daskalova, 'Consumer Welfare in EU Competition Law: What Is It (Not) About?' (2015) 11 *The Competition Law Review* 133.

welfare standards at first, and often interprets it broadly to include 'more than just price' (choice, quality, innovation)[65] and to protect the structure of the market.[66] Nonetheless, the CWS has become the well-established standard of EU competition law[67] and has been celebrated for making competition law analysis sounder.[68]

In many ways this welfarist turn in competition policy may be seen as a return to more classically liberalist ideals of markets and competition. While such a late return to more formal liberal ideas may seem surprising at first, (late) modernism's self-referentiality and self-reflexivity (whereby 'modernity becomes its own theme') can help to explain this clasp to the ideas of the first modernity and trends such as neoliberalism (and neo-conservativism). In fact, often the radicality of neo-liberal and neo-classical ideas – and the stringency and simplicity of early Chicago School ideas were indeed radical – can perhaps be seen as a symptom of modernity's uncertainty and self-questioning, which causes us to cling to a set of ideas or a truism, even while aware of their flaws and fundamental shortcomings.

Currently the pendulum seems to be swinging back from a purely welfarist rhetoric. In the debate on how to control or regulate the big tech giants, several authors argue for a larger set of policy considerations, including material justice and 'fairness'.[69] After decades of welfarist thinking, these demands are not easily transported into common doctrine or welfarist terms.[70] Here the old paradox between formal and material goals has arisen anew: While we desire material justice, distributive measures equally seem at odds with our idea that competition ought to represent something of a Darwinian struggle 'in which the most efficient succeed and the weak disappear'.[71]

IV. Applying the Theory of Reflexive Modernisation to New Forms of Concentration in Digital Markets

Lastly, this chapter looks at the impact of the paradox between liberal freedom and material justice on one current competition law issue: concentration and the

[65] Case C-209/10 *Post Danmark A/S v Konkurrencerådet* ECLI:EU:C:2012:172, [2012] ECR I-0000.

[66] Joined Cases C-501/06 P, C-513/06 P, C-515/06 P and C-519/06 P *GlaxoSmithKline Services Unlimited v Commission of the European Communities* ECLI:EU:C:2009:610, [2009] ECR I-09291.

[67] In 2005 then Competition Commissioner Neelie Kroes said: 'Our aim is simple: to protect competition in the market as a means of enhancing consumer welfare and efficient allocation of resources.' N Kroes, 'Delivering Better Markets and Better Consumer Choices' (speech 05/512, Brussels, 15 September 2005) ec.europa.eu/commission/presscorner/detail/en/SPEECH_05_512.

[68] See AD Melamed and N Petit, 'The Misguided Assault on the Consumer Welfare Standard in the Age of Platform Markets' (2019) 54 *Review of Industrial Organisation* 741.

[69] SM Colino, 'The Antitrust F-Word: Fairness Considerations in Competition Law' (2019) *Journal of Business Law* 329.

[70] For criticism of the proposed Digital Markets Act in this regard, see H Schweitzer, 'The Art to Make Gatekeeper Positions Contestable and Challenge to Know What is Fair: A Discussion of the Digital Markets Act Proposal' (2021) *Zeitschrift für Europäisches Privatrecht* 1. In the words of Daniel Crane, even the Neo-Brandeisians have 'grown up in a welfarist world'. DA Crane, 'How Much Brandeis Do the Neo-Brandeisians Want' (2019) 64 *The Antitrust Bulletin* 531.

[71] Whish and Bailey (n 6) 21.

rise of 'big tech'. While the prevalence of market power in a range of markets and high industry concentration does not automatically mean that a society is unequal, increases in overall concentration can generally be seen as a cause for inequality concerns.[72] High levels of concentration and economic power usually lead to great socio-economic discrepancies (in particular unequal bargaining power) and less equal societies.[73] Over the past decades we have witnessed the rise of super-dominant digital tech firms. To date competition policy has struggled to capture the nature and the manifestation of this new form of economic power.[74] For starters, these tech giants' economic activity often reaches across several markets. Thus, they are not classical monopolists, but rather take the shape of more diversified conglomerates or digital ecosystems.[75] In addition, some tech giants offer products and services for free and almost all of them benefit from large-scale data-related network effects. While competition law reforms and regulatory proposals to tackle big tech are well on their way and some have already been passed, the nature of these strategically relevant firms or digital ecosystems is still elusive and their virtues and harms are highly disputed: while some see them as dangerous and anticompetitive 'per se', others highlight far-reaching efficiencies (network effects), consumer welfare benefits (free digital products and services) and high innovative potential of the digital sector. This section considers both types of modernist reflexivity discussed above:[76] It first looks at competition law's approach to big tech and the imminent threat of concentration in the digital economy from the perspective of self-questioning, and then at the potential dangers of self-destruction that could be a result of rising concentration and inequality.

A. Self-Questioning: The Paradoxical Nature of Digital Bigness

With plans to regulate and control big tech, tensions between a very liberal notion of competition and more material or structuralist approaches to competition policy are on the rise again. In *The Moligopoly Hypothesis*, Petit sets out to

[72] Ennis, Gonzaga and Pike (n 13).

[73] See D Kennedy, 'Law Distributes I: Ricardo Marx Cls' (24 February 2021) ssrn.com/abstract=3813439; P Longman, 'The Case for Small-Business Cooperation' (1 November 2018) *Washington Monthly*, washingtonmonthly.com/2018/10/28/the-case-for-small-business-collusion/.

[74] A Gerbrandy, 'Conceptualizing Big Tech as 'Modern Bigness' and its implications for European Competition Law' (submission in reaction to the call for contributions Shaping Competition Policy in the Era of Digitalization, 2018) ec.europa.eu/competition/information/digitisation_2018/contributions/anna_gerbrandy.pdf, 2.

[75] See M Bourreau and A de Streel, 'Digital Conglomerates and EU Competition Policy' (2019) www.crid.be/pdf/public/8377.pdf; J Crémer, Y-A de Montjoye and H Schweitzer, 'Competition Policy for the Digital Era' (report for the European Commission, 2019) ec.europa.eu/competition/publications/reports/kd0419345enn.pdf; Monopolkommission, 'Empfehlungen für einen effektiven und effizienten Digital Markets Act' [2021] *Sondergutachten* 82, www.monopolkommission.de/images/PDF/SG/sg_dma_volltext.pdf; MG Jacobides and I Lianos, 'Ecosystems and competition law in theory and practice' (2021) 30/3 *Industrial and Corporate Change* 1199.

[76] See section II above.

analyse these strongly polarised attitudes towards big tech.[77] On the one hand he observes that 'neo-structuralists' see big tech firms as harmful conglomerates akin to monopolies that harm competition and have little legitimacy in the free market economy.[78] On the other side of the spectrum, 'welfarists' are not in favour of 'per se' structuralist reforms and think that competition law and regulatory measures alike require evidence of market power and harms to consumers.[79] Thus while some either praise or ignore the effects of concentration, others would either break up big tech firms or go to all necessary lengths to regulate them.[80] The dichotomy highlighted by Petit stems from two paradoxical interpretations about the nature of digital competition and the sources of the power the big tech firms hold.[81] On the one hand, big tech firms are seen as sinister amalgamators of power that prey on their consumers' weaknesses to gain access to the data, thereby monopolising the internet and eroding fundamental freedoms (autonomy, privacy). On the other, the size, financial strength, and conglomerate reach of the tech giants is seen to reflect fierce rivalry (amongst each other), extreme levels of innovation, disruption and numerous benefits for consumers that take the shape of free products and services and consumer-side network effects.[82] The theory of reflexive modernisation postulates that, despite the paradox, there is truth in each of these positions. In addition, the lesson of this theory seems to suggest that while such tensions may be irresolvable, they are also inherent to modernity and that more harm may come from ignoring either side of the debate. In fact, the current rise of concentration in the digital sphere may suggest that the evolution of competition law and its arrival at the consumer welfare standard may not have mitigated, but rather simply ignored and exacerbated competition law's central problem: power.

B. Self-Destruction: Consequences of Concentration and Inequality

According to the theory, one of the consequences of reflexive modernisation is that it begins to question and undermine the very promises on which it is based: While modernity is inherently incapable of fulfilling its promise of autonomy, prosperity and (formal) equality, to all individuals, it is its dedication to individualism and individual's strife for the ever-greater accumulation of wealth that becomes so pernicious that it erodes egalitarian promises.[83] This suspicion was first described by Hegel as the so-called 'tragedy of civil society',[84] but it is closely

[77] Petit (n 59).
[78] ibid 7–19.
[79] ibid 19–24.
[80] Eg, Melamed and Petit (n 66); Khan (n 46).
[81] Petit's hypothesis is thus that 'big tech firms, or perhaps just some of them, may simultaneously be monopolists and competitive firms'. Petit (n 59) 33.
[82] ibid 1–5.
[83] What Marietta Auer calls inherent self-harm (*immanente Selbstgefährdung*). Auer (n 16) 75.
[84] Hegel (n 18).

linked to economic arguments put forward by Schumpeter and his notion of 'creative destruction'.

Hegel's observation is that modern civil society and its dedication to the individual is only possible under conditions where real and ever-present chances of failure exist, and the allocation of scarce resources is inherently unequal (ie the mechanism of the free market). The same argument is used by Piketty to describe his discontent with 'competition' as primary means of allocation:

> [M]odern inequality is said to be just because it is the result of a freely chosen process in which everyone enjoys equal access to the market and to property and automatically benefits from the wealth accumulated by the wealthiest individuals, who are the most enterprising, deserving and useful.[85]

While this may seem like a simple and perhaps even fair consequence of autonomy and competition, Schumpeter argued that poverty and growing inequality would not be attributed to the failure, but instead the *success* of modern civil society, as a process of ever greater rationalisation and realisation of efficiencies through capitalist modes of production. This is part of his larger 'dematerialisation' argument:

> The capitalist process, by substituting a mere parcel of shares for the walls of and the machines in a factory, takes the life out of property …. Dematerialized, defunctionalized and absentee ownership does not impress and call forth moral allegiance as the vital form of property did.[86]

Using this argument Schumpeter postulated that modern society would become increasingly blind to growing concentration, since it would become harder to identify its harms. This argument is based on his famous concept of 'creative destruction'.[87] While this notion is prominently read as a justification for monopolies due to their innovative potential,[88] Schumpeter in fact used it to warn that we would become blind to these obvious signs of inequality since monopolies and oligopolies (or other forms of concentration) could always be justified in light of the greater efficiencies they created.[89]

[85] Piketty, *Capital and Ideology* (n 3) 1.

[86] Schumpeter (n 37) 139, 142.

[87] ibid 81.

[88] For instance, G Parker, G Pertopoulos and M Van Alstyne, 'Digital Platforms and Antitrust' (2020) Breugel Working Paper 06/2020, www.bruegel.org/2020/11/digital-platforms-and-antitrust/, 15.

[89] In 'Crumbling Walls' (ch 12), Schumpeter writes the following: 'A very common type of social criticism which we have already met laments the "decline of competition" and equates it to the decline of capitalism because of the virtues it attributes to competition and the vices it attributes to modern industrial "monopolies." In this schema of interpretation, monopolization plays the role of arteriosclerosis and reacts upon the fortunes of the capitalist order through increasingly unsatisfactory economic performance. We have seen the reasons for rejecting this view. Economically neither the case for competition nor the case against concentration of economic control is anything like as strong as this argument implies. And, whether weak or strong, it misses the salient point. Even if the giant concerns were all managed so perfectly as to call forth applause from the angels in heaven, the political consequences of concentration would still be what they are. The political structure of a nation is profoundly affected by the elimination of a host of small and medium sized firms the owner managers of which, together with their dependents, henchmen and connections, count quantitatively at the polls and have

Last, joining the arguments about creative destruction as well as the so-called 'dematerialisation' of our modes of production, Schumpeter suspected that this would ultimately lead to an erosion of legal institutions (property and contract) that form the foundation of our capitalist systems and of civil society.

> Thus, the capitalist process pushes into the background all those institutions, the institutions of property and free contracting in particular, that expressed the needs and ways of the truly 'private' economic activity. Where it does not abolish them, as it already has abolished free contracting in the labour market, it attains the same end by shifting the relative importance of existing legal forms – the legal forms pertaining to corporate business for instance as against those pertaining to the partnership or individual firm – or by changing their contents or meanings.

While Schumpeter must be read within the historical context in which he was writing – ie the great depression, rise of fascism and the possible decline of democracy – many of his ideas, not least those on creative destruction, have remained highly influential, justifying a closer look at his thoughts on how these processes would affect the overall development of capitalist societies. When looking at Schumpeter's suspicions and fears, it is striking that competition policy has indeed become less sceptical of concentration and power per se and that large corporations have, overall, become harder to control, whether by competition remedies or by other (distributive) means such as taxes. The fact that Schumpeter accredits this to the ever-more fleeting and intangible nature of the manifestations of power that can always be justified due to greater efficiencies, makes his analysis strikingly fitting to our current troubles with digital power and our inability to capture (quantify and legally identify) its nature and harms. In fact, several new notions of power have been introduced to try to detect and control negative manifestations of concentration in future. These include 'strategic market status',[90] 'intermediation power',[91] 'gatekeepers',[92] and theories of harm looking at 'conglomerate power'.[93] None of these concepts, however, fully encompasses the full extent or the diverse manifestations of digital power. The Digital Market Act's notion of 'gatekeeper' power, for example, only captures a very small group of norm-addressees and only a limited number of manifestations of economic power in the digital sphere. In addition, the EU has yet to expand competition law tools, in particular merger

a hold on what we may term the foreman class that no management of a large unit can ever have; the very foundation of private property and free contracting wears away in a nation in which its most vital, most concrete, most meaningful types disappear from the moral horizon of the people.' Schumpeter (n 37) 140.

[90] Term used by the UK Furman Report. J Furman, D Coyle, A Fletcher, D McAuley and P Marsden, 'Unlocking Competition: Report of the Digital Competition Expert Panel' (2019) www.gov.uk/government/publications/unlocking-digital-competition-report-of-the-digital-competition-expert-panel.

[91] Term put forward in the following report: H Schweitzer, J Haucap, W Kerber and R Welker, 'Modernising the Law on Abuse of Market Power' (report for the German Federal Ministry for Economic Affairs and Energy, 2018) ssrn.com/abstract=3250742.

[92] See Commission proposal, Digital Markets Act, COM/2020/842, Art. 3.

[93] Bourreau and de Streel (n 72).

control, to prevent the rise of more such gatekeepers in the future.[94] Without a firm notion of power and competition policy's grasp on it, economic concentration becomes ever less tangible, and its harms are difficult to detect, theorise and balance against the benefits produced by the digital economy. If Schumpeter is correct, this is not an accident but part of the nature of capitalist development that should not be left unchecked.

V. Conclusion

Using the theory of reflexive modernisation, this chapter looked at one of the central conflicts of modernity: the tension between formal, liberal freedom and substantive justice. It shows that modernisation is not a linear projection of any one set of ideas but is instead defined by the paradox between formal liberalism of the so-called first modernity and its substantive shortcomings (the critique of the second modernity). The theory of reflexive modernisation also suggests that modernity's inability to resolve this paradox will lead to its eventual demise, and that its original promises will fade and become meaningless. Such ideas were first expressed by Hegel and Schumpeter in their descriptions of the tragedy of civil society and creative destruction. The paradoxes of modernity thus lead not only to a mechanism of self-questioning but also one of self-destruction.

These paradoxes can be used to explain the polarised nature of the debate on the goals of competition law that has arisen time and again between structuralists and welfarists. This in turn explains why it is so difficult to include inequality considerations in the liberal competition paradigm, even though it too rests on the promise of (formal) equality and greater prosperity for all market participants, and indeed why liberal competition thinking persists despite its production of inequalities. There presently exists a very pressing real-world applicability of the theory of reflexive modernisation within the context of competition law: our inability to capture concentration and new manifestations of power in the digital sphere and the highly polarised debate on the harms and virtues of such manifestations and big tech. This chapter illustrated this dichotomy as a symptom of self-questioning and then looked at the possible self-destructive effects thereof as suggested in theory. Both Hegel and Schumpeter warned that modern capitalist societies would eventually end in poverty and destruction, because of the accumulation of wealth by the few. For Hegel this is the inherent demise of civil society, and for Schumpeter a feature of the process of creative destruction that will find ever new ways to justify monopolies or other discrepancies of power. A connection can be drawn between their expectations and growing concentration in the digital sphere. Hence, if digital bigness is left unchecked, it could lead to precisely the inequality and poverty Hegel and Schumpeter envisioned and this not in spite of, but because of its great innovative potential.

[94] See O Budzinski and J Mendelsohn, 'Regulating Big Tech: From Competition Policy to Sector Regulation?' (2021) Ilmenau Economics Discussion Papers, vol 27 no 154, ssrn.com/abstract=3938167.

3

A Cross-Country Analysis of the Relationship between Competition Law and Economic Inequality

AMIT ZAC, CAROLA CASTI, CHRISTOPHER DECKER, ARIEL EZRACHI*

I. Introduction

The past four decades have been prosperous. Global GDP per capita has grown by 76 per cent between 1980 and 2019 (in real terms), with higher growth (86 per cent) being achieved by the world's most industrialised countries.[1] However, over the same period, various indicators show that economic inequality levels have increased in many parts of the world. The latest UN Human Development Report notes that income inequality has risen since the 1980s, and that '[t]he global top 1 percent, the economic elite of rich and poor countries, made huge gains over 1980–2016'.[2] So, while the world and particularly industrialised countries have become considerably richer in aggregate, the spoils of this growth have not been distributed evenly and the gap between those with the highest and the lowest incomes has expanded.[3]

* This chapter forms part of a research project funded by the Leverhulme Trust, that explores the relationship between competition law enforcement and economic inequality. We are grateful to the trust and the project advisory board, for their support. We would also like to thank Anu Bradford and Adam Chilton for sharing their CLI database at an early stage of this project, and the editors of this book, Jan Broulík and Kati Cseres, for the insightful comments and thorough review of this chapter.

[1] World Bank, 'GDP per Capita' (2020) data.worldbank.org/indicator/NY.GDP.PCAP.KD?end=2019&start=1980.

[2] In 2017 the global top 1% owned more than 33% of total wealth while the bottom 50% owned less than 2%. United Nations, 'Human Development Report 2019: Beyond Income, Beyond Averages, Beyond Today: Inequalities in Human Development in the 21st Century' 131, hdr.undp.org/sites/default/files/hdr2019.pdf.

[3] ibid. In the US, for example, between 1980 and 2017 the pretax income share of the bottom 40% fell from about 13% to 8%, while the share of the top one per cent rose from about 11% to 20%. See also R Joyce and X Xu, 'Inequalities in the Twenty-First Century' (2019) ifs.org.uk/inequality/chapter/briefing-note/.

Economic inequality is driven by a wide range of variables, and affected by historical, legal, and economic context. In its quest to reduce inequality, the state may deploy a range of public policies and utilise both direct and indirect instruments, ranging from tax policies, credits, and subsidies to education and training. In this chapter, we consider the possible role competition law might play as an additional policy tool that could help reduce income and wealth inequality (economic inequality).

Despite the widely held view that competition law is related to economic inequality,[4] much less is known about the economic mechanism underlying this effect or about its scale. As such, this relationship remains largely unexplored empirically.[5] Our inquiry seeks to address this gap and explore whether competition law may be correlated with observed inequality trends. We seek to contribute to existing work in two ways. First, we outline a mechanism of how competition law could affect inequality via changes in prices, wages and the labour share. Second, we examine the relationship between competition laws and inequality by combining country-level panel-data with multiple competition law indices and various economic inequality metrics across a wide range of jurisdictions over an extended time period.

At the centre of our analysis are two competition law indices which track changes in the scope and perceived effectiveness of competition law across the world over several decades. We fit a linear panel-data model (OLS) to investigate the relationship between these indices and economic inequality. We include country fixed-effects, accounting for the time-invariant unobserved heterogeneity (by country), and the full set of time fixed effects (by year). We also account for geographical region trends[6] and an extensive set of macroeconomic time-varying factors such as the level of unemployment, economic development, and human capital.

This chapter comprises six sections. Section II provides a brief overview of existing scholarship and conceptually sets out the causal links between competition

[4] Eg, Carl Shapiro notes that 'antitrust enforcement does tend to reduce income inequality'. C Shapiro, 'Antitrust in a Time of Populism' (2018) 61 *International Journal of Industrial Organization* 714, 746. Similarly, Joseph Stiglitz notes the following: 'While market power has long been front and center in competition policy, recent advances have, as we have noted, provided new arguments for the importance of attacking it. It leads to inequality, and inequality leads to poorer economic performance, including lower growth and more instability.' JE Stiglitz, 'Towards a Broader View of Competition Policy' in T Bonakele, E Fox and L Mncube (eds), *Competition Policy for the New Era: Insights from the BRIC Countries* (Oxford, Oxford University Press, 2017) 17.

[5] Legal studies that do exist tend to focus on inequality in specific jurisdictions (for example the US or Europe) without using causal inference methods. Lina Khan and Sandeep Vaheesan, for example, argue that the failure of competition law (antitrust law) in the US to preserve competitive markets contributes to regressive wealth and income distribution, and that competition law is likely to have progressive distributive effects. LM Khan and S Vaheesan, 'Market Power and Inequality: The Antitrust Counterrevolution and Its Discontents' (2017) 11 *Harvard Law and Policy Review* 235.

[6] Eg, if North America, as a region, experienced a different trend over the observed period, such a trend will be absorbed by the time-trends.

law and economic inequality. Section III offers a description of the data. Section IV presents our economic specification and the results. Section V discusses the results and considers some implications of our findings. Section VI concludes.

II. The Link between Competition Law, Competition, and Inequality

One can conceptualise the causal chain between competition law and economic inequality through the intensity of competition (the competition dynamic). The first link of this chain concerns the impact that competition law has on the intensity of competition. The second link of this chain has to do with the impact that the intensity of competition has on economic inequality. In this section, we first elaborate on these two links before focusing our attention on the overall relationship between competition law and economic inequality.

A. Competition Law and the Intensity of Competition

A primary aim of competition law is to protect and enhance the competitive environment by tackling excesses of market power that allow firms to (individually or jointly) exploit their position to earn supernormal profits on a sustained basis, or to stifle the development of competition through foreclosing entry and expansion. From an empirical perspective, inquiries into the relationship between competition law and the intensity of competition (or market power as its counterpart) need to find a way to measure the strength of competition. One possible metric is the level of markups (price above marginal costs) that can be sustained in an industry or an economy over an extended period. Historically, the focus of markup studies has been on differences between prices and marginal costs in specific markets or industries. More recent studies have progressed to explore large, aggregated datasets to evaluate whether economies are becoming more or less competitive. For example, in a large cross-country study of global trends, De Loecker and Eeckhout examined 70,000 firms in 134 countries and found that average markups have increased significantly in advanced economies since the 1980s.[7] Other studies have qualified this result, noting that markup increases appear to be driven by the performance of only a relatively small group of firms, particularly those in the digital sector.[8]

[7] J De Loecker and J Eeckhout, 'Global Market Power' (2018) National Bureau of Economic Research Working Paper 24768, www.nber.org/papers/w24768.

[8] M Bajgar et al, 'Industry Concentration' (OECD, 2019) www.oecd-ilibrary.org/economics/industry-concentration-in-europe-and-north-america_2ff98246-en; International Monetary Fund, 'The Rise of Corporate Market Power and its Macroeconomic Effects' (2019) www.elibrary.imf.org/view/books/081/25771-9781484397480-en/ch002.xml.

Some commentators argue that increases in markups may be linked to low levels of competition law enforcement,[9] yet only a handful of studies have examined such links empirically. Kee and Hoekman,[10] for instance, investigated the effect of competition law adoption on the number of firms and industry markups in a panel of 42 countries over 18 years. While they identified evidence of competition laws promoting entry, they did not find that competition law has an effect on industry markups.

Other empirical studies use different proxies and indicators of competition intensity to explore its relationship with competition law. Khan and Vaheesan examined rising industry concentration levels in the US, which they linked descriptively (without the use of any causal inference methods) to the failure of antitrust law in the US to preserve competitive markets, especially in specific industries such as communications and health care.[11] Gutiérrez and Philippon investigated profit rates and found a connection between EU competition law (and other institutions) and increased market competition in the EU over the past two decades.[12] More broadly, competition law and its effective enforcement have been seen as crucial in protecting competition and enhancing consumer welfare in literature surveys and meta-analyses.[13] However, some of these studies concern only specific sectors or country-specific competition law reforms, which limits the generalisability of their results.

One study that tries to provide a more general picture is Besley et al,[14] covering a large sample of countries over 10 years. Using firm-level data, this study compares firms operating in tradable markets (ie those sectors that are subject to international competition, namely: Agriculture, Mining and quarrying and Manufacturing) with firms in non-tradable markets (ie all others). It found that profit margins of firms operating in non-tradable sectors are significantly lower in countries with wider competition policies (in terms of scope) compared to firms

[9] S Berry, M Gaynor and FS Morton, 'Do Increasing Markups Matter? Lessons from Empirical Industrial Organization' (2019) 33 *Journal of Economic Perspectives* 44; JB Baker, *The Antitrust Paradigm: Restoring a Competitive Economy* (Cambridge, MA, Harvard University Press, 2019).

[10] HL Kee and B Hoekman, 'Imports, Entry and Competition Law' (2007) 51 *European Economic Review* 831.

[11] Khan and Vaheesan (n 5).

[12] G Gutiérrez and T Philippon, 'How EU Markets Became More Competitive than US Markets: A Study of Institutional Drift' (2018) National Bureau of Economic Research Working Paper 24700, www.nber.org/papers/w24700. Although the empirical analysis only focusses on product market regulations (PMR) as their main proxy for policy changes, the authors specifically identify competition law as a main driver for the change.

[13] OECD, 'Evaluation of Competition Enforcement' (2013) www.oecd.org/officialdocuments/publicdisplaydocumentpdf/?cote=DAF/COMP/WP2(2012)7/FINAL&docLanguage=En; OECD, 'Factsheet on How Competition Policy Affects Macro-Economic Outcomes' (2014) www.oecd.org/daf/competition/2014-competition-factsheet-iv-en.pdf; OECD, 'Reference Guide' (2016) www.oecd.org/daf/competition/Ref-guide-expost-evaluation-2016web.pdf.

[14] T Besley, N Fontana and N Limodio, 'Antitrust Policies and Profitability in Nontradable Sectors' (2021) 3 *American Economic Review: Insights* 251.

operating in tradable sectors. The study relies, however, on the Total Scope Index Score developed by Hylton and Deng from 2007,[15] which is a measure of the scope of competition law that is less comprehensive than those employed in this chapter.

B. The Intensity of Competition and Economic Inequality

Two main mechanisms in the microeconomics literature support the proposition that low competition intensity may be associated with higher inequality (and high competition intensity with lower inequality). The first mechanism relates to *product markets*. Higher prices (resulting from market power) in essential product markets (like food and clothes) affect households in a regressive way, as poorer consumers tend to spend more of their disposable income on these products.[16] However, the effects do not stop there. The higher prices of products naturally reduce consumption, which in turn reduces the scale of production and subsequently leads to a reduction in the demand for labour (especially for low-skilled workers)[17] even if the labour market itself is competitive. To estimate this effect on wages, De Loecker, Eeckhout, and Mongey construct an oligopolistic framework for firm dynamics that quantitatively accounts for the general equilibrium implications of the rise in market power on product markets. They find that current levels of market power had an effect on equilibrium wages, and that quantitatively that effect is large (real wages as a share of GDP dropped by over 26 per cent between the 1980s and 2015).[18] The aggregated decline in wages manifests as a decline in the share of the overall income going to workers (labour share).[19]

The second mechanism relates to the direct effect on *labour markets*. Market power gains (in product markets) are unlikely to be shared with those on the lowest incomes via wages if employers have some market power in the labour market. When only a small group of employers are looking to hire employees in a geographic area, there is potential for monopsony or buyer market power. This

[15] KN Hylton and F Deng, 'Antitrust around the World: An Empirical Analysis of the Scope of Competition Laws and Their Effects' (2007) 74 *Antitrust Law Journal* 27.

[16] J Creedy and R Dixon, 'The Relative Burden of Monopoly on Households with Different Incomes' (1998) 65 *Economica* 285; J Hausman and E Leibtag, 'Consumer Benefits from Increased Competition in Shopping Outlets: Measuring the Effect of Wal-Mart' (2007) 22 *Journal of Applied Econometrics* 1157, who estimated an average 4% reduction in prices associated with greater retail competition (due to entry of low-priced outlets to the geographical market) in the US and found that households with an income below $10,000 benefitted disproportionately from competition (by approximately 50% more than the average household); CM Urzúa, 'Distributive and Regional Effects of Monopoly Power' (2013) 22 *Economía Mexicana Nueva Época* 279.

[17] J De Loecker, J Eeckhout and G Unger, 'The Rise of Market Power and the Macroeconomic Implications' (2020) 135 *The Quarterly Journal of Economics* 561.

[18] ibid; J De Loecker, J Eeckhout, S Mongey, 'Quantifying Market Power and Business Dynamism in the Macroeconomy' (2021) National Bureau of Economic Research Working Paper 28761, www.nber.org/papers/w28761.

[19] De Loecker, Eeckhout and Unger (n 17); De Loecker and Eeckhout (n 7).

monopsony (wage-setting power) effect is, from an economic perspective, identical to the analysis of monopoly power in product markets.[20] Since the early 1980s, the link between productivity growth (how much the individual worker produces) and real increases in wages appears to have declined.[21] That is to say that companies are sharing less of the gains than they used to.[22] This wage stagnation has been partly attributed to weakening competition in labour markets.[23] All in all, competition (or the lack of it) in both product and labour markets is expected to affect wealth, consumption, and income inequality.

The empirical relationship between the intensity of competition and the degree of inequality, at the macro-economic level was first investigated by Comanor and Smiley in 1975.[24] They found that up to a half of wealth holdings by the richest 2.4 per cent of American households at the time was entirely due to capitalised market power gains. Han uses a panel of 22 countries (18 developed) from between 1961 to 2004 and finds a positive effect of market power on the top 5, 1 and 0.1 per cent income shares, and the opposite effect on the lowest 10 per cent and 5 per cent income shares.[25] More recently, Ennis, Gonzaga and Pike investigated this relationship in eight OECD countries and found that, on average, market power increases the wealth of the richest 10 per cent by between 12 and 21 per cent, while it reduces the income of the poorest 20 per cent by 11 per cent or more.[26] In another paper, Gans et al focused on the effects of capital shareholding versus consumption in the US, exploring the conditions under which market power can

[20] S Naidu, EA Posner and G Weyl, 'Antitrust Remedies for Labor Market Power' (2018) 132 *Harvard Law Review* 536.

[21] L Mishel and R Eisenbrey, 'How to Raise Wages: Policies That Work and Policies That Don't' (2015) 45 *Stetson Law Review* 43; J Bivens et al, 'Raising America's Pay: Why It's Our Central Economic Policy Challenge' (2014) Economic Policy Institute Briefing Paper 378, www.epi.org/publication/raising-americas-pay/; J Uguccioni, A Sharpe and A Murray, 'Labour Productivity and the Distribution of Real Earnings in Canada, 1976 to 2014' (2016) CSLS Research Report 2016-15, www.csls.ca/reports/csls2016-15.pdf.

[22] B Bell, P Bukowski and S Machin, 'Rent Sharing and Inclusive Growth' (2018) IZA Discussion Paper 12060, www.iza.org/publications/dp/12060/rent-sharing-and-inclusive-growth.

[23] Weakening competition in labour markets could be a result of de-unionisation of the labour supply. D Card, 'The Effect of Unions on the Structure of Wages: A Longitudinal Analysis' (1996) 64 *Econometrica: Journal of the Econometric Society* 957; HS Farber et al, 'Unions and Inequality over the Twentieth Century: New Evidence from Survey Data' (2021) 136 *The Quarterly Journal of Economics* 1325. It could also follow from higher levels of concentration on the demand side, ie, employers. See J Azar, I Marinescu and M Steinbaum, 'Measuring Labor Market Power Two Ways' (2019) 109 *AEA Papers and Proceedings* 317. It may also be brought about by anti-competitive behaviour. AB Krueger and O Ashenfelter, 'Theory and Evidence on Employer Collusion in the Franchise Sector' [2021] *Journal of Human Resources* 1019; E Starr, JJ Prescott and N Bishara, 'Noncompetes in the US Labor Force' (2021) 64 *Journal of Law and Economics* 53.

[24] WS Comanor and RH Smiley, 'Monopoly and the Distribution of Wealth' (1975) 89 *The Quarterly Journal of Economics* 177.

[25] M Han and JH Pyun, 'Markups and Income Inequality: Causal Links, 1975–2011' (2021) 49 *Journal of Comparative Economics* 290.

[26] SF Ennis, P Gonzaga and C Pike, 'Inequality: A Hidden Cost of Market Power' (2019) 35 *Oxford Review of Economic Policy* 518.

transfer wealth from consumers to shareholders, and what impact these mechanisms had on income inequality. They found that the top 20 per cent consumed approximately as much as the bottom 60 per cent in the studied period, but had 15 times as much corporate equity. Because ownership is more skewed than consumption, increased markups increase inequality. The effects are increasing over time as corporate equity has become even more skewed relative to consumption.[27]

C. The Overall Relationship: Competition Law and Economic Inequality

The economic mechanism we emphasise in our research suggests that competition law affects market power through its impact on prices and wages. When competition laws are ineffective in mitigating market power in the long run, concentration levels, prices, markups and profits all increase while the demand for labour, wages and the labour share all decrease. Eventually, this dynamic leads to an increase in both income and wealth inequality.

Accordingly, most relevant to our investigation are studies that have sought to directly investigate the overall relationship between competition law and economic inequality. As far as we are aware, Dierx et al present the only empirical study on the relation between competition policy and distributional macroeconomic effects.[28] Using a mixed methods 'bottom-up' approach, the authors develop a model that connects competition policy, competition, and wealth distribution and therefore takes account of the two-part causal chain.[29] The authors investigated the effects of EU competition policy interventions on distributional outcomes across households with different skill levels and across different types of income earners (capital owners, wage earners, and benefit recipients). They found that liquidity-constrained households – ie less well-off individuals – increased their consumption after an intervention proportionally more than non-liquidity-constrained households (four times more after five years), which supports the notion that competition law enforcement could have a progressive effect. The study is illuminating as it highlights the economic mechanism at play: from the law to inequality via market competition.

[27] J Gans et al, 'Inequality and Market Concentration, When Shareholding is More Skewed Than Consumption' (2019) 35 *Oxford Review of Economic Policy* 550.

[28] A Dierx et al, 'Distributional Macroeconomic Effects of the European Union Competition Policy: A General Equilibrium Analysis' in M Martinez Licetti et al (eds), *A Step Ahead: Competition Policy for Shared Prosperity and Inclusive Growth* (Washington, DC, World Bank Group, 2017).

[29] Consumers' savings estimates are calculated by multiplying the foreseen reduction in prices (in comparison with the counterfactual of no competition policy intervention), the duration of such price reduction, and the turnover in the market affected by the decision.

III. Data Description

This section outlines the data that underpins our empirical analysis. We describe the two competition law indicators and the three measures of economic inequality used in our analysis. We also discuss the control variables we use to isolate the effect of competition law on inequality. Descriptive statistics for all variables are presented in Table 3.1.

Table 3.1 Overview of the variables[30]

Variable	Source	Obs	Mean	Std. Dev.	Min	Max
Competition law indices						
cli_overall_norm	Bradford & Chilton (2018)	2004	0.63	0.17	0.09	1
anti_monopoly (GCI)	World Economic Forum	1174	4.01	0.79	2.02	6.12
Inequality indicators						
gini_mkt	SWIID	2004	0.51	0.10	0.23	0.70
ehii	UTIP-UNIDO	741	43.75	7.10	26.93	58.92
top1_wealth	WID	1174	0.29	0.08	0.12	0.52
Controls						
gdp_pc	WDI	2004	13453	12608	598	125011
inflat	WDI	2004	18.35	150.59	0.02	4735
unemployment	WDI	2004	13.08	10.06	0.31	33.47
imp_gdp	WDI	2004	38.39	21.96	6.93	208.33
exp_gdp	WDI	2004	36.44	23.08	6.73	228.99
gov_exp	WDI	2004	16.90	4.22	4.99	33.41
life_exp	WDI	2004	67.94	9.42	45.09	82.59
inv	WDI	2004	22.56	5.82	1.17	57.99

Notes: The table reports the descriptive statistics of the sample used in the analysis in section IV.

[30] The *inflat* proxy presents high absolute values with respect to the max and the min in the original raw data, which are not the result of measurement errors. They refer to events such as the hyperinflation experienced by Peru and the deflation in Angola. However, in the econometric analysis, since we take the log transformation, these limited extreme values are automatically dropped out of the sample and the few outliers left are rescaled accordingly. The *cli_overall_norm* ranges from 0 to 1 and, similarly, when we run the model in log, its minimum values are not kept in the sample. In doing this, we decided to adopt a conservative approach, by keeping those countries which had already a competition law in place. We did not want our results to capture the shift in the adoption of antitrust law, which would have affected the main purpose and the implications of our analysis.

A. Competition Law Indices

A key challenge in the empirical analysis of competition law is how to accurately measure it in quantitative terms. In recent years, numerous competition law indices have been constructed to capture the goals, scope and effectiveness of competition laws in different jurisdictions over time. For the purposes of our analysis, we rely on two competition law indices: the Competition Law Index (CLI), and the World Economic Forum Global Competitiveness Index (GCI).[31] The two indices are the most comprehensive competition law indices available and allow for the use of panel data econometrics.

The CLI, which was developed by Bradford and Chilton, is the most comprehensive and current index of the scope of competition laws available to date and includes almost all countries (123 out of 126) that enacted competition laws between 1889–2010.[32] The CLI is of value as it allows for cross-country, time-series research on competition laws (ie panel data). The database includes aggregated dummy variables that capture the key elements of competition regulation: merger control; abuse of dominance; horizontal agreements; authority powers; and substance law (which refers to the aggregation of the three sub-categories of rules). Each element is based on a set of dummy variables (0/1) and aggregated into a 0–1 scale of the norm. We use the variable *cli_overall_norm*, which aggregates the five elements into a single overall CLI index 0–1 (0 = worst; 1 = best), measuring thus the scope of competition regulation (the 'size of the net': which actions are considered unlawful under the law).

The GCI contains data from 152 countries over a decade (2007–2017) covering a broad set of indicators. It offers a wide-ranging perspective on institutions, infrastructure, ICT adoption, macroeconomic stability, health, skills, product markets, labour markets, financial system, market size, business dynamism and innovation capability. For our analysis, we specifically use the antimonopoly policy indicator (*anti_monopoly*), which measures the perceived effectiveness of competition policy; it ranges from 1 to 7, indicating the worst and the best score, respectively. Like the CLI, the GCI allows for panel-data research on competition laws, albeit on

[31] Other competition law indices include the following: Nicholson's Antitrust Law Index. See MW Nicholson, 'An Antitrust Law Index for Empirical Analysis of International Competition Policy' (2008) 4 *Journal of Competition Law and Economics* 1009. This index classifies competition law regimes according to three headings: (i) Regime Structure (scope, structure, and available remedies), (ii) Merger Policy (notification, assessment criteria, and rights of private enforcement), and (iii) Anti-competitive Practices (dominance and restrictive trade practices). Voigt's index. See S Voigt, 'The Effects of Competition Policy on Development – Cross-Country Evidence Using Four New Indicators' (2009) 45 *Journal of Development Studies* 1225. The index provides another competition law index based on four indicators: (i) the substantive content of competition laws, (ii) the degree to which they incorporate an economic approach, (iii) the formal independence of the competition agencies that are to implement the competition laws, and (iv) the actual independence of the competition agencies.

[32] A Bradford and AS Chilton, 'Competition Law around the World from 1889 to 2010: The Competition Law Index' (2018) 14 *Journal of Competition Law & Economics* 393.

a more limited time horizon. The extent of overlap between the two indicators is minimal (2007–2010) and coincided with the financial crisis, which limits comparability. The GCI data is limited by the method of collection (survey of experts and practitioners) but allows for a closer look at how competition law enforcement interacts with inequality and goes beyond the 'law of the books' nature of the CLI.

B. Economic Inequality Indicators

For the purpose of our analysis, we use different and complementary proxies of economic inequality. They include the gross Gini index (*gini_mkt*), the EHII index (Estimated Household Income Inequality, *ehii*), and the top 1 per cent wealth share (*top1_wealth*). Again, like in the case of competition law indices, each measure captures a different aspect of economic inequality.

The Gini index is focused on income inequality. It can range from 0 (perfect equality in income distribution) to 1 (perfect inequality). In other words, it offers a proxy of distribution rather than absolute values. The index is taken from the SWIID (Standardized World Income Inequality Database)[33] and spans the period between 1960 and 2019.

The EHII proxy reflects wage inequality. It ranges from 0 (perfect equality) to 100 (perfect inequality). Being based on individual wage income only, it does not include income from self-employment nor from the agricultural sector. It is thus less comprehensive but more stable over time than the Gini index.[34] EHII comes from the UTIP-UNIDO (University of Texas Inequality Project – United Nations Industrial Development Organization) and covers a slightly shorter period than the Gini index (between 1963 and 2015).

The wealth inequality proxy measures the net personal wealth share held by the top 1 per cent group in a country. Personal wealth is the total value of non-financial and financial assets – eg housing, land, deposits, bonds, and equities – held by households, minus their debts. The indicator is expressed as a ratio which emphasises the right end tail of the wealth distribution. It has been taken from the World Inequality Database (WID)[35] and covers only the period between 1995 and 2018.

[33] The source of the Gini indices, the SWIID dataset, 'represents a particular choice in the balance between comparability and coverage: it maximizes comparability for the broadest available set of country-year observations'. F Solt, 'Standardizing the World Income Inequality Database' (2009) 90 *Social Science Quarterly* 231.

[34] It does not include capital income and other sources of financial gains, which depend to a large extent on the fluctuations of the stock markets (such as stock options realisations, wage or salary payout as a direct result of investments in venture capital). The EHII is calculated by first regressing the Deininger and Squire (DS) Gini index on the UTIP-UNIDO Theil pay inequality index (which measures the dispersion of wages within the manufacturing sector, as an indicator of sector specialisation) and other control variables (such as the manufacturing employment share and other dummies related to data structure). Predicted values are then used to construct the EHII indicator.

[35] See project website for more details: wid.world.

C. Control Variables

We include various controls typically associated with inequality in cross-country macroeconomic studies.[36] The main source for these variables is the World Development Indicators (WDI) repository maintained by the World Bank. We include GDP per capita (in constant US dollars, 2,000) (*gdp_pc*) to capture the level of economic development of a country and the inflation rate (*inflat*) to account for macroeconomic stability and monetary policy.[37] The total unemployment rate (*unemployment*) is also included. Increased unemployment has been found to disproportionately affect low-income groups and increase inequality, as more workers shift to the bottom of the income distribution.[38] The level of imports (*imp_gdp*) and exports (*exp_gdp*) as a percentage of GDP are included separately.[39] Public expenditure (*gov_exp*) as a percentage of GDP can be effective in reducing inequality, if efficiently allocated, by improving the living conditions of the bottom income earners through redistributive policies; on the other hand, if the public resources are not wisely employed, inequality might increase. We also include life expectancy in years (*life_exp*) as a proxy for human capital. We acknowledge that education would have been a better proxy and that it plays a crucial role in shaping inequality.[40] However, the limited amount of data and the presence of several missing values would have further reduced the size of our sample. In addition, life expectancy is strongly and positively correlated with education.[41] Finally, gross capital formation or physical investment (*inv*) as a percentage of GDP is added as

[36] RJ Barro, 'Inequality and Growth Revisited' (2008) Asian Development Bank Working Paper Series on Regional Economic Integration No 11, www.adb.org/sites/default/files/publication/28168/wp11-inequality-growth-revisited.pdf; MD Delis, I Hasan and P Kazakis, 'Bank Regulations and Income Inequality: Empirical Evidence' (2014) 18 *Review of Finance* 1811; O Causa, A De Serres and N Ruiz, 'Can Pro-Growth Policies Lift All Boats? An Analysis Based on Household Disposable Income' (2015) *OECD Journal: Economic Studies* 227; S Jauch and S Watzka, 'Financial Development and Income Inequality: A Panel Data Approach' (2016) 51 *Empirical Economics* 291.

[37] The effect of inflation on inequality is ambiguous. See, eg, O Coibion et al, 'Innocent Bystanders? Monetary Policy and Inequality' (2017) 88 *Journal of Monetary Economics* 70; D Furceri, P Loungani and A Zdzienicka, 'The Effects of Monetary Policy Shocks' (2018) 85 *Journal of International Money and Finance* 168. Inflation can be costly and harmful for the poor, who hold more illiquid assets. When prices increase, the real value of wages and cash decreases, while the value of financial assets (mostly held by the wealthy groups) increases, making the rich better insured and protected against uncertainty. However, lower interest rates can benefit borrowers (middle-class households with fixed-rate mortgage debt) to the detriment of savers. See M Doepke and M Schneider, 'Inflation and the Redistribution of Nominal Wealth' (2006) 114 *Journal of Political Economy* 1069.

[38] BM Van Arnum and MI Naples, 'Financialization and Income Inequality in the United States, 1967–2010' (2013) 72 *American Journal of Economics and Sociology* 1158.

[39] M Roser and JC Cuaresma, 'Why Is Income Inequality Increasing in the Developed World?' (2016) 62 *Review of Income and Wealth* 1.

[40] D Coady and A Dizioli, 'Income Inequality and Education Revisited: Persistence, Endogeneity and Heterogeneity' (2018) 50 *Applied Economics* 2747.

[41] The *life_exp* proxy is highly correlated with the education measure (ρ=0.85) and there is sufficient data for the required time periods of our analysis.

a control to capture differences in how the rate of returns of human and physical capital interact with inequality over time.[42]

IV. Econometric Specifications and Results

Our econometric estimation strategy is based on a log-log OLS model with two different specifications to account for year and country fixed effects (specification I) and regional time trends (specification II). By including country and time fixed effects, we seek to account for the time-invariant unobservable heterogeneity across the economies (such as their preferences towards inequality aversion, their historical and legal background, and cultural factors) and common macroeconomic shocks and potential global trends (such as global financial shocks). The interaction between geographical regions (according to the World Bank categorisation) and years captures region-time variant factors. This allows us to take account of the effects of changes (and shocks) over time among macro geographic regions. We also estimate robust standard errors and cluster them at the country level to correct for heteroskedasticity and correlation in the error terms. We estimate the model in logs to better account for outliers and to ease the interpretation of results in terms of elasticities. The econometric specifications are as follows:

Specification I

$$Y_{i,t} = \beta_0 + \beta_1 Comp_{i,t} + \sum X_{i,t} + \alpha_i + \gamma_t + \varepsilon_{i,t} \quad (1)$$

Specification II

$$Y_{i,t} = \beta_0 + \beta_1 Comp_{i,t} + \sum X_{i,t} + \alpha_i + \gamma_t + \delta_{j2} * \gamma_t + \varepsilon_{i,t} \quad (2)$$

Where i defines the country, j the region (according to the geographical areas categorised by the World Bank) and t the years; $Y_{i,t}$ is the inequality measure (Gini, EHII, WID index) and $Comp_{i,t}$ is the country-level competition law index (CLI or GCI). $\sum X_{i,t}$ are the control variables considered to be the co-founders of economic inequality (level of economic development, inflation, unemployment, imports, exports, public expenditure, life expectancy, and investment) and listed in Table 3.1; α_i refers to the country fixed effect; γ_t captures the time fixed effect; $\delta_j * \gamma_t$ measures the regional time trend term; and $\varepsilon_{i,t}$ is the error term.

Table 3.2 presents the results of the analysis of the relationship between the CLI, and the Gini and EHII wage inequality measures for all available countries

[42] O Galor and O Moav, 'From Physical to Human Capital Accumulation: Inequality and the Process of Development' (2004) 71 *Review of Economic Studies* 1001. According to this model, in the initial phase of industrialisation, physical capital tends to be the main booster of economic growth (also ensuring a higher rate of return), exacerbating income inequality, as the poor have a lower marginal propensity to save. As the economy develops, the rate of return on human capital increases, making human capital accumulation the main engine of growth.

in the CLI dataset.[43] We follow the two specifications detailed in equations 1 and 2 (equation 1: columns 1 and 2, equation 2: columns 3 and 4). As can be seen in Table 3.2, the associations between the CLI and the two inequality measures are mostly negative, but only one specification – concerning wage inequality (EHII) – is statistically significant. This likely reflects a weak correlation between the scope of law and income distribution at this level of aggregation. As discussed above, one of the links between competition law and income inequality goes through the effects of market power on the demand for labour, wages and the labour share. When firms exercise market power to set high prices, the demand for products and labour goes down together with the equilibrium wage (especially the low-skilled wages) and the labour share. The observed differences between the general income-based measures of inequality (gini_mkt) and the wage-based measures (EHII) might be related to the interaction between market power and the demand for labour. Addressing this interaction requires a more disaggregated analysis at the industry or firm level. In section V below, we offer more detail on our exploration of the labour share mechanism based on a cross-industry study.

Table 3.2 Log-log, CLI and income and wage inequality

	(1)	(2)	(3)	(4)
	log_gini_mkt	**log_ehii**	**log_gini_mkt**	**log_ehii**
log_CLI_overall_norm	−0.007	−0.007	0.001	−0.038*
	(0.006)	(0.017)	(0.008)	(0.020)
_cons	−0.569	3.503***	−0.137	3.132**
	(0.454)	(0.957)	(0.467)	(1.412)
Obs.	1527	764	1527	764
Controls	YES	YES	YES	YES
Country & Year FE	YES	YES	YES	YES
Region time trends	NO	NO	YES	YES
R-squared	0.971	0.931	0.976	0.949

While the Gini looks at the spread of income inequality in general, we wanted to further focus our attention on the way in which competition law might relate to extremes of inequality and in particular the top 1 per cent of wealth. This line of inquiry is driven by concerns that the share of global wealth held by the top 1 per cent has been rising over the past decade,[44] and suggestions that competition

[43] For the sake of brevity, we have not included the results for the control variables, including the country and region fixed effects.

[44] Evidence points toward a rise in global wealth concentration. For China, Europe, and the US combined, the top 1% wealth share has increased from 28% in 1980 to 33% 2019, while the bottom 75% share hovered around 10%. G Zucman, 'Global Wealth Inequality' (2019) 11 *Annual Review of Economics* 109.

law has been ineffective in stopping this from happening (as firms' profits rise). To do this, we compared the GCI with the changes in top 1 per cent wealth share.[45] As shown by Table 3.3, we found negative and statistically significant results, which we discuss below.[46]

Table 3.3 Log-log, GCI and top one per cent wealth ratio

	(1)	(2)
	log_top1_wealth	**log_top1_wealth**
log_GCI	−0.078*	−0.074*
	(.042)	(.042)
_cons	0.06	−0.313
	(1.534)	(2.084)
Obs.	1174	1174
Controls	YES	YES
Country & Year FE	YES	YES
Region-time trend	NO	YES
R-squared	0.943	0.951

V. Discussion of Results

The results presented in section IV offer several insights into the relationship between competition law and economic inequality. Overall, we observe a negative relationship between the competition law indices and the inequality measures in five of the six specifications, with the relationship being statistically significant in three specifications. While the analysis provides some support for a relationship between competition law and economic inequality, it is not conclusive, and should not be interpreted causally. We attribute this result to three main factors.

First, the analysis was undertaken at the macro-scale using country-level indicators of inequality and competition law. While such an approach is consistent with the standard approach of many macroeconomic studies of inequality – such as those which examine the relationship between economic growth and inequality – it is arguably less suited to this inquiry as effects of competition

[45] The cross-country data on top wealth shares coverage is limited in most countries to the middle of the 1990s, making the CLI (which covers data until 2010) less suited for an analysis with these proxies, and we can only report the results for the GCI.

[46] Our inquiry included other types of economic inequality measures which we do not report here, including the Gini income inequality measure (post tax), and the top income inequality shares (1–10 per cent). Overall, the results remain similar with a negative coefficient with statistical significance in some but not all specifications. We explore the potential reasons for our inquiry results in section V.

law tend to be at the microeconomic level (ie in specific markets or sectors). As such, while competition law could impact inequality in a specific sector (such as financial services) or market (such as gasoline markets), this effect could be lost in aggregated macroeconomic data. Put simply, one reason why we may not observe a strong relationship between competition law and inequality is because the macroeconomic scale of the analysis conceals some of the effects that competition law may generate at a smaller scale (sector, industry, relevant market). In another study, we address this limitation and carry out the analysis at a more granular scale, looking at the aggregate effects of competition law enforcement on UK households over a 15-year period.[47]

Second, the analysis presented in this chapter is based on a panel dataset that combined data for over 100 countries across several decades. Unsurprisingly, there is considerable heterogeneity in the data both across countries and over time. While we have attempted to control for such heterogeneity by introducing various controls (time fixed effects and geographic region time trends), it nevertheless remains the case that there are likely to be important differences between countries (and within countries over time) which could affect inequality and that are not accounted for in our analysis and might alter the results. More refined estimation strategies of causal effects are needed to reach conclusive results concerning the effects of competition law on economic inequality. A recent example of an alternative approach can be found in another study of ours,[48] which uses industry panel data to investigate the links between competition policy, competitive margins and changes in the labour share observed in many industrialised countries. The results indicate a strong statistically significant relationship between effective competition policy and the labour share, suggesting that weak competition policy may contribute to higher levels of economic inequality through the decline of the labour share.

Lastly, while our approach was driven by coverage of competition law indices (starting from the widest measures available) the differences between the indices limited our ability to capture meaningful effects of competition policies. For example, the CLI which measures the scope of law is based on the 'law of the books', and therefore does not capture a situation where the text of laws in a jurisdiction is stable over time but the level of enforcement of that law changes significantly. As such, it is less suited for examination of the way in which changes in the application of competition law relate to changes in economic inequality.[49] The GCI, on the other hand, is based on the perceptions of experts and practitioners about the effectiveness of the anti-monopoly enforcement in a country and may better

[47] C Decker et al, 'Competition Law Enforcement and Household Inequality' (2022) *Journal of Competition Law and Economics*.

[48] A Zac et al, 'Competition Policy and the Labour Share' (2022) ssrn.com/abstract=3824115.

[49] It may be more suited to other analysis of the development of the laws over time and areas of the world, such as A Bradford, AS Chilton and FM Lancieri, 'The Chicago School's Limited Influence on International Antitrust' (2020) 87 *The University of Chicago Law Review* 297.

reflect the actual working of competition law, but is sensitive to data errors resulting from the subjectivity of survey methods.

VI. Conclusion

While it is increasingly acknowledged that competition law could affect inequality levels, the specific ways and mechanisms through which a competition law regime might interact with economic inequality remain largely unexplored. Given the limitations of traditional tools, such as taxation and public expenditure, in tackling economic inequality, there is clear value in broadening our understanding of the possible interrelations between competition law and inequality.

In this chapter, we empirically investigated the relationship between competition law and economic inequality by taking advantage of large-scale global datasets that cover many countries over a long period. This is one of the first attempts to use large cross-country panel datasets to empirically test the intuition that a link between competition laws and economic inequality exists. Our approach has been the traditional one used in macro-inequality studies: we compared changes in different competition law indices to a number of macro-indicators of inequality over a large period of time (several decades) and across many countries (over 100).

Overall, we find some evidence of a negative relationship between competition law and inequality. However, while the relationship between competition law and inequality is consistently negative across most of the econometric specifications, it is not statistically significant in all cases. The precise relationship appears to be sensitive to factors such as the competition law index used, and the inequality measure applied. Given the considerable heterogeneity in the data and the macro-scale of the analysis, these results are neither surprising nor conclusive. Nevertheless, they suggest that competition law could have an impact on economic inequality. To fully understand the relationship between competition law and inequality, we recommend that further analysis be conducted, to test more precise transmission mechanisms at different scales such as the country, industry and household level.

PART II

Economic Inequality in Doctrines of Individual Jurisdictions

4

Antitrust and Inequality: The History of (In)Equality in Competition Law and Its Guide to the Future

ELEANOR M FOX AND PHILIPP BASCHENHOF*

I. Introduction

The inequality of wealth and income is increasing at a frightening pace across much of the world. At the same time, researchers are documenting increasing market power of large corporate players in concentrated markets. Market power may produce higher prices, less choice, less innovation, blocked opportunities, and lower wages. Studies link inequality of wealth and income with antitrust – the body of law charged with control of market power. Is antitrust (also called 'competition law') a cause of inequality of wealth and income? Is it a cure?

Many scholars and policymakers answer yes to both questions. They typically recommend more aggressive antitrust, more funding of the antitrust agencies, prioritisation of cases that could principally help the middle- and lower-income population, and exemptions from antitrust for smaller market players.[1] A separate body of scholarship questions whether antitrust has caused or could remedy inequality.[2]

There is a gap in the literature. No one has previously written the history of equality/inequality in antitrust: how has equality as a value been received into, or rejected by, antitrust? Is it a sympathetic or foreign element? How the value has been used in the past and is being used today can illuminate how it might be used

* The authors thank editors Jan Broulík and Katalin Cseres for their extraordinary attention to both concept and detail in this chapter. Their suggestions have helped improve this work enormously. They also thank Firoz Cachalia, Maarten Pieter Schinkel, and Christine Bartholomew for helpful and stimulating comments. They thank Edmund Brose, candidate for JD 2023 at New York University School of Law, for his excellent research assistance. Eleanor Fox is grateful to the Filomen D'Agostino and Max E Greenberg Foundation for research support.

[1] See Khan and Vaheesan (n 4) and (n 5), Valletti and Zenger (n 6) and (n 7), Ennis, Gonzaga and Pike (n 8) and (n 9), Hsu (n 10)–(n 12) below.

[2] See text at n 13 below.

in the future. It can clarify the receptivity, or not, of the antitrust ecosystem to equality. This chapter helps to fill the gap.

The chapter offers four country studies. The countries (or jurisdictions) were selected to illustrate the full range of approaches from antagonism to equality as relevant to antitrust to equality as a raison d'être of antitrust. The country studies become a laboratory for drawing recommendations and conclusions.

To give context to the country studies, this chapter briefly reviews the main points and claims in the literature on antitrust and inequality. It observes the multifaceted nature of the problem, including some difficulties in using antitrust to address the wealth/income gaps. After the country studies, the chapter synthesises the results, considers how equality can be integrated into antitrust in view of how it has been integrated in the past, and ends with recommendations and conclusions.

The chapter takes as a starting point the premises that inequality of wealth and income without significant mobility is rising dramatically, and that extreme and growing inequality without mobility threatens the legitimacy of the socio-economic fabric, undermining democracy and causing instability within nations and in the world.[3]

II. Main Points and Claims in the Literature

This section cuts a path through the growing body of literature on antitrust and inequality by, first, drawing from four seminal articles that illuminate the antitrust-inequality links, and, second, describing the literature that disputes the links. The four selected articles make a powerful case for a role for antitrust and give flavour, even passion, to the claims.

The section begins with the work of Lina Khan and Sandeep Vaheesan, who stress market power as a principal vehicle for transferring wealth to the very rich. While they focus on the US, their observations can fairly be generalised to the world. In their article *Market Power and Inequality: The Antitrust Counterrevolution and its Discontents*, they write:[4]

> In recent years, economic inequality has become a central topic of public debate in the United States and much of the developed world. … As top intellectuals, politicians,

[3] See UN Department of Economic and Social Affairs, 'Rising inequality affecting more than two-thirds of the globe, but it's not inevitable: new UN report', (21 January 2020, UN Press Release) ('Inequality is growing for more than 70 per cent of the global population, exacerbating the risks of divisions and hampering economic and social development … The study shows that the richest one per cent of the population are the big winners in the changing global economy, increasing their share of income between 1990 and 2015, while at the other end of the scale, the bottom 40 per cent earned less than a quarter of income in all countries surveyed. One of the consequences of inequality within societies … is slower economic growth. In unequal societies, with wide disparities in areas such as health care and education, people are more likely to remain trapped in poverty, across several generations').

[4] L Khan and S Vaheesan, 'Market Power and Inequality: The Antitrust Counterrevolution and its Discontents' (2017) 11 *Harvard Law and Policy Review*, 235.

> and public figures have come to recognize inequality as a major problem that must be addressed, they have offered a range of potential solutions [in fields such as tax, labour, trade, investment, and financial institutions].
>
> One underexplored theme in this larger debate is the role of monopoly and oligopoly power. Given the current distribution of business ownership assets in the United States, market power can be a powerful mechanism for transferring wealth from the many among the working and middle classes to the few belonging to the 1% and 0.1% at the top of the income and wealth distribution.[5]

Second, Tommaso Valletti and Hans Zenger document a 'significant body of empirical research showing increases in margins across a wide range of industries …'. They write in their article, *Increasing Market Power and Merger Control*:[6]

> A significant body of empirical research has documented a structural increase in margins across a wide range of industries and countries. On average, firms enjoy appreciably greater pricing power today than used to be the case in prior decades. Research also showed that this increase in mark-ups coincide[s] with a decline in the labour share of output, higher aggregate concentration, larger corporate profitability, and a slump in business dynamism ….[7]

Third, Sean Ennis, Pedro Gonzaga and Chris Pike, having constructed a model to measure the effect of market power on inequality, report a sizeable effect of market power on the middle class and the poorest segment of the population. Their article, *Inequality: A Hidden Cost of Market Power*,[8] concludes:

> This paper provides evidence that market power can contribute substantially to wealth inequality, augmenting wealth of the richest 10% of the population on average by 12% to 21%, depending on … saving behaviour, and reducing the income of the poorest 20% of the population by 11% or more. The groups of the population who are typically harmed by market power are the 0 to 80th percentiles, and interestingly the harm

[5] ibid 235–36.

[6] TM Valletti and H Zenger, 'Increasing Market Power and Merger Control' (2019) 5 *Competition Law & Policy Debate* 26.

[7] ibid, citing and drawing from authorities including D Autor et al, 'The Fall of the Labor Share and the Rise of Superstar Firms' (2020) 135 *Quarterly Journal of Economics* 2; J De Loecker, J Eeckhout and G Unger, 'The Rise of Market Power and the Macroeconomic Implications' (2020) 135 *Quarterly Journal of Economics* 561; C Shapiro, 'Antitrust in a Time of Populism' (2018) 61 *International Journal of Industrial Organization* 714; G Gutiérrez and T Philippon, 'Declining Competition and Investment in the U.S.' (2017) NBER Working Paper 23583. Robert E Hall and James Traina also find higher US markups since the 1980s but find less significant increases than De Loecker, Eeckhout and Unger. See RE Hall, 'Using Empirical Marginal Cost to Measure Market Power in the U.S. Economy' (National Bureau of Economic Research Working Paper, 2018) www.nber.org/papers/w25251; J Traina, 'Is Aggregate Market Power Increasing? Production Trends Using Financial Statements' (Working Paper, 2018 Stigler Center for the Study of the Economy and the State, University of Chicago Booth School of Business) research.chicagobooth.edu/-/media/research/stigler/pdfs/workingpapers/17isaggregate marketpowerincreasing.pdf.

[8] S Ennis, P Gonzaga and C Pike, 'Inequality: A Hidden Cost of Market Power' (2019) 35 *Oxford Review of Economic Policy* 518. (Study of eight countries: Canada, France, Germany, Korea, Japan, Spain, UK and US). See for data on rising corporate market power, U Akcigit et al., 'Rising Corporate Market Power: Emerging Policy Issues' (2021) www.imf.org/en/Publications/Staff-Discussion-Notes/Issues/2021/03/10/Rising-Corporate-Market-Power-Emerging-Policy-Issues-48619. See also, for work

appears to be particularly accentuated on a middle class comprised somewhere between the 20th to 60th percentiles.[9]

Fourth, Shi-Ling Hsu offers a nuance. Hsu is sceptical of the link between growing concentration and inequality, and sceptical that concentration has harmed consumers, but identifies a major shift in the capital-labour ratio as relevant to inequality. He writes in his article *Antitrust and Inequality: The Problem of Super-firms:*[10]

> [L]arge, consolidated 'super-firms' have grabbed ominously large market shares, limited consumer choices, and threatened to render local provision of goods and services anachronistic. … [Unrest has exploded into politics and] populist anger. … Monopoly or oligopoly rents transfer wealth from consumers to producers, which would seem to naturally lead to an increase in inequality.
>
> But the linkage between inequality and the rise of this new trend towards industrial concentration is not always so clear. For one thing, as Daniel Crane argues,[[11]] heterogeneity among consumers and producers render it extremely difficult to determine whether on net, industrial concentration redistributes wealth from poor to rich. On the consumer side, the rise of these super-firms that seek to dominate markets for internet search, retail, social media, telecommunications, electronics, and seemingly everything important have, despite their ominously large market shares, incontrovertibly produced enormous consumers surplus. …
>
> … [Still, antitrust law may] contribute to inequality in a subtle but important way: by contributing to a shift in the capital-labor ratio of some of the most dominant firms.[12]

Other scholars dismiss or qualify claims of linkages. They dispute the claim that concentration is increasing, or that it is increasing beyond a handful of markets that require large scale for better service (high tech, health care, energy, transportation, on-line retailing). They disagree with the broad generalisation that business concentration undermines competition and point to markets with few firms where competition is intense. They would not infer monopoly profits from higher prices, which may reflect higher quality or better service. They question whether, when higher mark-ups are observed, the increment is traceable to concentration

identifying market power as contributing to inequality, authorities in Valletti and Zenger (n 7) above and B Kavoussi, 'How market power has increased U.S. inequality' (3 May 2019, Washington Center for Equitable Growth) equitablegrowth.org/how-market-power-has-increased-u-s-inequality/; J Furman and P Orszag, '*A Firm-Level Perspective on the Role of Rents in the Rise in Inequality*' (2015 Presentation at A Just Society Centennial Event in Honor of Joseph Stiglitz at Columbia University); S Salop and J Baker, 'Antitrust, Competition Policy, and Inequality' (2015) 104 *Georgetown Law Journal* 1; E Saez and G Zucman, 'Wealth Inequality in the United States since 1913: Evidence from Capitalized Income Tax Data' (Working Paper, 2014 NBER), gabriel-zucman.eu/files/SaezZucman2014.pdf.

[9] Ennis, Gonzaga and Pike (n 8) 539.

[10] S-L Hsu, 'Antitrust and Inequality: The Problem of Super-firms' (2018) 63 *The Antitrust Bulletin* 104, 105. Footnotes omitted.

[11] [Authors' footnote] D Crane, 'Antitrust and Wealth Inequality' (2016) 101 *Cornell Law Review* 1171.

[12] Hsu (n 10) 105–06.

(as opposed to efficiency). They dispute the narrative that firms are currently making higher than normal profits. They do not believe that monopoly profits, when made, go systematically and disproportionately to the rich and high-income earners.[13]

For those of us who have not prepared the studies or closely examined the data, it is not easy to work through this briar patch of literature. There appears to be a tendency of scholars writing on antitrust and inequality to cite the narrative that fits predilections they have previously expressed for either more robust or more reluctant antitrust enforcement.[14] Fortunately, the discrepancy does not matter for the policy recommendations, as explained below.

III. Observations on the Complexity of the Problem

As background and for context, this chapter makes six initial observations.

First, there are many causes for the rising inequality gap. First among them are globalisation, technological advances, and the catapulting of super firms especially in the digital sector, where the power and sway of the super firms has been enhanced by the pandemic.[15] The world is witnessing 'The Rise and Rise of the

[13] See GA Manne, D Auer and S Bowman, 'Should ASEAN Antitrust Laws Emulate European Competition Policy?' (2021) 66 *The Singapore Economic Review Online* doi.org/10.1142/S0217590821430025; GJ Werden, 'Concentration and Rising Market Power: Fears and Facts', ch 5 in P Akman, O Brook and K Stylianou (eds), *Research Handbook on Abuse of Dominance and Monopolization* (Cheltenham, Edward Elgar, 2022); E Dorsey, GA Manne, J Rybnicek, K Stout and JD Wright, 'Consumer Welfare & the Rule of Law: The Case against the New Populist Antitrust Movement' (2020) 47 *Pepperdine Law Review* 861 (finding that the evidence for an increase in concentration is weak and that the underlying studies offer 'no insight into actual market power' nor competitiveness in the analysed markets, ibid 891–895); J Kennedy, 'Monopoly Myths: Are Markets Becoming More Concentrated?' (29 June 2020) Information Technology and Innovation Foundation (ITIF) itif.org/publications/2020/06/29/monopoly-myths-are-markets-becoming-more-concentrated? (finding that concentration is not increasing). See also *Crane* (n 11) and DW Carlton, 'Some Observations on Claims That Rising Market Power Is Responsible for US Economy Ills and That Lax Antitrust Is the Villain' (29 June 2020) ssrn.com/abstract=3638500. Carlton observes that concentration may have led to higher margins but not higher prices, questions whether mark-ups, where they exist, are as high as De Loecker and others calculate, questions whether it is market power (or technological change, etc) that has produced a declining labour share, and presents reasons to question most of the other linkages while suggesting that some concerns may be valid and warrant more investigation.

[14] cp Khan and Vaheesan (n 4) with Manne et al. and Dorsey et al. (n 13).

[15] See, for causes, AV Banerjee and E Duflo, *Good Economics for Hard Times* (New York, PublicAffairs, 2019) 236–62. The pandemic has shifted online any business activity that can thrive in that environment, sinking the financial fates of those who depend on brick-and-mortar business. But the pandemic has caused even more nuanced shifts in inequality – in the US, those who own stocks have profited, and the very rich own a disproportionate amount of the stocks. See R Gebeloff, 'Who Owns Stocks? Explaining the Rise in Inequality During the Pandemic' *NY Times* (New York, 26 January 2021) www.nytimes.com/2021/01/26/upshot/stocks-pandemic-inequality.html. Inequality of education is a basic contributing factor. So too is the failure of developed nations such as the US to manage globalisation to protect the losers. See J Stiglitz, *People, Power, and Profits: Progressive Capitalism for an Age of Discontent* (London, Allen Lane, 2019).

One Percent'.[16] It is also witnessing stagnation in the middle class and to some extent the fall of the standard of living of the people on the bottom rungs of the inequality ladder.[17] Antitrust has not *caused* the rise and rise or the fall and fall; the market has. The market, in the context of the new technologies and their global reach, pushes inexorably towards greater concentration of wealth and income; it plays into the hands of those who have the skills and money.[18] Antitrust has not *caused* the growth of market power. Indeed, antitrust is not charged generally with preventing the growth of market power. It generally prohibits market-power-creating mergers not justified by offsetting benefits, and dominant firms' exclusionary practices that create market power, do not benefit consumers, and are not normal responses to competition. In other words, antitrust is charged with controlling just a fraction of market power in specific circumstances. Nonetheless, in leading jurisdictions that purport to be models for the world, antitrust has stood by where market power has accumulated and flourished.[19]

Second, where economic power is created by mergers or anticompetitive conduct or is used to harm competition, that is a problem that antitrust ought to address, whether or not economic concentration is rising and whether or not economic concentration generally produces more power, higher markups, or disproportionate gains to the rich. When antitrust is successfully enforced against firms with market power, the enforcement generally helps people without power or privilege and thus tends to move the law in the direction of less inequality, which could slow the trend of constant increases in the inequality gap.

Third, in most jurisdictions, antitrust primarily addresses allocative, not distributive, problems. The question – how to close the wealth-and-income inequality gap – is distributive. Those who support the allocative-only view of antitrust's domain argue that non-economic factors are alien and importing them will shrink the pie, undermine incentives to invent and invest, and make 'everyone' worse off.

[16] S-L Hsu, 'The Rise and Rise of The One Percent: Considering Legal Causes of Wealth Inequality' (2015) 64 *Emory Law Journal Online* 2043.

[17] The financial fate of the poor and near poor and in general developing countries has been exacerbated by the pandemic in view of the closures of brick-and-mortar businesses, disruption of global value chains, and ascendancy of Internet and communications technologies when the poorer countries are already far behind in access and capabilities.

[18] See Hsu (n 10); see also T Piketty, *Capital in the Twenty-First Century* (Cambridge, MA, Harvard University Press, 2014). Piketty reports rising income inequality from 1970–2010. Since the publication of his book, he has questioned whether the past is a proxy for the future and has observed that wealth inequality is much less extreme than a century ago. T Piketty, 'About Capital in the Twenty-First Century' (2015) 105 *American Economic Review* 5, 48.

This constant tendency towards inequality is a phenomenon of all economic law in a capitalist society. It is exacerbated by the fact that the elite and the establishment have a big hand in moulding the law in their favour. For corporate law, see K Pistor, *The Code of Capital: How the Law Creates Wealth and Inequality* (Princeton, Princeton University Press, 2019).

[19] See A Zac, C Casti, C Decker and A Ezrachi, 'Competition Law and Income Inequality: A Panel Data Econometric Approach' (20 April 2021) ssrn.com/abstract=3402436 or dx.doi.org/10.2139/ssrn.3402436, finding a negative relationship between competition law and level of wage and income inequality. See A Zac, 'Economic Inequality and Competition Law: A Comparative Analysis of the USA Antitrust Model' (22 September 2020) Oxford Centre for Competition Law and Policy, Working paper CCLP(L)53, finding that US antitrust is linked to higher levels of inequality than EU competition law.

The subject of antitrust and its possible role in closing the wealth-income gaps is thus fraught with ideology.

Fourth, focus on wealth and income inequality obscures other equality problems that many people believe are of higher urgency: the problems of deep systemic poverty and the problem of raw corporate power. This accounts for the fact that much of the literature on inequality of wealth and income veers off to discuss, centrally, poverty and power.

Deep systemic poverty: the problem of poverty and of the people who are the worst off is different from the problem of the skewed spread of wealth and income as between, say, the 90 per cent and the 1 or 10 per cent. The skewed spread is a huge sociological, psychological, and political democracy problem. The constant flow of wealth to the elite and the hollowing out of the middle class undermines dignity, breeds personal disaffection and depression, and weakens democracy and its legitimacy.[20] The wealth/income gap is different from the poverty problem on three counts. Its causes are different, its effects are different, and its cures are largely different. The main causes of the skewed spread include inherited wealth, globalisation and technological advances – especially in high tech and data, the rise of superstars – entertainers and firms, and rags-to-riches financial successes (especially from globalisation and high-tech developments) such as Jeff Bezos with $200 billion net worth. The persistence of educational inequalities is a critical structural factor. The effects of the skewed spread on people are diffuse; they include disaffection and a feeling of a stacked deck, loss of control, and profound unfairness; but the problem is not typically where one will get her next meal. An obvious cure for extreme inequality of wealth would be a generous wealth tax on the very rich. This would immediately shrink the wealth gap without (directly) making the poor better off. Lifting up the bottom is urgent, and handicapping the top for the sake of doing so is not a consensus goal – even if a big tax on the rich would be a welcome source of money for the common good.

Raw corporate power: competition law is about power, its accumulation and abuse. In modern times it is about efficiency, but before it was about efficiency it was about power.[21] Competition law was envisioned as a way to preserve autonomy for the people.[22] As competition law turned towards an efficiency mission, and as (especially) Big Tech/Big Data got bigger and more invasive, people began to worry about grabs of power and manipulating power in dimensions society does not yet fully appreciate.[23]

[20] See Banerjee and Duflo (n 15); M Gal, 'The Social Contract at the Basis of Competition Law: Should We Recalibrate Competition Law to Limit Inequality?' in D Gerard and I Lianos (eds), *Reconciling Efficiency and Equity: A Global Challenge for Competition Policy* (Cambridge, Cambridge University Press, 2019).

[21] See EM Fox, 'The Modernization of Antitrust: A New Equilibrium' (1981) 66 *Cornell Law Review* 1140.

[22] ibid.

[23] See S Zuboff, *The Age of Surveillance Capitalism: The Fight for a Human Future at the New Frontier of Power* (London, Profile Books, 2019); T Wu, *The Curse of Bigness: Antitrust in the New Gilded Age* (New York, Columbia Global Reports, 2018).

These two problems and what to do about them are a better fit with antitrust than whether the ultra-rich are persistently winning more than middle- and lower-income earners and what to do about that.

Fifth, some tasks antitrust can and cannot do. Antitrust cannot do anything about acquired great wealth and cannot do anything significant about the fact that the 0.1 per cent earn 200 times more than the 90 per cent. But antitrust can do something significant about keeping markets open, thus enhancing mobility and helping people and firms without power. Thus, antitrust can help promote equality of opportunity. Promoting equality of opportunity implies, at least marginally, more income for those at the lower end of the continuum, even if it does not perceptibly rebalance the wealth/income charts.

Moreover, antitrust can help prevent growth of economic power through preventing some mergers, and can prevent use of dominant power to create more power, and both merger and monopoly litigations can prevent appropriation of income and wealth by those who tend to be at the top of the scale from those who are not. Antitrust has been doing this all along (preventing wealth transfers that often would have gone to the wealthier quadrant as a by-product of condemning anticompetitive behaviour and transactions), and yet we are experiencing an unprecedented widening of the inequality gaps, probably because the major causes of the attenuation – globalisation and technology – overwhelm the possible contribution of antitrust in distributing from the ultra rich to the rest.

Sixth, equality, like democracy, can be embedded in a law even without mention of the word. It can be the music behind the words. It can entail a vision of society in which people have opportunity to join the economic enterprise on their merits, in which they can expect to get a fair share of value in goods and services, and in which they do not feel dominated by corporate power. The case studies that follow capture the various ways in which each jurisdiction incorporates a notion of equality.

With this background, the chapter turns to the case studies of the history of antitrust and equality. For each selected jurisdiction, the authors ask how 'equality' or 'inequality' is received into the competition law. The past reception may be a good proxy for future possibilities of using antitrust to help close the inequality gap.

IV. Country/Jurisdiction Studies: How Equality Is Used in the Competition Law

A. Introduction

This part examines the use of an equality value in the competition law of selected jurisdictions. It does so through the lens of trying to understand whether and how a value of equality has shaped the substantive interpretations of the competition law in ways that might lessen the inequality gap in wealth or income, and how interpretations of the competition law of the jurisdiction might help to close the gap or prevent its widening. The words 'equality/inequality' are used only in this narrow sense. What vision of competition law and what rules of law and enforcement priorities tend to increase the inequality of wealth and income, and which tend to close the gap?

Each country study describes the adoption and evolution of the law (what role for equality, historically), and then assesses whether and how the value is 'in' the law. The value may be expressed by words other than equality. For example, conceiving of the antitrust law as 'democracy of the marketplace' expresses an equality value. So too does conceiving of the law as against power and privilege, and helping outsiders or people without power to contest the market. Enhancing opportunity for small and middle-sized business and entrepreneurs is an equality value – even though some owners of small business may be wealthier than owners of or stockholders in big business. Protecting the rights of workers is an expression of an equality value, even though employees of monopolistic enterprises sometimes profit from the increased market power and revenues of their employer.

The end of each country description assesses the competition law of the jurisdiction in terms of six categories: First, is an equality value embedded in the law? Second, is it a source of wisdom available to enforcers and jurists to decide priorities or reach outcomes in particular cases? Third, are consent decrees or clearances used as an occasion for imposing conditions that can help the less-well-off, such as benefiting workers by delaying the date of layoff? Fourth, is more equality a separate mandate that can warrant an antitrust exemption or trump? Fifth, does the jurisdiction's antitrust law alleviate inequality? Does it aggravate inequality? Is it neutral on equality? or does it just not help to remedy inequality? Sixth, would equality-leaning changes in competition law be feasible and likely to help close the inequality gap?

This section is largely descriptive. It provides the basis upon which to consider what competition law can and should do to help close the inequality gap, in sections V and VI below.

B. The United States

i. The Statutes and their Interpretation

At its origins, US antitrust law had a sympathetic relationship with equality. The symbiosis reached its high point in the 1960s. But the sympathetic relationship ended in the late 1970s, and, since the early 1980s, equality and all other non-market factors have been systematically expunged from US antitrust. Contemporary US Supreme Court caselaw, especially since the *Trinko* case in 2004,[24] has ushered in a

[24] *Verizon Communs Inc v Law Offices of Curtis V Trinko* 540 U.S. 398 (2004).

long wave of devotion to 'the market', even when 'the market' is comprised of only a few producers/suppliers. A backlash, however, is brewing. Public perception by the people that the market has not worked for them, and a consciousness of severe inequalities exacerbated by the coronavirus, has led to powerful popular rhetoric and growing Congressional support for turning the tide. Whether Congress will do so is question at the time of writing.

The Sherman Act, which is the principal and oldest US federal antitrust law, was adopted in 1890 during an age of revolutionary industrialisation. The growing transportation networks brought hundreds of small local monopolies into competition with one another. New investment poured into markets. Competition was cutthroat. Moguls began to form empires, both by new means of efficient production and by stamping out or buying up competitors. Small suppliers were squeezed out by conduct foul and fair. Farmers, shippers, and consumers were over-charged and underpaid.[25] The legislative history of the Sherman Act is replete with the myriad concerns that gave birth to the law. The legislative history focuses on the giant trusts, their predatory exclusions, their exploitations, and their looming power and control over life and wealth. Urging enactment, Senator Sherman famously spoke of the problems that 'agitate' 'the popular mind' 'that may disturb social order'.[26]

> [A]mong them all none is more threatening than the inequality of condition, of wealth, and opportunity that has grown within a single generation out of the concentration of capital into vast combinations.[27]

Some legislators worried that the trusts had the power to limit production and increase price oppressively.[28] Representative Mason worried: 'Even if the price of oil is reduced to one cent a barrel, it would not right the wrong done to the people by the trusts which have destroyed legitimate competition and driven honest men from legitimate business.'[29] The legislative history reveals 'a potpourri of … values', internally inconsistent, in the words of judge/Professor Robert Bork.[30] Congress left the development of the law to the courts.

[25] HB Thorelli, *The Federal Antitrust Policy: Origination Of An American Tradition* (Baltimore, The John Hopkins Press, 1955) 143–44. See *Brown Shoe Co v United States* 370 U.S. 294, 311–23 (1962); *Standard Oil Co v United States* 221 U.S. 1, 50 (1911).

[26] 21 Cong Rec 2460 (1890).

[27] ibid.

[28] ibid 2558.

[29] ibid 4100.

[30] R Bork, 'The Role of the Courts in Applying Economics' (1985) 54 *Antitrust Law Journal* 21, 24; Only later did Bork decide to narrow the objectives to total welfare, which he famously mis-labeled consumer welfare. The Court (also famously) picked up Bork's consumer welfare language as dictum in *Reiter v Sonotone Corp* 442 U.S. 330 (1970). The issue in *Reiter* was whether consumers could *ever* sue under the antitrust laws; not whether consumer welfare was the goal of the antitrust laws. Sonotone argued that the damage section of the Clayton Act was limited to business harm. For Bork's error in mis-labeling total welfare as consumer welfare, see C Shapiro, 'Antitrust: What went wrong and How to Fix it' (29 March 2021) Draft for ABA Antitrust Section Spring Meeting (on file with Haas School of Business, Berkeley).

In early years, the courts applied the Sherman Act inconsistently, unpredictably, and sometimes very conservatively, leading Congress to pass supplemental laws in 1914. The Clayton Act designated specific conduct as an antitrust violation, including certain exclusive dealing and acquisitions. The Federal Trade Commission Act created the Federal Trade Commission to monitor and prevent business abuse, to provide guidance to businesses, and to proscribe 'unfair methods of competition'. The central theme of the legislative history of the Clayton Act is freedom of economic opportunity.[31] The Clayton Act promised to open the field 'to scores of men who had been obliged to serve when their abilities entitled them to direct'.[32]

From the passage of the Clayton Act to mid-century, antitrust paled in the shadow of war, depression, and recovery.[33] In 1936 Congress passed the Robinson Patman Act to prevent price discrimination in favour of powerful big buyers that threatened to decimate mom and pop stores.[34]

Meanwhile, just when Hitler was using Germany's private monopolies to carry out his fascist programmes, a huge merger wave hit the US.[35] People feared that too much power was falling into the hands of too few businesses, impairing economic opportunity, depriving people of control over their lives, and threatening democracy.[36] The concerns produced the Celler-Kefauver Amendment to the Clayton Act,[37] toughening the merger law to stem increasing concentration in its

[31] See, eg, the remarks of Senator Reed:

> [W]e wrote it into our creed, that all men were created free and equal, and that all are entitled to life, liberty, and the pursuit of happiness. We construed "liberty" to mean not merely the right to walk upon the streets of cities … but liberty … to engage in commerce, to solve for one's self the problem of one's own happiness and success … So we began enacting legislation calculated to produce a condition which would leave open for all men, big and little, the opportunity to engage in the affairs of life.

51 Cong Rec 15867 (1914). Legislators also wished 'properly [to] control … the great industrial corporation that really has … the power to arbitrarily control prices and thus exact unjust profits from the people' 51 Cong Rec 9265 (1914) (remarks of Rep Morgan).

[32] Addressing a joint session of Congress on Trusts and Monopolies, President Wilson commented on a limitation on interlocking directorates: 'It will bring new men, new energies, and a new spirit of initiative, new blood, into the management of our great business enterprises. It will open the field of industrial development and origination to scores of men who have been obliged to serve when their abilities entitled them to direct'. Address by the President on Trusts and Monopolies before the Joint Session of Congress (20 January 1914), HR Doc No 625, 63d Cong, 2d Sess 5 (1914).

[33] See generally EF Goldman, *Rendezvous With Destiny* (New York, Knopf, 1952).

[34] See recounting of the legislative purpose in *Volvo Trucks N Am Inc v Reeder-Simco GMC Inc* 546 U.S. 164 (2006). The Robinson Patman Act was an amendment to the original s 2 of the Clayton Act, which then concerned only seller power, not buyer power.

[35] Frederic M Scherer, *Industrial Market Structure and Economic Performance*, 2nd edn (Boston, Houghton Mifflin, 1980) 49.

[36] See Goldman (n 33) 453. In 1938 President Franklin D Roosevelt told Congress: '[T]he liberty of a democracy is not safe if the people tolerate the growth of private power to a point where it becomes stronger than their democratic state itself.' 83 Cong Rec 5992 (1938).

[37] Ch. 1184, 64 Stat 1125 (1950) (current version at 15 U.S.C. §§ 18, 21 (1976), as amended by Pub L No 96-349, § 6(a), 94 Stat 1154 (1980)).

infancy, to disperse economic and political power, and to help ensure that a Hitler could never rise to power in America.[38]

Antitrust emerged from the 1960s as a body of law reflecting American political democracy.[39] It favoured dispersing economic power[40] and easing access to markets, all consistent with more equality.[41]

This pro-democracy, pro-diversity, power-dispersion orientation of the law was, however, to change dramatically in the late 1970s and more decisively with the coming of the Reagan administration in the early 1980s. In the mid-1970s, trade barriers fell, and foreign competition seriously challenged American business. The Supreme Court's Chief Justice Earl Warren, who had led the liberal, pro-outsider Supreme Court through the 1960s, and his most pro-equality associate justices, retired. Presidents Reagan and Nixon filled their places with justices aligned with the business establishment. The changes ushered in a revolution in US antitrust. Chicago School teaching – to trust the market and assume that firms were

[38] Representative Celler said:

> I want to point out the danger of this trend toward more and better combines. I read from a report filed with [the former Secretary of War] as to the history of the cartelization and concentration of industry in Germany: "Germany under the Nazi set-up built up a great series of industrial monopolies in steel, rubber, coal and other materials. The monopolies soon got control of Germany, brought Hitler to power and forced virtually the whole world into war." I do not want to see my country go the way of Japan or the way of Italy or the way of Germany or even the way of England.

95 Cong Rec 11486. See remarks of Senator Kefauver, 96 Cong Rec 16452 (1950). See also F Neumann, *Behemoth: The Structure and Practice of National Socialism* (Oxford, OUP, 1942) 22–23.

[39] See LA Sullivan, 'Antitrust, Microeconomics, and Politics: Reflections on Some Recent Relationships' (1980) 68 *California Law Review* 1. See also JF Brodley, 'Limiting Conglomerate Mergers: The Need for Legislation' (1979) 40 *Ohio State Law Journal* 867; JJ Flynn, 'Antitrust Jurisprudence: A Symposium on the Economic, Political and Social Goals of Antitrust Policy' (1977) 125 *University of Pennsylvania Law Review* 1182; E Fox, 'Antitrust, Mergers, and the Supreme Court: The Politics of Section 7 of the Clayton Act' (1975) 26 *Mercer Law Review* 389; LB Schwartz, 'On the Uses of Economics: A Review of the Antitrust Treatises' (1979) 128 *University of Pennsylvania Law Review* 244; LB Schwartz, 'Justice and Other Non-Economic Goals of Antitrust' (1979) 127 *University of Pennsylvania Law Review* 1076; LB Schwartz, 'Institutional Size and Individual Liberty: Authoritarian Aspects of Bigness' (1960) 55 *Northwestern University Law Review* 4. The Supreme Court summed up the interrelated political and economic values of antitrust legislation in *Northern Pac Ry v United States* 356 U.S. 1, 4 (1958):

> The Sherman Act was designed to be a comprehensive charter of economic liberty aimed at preserving free and unfettered competition as the rule of trade. It rests on the premise that the unrestrained interaction of competitive forces will yield the best allocation of our economic resources, the lowest prices, the highest quality and the greatest material progress, while at the same time providing an environment conducive to the preservation of our democratic political and social institutions.

[40] See, eg, *United States v Von's Grocery Co* 384 U.S. 270, 275 (1966) ('Like the Sherman Act in 1890 and the Clayton Act in 1914, the basic purpose of the 1950 Celler-Kefauver Act was to prevent economic concentration in the American economy by keeping a large number of small competitors in business'. (footnote omitted).

[41] The Supreme Court said, and repeated on a number of occasions: 'The fundamental purpose of the Sherman Act was to secure equality of opportunity and to protect the public against evils commonly incident to destruction of competition through monopolies and combinations in restraint of trade.' *Paramount Famous Lasky Corp v United States* 282 U.S. 30, 42 (1930).

efficient – was waiting in the wings. It finally made entrée into antitrust.[42] In a major case at the end of the 1970s, the Supreme Court began its long trek to overturn the Warren Court antitrust precedents, one by one.[43] The Supreme Court reversed the Warren Court cases that promoted ease of access of outsiders (firms not having power) and freedom from leverage by dominant firms.[44] It shifted course from favouring the unconnected and powerless to favouring incumbents, even monopolists. It did so on the basis of a philosophy to let the market work and to be wary of antitrust intervention on grounds that the market would spur firms on to greater heights of efficiency and innovation, and that antitrust intervention, except against price-fixing, would protect inefficient competitors from competition. At this point, the US (Supreme Court) antitrust severed its connection with equality. Also, it lost its resonance with much of the rest of the world. *Verizon v Trinko* (Supreme Court 2004)[45] is a clear example of the de-linkage of equality and antitrust in the US. After the AT&T breakup by consensual decree in 1981, federal communications regulation segregated regional markets for telecoms service, and regulated them. Then technology advanced, competition became feasible, and the regulation was lifted. Verizon's predecessor Bell Atlantic was the monopolist incumbent in north-eastern US and it alone owned the elements of the local loop, an essential input to new rivals who would begin to compete in the territory. As rivals began to enter the north-eastern market, Bell Atlantic purposely, sporadically disrupted service to its rivals in order to impugn their reliability and keep its customers from migrating.[46] When telephone users sued Bell Atlantic, which became Verizon, Verizon moved to dismiss on grounds, among others, that the disruptions constituted a refusal to deal, and under antitrust principles it had no duty to deal. The appellate court disagreed and declined to dismiss the complaint.[47]

On Verizon's appeal to the Supreme Court, New York and other states appeared as amici, friends of the Court. They noted that the new entrant telecom companies were at the mercy of the incumbent, whose ownership of the local loop gave it power of life or death over its rivals. Bell Atlantic threatened the entrants, they said, with 'death by a thousand cuts'. The Court, by Justice Scalia, turned the image on

[42] See R Posner, 'The Chicago School of Antitrust Analysis' (1979) 127 *University of Pennsylvania Law Review* 925.

[43] *Continental TV v GTE Sylvania* 433 U.S. 36 (1977), overruling *United States v Arnold, Schwinn & Co* 388 U.S. 365 (1967). See *Continental TV* at 53, disclaiming as a value the autonomy of independent businesspeople. See concurrence of Justice White, noting that autonomy of independent businesspeople was much more deeply embedded in the law than efficiencies and the new economics. ibid 68–69 (J White concurring).

[44] Eg, *State Oil Co v Khan* 522 U.S. 3 (1997); *Leegin Creative Leather Products Inc v PSKS Inc* 551 U.S. 877 (2007); *Ill Tool Works Inc v Indep Ink Inc* 547 U.S. 28 (2006). It recharted the course of leveraging by *Trinko* (n 45).

[45] *Verizon Commc'ns Inc v L Offs of Curtis V Trinko LLP* 540 U.S. 398 (2004).

[46] See complaint, *L Offs of Curtis V Trinko v Bell Atlantic Corp* (No. 1:00-cv-01910). See *Law Offs of Curtis V Trinko LLP* 305 F.3d 89 (2d Cir 2002), *rev'd*, 540 U.S. 398 (2004).

[47] 305 F.3d 89.

its head. The argument of death-by-a-thousand-cuts, he said, favoured the incumbent. Antitrust courts could not deal with such sprawling claims of responsibilities to entrants. False condemnations [type one errors] were especially costly, and:

> identification of [the thousand cuts] would surely be a daunting task for a generalist antitrust court. Judicial oversight under the Sherman Act would seem destined to distort investment and lead to a new layer of interminable litigation ….[48]

Famously, Verizon won the case. The Supreme Court dismissed the complaint. Discordant with the prior antitrust jurisprudence, it said that monopoly pricing is good because it attracts investment to the market,[49] and that antitrust courts are not tasked with pushing firms to compete in a better way 'whenever some other approach might yield greater competition'.[50] They have power only to stop prohibited conduct – the very category that the Court greatly narrowed.[51]

There is one US antitrust statute that was explicitly and incontestably redistributive (although it is not always called 'antitrust') – the Robinson Patman Anti-Price Discrimination Act of 1936. The Robinson Patman Act (and the predecessor it amended) 'was born of a desire by Congress to curb the use by financially powerful corporations of localised price-cutting tactics which had greatly impaired the competitive position of other sellers',[52] and to protect small sellers from the favourable deals given to powerful buyers. When the *Volvo Trucks*[53] case came to the Supreme Court shortly after *Trinko*, the Supreme Court read out of the Robinson Patman Act its central prohibition of price discrimination that harms competition between favoured and disfavoured buyers, in contrast to price discrimination that harms competition in a market and raises prices to consumers. It said that the Court must resist 'protection of existing competitors' and must bring the Robinson Patman Act into line with the primary concern of the antitrust laws – promoting interbrand competition.

The last time that a US federal court expressed the democracy goals of antitrust is in *LePage's v 3M*, wherein judge Delores Sloviter, for the Third Circuit Court of Appeals, upholding a monopoly violation in a loyalty rebate case, said:

> Section 2, the provision of the antitrust laws designed to curb the excesses of monopolists and near-monopolists, is the equivalent in our economic sphere of the guarantees

[48] *Verizon* 540 U.S. at 414.

[49] ibid 407. The Court said: 'The opportunity to charge monopoly prices – at least for a short period – is what attracts 'business acumen' in the first place; it induces risk taking that produces innovation and economic growth. To safeguard the incentive to innovate, the possession of monopoly power will not be found unlawful unless it is accompanied by an element of anticompetitive conduct'.

[50] ibid 416.

[51] There were a number of points on which Verizon might have prevailed or facts to which the Court's holding might have been limited, such as simultaneous regulation by a regulatory authority, but the holding was not so limited. The Court refused to recognise that there is an essential facilities doctrine but said the doctrine, if it exists, would have been inapplicable in any case because Verizon had already engaged in some dealing.

[52] *FTC v Anheuser-Busch Inc* 363 U.S. 536 (1960), quoted in *Volvo* 546 U.S. 164. The second part – buying power – is the heart of the amendment and is referenced in *Volvo*.

[53] *Volvo* 546 U.S. 164.

> of free and unhampered elections in the political sphere. Just as democracy can thrive only in a free political system unhindered by outside forces, so also can market capitalism survive only if those with market power are kept in check. That is the goal of the antitrust laws.[54]

3M, however, was decided before *Trinko*.

Another cut at the place of inequality in US antitrust jurisprudence involves a closer look at winners and losers. It is helpful to consider who (richer or poorer, privileged and powerful or not) tend to be the winners, and who tend to be the losers, in view of influential cases, case selection, and doctrines that determine coverage of the law. First, as to caselaw:

Predatory pricing – *Brooke Group v Brown and Williamson*:[55] This case makes it so difficult to prove a predatory pricing violation that a plaintiff never wins. This means that established companies can usually lower their prices deeply and selectively to target and destroy feisty new entrants with impunity. The lower end of the income/wealth/power scale tend to be the losers.

Professional associations – *California Dental Association v FTC*:[56] This case gives deference to professional associations in limiting activities of members of the profession – especially activities that entrants may need to make themselves known, such as truthful discount advertising. The lower end of the income/wealth/power scale tend to be the losers.

Vertical restraints that limit horizontal competition – *Ohio v American Express*:[57] American Express was permitted to 'gag' merchants who are presented with an American Express card at the check-out counter. American Express forced the merchants not to tell customers that they could use a cheaper card. A cheaper card would save the merchant money in the form of exchange fees and potentially reduce prices across all items in the store. Obviously, the gag order meant that American Express would get more card usage, therefore more revenues; and American Express claimed it would use the extra money to give premium card holders more frequent flier points and other benefits. The lower end of the income/wealth/power scale tend to be the losers.

Second, the section discusses case selection, which is also a matter of prioritisation.

Case selection is within the discretion of the antitrust agencies. The following incident arose at the start of the Reagan administration. In the District of

[54] *LePage's Inc v 3M*, 324 F.3d 141, 169 (3d Cir 2003).

[55] *Brooke Grp v Brown & Williamson Tobacco Corp* 509 U.S. 209 (1993). See, for a description of the conservative route the Court chose to take, siding with Professor Robert Bork rather than Professor Philip Areeda (who argued the case on opposing sides), E Fox, 'The Efficiency Paradox', in R Pitofsky (ed), *How the Chicago School Overshot the Mark* (Oxford, Oxford University Press, 2008).

[56] *Cal Dental Ass'n v FTC* 526 U.S. 756 (1999). See, for the conservative route the Court chose to take, with the majority arguing that the professional association's price gags on dentist's advertising of discounts could actually increase output of dental services by stemming deceptive ads and giving patients more confidence in the profession, Fox (n 55).

[57] *Ohio v American Express Co* 585 U.S. (2018).

Columbia, private lawyers represented indigent criminal defendants. The District of Columbia paid them a pittance for their work ($20 for out of court hours, $30 for in court hours). The pay scale was too low to induce sufficient representation. The lawyers who represented the indigent defendants, who were mostly public interest lawyers, called the situation to the attention of the Mayor, who advised the lawyers that they would have to call public attention to the situation before the D.C. Council would act on a more fitting pay scale. So the lawyers went on strike, refusing to accept more cases until the pay scale was raised. They marched with placards to attract the press. They got public attention; the D.C. Council finally acknowledged the indigent defendants' plight, and raised fees. The FTC sued the lawyers for price-fixing and for an illegal boycott per se, and it won. All of the lawyers' defences, including that they had no power and their acts were political action, failed.[58] The lower end of the income/wealth/power scale were clear losers. If ever a case epitomises the disregard of equality values, *Superior Court Trial Lawyers* is it.

Enforcement choices during the Trump administration included opening investigations against mergers of small cannabis firms, and against four auto companies for agreeing with California to adopt higher than federally-required auto emission standards.[59]

Not all enforcers would have made these choices and the Biden administration weighs in at the opposite end of the scale, but history reveals that prioritisation depends on the administration. Antitrust may be applied in disregard of distributional consequences.

Underenforcement may be even more material to this inquiry. On the underenforcement side, there is a common view that – on market grounds alone (having nothing to do with equality) – the antitrust laws are underenforced against large and dominant firms. There is a significant call in the US today for more aggressive enforcement of the antitrust laws to stem market power. Pending legislation would significantly increase agency funding, would shift burdens of proof to big firms, and would condemn many more acquisitions and exclusionary practices.[60]

Third, the section reflects on coverage and limits of the law where greater coverage could contribute to less inequality.

[58] *FTC v Superior Ct Trial Lawyers Ass'n* 493 U.S. 411 (1990).

[59] See E Fox in R Goodman, '11 Top Antitrust Experts Alarmed by Whistleblower Complaint Against A.G.Barr – and Office of Professional Responsibility's Opinion' (26 June 2020) *Just Security* www.justsecurity.org/71059/top-antitrust-lawyers-assess-john-elias-whistleblower-complaint-against-a-g-barr-including-office-of-professional-responsibilitys-letter/.

[60] See, eg, American Innovation and Choice Online Act, s 2992, 117th Cong (2021–2022); Open App Markets Act, s 2710, 117th Cong (2021–2022); Competition and Antitrust Law Enforcement Reform Act of 2021, s 225, 117th Cong (2021); Anticompetitive Exclusionary Conduct Prevention Act of 2020, s 3426, 116th Cong (2020); Consolidation Prevention and Competition Promotion Act of 2019, s 307, 116th Cong (2019). For a general summary see Department of Justice Antitrust Division contribution to Compendium of approaches to improving competition in digital markets, G7, convened by UK, 29 November 2021, assets.publishing.service.gov.uk/government/uploads/system/uploads/attachment_data/file/1036995/Compendium_final_format.pdf at 83–84.

First, under US antitrust law, dominant firms can charge excessive prices with impunity and can in most cases leverage their power with impunity. A number of jurisdictions prohibit dominant firms from excessive pricing, abusing a superior bargaining position, and using their leverage to get significant competitive advantages. The US does not. The losers from these acts are predominantly the lower end of the wealth/income/power distribution.

Second, workers are often the losers of both antitrust enforcement and non-enforcement, and workers are usually at the lower end of the wealth/income/power scale. US antitrust has not been particularly kind to workers. The first big antitrust injunction case ever brought was against Eugene Debs and his railway workers for boycotting trains that included a Pullman (sleeping) car. As background, there was an economic recession. Mr Pullman had just lowered the pay of his railroad workers by 25 per cent to 40 per cent and refused to reduce the rents for their sleeping quarters, which they could no longer afford. The railroad union went on strike to pressure Pullman to certify a bargaining unit. The US sued and won an injunction.[61] Debs' defeat spurred Congress to adopt the labour exemption from the antitrust laws, allowing labour to collectively bargain.[62]

Only recently, in this time of higher consciousness of the inequities visited on labour, have US antitrust authorities brought cases against rival employers who had agreed with one another not to solicit their employees (no-poach agreements).[63] These cases fit an efficiency paradigm, and traditional market theories justified the suits. The complaints do not invoke fairness or equity, although equity and efficiency coincide.

The gig economy, typified by Uber and Lyft drivers, has revealed the problem they face – independent contractors who have no bargaining power against their principals and who share many characteristics with employees. US antitrust has no countervailing power defence; therefore, as long as gig workers are recognised as independent contractors, they cannot legally combine to negotiate prices with the platform.[64] The drivers are usually at the lower end of the wage/wealth scales, and those at the lower end are systematically the losers.[65]

[61] *In re Debs* 158 U.S. 564 (1895).

[62] Clayton Act, § 6 (15 U.S.C. § 17).

[63] See Department of Justice (Antitrust Division), *No-Poach Approach* (Spring 2019) www.justice.gov/atr/division-operations/division-update-spring-2019/no-poach-approach.

[64] When Uber drivers in Seattle wanted to bargain together against Uber and the City of Seattle authorised gig drivers to do so, the Justice Department Antitrust Division weighed in on the side of Uber (and the Chamber of Commerce), arguing that the City had no authority to shield the drivers from the antitrust anti-price-fixing law. Marshall Steinbaum of the Roosevelt Institute 'called the federal government's decision to use antitrust law to block Uber drivers from negotiating better working conditions "galling"'. A Asher-Shapiro, 'Trump Administration Fights Effort to Unionize Uber Drivers', *The Intercept* (26 March 2018) theintercept.com/2018/03/26/uber-drivers-union-seattle/. The appellate court sided with Uber. *Chamber of Commerce v City of Seattle* 890 F.3d 769 (9th Cir 2018).

[65] Unlike the US, the competition law of the EU is sympathetic to gig workers. See *European Commission* (n 167–169).

Third, state-related acts are too easily immunised. US antitrust law provides for a state action defence and a companion doctrine of immunity for lobbying, even lobbying jointly with rivals for government action to protect an industry from competition. Not only is this doctrine available to shield private parties' strategies to advance their interests, but, unlike in the EU and some other jurisdictions, states of the US cannot be sued for use of state privileges to harm competition.[66]

Most restraints in these categories entrench the power of vested interests. The losers fall at the lower end of the wealth/income/power distribution.

ii. The Six Questions

Question One: Is an equality value embedded in the US antitrust law?

Equality was embedded in the US antitrust laws and was a particularly prominent value in the 1960s and early 1970s. It is not anymore.

Question Two: Is an equality value a source of wisdom available to enforcers and jurists to decide priorities or to reach outcomes in particular cases?

Yes, in theory.

Question Three: Are antitrust consent decrees or clearances used as an occasion for imposing conditions that advance equality – eg, to protect workers from layoffs?

No. US merger decrees do not give rights to workers targeted for lay off, and US antitrust philosophy is hostile to such conditions on grounds that they would undermine the cost savings from the merger. Occasionally a US court will include, in conditions of settlement or clearance, obligations that are not directly linked to the violation. For example, some media merger consent decrees include must-carry or access obligations that would probably not be won through litigation.[67] This is rare. Conditions not relating to the violation are criticised as deviating from antitrust. In general, inequality is not addressed in conditionality in US decrees.[68]

Question Four: Is more equality, or reducing the inequality gap, a separate mandate that can warrant an antitrust exemption or be used as a trump?

No.

Question Five: Does US antitrust alleviate inequality? Aggravate inequality? Or just not help to remedy it?

US antitrust just does not help remedy the inequality problem (except to the extent that enforcement naturally tends to dissipate power). But by standing by while market power is accumulated and used and erring on the side of

[66] See E Fox and D Healey, 'When the State Harms Competition – The Role for Competition Law' (2014) 79 *Antitrust Law Journal* 769. Many antitrust enforcers over time, both liberal and libertarian, have tried to narrow this gap.

[67] Eg *In re AOL (Time Warner)*, FTC File No 001-0105, Consent Agreement (14 December 2000).

[68] But see JB Baker and SC Salop, 'Antitrust, Competition Policy, and Inequality' (2015) 104 *The Georgetown Law Journal* 1 suggesting such conditionality as one way to address equality concerns.

non-intervention (see *Trinko, Brooke Group, California Dental, Ohio v American Express*), while pursuing antitrust litigation against powerless individuals fighting for the poor (see *Superior Court Trial Lawyers*), the US antitrust system could be seen as complicit.

Question Six: Would equality-leaning changes in competition law be feasible and likely to help close the inequality gap?

Legislative change in US antitrust law may be on the horizon. The change would be largely addressed to market and power problems but with positive spill-over effects on equality.

The change on the horizon to toughen US antitrust against power and abuses would potentially recalibrate and reverse some of the caselaw cited above. The law might finally, once again, be sufficient to prohibit anticompetitive exclusionary practices and mergers that have been treated as benign or even procompetitive. But the caution that US antitrust addresses allocative problems and is not distributive might remain intact. A critical mass of policy makers are concerned that admitting an equality factor into the antitrust equation will soften the antitrust law and prevent it from doing its job.

C. Germany

i. Introduction

The story of German competition law and its relation to equality is unique. The competition law of Germany reflects EU competition law, as Member State law must,[69] and it influenced EU competition law at its inception. But there are differences. EU law (treated in the next section) necessarily applies a top-down blueprint, to be adopted and implemented by all of its members; it is a product of combining influences – national and European. German competition law is rooted in; in particular, the Ordoliberal tradition. The Ordoliberal tradition has a unique relationship to power; it looks to the state to control powerful private interests.[70] In Germany, equality concerns generally align with the mandate to control economic power, public and private.[71] Ordoliberalism contrasts with laissez-faire liberalism, which is permissive of business acts and tends to see them sympathetically as the emanation of good market competition. Neoliberalism tends to facilitate 'the free market' without regard to its distributive consequences.

[69] Member States must apply EU competition law in all matters affecting Member State trade, except that they may go further in applying abuse of dominance law. Council Regulation (EC) No 1/2003 of 16 December 2002 on the implementation of the rules on competition laid down in Arts 81 and 82 of the Treaty [2003] OJ L1/1. Therefore, it is natural that there should be an absorption of EU law into national law.

[70] See ch 1 in this volume.

[71] See ibid.

This section looks at the underpinnings of German competition law, the influence of Ordoliberalism, and selected applications of the German competition law – namely, the *Facebook* case and treatment of small and middle-sized enterprises – that may suggest an affinity to concerns for equality.

ii. The Statutes and their Derivation; Ordoliberalism

Cartels and agreements between competitors were lawful in pre-WWII Germany. Only 'certain abusive effects' were considered illegal.[72] The early German anti-cartel law – the Verordnung gegen Missbrauch wirtschaftlicher Machtstellungen (Ordinance against the abuse of positions of economic power, 1923) – was designed to control, rather than eliminate, such agreements.[73] Overall, the pre-WWII 'German regulatory regime ... recognised cartels as a fundamental component of the German economy'.[74] With the beginning of the Nazi dictatorship in Germany in 1933, the limitations on anticompetitive agreements – weak as they were – were abolished. New legislation made cartels mandatory and empowered the Ministry of Economic Affairs to organise and monitor them.[75] This helped the Nazi regime organise German industry for war. At the Potsdam Conference following the surrender of Germany, the US, UK and USSR agreed that the German economy would 'be decentralised for the purpose of eliminating the ... excessive concentration of economic power as exemplified in particular by cartels, syndicates, trusts and other monopolistic arrangements'.[76] The ultimate purpose was to limit Germany's military capability so as to prevent future German aggression.[77] With the beginning of the Cold War, the US Government's strategy also facilitated a rapid economic recovery for West Germany, to prevent it from becoming part of the communist bloc.[78] Antitrust law was a tool for 'Germany's reintegration into the international economic community'.[79] With control over legislation restored, West-German policymakers built the country's new competition law on the basis of the Ordoliberal ideas of the Freiburg school in light of the specific post-war discourse surrounding the introduction of the Act Against Restraints of Competition (GWB) and the development towards a social market

[72] HL Buxbaum, 'German Legal Culture and the Globalization of Competition Law: A Historical Perspective on the Expansion of Private Antitrust Enforcement' (2005) 23 *Berkeley Journal of International Law* 474.

[73] ibid.

[74] ibid.

[75] See S Quack and ML Djelic, 'Adaptation, Recombination and Reinforcement: The Story of Antitrust and Competition Law in Germany and Europe' (2005) 4 spire.sciencespo.fr/hdl:/2441/26l5o52m2c857apcgdgcplhr3h/resources/2005-djelic-quack-story-of-antitrust-and-competition-law-in-germany-and-europe.pdf.

[76] Potsdam Agreement – Protocol of the Proceedings (1 August 1945).

[77] See Buxbaum (n 72).

[78] See ibid 478.

[79] ibid 478.

economy.[80] The new law, the GWB,[81] came into force on 1 January 1958 – the same day as the EEC Treaty of Rome.

What did Ordoliberalism entail? The answer illuminates Ordoliberalism's relation to equality.

Ordoliberalism originated in the 1930s at the University of Freiburg, Germany, against the background of the political and economic instability of the Weimar Republic and the germs of the soon-to-emerge Nazi dictatorship. Ordoliberals rejected fascism and socialism.[82] They considered 'a competitive economic system to be necessary for a prosperous, free and equitable society'.[83] They sought a '"third way" between democracy and socialism, between the American "West" and the Soviet "East."'[84] They believed that a free-market order 'could only exist within the framework of an economic constitution which must be "consciously shaped," carefully cultivated and protected by the State'.[85] Implementing this framework would contain private power; it 'would serve to guard against competitive distortions, to ensure the equitable distribution of resources in society, and to prevent undue government intervention in the market'.[86] '[T]he market had to function [and under this framework would be expected to function] in a way that all members of society perceived as fair and that provided equal opportunities for participation to all'.[87]

The GWB reflects the Ordoliberal underpinnings. Dominant power can be found at relatively low thresholds. Abuse of a superior bargaining position as well as abuse of a dominant position is a violation. Firms in positions of dominance and relative dominance have a panoply of duties to smaller firms and especially to small and middle-sized firms (SMEs) to treat them fairly and not to hinder their competition. Dominant firms must behave 'as if' they faced competition, and have duties to grant access, including – as applied today – to their networks and data.

Applications of the GWB reflect the Ordoliberal lineage; first the *Facebook* case on the abuse of a superior bargaining position and digital data, and second, the special protection of SMEs.

[80] See ibid 479. To obtain the legislation, the Ordoliberals made some compromises with industry. The original Ordoliberal 'Josten' draft of 24 June 1949 (B 136/700) provided for a total ban on cartels and for conduct-independent breakups of monopolies and of undertakings with significant economic power. These provisions were dropped. For the Ordoliberal coining of the term 'social market economy' ('soziale Marktwirtschaft') see A Müller-Armack, *Wirtschaftslenkung und Marktwirtschaft* (Kastel, 1947). See also LF Pace and K Seidel, 'The Drafting and the Role of Regulation 17' in KK Patel and H Schweitzer (eds), *The Historical Foundations of EU Competition Law* (Oxford, Oxford University Press 2013) ch 2.

[81] Gesetz gegen Wettbewerbsbeschränkungen (GWB) www.gesetze-im-internet.de/englisch_gwb/index.html (English translation).

[82] See DJ Gerber, 'Constitutionalizing the Economy: German Neo-Liberalism, Competition Law and the *"New" Europe*' (1994) 42(1) *The American Journal of Comparative Law* 63, 25.

[83] ibid 25.

[84] ibid 36.

[85] ibid 12 (emphasis added).

[86] ibid.

[87] ibid 38.

iii. Applications of Law

a. Abuse of Dominance Including Superior Bargaining Position – The *Facebook* Decision

The German *Facebook* case is a good example of law protecting the vulnerable from the powerful in the digital economy. The case goes significantly beyond EU abuse of dominance law.[88]

The Federal Cartel Office (FCO) spent several years investigating Facebook for abuse of dominance for misappropriating personal data and amassing hoards of it, to its great profit. Indeed, Germany was far ahead of the rest of the world in identifying data as a source of substantial market power and in proceeding against Big Tech. In its case against Facebook, the FCO found that Facebook had a dominant position in the market for private social networks with private users which allowed it to impose abusive business terms on the users.[89] The FCO found that since 2012, Facebook continuously had a market share of more than 90 per cent (and up to 97 per cent) of the relevant market, based on the number of daily active social network users in Germany.[90] It determined that Facebook abused that position by forcing users to give up their data to Facebook in order to use its services and also by taking personal data without consent from third party sites, all of which data Facebook combined to sell targeted advertising services. The FCO decreed that Facebook's terms of service violated the EU General Data Protection Regulation (GDPR), and that Facebook's appropriation of data without consent violated the GDPR, also violating the GWB.[91] Facebook's conduct, it said, undermined 'constitutional principles that protect the right to informational self-determination and the fundamental right to data protection'.[92] The FCO identified the violations as exploitative.

The Dusseldorf Higher Regional Court considered the GDPR separate from antitrust and reversed the FCO decision,[93] but, on appeal, the Federal Court of Justice (FCJ) restored the effect of the original FCO decision.[94] The FCJ emphasised that Facebook had deprived users of their constitutional 'right to informational self-determination'.[95] It had deprived them of 'genuine voluntary choice' and

[88] Under EU law, Member States are entitled to maintain national law governing single firm conduct that goes beyond the EU abuse of dominance violation. See Regulation (EC) 1/2003, Art 3(2).

[89] Bundeskartellamt, Decision B6-22/16 of 6 February 2019 (for an English translation, see www.bundeskartellamt.de/SharedDocs/Entscheidung/EN/Entscheidungen/Missbrauchsaufsicht/2019/B6-22-16.pdf?__blob=publicationFile&v=5).

[90] ibid para 392.

[91] ibid paras 526, 629–630.

[92] ibid para 529.

[93] Dusseldorf Higher Regional Court, Decision *VI-Kart 1/19 (V)* of 26 August 2019 ECLI:DE:OLGD:2019:0826:KART1.19V.00.

[94] *Bundesgerichtshof*, Decision of 23 June 2020 – KVR 69/19 ECLI:DE:BGH:2020:230620BKVR69.19.0.

[95] ibid paras 109–110.

'autonomous decision-making' in a market wherein, because of network and lock-in effects, 'competition [was] unable to effectively exercise its controlling function', including as to the scope of the collection of personal data.[96] Facebook's acts amounted to an illegal abuse. It was not important that users were not deprived of all choice, or that Facebook's service was not one that was 'vital for life', or whether Facebook had violated the GDPR.[97] For many consumers, access to Facebook was decisive for their participation in social life and public discourse, so that it would be unacceptable to expect them to refrain from using Facebook. The fundamental right to informational self-determination[98] – in particular in connection with the significance of the political, social and economic communication on the internet, and in light of the quantity and quality of the data processed by social networks – mandated a special level of user protection against inappropriate data collection by dominant social network operators such as Facebook.[99]

The FCJ rejected Facebook's argument that the indirect network effects of the relevant double-sided market constrained Facebook's scope of behaviour.[100]

[96] *Bundesgerichtshof*, Press Release No 080/2020 of 23 June 2020, 3 – for an English translation see www.bundeskartellamt.de/SharedDocs/Publikation/EN/Pressemitteilungen/2020/23_06_2020_BGH_Facebook.pdf;jsessionid=6F4791E8E59EC63B4ECBF4DDE2956026.1_cid378?__blob=publicationFile&v=3.

[97] *Bundesgerichtshof* (n 94) para 102. For a finding of abuse, it was enough that Facebook deprived users of their choice as to the level of personalisation of its service. Facebook collected user data outside of Facebook ('Facebook' data) and combined this with data collected on Facebook ('on-Facebook' data). It then used this data set to personalise its service, irrespective of whether users wanted to use a highly personalised version of Facebook or not. In a competitive market, this forced extension of a service (*'aufgedrängte Leistungserweiterung'*) would be impossible. Facebook would have to provide a less personalised option to users who only want to use Facebook's basic functionalities and do not wish to provide more data than is necessary for this narrower scope of services. The additional, involuntarily provided user data meant that it did not matter for the FCJ's finding of an exploitative abuse that Facebook provided its service free of charge.

[98] The right to *informational self-determination* was established by the German Federal Court of Justice (FCJ) in the 1983 *Volkszählungsurteil* decision (1 BvR 209/83, 1 BvR 269/83, 1 BvR 362/83, 1 BvR 420/83, 1 BvR 440/83, 1 BvR 484/83). The case concerned a proposed population census law which included provisions on the processing and use of the obtained information. The FCJ struck down the law as unconstitutional, holding that it infringed the *constitutional right to informational self-determination*. In the FCJ's opinion, this right is grounded in Art 1(1) of the German Basic Law (GG) ('Human dignity shall be inviolable. To respect and protect it shall be the duty of all state authority') in conjunction with Art 2(1) GG ('Every person shall have the right to free development of his personality insofar as he does not violate the rights of others or offend against the constitutional order or the moral law'). The FCJ held that limitations of the right to informational self-determination are only allowed in cases where the public interest prevails and the rule of law and principle of proportionality are complied with. The FCJ noted that the proposed census law would lead to a registration and cataloguing of individuals' personalities which is incompatible with respect for human dignity (Art 1(1) GG). The FCJ cautioned against a social order in which people do not know who knows what about them at any given point in time. In the FCJ's view, such a situation would pose a risk to the liberal-democratic order by discouraging individuals from developing their personalities, since they would not know whether their behaviour is being recorded and permanently saved as information. The FCJ found that the free development of individuals' personalities in (1983) modern conditions required the protection of individuals against unlimited collection, storing and processing of personal data and, as such, was covered by Art 2(1) in conjunction with Art 1(1) GG.

[99] *Bundesgerichtshof* (n 94) para 103.

[100] ibid para 43.

Facebook was wrong to suggest that it was constrained in its data collection and other conduct simply because it was forced to consider the effects of its conduct on the user side of the market in planning its conduct on the advertising side.[101] On the contrary, the FCJ found that the indirect network effects provided Facebook with a strong incentive to act in a way that favours only the advertising side and not the user side. Because Facebook capitalised on user data on the advertising side of the market, the price it could charge for its services increased with the quality and quantity of the provided user data. At the same time, no competitive force constrained or counteracted these incentives, since the indirect network effects in the relevant market were asymmetrical.[102]

The German *Facebook* case is an example of competition law protecting the 'ordinary person' against one of the most powerful businesses in the world economy.

b. Small- and Middle-sized Business: Protecting SMEs as Victims; Protecting SMEs from Liability

The GWB includes a number of provisions aimed at supporting SMEs. While owners of SMEs do not *necessarily* fall outside of the cohort of high wealth or income, they usually do, and therefore support for SMEs might be equated with more equality. Moreover, SMEs are the source of most jobs in the economy, especially in the German economy, and these jobs are not in the highest-paying categories.[103]

The support of SMEs by German competition law comes both in terms of specially protecting SMEs from exploitative and exclusionary abuses, and in terms of exempting them from liability or limiting their liability.

On the side of exempting and limiting liability of SMEs, the GWB exempts cartels of SMEs from the general prohibition of anticompetitive agreements where their 'subject matter is the rationalisation of economic activities through inter-firm cooperation' if the cartel does not significantly affect competition and the agreements 'serve to improve the competitiveness of … the [SMEs]'.[104] On the side of special protection against abuses, the GWB provides: 'undertakings with

[101] ibid.

[102] ibid 'asymmetrical' in the sense that the interactions did not affect both market sides to the same extent.

[103] More than 99% per cent of German companies are SMEs. In 2016, more than 58% per cent of all employees subject to social insurance in Germany were employed by SMEs. See German Ministry for the Economic Affairs and Energy, *Wirtschaftsmotor Mittelstand: Zahlen und Fakten zu den deutschen KMU* (2018) www.bmwi.de/Redaktion/DE/Publikationen/Mittelstand/wirtschaftsmotor-mittelstand-zahlen-und-fakten-zu-den-deutschen-kmu.pdf?__blob=publicationFile&v=1; See also J de Kok et al., *Do SMEs create more and better jobs?* (November 2011) 13 finding that '[i]n almost all [EU] Member States, average wages in SMEs are lower than in large enterprises' ec.europa.eu/growth/sites/default/files/docs/body/do-smes-create-more-and-better-jobs_en.pdf.

[104] GWB, Art 3.

superior market power in relation to small- and medium-sized competitors may not abuse their market position to impede such competitors directly or indirectly in an unfair manner'.[105] Moreover, SMEs with less than five per cent of the market may be freed from the obligations of joint and several liability if they are not the ring leader or a repeat offender and joint and several obligations would 'irretrievably jeopardise' their 'economic viability'.[106]

SMEs typically lack the scale to build an online platform for their own goods or services. They depend on large platforms. The German FCO protects the path of the SMEs to do business on the platforms, free of roadblocks.

For example, in *ASICS*,[107] a major running shoe company had a selective distribution system. It prohibited authorised retailers from using the ASICS trademarks on third-party websites for any purpose, including to guide customers to the authorised retailers' own websites; and it would not allow them to provide an interface to price comparison websites.[108] ASICS also prohibited its dealers from selling the running shoes through online marketplaces such as Amazon.[109]

Finding the restrictions illegal, the FCO said: '[S]mall and medium-sized retailers are reliant on the wide reach of online marketplaces …'. '[M]any of them would not or only with difficulties be able to be found by customers otherwise … [and be] unable to compensate for this loss of reach through other measures'.[110]

Another example can be found in the *HRS* case. The three leading online hotel booking services in Germany (HRS, Booking.com and Expedia), wanting to guarantee customers the best price, required their hotel clients ('partners') to agree to most favoured customer (MFN) clauses. HRS used *wide* MFN clauses. It

[105] GWB, Art 20(3). Note that the Art 19(1) prohibition of abuses of dominance contained applies 'to undertakings and associations of undertakings to the extent that [SMEs] as suppliers or purchasers of a certain type of goods or commercial services depend on them in such a way that sufficient and reasonable possibilities of switching to other undertakings do not exist'. Per Art 20(3) an *unfair impediment* occurs where an undertaking 'demands from [SMEs] with which it competes on the downstream market in the distribution of goods or commercial services a price for the delivery of such goods or services which is higher than the price it itself offers on such market' 'unless there is […] an objective justification'.

[106] GWB, Art 33d(3).

[107] Bundeskartellamt, Decision B2-98/11 of 26 August 2015 *ASICS and Others* (in German) www.bundeskartellamt.de/SharedDocs/Entscheidung/DE/Entscheidungen/Kartellverbot/2015/B2-98-11.html (own translation).

[108] ibid para 4.

[109] ibid briefly discussed by the FCO but said not to be essential to the present decision.

[110] ibid para 41. The EU caselaw appears to be in some tension. In *Oscar Bronner*, the Court declared that a small newspaper had no right to access the monopoly firm's distribution system. It was 'not impossible, or even unreasonably difficult' for other publishers to set up their own distribution. See Case C-7/97 *Oscar Bronner GmbH & Co KG v Mediaprint Zeitungs- und Zeitschriftverlag GmbH & Co KG and others* [1998] ECR I-7791 para 44. The *ASICS* decision has some affinity with pre-Reagan-era US antitrust law on vertical restraints. The law then protected the autonomy of dealers to sell where they wished. *United States v Arnold Schwinn & Co* 388 U.S. 365 (1967), rev'd *Continental TV Inc v GTE Sylvania* 433 U.S. 36 (1977). *Schwinn* was reversed because it protected non-economic values; other than efficiency; it interfered with the producers' choices for an efficient distribution system to wage effective interbrand competition.

prohibited hotel partners from offering a lower price than HRS both to customers who directly contacted the hotel partners to arrange a room booking and to guests who booked their stays through competing hotel booking services. By contrast, the narrow MFN clauses used by HRS's competitors (following the HRS decision) merely prohibited hotel partners from undercutting them on price in partners' direct offering, but not on competing booking services.

The FCO found that HRS's MFN clauses constituted an 'unfair hindrance' of SME hotels which were dependent on HRS to connect with customers online.[111] Among other things, this was because SME hotels could not 'reach a good ranking on the search engines when competing with the hotel portals and the large hotels'.[112] The fact that HRS's main competitors also used MFN clauses further strengthened the effect of these restraints.[113]

In the FCO's view, HRS's MFN clauses were 'anti-competitive even taking into account the problem of free riding and the possible reduction of search costs for hotel customers'.[114] They were 'not indispensable' to solving a potential free riding problem and did 'not allow consumers a fair share of the benefit'.[115] Thus, HRS's MFN clauses could not be justified under Art 101(3) TFEU.[116]

The FCO's decision reflects a concern for the protection of SMEs against 'unfair hindrances' by large platforms on whom they depend in the online distribution of their goods or services.

iv. Comment

German competition law, with its Ordoliberal underpinnings, is unique in its relation to equality. German law is founded on a philosophy to control power, and to preserve freedom from (more) government by preserving freedom from private power. In its application, German competition law prohibits exploitation by dominant firms and by firms with superior bargaining power. It is not reluctant to find both economic power and abuse of it, including by serious invasions of user autonomy and choice. In addition, German competition law is protective

[111] Bundeskartellamt, Decision B9-66/10 of 20 December 2013 *HRS-Hotel Reservation Service* (for an English translation see www.bundeskartellamt.de/SharedDocs/Entscheidung/EN/Entscheidungen/Kartellverbot/B9-66-10.pdf%3F__blob%3DpublicationFile%26v%3D3; unfair hindrance within the meaning of Art 20(1) in conjunction with Art 19(1) and (2) No 1 GWB.

[112] ibid para 237.

[113] ibid paras 9 and 48–51. The FCO and the FCJ later found that Booking.com's narrow MFN clause also violated Art 101(1) TFEU. The FCJ held that the only way to justify MFN clauses was under Art 101(3), and the narrow MFN clause used by Booking.com failed this justification. See Decision of 18 May 2021 – KVR 54/20 (Press Release, in German) www.bundesgerichtshof.de/SharedDocs/Pressemitteilungen/DE/2021/2021099.html. Unlike the FCO, many NCAs have accepted narrow MFN clauses as lawful.

[114] ibid para 154.

[115] ibid.

[116] ibid para 11.

of SMEs, which form the backbone of the German economy and are the biggest source of jobs, both by giving them special protection from abuses by firms with power and by limiting their exposure to liability when they might be the offenders. While some observers might regard German law as being too protective of small firms and too regulatory of conduct, defenders will point to the role of the law in organising an economic system designed to provide the structural underpinnings for a free and equitable society.[117]

v. The Six Questions

Question One: Is an equality value embedded in German competition law?

Yes.

Question Two: Is an equality value a source of wisdom available to enforcers and jurists to decide priorities or to reach outcomes in particular cases?

Yes.

Question Three: Are antitrust consent decrees or clearances used as an occasion for imposing conditions that advance equality?

No.

Question Four: Is more equality a separate mandate of higher standing that may warrant exemption or be used as a trump?

Yes. SMEs may come within exemptions.

Question Five: Does German competition law alleviate inequality? Aggravate inequality? Or just not help to remedy it?

It tends to alleviate inequality.

Question Six: Would equality-leaning changes in competition law be feasible and likely to help close the inequality gap?

German law already tilts in favour of SMEs and access to markets and data. It is unlikely for a more explicit equality principle to be absorbed into the law.

D. The European Union

i. Introduction

a. The History of EU Competition Law and Equality

Whereas US antitrust law valued equality in its first phase and disowned it in its second phase, EU law has followed a steady course. Equality is a basic EU Treaty value.[118] It is diffused into all EU law. While the most basic equality principle is

[117] See E Deutscher and S Makris, 'Exploring the Ordoliberal Paradigm: The Competition-Democracy Nexus (2016) 11(2) *Competition Law Review* 181–214.

[118] See Consolidated Version of the Treaty on European Union [2016] OJ C202/17; Art 6 of the Treaty provides that '[t]he Union is founded on the values of … equality'. See also Case T-612/17 *Google and Alphabet v Commission* ECLI:EU:T:2021:763 para 155 eur-lex.europa.eu/legal-content/

equality of treatment of all EU citizens regardless of their Member State,[119] the equality principle in EU law has a stronger purview.

EU law is driven by a goal of market integration. Pursuit of market integration is inherently inclusive,[120] and inclusivity is inherently pro-equality.[121] Market integration demands openness of and access to markets; thus contestability of markets. It demands a level playing field, not to be distorted by power and privilege, including state-granted privilege. The openness principle creates an environment that welcomes and incentivises outsiders (those not in the inner circle of power).[122] A second and third thread promotes equality independently from market integration. They derive from a posture on political economy and control of power. They are: equality of opportunity to contest markets on the merits, and a right not to be (excessively) exploited. Of course, EU competition law also prohibits mergers and dominant firm conduct that increases market power without offsetting benefits, which, even if not equality-leaning, can better distribute wealth.[123] Finally, EU law shows special regard for workers through exemptions or immunities.

The principal beneficiaries of these principles and concerns are not only the abstract 'market' (it will work better) but also people without power – the non-elite. The phrase 'non-elite' normally means people with less income and wealth. This section reviews the relevant EU Treaty and competition case law on equality.

ii. *The Treaties and Caselaw*

European Union competition law has its origin in the Treaty of Rome, adopted in 1957.[124] The Treaty of Rome evolved into the Treaty on European Union (TEU) and the Treaty on the Functioning of the European Union (TFEU).[125] Article 2 TEU identifies equality as one of the values on which 'the Union is founded'.[126] Also,

en/TXT/?uri=CELEX:62017TJ0612 citing Case C-242/95 *GT-Link* ECLI:EU:C:1997:376 para 41; Case C-82/01 P *Aéroports de Paris v Commission* ECLI:EU:C:2002:617, para 114; and Case T-228/97 *Irish Sugar v Commission* ECLI:EU:T:1999:246 para 140, for an application of 'the general principle of equal treatment, as a general principle of EU law' in EU competition law; The application of unequal ('dissimilar') 'conditions to equivalent transactions with other trading parties' is capable of constituting an abuse of dominance pursuant to Art 102(c) TFEU.

[119] ibid Arts 6 and 9.

[120] See EM Fox, 'Monopolization and Abuse of Dominance: Why Europe is Different' (2014) 59 *Antitrust Bulletin* 129. But see ch 5 in this volume, noting that the EU competition law's objective of tackling partitions of the single market may in some applications transfer wealth from poorer consumers to wealthier consumers.

[121] See C Pike, 'Rawlsian Antitrust' (15 April 2021) *Competition Policy International Antitrust Chronicle*, CCP Working Paper 21-04 papers.ssrn.com/sol3/papers.cfm?abstract_id=3832594.

[122] See Fox (n 120).

[123] ibid.

[124] Treaty Establishing the European Economic Community (Treaty of Rome) eur-lex.europa.eu/eli/treaty/teec/sign.

[125] In 1992, the 'Treaty on European Union' (TEU) was concluded in Maastricht, establishing the EU. In 2007, the Treaty of Lisbon renamed the Treaty of Rome the 'Treaty on the Functioning of the European Union' (TFEU).

[126] Consolidated version of the Treaty on European Union [2012] OJ C226/01 eur-lex.europa.eu/eli/treaty/teu_2012/oj.

equality is identified as a fundamental right in the EU Charter of Fundamental Rights.[127] While the prime meaning of equality is equality before the law, a broader idea of equality is diffused throughout EU law.[128]

The cases fall into three categories. First, exclusionary practices; second, excessive pricing; and third, exemptions and immunities. All of the outcomes benefit those who are the outsiders: people without power in the marketplace. Presumably, they are predominantly those with lesser wealth and income.

Mergers are not treated here because there is no special use of equality in EU merger analysis.[129] This does not discount the importance of merger enforcement. Merger enforcement prevents creation of market power, and market power contributes to worse distributions of wealth and income; therefore merger law features in the inequality debate.

a. Exclusionary Practices and Equal Opportunity to Compete

EU law has two special principles: equality of opportunity to compete on the merits, which is a right of outsiders (not the dominant firm),[130] and special responsibility of dominant firms not 'to impair genuine undistorted competition', which is a duty of the insider – the dominant incumbent.[131]

In *Michelin*,[132] the Court of Justice announced the principle that dominant firms have a special responsibility not to distort the market. It prohibited exclusive dealing contracts by dominant firms, lest they tie up the market and fence out rivals, depriving rivals of a fair opportunity to compete. The principle has been qualified so as not to undermine rules of good economic analysis,[133] and today the Court may require an antitrust plaintiff to link significant foreclosures of rivals in high barrier markets to harm to consumers; nonetheless the special responsibility principle has enduring power. It sets a tone and presumption. It accounts for stark differences in EU and US law, illustrated, for example, by two pairs of telecom cases that reached opposite results on nearly identical material facts. In the first pair, the EU case endorsed entrants' right of equal access to a scarce input supplied

[127] Charter of Fundamental Rights of the European Union [2012] OJ C326/391 eur-lex.europa.eu/eli/treaty/char_2012/oj. The Preamble to the Charter states that 'conscious of its spiritual and moral heritage, the Union is founded on the indivisible, universal values of [...] *equality* and solidarity'.

[128] See, eg, *Google and Alphabet* (n 118) and cases and other authorities cited therein.

[129] Contrast, for example, South Africa's attention to equality principles in merger analysis. See section IV.E. below.

[130] See, eg, Case C-1/12 *Ordem dos Técnicos Oficiais de Contas (OTOC) v Autoridade da Concorrência* ECLI:EU:C:2013:127 and *Google and Alphabet* (n 118).

[131] See Case C-322/81 *NV Nederlandsche Banden Industrie Michelin v Commission* [1983] ECR 3461 para 57; Dominant undertakings have 'a special responsibility not to allow [their] conduct to impair genuine undistorted competition on the [internal] market'.

[132] Case C-322/81 *NV Nederlandsche Banden Industrie Michelin v Commission* [1983] ECR 3461 para 57.

[133] Case C-413/14 P *Intel Corp v Commission* ECLI:EU:C:2017:632, paras 138–147. See also Case T-286/09 RENV Intel Corp v Commission ECLI:EU:T:2022:19.

by the incumbent, and the US case favoured the incumbent's freedom of action.[134] In the second pair, the EU case decreed rivals' right to be free of a margin squeeze imposed by the incumbent, and the US case upheld the incumbent's freedom of action.[135] The cases illustrate that EU law is outsider-leaning, and US antitrust is not.[136]

Equality of opportunity is a companion principle to special responsibility. This EU principle appears in many cases, and has particular relevance today to gatekeeping platforms.[137] In gatekeeper cases, a firm owns and runs a dominant platform and also does business on its own platform in competition with the firms it hosts. It has the power to use its leverage to outcompete the rivals, and it does so. The modern cases were foreshadowed by cases before the age of the Internet. In *OTOC*,[138] the Portuguese Order of Chartered Accountants, a professional body empowered by statute to oversee the accountancy profession, required accountants to log a certain number of hours of professional training and required them to take a substantial part of that training from it, the professional body. Firms that offered similar training complained that the OTOC had an unfair competitive advantage and denied equality of opportunity to the rivals. The Court agreed with the complainants.[139]

EU law condemns unfair use of leverage by dominant gatekeeping Big Tech/Big Data platforms. In *Google Shopping*,[140] Google, the search giant and gatekeeper, used its might in the general search market to outrun rivals in comparative shopping. It prominently positioned and displayed its own comparison-shopping services on its search results pages while it displayed competitors' services only as generic search results, which it algorithmically demoted. In *Google Android*,[141]

[134] Case T-486/11 *Orange Polska SA, formerly Telekomunikacja Polska SA v Commission* ECLI:EU:T:2015:1002, aff'd Case C-123/16 P *Orange Polska SA v Commission* ECLI:EU:C:2018:590; and *Verizon Commc'ns Inc v L Offs of Curtis V Trinko LLP* 540 U.S. 398 (2004).

[135] Case C-280/08 P *Deutsche Telekom v Commission* [2010] ECR I-9555 and *Pacific Bell Telephone Co v linkLine Commc'ns Inc* 555 U.S. 438 (2009). See discussion of the two pairs of cases in E Fox, 'Monopolization and Abuse of Dominance: Why Europe is Different' (2014) 59 *The Antitrust Bulletin* 129.

[136] Outside of the circles of power. Not a dominant or leading firm. Firms in the market that have no power, and firms that might enter the market if not deterred by power. See EM Fox, 'Outsider Antitrust: "Making Markets Work for People" as a Post-Millennium Developmental Goal' in T Bonakele, E Fox and L Mncube (eds), *Competition Policy for the New Era: Insights from the BRICS Countries* (Oxford, Oxford University Press, 2017).

[137] See, eg, *Google and Alphabet* (n 118).

[138] Case C-1/12 *Ordem dos Técnicos Oficiais de Contas (OTOC) v Autoridade da Concorrência* ECLI:EU:C:2013:127.

[139] ibid.

[140] Commission Decision of 27 June 2017 relating to proceedings under Article 102 of the Treaty on the Functioning of the European Union and Article 54 of the Agreement on the European Economic Area (AT.39740 – *Google Search (Shopping)*) ec.europa.eu/competition/antitrust/cases/dec_docs/39740/39740_14996_3.pdf, Case T-612/17 *Google and Alphabet v Commission* [2017] OJ C369/37 eur-lex.europa.eu/legal-content/EN/TXT/?uri=CELEX:62017TN0612: appeal dismissed by the General Court on 10 November 2021 ECLI:EU:T:2021:763 eur-lex.europa.eu/legal-content/en/TXT/?uri=CELEX:62017TJ0612.

[141] Commission Decision of 18 July 2018 relating to proceedings under Article 102 of the Treaty on the Functioning of the European Union and Article 54 of the Agreement on the European Economic

Google used leverage from its own Android smartphone operating system to preinstall its apps, which covered key search access points, on Android, further entrenching Google search. In *Google AdSense*,[142] Google imposed exclusivity contracts on third party website owners, entrenching Google as the exclusive ad broker and monopolising the search advertising intermediation market. The European Commission found all three sets of practices to be abuses of dominance. It applied a principal of access for outsiders, and imposed responsibilities on the dominant insider. The General Court affirmed *Google Shopping*.[143] Appeals of the other two cases to the General Court are pending.

Persistent abuses by Big Tech along with a general commitment to a digital single market led EU to craft the Digital Markets Act (DMA) and related regulation.[144] Under the DMA, covered platform gatekeepers will have specific duties not to use their gatekeeping advantages to the detriment of rivals and other users on their platform, and to grant rivals access to data to allow them to effectively compete.[145]

Area (AT.40099 – *Google Android*), appeal pending, Case T-604/18 *Google and Alphabet v Commission* [2018] OJ C445/21.

[142] Commission Decision of 20 March 2019 relating to proceedings under Article 102 of the Treaty on the Functioning of the European Union and Article 54 of the EEA Agreement (AT.40411 – *Google Search (AdSense)*).

[143] Case T-612/17 *Google and Alphabet v Commission* ECLI:EU:T:2021:763 eur-lex.europa.eu/legal-content/en/TXT/?uri=CELEX:62017TJ0612.

[144] See Proposal for a Regulation of the European Parliament and of the Council on contestable and fair markets in the digital sector (Digital Markets Act) COM/2020/842 final eur-lex.europa.eu/legal-content/en/ALL/?uri=COM:2020:842:FIN. See also Proposal for a Regulation of the European Parliament and of the Council on a Single Market For Digital Services (Digital Services Act) and amending Directive 2000/31/EC, COM(2020) 825 final eur-lex.europa.eu/legal-content/en/TXT/?uri=COM%3A2020%3A825%3AFIN.

[145] For example, Art 6(1)(a) DMA requires gatekeepers to 'refrain from using, in competition with business users, any data not publicly available, which is generated through activities by those business users, including by the end users of these business users, of its core platform services or provided by those business users of its core platform services or by the end users of these business users'. This is to prevent gatekeepers from taking 'advantage of [their] dual role to use data, generated from transactions by [their] business users on the core platform, for the purpose of [their] own services that offer similar services to that of [their] business users'. (Recital 43). Art 6(1)(j) DMA requires that gatekeepers who offer online search services 'provide […] any third party providers of online search engines, upon their request, with access on fair, reasonable and non-discriminatory terms to ranking, query, click and view data in relation to free and paid search generated by end users on online search engines of the gatekeeper, subject to anonymisation for the query, click and view data that constitutes personal data'. Art 6(1)(i) DMA requires gatekeepers to 'provide business users, or third parties authorised by a business user, free of charge, with effective, high-quality, continuous and real-time access and use of aggregated or non-aggregated data, that is provided for or generated in the context of the use of the relevant core platform services by those business users and the end users engaging with the products or services provided by those business users'. ibid. For an analysis of the DMA's provisions and their interaction with existing regulation and competition law see, eg, P Larouche and A de Streel, 'The European Digital Markets Act: A Revolution Grounded on Traditions' (2021) 12(7) *Journal of European Competition Law & Practice* 542–560 ssrn.com/abstract=3911361; H Schweitzer, 'The art to make gatekeeper positions contestable and the challenge to know what is fair: A discussion of the Digital Markets Act Proposal' (2021) forthcoming in *Zeitschrift für Europäisches Privatrecht* Issue 3; Centre on Regulation in Europe, Alexandre de Streel (coordinator), *Recommendations Paper: Digital Markets Act: Making Economic Regulation of Platforms fit for the Digital Age* (November 2020) cerre.eu/wp-content/uploads/2020/11/CERRE_DIGITAL-MARKETS-ACT_November20.pdf; P Baschenhof, 'The Digital

In the EU, the principle of equality of opportunity is most explicit in the case of state-granted privileges.[146] The EU Treaty requires SOEs and state-privileged entities to abide by the competition rules when they can do so consistently with their public service obligations, and requires Member States not to adopt measures inconsistent with the competition rules.[147] In one illustrative case, Greece gave its partly state-owned electricity company, DEI, the exclusive right to mine for lignite (brown coal), which was the cheapest and best primary fuel available in Greece and thus gave DEI a big competitive advantage over its electricity rivals. The rivals complained. The Court of Justice ruled that the allocation of the lignite to DEI in itself violated the Treaty. The action created 'inequality of opportunity between economic operators, and thus distorted competition'.[148]

How far does the EU principle of equality of opportunity go? This is not clear. When the condition of inequality is created by the state, the principle is strongest.[149] The state has no right to grant a privilege, except as needed to satisfy public service obligations. When a private firm has a competitive advantage as a result of its own achievements, it can usually use that advantage to compete,[150] unless it maintains a critical platform or facility and the firm's conduct deprives rivals of their right to competition on the merits.[151]

b. Excessive Pricing

Competition law that prohibits excessive pricing is paradigmatically distributive. It distributes from those who unfairly and excessively elevate their prices (corporations with dominant market power) to those who are the victims of the exploitation. EU law prohibits excessive pricing. The threshold for proving that

Markets Act (DMA): A Procompetitive Recalibration of Data Relations?' (2022) 101 *University of Illinois Journal of Law, Technology & Policy* ssrn.com/abstract=3970101.

[146] See E Fox and D Healey, 'When the State Harms Competition' (2014) 79 *Antitrust Law Journal* 769, 780–781 and especially footnote 56; ch 5 in this volume.

[147] Arts 106 (1) and (2).

[148] Case C-553/12 P *Commission v Dimosia Epicheirisi Ilektrismou AE (DEI)* ECLI:EU:C:2014:2083 para 44.

[149] See Fox and Healey (n 146). See also case T-791/19 *Sped-Pro v Commission* ECLI:EU:T:2022:67 in which the General Court annulled the Commission's decision to reject a small Polish transport company's claim against PKP Cargo – Poland's largest rail freight company, owned 50% by the State Railway company (PKP). Sped-Pro argued that its right to a fair trial would not be protected should the Polish NCA (rather than the Commission) consider its complaint. It feared that the Polish NCA would give preferential treatment to PKP Cargo, pointing to the NCA President's lack of independence from government and a history of mild and ineffective penalties against PKP. The GC observed that, since the Polish courts hearing a potential appeal against the NCA's decision lacked independence, they would not be in a position to balance any deficiencies in the Polish NCA's decision making. *Sped-Pro* shows how EU law protects small outsider entities against the fused political and economic power of the state and dominant incumbents controlled by it.

[150] See Case C-413/14 P *Intel v Commission* ECLI:EU:C:2017:632 para 133; Case C-209/10 *Post Danmark A/S v Konkurrencerådet* ECLI:EU:C:2012:172 para 21.

[151] See Case T-612/17 *Google and Alphabet v Commission* ECLI:EU:T:2021:763 para 150 eur-lex.europa.eu/legal-content/en/TXT/?uri=CELEX:62017TJ0612.

a price is excessive is high, lest the law interfere with the ordinary give and take of the market; yet the law does have teeth.[152] It tends to prohibit unconscionable price hikes.

Outrageous price hikes recur in the pharmaceutical market. The big pharma companies have significant opportunities to inflate their prices, especially as patents expire and price regulation no longer applies, and when the market is too small for generic companies to invest and try to compete with big pharma. Outrageous price hikes have occurred also in times of the pandemic, when certain goods and services are suddenly necessities and become scarce.[153] When this occurs, only the rich can afford the drugs and other necessities of life.

Recent examples of unconscionable price hikes, around the world and in the EU, involved Aspen Pharmacare. Aspen owned patents on six drugs for essential cancer treatments, and the patents expired. Aspen increased prices to European Member State healthcare agencies (the principal purchasers) by as much as 1,500 per cent.[154] The Commission opened an investigation and settled the case with Aspen's commitments to decrease prices by an average of 73 per cent and to continue to supply the drugs to cover the needs of European consumers for a period of five to ten years.[155]

c. Small Businesses

The EU law open market principle is helpful to SMEs. They are usually the ones that benefit from being able to contest markets on their merits.

Anticompetitive agreements between SMEs may violate the law if they appreciably affect trade between Member States. However, agreements between SMEs are recognised by the Commission as 'not normally [being] capable of affecting trade between Member States'.[156] SMEs often have low annual turnovers and market

[152] See the standards set in Case C-372/19 *Belgische Vereniging van Auteurs, Componisten en Uitgevers CVBA (SABAM) v Weareone World BVBA and Wecandance NV* ECLI:EU:C:2020:959.

[153] Typically, competition laws catch price gouging only when the exploiting company is dominant. Many jurisdictions enact special crisis anti-gouging laws. South Africa has condemned price gouging under its abuse of dominance law. See section E. below.

[154] In 2016, the Italian Competition Authority found that Aspen Pharmacare had violated Art 102 TFEU through unfair and excessive pricing practices of threatening to interrupt supplies of 'life-saving and irreplaceable' cancer drugs in price negotiations with the Italian Medicines Agency (AIFA) and increasing prices by 300 to 1,500% in Italy without 'any necessary economic justifications'. en.agcm.it/en/media/detail?id=1c53b769-446d-4e36-bfed-49e2f7454e03&parent=Press%20releases&parentUrl=/en/media/press-releases. The full decision in English may be found at en.agcm.it/dotcmsDOC/pressrelease/A480_eng.pdf.

[155] European Commission, *Antitrust: Aspen proposes 73% price reduction for six off-patent cancer medicines to remove Commission's excessive pricing concerns*, (14 July 2020) ec.europa.eu/commission/presscorner/detail/en/qanda_20_1339.

[156] Communication from the Commission: Notice on agreements of minor importance which do not appreciably restrict competition under Article 101(1) of the TFEU (De Minimis Notice) [2014] OJ C291/1, n 5, eur-lex.europa.eu/legal-content/EN/TXT/PDF/?uri=CELEX:52014XC0830(01)&from=EN.

shares, and therefore agreements between them often fall within the safe harbours set out in Commission guidelines and block exemptions.[157] In relation to vertical agreements between SMEs, the Commission has stated that it 'will normally refrain from opening proceedings for lack of sufficient interest for the European Union' even where such agreements 'meet the conditions for the application of Article 101(1)'.[158] Furthermore, EU legislation is in place that aims to protect SMEs in certain situations of imbalances in bargaining power and to ease SMEs' liquidity constraints and complications associated with transborder trade.[159]

d. Immunities for Workers

The treatment of workers is a significant factor in the inequality equation, because workers are historically exploited and get a constantly decreasing share of the gains of trade and the profits of business. Workers are vulnerable, and they are squeezed. Most jurisdictions take account of the weak bargaining position of workers and provide an immunity from antitrust, at least for collective bargaining by unions. In the EU, the relevant early case is *Albany*.[160] In *Albany*, the Court took account of social rights protected elsewhere in the Treaty (now they are protected also in the Charter of Fundamental Rights), and in the Agreement on Social Policy.[161] The Court noted that the objectives of the Agreement on Social Policy 'include improved living and working conditions, proper social protection, dialogue between management and labour, the development of human resources with a view to lasting high employment and the combatting of exclusion'.[162]

[157] See, eg, Commission Regulation (EU) No 330/2010 of 20 April 2010 on the application of Article 101(3) of the TFEU to categories of vertical agreements and concerted practices (Vertical Block Exemption Regulation), Arts 2(1), 2(2) and 3, eur-lex.europa.eu/eli/reg/2010/330/oj; Commission Regulation (EU) No 1217/2010 of 14 December 2010 on the application of Article 101(3) of the TFEU to certain categories of research and development agreements, Art 4(2)-(3) data.europa.eu/eli/reg/2010/1217/oj; and Commission Regulation (EU) 1218/2010 of 14 December 2010 on the application of Article 101(3) of the TFEU to certain categories of specialisation agreements, Art 4, data.europa.eu/eli/reg/2010/1218/oj. See also Commission Guidelines on Vertical Restraints [2010] OJ C130/1, paras 8–11 eur-lex.europa.eu/legal-content/EN/TXT/PDF/?uri=CELEX:52010XC0519(04)&from=EN.

[158] ibid Commission Guidelines on Vertical Restraints, para 11. See also Annex to the Communication from the Commission, *Approval of the content of a draft for a Communication from the Commission Notice Guidelines on vertical restraints* of 9 July 2021 C(2021) 5038 final, para 26 ec.europa.eu/competition-policy/system/files/2021-07/draft_vertical-guidelines_en.pdf. There may be sufficient interest, however, where the firms hold a dominant position. ibid.

[159] See, eg, Directive (EU) 2019/633 of the European Parliament and of the Council of 17 April 2019 on unfair trading practices in business-to-business relationships in the agricultural and food supply chain [2019] OJ L111/59; Directive 2011/7/EU of the European Parliament and of the Council of 16 February 2011 on combating payment in commercial transactions (recast) [2011] OJ L48/1.

[160] Case C-67/96 *Albany International BV v Stichting Bedrijfspensioenfonds Textielindustrie* [1999] ECR I-5751.

[161] Agreement on social policy concluded between the Member States of the European Community with the exception of the United Kingdom of Great Britain and Northern Ireland [1992] OJ C191/91.

[162] *Albany* (n 160) para 57.

The Court said:

> [T]he social policy objectives pursued by such agreements would be seriously undermined if management and labour were subject to Article [101 (1)] of the Treaty when seeking jointly to adopt measures to improve conditions of work and employment.[163]

Therefore, it held, collective negotiations between management and labour in pursuit of such objectives fall outside of Article 101(1) TFEU which condemns agreements that distort competition.

Who qualifies as 'labour' that is entitled to the immunity? In *FNV Kunsten*,[164] a collective labour agreement providing for minimum pay was concluded on behalf of both musicians employed by an orchestra and self-employed substitute musicians. The self-employed musicians claimed immunity. The Court of Justice declared that, although self-employed independent service providers do not get the collective bargaining exemption, there was a legitimate question as to whether the individuals were 'false self-employed'. Even if the individuals are treated as self-employed for tax and other reasons in their Member State, they may be 'in a situation comparable to that of employees' and thus treated as employees under EU law.[165] The Court asked: is the 'independence … merely notional, thereby disguising an employment relationship'? Is the relationship one of subordination so that the individual enjoys no more 'independence and flexibility than employees who perform the same activity, as regards the determination of the working hours, [and] the place and manner of performing the tasks assigned …?'[166]

The issue surfaces today in the context of the gig economy. Drivers for Uber, Lyft and other ride-sharing platforms want to be able to bargain collectively with the platform, which has exponentially greater bargaining power than the drivers. EU Vice President and Competition Commissioner Margrethe Vestager has defended the right of gig workers to 'team up on wages'.[167] The European Commission has published proposals for a new Directive to improve gig workers' working conditions and new Draft Guidelines to clarify the categories of collective agreements that fall outside the scope of Article 101 TFEU.[168] In the Draft Guidelines, the

[163] ibid para 59.

[164] Case C-413/13 *Kunsten Informatie en Media v Staat der Nederlanden* ECLI:EU:C:2014:2411.

[165] ibid para 31.

[166] ibid para 37.

[167] See J Espinoza, 'Vestager says gig economy workers should "team up" on wages' *Financial Times* (24 October 2019) www.ft.com/content/0cafd442-f673-11e9-9ef3-eca8fc8f2d65. For the objective of 'allowing … trade unions to coordinate bargaining between sectors so as to increase their gains at the expense of managers and capital suppliers' see ch 10 in this volume.

[168] Proposal for a Directive of the European Parliament and of the Council on improving working conditions in platform work of 9 December 2021, COM(2021) 762 final ec.europa.eu/social/BlobServlet?docId=24992&langId=en. If adopted, Art 4 of the Directive will create a rebuttable legal presumption of employment where a digital labour platform is 'controlling the performance of work' by a gig worker. See also Annex to the Communication from the Commission, *Approval of the content of a draft for a Communication from the Commission: Guidelines on the application of EU competition law to collective agreements regarding the working conditions of solo self-employed persons* of 9 December 2021, COM(2021) 8838 final ec.europa.eu/competition-policy/document/

Commission stated that it would not 'intervene against collective agreements between solo self-employed persons and their counterparts in cases where there is a clear imbalance in bargaining power, even where such persons are not 'in a situation comparable to that of workers'.[169]

US antitrust law is unsympathetic to the plight of gig economy workers. It is not likely that gig economy workers can successfully analogise themselves to employees. Even municipalities have been unsuccessful in trying to protect gig workers from antitrust.[170] The US has a strong principle against exemptions from antitrust. More equality or reducing seriously unequal bargaining power do not count as justifications.[171]

iii. Comment

Particularly as compared with US antitrust case law, EU law leans towards the outsider and against the incumbent. It 'cares' about use of power against the vulnerable. It expressly promotes equality of opportunity and therefore both empowerment and mobility. It fosters openness and access to markets as a primary principle. It prohibits excessive pricing. It prohibits abuse of dominance in a way sensitive to the openness and equality principles above.[172] It condemns power-creating mergers.[173] It condemns state and local regulation that unnecessarily excludes and exploits. Given the confluence of these objectives and strands of law, EU law predictably tends to push back on the growth of the wealth/income inequality gap. It is not surprising, therefore, that Amit Zac et al. conclude that the EU competition model is linked to lower levels of income inequality than is the US antitrust model.[174]

iv. The Six Questions

Question One: Is an equality value embedded in EU competition law?

Yes.

download/9c836e4a-29b1-4659-86a4-6946e368d8cb_en. The Guidelines clarify 'that certain categories of collective agreements fall outside the scope of Article 101 TFEU' and 'that the Commission will not intervene against certain other categories of collective agreements'.

[169] *Draft Guidelines on the application of EU competition law to collective agreements regarding the working conditions of solo self-employed persons* (n 168) Recital 35.

[170] See *Chamber of Commerce v Seattle* (n 64).

[171] See generally section IV.B. above.

[172] For the proposition that 'the constitutional structure of the EU demands a holistic approach to Article 102' and demands an integration of equality considerations into Art 102 TFEU analysis and enforcement, see ch 5 in this volume.

[173] The Commission could, however, be bolder in prohibiting anticompetitive mergers as opposed to accepting packages of spin-offs and conditions proposed by the merging firms.

[174] A Zac, C Casti, C Decker and A Ezrachi, 'Competition Law and Income Inequality: A Panel Data Econometric Approach' (April 2021) ssrn.com/abstract=3402436.

Question Two: Is an equality value a source of wisdom available to enforcers and jurists to decide priorities or to reach outcomes in particular cases?

Yes.

Question Three: Are antitrust consent decrees or clearances used as an occasion for imposing conditions that advance equality, such as benefits for workers or SMEs?

No.

Question Four: Is more equality, or reducing the inequality gap, a separate mandate that can warrant an antitrust exemption or be used as a trump?

Not as such, but workers' collective agreements are not covered by the law's prohibition, and SMEs fall within a safe harbour in various guidelines.

Question Five: Does EU competition law alleviate inequality? Aggravate inequality? Or just not help to remedy it?

It probably tends to alleviate inequality.

Question Six: Would equality-leaning changes in competition law be feasible and likely to help close the inequality gaps?

For exclusionary practices, the EU open-market principle already tilts in favour of outsiders. The DMA and related legislation does so too. More injunctions against power-creating mergers (in all jurisdictions) would advance both traditional competition and equality values.

E. South Africa

i. History and Evolution of the Competition Law in Terms of Equality

South Africa tells its own brutal story of inequality and its self-conscious use of competition law as a tool to correct it. In South Africa, competition law is one means to help lift up, empower, and provide mobility for the great majority of the population who were heinously excluded from economic life by the white supremacist government during the dark years of apartheid, 1948 to 1994. Apartheid was formally abolished only when Nelson Mandela was freed from prison. In the New South Africa, competition law was designed both for economic performance and for black empowerment and empowerment of poorer, weaker and excluded persons in general. More than any other nation in the world, South Africa has made a deliberate effort to consider how competition law and policy can provide greater equality and be a cornerstone of justice in society.

Predictably, equality is deeply embedded in South African competition law and its jurisprudence. It is a source of wisdom both to prioritise enforcement and to decide cases. The competition authorities use competition law decrees for extensive conditionality in favour of SMEs, small suppliers, workers, and historically disadvantaged persons (HDPs). The substantive law embodies targeted affirmative action for HDPs and SMEs. If the world wants a touchstone for how far competition law might go to advance equality, it is South Africa's.[175] This section first invokes the Constitution of the New South Africa. It then highlights South African jurisprudence that bears on the equality value, describes the recent 'equality' amendments to the Competition Act, and describes some of the most germane jurisprudence and policy. It then answers the six questions encapsulating how this jurisdiction treats equality.

The new Constitution was adopted upon the overthrow of apartheid. First among all enumerated rights in the Constitution – higher than freedoms of expression and of property – is equality. The Constitution authorises affirmative action in favour of historically disadvantaged people.

Then Deputy Chief Justice Dikgang Moseneke captured the depth of the Constitutional guarantee:

> The achievement of equality goes to the bedrock of our constitutional architecture. The Constitution commands us to strive for a society built on the democratic values of human dignity, the achievement of equality, the advancement of human rights and freedom. Thus the achievement of equality is not only a guaranteed and justiciable right in our Bill of Rights but also a core and foundational value; a standard which must inform all law and against which all law must be tested for constitutional consonance.[176]

The Competition Act of 1998 is one piece of this fabric wherein all law must play its role. Apartheid South Africa had a vibrant economy. It had many state-owned enterprises (these, not so vibrant) and many internationally competitive private firms, all run by whites. In the mid-1980s, boycotts and campaigns of divestment for combined instrumental (to end apartheid) and moral purposes isolated South Africa's economy and entrenched its monopolies. When apartheid fell, the new policymakers faced the question: what to do about industry? While nationalisation was seriously considered, the leaders believed it important to adopt a market system, with antitrust law, to re-integrate South Africa into the world. But what kind of antitrust? Should they take the occasion to break up the white monopolies and transfer control to black ownership? In the end, the new government feared that break-ups would cripple South African business and handicap the firms in their international competition. Therefore, it chose a more traditional path. The competition law draws significantly from the EU and also but somewhat less from the US, but speaks its own voice. The new act was expected to open the doors wide to black participation in the economy.[177]

[175] The South Africa trajectory is not without its critics. The critics charge that tilting the law to favour equality may create uncertainty and unpredictability, open the door to ministerial, commission and court discretion and thus undercut rule of law and invite politics and corruption, handicap efficiency, and chill innovation. See J Oxenham, M-J Currie and A Stargard, 'Changing South Africa's Competition Law Regime: A Populist Departure from International Best Practices' (2019) 10 *Journal of European Competition Law & Practice* 232–240.

[176] *Minister of Finance v Van Heerden* (CCT 63/03) [2004] ZACC 3, 2004 (6) SA 121 (CC) para 22. See, to the same effect, and holding that the Competition Act must be interpreted to address inequalities as required by the Bill of Rights, *Competition Commission of South Africa v Mediclinic Southern Africa (Pty) Ltd and Another* (CCT 31/20) [2021] ZACC 35 (15 October 2021).

[177] See Zuma (n 188) below.

The Competition Act of 1998 included in its Purposes:

(e) to ensure that small and medium-sized enterprises have an equitable opportunity to participate in the economy; [and]

(f) to promote a greater spread of ownership, in particular to increase the ownership stakes of historically disadvantaged persons.[178]

The Purposes clause, however, was not textually woven into the prohibitory provisions of the Act, leaving ambiguity in the law. As the cases arose, the Competition Tribunal construed the law faithfully to its purposes and leaned on the side of inclusiveness and more equality. Thus, the Tribunal found a violation when a dominant firm price-discriminated against Mr Foot, producer of wooden posts for grape vines and telephone poles. Sasol, the producer, overcharged Foot for his critical input (creosote) and drove him out of business (*Nationwide Poles*).[179] The Tribunal also found a violation when a medical insurance merger threatened to stem the development of a capitated insurance option for low income persons (*Medicross*).[180] It also found a violation when a monopolist steel producer sold steel to South African fabricators at import parity prices (very high) while selling the steel abroad at the much lower competitive world price (*Mittal*).[181] Every one of these cases was overturned on appeal on grounds that the conduct did not violate the prohibitory language of the Act, which did not specifically incorporate the equality goals.[182] In *Nationwide Poles*, Mr Foot had not proved that his exclusion harmed the market and consumers. In *Medicross*, the Commission had not proved that capitated insurance was a market. In *Mittal*, the South African buyer, Harmony Gold, had not proved that the high home price returned excessive profits to the South African monopolist.

In other respects, however, the Act was and is both explicitly and implicitly sensitive to the needs for greater equality. South Africa, like many other developing countries, has not adopted US antitrust standards, which are, as applied today, based on a goal of efficient allocation of resources regardless of distributional effects and that assume the free market will efficiently allocate resources.[183] South Africa seeks inclusive economic development and access of 'the people' (other than the elite and the powerful) to markets, especially to necessities.

[178] Competition Act 89 of 1998, Art 2 (S Afr) (updated through July 2019).

[179] *Nationwide Poles v Sasol Ltd* (72/CR/Dec03) [2005] ZACT 17 (31 March 2005), rev'd (49/CAC/Apr05) [2005] ZACAC 5 (13 December 2005). The Tribunal, by David Lewis, noted: 'The Competition Act is, itself, punctuated with references to the legislature's desire that the statute should promote market access and equality of opportunity particularly … where small enterprise is concerned.' Para 88. See also para 142.

[180] *Medicross Healthcare Group (Pty) Ltd v Competition Commission of South Africa* (11/LM/Mar05) [2005] ZACT 66 (13 October 2005), rev'd (55/CAC/Sept05) [2006] ZACAC 3 (6 April 2006).

[181] *Harmony Gold Mining Co v Mittal Steel Corp* (13/CR/Feb04) [2007] ZACT 21 (27 March 2007), reversed (70/CAC/Apr07) [2009] ZACAC 1 (29 May 2009). The Tribunal fined Mittal 5.5% of its annual turnover. Remedies Decision (13/CR/Feb04) [2007] ZACT 71 (6 September 2007).

[182] See (n 179–181) above. The *Mittal* case was remanded.

[183] See *Trinko*, 540 U.S. 398.

It makes no assumptions that the free market will deliver access or inclusion.[184] Thus, in South Africa, the unilateral conduct offence is based on abuse of dominance; it does not require monopoly. Dominance is conclusively presumed at 45 per cent of the market, and a plaintiff has the chance to prove that dominant power exists at lower levels. Equal opportunity to compete on the merits is a major value. The structure of the statute itself makes this clear.[185] An exclusionary act that 'is substantial or significant in terms of its effect in foreclosing the market to rivals' is illegal.[186] Moreover, mergers can be prohibited on public interest grounds, even if they do not harm competition.

But still, even with the formal repeal of the apartheid laws, the tilt towards inclusiveness of the Competition Act and the range of other laws,[187] and a sweeping Black Empowerment program, the radical transformation hoped for had not occurred. In 2017 then-President Jacob Zuma noted with urgency that Black South Africans still did not participate equally or close to equally in the South African economy. Zuma announced that the Competition Act would need to be amended to facilitate the transformation. He promised that the government would bring forward amendments to the Act to address the need to have a more inclusive economy and to de-concentrate the high levels of ownership and control we see in many sectors. '… In this way we seek to open up the economy to new players, give black South Africans opportunities in the economy and indeed help to make the economy more dynamic, competitive and inclusive. This is our vision of radical economic transformation.[188]

Minister of Economic Development Ebrahim Patel embraced the cause and promised that an amended law would include the following:

> 9. [Market inquiries] … [T]he competition authorities must be empowered to consider these questions proactively or at the request of key stakeholders …. Markets plagued by

[184] See E Fox, 'Competition, Development and Regional Integration: In Search of a Competition Law Fit for Developing Countries' in J Drexl, M Bakhoum, E Fox, M Gal and D Gerber (eds), *Competition Policy and Regional Integration in Developing Countries* (Cheltenham, Edward Elgar, 2012).

[185] See Competition Act, Art 8 (c), (d).

[186] *Computicket (Pty) Ltd v Competition Commission of South Africa* (170/CAC/Feb19) [2019] ZACAC 4 (23 October 2019) para 18.

[187] For South Africa's contract law and the extent to which equality principles inform its interpretation, see KE Davis and M Pargendler, 'Contract Law and Inequality' (9 March 2021) draft on file with authors, documenting the law of South Africa, Brazil, and Colombia. In the name of greater equality especially for historically disadvantaged persons, a divided South African Constitutional Court construed law on the running of a debtor's interest during trial in favour of the debtor – thus suspending interest. *Paulsen and Another v Slip Knot Investments 777 (Pty) Limited* (CCT 61/14) [2015] ZACC 5; 2015 (3) SA 479 (CC); 2015 (5) BCLR 509 (CC) (24 March 2015). Justice Madlanga, in the main judgment, expressed particular concern for debtors who had been affected by apartheid and were financially vulnerable. He said: 'We need to look at South Africa's socio-economic realities. A large percentage of the providers of credit are large, established and well-resourced corporates. … To many credit consumers, who fall on the wrong side of this country's vast capital disparities, astronomical interest may mean the difference between economic survival and complete financial ruin. [para 66] Entrepreneurship and the economic advancement of those with no history of being financially resourced must be given room to take root and thrive.' Para 75.

[188] Jacob Zuma, President of South Africa, *2017 State of the Nation Address* (9 February 2017).

over-concentration and untransformed ownership will be identified, investigated and appropriate measures applied to remedy these market features. These inquiries, and any remedies that result, will target the primary structural impediments to market entry and ownership by black South Africans.

10. The proposed amendments also will seek to incentivise firms to develop relationships and adopt strategies that would alter market structure, reduce concentrations by encouraging entry of historically disadvantaged South Africans (particularly those who own small and medium-sized enterprises), reduce barriers to entry, and expand ownership to ensure that more enjoy substantive economic citizenship.[189]

The Amendments were proposed and adopted.[190] They fall largely into five categories: First, dominant firms' abuses; second, exemptions for anti-competitive agreements and practices; third, mergers: 'transformation' was added to the list of public interests, and a process was introduced for mergers that threaten national security; fourth, market inquiries: power to investigate markets for distortions of competition was enhanced and strong remedies authorised; and 'distortion' was defined to include adverse impact on SMEs and HDPs; and fifth, institutional: the minister was given more powers of intervention. We show below how a number of the reforms (2018–2019) would or could contribute to equality.

ii. The Contribution to Equality by the Amendments

a. Dominant Firms

The amendments strengthen South Africa's ability to control dominant firm conduct that exacerbates inequality. It does so in categories including excessive pricing, buyer power, price discrimination, and exclusionary practices.

In excessive pricing cases, the amendments shift the burden of proof. If the plaintiff shows that the price was excessive (in accordance with specified factors), the defendant must prove that the price was reasonable. This shift of the onus overrules prior cases, including *Mittal.*[191] The amendment paved the way for the Tribunal's and Court's decisions in a recent case for price-gouging coronavirus masks, elaborated below.

Buying power. the Amendments prohibit exercise of monopsony power in sectors to be designated by the minister. The minister designated agro-processing, grocery retail, and on-line intermediation services. In the designated sectors a dominant firm may not impose unfair prices or other unfair trading conditions

[189] Background Note issued by the Minister of Economic Development, 25 May 2017. Emphasis added.

[190] On 13 February 2019, President Cyril Ramaphosa signed the Competition Amendment Bill in Law and on 12 July 2019, President Ramaphosa published a notice immediately bringing into force certain of the provisions of the Competition Amendment Act. The provisions brought into force do not include the national security provision in mergers or the buyer power and price discrimination sections of the abuse of dominance law.

[191] *Mittal*, 13/CR/Feb04 [2007].

on a supplier that is a SME or HDP.[192] Where the plaintiff makes a prima facie case, the dominant firm must prove that the prices or trading conditions are not unfair.[193] This section is about unequal bargaining power used to squeeze vulnerable suppliers.

In the category of price discrimination, the 1998 Act prohibits dominant firms from engaging in price discrimination likely to substantially prevent or lessen competition. The Amendments add to this provision. They also prohibit also dominant firm price discrimination that would impede SMEs and HDPs from participating effectively in the market. Moreover, plaintiffs can now easily make a prima facie case, shifting to dominant firm price-discriminators the burden to show that the discrimination did not impede the small firm's effective participation in the market. This amendment overrules the *Nationwide Poles* case.[194]

The amendments strengthen control over exclusionary acts in general. Exclusionary acts bear greatly on inequalities, because vulnerable firms and people are usually the victims of dominant firms' exclusionary acts. Some of those acts make the market work better and make people as consumers better off, some of them simply build moats around the dominant firm's power, and some have characteristics of both. The definition of illegal exclusionary acts under the South African Competition Act always included acts that impede or prevent a firm from entering and expanding in a market.[195] The definition is now expanded to include acts that impede a firm from *participating* in the market. 'Participation' is defined as the ability of or opportunity for firms to sustain themselves in the market.

b. Exemptions: Anticompetitive Agreements and Practices

Anticompetitive agreements and practices may be eligible for an exemption. Under the 1998 Act, an exemption could be granted if the agreement or practice promoted exports, promoted the ability of SMEs or HDPs to become competitive, stopped a decline in an industry, or fostered economic stability. The amendments add as grounds for exemption: promotion of the ability of SMEs and HDPs to participate (as well as enter and expand) in the market; and: 'competitiveness and efficiency gains that promote employment or industrial expansion'. They add also, as grounds for exemption: 'development, growth, [and] transformation' (along with stability) of an industry. 'Transformation' is a key concept and is principally about greater equality for HDPs.

[192] The category of historically disadvantaged persons refers to people who, before the current Constitution, were discriminated against on the basis of race, and entities owned or controlled by them. According to the minister's regulations, to qualify as an HDP, a firm may supply not more than 20% of the purchases of the dominant buyer for the good or service. In this way the advantages are limited to the smaller, and probably in most cases, the less advantaged, suppliers.

[193] See Commission website, www.compcom.co.za.

[194] *Nationwide Poles v Sasol Ltd* 71CR/Dec03 [2005] ZACT 17. See discussion in ElM Fox and M Bakhoum, *Making Markets Work for Africa: Markets, Development and Competition Law In Sub-Saharan Africa* (Oxford, OUP, 2019) 110–112.

[195] The acts are subject to justification.

c. Mergers

Public interest. Under the Competition Act of 1998, mergers were always subject to a public interest test. They could be prohibited even if the merger was not anticompetitive, and they could be approved even if it was anticompetitive. Enumerated public interests included employment and the ability of SMEs and HDPs to become competitive. The amendments embellish the SME/HDP clause. The authorities must consider the effect of the merger on the ability of SMEs and HDPs 'to effectively enter into, participate in or expand in the market'. Also, authorities must consider: 'the promotion of a greater spread of ownership, in particular to increase the levels of ownership by [HDPs] and workers in firms in the market'. The latter requirement to consider spread of ownership to HDPs has led to a practice in connection with big foreign firm takeovers for the merging parties to give stock or joint venture opportunities to selected HDPs.

In June 2021, for the first time, the Competition Commission prohibited an acquisition outright on public interest grounds. ECP, a private equity firm with a commitment to investing in Africa, proposed to buy Burger King South Africa from Grand Parade Investments. The acquisition posed no competition problems. For public interest commitments, ECP offered to increase the number of Burger King outlets in South Africa to at least 150, to increase the number of permanent employees by no less than 1,250 HDPs, to increase the value of payroll and employee benefits by no less than R120 million, to increase procurement from Black Empowerment enterprises in South Africa to at least R930 million a year, and within two years to allocate five per cent of the shares of the merged firm to a Black ownership structure. But the selling owners were more than 68 per cent Black and the acquirers were White investors. As reported in its press release, 'The Commission found that the merger would lead to a significant reduction in the shareholding of historically disadvantaged persons in the target firm, from more than 68 per cent to 0 per cent as a result of the merger.'[196] While appeal to the Competition Tribunal was pending, the private equity acquirer agreed to expanded commitments including more concrete commitments anchoring the promise of five per cent employee shareholding and sale of the Grand Food meat plant to historically disadvantaged persons, and the Commission agreed to unblock the deal.[197]

It remains uncertain what the competition law requires in terms of greater spread of ownership, and to what extent increase of jobs for HDPs and related

[196] Commission Prohibits Acquisition Between ECP Africa Fund, Burger King South Africa and Grand Foods, South Africa Competition Commission (Media Statement, 1 June 2021) www.compcom.co.za/wp-content/uploads/2021/06/COMMISSION-PROHIBITS-ACQUISITION-BETWEEN-ECP-AFRICA-FUND-BURGER-KING-SOUTH-AFRICA-AND-GRAND-FOODS-.pdf.

[197] See A Madubela, 'Burger King sale possibly back on the cards after revised conditions', *Fin24* (18 August 2021) www.news24.com/fin24/companies/retail/burger-king-sale-possibly-back-on-the-cards-after-revised-conditions-20210818.

commitments such as a large capital investment, increase of worker benefits, and increase of procurement from B-BBEEs (broad-based black economic empowerment) will be accepted as offsets against a net decrease in Black ownership. Clarity on parameters would help Black owners sell the businesses they have built and would stabilise the sales value of their businesses.

d. Market Inquiries

Before the amendments, the Commission could decide to conduct market inquiries where it had reason to believe that features of the market impeded, distorted or restricted competition. At the conclusion of any such inquiry, the Commission could make recommendations. The amendments give teeth to market inquiries by giving the Commission the power to order remedies, even significant structural remedies, on approval by the Tribunal. The amendments give the minister power to require market inquiries. In making its decision, the Commission must have regard to whether the structure of the market has an adverse effect on SMEs or HDPs. Effect on SMEs/HDPs is identified as a feature that may constitute a distortion of competition. As Minister Patel said, 'markets plagued by … untransformed ownership will be identified'.[198]

Comment. The Amendments are designed to give greater equality to HDPs and to SMEs, which is a category largely comprised of HDPs. They are designed to do so by easier access to the market, fairer access to inputs, protection against exploitation by unequal bargaining power, and – for a few – access to stock or joint venture opportunities that can be the price of a merger clearance. For South Africa, equality includes a better, fairer spread of ownership of the South African economy.

iii. Competition Law Enforcement and Priority Choices that Demonstrate South Africa's Commitment and Implementation

This section examines cases and initiatives that best tell the story of how South Africa incorporates the equality value in its competition law and policy. It focuses on conditionality of approval of big mergers and price gouging during the pandemic.

a. Cases – Mergers and Conditionality

Walmart/Massmart[199] is the starting point. The US giant Walmart, with a history of treating workers and small suppliers aggressively and unfairly, proposed to enter

[198] Patel (n 81).

[199] *Wal-Mart Stores Inc and Massmart Holdings Ltd* (73/LM/Dec10) [2011] ZACT 41 (29 June 2011).

the African market by buying the large South African supermarket firm Massmart. Workers feared layoffs and mistreatment, and small suppliers of Massmart feared that they would be displaced by the Walmart global value chain. The merger did not have anticompetitive aspects, and indeed promised lower prices to South African consumers. To get clearance for the merger, Walmart stated its intention to recognise the union, not to lay off workers for two years, and to give employment preferences to 503 employees who were laid off just before the merger agreement was signed, and it offered to invest R100 million (almost US$7 million) for capacity-building of the small suppliers.

The Tribunal approved the deal. The union appealed. The Appeal Court toughened up the conditions. It required double the capacity-building fund and required that all of the commitments be subject to court order. The court order required Walmart to recognise the union, to reinstate the 503 laid off employees, and to invest R200 million (US$13 million) in addition to R40 million already spent by Massmart, for capacity training of small suppliers with a view to their qualifying to enter Walmart's global value chain. In an ex post review, the capacity-building program was found to have made a positive contribution to job creation and local procurement.[200]

Walmart and Massmart merged before the amendments were adopted. Later, in the wake of the draft amendments, Pepsi Cola Corporation proposed to buy Pioneer Foods, one of the largest South African producers and distributors of branded food and beverages. The acquisition was not anticompetitive.[201] Incentivised by the amendments, Pepsi and Pioneer approached the Minister of Economic Development with a view towards negotiating a package of commitments that would be acceptable to the minister and thus to get the minister's blessing as they moved forward to scrutiny by the Tribunal. The minister and the merging parties negotiated, and the Tribunal accepted, the following conditions:

Pepsi/Pioneer promised to create a Black Empowerment workers fund of R1.6 billion. The merged firm would make no merger related retrenchments for five years. It would create 500 direct jobs and 2,500 indirect jobs within five years. It would invest R5.5 billion in production capacity within five years. It would promote local procurement and it would contribute R600 million to a development fund for education and SME and agricultural development.

Orders of the Tribunal approving mergers commonly forbid the merged firm from laying off workers for periods of years from two to five. The merging firms may be required to set up development funds to re-skill the redundant workers. A recent order that sets up such a fund also provides that the redundant employees 'could, alternatively, use their portion of the fund to start up small businesses ….'[202]

[200] T Mandiriza, T Sithebe and M Viljoen, *Ex-Post Review of the Wal-mart/Massmart Merger* (Competition Commission of South Africa Working Paper CC2016/03).

[201] *Simba (Pty) Ltd and Pioneer Food Group Ltd* (108/LM/Sep19) (5 March 2020).

[202] *Boundary Terraces 042 (Pty) Ltd v Bravo Group (Pty) Ltd.* (272/LM/Mar19) [2019] ZACT 74 (21 October 2019) para 29.2.

The order thus adopted a creative and market-friendly way to require employers to help their workers who face dismissal in a job-scarce economy.

As noted above, the Competition Commissioner has claimed that mergers must not decrease Black shareholding but should increase it.[203] Conditionally increasing Black shareholding for a greater spread of ownership may now become routine.

b. Cases – Price Gouging

The South African Competition Act prohibits abuse of a dominant position and provides that excessive pricing by a dominant firm is an abuse of a dominant position. In the early days of the coronavirus pandemic when scarcities of face masks and hospital equipment arose overnight, South Africa passed a law against price gouging. The law had not yet come into effect when stores and establishments of all sizes jacked up prices of necessities by hundreds of percentage points. One such store was Babelegi Workwear, a small establishment in Pretoria that had a supply of dust masks on hand and imposed a series of increases amounting to 888 per cent. Its margin on the masks increased from 23 per cent to 1,119 per cent over the complaint period. But Babelegi's share of face masks in the geographic area in which it sold was only 4.7 per cent. The Competition Commission brought a case against Babelegi for abuse of a dominant position. It found the offence very severe – exploiting people in need at a time of crisis – and it imposed a large fine, which included 1.5 times the improper gains. Babelegi appealed. Could Babelegi be held to have dominant market power? The Court, led by judge Dennis Davis, wrote a judgment that was sensitive to the outrageous conduct 'as firms seek to prey on desperate consumers in a time of disaster'.[204] Babelegi mimicked the behaviour of a monopolist; its behaviour was not constrained by any other sellers, maybe because panicked customers felt they had to take what they could get and pay what was demanded. The Court found that in these circumstances it was not necessary to define a market because the behaviour proved the power. The Court said:

> Competition law in South Africa has a more ambitious animating framework than that which has dominated the US antitrust law and even that of the European Union. *It is designed to ensure that markets work fairly and do not add to the economic disadvantage of millions of presently disadvantaged South Africans.* The manner in which I have sought to apply s 8 (1) gives expression to this objective which finds clear support in the Preamble and s 2 of the Act.[205]

However, because Babelegi had sold only a few boxes of masks at the inflated prices, and did so over a short time, the Court treated the case as de minimis and

[203] See (n 196–197) above.

[204] *Babelegi Workwear and Industrial Supplies CC v Competition Commission of South Africa* (186/CAC/JUN20) [2020] ZACAC 7 (18 November 2020) para 42.

[205] ibid para 68. Emphasis added.

lifted the Tribunal's penalty, and the judgment was a caution to others not to price gouge vulnerable customers in times of crisis.

c. Priorities

The South African Competition Commission prioritises matters that will help the less-well-off, that will level the playing field, and that will contribute to economic growth. Its priority areas include food and agro-processing, healthcare, and financial services. It investigated pharmaceutical companies for excessive pricing. It opens market inquiries where critical markets are not working, as in private healthcare and in medicines. It has issued Price Discrimination and Buyer Power Guidelines 'aimed at bringing more fairness for emerging entrepreneurs and small businesses' and, as to buyer power, 'to enhance the participation of small and medium businesses (SMEs) and historically disadvantaged persons (HDP) firms in the economy by protecting these firms from unfair exploitation by dominant buyers of their products'.[206]

iv. The Six Questions

Question One: Is an equality value embedded in the South African competition law?

Yes, and even more so since the 2018 Amendments.

Question Two: Is an equality value a source of wisdom available to enforcers and jurists to decide priorities or to reach outcomes in particular cases?

Yes.

Question Three: Are antitrust consent decrees or clearances used as an occasion for imposing conditions that advance equality, such as protection for workers?

Yes.

Question Four: Is more equality, or reducing the inequality gap, a separate mandate that can warrant an antitrust exemption or be used as a trump?

Yes.

Question Five: Does South African competition law alleviate inequality? Aggravate inequality? Or just not help to remedy it?

By intention, the first.

Question Six: Would equality-leaning changes in competition law be feasible and likely to help close the inequality gap?

South Africa has already been more aggressive than the rest of the world in using its competition law to try to remove the enormous inequalities that (in South Africa) were imposed by positive law. Professors Firoz Cachalia and Alexander Beyleveld, in chapter six in this volume, propose further movement in the same

[206] South Africa Competition Commission, *Commission Releases Buyer Power Guidelines that Give Boost to Small Business* (Press Release, 18 May 2020).

direction. They recommend changes in competition law that would require (not just authorise) the Commission to consider distributional effects in merger review, they propose more aggressive merger control in general to combat economic concentration, and, in market studies, they would give the Commission greater power to remedy distributional problems resulting from lack of competition.[207]

Figure 4.1 below summarises the findings of the case studies graphically. A textual summary is presented in the description of the four models section V below.

Figure 4.1 Consolidation of Country Case Studies

Is an equality value …				
	embedded in the competition law?	**a source of wisdom to prioritise and decide?**	**included in conditionality, as for merger clearance?**	**available for exemption?**
US	No	Yes	No	No
EU	Yes, in the form of openness and access and special responsibility	Yes	No	No
Germany	Yes, in the form of Ordoliberalism and abuse of superior bargaining power	Yes	No	Yes, especially for SMEs
South Africa	Yes, at the roots	Yes, emphatically	Yes. Commonly used to help workers, historically disadvantaged persons, SMEs	Yes, especially for SMEs, HDPs

V. Integrating Equality

A conference note of the Amsterdam Centre asks the key question about equality and competition law:

> Can equality concerns be better integrated into the current model of competition law, especially with respect to its efficiency-oriented paradigm? Would integration require revision of the law's deeper foundations and economic constitutional embedding?

[207] For more, see ch 6 in this volume.

Certain equality values are naturally integrated into competition law because competition in markets without entry barriers and without market power favours the people as against the privileged few. It gives people opportunity and access, and it produces competitive prices and the quantities of goods and services that people demand at cost including only a competitive return. Even efficiency-based law favours these conditions of competition. You do not need distributive goals to agree.

This section asks: do competition laws self-consciously include pro-equality distributive values. If not, should they? Is inclusion of distributive concerns compatible with the jurisdiction's competition law? The answers depend upon the jurisdiction.

This chapter has identified four models of competition law.

The first is the US model of today, defined by US Supreme Court jurisprudence (that is, not accounting for possible legislative change). According to this model, antitrust is a response to concerns that are allocative, not distributive. Moreover, the model emphasises freedom of firms, even dominant firms, except in the case of hard-core cartels, which are prohibited. Introducing considerations of equality including a more nearly equal distribution of wealth runs against the grain and (it is thought) would soften and degrade the law.

Equality was a value in US antitrust law until the end of the 1970s, but is no more (although Congress may be poised to change the direction of the law).

The second model is that of Germany. German competition law is rooted in Ordoliberalism and was shaped by the specific post-war discourse surrounding the introduction of the Act Against Restraints of Competition (GWB). Ordoliberalism stands against power, public and private, economic and political. The stance against the political and economic power of great corporations is a stance for greater equality. Germany has special regard for SMEs and protects more vulnerable players by proscribing abuse of superior bargaining power, whether under the rubric of abuse of dominance or abuse of economic dependency.

The third model is that of the EU. Equality is a value of the EU. The EU competition model is more congruent with equality than is US antitrust. Equality of opportunity and principles of access, openness, and contestability are inherent in the development of the EU single market and are deeply embedded in EU competition law. Principles against power and privilege are broadly rooted and include proscriptions of acts of Member States and of state-grantees of exclusive rights. Moreover, the EU is much more likely than the US under its current law to recognise new forms of market power and to control them. EU competition law, like German law, gives access for people and firms without power. But unlike German competition law, EU law has been influenced by neoclassical economic analysis as well as by Ordoliberalism, and principally protects markets, not equality.

The fourth model is that of South Africa. South Africa is virtually the reverse image of that of US law today. In South Africa, correcting inequality is one of the handful of major constitutional and societal missions of the nation. The Competition Act was adopted in post-apartheid South Africa in the hope of opening the markets to the heinously excluded majority and play a major role in radically transforming the society. When the transformation did not happen, South Africa adopted amendments to the Competition Act to give more and special benefits to historically disadvantaged persons. South Africa's initiatives are along the lines of enabling and empowering outsiders, not handicapping insiders. When faced with large mergers, the authorities usually clear them, mandating obligations to build capacities and skills of workers and small suppliers to spread ownership. Typically, the merging firms agree to retain redundant workers for several years, and, of more recent origin, they agree to set up capacity-building funds to train small suppliers with a view to their inclusion in global value chains. For merger clearance, the parties are induced to offer stock or an opportunity to partner in a joint venture to historically disadvantaged persons or small businesses. Increasing the spread of ownership is a mandate.

South Africa has a greater equality-consciousness in competition policy than the rest of the world.

In conclusion, antitrust does and can work in a positive way towards greater equality. In the US, unless Congress enacts radical reform, some greater equality may continue to be a by-product of better enforcement and priorities, but little more. In South Africa, at the other extreme, the project for more equality works hand in glove with antitrust. The law is consciously distributive. In the EU, equality and the single market goal nourish one another, and in Germany, equality and the Ordoliberal heritage nourish one another. We have seen a wide range of how antitrust can work for greater equality, from an embedded principle, to a source of wisdom for prioritisation and decisions, to affirmative action for disadvantaged persons, to benefits for workers caught in a free-market vice.

VI. The Objections to Including Equality as a Competition Law Value

Thus far this chapter has been largely descriptive. It has shown the various ways in which equality is incorporated into antitrust. Nonetheless, as telescoped in the observations on complexity in section III, a battery of objections have been made to the project. This section identifies six objections and gives responses.[208]

The first objection is: 'Competition law is about maximising consumer welfare or allocative efficiency. Equality is about distribution of the gains. The two concepts are apples and oranges. Let competition law be competition law.'

[208] See I Lianos, 'The Poverty of Competition Law: The Short Story' in D Gerard and I Lianos (eds), *Reconciling Efficiency and Equity: A Global Challenge for Competition Policy* (Cambridge, Cambridge University Press, 2019) 45, for a catalogue of the objections and his responses to them. See JD Wright et al., 'Requiem for a Paradox: The Dubious Rise and Inevitable Fall of Hipster Antitrust' (2018) 51 *Arizona State Law Journal* 293 (finding the objections conclusive against the inclusion of equality values).

This is indeed a claim made by many commentators. It raises the existential question about what antitrust law is and should be, and thus begs the question.[209]

The second objection is: 'Crediting equality will dilute the efficiency mission; it will protect inefficient competitors and recreate Robert Bork's dystopia, A Policy at War with Itself.'[210]

There are many ways to incorporate equality values in antitrust. No one is trying to use antitrust to achieve absolute equality of outcome of wealth or income, and many applications of equality values inhabit a space that serves both efficiency and equality.[211] This space is especially wide under US law today, where, as Professor Robert Pitofsky observed, the Chicago School 'overshot the mark'.[212] Also, in nations plagued by privilege, corruption and cronyism, an adjustment favouring lower barriers to entry and a clearer path for outsiders is needed to secure more efficiency (as well as equity).

Equality of opportunity to contest markets on the merits normally works in the same direction as allocative efficiency. At the other extreme, a competition law that lets dominant firms block opportunities for outsiders with impunity has strong inefficiency properties.

This does not mean that the objection has no merit. It can be treated as a helpful caution to assess and reassess whether any given nation's competition policy is truly helping the market work and protecting neither inefficiencies nor incumbents.

The third objection is: 'Incorporating equality in competition law introduces a soft element with no objective standards, undermining certainty and predictability, falling into an abyss of discretion and subjectivity, and opening the door to corruption.'

Standardless antitrust is indeed a danger to be avoided. The first point of departure is the facts: how is the equality value being incorporated into the law? In most instances studied above, the principles of incorporation are either clear or at least as clear as the incorporation of freedom, efficiency, and innovation. Some modes and extent of incorporation are more challenging than others, as in South Africa.[213] The South African Competition Commission has issued guidelines

[209] There are competing formulations of the goals of competition law such as making markets work and controlling market power for the people. Under this formulation, it is fair game, even mandatory, to assess who are the winners and who are the losers and to adopt rules of the game that not only are designed to limit power but are equitable to the great masses of people.

[210] R Bork, *The Antitrust Paradox: A Policy at War with Itself* (New York, Basic Books, 1978).

[211] See E Fox, 'Competition Policy at the Intersection of Equity and Efficiency: The Developed and Developing World' in D Gerard and I Lianos (eds), *Reconciling Efficiency and Equity: A Global Challenge for Competition Policy* (Cambridge, Cambridge University Press, 2019) 441.

[212] See EM Fox, 'The Efficiency Paradox' in R Pitofsky (ed), *How the Chicago School Overshot the Mark: The Effect of Conservative Economic Analysis on U.S. Antitrust* (Oxford, Oxford University Press, 2008).

[213] Critics have raised concerns. See Oxenham et al. (n 175).

for some provisions and are developing practices for others. Again, the objection is not without merit. It can be taken as a call to clarity and transparency, which are needed watchwords.

The fourth objection is: 'Efficiency-based competition law is the underpinning of international convergence, and international convergence is critical to garnering the cooperation of nations and facilitating trade. Embracing an equality value will undermine the hard-won consensus.'

The idea that nations have reached consensus on competition law and have done so based on pure efficiency goals is illusory. Most nations' competition laws embrace other goals and values. Efficiency-only rules most advantage the developed world because its firms are best poised to win the efficiency-only race; the developing world is the most disadvantaged.[214] Acceptance of an equality goal actually makes an international-standards project more attractive to developing countries, for they need the policy space for inclusive development.

The fifth objection is: 'The project will not work. Competition law imbued with equality will not produce equality.'

Contributions of an equality-conscious antitrust are not easy to measure or document, just as contributions to free speech from constitutional protections are not easy to measure or document.

It is useful to look separately at two prongs: opportunity, and distribution of wealth and income. For the first, incorporation of equality values sets an environment. It is a statement of what the society cares about. Children perform better in school and workers perform better at work when they are surrounded by a supportive environment (and they develop better self-esteem).[215] Market players can be expected to do better in the marketplace when they have confidence that, given their abilities, they will be given an equal chance to compete. Even monkeys refuse to play games when the rules are unfair.[216]

As for wealth and income, the return of illegally-appropriated monopoly profits is by definition a fairer distribution of wealth, and deterrence of illegal acts in getting and keeping monopoly implies retention of a fairer distribution of wealth.

[214] It will be argued that efficiency-only rules are best for developing countries too, on grounds that they need such rules to grow efficient businesses, and that they are likely to handicap themselves with equality rules, sheltering inefficient businesses from competition and pulling the whole society down economically. This argument is mostly based on stereotype but with a cautionary germ of truth. Developing countries need development; the scaffolding to grow to be efficient. A worst-case scenario for them is to step back and vacate their economic space to multinationals – the same firms that have systematically blocked their best paths to growth by strategic trade and competition policies. See M Wolf, *Why Globalization Works* (New Haven, Yale University Press, 2004); H-J Chang, *Kicking Away the Ladder: Development Strategy in Historical Perspective* (London, Anthem Press, 2003).

[215] See J Bruner, *The Process of Education* (Cambridge, MA, Harvard University Press 1960); E Seppala and K Cameron, 'Proof that Positive Work Cultures are More Productive' *Harvard Business Review Online* (1 December 2015) hbr.org/2015/12/proof-that-positive-work-cultures-are-more-productive.

[216] N Kristof, 'What Monkeys can Teach Us about Fairness' *NY Times* (New York, 3 June 2017), www.nytimes.com/2017/06/03/opinion/sunday/what-monkeys-can-teach-us-about-fairness.html.

South Africa goes further than western nations in using competition law to benefit redundant workers, squeezed small businesses, and historically disadvantaged persons.[217] South Africa pursues the devoutly wished for societal transformation after the end of apartheid. Policymakers stake their hopes on empowering the disempowered, even if it be one step at a time, to help break the back of an exclusionary society.

Will such measures, big and small, produce a greater measure of equality? Competition law enforcement will probably not shift the percentages on charts of wealth and income inequality. But if the measures incrementally empower and incentivise historically marginalised people and deter growth of monopoly power, that can be counted as success. If the measures disincentivise firms and decrease foreign investment, that is a negative. Policy makers need to promote the benefits and contain the risks by wise rules that nurture and do not trample on robust market competition.

The sixth objection is: 'There are better tools.'

If, in the equality debates, the sole objective was a more equal distribution of wealth, then a tax on the very wealthy and a generous subsidy for the poor could solve the problem overnight (if the legislature passed the necessary laws).[218] But that is not the project in the sites of competition law.

Taxation is static and disconnected from living life. Taxation *is* redistribution. If antitrust can do anything significant to advance a goal of greater equality, it can do it dynamically. It can empower people to enter and thrive in markets; it can create a business environment not stacked in favour of incumbents and powerful privileged firms. It can (continue to) return to victims the wealth that the abusers of market power have seized from them; and it should deter the private power acts that distribute away from the people in the first instance. For these tasks, nothing else can take the place of antitrust.

In sum, no objection categorically stands in the way of nations' embracing equality values in their competition laws; but arguments about clarity, effects, due process, and consciousness of trade-offs should be understood as helpful cautions.

VII. Recommendations

In view of the significance of an equality value in competition law,[219] of the role of free markets (uncabined power) in tending to increase the inequality gap,[220]

[217] Competition Act of 1998 (n 178).

[218] See Z Liscow, 'Equality, Taxation, and Law and Economics in the 21st Century' (February 2020, unpublished article on file with Yale Law School), arguing Congress may not be sympathetic to a wealth tax.

[219] See section IV above.

[220] See Piketty (n 18). See also Hsu (n 10)–(n 12), Khan and Vaheesan (n 4) and (n 5), Valletti and Zenger (n 6) and (n 7), and Ennis, Gonzaga and Pike (n 8) and (n 9).

and the role of antitrust in containing power, which tends also to limit inequality,[221] this section makes five recommendations. Most of them stand on their own ground, independent from a special focus on inequality. In other words, they are mostly recommendations to help make markets work better for the people. They are simply good antitrust.

First, it is important to appreciate the close connection between competition law and an equality value. The two are sympathetic and symbiotic in large measure – not in the sense that people should have equal income and wealth but in the sense that people should not be deprived by business power of a fair opportunity to compete, nor of the benefits of competition in terms of price or wages. Antitrust should be recognised as on the side of the people, not on the side of privilege and power. This appreciation is a necessary part of understanding the foundational platform of antitrust.

Second, the law needs to get better control over antitrust prohibitions against the creation, entrenchment, and abuses of market power. For some jurisdictions, this means that substantive standards for violation must be revised. It means rethinking what is substantial market power and considering whether current requirements for proof of monopoly or dominance blind the law to significant market power problems. It also means, in most jurisdictions, better policy on remedies; anticompetitive mergers should normally be enjoined.

Third, certain terminology and conceits should change, for they obscure who are the winners and who are the losers, they help entrench a system that protects incumbents and widens the inequality gap while purporting to be neutral, and they obscure what is at stake in not main-streaming equality-consciousness. Terminology and their related concepts should change in two categories.

Category one: the principle of Kaldor Hicks. If winners win more than losers lose, the conduct is called efficient and presumed good for 'everyone'. All that is required is that the winners *could* pay the losers and still come out ahead. But the losers still lose. Kaldor Hicks can still play a role, but good policy would also identify the losers and ask whether the poorer people persistently lose, and what to do about it.

Category two: aggregate consumer welfare. Because the welfare paradigm (consumer or total) counts euros or dollars or yens and not people, rich people have more votes. The pursuit of maximising consumer welfare maximises aggregate wealth (the rich win more) and not individuals' well-being. Identifying the winner-loser groups is critical to good policy. For example, if allowing resale price fixing in the name of helping producers control free riders rewards a richer clientele (who want more luxury leather belts from Leegin[222] or more free frequent flier miles from American Express[223]), but discounting benefits more individual people and predominantly poorer people, society might prefer freedom of discounting to freedom to fix resale prices.

[221] See Zac, Casti, Decker, and Ezrachi (n 19).
[222] See facts of *Leegin Creative Leather Products Inc v PSKS Inc* (n 44) above.
[223] See facts of *Ohio v American Express Co* (n 57) above.

Fourth, antitrust should normally keep its focus on market goals, while respecting jurisdictions that choose to lean further towards equality, such as protecting against exploitation by superior bargaining power, or giving extra rights to SMEs or historically disadvantaged people. The chapter does not recommend 'throwing' equality into a balance of factors. Keeping the focus on market goals lends more certainty, predictability, and stability to the analysis. Most equality-leaning goals (that are compatible with a market system) are a natural part of market analysis; for example, ability to contest markets on merits, preventing anticompetitive mergers, depriving monopolists of illegally-won gains, and freeing workers from employer agreements not to compete for them.

Fifth, priorities. Antitrust authorities should (continue to) prioritise cases that principally help the poorer or middle class and not the very rich. They should prioritise cases in markets particularly crucial to the poorer population, such as health care and medicines, food, transportation, energy, communications, and payment systems. The authorities do commonly prioritise these cases and sectors,[224] so this frequently made and important recommendation is not likely to produce observable change.

This leads, as a final point, to expectations. Apart from adopting principles for more aggressive antitrust to make markets work better, can we expect antitrust to become more equality-friendly? The answer is jurisdiction specific. The US might adopt legislation. Other jurisdictions are fairly well armed, or becoming so through regulation about to be adopted. It is not easy to see what more room they will find in the name of equality beyond just good sound antitrust. But perhaps it is enough that equality-consciousness can lead in the direction of good sound antitrust.

This is not a negative view of the future of equality in antitrust. As the chapter has shown, equality is already embedded in antitrust in most jurisdictions, and 'equality consciousness' is a positive and sympathetic orientation in framing the antitrust enterprise.

VIII. Conclusion

This chapter has examined the variety of ways in which jurisdictions have incorporated equality values in their competition laws. These range from embeddedness, equality as a source of wisdom including prioritisation, clearances or consent decrees as an occasion for imposing equality-leaning conditions, and affirmative

[224] See Report on ICN Agencies' Prioritisation and Initiation (Final 25 November 2021), ICN Agency Effectiveness Working Group, at 2.4: key sectors; OECD Policy Roundtable, Competition and Poverty Reduction 2013, DAF/COMP/G(2013)12, 7–8 www.oecd.org/daf/competition/competition-and-poverty-reduction2013.pdf. Tough issues may arise because most of the sectors essential to the poorer population are exactly the areas where scale may be needed for lower prices and the scale may naturally produce market power, so the effect of interventions to prevent market power in these sectors may be ambiguous.

action for vulnerable groups. The chapter has shown that incorporation can be done with relative clarity and predictability, and to a significant extent it is compatible with efficiency and can even increase it. Regard for equality, or less inequality without mobility, is a value choice to be made by each society.

Fighters for greater equality should neither underestimate nor overestimate the importance of pursuing greater equality in antitrust. One should not overestimate the role of antitrust in increasing equality because: 1) the principal causes of inequality – particularly technological developments in the wake of globalisation – are so strong and they constantly operate to increase the gap; and 2) although a form of equality may be inherent in most jurisdictions' competition laws, antitrust is not a robust instrument for pursuing equality more than already is built into the system, and antitrust enforcement is not likely to visibly reduce the inequality gap even though it can help push back its growth.

Also, one should not underestimate the importance of greater equality as a factor in antitrust. Picture us in a long narrow crew boat with many pairs of oars. We are rowing towards a better society. Antitrust is one of many pairs of oars. We must do our bit to row in the right direction. Every rower counts.

5

Economic Inequality and Abuse of Dominance in EU Competition Law

KONSTANTINOS V SIDIROPOULOS*

I. Introduction

Delineating clear-cut rules for provisions which regulate the unilateral conduct of market players with substantial market power is a far cry from being a straightforward task, because of their controversial nature and the fact that they are susceptible to divergent interpretations. The provision controlling the unilateral conduct of dominant firms in the EU legal order is currently Article 102 TFEU, which prohibits the abuse of a dominant position.[1] This is perhaps the most controversial area of EU competition law, and as such, has generated a voluminous body of bibliography aiming to contribute to the debate around the optimal application of Article 102.[2] The legal and academic interest in Article 102 has particularly increased since the European Commission ('Commission') launched the process

* All opinions expressed here are my own. I am grateful to Julian Nowag, Thomas Papadopoulos, Maria Kallidopoulou, Stavros Makris, and Liana Japaridze for sharing their views on a previous version of this chapter, as well as the participants at the conference 'Should Wealth and Income Inequality be a Competition Law Concern?', organised by the University of Amsterdam on 20–21 May 2021. I also thank Kati Cseres and Jan Broulík for valuable suggestions and comments to the draft. All errors and/or omissions remain my own.

[1] Consolidated Version of the Treaty on the Functioning of the European Union [2012] OJ C326/47, Art 102.

[2] Eg, C-D Ehlermann and I Atanasiu (eds): *What is an Abuse of a Dominant Position? European Competition Law Annual 2003* (Oxford, Hart Publishing, 2006); C-D Ehlermann and M Marquis (eds), *European Competition Law Annual 2007: A Reformed Approach to Article 82 EC* (Oxford, Hart Publishing, 2008); A Ezrachi (ed), *Article 82: Reflections on its Recent Evolution* (Oxford, Hart Publishing, 2009); E Rousseva, *Rethinking Exclusionary Abuses in EU Competition Law* (Oxford, Hart Publishing, 2010); LL Gormsen, *A Principled Approach to Abuse of Dominance in European Competition Law* (Cambridge, Cambridge University Press, 2010); P Akman, *The Concept of Abuse in EU Competition Law: Law and Economic Approaches* (Oxford, Hart Publishing, 2012); V Brisimi, *The Interface between Competition and the Internal Market: Market Separation under Article 102 TFEU* (Oxford, Hart Publishing, 2014); F Di Porto and R Podszun (eds), *Abusive Practices in Competition Law* (Cheltenham, Edward Elgar, 2018); C Fumagalli, M Motta and C Calcagno, *Exclusionary Practices: The Economics of Monopolisation and Abuse of Dominance* (Cambridge, Cambridge University Press, 2018); R O'Donoghue and J Padilla, *The Law and Economics of Article 102 TFEU*, 3rd edn (Oxford, Hart Publishing, 2020).

of reviewing the provision with the objective of introducing a more economically inspired approach to abuse of dominance.[3]

However, little attention has been paid so far to the influence of the EU's constitutional peculiarities on the interpretation of Article 102. This chapter discusses these peculiarities and highlights their implications for the concept of abuse of dominance.[4] The purpose is to shed light on issues that have generally been neglected in the literature, with a particular emphasis on the relevance of inequality considerations to the interpretation of Article 102.[5] Specifically, Article 102 is part of an overall Treaty framework, thereby reflecting the underlying principles and objectives of the EU Treaties. Therefore, the provision must be interpreted in a contextual manner. As such, certain Treaty provisions which do not directly relate to Article 102 may, nevertheless, have an impact on its interpretation. This illustrates the peculiar constitutional setting of the EU. Building on the role of Article 102 in the scheme of the EU Treaties, the chapter first endeavours to identify the potential relevance of economic inequality for the interpretation and application Article 102 in light of the EU Treaties, so as to subsequently assess whether the current state of the law, as developed by the case law of the EU courts, includes economic inequality as a relevant concern.

Adopting such a constitutional perspective reveals that the constitutional structure of the EU demands a holistic approach to Article 102. This constitutionally mandated holistic approach entails that inequality-related concerns and (re)distributive policy considerations may affect both the general interpretation and enforcement of Article 102 and its ad hoc application. In this regard, the application of the provision must at least avoid contradicting redistributive policy considerations and other (in)equality-related concerns that are aimed at establishing an internal market committed to a highly competitive social market. Turning then to the relevant case law, the way that inequality considerations are reflected in the rules applied by the EU courts to the unilateral conduct of dominant firms is examined. The analysis unveils that the designed legal tests ensure conformity with the constitutionally demanded holistic approach.

[3] Economic Advisory Group for Competition Policy (EAGCP), 'An Economic Approach to Article 82' (Brussels, July 2005) (EAGCP Report); Commission, 'DG Competition Discussion Paper on the Application of Article 82 of the Treaty to Exclusionary Abuses' (Brussels, December 2005) (Discussion Paper); Commission, 'Guidance on the Commission's Enforcement Priorities in Applying Article 82 of the EC Treaty to Abusive Exclusionary Conduct by Dominant Undertakings' (Communication) [2009] OJ C45/7 (Priorities Paper).

[4] See generally K Heyer, 'A World of Uncertainty: Economics and the Globalization of Antitrust' (2005) 72 *Antitrust Law Journal* 375, 399–400; D Evans, 'Why Different Jurisdictions Do Not (and Should Not) Adopt the Same Antitrust Rules' (2009) 10 *Chicago Journal of International Law* 161, 171–2; K Bernard, 'Is Full Transatlantic Competition Law Convergence Realistic, or Even Desirable' [2015] *Competition Policy International Antitrust Chronicle* 1, 5; A Ezrachi, 'Sponge' (2017) 5 *Journal of Antitrust Enforcement* 49, 51, illustrating that, despite the internationalisation of the discipline of competition law, there is significant divergence between the different competition law regimes, which reflects, inter alia, diverging normative choices.

[5] The chapter does not discuss in any depth the *stricto sensu* objectives pursued by Article 102.

In particular, the discussion documents that the designed legal tests successfully reconcile the market-oriented objectives of Article 102 with equality-related concerns and redistributive policies, thereby allowing the provision to operate according to the constitutional role imposed on it by the Treaties. Specifically, rationalising the relevant case law of the EU courts from the perspective of equality, the chapter identifies two distinct techniques for incorporating inequality concerns into the analysis of Article 102. The first technique incorporates inequality considerations in the analysis of Article 102 in an indirect manner. Under this technique, inequality-related concerns are factored in the legal tests developed by the EU courts for the assessment of the abusive conduct of dominant undertakings under Article 102. However, considerations unrelated to market competition also come directly into play in the application of Article 102. Particularly, under the second technique, certain non-specified socio-political values, which include (re)distributive policy considerations, come directly into play in the context of a proportionality analysis, exceptionally leading to the ad hoc exclusion of the application of Article 102. This technique is illustrated in the possibility of balancing non-competition objectives against a restriction of competition in the context of Article 102. Overall, both techniques reflect the holistic approach to Article 102 insofar as they allow concerns related to wealth (in)equality and (re)distribution to find their way into the analysis of Article 102.

The chapter is structured in the following manner. Section II offers some general and EU specific insights on the links between market dominance, competition law and economic inequality. Section III explores whether economic inequality should be a relevant concern under Article 102 by examining the role of the provision in the scheme of the EU Treaties (the constitutional perspective). Section IV turns to the discussion of the relevant case law in order to assess the actual relevance of economic inequality in the interpretation and application of Article 102. In this context, it first looks at the designed legal tests for the assessment of the unilateral conduct of dominant firms (indirect relevance of inequality) and then discusses the accommodation of services of general economic interest ('SGEI') and the concept of objective justification (direct relevance of inequality). The final section draws together the conclusions.

II. Market Dominance, Competition Law, and Inequality

The chapter aims to clarify whether economic inequality should be a relevant concern in the analysis of Article 102, and to subsequently explore whether economic inequality is actually reflected in the rules applied by the EU courts to the unilateral conduct of dominant firms. Before doing so, however, this section is dedicated to a discussion of certain inequality-inspired concerns for the adopted stance to abuse of dominance, followed by a brief reference to peculiar features of EU competition law that may reveal its predisposition of including redistribution and (in)equality considerations. This discussion will set the scene for the analysis to follow.

A. Inequality Concerns and Abuse of Dominance

Socio-political concerns that can potentially be relevant to any rule relating to the unilateral conduct of dominant companies may include: i) the fear of concentrated economic power because it can lead to political interference; ii) the reduction in the range of private discretion for the safeguarding of equality of opportunities to participate in the market; iii) the favourable treatment of small firms, either under the belief that they can contribute to society's welfare in economic terms or irrespective of economic considerations; and iv) income redistribution.[6]

All these concerns are conceptually and practically linked to one another: they all relate to the adverse effects of high levels of inequality on a society's political, social, and economic order. This chapter focuses on the relevance of these inequality-inspired concerns for the adopted stance to abuse of dominance based on a two-fold consideration. First, the origins of competition law lie very much in concerns about concentration of wealth,[7] while other socio-political issues can only remotely be relevant in the assessment of the unilateral conduct of dominant companies. Second, economically significant market power contributes to growing inequality, since the exercise of market power tends to raise the return to capital.[8]

The first of those concerns relates to the dangers that economic power poses to democracy.[9] In essence, the concern is that very concentrated economic power can invade the state, that is, market strength gives political strength which, in turn, can be exploited for economic and other purposes.[10] Undoubtedly, globally operating powerful firms can have direct effects on the political process and in the context of specific competition law investigations.[11] Additionally, evidence suggests that

[6] R Pitofsky 'The Political Content of Antitrust' (1979) 127 *University of Pennsylvania Law Review* 1051.

[7] E Fox and L Sullivan, 'Antitrust-Retrospective and Prospective: Where Are We Coming From? Where Are We Going?' (1987) 62 *New York University Law Review* 936, 977 and 981.

[8] J Baker and S Salop, 'Antitrust, Competition Policy, and Inequality' (2015) 104 *Georgetown Law Journal* 1, 11–13; S Ennis, P Gonzaga and C Pike, 'Inequality: A Hidden Cost of Market Power' (2019) 35 *Oxford Review of Economic Policy* 518, 520 and 539.

[9] E Muller, 'Democracy, Economics Development, and Income Inequality' (1988) 53 *American Sociological Review* 50, 62; T-C Ma, 'Antitrust and Democracy: Perspectives from Efficiency and Equity' (2016) 12 *Journal of Competition Law and Economics* 233, 234. See also M Vatiero, 'Dominant Market Position and Ordoliberalism' (2015) 62 *International Review of Economics* 291, 293, referring to the Ordoliberal perspective, which emphasises the dangers that economic power poses to democracy.

[10] See generally H Oliver, 'German Neoliberalism' (1960) 74 *The Quarterly Journal of Economics* 117, 127; R Pitofsky, (n 6) 1053; Baker and Salop (n 8) 6–10. See also J Stiglitz, *The Price of Inequality: How Today's Divided Society Endangers our Future* (New York, W W Norton, 2012) 36 and 148–82.

[11] F Maier-Rigaud, 'On the Normative Foundations of Competition Law – Efficiency, Political Freedom and the Freedom to Compete' in D Zimmer (ed), *The Goals of Competition Law* (Cheltenham, Edward Elgar, 2012) 166. See also L Zingales, 'Towards a Political Theory of the Firm' (2017) 31 *Journal*

competition law can foster democracy by improving income distribution.[12] Even so, by now there is a large degree of consensus worldwide that this, in principle, legitimate concern does not imply that the objective of competition law should be the elimination of market power per se. The *ratio* for not targeting market power is that, just as competition stimulates innovation, so does the expectation of being able to extract profits from investments in innovation, which are the result of the exercise of market power. Hence, the expectation to exercise market power has a pivotal role in maintaining the firms' incentives to invest, innovate, improve product quality, and introduce new goods.[13] Consequently, there is no justification for setting the elimination of market power as the objective of competition law.

The second concern of safeguarding equality of opportunities outlines the same fear of too much economic power being in the hands of too few people.[14] Thus, it reveals the same distrust of economic power.[15] However, the focus here is on diversity and on the equal opportunity for the unestablished to participate in the market.[16] Certainly, inequality is a natural by-product of a market economy in the sense that the market generates winners and losers. At the same time, however, inequality erodes the sense of a society giving everyone a fair opportunity to succeed.[17] Essentially, a competition policy protecting equality of opportunities entails a policy protecting the economic freedom to participate in the marketplace as an individual right.[18] In any event, it is argued that protecting opportunity and access for smaller firms is an efficient way to increase competition, and thus foster both efficiency and progressiveness.[19] In this regard, we should distinguish between protecting the equality of opportunity in this sense and protecting non-dominant firms *tout court*. Nevertheless, some commentators urge that protecting

of Economic Perspectives 113, eloquently illustrating the threat posed to the free market economy, economic prosperity, and democracy by the interaction of concentrated corporate power and politics.

[12] Ma, (n 9) 251, reaching this conclusion based on an econometric model. On the positive effects of competition law enforcement on democracy see, eg, W Adams, 'Antitrust and a Free Economy' (1977) 46 *Antitrust Law Journal* 794; D Barnes, 'Nonefficiency Goals in the Antitrust Law of Mergers' (1989) 30 *William & Mary Law Review* 787. Against N Peterson, 'Antitrust Law and the Promotion of Democracy and Economic Growth' (2013) 9 *Journal of Competition Law and Economics* 593, 620, arguing that the effect of competition law on democracy is insignificant.

[13] M Motta, *Competition Policy: Theory and Practice* (Cambridge, Cambridge University Press, 2004) 58.

[14] B Gates, 'Why Inequality Matters' (*Gates Notes*, 13 October 2014) www.gatesnotes.com/Books/Why-Inequality-Matters-Capital-in-21st-Century-Review, arguing that 'high levels of inequality are a problem' and that '[c]apitalism does not self-correct toward greater equality'.

[15] F Rowe, 'The Decline of Antitrust and the Delusion of Models: The Faustian Pact of Law and Economics' (1984) 72 *Georgetown Law Journal* 1511, 1567.

[16] Fox and Sullivan (n 7) 944, claiming that this has traditionally been the main concern of competition law.

[17] See generally T Piketty, *Capital in the Twenty-First Century* (Massachusets, Harvard University Press, 2014) 571, warning about the fact that growing inequality endangers the values of social justice on which democratic societies are grounded.

[18] P Behrens, 'The Ordoliberal Concept of "Abuse" of a Dominant Position and its Impact on Article 102 TFEU' in Di Porto and Podszun (n 2) 21.

[19] Fox and Sullivan (n 7) 987.

equality of opportunities can be a slippery objective, which may mean no more than protecting competitors (including non-efficient ones).[20]

The third listed consideration is the favourable treatment of small firms (the so-called small- and medium-sized enterprises (SMEs) because of their difficulty in raising capital and their insufficient access to information. Such a policy objective in and of itself would mean that any exclusionary practice carried out by a dominant firm would be prohibited, regardless of both the potential advantageous effects on consumers and the rivals' efficiency.[21] This approach would obviously be irrational, not least because it would de facto target market dominance. It is, however, argued that economic evidence suggests that SMEs are the most fertile source of economic growth, innovation and employment,[22] and thus it is important to ensure free market access.[23]

Lastly, a putative socio-political objective of Article 102 is the equitable distribution of income. In fact, all legal policies have more or less significant consequences for the distribution of wealth.[24] For example, it has been forcefully argued by many commentators that the adoption of more permissive antitrust rules in the US during the past four decades has increased the 'wealth gap', ie the unequal distribution of wealth.[25] It is, therefore, thought that greater competition law enforcement would generally improve the distribution of income and wealth.[26] However, it has also been stressed that the pursuit of income redistribution through competition law enforcement is likely to have limited results and that other policies, such as tax and subsidy schemes, are more effective in promoting distributional goals.[27] In

[20] On this long-running debate about Article 102 see, eg, C Ahlborn and C Grave, 'Walter Eucken and Ordoliberalism: An Introduction from a Consumer Welfare Perspective' (2006) 2 *Competition Policy International* 197, 214; L Parret, 'The Multiple Personalities of EU Competition Law: Time for a Comprehensive Debate on its Objectives' in Zimmer (ed) (n 11) 67.

[21] R Bork, *The Antitrust Paradox: A Policy at War with Itself* (USA, Free Press, 1993) 54, reproving this attitude.

[22] S Davis, Haltiwanger and R Jarmin, 'Turmoil and Growth: Young Businesses, Economic Churning, and Productivity Gains' (Report, Ewing Marion Kauffman Foundation, 2008) 6; S Mitchell, 'The View from the Shop – Antitrust and the Decline of America's Independent Businesses' (2016) 61 *Antitrust Bulletin* 498, stressing the need to bring back into competition policy a commitment to SMEs because they deliver distinct consumer benefits.

[23] J Brodney, 'The Economic Goals of Antitrust: Efficiency, Consumer Welfare, and Technological Progress' (1987) 62 *New York University Law Review* 1020, 1045; F Scherer, 'Antitrust, Efficiency, and Progress' (1987) 62 *New York University Law Review* 998, 1012 and 1014.

[24] H Hovenkamp, 'Antitrust Policy and Inequality of Wealth' [2017] *Competition Policy International Antitrust Chronicle* 1, recognising this even though he opposes the use of competition law as a wealth distribution device.

[25] See, eg, E Fox, 'We Protect Competition, You Protect Competitors' (2003) 26 *World Competition* 149, 152; Stiglitz, (n 10) 44–45; J Baker, 'Economics and Politics: Perspectives on the Goals and Future of Antitrust' (2013) 81 *Fordham Law Review* 2175, 2184.

[26] A Atkinson, *Inequality: What Can be Done?* (Massachusetts, Harvard University Press, 2015) 126–7; Baker and Salop (n 8) 18.

[27] K Elzinga, 'The Goals of Antitrust: Other than Competition and Efficiency, What Else Counts?' (1977) 125 *University of Pennsylvania Law Review* 1191, 1196. *cf* Baker and Salop (n 8) 10, arguing that 'despite the benefits from redistribution, existing programs do not appear to have offset the growing inequality in [the American] society'. Against D Crane, 'Antitrust and Wealth Inequality' (2016) 101

any event, although competition law is unlikely to take on the same importance as legal policies which have as their primary goal wealth distribution, it may certainly complement and support those policies.[28] This could be achieved, for instance, by interpreting and enforcing the relevant competition rules in line with these other legal policies.

B. EU Framework, Economic Inequality and Abuse of Dominance

It could legitimately be argued that EU competition law has the predisposition of including redistribution and (in)equality concerns,[29] not least because of the historical context in which it was born and the constitutional nature of its rules.[30] Influenced by the humanist values promoted by the German Ordoliberal School,[31] EU competition law is mandated with the concern about the potential misuse of accumulated economic power.[32] This entails a sceptical view of market forces, in the sense that 'self-regulated' markets can have undesirable outcomes.[33] More importantly, the EU competition rules are part of an overall Treaty framework,

Cornell Law Review 1171, 1228, claiming that '[w]ealth inequality does not belong to antitrust law's domain'.

[28] Ma (n 9) 251.

[29] *cf* ch 3 in this volume, finding that the EU competition model is linked to lower levels of income inequality than is the US antitrust model, which should perhaps not come as a surprise.

[30] For analysis of the historical factors influencing the drafting of Article 102 see, eg, H Schweitzer, 'The History, Interpretation and Underlying Principles of Section 2 Sherman Act and Article 82 EC' in Ehlermann and Marquis (eds) (n 2) 130–8; Rousseva (n 2) 13–21; Akman (n 2) 80–85. See also Ezrachi (n 4) 53–54, emphasising the constitutional nature of EU competition law.

[31] D Gerber, *Law and Competition in Twentieth Century Europe: Protecting Prometheus* (Oxford, Oxford University Press, 2001) 263ff; M Cole, 'Ordoliberalism and its Influence on EU Tying Law' (2015) 36 *European Competition Law Review* 255, 261. *cf* Ahlborn and Grave (n 20) 206, arguing that, over time, Ordoliberalism has inevitably lost influence over EU competition policy. But see Behrens (n 18) 5–7, arguing that Article 102 still reflects Ordoliberal ideas, but this is a refined version of the original Freiburg School's learnings. See also E Deutscher and S Makris, 'Exploring the Ordoliberal Paradigm: The Competition-Democracy Nexus' (2016) 11 *Competition Law Review* 181, 190–2, stressing that ordoliberals praised competition because it sets the boundaries of economic power and creates the preconditions for economic freedom and equality of opportunity.

[32] D Gerber, 'Constitutionalizing the Economy: German Neo-Liberalism, Competition Law and the "New" Europe' (1994) 42 *American Journal of Comparative Law* 25, 82; V Vanberg, 'The Freiburg School: Walter Eucken and Ordoliberalism' (2004) *Freiburg Discussion Papers on Constitutional Economics* 04/11, 12, asserting that the ordoliberals focused on economic power and its deprivation. See also ch 1 in this volume, tracing how the egalitarian understanding of competition put the concern about the adverse effect of concentrated economic power at the heart of the formative era of the Ordoliberal foundations of EU competition law.

[33] P Jebsen and R Stevens, 'Assumptions, Goals and Dominant Undertakings: The Regulation of Competition under Article 86 of the European Union' (1996) 64 *Antitrust Law Journal* 443, 452. *cf* E-J Mestmäcker, 'Competition Policy and Antitrust: Some Comparative Observations' (1980) 136 *Zeitschrift für die Gesamte Staatswissenschaft* 387, 389, arguing that competition is the most effective instrument to decentralise economic power.

and hence must be given content through their role in the scheme of the Treaties.[34] Thus, the behaviour of dominant firms may be analysed with respect to a broader range of concerns, which may include the above-mentioned (in)equality-related aims.[35]

Unquestionably, other legal policies, such as tax, subsidy schemes or labour, are better suited to effectively address issues of inequality and promote wealth distribution. In the EU, however, there only exists limited competence to pursue such other policies.[36] At the same time, the establishment of a 'highly competitive *social* market economy'[37] combined with the horizontal social clause enshrined in the Treaties,[38] demand a holistic approach to EU law. That is, an approach where economic and social policies are reconciled and integrated into one overall policy. Under this holistic approach, Article 102 should contribute to, or be consistent with, the promotion of distributional goals.

That being said, an effective response to these values may not necessarily be one where Article 102 is called on to specifically address inequality. Adopting inequality as an explicit policy focus of the prohibition contained in Article 102 is not necessary for satisfying the constitutionally required holistic approach. The design of rules that are consistent with these values and a forceful enforcement of the relevant provision would be sufficient and compatible with the constitutional requirement of a holistic approach to the competition rules.

III. Constitutional Perspective: Should Economic Inequality be a Relevant Concern?

The chapter now adopts a constitutional perspective, turning to the role of Article 102 in the scheme of the EU Treaties. The analysis illustrates that specific clauses in the EU Treaties mandate a holistic approach to the interpretation of Article 102, meaning that the application of the provision must at least avoid contradicting redistributive policy considerations and other equality-related concerns that are aimed at establishing an internal market committed to a highly competitive social market.

[34] I Samkalden and I Druker, 'Legal Problems Relating to Article 86 of the Rome Treaty' (1966) 3 *Common Market Law Review* 158; D Gerber, 'Law and the Abuse of Economic Power in Europe' (1988) 62 *Tulane Law Review* 57, 90.

[35] Jebsen and Stevens, (n 33) 449; B Hawk, 'Article 82 and Section 2' in *OECD, Paper on Competition on the Merits* (DAF/COMP(2005)27, 30 March 2006), 251.

[36] The fundamental principle governing EU competences is the principle of conferral, which commands that the Union shall act only within the limits of the competences conferred upon it by the Member States and that competences not conferred upon the Union remain with the Member States. On the distribution of competences between the EU and its Member States, see Consolidated Version of the Treaty on the European Union [2012] OJ C326/13, Art 5; TFEU, Arts 3–6.

[37] TEU, Art 3(3).

[38] TFEU, Art 9.

A. Holistic Approach under EU Law: Integrating Economic and Social Policies

The Lisbon Treaty came into force on 1 December 2009 and significantly amended the constitutional basis of the EU.[39] Of prominent – but contested – significance in this regard is the introduction to EU primary law of more socially motivated provisions and language,[40] often at the expense of market competition.[41] Particularly, the 50-year-old commitment to 'undistorted competition' has been moved from the Treaties 'proper' to a Protocol annexed to the Treaties.[42] In this regard, although this makes no formal legal difference,[43] it suggests a weakening of the aggressively competitive focus of the EU's overall policy.[44] These amendments appear to be highlighting that the EU is not just a market place but also a social agent.[45] This idea is certainly not novel: the EU has always struggled to reconcile and integrate the economic and the social.[46] Indeed, the EU institutions have often insisted on such an integrated policy and have always valued the social structure of the internal market.[47] In any event,

[39] [2008] OJ C115/1.

[40] Eg, TFEU, Art 9, establishing a horizontal social clause; Protocol No 26 on services of general interest annexed to the Consolidated versions of the Treaty on European Union and the Treaty on the Functioning of the European Union [2008] OJ C115/308, recognising the social usefulness of SGEI.

[41] On the relevance of this 'social push' to competition law see A Riley, 'The EU Reform Treaty and the Competition Protocol: Undermining EC Competition Law' (2007) 28 *European Competition Law Review* 703; B Van Rompuy, 'The Impact of the Lisbon Treaty on EU Competition Law: A Review of Recent Case Law of the EU Courts' [2011] *Competition Policy International Antitrust Chronicle*; I Lianos, 'Competition Law in the European Union after the Treaty of Lisbon' in D Ashiagbor, N Countouris and I Lianos (eds), *The European Union after the Treaty of Lisbon* (Cambridge, Cambridge University Press, 2012).

[42] Protocol No 27 on the internal market and competition annexed to the Consolidated versions of the Treaty on European Union and the Treaty on the Functioning of the European Union [2008] OJ C115/309.

[43] TEU, Art 51, providing that Protocols to the Treaties form an integral part thereof.

[44] See N Sarkozy, 'Conférence de Presse Finale à L'occasion du Conseil Européen à Bruxelles' (Paris, 23 June 2007), showing the heavy emphasis placed on this matter by the President of France at the time of the drafting of the Lisbon Treaty.

[45] In this vein, see, eg, Commission, 'Towards a Single Market Act: For a Highly Competitive Social Market Economy' (Communication) COM(2010) 608 final, 18–20.

[46] C Offe, 'The European Model of "Social" Capitalism: Can it Survive European Integration?' (2003) 11 *Journal of Political Philosophy* 437. *cf* S Weatherill, *EU Consumer Law and Policy*, 2nd edn (Cheltenham, Edward Elgar, 2013) 58–59, arguing that the Lisbon Treaty's amendments could be seen as having carried out an adjustment of the constitutional balance in favour of social policies and at the expense of unconstrained market competition.

[47] Eg, Case C-67/96 *Albany International BV v Stichting Bedrijfspensioenfonds Textielindustrie* ECLI:EU:C:1999:430, paras 54–55; Case C-438/05 *International Transport Workers' Federation and Finnish Seamen's Union v Viking Line ABP and OÜ Viking Line Eesti* ECLI:EU:C:2007:722, paras 78–79; Case C-341/05 *Laval un Partneri Ltd v Svenska Byggnadsarbetareförbundet, Svenska Byggnadsarbetareförbundets avdelning 1, Byggettan and Svenska Elektrikerförbundet* ECLI:EU:C:2007:809, paras 104–5; Commission (n 45) 4, claiming that 'the success of the European model depends on its ability to combine economic performance with social justice'. See also G Davies, 'The Consumer, the Citizen, and the Human Being' in D Leczykiewicz and S Weatherill (eds), *The*

with effect from 2009, EU primary law clearly favours a holistic approach, that is, one where economic and social policies are integrated rather than separated.[48] This entails that the approach to the EU competition rules may not ignore and/or contradict attempts to achieve distributional aims.

i. Highly Competitive Social Market Economy

Stating the objectives of the EU, Article 3 TEU now provides, inter alia, that '[t]he Union shall establish an internal market', referring to a '*highly competitive social market economy*, aiming at full employment and social progress'.[49] The fact that Article 3(3) TEU conceives the internal market as an all-embracing concept, in the sense that concerns other than market competition are relevant for its successful establishment and proper functioning, must somehow be taken into consideration in the analysis under Article 102.[50]

This, however, leaves open the question concerning the meaning of the vague legal concept of a 'highly competitive social market economy'. This concept has its origins in West Germany's social market economy.[51] It was an economic model that evolved during the Nazi German regime under the influence of a group of lawyers and economists,[52] the so-called Ordoliberals.[53] In essence, the concept of the social market economy was the result of a search for a post-Nazi order for West Germany,[54] and it became the political programme of the party in power in West

Images of the Consumer in EU Law (Oxford, Hart Publishing, 2016) 337, stating that to 'deny the need for such integrated policy, in an unspoken parody of old Chicago economics, is to see the Union as a break with the achievements of its states, as a market which should not be social'.

[48] Eg, TFEU, Arts 7–13.

[49] TEU, Art 3(3) (emphasis added).

[50] See also TFEU, Art 119, demanding 'the adoption of an economic policy which is based […] on the internal market', referring thus to Article 3(3) TEU which affirms that the EU should work to establish a highly competitive social market economy.

[51] See A Müller-Armack, *Wirtschaftslenkung und Marktwirtschaft* (Kastell, 1946) 88, where the German term 'Soziale Marktwirtschaft' first appeared in a publication. See also L Erhard, *Prosperity Through Competition* (Frederick Praeger, 1958), who is regarded to be the father of the social market economy, because he introduced the concept into the political sphere.

[52] Certain of the most important figures in the development of the concept include Franz Oppenheimer, Walter Eucken, Franz Böhm, Hans Grossmann-Doerth, Alfred Müller-Armack, Ludwig Erhard, Wilhelm Röpke, Alexander Rüstow, and Constantin von Dietze. On the intellectual similarities and differences between these leading personalities see Oliver (n 10) 117–9; Cole (n 31) 256–8.

[53] Gerber (n 31) 236–7, explaining that the term 'Ordoliberal' has been attributed to a broad stream of thought, featuring the basic ideas of the Freiburg School, but also the 'pure' economic liberalism of Friedrich von Hayek.

[54] H Rieter and M Schmolz, 'The Ideas of German Ordoliberalism 1938–1945: Pointing the Way to a New Economic Order' (1993) 1 *European Journal of the History of Economic Thought* 87, 98, explaining that an important background in the development of the social market economy model was that all the main figures shared an involvement in the anti-Nazi opposition and a desire to plan the rebuilding of Germany after the war.

Germany from 1949 to 1966,[55] which implemented the model for it to become the cornerstone of what is known as the 'German economic miracle'.[56]

West Germany's commitment to a social market economy, which may have inspired the similar concept in Article 3(3) TEU, refers to a viable economic and socio-political alternative to the Scylla of laissez-faire capitalism and the Charybdis of centrally planned socialism.[57] This model, which evolved from Freiburg School's Ordoliberalism,[58] aspires to combine private enterprise with state intervention in order to establish a competitive process that would maintain a balance between a high rate of economic growth, low levels of unemployment, good working conditions, social welfare and public services.[59] On this approach, it is the responsibility of the state to ensure simultaneously a functioning competitive order and social balance, by granting equal opportunity and protection to those unable to enter the free market labour force (because of old-age, disability or unemployment), as well as to foster distributive justice.[60]

Obviously, by placing social policy on a par with economic policy, social market economies challenge the perception that the capitalist system is inherently antagonistic to social goals.[61] Nonetheless, as emphasised in an essay already in 1957:

> The Social Market Economy is not primarily an economic order, but a leading idea or programme. An order is a concrete realisation, but a leading idea gives direction for human action.[62]

Therefore, the social market economy model is not a defined economic order, but an adjustable holistic and democratic social order that unifies supposedly conflicting

[55] N Giocoli, 'Competition versus Property Rights: American Antitrust Law, the Freiburg School, and the Early Years of European Competition Policy' (2009) 5 *Journal of Competition Law and Economics* 747, 775. See also L White, *The Clash of Economic Ideas* (Cambridge, Cambridge University Press, 2012) 235.

[56] This refers to the surprisingly quick recovery of West Germany's economy after the catastrophe of the Nazi regime and World War II.

[57] J Van Hook, *Rebuilding Germany: The Creation of the Social Market Economy, 1945–1957* (Cambridge, Cambridge University Press, 2004) 185. The socio-economic imperative of the model is often labelled the 'Third Way', see, eg, Oliver (n 10) 119; Ahlborn and Grave (n 20) 198. *cf* M Vatiero, 'The Ordoliberal Notion of Market Power' (2010) 6 *European Competition Journal* 689, 706, arguing that it is a different form of liberalism rather than a third way between capitalism and socialism.

[58] Gerber (n 31) 237, explaining that the terms 'Ordoliberalism' and 'social market economy' are rightly used interchangeably, although the supporters of the social market economy placed greater emphasis on the equitable distribution of market benefits.

[59] *cf* ibid 238.

[60] M Marktanner, 'Addressing the Marketing Problem of the Social Market Economy' in C Glossner and D Gregosz (eds), *60 Years of Social Market Economy: Formation, Development and Perspectives of a Peacemaking Formula* (Konrad-Adenauer-Stiftung, 2010) 172.

[61] *cf* S Hill, *Europe's Promise: Why the European Way is the Best Hope in an Insecure Age* (California, University of California Press, 2010) 19–24.

[62] K Zweig, *The Origins of the German Social Market Economy: The Leading Ideas and their Intellectual Roots* (Adam Smith Institute, 1980) 7, translating a quotation from H-J Seraphim in a paper written in German in 1957.

objectives, namely economic freedom and social justice.[63] Central to this socially committed market economy is the establishment of a genuine performance-based competition, which exists when the competition rules ensure that, under conditions of equal opportunity, the best performance is rewarded.[64] In other words, the state must, through measures that adhere to market principles, create an environment where a healthy level of competition prevails.[65]

Hence, the EU's commitment to an internal market based on a highly competitive social market economy is, first and foremost, an engagement to a holistic societal order. This is an order where economic and social policies are integrated for the EU to both achieve the objectives outlined in Article 3 TEU and comply with the founding values prescribed in Article 2 TEU. This holistic approach is fully consistent with the whole framework of the Treaties, and, especially so, with the TFEU's horizontal clauses.

ii. Horizontal Clauses

After the Lisbon revision, a new title was created in the EU Treaties which group together all horizontal clauses. These are provisions that have an overarching character, in the sense that they must be taken into account in all areas of the EU's activities. Their purpose is to streamline the Union's actions in a manner that would ensure consistency between different policies so as not to jeopardise the pursued objectives of one another.[66] Put differently, the aim is the safeguarding of certain values and objectives that are regarded to be central to EU's overall policy, irrespective of the area or activity concerned.[67]

The horizontal clauses are included into the introductory part (Title II) of the TFEU under the title 'Provisions Having General Application'.[68] Particularly, Article 7 TFEU provides that 'the Union *shall* ensure *consistency* between its policies and activities, *taking all of its objectives into account*'.[69] Moreover, the TFEU enumerates a series of principles and goals that should always be taken into consideration by the EU institutions, irrespective of the actual topic of the policy or

[63] A Müller-Armack, 'The Social Market Economy as an Economic and Social Order' (1978) 36 *Review of Social Economy* 325, 326.

[64] Vatiero, (n 9) 305. See also Marktanner (n 60) 174, claiming that '[t]he Social Market Economy's value system is based on market efficiency that rests on equal opportunity'.

[65] Giocoli (n 55) 770; C Talbot, 'Ordoliberalism and Balancing Competition Goals in the Development of the European Union' (2016) 61 *Antitrust Bulletin* 264, 267.

[66] See generally P Vielle, 'How the Horizontal Social Clause can be Made to Work: The Lessons of Gender Mainstreaming' in N Bruun, K Lörcher and I Schömann (eds), *The Lisbon Treaty and Social Europe* (Oxford, Hart Publishing, 2012) 109–10, explaining that the general idea of horizontal clauses originated from the gender mainstreaming approach expressed in what used to be Art 3(2) EC Treaty. The provision recognised that sex equality can only be reached when all EU's activities and policies are directed towards this goal.

[67] R Holtmaat, 'Horizontal Clauses' in C Tobler (ed), *The Lisbon Treaty* (Europa Institute of Leiden University, 2008) 40.

[68] TFEU, Arts 7–17.

[69] ibid Art 7 (emphasis added). This is mandatory language in treaty interpretation, and thus the Union has an obligation to take into account the stated objectives.

activity. Specifically, Title II refers to the following goals: the promotion of gender equality,[70] the promotion of employment and other social aims,[71] the combating of any form of discrimination,[72] the protection of the environment and the promotion of sustainable growth,[73] consumer protection,[74] animal welfare, and respect of traditions.[75,76]

Important in this context is the so-called horizontal social clause contained in Article 9 TFEU, which states that:

> In defining and implementing its policies and activities, the Union shall take into account requirements linked to the promotion of a high level of employment, the guarantee of adequate social protection, the fight against social exclusion, and a high level of education, training and protection of human health.

The said horizontal social clause must be understood in context with the model of a highly competitive social economy enshrined in Article 3(3) TEU. Indeed, Article 9 TFEU is perceived as the link between the general integration goal set out in the introductory provisions of the TEU and the Union's specific tasks and powers as outlined in the TFEU.[77] Thus, Article 9 TFEU instructs the implementation of the goal of an internal market based on a highly competitive social market economy into all EU activities and acts, including to the competition rules.[78]

Nevertheless, just as with the goal of constructing an internal market based on a highly competitive social market economy, the potential relevance of these horizontal provisions for the interpretation of Article 102 is challenging. This stems above all from the use of vague legal terms (eg, 'high level' and 'adequate'),[79] and from the ambiguous purpose of the Union's duty to 'take into account',[80] 'aim to',[81] 'pay full regard to',[82] or 'take care that'.[83,84] Even so, without setting measurable objectives or targets, especially Articles 7 and 9 TFEU expressly demand the integration of social policy matters into all of the EU policies as a general goal. As a

[70] TFEU, Art 8.
[71] ibid Art 9.
[72] ibid Art 10.
[73] ibid Art 11.
[74] ibid Art 12.
[75] ibid Art 13.
[76] See also ibid Arts 14–17, covering services of general economic interest, the principles of good governance and transparency, personal data protection, and the respect of churches and religious associations under their national law status.
[77] N Dimmel, 'A Study on Art 9 TFEU: Horizontal Social Clause' (Commissioned by the European Association of Service providers for Persons with Disabilities (EASPD), EU, 2014) 24–28.
[78] *cf* D Schiek et al, 'EU Social and Labour Rights and EU Internal Market Law' (Commissioned by the European Parliament's Committee on Employment Affairs (EMPL), EU, 2015) 16, stressing that '[t]he EU is now premised on an integrated approach to economic and social policies, and pursues socio-economic integration as a holistic aim'.
[79] TFEU, Art 9.
[80] ibid Art 7.
[81] ibid Art 8.
[82] ibid Art 13.
[83] ibid Art 14.
[84] *cf* Dimmel, (n 77) 32.

result, the analysis under Article 102 shall, insofar as this is possible, incorporate certain of these social concerns, including especially redistributive policy considerations. In any event, at the very least, Article 102 must be interpreted consistently with policies of a social nature, that is, in a manner that would not contravene the latter's objectives.[85]

Two conclusions may be drawn at this point, before concretely exploring the potential relevance of this analysis for the interpretation of Article 102. First, the horizontal clauses enshrined in the TFEU mandate a holistic approach to the interpretation of Article 102, thus providing a firmer legal basis for the conclusion that Article 102 must be interpreted in light of the EU's wider normative values. Second, the inclusion in the Treaties of the horizontal social clause may support the argument for a greater socio-economic balance post-Lisbon, giving prominence to the Union's commitment to employment and social balance.[86] As the following section illustrates, a market-oriented approach may contribute to the improvement of inequality, and thus to the establishment of a highly competitive social market economy.

iii. Industrial Policy: SMEs' Role and the Promotion of Entrepreneurship

SMEs appear to play a crucial role in the design and development of the EU's overall economic policy.[87] The reason for this does not seem to be what Bork described as 'the uncritical sentimentality in favor of the small guy'.[88] On the contrary, this approach is rather based on the utilitarian perception that the EU's economic success heavily depends on the growth of SMEs.[89] In fact, the Commission considers SMEs and entrepreneurship to be of pivotal importance in ensuring economic growth, job creation, innovation and social integration in the

[85] See generally J Nowag, *Environmental Integration in Competition and Free-Movement Laws* (Oxford, Oxford University Press, 2016) 156ff, offering a concrete framework of analysis in this regard.

[86] *cf* Commission 'Reforming Europe for the 21st Century: Commission Adopts its Formal Opinion before the Intergovernmental Conference' (IP/07/1044, Brussels, 10 July 2007). See also A Veldman and S de Vries, 'Regulation and Enforcement of Economic Freedoms and Social Rights: A Thorny Distribution of Sovereignty' in T van den Brink et al (eds), *Soveignty in the Shared Legal Order of the EU* (Intersentia, 2015) 65, arguing that the Lisbon Treaty considerably strengthened the social face of the EU.

[87] Eg, Council, 'The European Charter for Small Enterprises' (Annex III to the Conclusions of the Presidency of the Santa Maria Da Feira European Council of 19 and 20 June 2000); Commission, *Thinking Big for Small Businesses: What the EU does for SMEs* (EU, 2011); Commission, 'Single Market Act II: Together for a New Growth' (Communication) COM(2012) 573 final, 20; Commission, 'Staff Working Document Accompanying the Report on Competition Policy 2018' SWD(2019) 297 final, 32; Commission, 'An SME Strategy for a Sustainable and Digital Europe' (Communication) COM(2020) 103 final; Commission, 'Updating the 2020 New Industrial Strategy: Building a Stronger Single Market for Europe's Recovery' (Communication) COM(2021) 350 final, 9-10. See also Commission, 'Recommendation Concerning the Definition of Micro, Small and Medium-Sized Enterprises' [2003] OJ L124/36, regarding the definition of SMEs.

[88] Bork (n 21) 54.

[89] Commission, 'Towards a Single Market Act' (n 45) 12; Commission, *Thinking Big for Small Businesses* (n 87) 1; Commission, 'An Action Plan to Improve Access to Finance for SMEs' (Communication)

EU.[90] Hence, the EU institutions over the years have adopted numerous distinct measures in order to support SMEs' growth and encourage entrepreneurship.[91]

Specifically, a comprehensive framework for the EU policy on SMEs has been crafted.[92] This framework is grounded on the necessity to give full consideration to SMEs at the early stage of policy making and on promoting an entrepreneurial spirit among EU citizens.[93] This assists in the development of SME-friendly legislation, which, in turn, helps effectuate one of the EU's stated goals, namely to create a business friendly environment for existing SMEs and potential entrepreneurs.[94] In this context, the Commission has proposed a series of legislative and soft law measures and has adopted decisions under the state aid rules in order to facilitate SMEs' economic growth and their prospect for innovation.[95] These initiatives and decisions help SMEs and new entrepreneurs, in particular, by improving their access to finance;[96] simplifying the regulatory and fiscal environment in which they operate;[97] enabling them to create new business models and sell goods or provide services across borders;[98] and presenting business opportunities offered by the transition to a green and digital economy.[99]

COM(2011) 870 final, 1; Commission, 'A New Industrial Strategy for Europe' (Communication) COM(2020) 102 final, 2 and 3; Commission, 'Updating the 2020 New Industrial Strategy' (n 87) 9.

[90] Eg, Commission, 'Minimizing Regulatory Burden for SMEs: Adapting EU Regulation to the Needs of Micro-Enterprises' COM(2011) 803 final, 2; Commission, *Thinking Big for Small Businesses* (n 87) 11 and 16–18; Commission, 'An SME Strategy' (n 87).

[91] For a rich source of material see DG GROW's website at knowledge4policy.ec.europa.eu/organisation/dg-grow-dg-internal-market-industry-entrepreneurship-smes_en.

[92] Commission, '"Think Small First": A "Small Business Act" for Europe' (Communication) COM(2008) 394 final (Small Business Act); Commission, 'An SME Strategy' (n 87).

[93] ibid.

[94] Commission, 'EUROPE 2020: A Strategy for Smart, Sustainable and Inclusive Growth' (Communication) COM(2010) 2020 (EUROPE 2020) 4, 15, 19 and 30.

[95] Eg, Commission Regulation (EU) 651/2014 of 17 June 2014 declaring certain categories of aid compatible with the internal market in application of Articles 107 and 108 of the Treaty [2014] OJ L187/1, Art 1(1)(b), exempting from prior notification aids to SMEs in the form of investment aid, operating aid and SMEs' access to finance.

[96] Commission, 'An Action Plan to Improve Access to Finance for SMEs' (n 89); Commission, '2007–2013 Competitiveness and Innovation Framework Programme (CIP)', provided for financial instruments, which helped SMEs raise equity and debt financing; Commission, '2014–2020 Programme for the Competitiveness of Enterprises and SMEs (COSME)', aims to make it easier for SMEs to access loans and equity finance. See also Directive 2011/7/EU of 16 February 2011 on combating late payment in commercial transactions [2011] OJ L48/1, strengthening businesses' rights to prompt payment in order to protect SMEs in particular against late payment and to improve their competitiveness.

[97] Commission, 'Minimizing Regulatory Burden for SMEs' (n 90); Commission, 'Entrepreneurship 2020 Action Plan: Reigniting the Entrepreneurial Spirit in Europe' (Communication) COM(2012) 795 final, 10–19; Commission, 'Business Journey on the Single Market: Practical Obstacles and Barriers' SWD(2020) 54 final.

[98] Commission, 'Horizon 2020: The Framework Programme for Research and Innovation' (Communication) COM(2011) 808, providing for an 'SME Instrument' offering funding and support for innovation projects that help SMEs grow and expand their activities into other countries; Commission, 'Long Term Action Plan for Better Implementation and Enforcement of Single Market Rules' (Communication) COM(2020) 94 final, 2 and 5.

[99] Commission, 'Green Action Plan for SMEs: Enabling SMEs to Turn Environmental Challenges into Business Opportunities' (Communication) COM(2014) 440 final; Commission, 'An SME Strategy' (n 87).

The reason for the EU's commitment to support SMEs' development and entrepreneurial potential is primarily linked to their key role in shaping the EU's economy.[100] Starting with SMEs, there are several reasons why they are regarded as the backbone of the EU's economy.[101] First, SMEs represent the largest statistical group of businesses in the EU.[102] They also create the vast majority of new jobs and provide for most of the total private sector employment in the EU.[103] Additionally, based on a logic that replicates Arrow's economic model, SMEs in the EU are treated as an important source of innovation.[104] Finally, in accordance with the objective of constructing an internal market based on a highly competitive social market economy, SMEs are treated as main drivers for integration in the EU.[105] For the exact same reasons, the EU is committed to widely and actively promote entrepreneurship given that new market entrants are likely to be SMEs.[106]

That being said, SMEs are often prevented from achieving their full growth and potential due to their size. First, they often lack the financial resources to compete on equal terms and find it difficult to access the necessary funds for growth and innovation. Second, they are the first to be affected by regulatory, fiscal, and administrative market barriers, and are the most sensitive to changes in the business environment. Third, the smaller a firm is, the more it faces constraints to innovation or to the commercialisation of its innovations. In order therefore to address these structural problems, the best possible environment for SMEs' competitiveness needs to be created. Hence, the above-described initiatives are placing SMEs in the forefront of EU policymaking so that they can unveil their key role in the EU's economy as the main drivers of economic growth, employment, innovation, and social integration.

This approach is fully compatible with both the highly competitive social market economy envisaged in Article 3(3) TEU and the horizontal clauses contained in the TFEU. By placing SMEs and entrepreneurship at the centre of policymaking, the EU is indirectly addressing socio-political concerns, such as inequality, unemployment, and even social or gender exclusion. First, the adoption

[100] See, eg, Commission (n 45) 12; Commission, *Thinking Big for Small Businesses* (n 87) 1; Commission, 'Minimizing Regulatory Burden for SMEs' (n 90) 2; Commission, 'An SME Strategy' (n 87).

[101] Council, 'The European Charter for Small Enterprises' (n 87) 7; Commission, *Thinking Big for Small Businesses* (n 87) 1, emphasising that Europe's 23 million SMEs are the lifeblood of Europe's economy; Commission, 'An SME Strategy' (n 87).

[102] Commission, 'A New Industrial Strategy for Europe' (n 89) 2.

[103] Commission, 'An SME Strategy' (n 87), underlining that SMEs provide two out of three jobs. See also Commission, 'A New Industrial Strategy for Europe' (n 89) 9.

[104] Commission, 'Horizon 2020' (n 98) 9; Commission, 'Updating the 2020 New Industrial Strategy' (n 87) 9, claiming that SMEs have significant innovation potential, and they have the agility to bring revolutionary technological breakthroughs and service innovation to the market.

[105] Small Business Act (n 92) 2; Commission, 'Business Journey on the Single Market' (n 97).

[106] Commission, 'Europe's Next Leaders: The Start-up and Scale-up Initiative' (Communication) COM(2016) 733 final; Commission, 'A New Industrial Strategy for Europe' (n 89) 5 and 10.

of measures supporting SMEs itself is a strategy for inclusive growth, and thus promotes the redistribution of wealth. Second, being the most important sources of employment in the EU, SMEs promote Article 9 TFEU's objective of a 'high level of employment'. Finally, in encouraging people to become entrepreneurs, the Commission targets particularly certain groups, such as women, migrants, seniors or social economy enterprises.[107,108] Here again, economic and social policies are integrated into a holistic approach where entrepreneurship is supported in order to address, inter alia, other public policy concerns, such as wealth inequality.

Arguably, therefore, the EU's policy choice to create a supportive environment for SMEs emanates from provisions of a constitutional nature, namely Article 3(3) TEU and Articles 7–13 TFEU. This is because of the (actual or perceived) beneficial by-products of such a policy, ie improved distribution of income, employment growth, and overall social balance. In any event, this approach is clearly compatible with the EU's constitutional peculiarity of aiming to create a highly competitive social market economy. This implies that the interpretation and enforcement of the competition rules should, at the very least, not disregard the key role of SMEs in shaping the EU's economy. In fact, the Commission had previously stressed that a SME-friendly policy would only be successful if:

> At the same time, European and national competition rules [are] vigorously applied to make sure that small businesses have every chance to enter new markets and compete on fair terms.[109]

Thus, the competition rules could be enforced to keep markets open and accessible to SMEs and newcomers. Interestingly, as of late 2019, the design of a new strategy for SMEs is co-led by two of the Commission's executive vice-presidents, one of whom is also responsible for the competition portfolio.[110] This development illustrates the ongoing importance of SMEs in EU policymaking, while also indicating the interaction of competition policy with SMEs' growth and inequality-related concerns.

In fact, Margrethe Vestager has been re-appointed as Commissioner for Competition for a second term and has also been designated as one of the executive vice-presidents taking on responsibility for the 'a Europe fit for the digital age' agenda. This is interesting, not least because during her first term the Commission particularly targeted perceived abusive practices by industrial giants in the tech

[107] Commission, 'Social Business Initiative: Creating a Favourable Climate for Social Enterprises, Key Stakeholders in the Social Economy and Innovation' (Communication) COM(2011) 682 final, 2, defining a social enterprise as 'an operator in the social economy whose main objective is to have a social impact rather than make a profit for their owners or shareholders'. According to the Commission, social economy entities are mostly SMEs.

[108] Small Business Act (n 92) 5–6; Commission, 'Social Business Initiative' (n 107) 9–10; Commission, 'Entrepreneurship 2020 Action Plan' (n 97) 24–27.

[109] Council, 'The European Charter for Small Enterprises' (n 87) 12.

[110] See Ursula von der Leyen, 'Mission Letter to Margrethe Vestager (Executive Vice-President-designate for a Europe fit for the Digital Age)' (Brussels, 10 September 2019) 5.

sector.[111] There is also every indication that the Commission will continue the same trend.[112] Moreover, Commissioner Vestager has specifically communicated that, when considering regulation for the digital sector, her policy will draw on the insights gained from the Commission's enforcement of the competition rules during her previous term.[113] Particularly, she signals her anxiety that quasi-monopolistic tech companies inhibit promising ideas by small firms based on their economic power rather than their merit, thus blocking a path that delivers innovation to consumers.[114] For this reason, she expressly opposed an approach that would lead to the application of less stringent rules in the context of EU competition law.[115] In this context, the Commission acknowledges the dynamic capacities of small enterprises in answering to new market needs, considering that competition law tends to safeguard economic opportunities for SMEs by ensuring open markets.[116] SMEs rely heavily on online tools, and may therefore be disproportionately affected by abuses of dominant undertakings in this area.

Having unveiled the interconnection between Article 3(3) TEU's highly competitive social market economy, the TFEU's horizontal clauses, and the

[111] *Google Search (Shopping)* (Case AT.39740) C(2017) 4444 final, imposing a fine of €2.42 billion on Google for abusing dominance as search engine; *Google Android* (Case AT.40099) C(2018) 4761 final, fining Google €4.34 billion for illegal practices regarding Android mobile devices to strengthen dominance of Google's search engine; *Google Search (AdSense)* (Case AT.40411) C(2019) 2173 final, fining Google €1.49 billion for abusive practices in online advertising; *Qualcomm (Exclusivity Payments)* (Case AT.40220) C(2018) 240, fining Qualcomm €997 million for abuse of dominance in LTE baseband chipsets which prevented competition on the merits; *Qualcomm (Predation)* (Case AT.39711) C(2019) 5361, fining Qualcomm €242 million for engaging in predatory pricing; Commission, 'Antitrust: Commission Opens Investigation into Possible Anti-competitive Conduct of Amazon' (Press Release, 17 July 2019); *Broadcom* (Case AT.40608) C(2019) 7406 final, imposing interim measures on Broadcom in TV and modem chipset markets.

[112] See M Vestager, 'European Parliament Hearing' (Speech, 8 October 2019); Commission, 'Antitrust: Commission Opens Investigation into Possible Anticompetitive Conduct by Google in the Online Advertising Technology Sector' (Press Release, 22 June 2021). On the Commission's proposed new rules for digital platforms, see Commission, 'Proposal for a Regulation of the European Parliament and of the Council on a Single Market For Digital Services (Digital Services Act) and amending Directive 2000/31/EC' [2020] COM(2020) 825 final; Commission, 'Proposal for a Regulation of the European Parliament and of the Council on contestable and fair markets in the digital sector (Digital Markets Act)' [2020] COM(2020) 842 final, proposing an ambitious set of new rules for all digital services, including social media, online market places, and other online platforms that operate in the EU: the Digital Services Act and the Digital Markets Act.

[113] See M Kirk and F Liberatore, 'Towards Competition Law Based Regulation and Policy for the EU Digital Economy?' (*Global IP & Technology Law Blog*, 16 September 2019).

[114] M Vestager, 'Shaping Competition Policy in the Era of Digitisation' (Speech, Brussels, 17 January 2019); M Vestager, 'New Technology as a Disruptive Global Force' (Speech at the Youth and Leaders' Summit, Paris, 21 January 2019). See also M Vestager, 'Security and Trust in a Digital World' (Speech at CCBE Standing Committee, Copenhagen, 13 September 2019), referring to the ability of such firms 'to undermine democracy' and 'harm the fundamental values of our society'.

[115] M Vestager, 'The Champions Europe Needs' (Speech at the WELT Economic Summit, Berlin, 9 January 2019).

[116] See J Laitenberger, 'Competition Enforcement in Digital Markets: Using our Tools Well and a Look at the Future' (Speech at the 14th Annual Conference of the GCLC, Brussels, 31 January 2019) 4–5.

commitment to support SMEs and entrepreneurship, the issue to consider next is their potential relevance for the interpretation and enforcement of Article 102.

B. Relevance of Inequality-Related Concerns under Article 102

The above analysis is a far cry from being determinative of what it entails at the detailed level of interpretation and application of Article 102. This is because the content of the EU Treaties, just as with most constitutional arrangements, are an incomplete contract leaving space for interpretative choices.[117] Nevertheless, the Treaties do provide some guidance: they require the integration of economic and social policies for the completion of an internal market which has a 'social' element. This, in turn, provides more obvious support for the holistic perspective of Article 102, since, according to the scheme of the Treaties, its role is to achieve the completion of the internal market. Denying such an integrated policy would not sit comfortably with the text of the Treaties and would contradict the historical and political context in which EU competition law was created and has developed ever since.

Clearly, the commitment to a highly competitive social market economy in the context of establishing an internal market must guide the goals that Article 102 is constitutionally mandated to pursue. This is a direct consequence of the finding that Article 102 is part of a system which is employed as a means to achieve the integration of the internal market.[118] Article 102 therefore is a tool that must be interpreted and enforced in such a manner that it would either directly assist in the promotion of an internal market based on a highly competitive social market economy or – at the very least – be consistent with the particularities of this goal.

However, the question that arises is related to the unclear normative content of both the concept of a highly competitive social market economy and the TFEU's horizontal clauses for the analysis under Article 102. That is, it is necessary to discuss their relevance for the interpretation and enforcement of Article 102. Indeed, the prohibition contained in Article 102 may, depending on its interpretation and the intensity of its enforcement, have an effect of varying degree on certain distinctive elements of a highly competitive social market economy. Most notably, these include the inequality-related concerns that have been outlined above. Particularly, to the extent that competition law can restrain the concentration of wealth in the hands of a few firms, it may effectively enhance wealth

[117] S Makris, 'Openness and Integrity in Antitrust' (2021) 17 *Journal of Competition Law and Economics* 1, calling this phenomenon 'EU competition law's openness' and explaining its causes.

[118] See Commission, 'Towards a Single Market Act' (n 45) 4, stressing that the internal market 'is not an end in itself. It is a tool for implementing other policies'. This is clear at the constitutional level from Arts 2 and 3 TEU – and this has always been true (see the original Art 2 EEC).

distribution and protect SMEs.[119] On this approach, a loss of a certain degree of economic efficiency would be acceptable in order to ensure an internal market based on a highly competitive social market economy.[120]

In the context of Article 102, however, this cannot lead to a *contra legem* interpretation that would entail the de facto targeting of market power. This arises effortlessly from the very wording of the provision, which does not target dominance per se but stipulates the prohibition of the abuse of dominance. Moreover, targeting market dominance would itself contradict the concept of a highly competitive social market economy, as well as the policy choice to actively promote entrepreneurship. This is so because it would eliminate the firms' incentives to compete for market dominance on the basis of performance. Consequently, irrespective of the wording of Article 102, attempting to eliminate market power would not sit comfortably with an internal market committed to both a social market economy and a highly competitive one.

There are, however, specific approaches to Article 102 that could effectively respond to inequality-related concerns while being in tune with the wording of the provision. In this regard, to the extent that competitive markets are conducive to a more even distribution of income, competition law could be employed to contribute to this objective simply by making markets more competitive.[121] To this end, Article 102 could account for inequality concerns in the context of both its enforcement and its substantive interpretation.

Starting with enforcement, the Commission could exercise its administrative discretion to prioritise cases that would benefit the less advantaged EU citizens.[122] The Commission could, for instance, systematically direct its limited resources towards products and/or sectors that are most relevant and sensitive for middle- and lower-class consumers, such as healthcare products, the pharma sector, and supermarket retailing.[123] It might also attach a lower priority to the enforcement of Article 102 against a conduct that would likely benefit the disadvantaged. In a similar vein, the Commission could adopt a sufficiently interventionist approach, recognising both the concerns about wealth inequality and the fact that economically significant market power contributes to it.[124] In this regard, the Commission

[119] *cf* Ennis, Gonzaga and Pike (n 8) 539, showing that market power may contribute substantially to wealth inequality, and that policies that enhance competition can reduce inequality. See also Ma (n 9) 251, proving that an equity-based antitrust can have a significant effect on inequality and that lower inequality can significantly promote democracy.

[120] *cf* Ma (n 9) 239.

[121] L Khan and S Vaheesan, 'Market Power and Inequality: The Antitrust Counterrevolution and its Discontents' (2017) 11 *Harvard Law and Policy Review* 235, 294; Ennis, Gonzaga and Pike (n 8) 518. Against Crane (n 27) 1228.

[122] See generally O Brook and K Cseres, 'Policy Report: Priority Setting in EU and National Competition Law Enforcement' (2021), ssrn.com/abstract=3930189, offering a comprehensive mapping of the priority setting rules guiding the Commission and the NCAs.

[123] Similarly, Baker and Salop (n 8) 18.

[124] *cf* Ennis, Gonzaga and Pike (n 8) 539, showing that market power both increases wealth of the richest population and weakens the income of the poorest population.

would consider wealth inequality when striking the balance between the costs of under-enforcement versus over-enforcement, thus recognising greater harm from the exercise of market power.[125]

Such an interventionist enforcement would also be consistent with the important functions of SMEs for the economy and society.[126] This is because it would potentially increase the incentives of non-dominant firms to enter the market, invest and compete. This may be particularly valuable 'in a market environment where barriers to enter foreign markets frequently remain significant';[127] and such a market environment is still prevailing in the EU.

As a matter of substance, an approach that effectively responds to inequality concerns is one where Article 102 directly challenges dominant firms' pricing,[128] especially when the conduct is one of a super-dominant or quasi-monopolistic firm and/or targets less advantaged consumers.[129] With regard to the issue of directly controlling dominant firms' pricing, under EU law a dominant firm that exploits its position by charging supra-competitive prices may be found to violate Article 102.[130] Such a pricing exploitation may be challenged under both Article 102(a) and Article 102(c). That is, both the excessive pricing and the discriminatory pricing of a dominant firm may amount to an abuse of a dominant position.[131]

[125] Baker and Salop (n 8) 21.

[126] See generally C Lee and BZ Yuhua, 'SMEs, Competition Law and Economic Growth' (Commissioned by APEC, ISEAS-Yusof Ishak Institute, 2015), 11, stating that SMEs carry a range of important functions for the economy and society at large by, inter alia, introducing new ideas and processes, claiming niche markets, or simply providing goods and services in socially important contexts.

[127] Schweitzer (n 30) 162.

[128] See ch 4 in this volume, stressing that prohibiting excessive pricing is 'paradigmatically distributive', in that it distributes from those who unfairly elevate their prices (corporations with dominant market power) to those who are the victims of the exploitation. The Commission has rarely enforced Article 102 to standalone excessive pricing cases, because of both the practical difficulties and the conceptual concerns involved in pursuing such investigations. In practical terms, it is troublesome to set a standard for the identification of the dividing line between high and excessive prices, and thus to design an administrable legal test for exploitative pricing. In conceptual terms, dominant firms should also be permitted to fully take part in the competitive process, even to charge high prices so as not to reduce their investments incentives. On these issues see, eg, D Evans and J Padilla, 'Excessive Prices: Using Economics to Define Administrable Legal Rules' (2005) 1 *Journal of Competition Law and Economics* 97; M Motta and A de Streel, 'Exploitative and Exclusionary Excessive Prices in EU Law' in Ehlermann and I Atanasiu (eds) (n 2) 108–9; A Ezrachi and D Gilo, 'Are Excessive Prices Really Self-Correcting?' (2009) 5 *Journal of Competition Law and Economics* 249; C Calcagno and M Walker, 'Excessive Pricing: Towards Clarity and Economic Coherence' (2010) 6 *Journal of Competition Law and Economics* 891, 909–10; S Bishop and M Walker, *The Economics of EC Competition Law: Concepts, Application and Measurement*, 3rd edn (London, Sweet & Maxwell, 2010) 237–44.

[129] Priorities Paper (n 3), paras 20 and 30, saying that 'the stronger the dominant position, the higher the likelihood that conduct protecting that position leads to anti-competitive foreclosure', and that 'exclusionary conduct which maintains, creates or strengthens a market position approaching that of a monopoly can normally not be justified on the grounds that it also creates efficiency gains'.

[130] According to the wording of s 2 of the Sherman Act 1890, excessive pricing is not prohibited in the US. See, eg, M Gal, 'Monopoly Pricing as an Antitrust Offense in the U.S. and the EC: Two Systems of Belief about Monopoly?' (2004) 49 *Antitrust Bulletin* 343.

[131] See generally N Dunne, 'Regulating Prices in the European Union' (2018) 37 *Yearbook of European Law* 344. On excessive pricing see L Hou, 'Excessive Prices within EU Competition Law' (2011) 7

In this regard, despite the Commission's understandable reluctance to act as price regulator,[132] it has intervened against excessive pricing in certain instances, such as in the pharma sector.[133]

Furthermore, as illustrated in the next section, promoting the goal of consumer interests through consumer-related proxies under Article 102 may be compatible with the constitutional requirement to include inequality concerns into the analysis of the provision. Overall, designing rules that would promote the interests of the consumer while also giving due regard to SMEs' ability to effectively compete in the market is consistent with the EU's constitutional framework.[134]

IV. Is Economic Inequality a Relevant Concern under Article 102?

The analysis so far has examined the constitutional structure of the EU, demonstrating that the latter demands a holistic approach to Article 102. This constitutionally mandated holistic approach entails that values external to market competition, such as equality-related concerns and redistributive policy considerations, should be taken into account in the analysis of Article 102. This section turns to the discussion of the relevant case law in order to assess whether the designed legal tests successfully reconcile the market-oriented objectives of Article 102 with equality-related concerns and redistributive policies, thereby allowing the provision to operate according to the constitutional role imposed on it by the Treaties.

European Competition Journal 47. On discriminatory pricing see Motta, *Competition Policy: Theory and Practice* (n 13) 491–511.

[132] Commission, 'XXVIIth Report on Competition Policy' (1997) 29 (point 77), stipulating that 'the Commission is not and does not wish to act as a price regulator'; M Vestager, 'Protecting Consumers from Exploitation' (Brussels, 21 November 2016), stressing that '[t]he last thing we should be doing is to set ourselves up as a regulator, deciding on the right price'.

[133] *Aspen* (Case AT.40394) C(2021) 724 final. See Vestager (n 132), emphasising the Commission's 'responsibility to the public' to address excessive pricing, especially in sectors and products that are vital to the consumer, such as in the pharmaceutical industry; OECD, 'Excessive Pricing in Pharmaceutical Markets: Note by the European Union' (DAF/COMP/WD(2018)112, 23 November 2018). On the renewed interest of NCAs in pursuing excessive pricing investigations see *Incremento Prezzo Farmaci Aspen* (Case A480) AGCM decision of 29 September 2016, where the Italian competition authority imposed a fine on Aspen for excessive pricing; *Unfair pricing in respect of the supply of phenytoin sodium capsules in the UK* (Case CE/9742-13) CMA decision of 7 December 2016, where the UK's competition authority found that that Pfizer and Flynn had set excessively high prices; CMA, 'Pharmaceutical Company Accused of Overcharging NHS' (Press Release, 16 December 2016), where the CMA has issued a statement of objections alleging that Actavis UK has breached and continues to breach UK and EU competition law by charging excessive and unfair prices; CMA, 'Drug Company Accused of Abusing its Position to Overcharge the NHS' (Press Release, 21 November 2017), stating that the UK competition authority has provisionally found that Concordia abused its dominant position to overcharge the NHS by millions for an essential thyroid drug; CNMC, 'La CNMC incoa expediente sancionador contra el grupo Aspen y su distribuidor en España Deco Pharma por posibles prácticas abusivas' (Press Release, 3 February 2017), where the Spanish competition authority announced that it started a sanction procedure against Aspen for imposing excessive prices.

[134] *cf* Ma (n 9) 251.

Taking as granted that Article 102 is designed to pursue the objectives of protecting both the integrity of the internal market and consumer interest, this section illustrates the way that inequality considerations are reflected in the rules applied by the EU courts to the unilateral conduct of dominant firms.[135] The discussion unveils that the designed legal tests ensure conformity with the constitutionally demanded holistic approach, in the sense that inequality considerations are factored in the EU courts' case law on Article 102. Particularly, conceptualising the relevant case law on abuse of dominance, it is shown that inequality considerations are incorporated in the EU courts' analysis of Article 102 via two distinct techniques, an indirect and a direct one. Both techniques are examined in turn.

A. Indirect Relevance of Inequality

i. Internal Market Integration and Inequality

The concern for the establishment and well-functioning of the internal market has dominated the implementation of the competition rules, including Article 102. The EU competition rules were drafted as a legal complement to the provisions establishing the four economic freedoms: the abolished public barriers to trade should not be replaced by 'private barriers' created by anticompetitive conduct in the marketplace.[136] Article 102 is therefore a means to achieve the broader goal of the completion of the internal market, which, as already explained, is committed to be a highly competitive social market.[137]

The EU courts have from the outset treated EU competition policy as a powerful tool to achieve the goal of market integration.[138] This had an inevitable and

[135] For a detailed analysis of this claim see ch 2 of K Sidiropoulos, *The Influence of EU's Constitutional and Institutional Peculiarities on the Interpretation of Abuse of Dominance under Article 102 TFEU* (forthcoming, 2022).

[136] Eg, Joined Cases 56 and 58/64 *Établissements Consten S.à.R.L. and Grundig-Verkaufs-GmbH v Commission* ECLI:EU:C:1966:41, para 340; Joined Cases C-468 to 478/06 *Sot. Lélos kai Sia EE and Others v GlaxoSmithKline AEVE Farmakeftikon Proïonton, formerly Glaxowellcome AEVE* ECLI:EU:C:2008:504 (*Sot Lélos*), para 37.

[137] Commission, 'XXIXth Report on Competition Policy' (1999) 19, stating that '[t]he second [objective of competition policy] is the single market objective. An internal market is an essential condition for the development of an efficient and competitive industry'. See also I Lianos, 'Some Reflections on the Question of the Goals of EU Competition Law' (2013) UCL CLES Working Paper Series 3/2013, 42, arguing that the modifications introduced by the Lisbon Treaty 'confirm the importance of market integration in EU competition law'. *cf* K Cseres, 'The Controversies of the Consumer Welfare Standard' (2006) 3 *Common Market Law Review* 121, 151–2, arguing that 'the primacy of market integration among the policy goals of European competition law does not hold anymore'.

[138] See, eg, in the context of Article 101, *Consten and Grundig* (n 136), holding that 'an agreement [...] which might tend to restore the national divisions in trade between Member States might be such as to frustrate the most fundamental objecti[ves] of the [EU]. The Treaty, whose preamble and content aim at abolishing the barriers between States, [...] could not allow undertakings to reconstruct such barriers. Article [101](1) is designed to pursue this aim'; Case 19/77 *Miller International Schallplatten GmbH v Commission* ECLI:EU:C:1978:19, para 7, holding that a clause prohibiting exports (ie, an obligation to sell on the domestic market) constitutes, by its very nature, a restriction on competition;

significant impact on the outcome of certain cases on abuse of dominance, revealing that the integrity of the internal market is a standalone objective pursued by Article 102.[139] Indeed, Article 102 has often been applied to prohibit practices of dominant firms which either aimed at restricting cross-border trade or had the effect of partitioning national markets through any form of territorial restriction.[140] In this regard, Article 102 promotes the integration of markets in the EU by prohibiting restrictions on cross-border trade. In practice, this means removing barriers to entry for dominant firms' rivals, thus allowing a pluralistic market structure with diversified sources of supplies.[141] Pursuing the objective of internal market integration in the context of Article 102 ensures open and accessible markets with better prices and enhanced choice for consumers. Allowing for the existence of more buyers and sellers through the application of Article 102 combined with the EU initiatives creating a supportive market environment for SMEs improve the opportunities of small businesses to enter new markets and compete on fair terms.

Case C-319/82 *Société de Vente de Ciments et Bétons de l'Est SA v Kerpen & Kerpen GmbH und Co. KG* ECLI:EU:C:1983:374, para 6, holding that a contract that imposes on the purchaser restrictions on the territory into which goods can be resold has as its object the prevention of competition within the internal market. See also Commission Regulation (EU) 330/2010 of 20 April 2010 on the application of Article 101(3) of the Treaty on the Functioning of the European Union to categories of vertical agreements and concerted practices [2010] OJ L102/1, Art 4(b); Commission Regulation (EU) No 1217/2010 of 14 December 2010 on the application of Article 101(3) of the Treaty on the Functioning of the European Union to certain categories of research and development agreements [2010] OJ L335/36, Art 5(d)-(g); Commission Regulation (EU) 1218/2010 of 14 December 2010 on the application of Article 101(3) of the Treaty on the Functioning of the European Union to certain categories of specialisation agreements [2010] OJ L335/43, Art 4(c).

[139] Eg, Joined Cases 40 to 48, 50, 54 to 56, 111, 113 and 114/73 *Coöperatieve Vereniging "Suiker Unie" UA and others v Commission* ECLI:EU:C:1975:174 (*Suiker Unie*), paras 396–400; Case 26/75 *General Motors Continental NV v Commission* ECLI:EU:C:1975:150, paras 11–12; Case 27/76 *United Brands Company and United Brands Continentaal BV v Commission* ECLI:EU:C:1978:22 (*United Brands*), paras 157–61; Case 226/84 *British Leyland Public Limited Company v Commission* ECLI:EU:C:1986:421, paras 16, 21 and 24; *BPB Industries plc* (Case IV/31.900) Commission Decision 89/22/EEC [1988] OJ L10/50, upheld in Case T-65/89 *BPB Industries Plc and British Gypsum Ltd v Commission* ECLI:EU:T:1993:31, paras 119–22; *AAMS* (Case IV/36.010-F3) Commission Decision 98/538/EC [1998] OJ L252/47, upheld in Case T-139/98 *Amministrazione Autonoma dei Monopoli di Stato (AAMS) v Commission* ECLI:EU:T:2001:272; *Deutsche Post AG – Interception of Cross-Border Mail* (Case COMP/C-1/36.915) Commission Decision 2001/892/EC [2001] OJ L331/40; *Sot Lélos* (n 136), para 66; *Romanian Power Exchange/OPCOM* (Case AT.39984) [2014] OJ C134/7, paras 36, 129 and 230.

[140] For recent Commission decisions illustrating this see *Upstream Gas Supplies in Central and Eastern Europe* (Case AT.39816) [2018] OJ C(2018) 3106 final (*Gazprom*), para 61; *AB InBev Beer Trade Restrictions* (Case AT.40134) [2019] C(2019) 3465 final, paras 89–93, stating that partitioning of the internal market by restricting cross-border trade is an abuse 'by nature'. See also *Baltic Rail* (Case AT.39813) [2017] C(2017) 6544 final, paras 114–26 and 323, explicitly linked the decision's outcome to its persistent efforts to complete the internal market for rail services.

[141] See Joined Cases C-468 to C-478/06 *Sot. Lélos kai Sia EE and Others v GlaxoSmithKline AEVE Farmakeftikon Proïonton, formerly Glaxowellcome AEVE* ECLI:EU:C:2008:180 (*Sot Lélos*), Opinion of AG Colomer, para 88, stressing that the free movement case law is relevant, at least inasmuch as it concerns practices on the part of dominant firms which have the aim or effect of partitioning national markets. *cf* P Akman, 'The Role of "Freedom" in EU Competition Law' (2014) 34 *Legal Studies* 183, 211, arguing that this may have led to the misinterpretation of the relevant case law as being exclusively concerned with the maintenance of rivalry.

This approach integrates (re)distributive policies into Article 102, consistently with Articles 7 and 9 TFEU, and the commitment to a highly competitive social market economy.[142] First, insofar as the application of Article 102 makes sure that small businesses participate in market competition, it promotes inclusive growth and redistribution of wealth.[143] Second, enabling SMEs to effectively present their product and services on the market promotes Article 9 TFEU's objective of a 'high level of employment', since they are the most important source of employment in the EU. Finally, this approach gives due regard to the key role of SMEs in shaping the EU's economy. Overall, this indicates that wealth inequality concerns are indirectly relevant into the analysis of Article 102.

In certain cases, however, a dominant firm's practice that prevents parallel trade may have desirable redistributive effects. This is the case, for example, when a dominant firm charges higher prices to consumers in prosperous Member States and offers lower prices to those located in poorer Member States.[144] Prohibiting such a pricing policy under Article 102 based on a finding of a market partitioning effect may result in transferring wealth from poorer consumers to richer ones, since consumers located in poorer Member States would have to pay a higher proportion of their income.[145] Even so, redistribution of income is not wholly irrelevant in this context. Particularly, practices of dominant firms that restrict parallel trade may be found compatible with Article 102 if they are reasonable and proportionate to ensure a legitimate economic or public interest.[146] Hence, claims based on redistributive justice or on securing an adequate and continuous supply of products may rebut the prima facie illegality of a practice that limits parallel trade.[147]

Altogether, the objective of market integration has distributive/allocative implications. Without saying that this is a coherent redistributive policy that tackle wealth and income inequality or that it addresses in a targeted way the problem of wealth inequality, pursuing the internal market objective under Article 102 indirectly complements policies that specifically aim to achieve wealth redistribution and other equality-related objectives. Therefore, the objective of protecting the integrity of the internal market is reconciled with the constitutionally required holistic approach to Article 102, since pursuing this objective is consistent with promoting policies of a social nature.

[142] Fox and Bazenov (n 128), emphasising, in the EU context, that the 'pursuit of market integration is inherently inclusive', and 'inclusivity is inherently pro-equality'.

[143] ibid, arguing that market integration demands openness of and access to markets, and thus contestability of markets.

[144] See *United Brands* (n 139), 209–13, where the firm charged the lowest price for bananas destined for Ireland and the highest for those heading to West Germany.

[145] See also R Whish and D Bailey, *Competition Law*, 8th edn (Oxford, Oxford University Press, 2015) 808–9, criticising the judgment in *United Brands* on this ground.

[146] *cf* TFEU, Art 36.

[147] *Sot Lélos* (n 136), paras 69–77.

ii. Protection of Consumer Interest and Inequality

a. Analysis of the Case Law: Tests Reflecting a Plurality of Consumer-Related Objectives

According to the relevant case law, the legal tests to establish liability under Article 102 vary from one practice to another, meaning that there is a spectrum of tests to assess the unilateral conduct of dominant firms. All these tests have one element in common, namely they are all designed to ultimately promote consumer interests. This is achieved by means of multiple consumer-related proxies, each of which expresses different forms of consumer harm.

In this context, the EU courts consider the interests of consumers as being about much more than just low prices, treating as relevant proxies in this respect: consumer choice and unrestricted market entry, dynamic efficiency and innovation, as well as consumer surplus and productive efficiency.[148] It is apparent from the applied tests under Article 102 that, depending on the nature of the practice concerned and the facts of each individual case, certain of these proxies are more relevant than others in the zeal for protecting consumer interest.

First, in certain instances, having in mind that competition in the market means a structure of decentralised economic power, the EU courts consider that diminishing the available choices to an unacceptable level might be more troubling than the effects of a conduct on prices.[149] In this regard, consumer choice exists only insofar as there are reasonable options of suppliers to choose from. Hence, protecting consumer choice entails ensuring unrestricted market entry, namely securing the freedom of non-dominant firms to access the market and trade on the merits without artificial obstacles constructed by dominant firms.[150]

In cases concerning exclusivity rebates and tying practices, for example, the designed tests are predominantly based on consumer choice and unrestricted market entry. According to the case law, these practices tie customers to the dominant firm, thereby denying both consumer choice and rivals' market presence.[151] The EU courts have enshrined a presumption of illegality for these business practices, considering that the competitive process will, in principle, be distorted.[152]

[148] E Buttigieg, *Competition Law: Safeguarding the Consumer Interest: A Comparative Analysis of US Antitrust Law and EC Competition Law* (The Netherlands, Wolters Kluwer, 2009) 382.

[149] See n 151 and n 152 below. *cf* Fox and Sullivan (n 7), arguing that '[a]ntitrust is rooted in a preference for pluralism, freedom of trade, access to markets, and freedom of choice'.

[150] *cf* E Fox, 'What is Harm to Competition? Exclusionary Practices and Anticompetitive Effect' (2002) 70 *Antitrust Law Journal* 371, 395.

[151] Eg, Case 85/76 *Hoffmann-La Roche v Commission* ECLI:EU:C:1979:36, para 90; Case 322/81 *NV Nederlandsche Banden Industrie Michelin v Commission* ECLI:EU:C:1983:313 (*Michelin I*), paras 85–86; Case T-83/91 *Tetra Pak International SA v Commission* ECLI:EU:T:1994:246 (*Tetra Pak II*), paras 137 and 213; Case T-201/04 *Microsoft Corp v Commission* ECLI:EU:T:2007:289, para 1088; Case T-286/09 *Intel Corp. v Commission* ECLI:EU:T:2014:547, paras 72–73, 76–77, 86 and 90; Case C-413/14P *Intel Corp. v Commission* ECLI:EU:C:2017:632, para 137.

[152] For exclusivity arrangements see, eg, *Suiker Unie* (n 139), para 518; *Hoffmann-La Roche* (n 151), paras 89–90; *Michelin I* (n 151), para 71; *BPB Industries* (n 139), para 120, upheld on appeal in Case

This approach is based on the assumption that the implementation of tying and exclusivity rebates on the part of dominant firms is a manifestation of inefficient behaviour exhibited by firms lacking the motivation to use their resources efficiently due to the absence of effective competitive pressure.[153] In other words, the dominant firms' preference for these practices and their potential impact on the market are considered to be the product of market power, rather than being the result of competition on the merits.[154] In this context, therefore, the prevailing proxies are consumer choice and unrestricted market entry, but other proxies are also relevant, such as the different forms of efficiencies and innovation.[155]

Second, in certain other instances, the identification of a distortion of the competitive process is based primarily on the actual or prospective effects of the examined conduct on innovation and dynamic efficiency. That is, in some cases innovation and dynamic efficiency are the critical proxies that guide the assessment of the dominant firm's conduct. Examples of dominant firms' conduct that are assessed in this way involve the refusal to supply goods or services,[156] the refusal to access an essential facility,[157] and the refusal to license IP rights to prevent the development of a new product or to limit the development of a new market.[158]

It is well-established in EU competition law that an undertaking enjoys the freedom to choose its trading partners, irrespective of its market power.[159]

C-310/93P ECLI:EU:C:1995:101; Case T-219/99 *British Airways plc v Commission* ECLI:EU:T:2003:343, paras 244–5, upheld on appeal in Case C-95/04P ECLI:EU:C:2007:166; Case T-57/01 *Solvay SA v Commission* ECLI:EU:T:2009:519, paras 316–7 and 365; Case T-66/01 *Imperial Chemical Industries Ltd v Commission* ECLI:EU:T:2010:255, paras 296 and 315; Case T-155/06 *Tomra Systems ASA and Others v Commission* ECLI:EU:T:2010:370, para 209, upheld on appeal in Case C-549/10P ECLI:EU:C:2012:221; Case C-23/14 *Post Danmark A/S v Konkurrencerådet* ECLI:EU:C:2015:651 (*Post Danmark II*), para 27; Case T-286/09 *Intel* (n 151), para 85; Case C-413/14P *Intel* (n 151), para 137. For tying practices see, eg, Case T-30/89 *Hilti AG v Commission* ECLI:EU:T:1991:70, paras 100–1; *Tetra Pak II* (n 151), paras 136–7, confirmed on appeal in Case C-333/94P ECLI:EU:C:1996:436, para 37; *Microsoft* (n 151), para 868. See also *Microsoft* (Case COMP/C-3/37.792) [2004] OJ L32/23, para 841; *Microsoft (Tying)* (Case COMP/C-3/39.530) [2009] OJ C242/2 (*Microsoft II*), para 34; *Google Android* (n 111), para 749.

[153] *cf* T van der Vijver, 'Article 102 TFEU: How to Claim the Application of Objective Justifications in the Case of *prima facie* Dominance Abuses?' (2013) 4 *Journal of European Competition Law and Practice* 121, 129.

[154] This is implicit in, eg, *Tetra Pak II* (n 151), paras 137 and 213; *Microsoft* (n 151), para 1088; *Imperial Chemical* (n 152), para 315, holding that these practices 'are not based on an economic transaction which justifies this burden or benefit'.

[155] Eg, *Microsoft* (n 151), para 1159, clarifying that relevant efficiencies are not confined to economic considerations in terms of price and cost but may consist of technical improvements in the quality of the goods or services. In the context of assessing the merits of efficiency claims see C-95/04P *British Airways* (n 152), para 86; Case C-209/10 *Post Danmark A/S v Konkurrencerådet* ECLI:EU:C:2012:172 (*Post Danmark I*), paras 40–41; C-413/14P *Intel* (n 151), para 140.

[156] Eg, Joined Cases 6, 7/73 *Istituto Chemioterapico Italiano S.p.A. and Commercial Solvents Corporation v Commission* ECLI:EU:C:1974:18 (*Commercial Solvents*); Case T-301/04 *Clearstream Banking AG and Clearstream International SA v Commission* ECLI:EU:T:2009:317.

[157] Eg, Case T-851/14 *Slovak Telekom v Commission* ECLI:EU:T:2018:929.

[158] Eg, Joined Cases C-241, 242/91P *Radio Telefis Eireann (RTE) and Independent Television Publications Ltd (ITP) v Commission* ECLI:EU:C:1995:98 (*Magill*).

[159] Case C-7/97 *Oscar Bronner GmbH & Co KG v Mediaprint* ECLI:EU:C:1998:264, Opinion of AG Jacobs, para 57.

In principle, thus, a dominant firm cannot be obliged to supply others with goods or services.[160] Depending on the facts of the case, however, it is sometimes appropriate to restrict, with the appropriate compensation, the dominant undertaking's freedom to refuse to supply a trading partner. This is the case, for instance, where: i) access to a facility is a precondition for competition on a related market for goods or services for which there is a limited degree of interchangeability;[161] ii) the exercise of IP rights by a firm holding a monopoly over a product, service or facility will lead to a permanent restriction of competition on a related market;[162] iii) duplication of the facility is impossible or extremely difficult owing to physical or geographical constraints or is highly undesirable for reasons of public policy;[163] or iv) the cost of duplicating a facility constitutes itself an insuperable barrier to entry.[164] Consequently, under certain exceptional circumstances, a dominant firm may infringe Article 102 by refusing to deal, but this would require an *in concreto* examination of all the relevant circumstances of the case.

The most pertinent relevant proxies in these cases are innovation and dynamic efficiencies. That is, the assessment is focused on the effects of the conduct in question on efficiencies resulting from R&D and innovation.[165] Ultimately, this promotes the interests of the consumer, who benefits from the introduction of new or improved products or processes.

The predominantly employed proxies in all the above-mentioned tests are concentrated on market effects other than near-term efficiencies associated with price, output, and production costs. Therefore, it is not always necessary to identify a direct link between a business practice and the reduction of consumer surplus in order to find a breach of Article 102. The EU courts have generally dismissed the importance of consumer welfare in terms of price and output effects; and, in fact, have never explicitly used the term in an Article 102 case.[166] Nevertheless, consumer surplus and production efficiency are not irrelevant in Article 102 cases. On the contrary, they are taken into account across the spectrum of the designed legal tests.

First, certain tests under Article 102 are focused on the structure of cost and profitability of the dominant undertaking, thereby considering the actual or likely results of the conduct under investigation on price and/or output. The most obvious examples of such unilateral exclusionary practices are predatory pricing and margin squeeze.[167] Particularly, the legal frameworks for analysing both these

[160] Case 238/87 *AB Volvo v Erik Veng (UK) Ltd* ECLI:EU:C:1988:477, para 11.

[161] Eg, Case C-280/08P *Deutsche Telekom AG v Commission* ECLI:EU:C:2010:603, para 234.

[162] Eg, *Magill* (n 158).

[163] Eg, *E.ON Gas* (Case COMP/39.317) [2010] C(2010) 2863 final, paras 36–41.

[164] *cf Oscar Bronner*, Opinion of AG Jacobs (n 159), para 66.

[165] *Microsoft* (n 151), paras 648, 656 and 658.

[166] Akman (n 2) 135. This remains true for more recent cases as well, even though the Commission uses the term more actively in its documents.

[167] For predatory pricing see, eg, Case C-62/86 *AKZO Chemie BV v Commission* ECLI:EU:C:1991:286, paras 71–72; C-333/94P *Tetra Pak* (n 152), para 41; Case T-340/03 *France Télécom SA v Commission* ECLI:EU:T:2007:22, paras 130 and 195, upheld on appeal in Case C-202/07P, paras 33 and 36. For margin

pricing policies have as benchmarks the dominant firm's production costs and the price charged for the product or service.[168] Hence, the effects on near term productive efficiencies and the immediate interests of consumers in terms of price and output are examined. However, other consumer-related proxies are also considered in this context. For instance, in the case of predatory pricing, consumer choice is also a relevant proxy to the extent that it is not necessary to prove the possibility of recoupment in order to establish an abusive predatory pricing practice.[169]

Similarly, near-term efficiencies associated with price, output and production costs are the predominant proxies underpinning the presumption of legality for the assessment of quantity rebates and price discrimination under Article 102.[170] Starting with quantity rebates, they fall in principle outside the scope of Article 102 because they reflect cost savings made by a dominant firm in the context of a particular transaction. These savings may safely be regarded to stem from the dominant firm's superior efficiency, and hence the dominant firm is entitled to pass them on to customers in the form of lower prices. As regards price discrimination, charging differentiated prices alone is regarded compatible with Article 102 because it entails cost savings which may result in an increase of output.[171] This may potentially allow new consumer/customers to be reached and increase market participation.[172] Hence, price discrimination has beneficial effects to allocative and productive efficiencies when it is not part of an exclusionary device.

Finally, the proxies of consumer surplus and production efficiencies directly come into play in all Article 102 cases in the context of assessing efficiency claims.[173]

squeeze see, eg, Case T-5/97 *Industrie des Poudres Sphériques v Commission* ECLI:EU:T:2000:278, para 180; Case T-271/03 *Deutsche Telekom AG v Commission* ECLI:EU:T:2008:101, para 237, on appeal in C-280/08P (n 161), paras 177, 252–3; Case C-52/09 *Konkurrensverket v TeliaSonera Sverige AB* ECLI:EU:C:2011:83 (*TeliaSonera*), paras 32–46, 64–66, 74 and 112; Case T-398/07 *Kingdom of Spain v Commission* ECLI:EU:T:2012:173, paras 67–68; *Slovak Telekom* (n 157), paras 230–4, 243 and 252–5.

[168] Similarly on excessive pricing see *United Brands* (n 139), paras 248–52.

[169] C-202/07P *France Télécom* (n 167), para 112. In this vein P Nihoul, 'Freedom of Choice: The Emergence of a Powerful Concept in European Competition Law' (2012) 3 *Concurrences Review* 55, 59.

[170] For the assessment of quantity rebates see, eg, Case C-163/99 *Portuguese Republic v Commission* ECLI:EU:C:2001:189, para 50; Case T-203/01 *Manufacture Française des Pneumatiques Michelin v Commission* ECLI:EU:T:2003:250 (*Michelin II*), para 58; Case T-219/99 *British Airways* (n 152), para 246, on appeal in C-95/04P (n 152), para 84; T-155/06 *Tomra* (n 152), para 212; *Post Danmark II* (n 152), para 27. For the assessment of discriminatory practices see, eg, Case C-209/10 *Post Danmark I* (n 155), paras 30–39; Case C-525/16 *MEO – Serviços de Comunicações e Multimédia SA v Autoridade da Concorrência* ECLI:EU:C:2018:270, paras 25–26 and 31.

[171] *cf* Fumagalli, Motta and Calcagno (n 2) 191, arguing that it may also give greater incentives to invest, and thereby result in dynamic efficiency gains.

[172] ibid. The fact that price discrimination is subject to a legality rule under Article 102 is compatible with the economic interpenetration desired by the EU Treaties, because it may lead to increasing market participation.

[173] See, eg, *United Brands* (n 139), para 184; Case 311/84 *Centre belge d'études de marché – Télémarketing (CBEM) v SA Compagnie* ECLI:EU:C:1985:394, paras 26–27; *Magill* (n 158), para 55; Case T-228/97 *Irish Sugar plc v Commission* ECLI:EU:T:1999:246, para 189; T-340/03 *France Télécom* (n 167), para 217; *Microsoft* (n 151), paras 1091–167; Case T-193/02 *Laurent Piau v Commission* ECLI:EU:T:2005:22, paras 117–9; C-95/04P *British Airways* (n 152), paras 69 and 85–87; *TeliaSonera* (n 167), paras 75–76; *Post Danmark I* (n 155), paras 40–41; C-413/14P *Intel* (n 151), para 140. See also Priorities Paper (n 3), paras 28–31.

The relevant efficiencies, however, are not confined to economic considerations in terms of price and cost but may also consist of technical improvements in the quality of the goods or services.[174] In this regard, one may legitimately question the usefulness of the consumer surplus proxy when applied, for example, to multi-sided platforms usually resulting in 0€ markets for final consumers.[175] Even so, consumer surplus and production efficiency remain relevant, despite the fact that the EU courts have also consistently placed value on other aspects of consumer interest, including choice and innovation.[176]

All in all, the different proxies that the EU courts employ to find a distortion of the competitive process under Article 102 denote the plurality of consumer-related objectives pursued by the provision. In this regard, the EU courts consider that a 'Chicago-oriented' approach to Article 102, where static efficiencies are the only relevant concerns for its application, takes an unduly narrow view of the benefits of undistorted competition.[177] This approach seeks to keep markets contestable, open and accessible to newcomers so as to protect consumer interest.[178] The following section explains that economic inequality considerations are factored in the legal tests applied by the EU courts in abuse of dominance cases.

b. Economic Inequality is Factored in the Designed Legal Tests

Pursuing the objective of protecting consumer interest as described above is compatible with the idea that the application of Article 102 must avoid contradicting (re)distributive policy considerations that are aimed at establishing an internal market committed to a highly competitive social market.

First, the objective of protecting consumer interests may overall help address inequality in the context of the application of Article 102. This is so to the extent that Article 102 does not permit a dominant firm's conduct that would harm consumers while benefiting wealthy businesses and shareholders.[179] It must be stressed in this context that protecting consumer interest may in principle increase inequality

[174] Eg, *Microsoft* (n 151), para 1159. This is consistent with the provision of Article 101(3) TFEU, which has been used as a model for the progressive development by the CJEU of a second stage of analysis under Article 102.

[175] *cf* A Ezrachi, 'EU Competition Law Goals and the Digital Economy' (2018) *Oxford Legal Studies Research Paper* 17/2018, 6; J Crémer, Y-A de Montjoye and H Schweitzer, 'Competition Policy for the Digital Era' (Report commissioned by the Commission, EU, 2019) 20–22.

[176] *cf* V Daskalova, 'Consumer Welfare in EU Competition Law: What Is It (Not) About?' [2015] *Competition Law Review* 131, 151–2.

[177] W Wils, 'The Judgment of the EU General Court in Intel and the so-called "More Economic Approach" to Abuse of Dominance' (2014) 37 *World Competition* 405, 414.

[178] J Laitenberger, 'Enforcing EU Competition Law: Principles and Illustrations' (Brussels, 29 May 2018); Crémer, de Montjoye and Schweitzer (n 175) 14. *cf* F Etro and I Kokkoris, 'Toward an Economic Approach to Article 102 TFEU' in F Etro and I Kokkoris (eds), *Competition Law and the Enforcement of Article 82* (Oxford, OUP, 2010) 35, arguing that EU's approach to exclusionary practices is 'linked to a naïve version' of the post-Chicago School, which considers that market failures are not necessarily self-correcting.

[179] Baker and Salop (n 8) 16–17.

in instances where customers/consumers are wealthier than suppliers.[180] In any event, consistently with the definition of dominance,[181] the Commission has tended to enforce Article 102 against firms holding extreme market power, where their unequal and asymmetrical position compared to both their rivals and their customers and consumers were guaranteed.[182]

Second, protecting consumer interest under Article 102 incidentally protects SMEs from strategic and inefficient conduct where a dominant firm invests in an exclusionary fight. This is the case, for example, when a dominant firm charges predatory prices, grants exclusivity rebates, or implements tying practices. In such cases, SMEs' economic freedom would be eliminated because of a dominant firm's significant market power, rather than being the result of competition on the merits and superior performance.[183] It is worth recalling that, under a socially committed market economy, the competition rules must ensure a performance-based competition, where performance based on merits is rewarded. Thus, prohibiting these practices is justifiable in this context.[184] Be this as it may, by incidentally protecting SMEs, Article 102 also indirectly promotes the SMEs' beneficial by-products of improved distribution of income, employment growth, and overall social balance.

Overall, the designed tests for assessing the unilateral conduct of dominant firms are consistent with the constitutionally required holistic approach to Article 102. Particularly, the employed tests are compatible with equality-related concerns, and thus Article 102 indirectly accounts for inequality considerations. Therefore, Article 102 assists in the promotion of an internal market based on a highly competitive social market economy through the requirement of consistency between EU's policies.

B. Direct Relevance of Inequality

The previous section showed that the legal tests applied by the EU courts for the assessment of the unilateral conduct of dominant firms incorporate into the analysis

[180] Crane (n 27) 1175.

[181] *United Brands* (n 139), para 65. *cf Virgin/British Airways* (Case IV/D-2/34.780) Commission Decision 2000/74/EC [2000] OJ L30/1, which is the only finding of dominance under Article 102 where the firm held a market share of below 40%. See also Priorities Paper (n 3), para 14, stipulating that 'dominance is not likely if the undertaking's market share is below 40 % in the relevant market'.

[182] For recent enforcement actions see n 111. For an example of a Commission decision rejecting a complaint that was based on the identification of dominance in a narrowly defined market see *Greek Horse Race Betting* (Case AT.40265) [2016] C(2016) 5841 final. For a case where judicial review guaranteed the high threshold for the identification of dominance see Case T-691/14 *Servier SAS and Others v Commission* ECLI:EU:T:2018:922, para 1607, annulling the Commission's finding of dominance in a narrowly defined relevant market.

[183] See Deutscher (n 32), rightly stating that 'the Court consistently condemned dominant firm conduct that tends to make it more difficult for smaller firms to compete at arm's length – such as tying, predatory pricing, exclusive dealing, and rebates – as obstacles to economic opportunities of smaller, independent competitors'.

[184] *cf* Talbot (n 65) 267.

of Article 102 equality-related considerations. As such, inequality concerns are in this context indirectly relevant to the analysis of abuse of dominance in that they are already factored in the tests for the assessment of the behaviour of an undertaking holding a dominant position. This section deals with a different technique that is (or may be) used to incorporate inequality considerations into the analysis of Article 102. In this context, inequality considerations come directly into play leading to the ad hoc non-application of Article 102, instead of only being indirectly relevant in the design of the relevant legal tests.

In this regard, this section first discusses the accommodation of services of general economic interest ('SGEI') into the analysis conducted under Article 102. Then, it turns to consider the existence of a *Wouters*-like rule and the concept of objective justification under Article 102. Hence, the section explores the possibility of balancing non-competition objectives, including (re)distributive policy considerations, against a restriction of competition.

i. SGEI under Article 106(2) TFEU

Article 102 is addressed to undertakings and, in principle, applies to anticompetitive conduct engaged in by undertakings on their own initiative. Nevertheless, the EU's particular feature of being a market without a state generates one of its competition law peculiarities, namely the concern about the compatibility of the Member States' activities with the rules of competition law. Member States often intervene in economic matters for socio-political reasons, such as to address income inequality through different taxation schemes and other redistributive policies.[185] However, this state involvement in economic activities may distort competition.[186] Thus, in order not to deprive the EU competition rules of their effectiveness, Article 106(1) TFEU imposes a prohibition addressed to Member States, which ensures their adherence to, inter alia,[187] the competition rules.[188] In this regard, Article 106(1) TFEU has particularly been applied in conjunction with Article 102 in order to determine whether the granting of exclusive or special rights to an undertaking by a Member State has led to an abuse of dominance which may be attributed to that Member State.[189]

[185] See generally JLB Sierra, *Exclusive Rights and State Monopolies under EC Law: Article 86 (former Article 90) of the EC Treaty* (A Read tr, Oxford University Press 1999); OECD, 'Regulating Market Activities by the Public Sector' (DAF/COMP(2004)36, 1 February 2015).

[186] *cf* TFEU, Art 119. See also Case C-198/01 *Consorzio Industrie Fiammiferi (CIF) v Autorità Garante della Concorrenza e del Mercato* ECLI:EU:C:2003:430, para 47, stressing the importance of Art 119 TFEU.

[187] According to its wording, the provision is not limited in its scope only to the competition rules.

[188] In this vein, eg, Case C-13/77 *SA G.B.-INNO-B.M. v Association des détaillants en tabac (ATAB)* ECLI:EU:C:1977:185, para 31. For a good discussion of the relevant case law see Joined Cases C-94 and C-202/04 *Cipolla and Others* [2006] ECLI:EU:C:2006:76, Opinion of AG Maduro, paras 31–40.

[189] Eg, Case C-41/90 *Klaus Höfner and Fritz Elser v Macrotron GmbH* ECLI:EU:C:1991:161; Case C-260/89 *Elliniki Radiophonia Tiléorassi AE and Panellinia Omospondia Syllogon Prossopikou v Dimotiki Etairia Pliroforissis and Sotirios Kouvelas and Nicolaos Avdellas and Others* ECLI:EU:C:1991:254; Case C-179/90 *Merci convenzionali porto di Genova SpA v Siderurgica Gabrielli SpA* ECLI:EU:C:1991:464;

However, to ensure the ability of Member States to organise certain matters of public interest in their own territory in a manner that better fits the situation of their citizens, Article 106(2) TFEU restricts the scope of application of the competition rules.[190] In this context, Article 106(2) TFEU shows tolerance to national interests by allowing for a derogation from the competition rules, in an attempt to strike a balance between the market-oriented objectives of EU competition law and the Member States' interest in providing quality, safe and affordable SGEI.[191] The underlying idea is that an undertaking that has been entrusted with the performance of SGEI may not effectively do so if it is subjected to a fully competitive market.[192] Examples of such services may include: the operation of a universal postal service;[193] the provision in certain sectors of non-economically viable services (eg, mooring services in ports);[194] waste processing;[195] pension schemes fulfilling a social function;[196] ambulance services;[197] and the provision of private medical insurance.[198]

Even so, Article 106(2) TFEU does not exempt undertakings entrusted with SGEI per se from the competition rules. The provision provides for a derogation from the application of the competition rules for these undertakings only to the extent that the application of competition law would obstruct the performance, in law or in fact, of the tasks assigned to them. Additionally, it is not possible to rely on this derogation if the development of trade would be affected to such an extent that it would be contrary to the interest of the EU. Indeed, being a derogation from the application of Articles 101 and 102, the EU courts have ruled that

Case C-18/88 *Régie des télégraphes et des téléphones v GB-Inno-BM SA* ECLI:EU:C:1991:474; Case C-320/91 *Criminal proceedings against Paul Corbeau* ECLI:EU:C:1993:198; Case C-49/07 *Motosykletistiki Omospondia Ellados NPID (MOTOE) v Elliniko Dimosio* ECLI:EU:C:2008:376; Case C-553/12P *Commission v Dimosia Epicheirisi Ilektrismou AE (DEI)* ECLI:EU:C:2014:2083.

[190] T Prosser, 'EU competition law and public services' in E Mossialos et al (eds), *Health Systems Governance in Europe: The Role of European Union Law and Policy* (Cambridge, Cambridge University Press, 2010).

[191] Commission, 'Green Paper on Services of General Interest' COM(2003) 270 final, para 17, defining SGEI as 'services of economic nature which the Member States or the [Union] subject to specific public service obligations by virtue of a general interest criterion'. For a similar definition see Commission, 'A Quality Framework for Services of General Interest in Europe' (Communication) COM(2011) 900 final, 3. See also TFEU, Art 14; Protocol No 26 (n 40), Art 1, establishing SGEI as 'shared values of the Union', thus recognising their important social usefulness.

[192] For an analysis focusing on healthcare access see ch 9 in this volume.

[193] Eg, *Corbeau* (n 189), para 15; Joined Cases C-147, 148/97 *Deutsche Post AG* ECLI:EU:C:2000:74, para 44.

[194] Case C-266/96 *Corsica Ferries France v Gruppo Antichi Ormeggiatori del porto di Genova and Others* ECLI:EU:C:1998:306, para 45.

[195] Case C-203/96 *Chemische Afvalstoffen Dusseldorp and Others v Minister van Volkshuisvesting, Ruimtelijke Ordening en Milieubeheer* ECLI:EU:C:1998:316, para 67; Case C-209/98 *Entreprenørforeningens Affalds/Miljøsektion (FFAD) v Københavns Kommune* ECLI:EU:C:2000:279, para 75.

[196] *Albany International* (n 47), para 105.

[197] Case C-475/99 *Firma Ambulanz Glöckner v Landkreis Südwestpfalz* ECLI:EU:C:2001:577, para 55.

[198] Case T-289/03 *British United Provident Association Ltd (BUPA), BUPA Insurance Ltd and BUPA Ireland Ltd v Commission* ECLI:EU:T:2008:29, paras 206–7; Case C-437/09 *AG2R Prévoyance v Beaudout Père et Fils SARL* ECLI:EU:C:2011:112, paras 80–81.

Article 106(2) TFEU must be construed narrowly.[199] Ultimately, the scope of the derogation contained showed in Article 106(2) TFEU depends on the EU courts' appreciation of the proper degree of discretion that should be left to Member States in this area.[200]

Considering that Article 106(2) TFEU is a derogation from the Treaty rules, it may be argued that the EU courts have shown willingness to accept claims that undertakings were shielded from the competition rules by virtue of that provision. This is evidenced in *Albany*, where the Court of Justice was faced with the question of whether the exclusive right conferred on a sectoral pension fund to manage a supplementary pension scheme could fall within Article 106(2) TFEU.[201] The Court was quick to assert that by exercising the exclusive rights granted to it, the dominant undertaking would be led to abuse its dominant position.[202] Thus, the focus was on the possible application of the derogation provided under Article 106(2) TFEU.[203] In this regard, the Court pointed out that the supplementary pension scheme fulfilled an essential social function within the Dutch pension system,[204] concluding that the removal of the exclusive right conferred on the sectoral pension fund might render impossible the performance of the SGEI entrusted to it under economically acceptable conditions.[205]

The derogation contained in Article 106(2) TFEU and the discretion for the provision of affordable SGEI enable Member States to pursue redistributive policies. SGEI are funded through national taxes and/or other schemes, which are generally designed to result in progressive redistribution. The discretionary space entitled to Member States when providing, executing, and organising SGEI, ensure their ability to promote greater social equity through more effective public policies that improve citizen access to services of general economic interest irrespective of their income and/or geographic location.[206] The intense political sensitivity of the issue is revealed by the fact that the Lisbon Treaty further reinforces the commitment of the EU and the Member States to support undertakings providing SGEI.[207] Particularly, the newly adopted Protocol No 26 annexed to the Treaties

[199] Case C-127/73 *Belgische Radio en Televisie and société belge des auteurs, compositeurs et éditeurs v SV SABAM and NV Fonior* ECLI:EU:C:1974:25, para 19; Case C-157/94 *Commission v Netherlands* ECLI:EU:C:1997:499, para 37.

[200] A Ezrachi, *EU Competition Law: An Analytical Guide to the Leading Cases*, 5th edn (Oxford, Hart Publishing, 2016) 349, illustrating the broad protection offered by the CJEU's interpretation of Art 106(2) TFEU.

[201] *Albany International* (n 47).

[202] ibid paras 94–97.

[203] ibid para 98.

[204] ibid para 105.

[205] ibid para 111.

[206] *cf* W Sauter, 'Services of General Economic Interest and Universal Service Obligations as an EU Law Framework for Curative Health Care' (2007) TILEC Discussion Paper 29.

[207] TFEU, Art 14; Protocol No 26 (n 40), Art 1, introducing a new legal basis for legislation concerning SGEI and interpretative provisions aimed at emphasising the importance attached by Member States to SGEI. See also Charter of Fundamental Rights of the European Union [2012] OJ C326/391 (CFREU), Art 36, stipulating that the EU recognises and respects access to SGEI.

emphasises the 'essential role and the wide discretion of national, regional and local authorities' in the provision of SGEI.[208]

All in all, the EU seems to be offering a sufficiently accommodating treatment to economic services with an important social dimension under Article 102. As a result, Member States are also allowed a wide discretionary space to promote policies of a redistributive nature via the market, without the constraints imposed by Article 102.[209] Article 106(2) TFEU embodies values of socio-political importance to Member States, which may act as ad hoc benchmarks against which EU institutions may exceptionally oppose competition law intervention so as to safeguard these values. Article 106(2) TFEU corroborates the holistic approach already discussed insofar as it ensures that inequality concerns are taken into account in the application of Article 102. Under Article 106(2) TFEU, however, these concerns directly come into play by determining the *in concreto* application of Article 102 in specific cases.

ii. The Wouters Doctrine and Objective Justification

The EU courts have also embraced the direct relevance of non-market-related values outside the scope of Article 106(2) TFEU irrespective of whether the undertakings concerned are entrusted with SGEI. Particularly, in a series of Article 101 judgments, the EU courts weighed restrictive competitive effects of agreements or decisions against the non-economic benefits resulting from them.[210]

This is well illustrated by the *Wouters* judgment, which concerned the conformity with Article 101 of a rule of the Dutch Bar Council prohibiting the partnership between lawyers and non-lawyers.[211] The judgment establishes that values of public interest that are of non-economic nature may be balanced against an identified competitive restriction.[212] In cases where the former outweighs the latter,

[208] Protocol No 26 (n 40), Art 2. See also CFREU, Art 36, reiterating this point.

[209] For an even wider discretionary space allowed to Member States see Case C-364/92 *SAT Fluggesellschaft mbH v Eurocontrol* ECLI:EU:C.1994:7, para 30; Case C-343/95 *Diego Calì & Figli Srl v Servizi ecologici porto di Genova SpA (SEPG)* ECLI:EU:C:1997:160, paras 22–25; Case C-67/96 *Albany International BV v Stichting Bedrijfspensioenfonds Textielindustrie* ECLI:EU:C:1999:28, Opinion of AG Jacobs, para 314; Case C-113/07P *SELEX Sistemi Integrati SpA v Commission* ECLI:EU:C:2009:191, paras 66–85, according to which Article 102 is not applicable to activities relating to the exercise of public powers or official authority. *cf* JW van de Gronden, 'Services of General Interest and the Concept of Undertaking: Does EU Competition Law Apply?' (2018) 41 *World Competition* 197, providing an alternative approach that would offer further scope for activities to be exempted from the reach of EU competition law.

[210] Whish and Bailey (n 145) 138–40, arguing that this jurisprudence recognises the idea of 'regulatory ancillarity', referring to the fact that the restrictions of competition in these cases were ancillary to a regulatory function. For a general discussion of the concept of ancillarity under Article 101(1) see Commission, 'Guidelines on the Application of Article 81(3) of the Treaty' [2004] OJ C101/97, paras 28–31.

[211] Case C-309/99 *Wouters and Others v Algemene Raad van de Nederlandse Orde van Advocaten* ECLI:EU:C:2002:98.

[212] *cf* Commission, 'White Paper on Modernisation of the Rules Implementing Articles 85 and 86 of the EC Treaty' [1999] OJ C132/1, para 57, claiming that the purpose of Article 101(3) is 'to provide a

Article 101(1) would not apply at all.[213] The *Wouters* doctrine has been confirmed by subsequent judgments and has been extended to cover cases dealing with the integrity of legal profession and sports.[214]

Even though this case law concerns Article 101, the reasoning process is clearly transplantable to situations under Article 102. In fact, in certain of these cases the parties involved are, most likely, dominant players in their respective markets. To the extent that the values and interests considered under this case law are not specific to Article 101, there is no rational reason to exclude non-economic variables from the analysis under Article 102.[215] Hence, the *Wouters* doctrine offers a tool allowing the EU courts to balance restrictions of competition against a range of values of public interest under both Articles 101 and 102.[216]

Indeed, the CJEU has previously addressed claims by dominant firms that their particular course of action is objectively justified by public interest considerations of a non-economic nature. Particularly, in both *Hilti* and *Tetra Pak II*, the undertakings concerned attempted to justify their allegedly abusive tying practices on grounds of safety and public health considerations.[217] In both cases, the General Court held that in the particular circumstances of these cases:

> it is clearly not the task of an undertaking in a dominant position to take steps on its own initiative to eliminate products which, rightly or wrongly, it regards as dangerous [...].[218]

In *Hilti* particularly, this was so because in the relevant Member State there existed laws in relation to these issues as well as public authorities vested with powers to enforce them.[219] However, in none of these cases the EU courts excluded, as a

legal framework for the economic assessment of restrictive practices and not to allow application of the competition rules to be set aside because of political considerations'. Perhaps, then, non-economic values are to be considered under Article 101(1).

[213] See generally G Monti, 'Article 81 EC and Public Policy' (2002) 39 *Common Market Law Review* 1057. *cf* I Forrester, 'Where Law Meets Competition: Is Wouters Like a Cassis de Dijon or a Platypus' in C-D Ehlermann and I Atanasiu (eds), *European Competition Law Annual 2004: The Relationship Between Competition Law and the (Liberal) Professions* (Oxford, Hart Publishing, 2006).

[214] Case C-519/04P *David Meca-Medina and Igor Majcen v Commission* ECLI:EU:C:2006:492, paras 43 and 46–55; Case C-1/12 *Ordem dos Técnicos Oficiais de Contas v Autoridade da Concorrência* ECLI:EU:C:2013:127, paras 94–95; Case C-136/12 *Consiglio nazionale dei geologi and Autorità garante della concorrenza e del mercato* ECLI:EU:C:2013:489, paras 52–57.

[215] See especially Case 6/72 *Europemballage Corporation and Continental Can Company Inc. v Commission* [1973] ECLI:EU:C:1973:22 (*Continental Can*), para 25, holding that the competition provisions in the Treaty are pursuing the same aim. See also Joined Cases C-501, 513, 515 and 519/06P *GlaxoSmithKline Services Unlimited v Commission* ECLI:EU:C:2009:610, para 63; Case C-8/08 *T-Mobile Netherlands BV, KPN Mobile NV, Orange Nederland NV and Vodafone* ECLI:EU:C:2009:343, para 38.

[216] *cf* S Weatherill, *The Internal Market as a Legal Concept* (Oxford, Oxford University Press, 2017) 108, naming this a '*Cassis*-inspired approach' to stress the functional similarities between the approach in *Wouters* and the *Cassis de Dijon* formula encountered in free movement law. On the similarities between *Wouters* and free movement law see also R O'Loughlin, 'EC Competition Rules and Free Movement Rules: An Examination of the Parallels and their Furtherance by the ECJ Wouters Decision' (2003) 24 *European Competition Law Review* 62.

[217] T-30/89 *Hilti* (n 152), para 33; T-83/91 *Tetra Pak II* (n 151), para 79.

[218] T-30/89 *Hilti* (n 152), para 118, upheld on appeal in Case C-53/92P ECLI:EU:C:1994:77; T-83/91 *Tetra Pak II* (n 151), paras 83–84 and 138, upheld on appeal in Case C-333/94P ECLI:EU:C:1996:436.

[219] T-30/89 *Hilti* (n 152), para 118. Similarly see, in the context of Article 101, Case C-68/12 *Protimonopolný úrad Slovenskej republiky v Slovenská sporiteľňa a.s.* ECLI:EU:C:2013:71, para 20.

matter of principle, the relevance of these or similar non-economic considerations. On the contrary, the General Court considered at length the dominant firms' claims relating to safety and public health before concluding that the relevant practices constituted abuses.[220] In any event, based on these judgments, the Commission has affirmed that non-economic concerns of this kind are directly relevant in the context of objectively justifying a conduct under Article 102.[221] Depending therefore on the circumstances of each case, values not related to market competition may be directly relevant to the assessment of the unilateral conduct of a dominant firm. In this regard, successful reliance on such non-economic considerations would lead to the ad hoc exclusion of the application of Article 102. However, a successful claim based on such considerations would be an exceptional occasion.

The case law on the *Wouters* doctrine and the concept of objective justification under Article 102 has not so far addressed issues relating to (re)distributive policy considerations. Considering, however, that these judge-created legal constructs enable public policy considerations that are unrelated to market competition to find their way into the analysis, there is no reason to believe that the EU courts should or would ignore claims based on redistributive justice. Hence, in the context of these mechanisms, inequality-related considerations may, in principle, come directly into play in the context of a proportionality analysis, exceptionally leading to the ad hoc exclusion of the application of Article 102. After all, this would ensure that Article 102 is interpreted and enforced in a manner that would not in the specific context contravene other distinct objectives that are pursued by the EU. This provides for the ad hoc reconciliation of the economic objectives of Article 102 with other policies of a social nature that the EU is committed to pursue.[222]

Altogether, the *Wouters* doctrine and the concept of objective justification under Article 102 reflect the holistic approach to competition law insofar as they include values unrelated to market competition in the analysis of the competition rules. In this context, just as under the framework of Article 106(2) TFEU, these values come directly into play in an ad hoc manner potentially leading to the exclusion of the application of Article 102.[223] The direct relevance of (re)distributive policy considerations in the application of Article 102 provides a certain degree of flexibility and displays tolerance to national public interests. Indeed, the fact that socio-political values act as ad hoc benchmarks in the analysis of Article 102 entails that they cannot be a priori specified in an exhaustive manner.[224] However,

[220] T-30/89 *Hilti* (n 152), paras 102–119; T-83/91 *Tetra Pak II* (n 151), paras 136–141.

[221] Priorities Paper (n 3), para 29.

[222] See, eg, S Holmes, 'Climate Change, Sustainability, and Competition Law' (2020) 8 *Journal of Antitrust Enforcement* 354, 388–9, arguing that sustainability could be used as a 'shield' against the use of Article 102, in the sense that a behaviour that would otherwise be abusive can be objectively justified if a firm engages in a proportionate behaviour to tackle environmental or climate change issues.

[223] *cf* Weatherill, *The Internal Market as a Legal Concept* (n 216) 108–9, arguing that functionally *Albany* and *Wouters* 'share an ambition to prevent a rigid application of competition law serving to disable pursuit of other distinct and worthwhile objectives'.

[224] *cf* ibid 109, concluding in this regard that '[t]he internal market is malleable as a legal concept'.

it should be recalled that only exceptionally they would lead to a derogation from the application of Article 102.[225]

V. Conclusion

This chapter finds that the constitutional structure of the EU demands a holistic approach to Article 102 TFEU. This constitutionally mandated holistic approach entails that inequality-related concerns and (re)distributive policy considerations may affect both the general interpretation and enforcement of Article 102 and its ad hoc application. Moreover, the discussion of the relevant case law documents that the designed legal rules successfully reconcile the market-oriented objectives of Article 102 with policies of a (re)distributive nature, thereby allowing the provision to operate according to the constitutional role imposed on it by the Treaties.

Conceptualising the EU courts' case law on abuse of dominance, it is demonstrated that two distinct techniques are employed for incorporating inequality concerns into the analysis of Article 102. The first technique incorporates inequality considerations in the analysis of Article 102 in an indirect manner. Under this technique, inequality-related values influence the design of the relevant tests and the Commission's enforcement choices, thus satisfying the constitutionally demanded consistency between EU's policies. However, considerations unrelated to market competition also come directly into play in the application of Article 102. Particularly, certain non-specified socio-political values, which include (re)distributive policy considerations, come directly into play in the context of a proportionality analysis, exceptionally leading to the ad hoc exclusion of the application of Article 102. Overall, both techniques reflect the holistic approach to Article 102 because they allow concerns related to wealth (in)equality and (re)distribution to find their way into the analysis of Article 102.

The relevance of wealth (in)equality and (re)distribution in the analysis of Article 102 does not contradict or replace the provision's economic objectives. In fact, to the extent that equality-related values are indirectly relevant for the interpretation of Article 102, the holistic approach is guiding the objectives pursued by the provision through the requirement of consistency between EU's policies. Turning to the direct relevance of these values, the practical amalgamation of the holistic approach with the ultimate goals pursued by Article 102 is ensured via the application of the principle of proportionality. In any event, the indirect relevance of equality and the ad hoc nature of the considerations that may exclude the application of Article 102, preclude the possibility of viewing them as goals pursued by Article 102.

[225] For an unsuccessful claim based on the *Wouters* doctrine see Case T-90/11 *Ordre national des pharmaciens (ONP) and Others v Commission* ECLI:EU:T:2014:1049, para 348.

6

Exploring Legal and Policy Options to Address the Competition-Inequality Nexus: The Case of South Africa

FIROZ CACHALIA AND ALEXANDER BEYLEVELD*

I. Introduction

In discussing some of the ways in which competition, and competition law and policy, could, and possibly should, play a role in addressing economic inequality in South Africa, it is important to understand that economic inequality in South Africa runs very deep. The top 10 per cent owned 87 per cent of aggregate national wealth and approximately 65 per cent of aggregate (pre-tax) annual national income accrued to the top 10 per cent of income recipients in 2017.[1] South Africa's colonial and Apartheid history of racial capitalism, moreover, has resulted in socio-economic inequality remaining highly racialised.[2] It is worth noting, however, that overall economic inequality has increased substantially since South Africa's transition to democracy in 1994, with the top one per cent wealth share increasing from a little under 50 per cent in 1994 to consistently being within the 54 to 58 per cent

* We are indebted to Kati Cseres and Jan Broulík for their tireless work as editors, especially for all the comments they provided on the various drafts leading up to this published version. Their guidance and insights have been most valuable. We are also grateful to Eleanor Fox who provided useful feedback on an early version of this chapter.

[1] A Chatterjee, L Czajka and A Gethin, 'Estimating the Distribution of Household Wealth in South Africa' [2020] WID.world Working Paper 2020/06; F Alvaredo and AB Atkinson, 'Colonial Rule, Apartheid and Natural Resources: Top Incomes in South Africa, 1903-2007' [2010] Centre for Economic Policy Research Working Paper Series 8155. The data contained in this paper have subsequently been updated for the World Inequality Database. See A Robilliard, '2020 DINA Update for Countries of the Africa Region' [2020] World Inequality Lab Technical Note 2020/03. The updated data are available on the website of the World Inequality Database. See wid.world/country/south-africa/ accessed 13 December 2021.

[2] See in this regard NS Makgetla, 'The Structural Dimensions of Inequality in South Africa: The Systemic Underpinnings of Inequality in South Africa' in Michael Nassen Smith (ed), *Confronting Inequality: The South African Crisis* (Johannesburg, Jacana Media, 2018); B Fine and Z Rustomjee, *The Political Economy of South Africa: From Minerals–Energy Complex to Industrialisation* (Johannesburg, Wits University Press, 1996) 111–112.

range in the 2010s and the top 10 per cent income share rising from approximately 47 per cent to consistently being in the 60 to 65 per cent range in the 2010s.[3]

While economic inequality has grown virtually everywhere around the world since 1994, both the absolute level of inequality and the rate at which it has grown is almost unprecedented in South Africa when viewed in comparative perspective. Consider the example of Brazil, another country known for its notoriously high levels of inequality. In 1994, the share of income accruing to the top 10 per cent in Brazil stood at around 55 per cent.[4] During the course of the next 20 years, that figure grew to around 56 per cent.[5] In India, the top 10 per cent share grew very rapidly from around 39 per cent to around 57 per cent, but remains significantly lower than the corresponding figure in South Africa.[6] In Russia, this figure grew from about 40 to 46 per cent.[7] In China, it went from approximately 34 per cent to 42 per cent.[8] In richer countries, inequality also grew in significant ways in this

[3] See Chatterjee, Czajka and Gethin (n 1); Alvaredo and Atkinson (n 1); Robilliard (n 1). We should add here that the tale of rising economic inequality has obviously not been the only story of importance in democratic South Africa. Access to education has been greatly extended, for example. Moreover, many measures have been taken, with varying levels of success, to address the legacies of apartheid, especially insofar as discrimination is concerned. These measures have enabled a significant number of black South Africans to access high income jobs and to begin accumulating the kind of wealth that the apartheid regime essentially outlawed. This has had important implications for the racial makeup of the top parts of economic distributions. Data on the top 10% of the income distribution make this clear: the share of black people in the top 10% increased from around 11% in 1993, to 18% in 1995, to 22% in 1996, to 25% in 2000, to 27.5% in 2008, and then, by 2017, it had increased further still to a figure in excess of 30%. While white people still make up a disproportionate share of the top 10%, then, its racial composition has changed in significant ways: the share of white people in the top 10% fell by about a third between 1993 and 2017, whereas the share of black people in the top 10% increased by 250% or more. See further in this regard J Seekings and N Nattrass, *Class, Race, and Inequality in South Africa* (New Haven, Yale University Press, 2005); A Finn, M Leibbrandt and I Woolard, 'Income and Expenditure Inequality: Analysis of the NIDS Wave 1 Dataset' [2009] NIDS Discussion Paper 2009/05; R Zizzamia, S Schotte and M Leibbrandt, 'Snakes and Ladders and Loaded Dice: Poverty Dynamics and Inequality in South Africa between 2008-2017' [2019] WIDER Working Paper 2019/25.

[4] See L Chancel and T Piketty, 'Countries with Regional Imputations on WID.World' [2020] World Inequality Lab Technical Note 2020/13. The full set of data is available on the website of the World Inequality Database. See wid.world/country/brazil accessed 13 December 2021.

[5] M De Rosa, I Flores and M Morgan, 'Inequality in Latin America Revisited: Insights from Distributional National Accounts' [2020] World Inequality Lab Technical Note 2020/02. The full set of data is available on the website of the World Inequality Database. See wid.world/country/brazil/ accessed 13 December 2021.

[6] See L Chancel and T Piketty, 'Indian Income Inequality, 1922-2015: From British Raj to Billionaire Raj?' (2019) 65 *Review of Income and Wealth* S33. The full set of data is available on the website of the World Inequality Database. See wid.world/country/india/ accessed 13 December 2021.

[7] See F Novokmet, T Piketty and G Zucman, 'From Soviets to Oligarchs: Inequality and Property in Russia 1905-2016' (2018) 16 *Journal of Economic Inequality* 189. The data contained in this paper have subsequently been updated for the World Inequality Database. See T Neef, '2020 DINA Update for the Russian Federation 2020 DINA Update for the Russian Federation' [2020] World Inequality Lab Technical Note 2020/05. The full set of data is available on the website of the World Inequality Database. See wid.world/country/russian-federation/ accessed 13 December 2021.

[8] See T Piketty, L Yang and G Zucman, 'Capital Accumulation, Private Property, and Rising Inequality in China, 1978-2015' (2019) 109 *American Economic Review* 2469. The data contained in this paper have subsequently been updated for the World Inequality Database. See M Jenmana, R Moshrif and L Yang, '2020 DINA Update for Asia' [2020] World Inequality Lab Technical Note 2020/08. The full set of data is available on the website of the World Inequality Database. See wid.world/country/china accessed 13 December 2021.

period. This is true for countries known for their low levels of inequality such as Denmark and Norway, where top 10 per cent shares grew from about 29 per cent to about 33 per cent and approximately 28 per cent to 31 per cent respectively.[9] It is also true for richer countries with higher levels of inequality such as the US, where the share of the top 10 per cent grew from around 39 per cent to 46 per cent.[10] These trends are captured in Figure 6.1.

Figure 6.1 Top 10 per cent pre-tax income shares in various countries: 1994 vs 2017

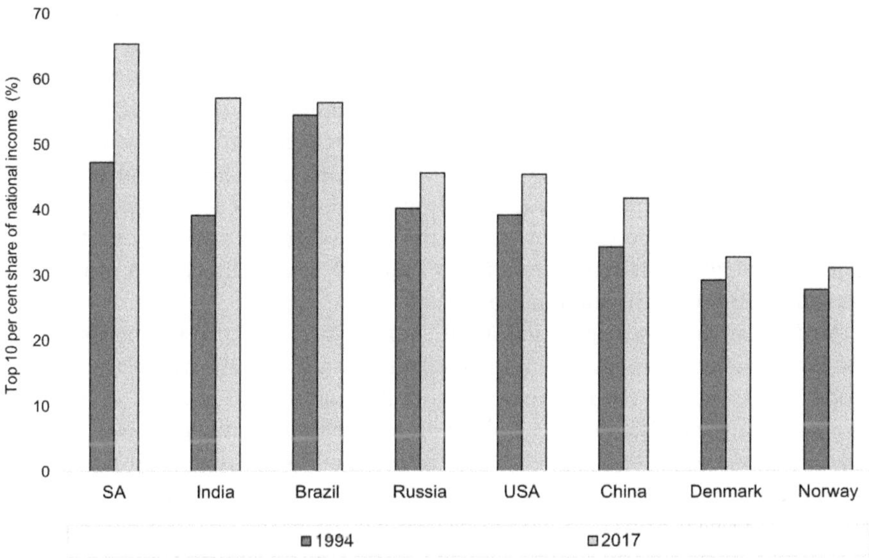

Data source: World Inequality Database (WID.world)

Similarly, *wealth* inequality in contemporary South Africa is very high. In 2015, the top 10 per cent owned around 87 per cent of aggregate national wealth, whereas the bottom 50 per cent share stood at approximately *negative* three per cent.[11]

[9] T Blanchet, L Chancel and A Gethin, 'Why Is Europe More Equal Than the United States?' [2020] WID.world Working Paper 2020/19. The data contained in this paper have subsequently been updated for the World Inequality Database. See M Morgan and T Neef, '2020 DINA Update for Europe' [2020] World Inequality Lab Technical Note 2020/04. The updated data are available on the website of the World Inequality Database. See wid.world /country/denmark/ and wid.world/ country/norway/ both accessed 13 December 2021.

[10] E Saez and G Zucman, 'The Rise of Income and Wealth Inequality in America: Evidence from Distributional Macroeconomic Accounts' (2020) 34 *Journal of Economic Perspectives* 3. The data contained in this paper have subsequently been updated for the World Inequality Database. See G Zucman, 'US Distributional National Accounts: Updates' [2020] Technical Note. The full set of data is available on the website of the World Inequality Database. See wid.world/country/usa/ accessed 13 December 2021.

[11] See Chatterjee, Czajka and Gethin (n 1).

At the same time, the top 10 and bottom 50 per cent shares in China, while also very high, stood at around 67 and 6 per cent respectively.[12] In the US, inequality was even higher than in China, but still quite significantly lower than in South Africa, with the top 10 and bottom 50 per cent shares at about 73 and 1 per cent respectively.[13]

Despite South African economic inequality being comparatively high, it is important to understand that rising inequality is not a challenge which is unique to South Africa. As Figure 6.1 begins to show, rising within-country inequality has been a *global* phenomenon of a *systemic* nature. While very different policy choices have been made in different parts of the world – and while it is true that inequality has grown at very different rates in different countries – economic inequality has risen virtually everywhere.[14] Moreover, there are numerous underlying causes of rising domestic inequality, many of which are associated with forms of economic globalisation. These include a country's openness to trade, the extent of capital market liberalisation, as well rapid technological changes – phenomena such as digitalisation, the consequent rise of the data economy and the onset of the so-called Fourth Industrial Revolution – many of which threaten to exacerbate inequalities, if they have not done so already.[15]

Aside from acknowledging its causal complexities, it is also important for us to make explicit why rising economic inequality matters in the first place. We see at least three reasons. The first reason is moral in nature and goes to questions of justice and fairness. The extent to which an economic system yields 'just' or 'fair' outcomes is a matter for considerable debate. When do outcomes become 'unfair' or 'unjust'? Are we only concerned with distributional shifts that are detrimental to equality of opportunity or intergenerational mobility? Or should we determine whether inequality is justifiable by applying a Rawlsian lens,[16] or perhaps with reference to the notion of 'substantive equality' in the sense that this term is deployed in South African constitutional law and scholarship?[17] We do not offer extensive answers to these questions in this chapter, but it seems clear to us that present levels of economic inequality in South Africa are unjust and unfair from numerous moral standpoints, albeit that there is room to debate the exact extent to which this is the case.

[12] See Piketty, Yang and Zucman (n 8); Jenmana, Moshrif and Yang (n 8).

[13] See Saez and Zucman (n 10); Zucman (n 10).

[14] For an extensive overview of inequality trends within countries around the world, see the second chapter of AD Beyleveld, *Taking a Common Concern Approach to Economic Inequality: Implications for (Cooperative) Sovereignty over Corporate Taxation* (Leiden, Brill, 2022).

[15] On the varying causes of rising inequality, see, eg, JD Ostry, P Loungani and A Berg, *Confronting Inequality: How Societies Can Choose Inclusive Growth* (New York, Columbia University Press, 2019) 23.

[16] In this regard, see, eg, C Pike, 'Rawlsian Antitrust' [2021] Centre for Competition Policy Working Paper 21-04.

[17] On this notion, see, eg, C Albertyn, 'Contested Substantive Equality in the South African Sonstitution: Beyond Social Inclusion Towards Systemic Justice' (2018) 34 *South African Journal on Human Rights* 441. There are also various other perspectives on why inequality matters. See, eg, TM Scanlon, *Why Does Inequality Matter?* (Oxford, Oxford University Press, 2018).

The second problem we see with present levels of economic inequality is that it appears to be harming the level and sustainability of economic growth in South Africa. While it seems to be the case that some economic inequality is acceptable – or even desirable – from a growth perspective, inequality levels currently observed in South Africa are probably highly detrimental to growth, as well as to its poverty alleviating effects.[18]

The third problem, and the one we emphasise most here, is the impact of rising economic inequality on the very functioning of South Africa's constitutional democracy. In his cross-national study of richer democracies, Frederick Solt proposes that 'greater inequality increases the relative power of the wealthy to shape politics in their own [favour] against rival arguments that focus on the effects of inequality on citizens' objective interests or the resources they have available for political engagement'.[19] Solt concludes that higher levels of income inequality are only detrimental to the political interest of poorer segments of the population.[20] We are persuaded by his argument that greater *economic* inequality yields greater *political* inequality.[21]

Christian Houle studies an even broader range of democracies – 140 of them, including South Africa.[22] Houle makes the valid point that 'democracy and political equality, although related, are distinct concepts' and then comes to the conclusion that 'economic inequality tends to increase political inequality, even when one controls for the level of democracy'.[23] As for causal mechanisms, Houle identifies at least four: economic inequality increases the resources of the rich relative to the poor; it widens the gap in policy preferences across income groups; it reduces participation; and it depresses support for democracy.[24]

[18] According to one study, 'growth and inequality codetermine one another in South Africa' in that '[g]rowth determines inequality' and 'inequality impacts growth' with '[b]oth associations [being] benevolent, in the sense that growth lowers inequality, and falling inequality in turn serves to stimulate growth'. See JW Fedderke, 'Growth and Inequality: The South African Case in International Context – The Central Role of the Labor Market' (2019) 3 *Journal of Development Perspectives* 191, 191. Grigoli and Robles come to more intricate conclusions in their extensive cross-country study. The authors find 'pervasive evidence of nonlinearities' in their dataset and 'identify an inequality overhang level in that the slope of the relationship between income inequality and economic development switches from positive to negative at a net Gini of about 27 percent'. South Africa has a net Gini coefficient well more than twice that, which suggests that inequality is not only a drag on growth, but a significant one. On the non-linear relationship between inequality and growth, see further F Grigoli and A Robles, 'Inequality Overhang' IMF Working Paper (2020) www.imf.org/en/ Publications/ WP/Issues/2017/03/28/Inequality-Overhang-44774 accessed 7 March 2022. On the extent to which inequality affects the extent to which growth alleviates poverty, see F Bourguignon, 'The Poverty-Growth-Inequality Triangle?' in Research Department, Agence Française de Développement (ed), *Poverty, Inequality and Growth: Proceedings of the AFD-EUDN Conference, 2003* (Paris, Maggelan, 2004) 85–98.

[19] F Solt, 'Economic Inequality and Democratic Political Engagement' (2008) 52 *American Journal of Political Science* 48, 48.

[20] ibid 48.

[21] ibid 48.

[22] C Houle, 'Does Economic Inequality Breed Political Inequality?' (2018) 25 *Democratization* 1500.

[23] ibid.

[24] ibid.

We view all of these factors as potentially being applicable to South Africa. As economic inequality has grown, it may be difficult to deny that the rich – especially the top one per cent of the income and wealth distributions – have become even more politically powerful vis-à-vis everyone else.[25] It may also be leading to a widening gap in policy preferences between the rich and everyone else, and there is also evidence to suggest that ever since South Africa's transition to democracy, during which period economic inequality has risen significantly, political participation has decreased and so has the support for democracy.[26]

Tim Wu has drawn attention to growing concentration of wealth and power in the US, particular in the 'platform economy', and its deleterious impact on democracy. He writes that '[w]hat … must [be realised] is that, once again, we face what Louis Brandeis called the "Curse of Bigness," which, as he warned, represents a profound threat to democracy itself'.[27] For us, although the contexts are different, this rings true. The coalescence of the economic and the political in South Africa implies that as economic concentration fuels growing economic inequality, that growing economic inequality will almost inevitably be converted into greater *political* inequality, which will in turn tend to be leveraged in ways which lead to further economic concentration (or at the very least reinforce existing levels of concentration), all of which tends to impede the realisation of the aspirational vision of the South African Constitution for the vast majority of those to whom it applies as economic and political elites act in concert in ways which disproportionately benefits themselves. Over time, this will (and to a large degree already has) lead to mass-disillusionment and possibly to constitutional democracy itself losing legitimacy because its central value of political equality is proved to be hollow.

Against this particular backdrop, and given too that the extent of competition in an economy has increasingly been identified as one among the many causes of economic inequality, the aim of this chapter is to explore to what extent income and wealth inequality considerations could, and arguably should, inform the development and implementation of *competition* law and policy *in South Africa*. We seek to achieve this aim by adopting a two-part structure. First, we examine what we refer to as the 'competition-inequality nexus', unpacking the relationship

[25] Standing explains that in a system of 'Rentier Capitalism' – a kind of system that becomes likely as economic inequality rises – '[p]owerful rentiers have ways of capturing the state and commodifying politics, while politicians can use rental income to indulge in clientelistic practices that help them stay in office'. See G Standing, *The Corruption of Capitalism: Why Rentiers Thrive and Work Does Not Pay* (London, Biteback, 2016) 241. In the South African case, this helps explain the country's experience with the phenomenon described as 'state capture'.

[26] See, eg, D Dryding, 'Are South Africans Giving Up on Democracy?' [2020] *Afrobarometer Dispatch* 372, available at afrobarometer.org/sites/default/files/publications/D%C3%A9p%C3% AAches/ab_r7_dispatchno372_are_south_africans_giving_up_on_democracy.pdf accessed 13 December 2021. Recently, turnout during the 2021 local government elections in South Africa hit a record low for all elections that have been held since 1994.

[27] T Wu, *The Curse of Bigness: Antitrust in the New Gilded Age* (New York, Columbia Global Reports, 2018) 13.

between the extent of *competition* (as opposed to competition *law and policy*), on the one hand, and the extent of economic inequality, on the other, with an appropriate level of specificity for the discussions that follow later in the chapter (section II). Section II makes it clear that there is a relationship between the level of competition and inequality observed in an economy plausibly exists, including in South Africa, and it is this relationship that serves as the motivation for examining competition law and policy in South Africa with a view to interrogating to what extent current and potential future iterations of law and policy could contribute to addressing certain outcomes that stem from the competition-inequality nexus in the next section (section III).

Ultimately, we conclude that competition law is no panacea, but that it has the potential of being utilised as one among many imperfect tools that, when deployed in a carefully coordinated way, could contribute to the reduction of economic inequality in South Africa, which may in turn improve the functioning of South Africa's constitutional democracy, simultaneously – perhaps even as a result – rendering South Africa a more economically just and fair country with improved levels of economic growth.

II. Unpacking the Competition-Inequality Nexus

In recent times, scholars have repeatedly found evidence for the proposition that deviations from 'perfectly competitive' markets may contribute to rising economic inequality.[28] Sean Ennis, Pedro Gonzaga and Chris Pike, for example, have examined the extent to which market power, which the authors define 'as the ability to drive prices and returns above competitive levels', contributes to rising economic inequality.[29] The authors explain that '[t]he existence of market power has a dual effect on the income distribution, not only generating higher economic profits for business owners, but also imposing higher prices on consumers'.[30] As such '[t]he wealthy, while paying more for goods, will at the same time receive higher profits from market power, due to their generally higher ownership of the stream of corporate profits and capital gains'.[31] This leads to a situation where '[t]he increased margins charged to customers as a result of market power will disproportionately

[28] See, eg, J Stiglitz, *The Price of Inequality: How Today's Divided Society Endangers Our Future* (New York, WW Norton, 2012); J Stiglitz, 'Inequality, Stagnation, and Market Power: The Need for a New Progressive Era' [2017] Roosevelt Institute Working Paper; J Gans et al, 'Inequality and Market Concentration, When Shareholding Is More Skewed than Consumption' (2019) 35 *Oxford Review of Economic Policy* 550.

[29] SF Ennis, P Gonzaga and C Pike, 'Inequality: A Hidden Cost of Market Power' (2019) 35 *Oxford Review of Economic Policy* 518, 518.

[30] ibid 519.

[31] ibid.

harm the poor, who will pay more for goods without receiving a counter balancing share of increased profits'.[32]

In the same paper, Ennis, Gonzaga and Pike attempt to quantify the relationship between market power and rising inequality in a wide range of OECD countries:[33] their paper provides evidence that market power could conceivably contribute substantially to wealth *and* income inequality, augmenting the *wealth* of the richest 10 per cent of the population on average by 12–21 per cent and reducing the *income* of the poorest 20 per cent of the population by 11 per cent or more.[34] As the authors note, persons who are typically harmed by market power fall within the bottom 80 per cent of the income distribution, with those falling between the 20th and 60th percentiles suffering most in relative terms.[35]

For us, the first set of questions that the paper by Ennis, Gonzaga and Pike – and other similar papers – occasioned us to ask are definitional in nature. When the authors, for example, assert that '[t]he existence of market power has a dual effect on the income distribution, not only generating higher economic profits for business owners, but also imposing higher prices on consumers', it is not immediately clear whether they are referring to income or wealth or both. While they refer to the 'income distribution', the notion of 'higher economic profits for business owners' does not directly relate to the distribution of *income*, but rather to various forms of *wealth* owned by shareholders. While a closer reading of Ennis, Gonzaga and Pike does provide one with a better sense of what definitions they ascribe to different terms, definitional specificity is clearly helpful when discussing the extent to which a lack of competition may affect economic distributions. For this reason, we begin with providing some baseline definitions (section II.A). With these definitions in place, we proceed to unpack how what we call the 'competition-inequality nexus' operates (section II.B).

A. Definitions

First, let us begin by clarifying that when we refer to the 'competition-inequality nexus' without any caveats, we are referring to the extent to which the *level* of economic competition in a given 'national' economy contributes to the *level* of economic inequality among the inhabitants of the state or country that exercises its sovereignty over that economy. This is distinct from what one might call the 'inequality-competition' nexus, that is the extent to which the level of economic inequality among the inhabitants of the country that exercises sovereignty over a given economy contributes to the level of economic competition in that 'national'

[32] ibid.
[33] South Africa is *not* an OECD country.
[34] Ennis, Gonzaga and Pike (n 29) 532–539.
[35] ibid.

economy. The focus of this chapter is, for the most part, on the former of the two hypothetical constructs, not the latter.

Unless qualified, the phrase 'level of economic competition' as relied on in the two definitions above refers to the extent to which markets in a 'national' economy generally tend to deviate from 'perfect' competition. Here, we use 'perfect competition' loosely. The concept refers to product markets where no actor in that market, whether buyer or seller, possesses 'market power', which in turn means no actor possesses the ability to affect prices in that product market through their own conduct. Other standard 'perfect competition' assumptions apply too: perfectly competitive markets have no or few barriers to entry or exit, and all buyers and sellers have more or less full access to the information relevant to their production and consumption decisions. In reality, very few perfectly competitive markets exist. That said, the construct of a perfectly competitive market can helpfully be placed on the one end of a continuum, with deviations from that construct progressively stretching to a complete lack of competition; that is, to a situation where a market consists of a perfect monopoly.

As for 'level of economic inequality', it refers to the manner in which income and wealth are distributed in a given country in a quantitative sense and the extent to which that state of affairs is justifiable in a qualitative sense. A country with no economic inequality in a quantitative sense would be one where all persons possess the same amount of wealth and receive the same amount of income. On the opposite end of the scale is a country where one individual possesses all wealth and receives all income. We will be careful here to distinguish between 'income', which is an annual flow of money, from 'wealth', which is a stock at a given point in time, and consists of tangible and intangible assets, and includes real estate or land, shares in companies, savings and pensions, and so forth. We feel the need to point out the obvious here: despite serious attempts, no country has ever managed to attain *perfect equality* in a *quantitative* sense. We are accordingly again dealing with a broad spectrum of possible outcomes – a spectrum which becomes even more complicated when viewed *qualitatively*, for example by adding considerations of justice, fairness or equity into the mix – and we should therefore be careful not to think in binary terms.

It is also important for us to note that when we speak of the manner in which the competition-inequality nexus operates, we are generally speaking about the *quantifiable* effects the state of competition in the South African economy has on economic distributions. In looking at how the nexus operates, then, it is not our aim to suggest that all shifts in economic distributions towards one end of the spectrum are necessarily problematic, or that the underlying causes of all shifts can and/or should be addressed by competition law and policy. Which effects are problematic and what competition law and policy should do about them should be approached with a fair deal of caution, especially given that we are working with an imprecise and contestable understanding of what levels of economic inequality are desirable and justifiable in South Africa in both quantitative and qualitative senses.

B. The Competition-Inequality Nexus

We have already described the level of economic inequality in the introduction above, so we begin this section with a discussion on the level of economic competition that is observed in the South African economy (sub-section II.B.i). We then take a closer look at the mechanisms through which the competition-inequality nexus operates (sub-section II.B.ii). What we ultimately hope to show is that to the extent that competition law and policy lead to greater levels of competition, they may have a role to play in addressing economic inequality by containing 'market power'.

i. The Level of Economic Competition in the South African Economy

A recent study conducted by Thembalethu Buthelezi, Thando Mtani and Liberty Mncube constitutes a good illustration of the extent of product market concentration in South Africa.[36] The authors begin their paper with the oft-made observation that for much of its history, South Africa's product markets and capital ownership have been abnormally concentrated.[37] They also note that high market concentration has been characteristic not only of scale-dependent products but also consumer products,[38] and proceed to demonstrate that at least 70.45 per cent of South African sectors have defined markets with *dominant firms*.[39]

Buthelezi and his co-authors also use the Herfindahl–Hirschman index (HHI) as a proxy for product market *concentration*.[40] As the authors point out, the US Department of Justice considers markets with HHI scores below 1,500 to be 'un-concentrated', those with scores between 1,500 and 2,500 to be 'moderately concentrated', and those with scores above 2,500 as 'highly concentrated'.[41]

[36] T Buthelezi, T Mtani and L Mncube, 'The Extent of Market Concentration in South Africa's Product Markets' (2019) 7 *Journal of Antitrust Enforcement* 352.

[37] ibid. See also, eg, the discussions in N Chabane, S Roberts and A Goldstein, 'The Changing Face and Strategies of Big Business in South Africa: More Than a Decade of Political Democracy' (2006) 15 *Industrial and Corporate Change* 549; J Klaaren, 'Laying the Table: The Role of Business in Establishing Competition Law and Policy in South Africa' (2018) 33 *International Review of Applied Economics* 119.

[38] Buthelezi, Mtani and Mncube (n 36) 352.

[39] ibid 356. The authors rely on s 7 of the Competition Act 89 of 1998 (Competition Act or Act) in order to determine dominance. Section 7 requires a definition of the relevant market and a computation of market shares. If the market share of a firm is found to be more than 45%, a dominant position is presumed. See Buthelezi, Mtani and Mncube (n 36) 355. Section 7 also establishes two other methods for determining dominance, both of which require a market share of less than 45%. As such, the 70.45% figure is likely on the conservative side.

[40] As the authors explain, '[t]he HHI takes account of the differences in the sizes of market participants, as well as their number', it 'gives a score that can range from close to zero (when a market is occupied by a large number of firms of relatively equal size) to 10,000' and it 'takes the value of 10,000 in the monopoly case and declines as the level of concentration decreases'. See Buthelezi, Mtani and Mncube (n 36) 354–355.

[41] Buthelezi, Mtani and Mncube (n 36) 355.

They also explain that in the UK any relevant market with a post-merger HHI exceeding 1,000 may be regarded as 'concentrated' and any relevant market with a post-merger HHI exceeding 2,000 as 'highly concentrated'.[42]

Within this context, Buthelezi and his co-authors show that the average HHI for priority sectors in the South African economy between 2009 and 2016 all exceed 2,700,[43] with the financial services sector recording the lowest score on the spectrum (2,788) and the information and communication technologies sector recording the highest score on the spectrum (3,539).[44] By US and UK standards, this would mean that product markets in *all* of South Africa's priority sectors are highly concentrated, with concentration in most priority sectors significantly exceeding the thresholds for what constitutes 'highly concentrated'.

Not only are South African markets characterised by high levels of dominance and concentration, but they are also characterised by high and increasing *mark-ups*. As illustrated by the work of the likes of Vimal Thakoor, mark-ups have risen dramatically from already high levels since South Africa's transition to democracy in 1994:[45] '[o]n average, elevated market concentration has translated into higher prices, as firms have leveraged their market power to hike [mark-ups], albeit with heterogeneous effects across industries' and that '[n]etwork industries have passed on their inefficiencies to the broader economy, including through regulated prices and unreliable services'.[46] According to Thakoor, mark-ups in South Africa have increased by nearly 25 per cent since 2000, this compared to a global average increase of six per cent during the same period of time.[47]

Against this backdrop, we turn next to analysing the mechanisms through which the competition-inequality nexus operates in South Africa.

ii. How the Competition-Inequality Nexus Operates

While to our knowledge no economic study has been conducted on the extent to which the competition-inequality nexus operates in South Africa, we look at the Ennis, Gonzago and Pike model discussed above,[48] and add a number of

[42] ibid 355–356.

[43] For how the authors define 'priority sectors', see ibid 355.

[44] See Table 1 in Buthelezi, Mtani and Mncube (n 36) 358.

[45] V Thakoor, 'Market Power, Growth, and Inclusion: The South African Experience' (International Monetary Fund 2020) IMF Working Papers WP/20/206.

[46] Thakoor (n 45) 5.

[47] ibid 8.

[48] Buthelezi and his co-authors also allude to this mechanism, noting that '[i]llegitimate market power is often associated with creating barriers to entry, keeping outsiders out of markets and is a major source of inequality', clarifying further that '[t]he monopolist's monopoly rents come at the expense of consumers: as monopolies raise their prices, their profits increase while the well-being of consumers and workers decrease'. See Buthelezi, Mtani and Mncube (n 36) 353. An additional question of importance – one which we do not address in this chapter – goes to the extent to which competition enforcement since the adoption of the Competition Act has done enough to countract rising mark-ups. In principle, competition law enforcement that leads to lower mark-ups is likely to result in less

additional observations of our own. We also acknowledge that there remains a live debate about the extent to which models such as the Ennis, Gonzago and Pike model hold,[49] but, for the reasons discussed below, it at the very least seems plausible to us that the model does hold, and that it holds for South Africa specifically. Additionally, we see no reason for this model to be inconsistent with other identified causes of rising economic inequality.[50]

With these caveats out of the way, we start from the product market perspective with the idea that a firm with market power sets prices at levels higher than they would in a perfectly competitive market. This results in that firm realising higher profits than it otherwise would. When the economy as a whole is characterised by markets of this type, everyone that buys a particular product – wealthy and poor, income-rich and income-poor, and everyone else that falls between these extremes – faces higher prices than they otherwise would. The higher profits, however, do not accrue to everyone; rather, they accrue only to those with a financial interest in the firms that are realising higher profits than they otherwise would.

This has a number of important implications that we should unpack carefully. First, while all consumers likely face higher prices when firms wield market power, consumers are not a homogenous group. Simply put for current purposes, poor consumers, rich consumers and all consumers in between these two extremes do not necessarily face the same effective prices, even for roughly the same products.[51] As we return to this issue later in this chapter, the example of data services is apt. Poorer consumers tend to buy smaller amounts of mobile data than richer consumers do. Small amounts of mobile data, in turn, may carry higher mark-ups than larger amounts of data.[52] The pricing of data services firms with market power, then, may operate in a similar manner to a regressive tax – they may impose a disproportionate burden on those lower down the income distribution.[53]

Second, it is important to understand that, legally speaking, *profits* generally accrue to *companies or other forms of juristic persons*.[54] What is 'owned' in

unequal economic outcomes and this should be taken into account when thinking about how best to address the competition-inequality nexus.

[49] See, eg, L Taylor with O Ömer, *Macroeconomic Inequality from Reagan to Trump: Market Power, Wage Repression, Asset Price Inflation, and Industrial Decline* (Cambridge, Cambridge University Press, 2020).

[50] Including, eg, those proffered in Taylor and Ömer (n 49).

[51] There are numerous ways in which this may occur. Orhun and Palazzolo, for example, have illustrated how liquidity constraints faced by poorer households prevents them from purchasing groceries in bulk, which results in them paying higher prices than richer consumers for the same goods because richer consumers have the necessary liquidity to buy groceries in bulk. See further AY Orhun and M Palazzolo, 'Frugality Is Hard to Afford' (2019) 56 *Journal of Marketing Research* 1. We discuss a different example of this – relating to different prices faced by South African consumers in mobile data markets – in section III.C.ii below.

[52] See further the discussion in section III.C.ii below.

[53] It is perfectly conceivable, of course, that pricing of firms with market power could instead be progressive in other product markets.

[54] This flows from the fact that incorporation entails the creation of separate legal personality and the corporation or a similar form is the most frequently used legal device to bring firms into legal existence,

a legal sense are *shares or some other form of equity or debt*; that is, *wealth*, and not *income*.[55] To the extent that these forms of *wealth* generate *income* for their owners,[56] for example through the firm in question paying a dividend to its shareholders, 'higher economic profits' go to the question of income distribution.[57] However, it is quite possible that no income comes of a particular form of wealth in a given year, for example because a given company retains its earnings or because it makes a loss. In these instances, higher economic profits may leave the *income* distribution unaffected, at least for the year in question. Whether this is the case, of course, depends on whether shareholders hang onto their shares or sell them;[58] it also depends on the value of the company in question and how much it fluctuates over time.[59]

Increased economic profits may also affect the distribution of *wealth*, especially given that product prices are higher than they would be if markets were more competitive. Considering that in South Africa in 2017 the top one per cent of the wealth distribution owned around 99.8 per cent of total stocks and bonds, leaving the bottom 90 per cent with a cumulative share of 0.2 per cent,[60] which, at 34.6 per cent of total national wealth, accounted for the largest share of total wealth amongst all asset classes – then the fact that companies earn higher profits is likely to result in individuals at the upper end of the wealth distribution

at least in South Africa. We accept that other forms of entities, such as partnerships, may entail different (although similar) implications.

[55] On the distinction between income and wealth, see generally T Blanchet et al, 'Distributional National Accounts Guidelines: Methods and Concepts Used in the World Inequality Database' [2021] World Inequality Lab Guidelines. This distinction is important in the competition law context since it helps explain how market power contributes to wealth inequality *and* income inequality. As Abhijit Banerjee and Esther Duflo observe: '[M]onopolies or near monopolies make more profits, and those tend to be distributed to shareholders'. The pair go on to suggest that 'the increase in concentration thus helps explain why wages are not keeping pace with GDP'. See AV Banerjee and E Duflo, *Good Economics for Hard Times* (New York, PublicAffairs, 2019) 242.

[56] The mere fact that one owns certain wealth does not automatically mean that one will receive income in a given period.

[57] While shares are considered to be wealth, dividends paid to shareholders constitute income.

[58] If shareholders sell their shares, *income* flows from the sale. What happens to the wealth they owned depends on what they do with the income that flows from the sale of the shares – they may acquire other (more or less valuable) forms of wealth or they may spend the income on consumables – they may also do a combination of both.

[59] We note here Piketty's propositions about circumstances under which r > g, that is when 'r' – the rate of return on capital (as defined by Piketty) – exceeds 'g' – the growth rate of an economy – capital becomes relatively more important within that economy vis-à-vis other factors. Since wealth has historically tended to be more unequally distributed than income, it therefore follows that when r > g, and capital is accordingly becoming more important, the distribution of income will become more unequal. See further T Piketty, *Capital in the Twenty-First Century* (Cambridge MA, Harvard University Press, 2014) 336–76. As we understand it, Piketty's analysis shows that in order to understand the logic of r > g, one must also look to financial markets. This should be borne in mind when attempting to understand the competition-inequality nexus and the extent to which competition law may be a useful tool for addressing inequality – we would caution against a view of these issues that obscures the dynamics and drivers of inequality in a capitalist economic system.

[60] See Chatterjee, Czajka and Gethin (n 1) 21.

seeing their wealth grow by more than those at the lower ends of the distribution. Simultaneously, it is conceivable that consumers paying higher prices than they otherwise would affects saving propensities unevenly, with those at the lower end of the *income* distribution being affected disproportionately in the sense that it becomes more difficult for them to save and therefore convert income *into* wealth. When prices are regressive, the uneven nature of this effect would be compounded.

All of this should naturally be viewed with a good understanding of initial levels of economic inequality, as well as the relative shares of income accruing to labour and capital respectively, or where product market factors meet labour market factors. The relevance of the labour-capital income ratio is rooted in the (empirically sound) assumption that capital income is always less evenly distributed than labour income.[61] When this assumption holds, a shift toward a greater portion of total income accruing to capital and a lower portion of total income accruing to labour implies that income inequality will necessarily rise.[62]

In this context, Polus, Kopiński and Tycholiz argue that in the South African context 'capital concentration in the capital-intensive sectors, magnified by consolidation and mergers, yields economic structures that favour capital over labour', which 'in turn limits wealth accumulation in large swathes of the population, and, through the accrual mechanism, multiplies wealth in the hands of the owners of economic capital'.[63] Their argument is congruent with empirical evidence on the labour share of income, which according to one estimate fell by almost 10 per cent in the period 1995 to 2013,[64] as well as the fact that, as shown above, the wealth share of the bottom 50 per cent of the distribution has consistently been negative since 1994. This is mostly *indirectly* relevant to how the competition-inequality nexus operates, but it serves as important context. The fact that wealth concentration in South Africa is particularly high and that the South African economy is particularly capital intensive reinforces the extent to which a lack of competition may be converted into higher levels of economic inequality.[65]

Additionally, a lack of competition in product markets also seemingly plays a role in rendering *labour incomes themselves* more unequal. There is strong

[61] In this regard, see generally Piketty (n 59).

[62] Again, see generally Piketty (n 59).

[63] A Polus, D Kopiński and W Tycholiz, 'Reproduction and Convertibility: Examining Wealth Inequalities in South Africa' (2020) 42 *Third World Quarterly* 292, 301.

[64] ILO and OECD, 'The Labour Share in G20 Economies' [2015] Report prepared for the G20 Employment Working Group 6.

[65] That said, we note that there are other ways to address this problem outside of the competition realm. If stocks and bonds were to be become more equally distributed – as a result of redistributive policies, for example – then the manner in which the competition-inequality nexus operates would change, and the role of competition law in addressing it may shift. We return to this point in section III.D below.

evidence to suggest that workers in South Africa are strongly sorted by firm rent, ie 'workers who are highly paid *anywhere* are concentrated at high-rent firms'.[66] In other words, even if a particular worker's labour income is supressed by the market-power-wielding firm they work for, they are still highly likely to receive a significantly higher income than a worker at a firm *that does not possess market power*. According to one estimate, these between-firm wage-differentials account for the majority of labour income inequality in South Africa, ie for around 53–58 per cent for the 2011–2017 period.[67]

All the mechanisms identified above act in concert. While some of the evidentiary pieces of the puzzle remain missing – which warrants some caution when drawing conclusions – it seems to us that there is a good case to be made out that sub-optimal levels of competition in South Africa – that is, an economy characterised by high levels of product market concentration, a large number of markets where the largest firms hold market power and high mark-ups – has contributed to rising economic inequality in democratic South Africa. We turn next to some of the reasons we see this development as being harmful.

III. Some Options for Addressing Competition-Inequality Nexus in South Africa

We turn now to the role of South African competition law and take a look briefly at existing debates on what the rationales and scope of competition law and policy should be as a general proposition (section III.A). Next, we turn to the actual rationales and scope of South African competition law and policy and attempt to situate the approaches taken by the Competition Act, Competition Commission (Commission), Competition Tribunal (Tribunal) and Competition Appeal Court (CAC) within the broader debate discussed in section III.A (section III.B). We then turn our attention to two existing tools in South African competition law and policy which seem promising for addressing the competition-inequality nexus: merger control and market inquiries (section III.C). Having discussed these tools in section III.C, we then provide a preliminarily answer to the questions of what an appropriate role for competition law and policy is when addressing the competition-inequality nexus in South Africa and what changes to existing law and policy this may require (section III.D).

[66] See I Bassier, 'The Wage-Setting Power of Firms: Rent-Sharing and Monopsony in South Africa' [2019] WIDER Working Paper 2019/34.

[67] A Kerr, 'Measuring Earnings Inequality in South Africa Using Household Survey and Administrative Tax Microdata' [2021] WIDER Working Paper 2021/82 12.

A. The Rationale and Scope of Competition Law and Policy: A Tale of Two Paradigms

i. The Narrow Paradigm: Efficiency and Consumer Welfare

On the one end of our spectrum, we have a paradigm the genesis of which is most often attributed to the so-called Chicago School and US professor, solicitor general and judge, Robert Bork.[68] This paradigm, which could also be referred to as the 'welfare economics paradigm', focuses on what has often been dubbed, erroneously in our view,[69] the 'economic goals' of competition law; that is, from the perspective of this paradigm, competition law is supposedly value neutral and objective and should thus be applied in a technocratic way.[70] This paradigm, which has constituted the mainstream way of thinking in the US for decades now, is rooted in the idea that competition law should concern itself exclusively with 'efficiency' and 'consumer welfare'.

We have no intention of contesting the meaning of either of these concepts or adding to existing debates on this score. For us, the point is simply that from the perspective of this paradigm, the competition-inequality nexus is entirely irrelevant; the extent to which the level of competition in an economy affects the level of economic inequality is beyond its proper scope. Robert Bork himself was explicit about this in *The Antitrust Paradox*,[71] and it does not seem to us that proponents of the consumer welfare standard have deviated from Bork's arguments on this front. In any event, as will become clear below, we need not say much more about the narrow paradigm because South African competition law takes a broader view on the proper scope of competition law.

ii. The Broader Paradigm: Competition Law and Policy as Social Regulation and the Potential Incorporation of Inequality Concerns

We borrow the term 'social regulation' from Ioannis Lianos's paper 'Competition Law as a Form of Social Regulation'.[72] This type of competition law encompasses a range of different conceptions. However, the animating idea is essentially that competition law and policy are part 'economic' regulation – in the neoclassical

[68] The resource most often associated with this paradigm is RH Bork, *The Antitrust Paradox: A Policy at War with Itself* (New York, Basic Books, 1978). As Wu explains, however, the ideas contained in Bork's 1978 book had been finessed over a period spanning more than a decade. According to Wu, it was in fact Bork's 1966 paper, 'Legislative Intent and the Policy of the Sherman Act' which was the key, and 'arguably the most influential single antitrust paper in history'. See Wu (n 27), ch 4.

[69] We explain why in section III.B below.

[70] See, eg, JF Brodely, 'The Economic Goals of Antitrust: Efficiency, Consumer Welfare, and Technological Progress' (1987) 62 *New York University Law Review* 1020.

[71] See Bork (n 68) 110–112.

[72] See I Lianos, 'Competition Law as a Form of Social Regulation' (2020) 65 *Antitrust Bulletin* 3.

price theory sense – but that other 'non-economic' or 'social' regulatory goals also fall within the remit of competition law and policy.[73] Examples of 'social' regulatory goals that fall within the remit of the broader paradigm conceivably include a long list of considerations. For example, a number of developing countries have allowed industrial policy objectives and the desire to become internationally competitive in export-oriented sectors to influence the manner in which they implement competition laws and policies.[74] Elsewhere, arguments have been made for incorporating a variety of other factors into competition law and policy, including considerations or environmental protection,[75] as well as privacy protection.[76]

As we will see in the next section, South Africa has opted for a version of the broader paradigm.[77] We will also see that the particular version South Africa has opted for already enables it to address the competition-inequality nexus through competition law and policy, albeit that to do so is not mandatory and depends a great deal on how existing rules are interpreted and enforced.

B. The Rationale of Competition Law and Policy in Contemporary South Africa

The Competition Act contains a unique preamble which incorporates multiple goals. It provides that

> [t]he people of South Africa recognise … [t]hat apartheid and other discriminatory laws and practices of the past resulted in excessive concentrations of ownership and control within the national economy … [t]hat the economy must be open to greater ownership by a greater number of South Africans [and] … [t]hat an efficient, competitive economic environment, balancing the interests of workers, owners and consumers and focussed on development, will benefit all South Africans.[78]

It also requires regulation of 'the transfer of economic ownership in keeping with the public interest'.[79]

The purpose of the Act is to promote and maintain competition in the Republic in order, amongst other things, 'to promote the efficiency, adaptability and development of the economy; … to ensure that small and medium-sized enterprises

[73] See generally Lianos (n 72).

[74] For examples, see generally A Ciani et al, *Making It Big: Why Developing Countries Need More Large Firms* (Washington DC, World Bank Group, 2020).

[75] See, eg, S Kingston, 'Integrating Environmental Protection and EU Competition Law: Why Competition Isn't Special' (2010) 16 *European Law Journal* 780.

[76] See, eg, K Kemp, 'Concealed Data Practices and Competition Law: Why Privacy Matters' (2020) 16 *European Competition Journal* 628.

[77] As the South African case makes clear, this alone obviously does not result in more even distributional outcomes.

[78] Preamble to the Competition Act as amended by s 22 of Act 39 of 2000.

[79] ibid.

have an equitable opportunity to participate in the economy; … [and] to promote a greater spread of ownership, in particular to increase the ownership stakes of historically disadvantaged persons'.[80] The substantive provisions of the Act have to be understood, interpreted and enforced within the context provided by the preamble.

Although very aware of the scope of its mandate, the Commission has not explicitly taken a position on its role in addressing the competition-inequality nexus as conceived of in this chapter. It has frequently made vague references to 'inclusion' as opposed to the actual reduction of economic *inequality*. Although 'inclusion' and 'inequality' overlap, these notions are clearly distinct and semantic differences on this front may conceal deeper conceptual differences which require analysis.

To this end, in its strategic plan for 2015–2020, under the broader heading of 'effective competition enforcement and merger regulation', the Commission indicated that it 'intend[ed] to use its regulatory instruments to contribute to a growing and *inclusive economy*'.[81] The Commission continued to indicate that it aimed to achieve this by 'creating an enabling environment for small, medium and micro enterprises, promoting job creation and preventing job losses, preventing further concentration and supporting competition in industries which have the potential to drive economic growth in South Africa', adding that '[a]s such, the balance between efficiency and public interest is taken into account in its decision-making'.[82]

For the Commission, a balanced approach of this kind includes 'the imposition of innovative remedies which have positive material impact in the market … [and] imposing conditions in merger decisions which address competition and public interest considerations and monitoring compliance with those decisions'.[83] The outcomes the Commission hoped to achieve by taking such an approach were, amongst other things, the realisation of '[e]fficient and effective merger regulation' but also '[i]mproved public interest outcomes in markets (relating to jobs, industrialisation, exports, development of black-owned businesses and SMEs'.[84]

The Commission also customarily acknowledges that inequality forms part of the *context* in which it operates. For example, in its 2019–20 annual report, the Commissioner writes in the overview that '[o]ur economy continues to be characterised by stagnant growth, persistent high levels of unemployment and *increasing inequality* – which is gendered and racialised', that '[a]ll these challenges are certainly amplified by the impact of COVID-19', that '[i]t is therefore time for all of us to stand united, not only in fighting the pandemic but also in ensuring that

[80] Section 2 of the Competition Act as amended by Act 18 of 2018. Emphasis added.

[81] Competition Commission, *Strategic Plan: 2015-2020* (30 January 2015) 18 www.compcom.co.za/wp-content/uploads/2019/10/Strategic-Plan-2015-2020_Signed.pdf accessed 13 December 2021.

[82] ibid 18–19.

[83] ibid 19.

[84] ibid.

the impact on the economy is minimised and that the economy recovers' and that this accordingly 'calls for a focused approach to our mandate, even as we reflect on our performance, to offer renewed ideas and appropriate solutions that would direct our country towards economic recovery, most importantly *inclusive* growth and transformation'.[85] In other words, against the *backdrop* of high and rising inequality, the Commission appears to seek to promote *inclusion*.

What seems clear to us is that the Commission is aware of the role inequality plays in the South African economy broadly speaking and of the role of competition (or rather the lack thereof) in its production and re-production. However, it has neither articulated a clear role of its understanding of the causal mechanisms that drive economic inequality from a competition perspective, nor translated the understanding it has in this regard into explicit steps which address the competition-inequality nexus.

C. Tools Available for Addressing the Competition-Inequality Nexus in South Africa

In this section we examine two of the tools already available to the Commission, Tribunal and Competition Appeal Court (CAC) which could be used to affect the manner in which the competition-inequality nexus operates: merger control and market inquiries. However, the importance of other available tools should not be neglected: the competition authorities could also rely on the prohibitions of restrictive horizontal and vertical practices in the Competition Act, as well as the Act's prohibitions related to abuse of dominance and price discrimination by dominant firms.[86]

i. Merger Control

In contemporary South African competition law, when required to consider a merger, the Commission or Tribunal must initially determine whether or not the merger is likely to substantially prevent or lessen competition, by assessing certain enumerated factors specified in the Act.[87] In the event that it 'appears that the merger is likely to substantially prevent or lessen competition' then Commission or the Tribunal must also determine 'whether or not the merger is likely to result in any technological, efficiency or other pro-competitive gain which will be greater than, and offset, the effects of any prevention or lessening of competition, that

[85] Competition Commission, *Annual Report 2019-20: Competition Regulation for a Growing and Inclusive Economy* 14, available at www.compcom.co.za/wp-content/uploads/2021/02/CC_Annual-Report-2019_20s.pdf accessed 13 December 2021. Emphasis added.

[86] For a discussion on some of these tools, see IV.E in ch 4 in this volume.

[87] Competition Act, s 12A(1), as amended by Act 18 of 2018.

may result or is likely to result from the merger, and would not likely be obtained if the merger is prevented' *and* 'whether the merger can or cannot be justified on *substantial public interest grounds* by assessing [certain enumerated factors]'.[88] Since the 2018 amendment of the Act, even in the event that that a merger is *not* likely to substantially prevent or lessen competition, the Commission or Tribunal must still determine whether the merger can or cannot be justified on substantial public interest grounds by assessing the enumerated factors.[89]

According to section 12A(3) of the Act, the Commission or Tribunal must consider the effect that the merger will have on, amongst other things, 'the promotion of a greater spread of ownership, in particular to increase the levels of ownership by historically disadvantaged persons and workers in firms in the market'.[90] As things stand, then, we already see some limited scope for the Commission to consider the impacts of particular proposed mergers on the competition-inequality nexus. As things stand, it is mandatory for the Commission to consider *the promotion of a greater spread of ownership*, in particular to increase the levels of ownership by historically disadvantaged persons and workers in firms in the market in determining whether it is in the public interest for a merger to be approved. While the relevant provision in the Act is open to interpretation, it seems fairly clear that looking at whether a proposed merger would promote the greater spread of ownership in a given market could potentially contribute to reducing concentration and market power, and therefore economic inequality.

Six large mergers have been prohibited by the Tribunal since 1999.[91] Of these six decisions, two have been overturned on appeal to the CAC,[92] and one was approved at a later stage by the Tribunal, albeit with conditions.[93] One of the cases overturned on appeal by the CAC is particularly interesting for different reasons. It is illustrative of a case where the Tribunal prohibited a merger based on reasoning that was distributional in nature, but where its decision was subsequently overturned by a formalistic application of the law by the CAC. The case in question

[88] Competition Act, s 12A(1)(a) and (b), as amended by Act 18 of 2018. Emphasis added.

[89] See Competition Act, s 12A(1A), as amended by Act 18 of 2018.

[90] Emphasis added.

[91] A list of all the large mergers considered by the Tribunal is published on its website. The list we rely on was current as at 2 September 2021.

[92] The first of which, the *Medicross* merger, is discussed immediately below. The second of these decisions is the *Mediclinic* merger discussed further below. As discussed further below, the CAC *Mediclinic* decision has subsequently been reversed by the Constitutional Court.

[93] The proposed merger involved Telkom and Business Connexion Group, both of which were listed ICT firms at the time of the proposed merger. The merger was initially prohibited by the Tribunal in 2007. See Competition Tribunal's reasons for decision in the proposed *Telkom SA Ltd and Business Connexion Group Ltd* large merger (51/LM/Jun06) [2007] ZACT 55 (20 August 2007), available at www.saflii.org/za/cases/ZACT/2007/ 55.html accessed 13 December 2021. The merger was later approved with conditions. See Competition Tribunal's reasons for decision in the proposed *Telkom SA Ltd and Business Connexion Group Ltd* large merger (Dimension Data (Pty) Ltd as intervening party) (LM065Aug14) [2015] ZACT 112 (12 October 2015), available at www.saflii.org/za/cases/ZACT/2015/112.html accessed 13 December 2021.

was the *Medicross* merger.[94] At the Tribunal level, the matter was decided by then Chairperson of the Tribunal, David Lewis. In his book, *Thieves at the Dinner Table*, Lewis spends a fair deal of time unpacking this case.[95]

He begins his discussion by noting that 'South Africa has a deeply segmented health care system comprising, on the one hand, a relatively well-resourced, comprehensive private health care system with excess capacity and, on the other hand, an under-resourced and over-used public health care system', continuing to add that while '[t]his problem, although by no means uniquely South African, is rooted in income distribution and so is naturally exacerbated by South Africa's unusually skewed distribution'.[96] For Lewis, this 'greatly limit[ed] the number of people who [could] afford the insurance premiums that effectively fund access to private health care', with '[o]ne possible solution [being] for the sophisticated private health care insurance system to develop insurance products that a significantly greater proportion of the population [could] afford, thus somewhat relaxing the burden imposed on public health care and increasing capacity utilisation in the private system'.[97]

It is against this backdrop that the Tribunal had to consider a merger between two of only three firms in what it saw as the market for *capitated* managed care in the world of private health insurance. According to Lewis, '[m]anaged care … may well have succeeded in lowering the costs of health care', and '[a]ssuming that managed care [had] actually reduced cost[s], in countries with flatter income distributions this was well have enabled a greater proportion of the population to afford private health care insurance'; in South African circumstances, however, 'the distance between those who [could] afford any form of private health insurance and those who [could not was] so great that the best that managed health care as a mechanism of cost reduction [could] achieve [was] to lower costs pertaining to that part of the population already insured'.[98] Or, simply put, for Lewis, '[i]ts impact could not be sufficiently great as to swell the ranks of those to whom private health care insurance [was] an affordable option'.[99] Only *capitated* managed care could potentially achieve this.[100]

As such, '[the Tribunal] had to be satisfied that the post-merger market structure encouraged innovation on the part of the participants', and '[t]hese features

[94] Competition Tribunal's reasons for decision in the proposed *Medicross Healthcare Group (Pty) Ltd and Prime Cure Holdings (Pty) Ltd* large merger (11/LM/Mar05) [2005] ZACT 66 (13 October 2005), available at www.saflii.org/za/cases/ZACT/2005/66.html accessed 13 December 2021 (*Medicross* Tribunal Decision); *Medicross Healthcare Group v Prime Cure Holdings* [2006] ZACAC 3 (6 April 2006), available at www.saflii.org/za/cases/ZACAC/2006/3.html accessed 13 December 2021 (*Medicross* CAC Decision).

[95] The discussion starts at D Lewis, *Enforcing Competition Rules in South Africa: Thieves at the Dinner Table* (Cheltenham, Edward Elgar, 2013) 96.

[96] Lewis (n 95) 97.

[97] ibid.

[98] ibid.

[99] ibid.

[100] See further Lewis (n 95) 98.

played a significant part in the Tribunal's decision to prohibit the merger'.[101] As the Tribunal put it:

> There is undoubtedly significant room and an urgent requirement for experimentation and innovation. We have little doubt that a significant merger in this embryonic market will slow the pace of innovation, it will reduce the number of alternative modes of provision on offer, and it will likely slow the pace at which new forms and concepts of low-income healthcare insurance are introduced.[102]

The CAC, however, ended up reversing the Tribunal decision on appeal. Lewis characterises the grounds on which it did so as 'indicative of the rather mechanistic, unimaginative approach that the Competition Appeal Court has adopted in its task of building a new body of competition jurisprudence'.[103] He also adds that they were 'indicative of the lack of deference the Competition Appeal Court accorded to the Tribunal as fact-finder, despite assertions to the contrary'.[104] Finally, Lewis draws attention to the fact that 'the Court held that [the Tribunal] had misdirected [itself] by adopting a "cautious and circumspect" approach towards this merger as a result of conflating the public interest test [it was] mandated to undertake with its "primary task" – that of deciding whether the merger was likely to substantially lessen competition – and, moreover, that the public interest ground [the Tribunal] invoked did not fall within the ambit of that specified by the Act', adding that '[t]he Court's conclusion arose from its reference – in a preamble to [the Tribunal's] competition evaluation outlining conditions in the health care sector – to the need for circumspection in dealing with a market in which "public interest" is as deeply implicated as the one in which the product is concerned with access to health care'.[105] Ultimately, Lewis makes an important point. As he puts it, the CAC has often refused 'to take account of the social content of competition law'.[106]

We agree with much of what Lewis has to say on this score, but we think there are a number of additional points that should be made. What the *Medicross* case illustrates quite clearly is that the CAC has interpreted the purview of South Africa's competition authorities in a very narrow way. In essence, while South African competition law as legislated and applied by the Commission clearly follows the broader paradigm described above, the CAC has on occasion interpreted its mandate as falling within the narrow paradigm. This sort of narrow interpretation may well have proven to be a serious impediment to any attempts by the Commission to explicitly address the competition-inequality nexus.

Indeed, interpretation of this kind would almost necessarily deter the Commission (and the Tribunal) from straying beyond their supposed purview, which the CAC had defined in a very narrow way. The differing approaches adopted

[101] Lewis (n 95) 99.
[102] *Medicross* Tribunal Decision, para 194.
[103] Lewis (n 95) 100.
[104] ibid.
[105] ibid.
[106] Lewis (n 95) 101.

by the Tribunal and the CAC certainly resulted in a different outcome to the *Medicross* case, but our broader point is that the kind of reasoning adopted by the CAC could have broader systemic impacts, including through having a so-called chilling effect on the Commission as investigator, and potentially through thwarting well-intentioned efforts by the legislature to adopt a broader view of the proper scope of competition regulation.

We note, however, that beyond this sort of merger generally not being in the 'public interest', the South African Constitution explicitly states that '*[e]veryone* has the right to have access to … health care services' in its Bill of Rights.[107] Moreover, the Constitution specifically mandates that '[w]hen interpreting any legislation, and when developing the common law or customary law, every court, tribunal or forum must promote the spirit, purport and objects of the Bill of Rights'.[108] Instead of referring to the general 'public interest' – a term which has a particular meaning in the Competition Act – then, the Tribunal may have been on more solid ground had it taken the position that the matter that was before it implicated constitutional rights of significant importance and that the Constitution mandates that this be taken into account when the Tribunal, and indeed the CAC, interprets the Competition Act. The Constitutional Court, moreover, has itself been clear that the South African Constitution is rooted in the idea of transformation. As the late Chief Justice Pius Langa once wrote:

> Transformation then is a social and an economic revolution. South Africa … has to contend with unequal and insufficient access to housing, food, water, healthcare and electricity'. As former Chief Justice Chaskalson wrote in *Soobramoney v Minister of Health, KwaZulu-Natal*, "[f]or as long as these conditions continue to exist that aspiration [that is, of substantive equality] will have a hollow ring. The provision of services to all and the levelling of the economic playing fields that were so drastically skewed by the apartheid system must be absolutely central to any concept of transformative constitutionalism.[109]

In the same article, Langa continued to note that

> [i]t is when adherence to the word is taken too far, when the upholding of a law obscures or ignores that law exists to try, however difficult, to ensure justice, that formalism becomes dangerous. … It is this type of conservative or formalist approach to law that is inconsistent with a transformative Constitution. At the heart of a transformative Constitution is a commitment to substantive reasoning, to examining the underlying principles that inform laws themselves and judicial reaction to those laws. Purely formalist reasoning tends to avoid that responsibility.[110]

[107] South African Constitution of 1996 (Constitution), s 27(1). Emphasis added.

[108] Constitution, s 39(2).

[109] P Langa, 'Transformative Constitutionalism' (2006) 17 *Stellenbosch Law Review* 351, 352.

[110] ibid 357. On transformative constitutionalism, see also S Ngcobo 'South Africa's Transformative Constitution: Towards an Appropriate Doctrine of Separation of Powers' (2011) 22 *Stellenbosch Law Review* 37; D Moseneke 'The Fourth Bram Fischer Memorial Lecture: Transformative Adjudication' (2002) 18 *South African Journal on Human Rights* 309.

We see the reasoning of the CAC in *Medicross* as having done exactly that. In failing to take the social content of competition law into account through applying formalistic reasoning, the CAC shirked its responsibility to help give effect to the Constitution's transformative vision of a nation where the attainment of substantive equality is closer to being a reality.

The Constitutional Court, however, has recently vindicated the approach we advocate for in its judgment relating to a different case in the healthcare sector.[111] In this matter, the Tribunal again sided with the Commission in prohibiting a large merger in the healthcare sector.[112] The majority of the CAC, while notionally acknowledging the right to have access to healthcare services, again overturned the Tribunal decision.[113] This time, however, the CAC decision was appealed to the Constitutional Court, where the CAC's interpretation of the Act was faulted on the basis that it failed to adopt the correct interpretive approach to statutes as set out in Constitutional Court judgments.[114] According to the Court, the CAC's approach failed 'to advance the purpose of the Act and to promote the spirit, purport and object of section 27 of the Constitution'.[115] The Court then proceeded to overturn the CAC decision. In so doing, it wrote as follows:

> Mediclinic's predicted post-merger tariff hike, in this country of huge inequalities and in this distressed economy, would not have been understood and treated as insignificant or miniscule as the Appeal Court seems to have perceived it. To a wealthy South African, the percentage by which tariffs would go up after the merger is understandably negligible and inconsequential. But, not so to an average South African who is not even a member of any medical scheme, not that members of medical schemes necessarily find these high tariffs any easier to live with. Maintaining or increasing the scope for choice of essential and much-needed services with particular regard to the plight of the financially under-resourced or the vulnerable, should always be at the back of the decision-makers' minds when dealing with mergers. This is, after all, one of the key demands of the Preamble and purpose of the Act.[116]

The Court also stressed that:

> [i]t bears repetition, that South Africa is at present the land of gross economic inequalities. Its wealth or economic ownership and control is concentrated in the hands of a few.

[111] *Competition Commission of South Africa v Mediclinic Southern Africa* (CCT 31/20) [2021] ZACC 35 (15 October 2021), available at www.saflii.org/za/cases/ZACC/2021/35.html accessed 13 December 2021 (*Mediclinic*, CC Decision).

[112] On this occasion the Tribunal did briefly contemplate the fundamental rights aspects of the case in reaching its decision. See further Competition Tribunal's reasons for decision in the proposed *Mediclinic Southern Africa and Matlosana Medical Health Services* large merger (LM124Oct16) (30 January 2019), available at www.comptrib.co.za/case-detail/7250 accessed 13 December 2021, para 441.

[113] See *Mediclinic Southern Africa (Pty) Ltd v Competition Commission* (172/CAC/Feb19) [2020] ZACAC 3 (6 February 2020), available at www.saflii.org/za/cases/ZACAC/2020/3.html accessed 13 December 2021, para 136.

[114] *Mediclinic*, CC Decision, para 55.

[115] ibid. See further *Mediclinic*, CC Decision, para 71.

[116] *Mediclinic*, CC Decision, para 73.

> And in the private health care services sector, Mediclinic is one of the three dominant groups at a national level. Grounding the substantiality of lessened competition on a tariff hike, as "insignificantly" low as the predictive percentage is to the opulent, and with due regard to the already high and ever-escalating costs in the private health care services sector, the already dominant position of a company seeking to take over and the constitutional imperative to fulfil the right of access to health care services do, all things considered, justify the discretionary choice of prohibition as a remedy in this matter. This is supported by the Tribunal's finding that the constitutionally-inspired public interest consideration would be harmed rather than advanced by the proposed merger.[117]

In essence, the Constitutional Court has taken the kind of approach we have argued in favour of above. It has made it clear that fundamental rights must be taken into consideration when interpreting the Act and that South Africa's high levels of economic inequality may serve as an important context when considering proposed mergers. Equally importantly, the approach adopted by the Court is likely to require that South Africa's competition authorities, especially the CAC, apply the Act more expansively, especially when fundamental rights are implicated. This places the Commission on firmer ground should it wish to use merger control as a tool to address the competition-inequality nexus. We do, however, remain of the view that it would be preferable for the Commission to be given a more explicit legislative mandate to address the competition-inequality nexus. We return to this point below.

ii. Market Inquiries

When the Act was amended in 2009, provisions were inserted that enabled the Commission to conduct what is called a 'market inquiry', that is, 'a formal inquiry in respect of the general state of competition, the levels of concentration in and structure of a market for particular goods or services, without necessarily referring to the conduct or activities of any particular named firm'.[118] The Act further states that '[a]n adverse effect on competition is established if any feature, or combination of features, of a market for goods or services impedes, restricts or distorts competition in that market' and proceeds to indicate that '[a]ny reference to a feature of a market for goods or services *includes*',[119] amongst other things: 'the structure of that market or any aspect of that structure, including … the level and trends of concentration and ownership in the market' and 'the outcomes observed in the market, including … levels of concentration and ownership'.[120]

Amongst other things, '[i]n a market inquiry, the Competition Commission must decide … whether any feature, including structure and levels of concentration,

[117] *Mediclinic*, CC Decision, para 81.
[118] Competition Act, s 43A(1), as amended.
[119] Emphasis added.
[120] Competition Act, s 43A(3), as amended.

of each relevant market for any goods or services impedes, restricts or distorts competition within that market'.[121] Moreover, in making its decision in this regard, the Commission 'must have regard to the impact of the adverse effect on competition on small and medium businesses, or firms controlled or owned by historically disadvantaged persons'.[122] In the event that the Commission

> decides that there is an adverse effect on competition, it must determine … the action that must be taken … [,] whether it must make recommendations to any Minister, regulatory authority or affected firm to take action to remedy, mitigate or prevent the adverse effect on competition … [and] if any action must be taken [by such Minister, regulatory authority or affected firm], the action that must be taken in respect of what must be remedied, mitigated or prevented.[123]

Since the 2018 amendment, the Act also expands further on what actions must be taken in this regard. Specifically, the Act states that '[s]ubject to the provisions of any law, the Competition Commission may, in relation to each adverse effect on competition, take action to remedy, mitigate or prevent the adverse effect on competition', which may include a recommendation to the Tribunal, who may in turn make an appropriate order.[124]

Here, too, the Commission may already be able to examine the distributional impacts of concentration in a given market. This is because it is open to look into an *open* list of 'the outcomes observed in the market'.[125] To the extent that increased concentration can be shown to result in certain distributional *outcomes*, for example, the Commission could examine these outcomes as part of an inquiry into an *entire* market (as opposed to merely examining it from the perspective of a *particular merger*). The Commission also has broad discretionary powers in this regard that could include ministers and other regulatory authorities, thus potentially leading to better co-ordination across different parts of the South African economic policy apparatus as a whole.

Market inquiries, being a relatively new possibility, the Commission has thus far only initiated six of them, five of which have been completed in their entirety. Perhaps the most useful illustration of the potential of market inquiries thus far is the Commission's data services market inquiry, in respect of which the Commission published its final report on 2 December 2019.[126] The DSM Inquiry was initiated in August 2017, at the request of the Minister responsible for administration of the Competition Act, and after persistent concerns were expressed by the South African public about the high level of data prices and the importance of

[121] ibid, s 43C(1)(a), as amended.
[122] ibid, s 43C(2), as amended.
[123] ibid, s 43C(3), as amended.
[124] ibid, s 43D(1) and (2), as amended.
[125] See ibid, s 43A(3)(b), as amended.
[126] The Commission, of course, only published the non-confidential version of this report. We refer to this non-confidential version of the report as the 'DSMI Report'. We refer to the inquiry in general as the 'DSM Inquiry'.

data affordability for the South African economy and consumers.[127] The purpose of the DSM Inquiry as set out in its terms of reference was 'to understand what factors or features of the market(s) and value chain may cause or lead to high prices for data services, and to make recommendations that would result in lower prices for data services'.[128]

Of particular interest for current purposes, perhaps, is that the Commission dedicated more than 50 pages of its report to discussing '[t]he structure of data prices and "anti-poor" pricing'.[129] The main takeaway from this section of the DSMI Report is that the Commission found that 'the pricing structures in the industry, and particularly for Vodacom and MTN, are anti-poor, whether viewed at a headline or effective price level', that 'poorer consumers in South Africa are being exploited through higher prices and inferior services' and that this is 'most likely due to the fact that they have no alternatives for data services in contrast to wealthier consumers, and that partitioning strategies used by the dominant operators seek to exploit this position'.[130] As a result, the DSM Inquiry ultimately resulted in a number of novel recommendations. As the Commission summed up in the DSMI Report:

> The Commission has identified a final package of recommendations that provide immediate relief to high data prices, especially for low-income consumers .... The full implementation of this package of remedies will not only lower prices for all consumers, and particularly the poor, but will lead to greater economic and social inclusion moving forward as the country moves into the digital age.[131]

These findings and recommendations illustrate that the Commission has already potentially used the market inquiry tool on at least one occasion in a manner which affects the operation of the competition-inequality nexus, albeit that it did not do so in a concerted or comprehensive fashion. This is apparent from the fact that the Commission made recommendations, in an attempt to provide 'immediate relief on data pricing', as to the 'level and structure of pricing',[132] which included the recommendation that 'Vodacom and MTN must independently reach agreement with the Commission to cease ongoing partitioning and price discrimination strategies that may facilitate greater exploitation of market power and anti-poor pricing'.[133] Moreover, the Commission did subsequently reach agreement with both Vodacom and MTN, which has resulted in data prices falling significantly over time.[134] Given, however, that large volumes of data pertinent to determining

[127] DSMI Report, 13, para 1.
[128] ibid.
[129] See DSMI Report, 119–171.
[130] DSMI Report, 170 and 171, paras 466 and 468. Vodacom and MTN are the two data services providers with the largest market shares in the South African market.
[131] DSMI Report, 29, para 46.
[132] See DSMI Report, 266–270.
[133] DSMI Report, 266, para 723.3.
[134] See, eg, in this regard, L Buthelezi 'Vodacom Slashes its Data Prices Further in Agreement with the Competition Commission' (fin24, 7 April 2021), available at www.news24.com/fin24/companies/ict/

whether these price reductions have in fact been 'pro-poor' are redacted from the DSMI Report, we cannot draw conclusions with any real certainty as to how the Commission's recommendations as implemented have affected the manner in which the competition-inequality nexus operates.

Regardless of whether price changes have been 'pro-poor', the fact remains, as the Commission found in the DSMI Report, that Vodacom and MTN are dominant in the data services market.[135] It also seems quite plausible to us that the lowering of prices was already on the cards, and that through lowering their prices in the ways that they have, Vodacom and MTN may in fact be further cementing their dominant position in the market. It may be precisely for this reason that the recommendations in the DSMI Report have not been challenged in the Tribunal. Speculation of this sort aside, the DSM Inquiry has not changed the fact that what profits do still accrue to shareholders in this market are very unevenly shared. It does still seem quite possible, however, that the DSM Inquiry has resulted in a situation where inequality is now lower than it otherwise would have been. The DSM Inquiry also illustrates quite clearly that market inquiries show some promise in relation to addressing the competition-inequality nexus.

All of this said, however, market inquiries exhibit a number of potential shortcomings. For one thing, they are susceptible to being challenged in the Tribunal and CAC. It seems plausible to us that the Commission's recommendations in the DSMI Report may have been set aside if litigation had ensued. After all, the DSM Inquiry's terms of reference (ToR) indicated that '[t]he outcome of the market inquiry will be to make recommendations on any matter covered in this ToR, including … [r]ecommendations to government as to how the market could be made more competitive and inclusive and how data prices can be brought down in order to secure South Africa's position as a low-data-cost economy'.[136] It could easily be argued that the ToR already suggested that remedial action beyond the Commission's remit may be taken, especially given that the Competition Act provides that '[s]ubject to the provisions of any law, the Competition Commission may, in relation to each adverse effect *on competition*, take action to remedy, mitigate or prevent the adverse effect *on competition*'.[137] As laudable as the goal of reversing anti-poor pricing is, it is not immediately apparent how requiring firms to lower their prices to this end is aimed at remedying an adverse effect *on competition*. Nor is it immediately apparent how anti-poor pricing is even an adverse effect *on competition* in the first place. Indeed, the fact that the Commission can only take action in order to remedy, mitigate or prevent the adverse effect *on competition* seems to us to be another one of this tool's current shortcomings. As such, we think it prudent for the legislature to provide the Commission with a more explicit

vodacom-slashes-its-data-prices-further-in-agreement-with-the-competition-commission-20 210407 accessed 13 December 2021.

[135] See, eg, DSMI Report, 265, para 719.1.

[136] DSMI Terms of Reference (18 August 2017), published in *Government Gazette* 41054, 9, para 3.4.1.

[137] Competition Act, s 43D(1). Emphasis added.

mandate to address the competition-inequality nexus. Against the backdrop of the Constitutional Court's recent approach to interpreting competition law,[138] a more explicit legislative mandate should suffice to give the Commission the necessary tools to effectively address the competition-inequality nexus without fundamentally changing South African competition law as it currently stands.

IV. Conclusion: What Role for Competition Law and Policy in Reducing Economic Inequality in South Africa?

In this chapter, we have given thought to some of the legal and policy options available to South African authorities in the *competition* space to address what we have called the competition inequality nexus. As we conclude, then, we think that it is important to point out that we have not situated these options within a broader legal and policy framework geared at the reduction of economic inequality in South Africa. While this is perhaps not the appropriate forum for discussing the type of overarching framework necessary for the reduction of economic inequality in any detail, we feel that it is necessary for us to clarify that we think that in relation to the immense amount of work that needs to be done in order to reduce economic inequality in South Africa specifically, it would not be realistic and probably be counterproductive to expect competition law and policy to do most of the heavy lifting. At the same time, competition law and policy should be enforced having regard to distributive goals where possible and enforced in such a manner that it complements efforts made to reduce inequality through other policy instruments.

We also find it necessary to reiterate that the nexus runs the other way as well: reducing economic inequality will likely in and of itself result in more competitive markets in South Africa. As such, we should not only be looking to incorporate distributional concerns into the existing paradigms of competition law and policy, but we should also be thinking about what other types of inequality-reducing policies will mean for the competitiveness of markets. For example, the goal of encouraging more competitive markets could perhaps be a consideration in the formulation of tax law and policy. In a country such as South Africa where pre-existing or initial levels of inequality are extraordinarily high, it is difficult to see how economic inequality – especially wealth inequality – can be reduced without resorting to redistribution through taxation, albeit that this sort of redistribution in contemporary South Africa comes with its own set of limitations.

Regardless, the point is that this is but one among many examples of the types of policies that will be necessary to reduce economic inequality in South Africa and, more importantly, that there is a need for cooperation among the different parts of the South African government responsible for different types of law

[138] See the discussion under C.i above.

and policy, as well as cooperation with the international community, in order to reduce economic inequality. This makes the reduction of economic inequality an extremely complex task.

While it is our argument that inequality reduction needs to be prioritised we recognise that there are also other goals worth pursuing; there are choices to be made and potential trade-offs to be considered. One example comes from the fact that South Africa is very much still a middle income 'developing' country, which some characterise as 'an emerging market'. In order to achieve 'inclusive growth' which addresses high levels of poverty and unemployment, improving the South African economy's international competitiveness will remain an important policy objective. It is arguable that, in this light, South Africa should have its own national champions that are able to capitalise on economies of scale to leverage access to large foreign markets, and to be able to compete with large foreign players in South African markets. The Competition Act does already require the Commission to contemplate the ability of national industries to compete in international markets when considering whether to permit a particular merger in the public interest and when conducting market inquiries. An approach which is permissive of greater concentration in some markets in order to develop national champions is obviously potentially in conflict over the short to medium term with the goal of reducing economic inequality.

All of this said, we are of the view that competition law and policy has a role to play in reducing economic inequality. As Tim Wu puts it in the context of the US, '[i]t is true that antitrust alone will not cure the curse of bigness or eliminate the excesses of private power', but 'it strikes at the root, and getting the engines of the law restarted is an important part of dealing with a problem that has reached Constitutional dimensions'.[139] Albeit that South African competition law and policy was not, as in the case of the US, initially conceived of as being a check on the kind of concentration of private power that would be harmful to democracy,[140] we think that similar logic applies in the South African context. Competition law and policy are among the few tools that strike 'proactively' at the root of the problem of growing socio-economic inequality, which, as we see it, undermines the fundamental value of political equality in a constitutional democracy, and thereby its very legitimacy.

Since economic concentration and the uneven distribution of power it engenders is harmful to democracy, and is unjust for other reasons,[141] we are of the view that competition law should not be blind to adverse distributive outcomes by continuing to profess to being an ostensibly technical, normatively empty discipline concerned only with 'efficiency' and consumer prices. To give effect to this

[139] Wu (n 27) 15. See also Wu (n 27) 18.
[140] In this regard, see generally Wu (n 27).
[141] On this point, see, eg, Pike (n 16) and Scanlon (n 17). See also generally MJ Sandel, *The Tyranny of Merit: What's Become of the Common Good?* (London, Penguin Books, 2020).

view, laws and policies could be amended to allow the Commission and other actors to explicitly consider the competition-inequality nexus in relation to their existing tasks and functions. Examples of how this could be done include further broadening the public interest standard to be considered in merger proceedings, or by explicitly enabling the Commission to consider the competition-inequality nexus when conducting market inquiries and to make appropriate recommendations based on their findings. These would not constitute radical alterations of the existing legal and policy paradigm. It would simply mean adding an additional factor to the list of factors the Commission and others are already obliged or may consider when scrutinising mergers and conducting market inquiries. While it is possible that the Commission may already have the power to address the competition-inequality nexus to a degree, an explicit legislative mandate would go a long way to providing legal certainty and may insulate future Commission decisions from overly formalistic judicial review.

We should also point out, as the likes of David Lewis has, that there is a good case to be made that perhaps not all markets warrant the same type of scrutiny or treatment. In the same way that the market for silk scarves is not the same as the market for healthcare services, the data services market is not the same as the market for luxury watches, and the market for education services is not the same as the market for yachts. Beyond the general proposition that economic concentration contributes to an unequal distribution of power and to higher levels of political inequality, it may also be worth making the broad set of human rights contained in the South African Constitution a more explicit part of competition analysis. Nobody is constitutionally guaranteed a silk scarf, a luxury watch or yacht. The Bill of Rights does, however, guarantee everyone the right to access to healthcare services, and to basic and further education, amongst a variety of other things. Where economic concentration contributes directly to increasing differences between different parts of the economic distributions in the extent to which they realise their constitutional rights, lawmakers, policymakers and adjudicators should acknowledge as much. A good argument can indeed be made that they are constitutionally obliged to do exactly that.

Ultimately, competition law is no panacea, but it seems to us that it has the potential of being utilised as one among many imperfect tools that, when deployed in a carefully coordinated and thoughtful way, may contribute to the successful reduction of economic inequality in South Africa, which may in turn improve the functioning of South Africa's constitutional democracy.

7

How Concerns of Economic Inequality and Poverty are Reflected in Efficiency-Based Competition Laws: A Developing Country Perspective

BARBARA DUFKOVÁ*

I. Introduction

Rising economic inequality is becoming a troubling issue in an increasing number of economies around the world. Whereas it has long been seen as a concern in developing countries that have undergone rapid economic growth, recent studies suggest that economic inequality is also of concern to developed countries.[1] The opening of the gap between the rich and the poor in developed countries is attributed, inter alia, to the lack of competition and extensive market power stemming from the concentration of wealth in the hands of a few privileged economic actors.[2] Market power generates higher economic profits for business owners, but at the same time, it imposes higher prices on consumers. Increased margins disproportionately harm the poor, who pay more for goods without receiving a counter-balancing share of increased profits.[3]

Against the context outlined above, this chapter explores whether and how competition law, as a primary regulatory tool to remedy market failures, should

* PhD candidate at the Faculty of Law, Charles University and Predoctoral Research Fellow at Peace Research Center Prague.

[1] See, eg, Department of Economic and Social Affairs (UNDESA), *The World Social Report 2020* (United Nations 2020) www.un.org/development/desa/dspd/world-social-report/2020-2.html.

[2] See, eg, JE Stiglitz, 'America Has a Monopoly Problem – and It's Huge' (23 October 2017) *The Nation*, or D Wessel, 'Is Lack of Competition Strangling the U.S. Economy?' [2018] *Harvard Business Review* 106. See also S Ennis et al, *Inequality: A hidden cost of market power* (OECD 2017) www.one.oecd.org/document/DAF/COMP(2015)10/en/pdf.

[3] S Ennis and Y Kim, 'Market Power and Wealth Distribution' in MM Licetti et al (eds), *A Step Ahead: Competition Policy for Shared Prosperity and Inclusive Growth* (Washington, DC, World Bank Publications, 2017).

reflect concerns of economic inequality. Empirical evidence suggests that economic inequality can rise despite the enforcement of efficiency-based competition laws.[4] This makes a case for the argument that a closer examination is needed of the relationship between competition law and economic equality and the potential reflection of equality considerations in the enforcement of the law. The experience of developing countries that have recently introduced competition laws can be instructive because they have already faced the need to make their competition laws more responsive to issues connected to economic inequality.

In their quest for integration into the global economy, many developing countries have adopted policies to promote economic growth and development, including competition law.[5] However, in developing such policies, it has been realised that competition law based solely on efficiency considerations can potentially exacerbate the negative impact of rapid economic growth on equality. Hence, developing countries have been advised to bear in mind the distributional effects of competition law.[6]

How to practically implement general recommendations has been left to developing countries. In this context, the purpose of the present chapter is to elucidate how developing countries have attuned their competition laws to the economic inequality that characterises their economies and the model that emerges to see whether this model offers useful lessons for developed countries. To this end, Vietnam's competition law system is used as an example, primarily because of its developing country status, rapid economic growth in recent years and fairly long history of competition regulation.

To examine the topic described above, the chapter proceeds as follows: section II describes competition law's redistributive effects and their implications for developing countries. It critically assesses the 'orthodox' model of competition law based on economic efficiency and identifies policy areas where this model proves inadequate for developing countries because of their developmental needs (ie lifting people out of poverty and securing inclusive economic growth). Section III sketches how redistributive considerations can be incorporated into competition law and its enforcement. Following this, section IV examines the

[4] The term is used to describe competition laws built on a presumption that only market equilibrium achieved under perfect competition promotes economic efficiency of the markets and consumer welfare. The increase in economic efficiency and consumer welfare are recognised as the only legitimate goals of competition law. See, eg, I Lianos et al, 'Is There a Tension Between Development Economics and Competition?' in DD Sokol et al (eds), *Competition Law and Development* (Stanford, Stanford University Press, 2013) 35.

[5] EM Fox, 'Competition, Development and Regional Integration: In Search of a Competition Law Fit for Developing Countries' in J Drexl et al (eds), *Competition Policy and Regional Integration in Developing Countries* (Cheltenham, Edward Elgar Publishing, 2012) 285.

[6] See, eg, DD Sokol, TK Cheng, and I Lianos, *Competition Law and Development* (Stanford, Stanford University Press, 2013); J Drexl, M Bakhoum, EM Fox, MS Gal and DJ Gerber, *Competition Policy and Regional Integration in Developing Countries* (Cheltenham, Edward Elgar Publishing, 2012); MS Gal, M Bakhoum, J Drexl, EM Fox and DJ Gerber, *The Economic Characteristics of Developing Jurisdictions: Their Implications for Competition Law* (Cheltenham, Edward Elgar Publishing, 2015).

provisions of Vietnam's competition law and patterns of its enforcement to identify whether and how they reflect redistributive considerations. Section V summarises the methods used to infuse equity into Vietnam's competition law and evaluates whether its experience is transferrable to other developing or developed countries. Finally, section VI concludes.

II. Redistributive Effects of Competition Law and Implications for Developing Countries

The relations between economic development (or growth), competition law and economic equality are complex. Cheng observed that the key to economic growth is the ability to create more output for the economy with existing resources.[7] In this context, competition is thought to promote investment, spur on productivity gains and encourage innovation.[8] Yet, competition does not mandate that the additional income generated by economic growth is distributed fairly and equally in the economy.[9] In particular, there is no guarantee that it will accrue to the poorest people. In some cases, increased competition can even be detrimental to the poor (eg by driving them out of the labour, product or services market).[10]

Given its complexity, since competition law serves as a major regulatory tool to address competition, policymakers should be mindful of the effects that it can have on economic equality and poverty.[11] Developing countries have been discouraged from 'blindly' copying competition laws from developed countries.[12] In particular, the general transferability of the US or EU models has been questioned because those models pursue narrow regulatory objectives.[13] Under US or EU efficiency-based models, the behaviour of market actors is evaluated through a

[7] TK Cheng, *Competition Law in Developing Countries* (Oxford, Oxford University Press, 2020) 70.

[8] ibid 44.

[9] F Cingano, 'Trends in Income Inequality and its Impact on Economic Growth' (2014) OECD Social, Employment and Migration Working Paper No 163, 5, 28.

[10] DD Sokol et al, 'Introduction' in DD Sokol et al (eds), *Competition Law and Development* 7 (Stanford, Stanford University Press, 2013). See also DJ Gerber, 'Economic Development and Global Competition Law Convergence' in DD Sokol et al (eds), *Competition Law and Development* (Stanford, Stanford University Press, 2013) 29. See also MW Dowdle, 'On the Public-Law Character of Competition Law: A Lesson from Asian Capitalism' (2015) 38 *Fordham International Law Journal* 301, 318.

[11] The existence of a relationship between competition law and income inequality is confirmed by empirical studies. For example, a recent analysis of data from a large sample of countries over the period of 1960–2010 found a negative relation between competition law and income inequality. See ch 3 this volume.

[12] Lianos et al (n 4).

[13] A Bhattacharjea, 'Who Needs Antitrust? Or, Is Developing-country Antitrust Different? A historical-comparative analysis' in DD Sokol et al (eds), *Competition Law and Development* (Stanford, Stanford University Press, 2013) 35.

purely economic lens; other regulatory or policy considerations are disregarded.[14] Thus, in such cases, the role of competition law is simply to ensure that the behaviour of market players does not disrupt efficient market equilibrium.[15]

Because of the specific characteristics of developing countries, the application of competition laws based purely on efficiency considerations in developing countries may not only fail to address market-related pain points those jurisdictions face but also even aggravate them.[16] Fox observes that developing countries differ from developed ones in at least two fundamental ways. First, they lag behind in terms of market and institutional development. Second, they face a much greater array of challenges that must be overcome to secure economic growth.[17]

Poverty and economic inequality are especially relevant from a competition law perspective because they influence the structure of the markets, consumption patterns or the development of entrepreneurship.[18] As noted by Cheng, a low level of income generally means that the domestic market is small when measured in terms of purchasing power.[19] Consumers have little income to spare for more sophisticated manufacturing products, and they spend most of their resources on basic necessities, such as food, clothing or housing. This affects the structure of the economy because producers who are active in the domestic market focus on producing basic necessities rather than products with higher added value.[20] Relatedly, markets are likely to be more concentrated.[21] Income inequality becomes particularly salient in view of the frequent stratification of economies between a large public or state-owned sector and a small privately owned sector, including the informal sector formed by unregistered businesses.[22] Although these mostly family-run businesses are often perceived as low in productivity and engaging in unfair competition with formal enterprises if unregistered, they are

[14] DJ Gerber, 'Adapting the Role of Economics in Competition Law: A Developing Country Dilemma' in MS Gal et al (eds), *The Economic Characteristics of Developing Jurisdictions: Their Implications for Competition Law* (Cheltenham, Edward Elgar Publishing, 2015) 251. See also Lianos et al (n 4) 35, or Gerber (n 10) 28.

[15] I Maher, 'The Institutional Structure of Competition Law' in MW Dowdle et al (eds), *Asian Capitalism and the Regulation of Competition: Towards a Regulatory Geography of Global Competition Law* (Cambridge, Cambridge University Press, 2013) 55.

[16] H Ergas, 'Should Developed Countries Require Developing Countries to Adopt Competition Law? Lessons from the Economic Literature' (2009) 5(2) *European Competition Journal* 347, A Singh, 'Competition and Competition Policy in Emerging Markets: International and Developmental Dimensions' (2002) United Nations Conference on Trade and Development (UNCTAD) G-24 Discussion Paper Series No 18 unctad.org/system/files/official-document/gdsmdpbg2418_en.pdf 16, or M Williams, *Competition Policy and Law in China, Hong Kong and Taiwan* (Cambridge, Cambridge University Press, 2005) 71.

[17] Fox (n 5) 273.

[18] Cheng (n 7), or MM Dabbah, *International and Comparative Competition Law* (Cambridge, Cambridge University Press, 2012) 301.

[19] Cheng (n 7) 257.

[20] ibid 258–259.

[21] MS Gal and EM Fox, 'Drafting Competition Law for Developing Jurisdictions: Learning from Experience' in MS Gal et al (eds), *The Economic Characteristics of Developing Jurisdictions: Their Implications for Competition Law* (Cheltenham, Edward Elgar Publishing, 2015) 343.

[22] Dowdle (n 10) 318.

also important from a development perspective; they generate employment and function as a 'social safety net'.[23] At the same time, their position in the economy can make them vulnerable to the abuse of market power by dominant state-owned enterprises (SOEs) or large business groups.[24] For example, Cheng observes how small businesses in the agricultural sector are often 'squeezed' between powerful sellers of agricultural inputs and powerful buyers of agricultural produce, which makes them price takers on both sides of the market.[25] The imposed high purchasing price of agricultural input and low selling prices of their agricultural produce increase economic inequality and prevent these small businesses from escaping the perpetuating circle of poverty. This is where a regulatory intervention to curtail the monopoly and monopsony power of buyers and sellers becomes necessary.

Despite the necessity of regulation, practices that exploit or increase economic inequality in developing countries are not necessarily considered a regulatory priority under the strict efficiency-based competition law. Under the efficiency-based model, economic entities that engage in such practices can theoretically evade intervention by a competition authority entirely. As developing countries usually use the efficiency-based model as a referential framework for their competition laws, the question is how to tailor that model so that it reflects those different needs and pain points of developing countries linked to poverty and economic inequality.

III. Ways of Reflecting Economic Inequality and Poverty Concerns in Competition Law and Its Enforcement

The literature on competition law and economic development offers a variety of specific suggestions as to how to make competition law more equitable. Prior to categorising these various suggestions, methodological observation is needed. Most of the suggestions seem to be based on an implicit consensus that the best way to reduce economic inequality is to give greater support to the poor. Such support can take various forms, such as redirecting the additional income from the wealthy to the poor or promoting ease of access to markets. These suggestions seem to support a specific distributive justice model that is especially akin to Rawls' justice as fairness model and its difference or maximin principle.[26] This principle

[23] SJ Evenett, 'Competition Law and the Economic Characteristics of Developing Countries' in MS Gal et al (eds), *The Economic Characteristics of Developing Jurisdictions: Their Implications for Competition Law* (Cheltenham, Edward Elgar Publishing, 2015).

[24] MS Gal and M Bakhoum, 'Introduction' in MS Gal et al (eds), *The Economic Characteristics of Developing Jurisdictions: Their Implications for Competition Law* (Cheltenham, Edward Elgar Publishing, 2015).

[25] Cheng (n 7) 150.

[26] J Rawls, *A Theory of Justice* (Oxford, Oxford University Press, 1999) 266–267. The least advantaged group includes '*those belonging to the income class with the lowest expectations*'. J Rawls, *Justice as Fairness: A Restatement* (Cambridge, MA, Harvard University Press, 2001) 59. See also I Lianos,

posits that economic inequalities are to be arranged to the greatest benefit of the least advantaged groups.[27] The reliance in the literature on the 'justice as fairness' model is presumably justified in that poverty alleviation is key to economic development and the allocation of economic surplus to the most vulnerable – likely including the poor – is a direct way to achieve it.[28] Yet, it should be borne in mind that the support of the least advantaged groups is not necessarily a priority under other models of distributive justice.[29]

Without having the ambition of evaluating the axiological and moral values of the underlying concepts of fairness, this chapter follows the implicit assumption of the literature on competition law and development that closing the economic inequality gap in developing countries is best achieved by allocating greater support to the poor and protecting their interests. This is also justified in that alternative models of distributive justice also lend support to redistribution to the benefit of the poor.[30] For example, under the utilitarianism model, which promotes distribution that maximises overall welfare, the greatest maximisation of utility would be achieved by support of the poor because of the principle of the diminishing marginal value of money.[31] Similarly, luck egalitarianism, which promotes distribution that leads to equal economic opportunities for all, affords greater support for the poor, where it is presumed that the rich are generally advantaged and the poor disadvantaged through no choice of their own.[32]

'Competition Law as a Form of Social Regulation' (2020) 65(1) *The Antitrust Bulletin* 3, 14 or 30, or MS Gal, 'The Social Contract at the Basis of Competition Law: Should We Recalibrate Competition Law to Limit Inequality?' in D Gerard and I Lianos (eds), *Reconciling Efficiency and Equity: A Global Challenge for Competition Policy* (Cambridge, Cambridge University Press 2019).

[27] ibid.

[28] EM Fox, 'Economic Development, Poverty, and Antitrust: The Other Path' (2007) 13 *Southwestern Journal of Law and Trade in the Americas* 211. See also D Gerard and I Lianos, 'Introduction' in D Gerard and I Lianos (eds), *Reconciling Efficiency and Equity: A Global Challenge for Competition Policy* (Cambridge, Cambridge University Press, 2019) 4.

[29] For an overview of other potential models of distributive justice see, eg, J Lamont and CH Favor, 'Distributive Justice' in EN Zalta (ed), *The Stanford Encyclopedia of Philosophy* (Stanford, 2017) plato.stanford.edu/archives/win2017/entries/justice-distributive, referring to, eg, welfare-based theories such as utilitarianism (which promotes distribution that maximises the sum of all satisfied preferences, ie increasing the overall welfare), the equality of opportunity and luck egalitarianism theories (which shift focus from the outcome to the initial disadvantages resulting in inequality, and under which equality would be satisfied as long as people have equal economic opportunities even if those do not result in them having the same material goods or services and under which distributive inequalities are only just when they flow from one's choices or from factors for which one can reasonably be held responsible), desert-based theories (arguing that people deserve varying levels of income by providing goods and services desired by others – distributive systems are just insofar as they distribute income according to the different levels earned or deserved by the individuals in the society for their productive labours, efforts or contributions), libertarian theories (seeing as just the outcomes arrived at by separate just actions of individuals) etc. See also Lianos (n 26) 31.

[30] For an overview see, eg, C Knight, 'Theories of Distributive Justice and Post-Apartheid South Africa' (2014) 41(1) *South African Journal of Political Studies*.

[31] Under this principle, a given amount of money tends to produce more utility when used by a poor person than it does when used by a rich person. Knight (n 30) 32.

[32] Knight (n 30) 34.

There are three general approaches which developing countries' policymakers can take towards equity considerations in competition laws that can be distilled from the literature: the policymakers can: (i) disregard any potential distributional consequences and leave redistribution to other policies; (ii) use competition law as a tool of redistribution; or (iii) reflect equity considerations in the applicable standards and promote them in enforcement.[33]

First, competition law can disregard that its enforcement has some distributional consequences. This approach honours the economic foundations of competition law because it implies that economic principles are universally applicable and wealth distribution under perfect competition is the most efficient.[34] Where such distribution under perfect competition is optimal in view of the reduction of poverty and economic inequality, disregarding distributional consequences can be instrumental. However, where the enforcement of such narrowly focused competition law results in suboptimal wealth distribution, this approach may not be efficient from a public policy perspective. This is because suboptimal wealth distribution would need to be remedied or offset by other regulatory tools. However, the harm that has already been inflicted on the welfare of the poor may not be easily remediable. Lianos observes that economic regulation is not available in all sectors or markets and may lack sophisticated techniques to target and remedy the harm that was inflicted.[35] In addition, the regulatory process is traditionally burdensome and more prone to the risk of industrial capture compared with the flexible and universally applied competition law.[36] These points may all result in inefficient use of notoriously scarce public resources because reflecting equity concerns in competition law may have provided a cheaper institutional alternative.[37]

Second, competition law can directly address economic inequality and poverty by shifting wealth from the rich to the poor.[38] To this end, competition law can explicitly stipulate that the reduction of economic inequality and poverty is one of its goals. These considerations can also be incorporated into the text of the law as grounds for exemptions from general prohibitions. For example, an otherwise prohibited merger would be approved if it provided employment benefits or contributed to socio-economic development or technical or technological progress.[39] This would allow the enforcement authority to prioritise equity-infused

[33] For other potential ways see, eg, I Lianos, 'The Poverty of Competition Law: The Short Story' in D Gerard and I Lianos (eds), *Reconciling Efficiency and Equity: A Global Challenge for Competition Policy* (Cambridge, Cambridge University Press, 2019) 46–48.

[34] See, eg, DD Sokol, 'Antitrust, Industrial Policy, and Economic Populism' in D Gerard and I Lianos (eds), *Reconciling Efficiency and Equity: A Global Challenge for Competition Policy* 281–290 (Cambridge, Cambridge University Press, 2019), or DD Sokol, 'Tensions between Antitrust and Industrial Policy' (2015) 22 *George Mason Law Review* 1247.

[35] Lianos (n 33) 63.

[36] ibid 63–64.

[37] ibid 63.

[38] *cf* Cheng (n 7) 156 or 315 who is rather sceptical towards this approach.

[39] *cf* Cheng (n 7) 437.

goals over efficiency-related concerns. Alternatively, practices that are found to harm the poor in a developing country can be qualified as anti-competitive even if they do not have such effects and classifications in developed countries. Nonetheless, using competition law to directly shift wealth from the rich to the poor is open to criticism on the grounds that it transforms competition law into a tool for redistribution when there are other, arguably more effective tools, such as taxation, economic regulation or redistribution schemes.[40] For example, taxation is often justified as superior to competition law because it is more direct, more targeted and more efficient in redistributing wealth.[41] According to Lianos, these arguments are based on the assumption that the economic system is designed such that it would be possible to eliminate the disparities of economic power that lead to wealth and income inequality by introducing changes in the tax schedule to improve the position of the weaker parties.[42]

Third, competition law can reflect equity-related concerns by prioritising equity and poverty considerations in enforcement. This involves adjusting the applicable standards so that the enforcement of the law does not detrimentally affect the poor.[43] Those standards that promise to be the most beneficial to poor consumers and small- and medium-sized enterprises (SMEs), which are the most vulnerable groups from an equity perspective, can be prioritised and promoted in enforcement. For example, irrebuttable presumptions of dominance can be established to facilitate enforcement against powerful monopolies. Alternatively, certain agreements can be designated as per se infringements to shift the burden of proof for the benefit of the enforcement agency, although they are not treated as such in the efficiency-based model. As opposed to the approach that uses competition law as a tool of redistribution, this does not require that redistributive objectives are explicitly mentioned in the law.

IV. Reflecting Economic Inequality and Poverty in Vietnam's Competition Law

The examination of Vietnam's competition law illustrates that policymakers can combine the approaches to reflecting economic inequality and poverty concerns in competition law identified in section III. Vietnam was chosen for the case study not only because of its economic status but also because of its fairly long history

[40] See generally Sokol (n 34). For an opposing view see Dowdle (n 10) 351 suggesting that using the market for redistribution in developing countries can be more effective than public tax or redistribution schemes.

[41] L Kaplow, 'On the Choice of Welfare Standards in Competition Law' in D Zimmer (ed), *The Goals of Competition Law* (Cheltenham, Edward Elgar, 2012) 7–25.

[42] Lianos (n 33) 61.

[43] Cheng describes this as a harm avoidance principle. Cheng (n 7) 143.

of competition regulation. As of June 2020, Vietnam has been classified as a lower middle income country in the World Bank classification.[44] In the last decades, it has undergone a tremendous economic transformation.[45] Although the poverty rate measured at the national poverty line dropped from more than 50 per cent in 1980s to 9.8 per cent in 2016,[46] there are concerns that in the past decade, the poverty rate has been decreasing at a slower pace and growth has begun to be less inclusive.[47]

Given its impact on economic growth and development, competition law may have played a role in some of these trends. This hypothesis can be justified in that competition regulation is not a new phenomenon in Vietnam. Vietnam enacted its first competition law in 2004 ('VCL 2004').[48] After 14 years, this was replaced with a new competition law that took effect in 2019 ('VCL 2018').[49] The change in law was also accompanied by a change in the enforcement structure and agencies.[50] The new law was adopted to remedy some deficiencies identified in relation to the first one. In particular, it was hoped that VCL 2018 would introduce a more effects-based approach into the enforcement of the law.[51] Looking at Vietnamese experience is also useful considering that both VCL 2004 and VCL 2018 allegedly drew inspiration from the economics-based model.[52] The analysis below examines the aspects of VCL 2018 that are relevant from a redistributive perspective.

[44] The World Bank, 'The World Bank List of Economies: Vietnam' databank.worldbank.org/data/download/site-content/CLASS.xls.

[45] K Schwab (ed), 'The Global Competitiveness Report' (2019) The World Economic Forum www3.weforum.org/docs/WEF_TheGlobalCompetitivenessReport2019.pdf.

[46] O Pimhidzai, 'Climbing the Ladder: Poverty Reduction and Shared Prosperity in Vietnam' (2018) The World Bank Report openknowledge.worldbank.org/bitstream/handle/10986/29684/124916-WP-PULIC-P161323-VietnamPovertyUpdateReportENG.pdf?sequence=1&isAllowed=y. The study reported that only 2% of the population lived in extreme poverty.

[47] NH Quyen, *Reducing rural poverty in Vietnam: issues, policies, challenges* (2019) Mekong Development Research Institute www.un.org/development/desa/dspd/wp-content/uploads/sites/22/2019/03/Reducing-rural-poverty-in-Vietnam-Issues-Policies-Challenges.pdf.

[48] Vietnamese Law on Competition, Law No 27/2004/QH11 of 3 December 2004, in force from 1 July 2005.

[49] Vietnamese Law on Competition, Law No 23/2018/QH14 of 12 June 2018, in force from 1 July 2019.

[50] Under VCL 2004, the 'investigative' and 'adjudicative' powers were separated between the Vietnam Competition Administrative Department (VCAD) and the Vietnam Competition Council (VCC). Under VCL 2018, an authority charged with enforcement of the law is the VCC, which acts on the basis of recommendations by the VCAD (later renamed as Vietnam Competition and Consumer Authority). See LH Luu, 'Vietnam's Competition Law Adoption: From Passive to Active' in S Van Uytsel et al (eds), *Research Handbook on Asian Competition Law* (Cheltenham, Edward Elgar Publishing, 2020) 137, or A Pham, 'The Development of Competition Law in Vietnam in the Face of Economic Reforms and Global Integration' (2006) 26 *Northwestern Journal of International Law & Business* 547, 557.

[51] OECD, *OECD Peer Reviews of Competition Law and Policy: Viet Nam* (2018) www.oecd.org/daf/competition/VietNam-OECD-Competition-Review-2018-ENG.pdf.

[52] Luu (n 50) 134, or Pham (n 50) 547. See also J Gillespie, 'Localized Global Competition Law in Vietnam: A Bottom-up Perspective' (2015) 64(4) *The International and Comparative Law Quarterly* 935, 938, or NT Hoa, 'How large is Vietnam's informal economy?' (2019) 39(1) *Economic Affairs* 81.

A. Goals of VCL 2018

As suggested above, the general position of a competition law towards equity and redistributive issues can at times be derived from the goals of the law. Gal and Fox recommend that competition law in developing countries should not be a priori opposed to pursuing goals other than increasing economic efficiency or consumer welfare. Rather, a multiplicity of goals should be recognised to ensure that weight is given to redistributive concerns and economic development is inclusive.[53]

Policymakers in Vietnam seem to have embraced this recommendation. VCL 2018 stipulates that the state's policies on competition shall aim to create and maintain a healthy, fair and transparent competition environment, enhance accessibility to markets, improve efficiency and social welfare and protect consumers' interests.[54] It is stated that competition must be conducted following the principles of honesty and fairness and shall not infringe upon the interests of the state, public interests and legitimate rights and interests of enterprises and consumers.[55]

Competition policy in Vietnam not only aims to create and maintain a healthy competition environment and enhance economic efficiency but also accords equal emphasis to securing fairness and improving social welfare. The imperative to reflect the interests of the state, public interests and interests and rights of enterprises or consumers in competition law suggests that the enforcement authority, ie, Vietnam Competition and Consumer Authority (the 'VCA'), will examine and balance interests that are not purely efficiency related.[56] Such balancing becomes especially important in view of the socio-political framework in which competition law in Vietnam operates. Vietnam declares itself to be a 'socialist market economy', which suggests that concerns related to sustainable economic development play a significant role.[57] Equity-driven (instead of purely efficiency-driven) competition law is in accordance with those developmental goals. Hence, the overarching regulatory framework of competition, as articulated in the goals of the law, seems to afford the VCA great leeway to reflect and accord weight to equity-related considerations in the enforcement of VCL 2018.

[53] Gal and Fox (n 21) 296.

[54] VCL 2018, Art 6.

[55] ibid, Art 5(2).

[56] HL Luu, 'Chapter 13: Vietnam', in K Groshinski and C Davies (eds), *Competition Law in Asia Pacific: A Practical Guide* (Alphen aan den Rijn, Kluwer Law International, 2015) 715–766.

[57] This follows from the understanding of the term as 'an economic model of a society in its transition from a low economic level to a higher level, toward a new society – the socialist regime. It is a well-organized market economy, under the leadership of the Communist Party and management of the socialist State. It limits weaknesses arising from the spontaneity of the market, so as to better serve the interests of a majority of the population and the sustainable development of the entire nation.' See The Embassy of the Socialist Republic of Vietnam in the United States of America, 'Socialist-Oriented Market Economy: Concept and Development Solution' (2003) vietnamembassy-usa.org/news/2003/11/socialist-oriented-market-economy-concept-and-development-soluti. See also TT Nguyen, 'Competition Law in Vietnam, A Paper or Young Tiger?' (2012) 57(3) *The Antitrust Bulletin* 409, 414.

B. Anti-competitive Agreements

i. Cartels

From the perspective of a country struggling with poverty and economic inequality, a competition law approach to cartels is of paramount importance because cartel behaviour usually directly impinges on consumer welfare, including that of poor consumers.[58] Products affected by cartel agreements are sold for higher prices than under the conditions of perfect competition, and their output is reduced. Cartels are said to diminish social welfare, create allocative inefficiency and transfer wealth from consumers of the products concerned to the participants in the cartel.[59] Hence, cartelisation in relation to products on which the poor spend most of their income, such as food, or that are crucial for economic development, such as healthcare or education, threatens to jeopardise poverty alleviation and increase economic inequality.[60] It has been recommended that developing countries should take a tough stance towards cartels; that is, a per se approach – which relieves the enforcement agency of the obligation to analyse their effect on competition – to the most serious cartel infringements is advised.[61]

This insight seems to have been followed in Vietnam. VCL 2018 provides a list of anti-competitive agreements that are prohibited per se.[62] This marks a shift from the approach under VCL 2004, which prohibited some of the enumerated agreements, including price-fixing or horizontal market-sharing agreements, only where the parties to those agreements had more than 30 per cent market share.[63] This approach may have been justified on the grounds that cartels can play some role in replacing inefficient enforcement of contracts by courts.[64] Richman observes that where institutionalised enforcement is not reliable, private merchants resort to coordinated measures akin to a group boycott to punish the parties who breach contracts.[65] On this account, group boycotts that are usually considered hardcore cartels can be regarded as a procompetitive solution to court failures.

[58] Bhattacharjea (n 13) 62.

[59] A Jones and B Sufrin, *EU Competition Law: Text, Cases, and Materials*, 6th edn (Oxford, Oxford University Press, 2016) 650.

[60] ibid. See also Cheng (n 7) 335.

[61] O Budzinski and MHA Beigi, 'Generating instead of Protecting Competition' in MS Gal et al (eds), *The Economic Characteristics of Developing Jurisdictions: Their Implications for Competition Law* (Cheltenham, Edward Elgar Publishing, 2015) 233, or DD Sokol and A Stephan, 'Prioritizing Cartel Enforcement in Developing World Competition Agencies' in DD Sokol et al (eds), *Competition Law and Development* (Stanford, Stanford University Press, 2013).

[62] VCL 2018, Arts 11 and 12. Other enumerated and unenumerated agreements are only prohibited if they adversely affect or are capable of adversely affecting competition in the Vietnamese market.

[63] VCL 2004, Arts 9 and 10.

[64] BD Richman, 'Contracts and Cartels, Reconciling Competition and Development Policy' in DD Sokol et al (eds), *Competition Law and Development* (Stanford, Stanford University Press, 2013) 155–166.

[65] ibid.

The change in law may have been instigated by the observation that cartel activity is widespread in Vietnam.[66] The adopted per se approach promises to facilitate enforcement against suspected cartels because it shifts the burden of proof for the benefit of the VCA. Prohibiting the most serious competition law infringements regardless of the market share of the enterprises involved also promotes competition advocacy and provides enterprises with clear boundaries that clarify what conduct is anti-competitive. Yet, as further explained below, even agreements that are prohibited per se can theoretically capitalise on an exemption where the parties show that the benefits of the cartel outweigh its harm to competition and consumers.

ii. Vertical Agreements

A competition law approach to vertical agreements is relevant from the perspective of inequality and poverty, inter alia, because of these agreements' potential relevance to and for SMEs. It has been suggested that vertical agreements help SMEs develop to become more competitive vis-à-vis larger enterprises.[67] Nevertheless, it has also been observed that the effects of vertical agreements can be more serious in concentrated markets, where they have greater potential to foreclose rivals and deter market entry.[68] Given their mixed effects, the competition law response to vertical agreements is expected to alternate between the effects-based and per se approaches. The per se approach provides greater legal certainty but risks punishing or deterring agreements that would otherwise be beneficial for SMEs. The effects-based approach puts greater demands on the depth of analysis required to establish that an anti-competitive vertical agreement has been concluded, but it is more responsive to the specifics of a case.

In general, it is recommended that developing countries favour a rules-based approach over a case-by-case approach.[69] Competition law should incorporate clear rules and precise standards that do not leave space for too much discretion.[70] This recommendation is justified in that the enforcement agencies in developing countries are usually financially constrained and lack personnel.[71] This lack of resources prevents them from performing extensive and complex analyses. In contrast, the rules-based approach relieves them from any such obligation. In addition, clear rules provide enterprises with greater certainty regarding the

[66] M Furse, 'Competition Law in Vietnam: A Critique' (2010) 33 (1) *World Competition* 163, 176.
[67] Nguyen (n 57) 424.
[68] Cheng (n 7) 347.
[69] Budzinski and Beigi (n 61) 232, or Cheng (n 7) 481.
[70] JO Haley, 'Competition Law for the Asia-Pacific Economic Cooperation Community: Designing Shoes for Many Sizes' (2002) 1 *Washington University Global Studies Law Review* 001, 12, Gal and Bakhoum (n 24), Sokol et al (n 10) 2, Budzinski and Beigi (n 61) 233, or TK Cheng, 'Convergence and Its Discontents: A Reconsideration of the Merits of Convergence of Global Competition Law' (2012) 12(2) *Chicago Journal of International Law* 433, 475.
[71] Cheng (n 7) 319.

requisite standards of conduct. Only after gaining experience with the application of the law on the side of both the regulatory agencies and the enterprises is it recommendable to venture to more case-by-case approaches.[72]

The general recommendation does not seem to have been followed in Vietnam in relation to vertical agreements, presumably because of their mixed effects on competition, and the country has opted for the effects-based approach. VCL 2018 explicitly enumerates vertical agreements containing hardcore restrictions as vertical agreements that are potentially anti-competitive; it also incorporates a general catch-all clause targeting unenumerated agreements.[73] However, it adds that such vertical agreements will only be prohibited if they cause or are capable of causing significant anti-competitive effects on the market.[74] The effects-based approach can be viewed positively in that it allows the VCA to evaluate the role of a vertical agreement in a specific business relationship. Where a vertical agreement has been concluded mainly to remedy deficient or missing legal institutions, such as inefficient contract enforcement, a more lenient approach can be adopted. Thus, until a more robust legal framework is established, enterprises will not be discouraged from entering into business relationships that encourage entrepreneurship and promote inclusive growth.[75] In line with the effects-based approach, vertical agreements can also be sanctioned as an abuse of dominance when entered into by dominant enterprises.[76]

iii. Exemptions

Granting exemptions from the general prohibition of anti-competitive agreements in Vietnam follows a different logic than the effects-based approach to vertical agreements. In this case, VCL 2018 relies on the rules-based approach and establishes an ex ante approval mechanism under which an otherwise anti-competitive agreement can be declared compliant with competition law.

As a general rule, both horizontal and vertical agreements can benefit from an exemption under VCL 2018.[77] Exempted agreements need to benefit consumers and meet one or more of the other enumerated criteria.[78] Interestingly, one of those criteria is that the agreement relates to conditions for contract performance,

[72] Budzinski and Beigi (n 61) 234.
[73] VCL 2018, Art 12(4).
[74] ibid.
[75] Hoa (n 52).
[76] See VCL 2018, Art 27(1)(b), which prohibits imposing an unreasonable buying or selling price of goods or services or fixing a minimum resale price that causes or is likely to cause damage to customers.
[77] VCL 2018, Art 14.
[78] These include, eg, the promotion of technical or technological progress, improving the quality of goods and services, strengthening the competitiveness of Vietnamese enterprises in the international market, or agreeing on conditions for contract performance, delivery and payment but not related to price and price factors (see VCL 2018, Art 14(1)).

delivery and payment.[79] This seems to confirm Richman's hypothesis that competition law can sometimes be used to remedy inefficient enforcement of contracts by courts, which may be the case in Vietnam.[80] Even hardcore cartels can theoretically benefit from an exemption. This corresponds to the EU approach.[81] The difference is that, in Vietnam, the exemption must be granted by the VCA in advance, and it only lasts for a limited period. This was the case in the nascent years of EU competition law enforcement prior to modernisation.[82] Although the ex ante approval system is more demanding regarding the enforcement capacity of the VCA, which can be overwhelmed with requests for exemption, it promises to provide clearer guidance to the enterprises in terms of the scope of the prohibitions. This system also helps the VCA to establish coherent case law regarding the interpretation of the criteria for potential exemptions. This is particularly useful if, in the future, Vietnam switches to a self-evaluative framework as the EU did.

C. Abuse of Dominance

Abuses of excessive market power deserve particular attention in developing countries, where markets tend to be monopolised and where harm to poor consumers and SMEs because of abusive practices increases economic inequality.[83] Hence, a tough competition law response to abuse of dominance is recommended.[84] Increased competition promises to curb excessive market power, preventing the gap between the rich and the poor from widening.

Vietnam indeed seems to possess some of the characteristics typical of developing countries that make them vulnerable to abuses of dominance.[85] Because of its geographical conditions and poor infrastructure and transportation, the markets are rather local and fragmented.[86] Relevant markets as identified in competition law analysis are more concentrated, and enterprises in such markets tend to have greater market power. Such a natural tendency for market concentration is further reinforced in that some strategic markets continue to be dominated by SOEs, which played a crucial role in the command economy era prior to the

[79] VCL 2018, Art 14(1).

[80] Richman (n 64). In the World Bank's database 'Doing Business', in 2020 on the criteria 'Enforcing Contracts' Vietnam was ranked on the 68th position out of the 190 countries included in the database. On the scale of 0-100, it received the score of 62.1. See World Bank, 'Doing Business' (2020) www.doingbusiness.org/en/data/exploreeconomies/vietnam.

[81] Communication from the Commission – Notice – Guidelines on the application of Article 81(3) of the Treaty [2004] OJ C101/08 para 46. See also R Whish and D Bailey, *Competition Law*, 9th edn (Oxford, Oxford University Press, 2018) 159.

[82] G Lusty and S King, 'Article 101(3)', in D Bailey and LE John (eds) '*Bellamy & Child, European Union Law of Competition*', 8th edn (Oxford, Oxford University Press, 2018) 205–256, 3.006.

[83] See, eg, Ennis and Kim (n 3).

[84] Budzinski and Beigi (n 61) 242.

[85] Gal and Fox (n 21) 331–332.

[86] Furse (n 66) 165.

introduction of market-oriented policies in 1986.[87] The importance of these enterprises for Vietnam's socialist market economy is recognised even by VCL 2018; these enterprises continue to play a central role in the state's macroeconomic policy. They can be or are used as a tool to safeguard social security and stability, secure employment opportunities and deliver basic goods.[88] This means that profit maximisation is not their sole objective, and this goal can be overshadowed by redistribution tasks. VCL 2018 expressly entrusts control over enterprises in state-monopolised sectors in relation to, for example, the price, quantity and scope of goods and services provided to the state.[89] As these are usually the sectors charged with the production of basic goods and services, it is for the state – rather than the free market – to ensure that these goods and services are provided to all.

Despite its support of SOEs, VCL 2018 makes it clear that when such enterprises act outside of the state monopoly domain, they are subject to the general prohibition of the abuse of dominance. This corresponds to the view that the private sector plays an indispensable role in driving economic growth and excessive reliance on the state sector distorts market competition.[90] Therefore, policymakers in Vietnam seem to show a determination to enforce the prohibition against abusive practices regardless of whether the enterprise is privately or publicly owned. Indeed, VCL 2018 allows the VCA to take a tougher stance towards unilateral practices if required. This can be inferred not only from the tests it uses to determine dominance, but also from the incorporation of specific rules applicable only to 'monopolies'.

As regards the tests used to determine dominance, VCL 2018 relies primarily on market shares. Enterprises with a market share of 30 per cent or higher are presumed to have a dominant position. Cheng suggests that the 30 per cent threshold is too low, especially considering the expected higher concentration of Vietnam's markets.[91] Joined with the irrebuttable nature of the presumption,[92] concerns have been voiced that this can lead to the overregulation of unilateral practices in Vietnam.[93]

In the absence of a requisite market share that would trigger the application of the presumption, a dominant position can also be inferred from an undertaking's market power: where the undertaking possesses a 'significant market power', it is to be considered dominant.[94] This alternative test of dominance enables the

[87] LN Dang et al, 'State-Owned Enterprises Reform in Viet Nam: Progress and Challenges' (2020) ADBI Working Paper Series No 1071.

[88] See, generally Dowdle (n 10) 352.

[89] VCL 2018, Art 28.

[90] Pham (n 50) 548.

[91] Cheng (n 7) 369.

[92] Mayer Brown, 'Vietnam Competition Law Series, Abuse of Dominance in Vietnam' (2018) www.mayerbrown.com/-/media/files/perspectives-events/publications/2018/12/vietnam-competition-law-series--issue-3-abuse-of-d/files/vietnamcompetitionlawseriesissue3pdf/fileattachment/vietnamcompetitionlawseriesissue3pdf.pdf.

[93] Nguyen (n 57) 429.

[94] VCL 2018, Art 24(1).

VCA to find dominance where the undertaking has a market share of less than 30 per cent.[95] For example, the test examines potential competition in the market, the financial strength of the enterprise or the countervailing buyer power.[96] The examination of the countervailing buyer power seems to be especially important from the perspective of a developing country; in such a context, countervailing buyer power issues can be particularly troubling.

As regards specific approach to 'monopolies', VCL 2018 subjects them to stricter regulation than 'regular' dominant enterprises. It defines monopolies as those dominant enterprises that have no competitors for the goods they trade or services they provide in the relevant market – that is, enterprises that have 100 per cent market share.[97] The stricter approach is reflected in that in addition to being prohibited from engaging in conduct that is also prohibited for non-monopolistic dominant enterprises, monopolies are proscribed from imposing unfavourable conditions on customers and exploiting the monopoly power to unilaterally modify or cancel the contracts signed without plausible reasons.[98]

The presumption of dominance based on 30 per cent market share – representing an alternative test to determine dominance that examines the existence of 'significant market power' or special abuses related to monopolies – promises to make it easier for the VCA to establish an abuse of dominance or monopoly case.[99] Nevertheless, the VCA is still obligated to establish real or potential harmful effects on competition of allegedly abusive conduct.[100] Cheng suggests that this obligation relativises the effect of presumptions of dominance and that a rebuttable presumption of abuse where abusive behaviour occurs would be more appropriate.[101] In this context, Cheng also points out that it is not possible to put forward any universally applicable defences to justify the allegedly abusive practices in Vietnam, in contrast to EU law, for example, in the form of the 'objective necessity defence' or 'meeting competition defence'.[102] Where the impossibility of putting forward such defences would be joined with a rebuttable presumption of abuse, the resulting regulatory setup may be unduly strict. From this perspective, the current approach may be considered adequate.

[95] Cheng (n 7) 368.

[96] VCL 2018, Art 26(1).

[97] ibid, Art 25.

[98] ibid, Art 27(2). Furse (n 66) 171.

[99] Luu (n 50) 142.

[100] VCL 2018 requires that the actual or potential effect of the conduct on competition is established. A mere proof of the actual conduct (ie the abuse) is not sufficient (see VCL 2018, Art 3(5)).

[101] Cheng (n 7) 369.

[102] Cheng (n 7) 374. For EU law, see Communication from the Commission – Guidance on the Commission's enforcement priorities in applying Article 82 of the EC Treaty to abusive exclusionary conduct by dominant undertakings [2009] OJ C45/02 paras 28–31. See also Whish and Bailey (n 81) 217.

D. Economic Concentrations

Recommendations vary in relation to merger control for developing countries. It is sometimes asserted that developing countries do not need merger control at all.[103] In such cases, it is argued that mergers are necessary to allow domestic firms to grow and become internationally competitive, given the small domestic markets that developing countries usually have.[104] In addition, it is pointed out that merger control can deter foreign direct investment, which is crucial for developing countries.[105] Others insist that even developing countries need merger control by asserting that it is necessary to prevent circumvention of anti-cartel policy and to prevent the creation of too many dominant firms.[106] In such cases, developing countries are advised to focus on whether a merger gives rise to a dominant undertaking (ie a unilateral-effects theory of harm) rather than on whether there is a risk of increased coordination in the market after the merger (ie a coordinated-effects theory of harm).[107] Hence, merger activity should be viewed more critically in a way that can lead to the creation of market power, which is notoriously detrimental to inclusive economic development.[108]

Vietnam's policymakers have decided to regulate mergers through competition law. Under VCL 2004, they seem to have strictly followed the advice to focus on the risks connected with the potential creation of market power. VCL 2004 prohibited all concentrations in which the combined market share of the enterprises was more than 50 per cent of the relevant market,[109] and it subjected concentrations between enterprises with a combined market share of 30–50 per cent to a notification obligation.[110] Although the general prohibition of mergers above 50 per cent market share was lifted by VCL 2018, the notification obligation remained linked to market shares.[111] The market share threshold is considered problematic by some commentators because its determination depends on the definition of the relevant market, which is usually not clear-cut and requires sophisticated economic analyses.[112] In addition to the market share threshold,

[103] For the summary of the discussion see, eg, Cheng (n 7) 398–399.

[104] P Brusick and SJ Evenett, 'Should Developing Countries Worry about Abuse of Dominant Power' (2008) 2 *Wisconsin Law Review* 269, 287.

[105] Cheng (n 7) 399.

[106] Budzinski and Beigi (n 61) 240.

[107] Cheng (n 7) 419.

[108] Budzinski and Beigi (n 61) 241.

[109] VCL 2004, Art 19. See also Furse (n 66) 173–174.

[110] VCL 2004, Art 20. No notification was required if a post-transaction market share was less than 30% or where the post-transaction enterprise remained an SME.

[111] The threshold is set at 20% of the combined market share of the merging parties in the relevant market. See Art 13.1 of the implementing Decree 35/2020/ND-CP ('Decree 35').

[112] This was at the cause of the investigation of Grab's acquisition of Uber's operations in Southeast Asia in consideration of Uber having a 27.5% share in Grab, where the parties had differing views as to what the post-transaction market share would be. See VCA, *Annual Report for 2018* (2019).

VCL 2018 adds other criteria that trigger the notification obligation, which relate to the assets, revenue and value of the transaction.[113] Economic concentrations will be prohibited if they restrict or are capable of significantly restricting competition in the Vietnamese market,[114] and both unilateral and coordinated effects are relevant.[115]

Although the evaluative benchmarks do not generally differ from those used under the efficiency-based model, VCL 2018 includes provisions that explicitly allow for the enforcement of concerns related to economic development, such as national competitiveness or the protection of SMEs. Indeed, merger control is considered an area of competition law where economic efficiency often needs to be balanced with the goals of other public policies, such as industrial policy.[116] As mentioned in relation to the goals of VCL 2018, the law explicitly authorises the VCA to consider public interest and industrial policy, and it anticipates balancing of objectives on a regular case-by-case basis.[117] Public policy interests can also be projected into the evaluation of positive effects of a concentration, such as its positive impact on the development of industries, science and technology; the development of SMEs; or the enhancement of Vietnamese enterprises' competitiveness in the international market.[118] This gives the VCA authority to accord greater weight in balancing the prospective effects of an economic concentration to concerns related to economic development rather than to simply economic efficiency.

E. Enforcement Priorities

Competition authorities in developing countries are advised to concentrate their enforcement efforts in sectors where the increased competition makes a particular contribution to poverty alleviation and reduction of economic inequality.[119] These are the sectors where the poor households spend a significant proportion of their income or where small entrepreneurs or SMEs face dominant counterparties that exploit their power, such as agriculture, health care, education or electricity.[120] An additional benefit of focusing on such sectors that are 'visible' to the public is that it promises to support accountability of the enforcement agency and competition advocacy, which are regarded as crucial in rooting competition culture in a society.[121]

[113] See Decree 35, Art 13.1.
[114] VCL 2018, Art 30.
[115] ibid, Art 31.
[116] Sokol, 'Tensions between Antitrust and Industrial Policy' (n 34) 1256–1258.
[117] VCL 2018, Arts 5(2) or 6(1) or (3).
[118] ibid, Art 32.
[119] Budzinski and Beigi (61) 238, or Cheng (n 7) 147.
[120] Cheng (n 7) 148 or 315, Evenett (n 23) 23, or Bhattacharjea (n 13) 63.
[121] Bhattacharjea (n 13) 61.

In Vietnam, the generally low level of enforcement seems to be an issue. The enforcement against both anti-competitive agreements and abuse of dominance has been rather scarce. From 2006 until 2018, the initial investigations were launched in 99 cases; formal investigations were launched in nine cases, leading to six infringement decisions.[122] The focus of the investigations varied from building ceramics, film, milk, gas or cement sectors in 2014[123] to milk, beer, seaport, maritime, banking or electricity sectors in 2015;[124] fishing vessel insurance, pay TV, film, tourism, sugar, steel and gas, TV rights or advertising markets in 2016; sugar market in 2017;[125] automobile, motorbike, sugarcane, petrol, platforms market, distribution of movies, tourism agricultural products or postal markets in 2018;[126] and pork markets in 2019.[127] Some investigations were carried out in sectors that can be considered 'essential' for the poor, small entrepreneurs or SMEs, such as sectors of agricultural products (eg sugar or milk market) or education (eg student insurance), sectors of building materials (eg cement or steel market), energy (eg gas) or communication (eg postal market).

Cases that resulted in a formal decision included finding a price-fixing agreement between 19 insurance companies in 2010[128] and fixing student insurance fees by 12 companies providing student insurance in 2011.[129] Abuse of dominance cases concerned the exclusivity agreements by an accommodation booking platform with various hotels and a refusal to supply aviation fuel to Jetstar by Vinapco.[130] Regarding merger decisions, although the enforcement in the merger review is largely determined by the notifications for approval, on its own initiative, the VCA reviewed several concentrations that did not trigger the notification obligation. For example, in 2018, it reviewed concentrations in the film production, car manufacturing, plastics and supermarkets sectors.[131] In 2019, it looked into mergers in the agricultural and pharmaceutical sectors.[132] The challenge of the Grab/Uber acquisition was also launched on the VCA's initiative.[133]

The above suggests that although some investigations are taking place, they seldom lead to infringement decisions. This is likely the result of resolving the

[122] VCA, *Annual Report for 2018* (2019).
[123] VCA, *Annual Report for 2014* (2015).
[124] VCA, *Annual Report for 2015* (2016).
[125] VCA, *Annual Report for 2017* (2018).
[126] VCA, *Annual Report for 2018* (2019).
[127] VCA, *Annual Report for 2019* (2020). The Annual report for 2018 envisaged conducting case investigations in automobile production and trading sectors, pharmaceutical distribution, steel production and trading, retail and beer, wine and soft drinks.
[128] VCA, *Annual Report for 2013* (2014).
[129] The parties voluntarily terminated the agreement once they discovered it was anti-competitive, but they were still held liable to pay administrative fees. See Mayer Brown, 'Vietnam Competition Law, Key Changes in 2019' (2019) www.mayerbrown.com/-/media/files/perspectives-events/publications/2019/02/vietnam_competition_law_key_changes_in_2019.pdf.
[130] ibid.
[131] VCA, *Annual Report for 2018* (2019).
[132] VCA, *Annual Report for 2019* (2020).
[133] VCA, *Annual Report for 2018* (2019).

issue by other means, such as settlement with the parties or through some administrative intervention.[134] Low enforcement is also symptomatic of merger control. Several significant economic transactions were carried out without notification, including the above-mentioned Grab/Uber acquisition.[135]

A lower level of enforcement should not necessarily be considered negatively. Indeed, the scarcity of cases is not an indication of whether competition law is efficient. As explained above, an 'optimal' level of competition can differ among countries and depends, inter alia, on their needs and strategies to achieve economic growth and development. Investigations were carried out in sectors that are important from a distributional perspective, such as agricultural products, building materials, energy or communications or pharmaceutical products. In addition, the SOEs do not seem to be shielded from enforcement. This is important given that SOEs traditionally occupy sectors that provide basic products such as food, energy or telecommunication. Therefore, it may be that a lower level of enforcement corresponds to Vietnam's competition-related needs and priorities.

V. Vietnam's Experience and Its Transferability to Developed Countries

The case study on competition law in Vietnam illustrates how the aim of reducing economic inequality and poverty can be implemented in competition law and its enforcement. Policymakers in Vietnam seem to have prepared the ground for both approaching competition law as a tool for redistribution if necessary, and reflecting equity-related concerns in a more nuanced way in the applicable standards and their enforcement.

The first of those approaches is reflected in that VCL 2018 may be conceived as yet another tool to directly address developmental concerns. This stems not only from the goals of VCL 2018 but also from the possibility accorded to the VCA to abstain from promoting increased competition in markets where this would be detrimental to other public interests. The 'state management of competition' established by VCL 2018 implies that competition law will be an instrument to guide and control the market economy, which is but a part of Vietnam's 'socialist market economy'.[136] Thus, the state's policies on competition can play a role in enhancing social welfare.[137] One of the means of exercising this control is through SOEs or enterprises operating in state-monopolised domains, which are governed by the state.[138] Since SOEs assume important roles in securing social welfare and

[134] Gillespie (n 52) 944.

[135] Other examples include a merger between Viettel and EVN Telecom and a merger between Jetstar Pacific Airline and Vietnamese Airlines. See Mayer Brown (n 129).

[136] VCL 2018, Art 7.

[137] ibid, Art 6(3).

[138] ibid, Art 28.

delivering the essential goods necessary to lift people out of poverty, through the VCA, the state can put the enforcement of competition law on the side-lines, where such roles would be endangered by increased competition. All this implies that competition law in Vietnam may be used selectively and purposefully to deliver the desired objectives, including enhancing social welfare. This corresponds to a 'functionalist' approach to law that perceives law as just another tool to achieve public policy goals.[139] In this view, competition law would acquire a rather public-law character in that it is addressed to administrative authorities rather than to enterprises. Rather than giving instructions to market actors themselves on how to behave in the market, it gives instructions on how to weigh various public policy interests that arise in terms of the conduct of market actors.[140]

As regards the second approach, VCL 2018 also allows for reflecting developmental concerns indirectly through enforcement. It does so by modifying the analytical approaches promoted under the purely efficiency-based model. Although it does not explicitly state that these modifications are intended to promote inclusive economic development, they are likely expected to have such an effect. VCL 2018 also authorises the VCA to avoid enforcement motivated purely by economic efficiency that is detrimental to poor consumers or SMEs – that is, the expected beneficiaries of inclusive economic growth. It also allows the VCA to prioritise enforcement practices that are expected to be the most harmful to those sensitive groups. This includes establishing a per se framework for hard-core cartels, incorporating a more lenient approach to vertical agreements, taking a tougher stance towards abuses of market power by establishing irrebuttable presumptions of dominance and not allowing any defences to justify the alleged abuses, screening economic concentrations of a relatively low transaction value, or leading to a relatively low combined market shares post-transaction to minimise the risk of creating dominant enterprises.

Vietnam's model, which reflects its needs related to combating economic inequality and poverty in competition law, seems to be adequate in view of its socio-economic and political environment. Policymakers seem to have acknowledged that competition law has redistributive effects, which need to be reflected in view of Vietnam's socialist political system and its developmental goals. Although the regulation is informed by the efficiency-based model and relies on analytical frameworks of the EU regime, it contains mechanisms allowing the VCA to divert from this model where necessary. A noteworthy feature is also a marked tendency to move from a formalistic approach towards a more effects-based approach. For example, the 30 per cent market share benchmark used to define some prohibited anti-competitive agreements under VCL 2004 was replaced by a by-effect approach

[139] See, eg, JKM Ohnesorge, 'Developing Development Theory: Law and Development Orthodoxies and the Northeast Asian Experience' (2007) 28 *University of Pennsylvania Journal of International Law* 219. This approach to law is said to be common in Asian jurisdictions.

[140] See generally Dowdle (n 10) 377.

of VCL 2018. Agreements are only prohibited if they have a significant restraining effect on competition, save for the hardcore cartels, which are prohibited per se. The formalistic benchmark of 30 per cent market share to establish dominance, which was the only test available to determine dominance under VCL 2004, was accompanied by a 'significant market power' test under VCL 2018. The prohibition of economic concentrations where the combined market share of enterprises is more than 50 per cent established by VCL 2004 was abandoned under VCL 2018 and replaced by the obligation to examine whether a concentration restricts or is capable of significantly restricting competition. All these changes suggest that the VCA is progressively gaining increased capacity to handle more complex cases.

Although Vietnam's model seems to fit the country's socioeconomic and political needs, it does not seem to be easily transferred or transplanted. This is because Vietnam's economic system – that is, a socialist market economy – significantly limits the role that competition can play. Instead of considering it as a self-regulatory phenomenon, Vietnam subordinates it to control by the state. Thus, Vietnam's approach is informative for jurisdictions where the state assumes a central role in the economy and economic development depends on state-led rather than private initiatives. This is the case for some other Asian economies that are described as 'developmental states'.[141] Yet, in developing economies that rely on free markets with less governmental intervention as the main driver of economic growth, the reliance on competition law for wealth transfer from the rich to the poor may need an additional justification and explanation for why other more direct distributional tools are set aside.

Despite its potential limitations, Vietnam's approach is methodologically instructive to other developing countries, including in relation to the transition from a rules-based towards a more effects-based analytical approach. Where economic inequality and poverty are the main concerns, countries should first identify the main market-related sources of such economic inequality and poverty. For example, sectors that provide necessities for poor consumers or entrepreneurs are occupied by large monopolies, private or state-owned, that abuse their position. The rise of these monopolies is facilitated by the fragmented and concentrated nature of the markets stemming from the great urban–rural divide. The prevalence of the informal economy outside of any governmental support or social welfare system further adds to the vicious circle of poverty. Upon identification of the main drivers of economic inequality and poverty, applicable rules shall be chosen. Policymakers can draw from the pool of shared competition law knowledge or 'best practices' that are traditionally informed by efficiency-based models. Where necessary, such rules should be adjusted to facilitate enforcement against behaviour that is expected to aggravate economic inequality. This can be done by incorporating clear-cut rules that rely on experience that the specified

[141] YW Chu, 'The Asian Developmental State: Ideas and Debates' in WY Chu (ed), *The Asian Developmental State, Reexaminations and New Departures* (London, Palgrave Macmillan, 2016).

conduct almost always harms the poor or otherwise widens economic inequality. Where the effects of the conduct are more nuanced, which is likely to be the case as a country progresses in its economic development, straightforward rules can be accompanied by rules that allow the enforcement authority to engage in a more complex analysis. VCL 2018 not only provides examples of concrete modifications to the purely efficiency-based model that can be implemented but also documents such progressive transformation from a rules-based approach towards a more effects-based approach.

Regarding the replicability of Vietnam's model in developed countries, substantive and methodological aspects need to be differentiated. From a substantive perspective, replicability might depend on the source of economic inequality. Because poverty is the main source of economic inequality, Vietnam's approach can be instructive. However, given the metrics used to differentiate between developing and developed countries, the poverty level is presumed to be rather low in developed countries.[142] This means that economic inequality is likely to be linked to other sources. At that point, the implicit reliance on the implied model of distributive justice, which favours helping the poor as the least advantaged group, can be problematic. To reduce economic inequality, the income achieved by increased competition can be allocated in a different way, which would be preferable in developed country settings. Such income can be allocated to a different group of consumers or follow a different distributional logic anchored in a distinct model of distributive justice.[143] For example, a utilitarian model would require maximising the total utility rather than strictly the income or wealth of a particular group.[144] Following a desert-based model of distributive justice – which advocates the distribution of wealth based on how the individual contributes to providing goods or services that are desired by others – would require a system that distributes income according to the different levels earned or deserved by the individuals according to their economic contributions to the society.[145] This illustrates that once the decision on the allocation of the surplus is integrated into competition law rather than left out, as in the efficiency-based model,[146] the advocated distributional model may need to be justified by the answerable political representation.

If inspiration is to be drawn from Vietnam's experience, it is necessary to consider that the Vietnamese system seems to implicitly follow the model of distributive justice, which supports the allocation of economic surplus to the least advantaged group. Where this model conforms to the redistributive policy needs of a developed country, from a methodological perspective, Vietnam's approach

[142] The classification of countries as developing or developed relies, inter alia, on the income criterion such as the gross national income (GNI), which is also used as an indicator of poverty. See, eg, United Nations Economic Commission for Europe, '*Guide on Poverty Measurement*' (United Nations, 2017) ec.europa.eu/eurostat/ramon/statmanuals/files/UNECE_Guide_on_Poverty_Measurement.pdf.

[143] Gerard and Lianos (n 28) 4.

[144] Knight (n 30) 32.

[145] Lamont and Favor (n 29).

[146] Gerard and Lianos (n 28) 4.

can serve as a point of reference. This can be the case, for example, where economic inequality that needs to be reduced is not drawn along 'rich–poor' lines but by appurtenance to a particular disadvantaged community. For example, authors have observed that 'ethnic' cartels exist in Malaysia, which often pose barriers to the participation of indigenous communities in the economy.[147] Competition law can respond by supporting affirmative action policies targeted at encouraging greater participation of those groups in the economy and by paying special attention to competition-law enforcement in markets where ethnic cartels are expected to operate. This parallels the approach of Vietnam's competition law in its goals' multiplicity, which facilitates enforcement against some anti-competitive agreements and an enforcement focus targeted at practices that are believed to be particularly harmful to the poor.

Given the characteristics outlined above, the granular experience from Vietnam's model can be shared with other countries where there is congruence in the distributional models pursued. Paradoxically, such experience sharing between Vietnam and developed countries reverses the direction of transfers, as witnessed in the past. Where the introduction of competition law in developing countries was connected to transplanting foreign concepts from developed countries, the reflection of distributional concerns in developed countries can draw on the experience of developing countries that already had to tailor those transplanted concepts to meet their need to secure inclusive economic development.

VI. Conclusion

This chapter examined how concerns about economic inequality and poverty can be reflected in competition laws that are being introduced in developing countries and whether developed countries can find inspiration in some of these approaches. It considered the example of Vietnam as representative of a developing country that underwent rapid economic growth and has a fairly long history of competition law. It found that Vietnam's competition law comprises mechanisms that allow the enforcement agency to use competition law as a tool to address economic inequality and poverty. It also found that the efficiency-based approaches transplanted to Vietnam, especially from the EU competition law, were modified so that the law is more responsive to Vietnam's distributive concerns. This chapter considered this approach adequate in view of Vietnam's socio-economic and political environment.

[147] H Ahamat, NA Rahman and AMH Mohamed, 'Competition Law and Affirmative Action in Malaysia: Complementarity or Conflict?' (2015) 23 *Pertanika Journal of Social Sciences and Humanities* 13, 19 or 23. Reference to Malaysia is being made with the acknowledgement that Malaysia is classified as an upper-middle income country in the World Bank classification as of June 2020. The World Bank, 'The World Bank List of Economies: Malaysia' (June 2020) databank.worldbank.org/data/download/site-content/CLASS.xls.

Despite the adequacy of the approach, however, the chapter questioned whether Vietnam's model is generally replicable. This is because of Vietnam's specific economic system – namely, that of a socialist market economy advocating for the direct involvement of the state in the economy. In addition, Vietnam's approach seems to be grounded in a specific model of distributive justice that does not need to be universally shared, especially not in developed countries. Nonetheless, the chapter recognised the usefulness of Vietnam's experience from a methodological perspective. In addition to illustrating a progressive transfer from a rules-based to a more effects-based approach, Vietnam's model proposes potential tools that can be used where policymakers want to employ competition law to afford greater protection to a particular economic group, however defined, that is recognised as deserving preferential treatment from a redistributive perspective.

PART III

Specific Problems and Markets

8

Network Externalities, Income Inequality and the Role of Competition Law

MITJA KOVAC AND ELISABETH WIELINGER*

I. Introduction

It is hard to overstate the effect of income inequality on the social fabric's existence and stability. The super-fast economic changes spurred by the worldwide integration of markets and related explosion of social inequality entail some of the modern world's most challenging developments. Namely, social inequality creates a heaven-like environment for all sorts of populisms, extremisms, calls for trade protection, restrictions on immigration, union protectionism, numerous anti-competitive measures, and useless government subsidies. As a result and as seen multiple times in history, it constitutes a very real threat to the fragile social fabric.[1]

What then should be done about today's rising income inequality? What is the optimal policy intervention? Conventional economic literature states income inequality should be exclusively regulated after it has occurred through the ex post tax-and-transfer system, not through the legal system.[2] Hence, conventional economic wisdom holds that the legal system should focus only on efficiency and that efficiency-equality trade-offs should be made solely in the tax system; income inequality arguments are considered irrelevant in competition law, contract law,

* The authors acknowledge financial support from the Slovenian Research Agency (research core funding No P5-0128).

[1] It should also be stressed that in countries that experienced the most severe economic depression real household incomes dropped more substantially at the lower end of the income distribution.

[2] Conventional wisdom suggests that redistribution through the legal system causes the same labour distortions as the tax system, but in addition triggers distortions by interfering with the legal system's specific goals, such as achieving optimal precaution; S Shavell, 'A Note on Efficiency vs Distributional Equity in Legal Rulemaking: Should Distributional Equity Matter Given Optimal Income Taxation?' (1981) 71 *American Economic Review Papers and Proceedings* 414, 418. See also L Kaplow and S Shavell, 'Should Legal Rules Favour the Poor? Clarifying the Role of Legal Rules and the Income Tax in Redistributing Income' (2000) 29 *Journal of Legal Studies* 821, 835.

property law, tort law, employment law, patent law or any other field of law except tax law. However, De Geest argues that the 'actual source of income inequality are unjustified rents which should be prevented from occurring in the first place and not merely after they have already been generated'.[3] Therefore, the ex post tax-and-transfer system might not be the best institutional mechanism for reducing the inequality caused by rent-seeking behaviour since it addresses income inequality merely after it has already occurred, whereas the legal system, intervening ex ante, may be generally superior at preventing unjustified rents because, compared to the tax system, it has two intrinsic advantages: it corrects price distortions and rent-seeking behaviour, and avoids the labour distortion associated with the tax system.[4]

This chapter joins this critical debate and suggests that a substantial amount of inequality could be prevented ex ante also through competition law. The chapter focuses on virtual hardware-software network externalities, lock-in effects and related marketing techniques as particular sources of rents which may lead to income inequality. Moreover, it is assumed in the chapter that legal interventions to correct inefficiencies (ie market failures) are simultaneously also interventions mitigating inequality where the promotion of efficiency also promotes equality. The ensuing rents actually lead to inequality since the increase in the producer surplus from the exercise of market power primarily accrues to top executives and shareholders, who on average are wealthier than the median consumer. The unprecedented progress seen in artificial intelligence and other high-technologies means a growing share of today's advanced economies is held by sectors that exhibit network and lock-in effects, which make it very difficult for entrants to compete against incumbents, and a monopoly might persist despite the absence of any barriers to entry. In such an environment, particular attention should also be paid to the incumbent's potential rent-extracting capacity. Namely, income inequality is not only caused by talent and labour effort differences but also to a considerable extent by 'rents' – profits – that would not have been made in a perfectly competitive and transparent economy. These rents are in turn made possible by (often subtle) market failures (like network externalities, lock-in effects, asymmetric information, exploitation of behavioural shortcomings, cartels, predatory pricing). The presence of network externalities thus amplifies the ability of the firms in such industries to employ lock-in effects and other marketing techniques (eg razor-blade marketing models) in order to effectively extract rents from consumers. This rent-extracting capacity of industries with network externalities has in our view not been considered seriously enough by early law and economics literature.[5]

[3] G De Geest, 'Removing Rents: Why the Legal System is Superior to the Income Tax at Reducing Income Inequality' (2013) George Washington University Legal Studies Research Paper No 13-10-02, 3, ssrn.com/abstract=2337720.

[4] ibid.

[5] See, eg, HW Page and JE Lopatka, 'Network Externalities' in G De Geest and B Bouckaert (eds), *Encyclopaedia of Law and Economics* (Cheltenham, Edward Elgar, 2000); N Economides, 'Public Policy

Still, we believe that network externalities and lock-in effects are a major source of undesirable inequality and that greater intervention is therefore needed.

It is helpful to state several caveats at the outset. This chapter omits the discussion on whether statistics on income inequality provide clear-cut guidance for social policy or even a clear picture of income inequality,[6] and instead views the problem of inequality as undisputable. The chapter also does not discuss the perplexing issue of whether inequality is at all inefficient and what might be an 'optimal' amount of inequality in a particular society. Further, given the limited scope of the chapter we focus merely upon two sources of EU competition law.

This chapter is structured as follows. Section II contrasts ex post and ex ante approaches to redistribution. Section III advocates ex ante competition law interventions against the rent-extraction enabled by network externalities and by lock-in effects as a suitable remedy to income inequality. Section IV examines relevant case law and offers a critical analysis of current competition law enforcement practices. Section V concludes.

II. Interventions to Reduce Inequality: Ex Post Redistribution through Taxes versus Ex Ante Prevention through Law

This section provides a synthesis of arguments advanced in legal-economic literature about how to best redistribute income in society. It first introduces the traditional view, which favours the ex post tax-and-transfer system. Subsequently, it contrasts this view with more recent arguments for why it might be more efficient to redistribute income and remove the causes of rents and inequality ex ante through the legal system.

A. Conventional Economic Wisdom: Ex Post Redistribution through Taxes

Conventional (legal-)economic literature advances the tax system, not the legal system, as the optimal mechanism for redistributing income. Shavell and Kaplow in their seminal, widely cited article support this view with the double distortion

in Network Industries' in P Buccirossi (ed), *Handbook of Antitrust Economics* (Boston, The MIT Press, 2008) 469. However, for a more cautious approach see, eg, D Rubinfeld, 'Antitrust Enforcement in Dynamic Network Industries' (1998) 43 *The Antitrust Bulletin* 859.

[6] Posner, for example, argues that by taking a snapshot of incomes for one year, scholars misleadingly compare people in different stages of their life cycle. For instance, he emphasises that statistics places a young lawyer who has just joined a firm and a senior partner in the same firm in different income classes, yet both may earn the same amounts in their lifetimes (or the young lawyers might earn even more). RA Posner, *Economic Analysis of Law*, 8th edn (New York, Wolters Kluwer, 2011) 627.

argument: using the tax-and-transfer system as well as the legal system to address inequality might trigger certain economic distortions, but use of the legal system in addition will undermine its other social functions.[7] They argue that 'using legal rules to redistribute income distorts work incentives fully as much as the income tax system and also creates inefficiencies in the activities regulated by the legal rules'.[8] Consequently, 'redistribution through legal rules offers no advantage over redistribution through the income tax system and typically is less efficient'.[9] This line of argument is further developed by Cooter and Ulen who provide several more reasons supporting the supremacy of taxation and transfers:[10] a) income tax targets inequality precisely, whereas redistribution by private legal rules relies on crude averages; b) the distributive effects of the reshuffling of private rights are hard to predict; c) the transaction costs of redistribution through private legal rules are typically high; and d) redistribution by private law distorts the economy (incentives) more than progressive taxation does.

A logical implication of this view is that 'it is appropriate for economic analysis of legal rules to focus on efficiency and to ignore the distribution of income in offering normative judgments'.[11] Thus, an effective and smart legal system should – except in special circumstances[12] – not focus on inequality but exclusively on efficiency. If efficiency needs to be traded for equity, it should be effectuated through progressive taxation and ex post social welfare programmes.[13] This has become a foundational law-making principle in legal-economic thinking, as evidenced by its adoption by leading law and economics textbooks.[14]

B. Superiority of Ex Ante Legal Intervention

Generations of lawyers from Roman times onwards[15] have intrinsically always felt that legal rules, despite economists' objections, are the right way of pursuing distributive justice and tackling the ruinous inequality problems. Their analytical justification nevertheless remained tautological or based on general standards of

[7] L Kaplow and S Shavell, 'Why the Legal System is Less Efficient than the Income Tax in Redistributing Income' (1994) 23 *Journal of Legal Studies* 667.

[8] ibid 668.

[9] ibid 667.

[10] R Cooter and T Ulen, *Law and Economics* (New York, Pearson, 2014). See also Posner (n 6) 9ff.

[11] Kaplow and Shavell (n 7) 677.

[12] Cooter and Ulen (n 10); Posner (n 6) 8.

[13] Kaplow and Shavell (n 7) 677. See also Kaplow and Shavell (n 2) 825.

[14] See Cooter and Ulen (n 10); Posner (n 6); S Shavell, *Foundations of Economic Analysis of Law* (Cambridge, Harvard University Press, 2004); HB Schäfer and C Ott, *The Economic Analysis of Civil Law* (Cheltenham, Edward Elgar, 2004); D Wittman, *Economic Foundations of Law and Organization* (Cambridge, Cambridge University Press, 2006); J Leitzel, *Concepts in Law and Economics: A Guide for the Curious* (Oxford, Oxford University Press, 2015).

[15] See, eg, MT Cicero, *De Officis* (AP Peabody tr, Boston, Little, Brown, and Co., 1887).

morality, good faith and ethical behaviour. In economic thinking about redistribution, the opposing arguments presented above have, at least in the last decades, been the dominant ones.

Yet, these arguments have been forcefully challenged by De Geest,[16] who advocates an 'ex ante approach' that – rather than remedying income inequality only after it has arisen – tries to prevent it from occurring in the first place. De Geest associates the ex ante approach with the problem of 'rents'.[17] These are 'profits that would not have been earned in a perfectly competitive and transparent economy'.[18] He argues that if 'inequality is not caused by differences in efforts or talents but by rent-seeking behaviour, then ex ante legal intervention is superior'.[19] The legal system then in his view holds an information advantage over the tax-and-transfer system in combating inequality:[20] The law intervenes at an ex ante stage, where there is less information required than at an ex post stage, where the symptoms have to be removed.[21] Hence, as De Geest's argument goes, to effectively address the rents and inequality problem, the legal system needs merely information on the total amount of rents, and not on individually received rents and consequent inequality.[22]

Moreover, the ex post tax-and-transfer system leaves unaffected the source of inequality and the price distortions associated with rents. In other words, it cannot address the causes of inequality and cannot in line with Kenneth Arrow's insight achieve perfect markets and their efficient outcomes by adjusting the starting positions of market participants.[23] Arrow namely shows that when one is trying to address the excesses of competitive markets one should not interfere with the markets themselves but should adjust the starting blocks.[24] The markets will then find every possible opportunity to make everybody better off from their revised starting points. In summary, whenever legal rules reduce rents, the trade-offs between income inequality and efficiency should be made in the legal – rather than tax – system.[25]

[16] De Geest (n 3).

[17] We believe that the prevention of rents might be the most understated, overlooked function of legal systems ever since ancient Roman law.

[18] De Geest (n 3) 8.

[19] ibid 9.

[20] ibid 10. See also E Erjavec and M Kovac, 'Public Law, Higher Education and the Ex-ante Removal of the Causes of Inequality' (2018) 1 *Sorbonne Student Law Review* 230.

[21] De Geest (n 3) 10.

[22] ibid.

[23] KJ Arrow, 'General Economic Equilibrium: Purpose, Analytic Techniques, Collective Choice' (1974) 64 *The American Economic Review* 253. See also KJ Arrow and G Debreu, 'Existence of an Equilibrium for a Competitive Economy' (1954) 22 *Econometrica* 265.

[24] Arrow (n 23).

[25] De Geest (n 3). He also emphasises that from an analytical perspective, rents are implicit commodity taxes causing labour and price distortions.

III. Network Externalities and Lock-In Effects

A. Network Externalities and Competition: An Introduction

A number of markets – especially digital ones – are characterised by the presence of 'network externalities', ie situations in which a consumer's utility in the consumption of a good increases directly with the number of other people consuming the same good, the larger the firm's output is, the more valuable that output is to customers.[26] The more subscribers there are, the more valuable the service is to each one, or at least to many of them.[27] Each new user of the product thus derives private benefits from, but also confers external benefits (network externalities) on existing users.[28] As a result, markets with strong network externalities are 'winner-take-most' markets.[29] They are prone to 'market-tipping', which means that, once a certain firm manages to gain a certain advantage in consumer preferences, it may become more and more popular and its rivals will be driven out from the market.[30] Such markets thus often suffer from sustained dominance of firms.[31]

The literature suggests that even though network externalities and market-tipping are important phenomena, it is premature to generally conclude that they are inevitably associated with anti-competitive practices.[32] For instance, initial stages of a given product life may by associated with intense promotional activities of various types and aggressive pricing as firms attempt to increase their market share.[33] Large profits made by a firm after its product has become the dominant standard might then merely cover the cost incurred during the standards war and should thus not pose any concern for the competition authority.[34] Moreover, Posner

[26] Posner suggests that economies of scale in consumption, more commonly referred to as network externalities, describe the situation in which the larger the firm's output is in such a network industry the more valuable that output is to its customers. Posner (n 6) 413. He also suggests that 'information technology service is worthless if there is only one subscriber since he has no one to connect to'. Posner (n 6) 413.

[27] Each additional subscriber confers a benefit on the other subscribers who might want to contact him. Posner (n 6) 413.

[28] Page and Lopatka (n 5).

[29] Economides (n 5) 483. See also N Economides and F Flyer, 'Compatibility and Market Structure for Network Goods' (1998) NYU Stern School of Business Discussion Paper No 98-02, ssrn.com/abstract=81268.

[30] M Motta, *Competition Policy: Theory and Practice* (Cambridge, Cambridge University Press, 2009) 84.

[31] The initial firm in an industry can persist in being dominant, even when superior technologies come along, because it has a large installed base – an entrant with a better technology then faces the disadvantage of not having an installed base. KW Viscusi, JE Harrington and JM Vernon, *Economics of Regulation and Antitrust*, 4th edn (Cambridge, The MIT Press, 2005) 335.

[32] ibid.

[33] ibid. See also P Rey, P Seabright and J Tirole, 'The Activities of a Monopoly Firm in Adjacent Competitive Markets: Economic Consequences and Implications for Competition Policy' (2002) IDEI Working Paper 132, ideas.repec.org/p/ide/wpaper/660.html.

[34] Motta (n 30) 85. See also J Farrell and P Klemperer, 'Coordination and Lock-In: Competition with Switching Costs and Network Effects' (2006) ssrn.com/abstract=917785.

argues the presence of network externalities may actually stimulate competition.[35] Traditional law and economics literature namely suggests that the more protection from competition is enjoyed by the firm that succeeds in obtaining a monopoly, the more competition there might be to become the monopolist; and provided that the only feasible means of obtaining the monopoly are socially productive, such competition might be desirable.[36] Further, the existence of only one network in the market might benefit consumers since they will 'be able to enjoy more communication possibilities or complementary services, whereas under competing networks they will not be able to'.[37] The presence of network externalities hence does not necessarily mean these markets will naturally show excess inertia or the persistence of dominance, or that new entries per se would always be beneficial.[38] Katz and Shapiro suggest the dynamics of industries subject to network externalities differ fundamentally from those of conventional industries and thus a regulator should also take the future benefits of such network externalities into account.[39]

There is no agreement on how well the current tools of competition law account for network externalities. Faull and Nikpay, for example, suggest that no revision might be necessary.[40] Jones and Sufrin, in contrast, argue that network externalities pose particular problems for competition law and emphasise the shortcomings of the traditional definition of markets, stressing that competition

[35] Posner (n 6) 628.

[36] Namely, a firm that 'will have the protection both of intellectual property law and economies of scale in consumption if it is the first to come up with an essential component of IT product or service will have a particularly lucrative monopoly, and this prospect should accelerate the rate of innovation'. Posner (n 6) 628.

[37] Motta (n 30) 85.

[38] Motta offers an example where due to consumers' expectations a new standard which does not offer any advantages over the previous one affirms itself in the industry – this then leads to the stranding of those consumers who have locked themselves into old, obsolete technology (duplication of purchases will follow soon). Motta (n 30) 85. See also ML Katz and C Shapiro, 'Systems Competition and Network Effects' (1994) 8 *Journal of Economic Perspectives* 93.

[39] They argue that in the presence of network externalities a consumer in the market today also cares about the future success of the competing products and, so long as the good is durable (or there is technology-specific human capital investment), the total benefits derived from it will depend in part on the number of consumers who adopt compatible products in the future. Katz and Shapiro (n 38) 824. Further, Arrow points out that interest group pressures make government responses less likely to favour efficiency than powerful incumbent producers. KJ Arrow, 'Vertical Integration and Communication' (1975) 6 *Bell Journal of Economics* 173, 183. See also SJ Liebowitz and SE Margolis, 'Are Network Externalities a New Source of Market Failure?' (1995) 17 *Research in Law and Economics* 1, 22; MG Vita and CP Wellford, 'Regulating the Electromagnetic Environment: Alternative Approaches to Policy' in JR Fleming and HA Gemery (eds), *Science, Technology, and the Environment: Multidisciplinary Perspectives* (New York, University of Akron Press, 1994) 238. Page and Lopatka, for example, defend antitrust's current reluctance to intervene on economic grounds. Page and Lopatka (n 5) 952–80.

[40] 'In conclusion, there seems to be no important conflict between innovation and competition policy aimed at product market and there seems to be no fundamental flaw in competition policy. Competition policy, by defending competition markets, will in general have a positive impact on both static and dynamic efficiency. Companies under competition pressure will be less complacent and will have more incentive to innovate and gain market share. Product market competition and a strict competition policy generally work as an incentive to promote innovative effort.' J Faull and A Nikpay, *The EC Law of Competition*, 2nd edn (Oxford, Oxford University Press, 2007) 1.129. However, it is

between undertakings is often not on price but on innovation and pointing to the competition for markets instead of standard competition in markets.[41] They also suggest that application of competition rules might be 'revised to allow for the dynamic competition' in markets with network externalities.[42] There is nevertheless a general consensus among competition lawyers that competition authorities must be sensitive to the special characteristics of new economy markets and refrain from moving against dominant positions that are only ephemeral.[43] What should constitute a particular concern in any competition policy are then practices that give a network monopolist greater insulation from competition than is inherent in its control of the network.[44]

B. Network Externalities, Lock-In Effects, and Inequality

Network externalities may hold legal implications if they lead to a dominant position, the existence of which is a condition for applying the rules against the abuse of a dominant position.[45] Alternatively, a firm which enjoys network externalities may employ exclusionary contracts that can drive out a more efficient firm or deter one from entering.[46] However, firms may employ various techniques that currently do not constitute a breach of competition law to adversely influence consumers' expectations concerning a new technology and, thereby, to cause a potential new firm that is attempting to enter the market to fail. For example,

noted that there has been much debate over the extent to which 'ordinary' competition law can be satisfactorily applied to the new economy. See, eg, LJ Temple, *European Community Antitrust Law: Innovation Markets and High Technology Industries* (New York, Fordham, 1996) 519; C Veljanovski, 'EC Antitrust in the New Economy: Is the European Commission's View of the Network Economy Right?' (2001) 22 *European Competition Law Review* 115; R Lind and P Muyset, 'Innovation and Competition Policy: Challenges for the New Millennium' (2003) 87 *European Competition Law Review* 91, 112.

[41] They also show that markets may 'tip towards one firm whose product become the standard, rendering the firm dominant and competition will be aimed at replacing the dominant firm'. A Jones and B Sufrin, *EC Competition Law: Text, Cases and Materials*, 4th edn (Oxford, Oxford University Press, 2010) 55.

[42] Jones and Sufrin (n 41) 55.

[43] See, eg, D Teece and M Coleman, 'The Meaning of Monopoly: Antitrust Analysis in High-Technology Industries' (1998) 43 *The Antitrust Bulletin* 801; C Ahlborn, DS Evans and AJ Padilla, 'Competition Policy in the New Economy: Is European Competition Law up to the Challenge?' (2001) 5 *European Competition Law Review* 156, 164.

[44] Network externalities may give the monopolist a cost advantage that exceeds the benefit of superior new technology. Economides (n 5) 511. See also ML Katz and C Shapiro, 'Technology Adoption in the Presence of Network Externalities' (1986) 94 *Journal of Political Economics* 822; MP Howard, 'Exclusive Dealing' (1982) 25 *Journal of Law and Economics* 1; SM Besen and J Farrell, 'Choosing How to Compete: Strategies and Tactics in Standardization' (1994) 8 *Journal of Economic Perspectives* 117; J Farrell and G Saloner, 'Installed Base and Compatibility: Innovation, Product Preannouncements and Predation' (1986) 76 *American Economics Review* 940, 955.

[45] R van den Bergh, *Comparative Competition Law and Economics* (Cheltenham, Edward Elgar, 2017).

[46] C Shapiro, 'Exclusivity in Network Industries' (1999) 8 *George Mason Law Review* 1, 11.

incumbents will want to ensure that new products cannot be made compatible with theirs.[47] Of course, such an incumbent firm may, as Motta suggests, engage in anti-competitive practices[48] or may advertise that the 'new entrant is making very slow progress in building a customer base or that the incumbent's market share is high and growing'.[49] Economic literature suggests that such announcements likely have 'an impact on the expectation of consumers about the viability of the entrant, and should therefore be carefully monitored by the competition authorities, and promptly punished if false'.[50]

Another potential legal implication derives from the distinction between penetration and predatory pricing.[51] Predatory pricing is highly relevant in competition law since such aggressive pricing can deter the entry of new firms and can keep an entrant from acquiring the critical mass it needs to effectively compete with an existing firm that enjoys the network externalities.[52] Yet, one complicating matter is that from an economic perspective 'penetration pricing'[53] is a legitimate business strategy in markets with network externalities, which actually enables potential new firms to enter the market and thus generates effective competition. In such circumstances, literature suggests that one should then expect 'below-cost pricing even when predation is not the intent'.[54] Viscusi, Harrington and Vernon correctly observe that this then points to the serious competition law challenge of distinguishing desirable penetration pricing from undesirable, inefficient predatory pricing.[55]

In addition, firms enjoying network externalities are also in a better position than other firms to employ 'razor-blade' marketing models that create 'lock-in' effects, which exacerbate the previously discussed inefficiencies in such network industries and reinforce the dominant position of such a firm.[56] These models are praised by marketing literature as a great tool to 'create value' for business.[57] Yet, they are created deliberately to extract rents from consumers. For example,

[47] Motta (n 30) 83.

[48] For example, 'faced with an entrant which offers a product with new features, an incumbent might want to announce that soon it will introduce an upgrade of its product that incorporates these new features even if this is not true'. ibid 83.

[49] Such announcements will have an impact on consumers' expectation about the entrant's viability. ibid 83.

[50] ibid 84.

[51] Viscusi, Harrington and Vernon (n 31).

[52] ibid 336.

[53] Penetration pricing refers to initially pricing low, even below marginal costs, so as to build an installed base. ibid 336.

[54] ibid 336.

[55] ibid 336.

[56] Razor-blade pricing and marketing strategy are designed to generate a reliable, recurring income by locking a consumer onto a platform or proprietary tool for a long period. The razor-blade model is a pricing strategy in which one good is sold at a discount or loss and a companion consumable good at a premium to generate profits. G De Geest, *Rents: How Marketing Causes Inequality* (New York, Beccaria Books, 2018).

[57] Lock-in effects are apparently a widespread practice employed by marketers in modern markets while the razor-blade model is taught at business schools. De Geest (n 56). See also P Kotler and KL Keller, *Marketing Management* (New York, Pearson Prentice Hall, 2012) 124–43.

once you are locked in a certain operating system, ie software that controls the operation of an IT device, the network externality effect induces you to pay a monopoly price for all subsequent apps, upgraded software and updated versions of the operating system.[58] Such lock-in effects are currently still legal, even if they are deliberately created as a marketing technique and as part of a business plan that is designed to extract rents (and, thus, to bring about income inequality).[59] Strikingly, as De Geest notes, such marketing techniques and lock-in effects in fact create a monopoly position which the consumer voluntarily steps into.[60] For example, nearly everyone uses Google because it does the best job at sorting the most useful sites. However, Google can only do this because nearly everyone uses Google, giving Google more information on search behaviour than any other search engine.[61] This network externality then creates a (quasi-) monopoly that enables Google to extract rents – profit that could not have been made in a perfect market. Similarly, network externality in the operating system market provided Microsoft with a pricing power that was close to that of a monopolist, which it used to achieve enormous profits.[62]

Network externalities are thus not innocent from an economic point of view since they naturally distort competition and may lead to a 'natural monopoly' and extreme market power. The returns from market power would only reduce income inequality if they were funnelled to people on below-average incomes. Yet, in reality, these rents go disproportionately to the wealthy – increases in the producer surplus from the exercise of market power accrue primarily to shareholders and the top executives, who on average are wealthier than the median consumer.[63] That is to say that rents from network externalities exacerbate income inequality. The ex ante role of competition law in removing rents as the source of inequality (ie taking network externality and lock-in effects seriously) may thus be instrumental in reducing inequality. The standard economic approach in choosing the optimal levels of legal intervention is, as De Geest suggests, only to consider the administrative costs associated with the legal system and the price distortion costs,

[58] A software company may say, 'buy my overpriced upgrade for your software or lose you data or build up a new administrative system from scratch'. De Geest (n 56) 176.

[59] These marketing techniques generally escape competition law scrutiny provided that a firm does not hold a monopoly position in the primary market. In terms of an example, US antitrust courts say that there is no monopoly problem because we should not look at the apps market but at the entire IT market. AD Goldfine and KM Vorrasi, 'The Fall of the Kodak Aftermarket Doctrine: Dying a Slow Death in the Lower Courts' (2004) 72 *Antitrust Law Journal* 209, 231.

[60] De Geest also suggests that, to make things worse, intellectual property law has no special rules for network externalities either, so it may unintentionally create network externality problems by granting patents to certain standards. De Geest (n 56) 178.

[61] De Geest (n 56) 178.

[62] De Geest suggests that the difference between the profits which Microsoft made and the profits that were strictly needed to recoup the investment are rents. De Geest (n 56) 178.

[63] EN Wolff, 'Household Wealth Trends in the United States, 1962–2013: What Happened over the Great Recession?' (2014) NBER Working Paper No 20733, www.nber.org/papers/w20733, 49 table 1. See also WS Comanor and RH Smiley, 'Monopoly and the Distribution of Wealth' (1975) 89 *Quarterly Journal of Economics* 177, 189.

whereas the rents are left out of the equation because they are seen by existing literature as zero-sum effects[64] and because the tax system is believed to be superior at redistributing income.[65] However, the extraction of rents and consequent income inequality should be taken into account while determining the optimal antitrust intervention in relation to network externalities.[66] In other words, the distributive aspects might also be a concern of competition law.[67]

IV. Case Law Analysis and Policy Suggestions

This section considers several recent cases that involved the issue of network externality and offers some suggestions for improved regulatory policy.

A. Case Law Analysis

EU competition law considers network externalities in the context of investigations into market power chiefly as potential barriers to market entry and as the problem of switching costs. The European Commission ('the Commission') and the General Court ('the Court') have addressed network externalities in several decisions. This section gives a comprehensive overview of selected decisions, followed by a critical analysis of whether the Commission and the Court have addressed potentially harmful network externalities in a coherent manner.

In the context of the *Microsoft/Skype*[68] merger, the Commission examined the concerns of third-party market participants that the existence of network externality in the consumer communications markets was acting as a barrier to expansion. That is to say, the more users a provider of communications has, the better its chances of expanding its user base. However, the Commission assumed that the

[64] M Roe, 'Rents and Their Corporate Consequences' (2001) 53 *Stanford Law Review* 1463, 1494.

[65] In reality, however, the tax system leaves the price distortions associated with the rent unaffected. De Geest (n 3) 11.

[66] Of course, when one considers the rents and income inequality caused by network externalities, there is a trade-off since the legal system can correct such inefficiencies (ie market failures) only by incurring administrative costs. De Geest (n 3) 31. See also T Blumkin and Y Margalioth, 'On the Limits of Redistributive Taxation: Establishing a Case for Equity-Informed Legal Rules' (2005) 25 *Virginia Tax Review* 1, 19; T O'Reilly, 'Principles of Efficient Tax Law: Apocrypha' (2008) 27 *Virginia Tax Review* 583, 630; C Jolls, 'Behavioral Economic Analysis of Redistributive Legal Rules' (1998) 51 *Vanderbilt Law Review* 1653, 1677; C Shapiro and EF McClennen, 'Law and Economics from a Philosophical Perspective' in P Newman (ed), *The New Palgrave Dictionary on Economics and the Law*, vol 2 (London, MacMillan, 1998) 460; B McDonnell, 'The Economists' New Arguments' (2003) 88 *Minnesota Law Review* 86, 118; BD Galle, 'Is Local Consumer Protection Law a Better Redistributive Mechanism than the Tax System?' (2010) 65 *New York University Annual Survey of American* Law 525, 543.

[67] See also JB Baker and SC Salop, 'Antitrust, Competition Policy, and Inequality' (2015) 104 *Georgetown Law Journal Online* 1, 11–13; JE Stiglitz, *The Price of Inequality: How Today's Divided Society Endangers our Future* (New York, W. W. Norton & Company, 2013).

[68] Case No COMP/M.6281 *Microsoft/Skype* para 91ff.

network externalities were reduced by the fact that most consumers of communications services made the majority of their voice and video calls to a small number of family and friends that establish their 'inner circle'. This was evidenced by Facebook data showing that users engaged in regular two-way interaction with only four to six people. The Commission was thus convinced that it was not too difficult for these groups to move between communications services. Further, it found that consumers to some extent practised 'multi-homing' – ie concurrently using the same services of multiple providers, which was apparently regarded as an additional mitigating factor.

The Court upheld this assessment in an appeal by Cisco Systems Inc and Messagenet SpA (further referred to as 'plaintiffs') against the Commission's clearance of the merger.[69] It dismissed as unfounded the plaintiffs' argument that the network externalities had further strengthened the dominant position of the new entity in a 'narrow market' (referring to the segment of video calls on Windows-based PCs). First, the Court found there were no technical or economic constraints which prevented users from downloading several communications applications on their device, especially as the software concerned was free, easy to download, and took up little space on their hard drives. Second, picking up on the Commission's findings on multi-homing, it noted there was no obstacle to users continuing to use several communications programmes at the same time. Finally, the Court acknowledged that the Commission did not contest the sheer existence of network externalities and further agreed with the assessment that there were network externalities and that they were creating barriers to entry, but that these barriers were not significant enough.

The Commission also assumed direct network externalities in consumer applications in the context of the *Facebook/WhatsApp*[70] merger and adopted a similar approach. Most notably, it argued that the existence of network externalities as such did not a priori indicate a competition problem in the market affected by the merger. Such externalities may however raise competition concerns if they enable the merged entity to foreclose competitors and make it more difficult for competing providers to expand their customer base. Network externalities would thus have to be assessed on a case-by-case basis. As concerns the mentioned merger, the Commission found three reasons against network externalities posing a concern. First, it restated its argument presented in *Microsoft/Skype* that consumer communications apps were then a fast-moving sector, where customers' switching costs and barriers to entry/expansion were low. In this market, it was considered unlikely that a dominant undertaking would not face competitive pressure, even if it relied on network externalities. This view was supported by the long track

[69] Case T-79/12 *Cisco Systems, Inc. and Messagenet SpA v European Commission* ECLI:EU:T:2013:635, para 75ff.

[70] Case No COMP/M.7217 *Facebook/WhatsApp* para 127ff.

record of entries by new players. Second, the use of a communications app arguably does not exclude the use of a competing one by the same user. Multi-homing was possible and indeed practised: the parallel use of apps worked smoothly since a user did not have to log in each time when switching apps, and messages were automatically delivered onto a user's device. The Commission further examined whether the merger was likely to reinforce network externalities and concluded that this was not the case because the user groups of Facebook and WhatsApp already overlapped to a large extent.

The Commission and the Court have also considered network externalities as a source of market power in a non-merger context. In *Google Search (Shopping)*,[71] Google was fined €2.42 billion for abusing its market dominance as a search engine by giving an illegal advantage to another Google product, its comparison-shopping service. In the context of investigations into Google's market power, the Commission noted that even if a significant number of users of Google's general search service were to practise multi-homing, the switching costs were in any event only one possible type of barrier to entry and expansion.[72]

Google then filed an action against this decision, which was largely dismissed by the Court.[73] It confirmed the Commission's findings on the relevance of network externalities, providing the following:

> the rationale and value of a general search engine lie in its capacity to be open to results from external (third-party) sources and to display these multiple and diverse sources on its general results pages, sources which enrich and enhance the credibility of the search engine as far as the general public is concerned, and enable it to benefit from the network effects and economies of scale that are essential for its development and its subsistence in a market in which, by their very nature, few infrastructures of that kind can subsist, given those network effects. A very large number of users is needed to reach the critical mass capable of compensating for the service being free of charge on one side of the market and generating advertising income on its other side. Accordingly, for a search engine, limiting the scope of its results to its own entails an element of risk and is not necessarily rational, save in a situation, as in this case, where the dominance and barriers to entry are such that no market entry within a sufficiently short period of time is possible in response to that limitation of internet users' choice.[74]

The fact that Google – in contrast to its earlier approach that had led to the success of its search engine – favoured its own specialised results over third-party results, therefore according to the Court necessarily involves a certain form

[71] Case No AT.39740 *Google Search (Shopping).*

[72] ibid, para 314. Barriers to entry and expansion could also derive for instance from network externalities and were found to be present in this case: direct network externalities stemmed from the fact that a substantial minority of users of a general search engine derived a benefit from search advertisements. Case No AT.39740 *Google Search (Shopping)* para 295ff.

[73] Case T-612/17 *Google LLC, formerly Google Inc. and Alphabet, Inc. v European Commission (Google Shopping)* ECLI:EU:T:2021:763.

[74] ibid, para 178.

of abnormality.[75] With no justification provided by Google,[76] it does not constitute competition on the merits.[77]

These recent cases indicate the EU competition authorities are taking network externalities much more seriously than suggested by early law and economics scholarship. These three cases may be seen as circumstantial evidence that legal systems and in particular competition law is not, as argued by Economides, ill equipped to 'deal with complex technical matters' or that the legal system has 'tremendous inertia to new ideas and models'.[78] Instead, it seems the law can adequately address the competition concerns associated with network externalities. Still, it remains to be seen whether these recent cases were merely sporadic reactions to the growing market power[79] of Big Tech or whether we are indeed witnessing a change in the paradigm in the EU's competition law enforcement. It also remains to be seen whether the issue of rent extraction and consequent income inequality will be considered while designing the optimal antitrust intervention with respect to network externalities.

B. Policy Suggestions

What could competition law do to reduce the network externalities and lock-in effects? Generally, we do not need to change the existing paradigm, but only to enforce the current one more intensively in cases concerning network externalities and lock-in effects. More specifically, in relation to the network externalities and lock-in effects one could design several policy responses including the following ones.

First, competition law and enforcement thereof should take evidence-based consumer behaviour into account, instead of strictly relying on theoretical economic concepts. In other words, neither the existence of alternative products or providers, nor the absence of technical or economic constraints to switching has prevented firms like Facebook, Google etc from obtaining quasi monopoly status. This is particularly crucial in the area of controlling mergers, where the effective application of competition law can ex ante prevent the reinforcement of network externalities.

Second, competition law should start to take network externalities and lock-in effects more seriously.[80] Competition law should adopt a more interventionist

[75] ibid, para 179.
[76] ibid, para 179.
[77] ibid, para 185.
[78] Economides (n 5) 511.
[79] Google, for example, is itself a market.
[80] Cafara et al suggest that this policy change already started in the EU. C Caffarra, O Latham, M Bennett, F Etro, EFP Régibeau and R Stillman, 'Google Android: European "Techlash" or Milestone in Antitrust Enforcement?' (2018) *VoxEU*, voxeu.org/article/google-android-european-techlash-or-milestone-antitrust-enforcement.

standard with regard to network externalities and lock-in effects. It should recognise certain conduct that makes use of network externalities (size of rents as a potential indicator) and lock-in effects as a competition law offence. Competition law could reduce the market power of companies that enjoy network externalities (and lock-in effects). De Geest even suggests a 'one-click-switching' feature allowing consumers to effortlessly switch between different firms and products.[81] Under such a 'one-click-switching' obligation, a company is supposed to make it possible for its customers to switch between different firms and products by clicking just once.

Unfortunately, such nudging, information disclosure or one-click-switching might not be effective at all since behavioural law and economics findings suggest that consumers suffer from various limitations while attempting to make rational decisions. They may be subject to the status quo bias, which refers to the phenomenon where consumers tend to stick to the state of affairs they perceive as the current baseline rather than opting for an alternative one.[82] For instance, if a consumer's usual (ie default) way of purchasing goods has been to use a certain product, then they will stick with that product even if the alternative might be better. Hence, if changing the status quo requires an action while maintaining the status quo involves a mere omission, consumers will then prefer omission over action.[83] Moreover, such consumer default decision-making forms a reference point and any departure from this reference point (ie the consumer's usual way of purchasing goods) is regarded as a loss.[84] Since losses generally loom larger than gains, people are generally loss-averse, making any departure from the status quo unlikely.

Nevertheless, it is stressed that the proposed ex ante competition law focus on network externalities and lock-in effects should not be regarded as the sole or only possible regulatory tool for tackling income inequality. We argue that an effective policymaker should, while tackling the inequality problem, design their policy in line with the golden Tinbergen rule – N problems require N solutions. This rule, employed in the natural sciences as a general research maxim, was formulated by the Dutch economics Nobel laureate Jan Tinbergen in 1952, and is generally interpreted as meaning that 'for each policy objective, at least one policy instrument is needed – there should be at least the same number of instruments as there are targets'.[85] Hence, a smart, enlightened policymaker should identify different

[81] De Geest (n 56) 276. See also Jones and Sufrin (n 41) 431.

[82] W Samuelson and R Zeckhouser, 'Status Quo Bias and Decision Making' (1988) 1 *Journal of Risk and Uncertainty* 7, 59.

[83] See, eg, M Schweitzer, 'Disentangling Status Quo and Omission Effects: An Experimental Analysis' (1994) 58 *Organizational Behaviour and Human Decision Processes* 457; Z Eyal and D Teichman, *Behavioral Law and Economics* (Oxford, Oxford University Press, 2020).

[84] A Tversky and D Kahneman, 'Prospect Theory: An Analysis of Decision under Risk' (1979) 47 *Econometrica* 263.

[85] J Tinbergen, *On the Theory of Economic Policy* (Amsterdam, North-Holland, 1952).

sources of market failures/rents/inequality and to each of them apply specific, ex ante or ex post (or combination of both) regulatory instruments.[86]

If, however, inequality is caused by differences in efforts or talents (competitive forces) then such inequality should be allowed and might eventually, according to specific, efficiently justified, normative preferences of a national lawmaker, be tackled only with ex post tax-and-transfer system of redistribution suggested by economics. We argue that competition law should only be used to correct inequality that arises from rents, but not from other sources like effort or talents. The potential ex post intervention should only be done in line with the previously emphasised economic principles. In other words, the ex post pursuit of distributive justice should not occur by modifying or reshuffling private legal rights but only via progressive taxation and social welfare programmes.

V. Conclusion

This chapter argues that competition law should target the sources of market failures in a more systematic way than it currently does. Namely, many undetected monopolies (or quasi-monopolies) and market failures are caused by network externalities and related lock-in effects. These omnipresent network externalities and lock-in effects might be one of the more substantive sources of income inequality and a serious threat to effective competition. The inquiry into these phenomena could also be a concern for competition law.

Network externalities and lock-in effects together with the resulting unjustified rents are far from harmless and may distort the economy and allocation of wealth. As concerns the inequality that arises from network externalities and lock-in effects, we also argue that a competition law intervention might be superior to ex post taxes for fixing the distributive distortions. There is no need to change the existing competition law paradigm – it would be enough to enforce the current one more intensively in cases involving network externalities and lock-in effects. Only the reduction of rents might perhaps be adopted as an explicit goal. Competition law should be used to correct exclusively inequality that arises from rents and not from other sources like effort or talents.

[86] Numerous rules in contract law might be interpreted exactly in that way. For example, doctrines of mistake, fraud, duress, misrepresentation, unjustified enrichment, *culpa in contrahendo*, and good faith can also have such an ex ante function. However, this does not imply that legal rules should, while drafted, be ex ante primarily concerned with redistribution goals. On the contrary, legal rules should still be designed in line with economic suggestions – such rules would actually then maximise social wealth and ex ante tackle the notorious rents and inequality problems.

9

Competition Law, Inequalities and Healthcare: Insights from EU and National Frameworks

MARY GUY*

I. Introduction

It is well-established[1] that healthcare is a sector which is characterised not only by high levels of spending, but also by expanding demand of caring for an ageing population, and by the increasing expectations of patients over time (suggesting a more consumer-like mindset).[2] Healthcare spending continued to outpace economic growth during the 1990s and 2000s, notwithstanding the economic downturn of 2008–2009. The effects of the COVID-19 pandemic arguably entrench this, with notable estimated increases in health spending to GDP ratio across OECD countries (from 8.8 per cent in 2019 to 9.7 per cent in 2020) combining with a reduction in economic activity.[3] It is common ground that COVID-19 is producing not merely an economic crisis, but also exacerbating existing inequalities and developing new inequalities with regard to healthcare access and affordability. This suggests that the focus in responding to the pandemic needs to include how to minimise health inequalities for future generations.[4]

* I am grateful for feedback from the conference, 'Should wealth and income inequality be a competition law concern?' University of Amsterdam, 20–21 May 2021, and to the editors for comments on earlier drafts.

[1] See B Nikolić, 'Applicability of European Union Competition Law to Health Care Providers: The Dividing Line between Economic and Noneconomic Activities' (2021) 46(1) *Journal of Health Politics, Policy and Law* 49.

[2] For further discussion, see J Tritter, M Koivusalo, E Ollila and P Dorfman, *Globalisation, Markets and Health Policy – Redrawing the Patient as Consumer* (Abingdon, Routledge, 2010).

[3] OECD, Health at a Glance 2021, ch 7, Health Expenditure. www.oecd-ilibrary.org/sites/ae3016b9-en/1/3/7/index.html?itemId=/content/publication/ae3016b9-en&_csp_=ca413da5d44587bc56446341952c275e&itemIGO=oecd&itemContentType=book accessed 20 February 2022.

[4] See, eg, C Bambra, R Riordan, J Ford, F Matthews, 'The COVID-19 pandemic and health inequalities' (2020) 74 *BMJ Journal of Epidemiology and Community Health* 964.

These factors combine to generate concerns about the long-term sustainability of healthcare systems based on the principle of solidarity (including universal access to healthcare), and about the affordability of, and access to healthcare. This has clear negative implications for population health and individual needs, particularly for those in lower socio-economic groups.[5]

Introducing marketisation and competition reforms into healthcare at the national level, and the linking of this with application of competition law at national and EU levels, has been seen as a way of attempting to address these concerns. This is evidenced by the range of competition reforms in healthcare taking place between, broadly, the 1980s and the first decades of the twenty-first century – with those in the US in turn influencing the Netherlands and England. This period has coincided with a focus on efficiency rather than equity within wider competition policy, although the focus may now be shifting in favour of questions of equity, and re-evaluation of the goals of competition law.[6] Certainly, taking equity as a starting-point for competition reforms in healthcare implies that a different approach may be needed.[7] Nevertheless, the dynamic between efficiency and equity continues to characterise approaches to competition reforms in healthcare in the US and Europe,[8] where questions of solidarity predominate,[9] and the concept of healthcare access being determined by clinical need, not the ability to pay, underpins healthcare system organisation.

Competition reforms in healthcare are generally framed around claims of improved efficiency or quality, and less explicitly linked with scope for addressing inequalities, or engaging with questions of healthcare access and affordability. However, it might be considered that there is scope for overlap: if a healthcare service is delivered more efficiently, this may have positive implications for addressing inequality.

[5] Suggesting a link with health inequalities, which can be defined as '… the systematic, avoidable and unfair differences in health outcomes that can be observed between populations, between social groups within the same population or as a gradient across a population ranked by social position'. G McCartney, F Popham, R McMaster, A Cumbers, 'Defining health and health inequalities' (2019) 172 *Public Health* 22.

[6] See, eg, I Lianos, 'Competition Law as a form of Societal Regulation' (2020) 65(1) *The Antitrust Bulletin* 3.

[7] M Guy, Competition Policy in Healthcare – Frontiers in Insurance-Based and Taxation-Funded Systems (Cambridge, Intersentia, 2019) 17.

[8] For further discussion, see TS Jost, D Dawson and A Den Exter, 'The Role of Competition in Health Care: A Western European Perspective' (2006) 31(3) *Journal of Health Politics, Policy and Law* 687. T Greaney and O Odudu, 'Introduction to Antitrust and the provision of healthcare in the United States and the European Union – Common Challenges', ch 16 in D Orentlicher and TK Hervey (eds), *The Oxford Handbook of Comparative Health Law* (Oxford, Oxford University Press, 2021).

[9] In contrast to US healthcare, where equity has been deemed subservient to efficiency. M Gaynor, 'Competition in Hospital Services', OECD Directorate for Financial and Enterprise Affairs Competition Committee, Working Party No 2 on Competition and Regulation, DAF/COMP/WP2(2012)3, 06.02.2012.

Certainly, the motivation for competition reforms in national healthcare systems is typically framed in terms of ensuring future sustainability,[10] with a focus on improving efficiency, which may be read as a means to engage with questions of healthcare access and affordability as a proxy for health inequalities. Efficiency has further been linked with distributional aims,[11] and seen as encompassing quality,[12] with attempts being made to align interpretations of quality by healthcare professionals and the competition context.[13]

Given the absence of an explicit focus on healthcare access and affordability, it may seem unsurprising that analysis of the effects of competition reforms in healthcare on equity appear limited. However, there is some evidence to suggest that fixed-price competition based on quality in the English National Health Service (NHS) potentially generated a slight improvement in a small reduction in social inequalities in accessing non-emergency hospital admissions.[14]

Although competition reforms in healthcare have taken place against a wider backdrop of a focus on efficiency rather than equity, it is nevertheless possible to revisit cases and policy to identify and evaluate where competition law has attempted to engage with economic inequality in a healthcare context.[15] These attempts have been framed in terms of two categories of concepts. First, in the juxtaposition of 'competition' and 'solidarity', with the latter (which can be linked with wider concepts of equality and universal access) indicating potential limits for competition law to engage with economic inequalities in healthcare. Second, in framings primarily such as 'accessibility' and 'affordability', although questions of 'quality' are considered to have linkages with these concepts as well.

Whether and *how* competition law *can*, and *should*, concern itself with economic inequality in the healthcare sector are questions which arguably have yet to yield clear answers, despite various levels of engagement at national and EU levels. When confronted with acknowledged problems, such as the prevalence of market power (of public or private providers) in the healthcare sector operating

[10] Nikolić (n 1).

[11] A Donabedin, *An Introduction to Quality Assurance in Health Care* (Oxford University Press, 2003) 10, cited in T Stavroulaki, 'The Curious Case of Competition Law and Health Equity' *Competition Policy International Antitrust Chronicle* December 2019.

[12] W Sauter, 'The Impact of EU Competition Law on National Healthcare Systems' (2013) 38(4) *European Law Review*, 457, 459.

[13] T Stavroulaki, 'Connecting the Dots: Quality, Antitrust and Medicine' (2019) 31(2) *Loyola Consumer Law Review* 175.

[14] R Cookson, M Laudicella and P Li Donni, 'Does hospital competition harm equity? Evidence from the English National Health Service' (2013) 32(2) *Journal of Health Economics* 410. R Cookson, M Laudicella, P Li Donni and M Dusheiko, 'Effects of the Blair/Brown health reforms on socioeconomic equity in health care' (2012) 17(1) *Journal of Health Services Research and Policy* 55. R Cookson, M Dusheiko, G Hardman and S Martin, 'Competition and inequality: evidence from the English National Health Service 1991–2001' (2010) 20 *Journal of Public Administration Research and Theory* 181.

[15] In line with contributions regarding competition policy more generally. See, eg, ch 1 in this volume.

to the detriment of patients,[16] part of the difficulty lies in the sequencing of the *whether* and *how* questions when considering responses.

On the one hand, it might be considered that the *ability* of competition law to address economic inequality in general (and the healthcare sector in particular) is determinative, and thus the questions of *whether/how* competition law *can* engage is effectively the starting point. *Whether/how* competition law *should* then become normative considerations which follow from *whether/how* it *can*. This might be illustrated to a certain degree by the experience at both national and EU levels of investigating abuse of dominance claims by pharmaceutical companies, thus limiting the potential consequence of the anticompetitive conduct, namely reducing access to particular medicines.[17] The questions of *whether/how-can* are answered in broad terms by the applicability of competition law being uncontroversial in this context, which might be attributed in part to the global character of the pharmaceutical market – coupled with the scope for interaction between competition law and pharmaceutical regulation.[18] The questions of *whether/how* competition law *should* engage with economic inequalities in healthcare can then follow by making use of the pre-existing 'toolbox' of competition law and exceptions, which may form one solution among several to a given problem (eg limited access to medicines).[19] However, this is not the case for other, less ancillary, aspects of healthcare provision, which may attract differing political sensitivities, and be of a local or national character.[20] The EU competition law framework, defined by the 'undertaking' concept and the Services of General Economic Interest (SGEI) exception mechanism,[21] provide a reference framework for leading questions of *whether/how-can* with healthcare provision typically seen as subject to EU competition law, but less clarity emerging regarding healthcare purchasing activities.[22] In response to COVID-19, the response at national and EU levels has been to relax

[16] O Odudu, 'Health Care Services and EU Competition Law' ch 17 in D Orentlicher and TK Hervey (eds), *The Oxford Handbook of Comparative Health Law* (Oxford, Oxford University Press, 2021).

[17] Notable examples are Aspen being investigated by the European Commission (as well as the Italian competition authority), and Pfizer/Flynn investigated by the UK Competition and Markets Authority (CMA). See, respectively, European Commission, 'Press Release: Antitrust: Commission accepts commitments by Aspen to reduce prices for six off-patent cancer medicines by 73% addressing excessive pricing concerns', 10 February 2021, ec.europa.eu/commission/presscorner/detail/en/ip_21_524 accessed 20 February 2022, and CMA, 'CMA finds Pfizer and Flynn £90 million for drug price hike to NHS', 7 December 2016 www.gov.uk/government/news/cma-fines-pfizer-and-flynn-90-million-for-drug-price-hike-to-nhs accessed 20 February 2022.

[18] For discussion, see, eg, D Danieli, 'Excessive Pricing in the Pharmaceutical Industry: adding another string to the bow of EU competition law' (2021) 16 *Health Economics, Policy and Law*, 64–75.

[19] In this particular example, it might be considered that the effect is the same, regardless of which questions are posed first, the *whether/how-can* questions, or the *whether/how-should* questions.

[20] Guy (n 7) 2.

[21] For consideration of the SGEI mechanism more generally, see ch 5 in this volume.

[22] See, eg, JW van de Gronden and CS Rusu, 'EU competition law and policy and health systems' in TK Hervey, CA Young and LE Bishop (eds), *Research Handbook on EU Health Law and Policy* (Cheltenham, Edward Elgar, 2017) 267.

applicability of predominantly the prohibition on anticompetitive agreements[23] and the state aid rules[24] (via Articles 101(3) and 107(3) TFEU). These relaxation frameworks extend to the whole economy, but might be expected to have different implications for the healthcare sector, given that the disruption for this sector may be considered to be of a different scope and scale to that experienced in other sectors.

On the other hand, however, the relative rigidity of the rules governing the applicability of competition law,[25] and the complexities inherent in introducing competition reforms in healthcare may indicate that the question of *how* competition law *should* engage with economic inequalities in healthcare can be subservient to the question of *whether it should*. In other words, a (political) decision to introduce competition reforms in healthcare is effectively answering the question of *whether* competition law *should* engage with economic inequalities in healthcare (albeit perhaps indirectly) as a first step. The questions of *whether* and *how* it *can* are then linked. Experiences from both England and the Netherlands of tensions between government and competition authority perspectives on competition reforms in healthcare[26] illustrate some of the complexities which can arise in this regard. The introduction of legislation in England and the Netherlands[27] to incorporate and develop competition in healthcare may be read as competition law being deemed to engage with questions of economic inequality in healthcare (by answering the *whether* it *should* question in the affirmative).

This chapter makes use of a matrix framework of *whether* and *how* competition law *can* and *should* address economic inequalities in the healthcare context to evaluate approaches taken at EU and national levels as follows. Section II considers in overview *how* competition *can* work in a healthcare system, juxtaposing this with *how* a competition policy framework *can* serve to regulate this, indicating engagement with the *whether-can/should* question. Section III examines the EU competition law framework, and the recourse to the SGEI exception in light of the wider *how* and *whether* questions, particularly when juxtaposed with the temporary relaxation of the antitrust and state aid rules to respond to COVID-19. Section IV considers the Health and Social Care Act 2012 (HSCA 2012) competition

[23] European Commission, 'Communication from the Commission Temporary Framework for assessing antitrust issues related to business cooperation in response to situations of urgency stemming from the current COVID-19 outbreak' [2020] C116I/02), *Official Journal of the European Union*, C 116I, 8 April 2020.

[24] European Commission, 'Communication from the Commission – Temporary Framework for State Aid Measures to support the economy in the current COVID-19 outbreak' (Consolidated Version) C(2021) 564 of 28 January 2021.

[25] See further on the distinction between introducing competition and competition policy, Guy (n 7) Introduction.

[26] For a discussion, see Guy (n 7) ch 3.

[27] Via the Dutch Health Insurance Act 2006 (*Zorgverzekeringswet*), the Dutch Healthcare (Market Regulation) Act 2006 (*Wet Marktordening Gezondheidszorg*), the Health and Social Care Act 2012 and the National Health Service (Procurement, Patient Choice and Competition) Regulations (No 2) 2013.

framework in England. This offers important insights on the *how* and *whether* questions in view of the limited scope for competition within a taxation-funded system (the NHS) and in light of the current Health and Care Bill legislative proposals to repeal the HSCA 2012 competition framework, and recent relaxation of the anticompetitive agreements prohibition in response to COVID-19. Section V concludes.

II. Framing Healthcare Access and Affordability in Competition and Competition Policy

An obvious, but useful, starting-point for any discussion of competition in healthcare is to recall that healthcare comprises myriad services, which leads to the implication that '… there is therefore no presumption that the desirability or feasibility of competition will be the same for all types of healthcare in all situations'.[28] Consequently, distinctions emerge between categories based on assessments of the scope for competition, including ancillary activities such as pharmacy distribution ('good'), more focused healthcare services included within hospital care or primary care ('average'), and emergency or trauma services being seen as separate again because conditions for competition are unlikely to be met.[29] While such distinctions do not clearly reference inequalities, they nevertheless suggest scoping for competition, which can underpin the positive and normative questions of *whether/how* competition law *can* and *should* address inequalities in a healthcare context.

A further consideration is the varying scope for competition according to the type of healthcare system, with insurance-based and taxation-funded representing two broad categories, and many European healthcare systems falling within these. Thus, it has been noted that there is greater scope for competition within an insurance-based system than a taxation-funded one in view of the greater scope for demand-driven competition in the former as distinct from the supply-driven nature of the latter, where governments are likely to determine the precise levels of benefits.[30]

How economic inequalities are addressed in the healthcare sector can be linked with the concept of universal health coverage, which means that '… all individuals

[28] Office of Health Economics (OHE), *Competition in the NHS* (London, Office of Health Economics 2012), 8.

[29] European Commission Expert Panel on Effective Ways of Investing in Health (EXPH), 'Competition among health care providers in the European Union – Investigating Policy Options', 17.02.2015, Table 4: 'Propensity to fulfil conditions for effective competition in health systems', 72, ec.europa.eu/health/sites/default/files/expert_panel/docs/008_competition_healthcare_providers_en.pdf accessed 20 February 2022.

[30] L Hancher and W Sauter, *EU Competition and Internal Market Law in the Health Care Sector* (Oxford, Oxford University Press, 2012)8.25, 232.

and communities receive the health services they need without suffering financial hardship'.[31] The relevance of this principle for addressing economic inequalities in the healthcare context is clear, and the challenge lies in sustaining and enhancing universal systems.[32] Universal access to healthcare becomes disaggregated across different financing methods, which can be described in broad terms as compulsory packages of healthcare access (whether taxation-funded or insurance-based), and out-of-pocket expenses. Compulsory packages are thought to equate to 75 per cent, and out-of-pocket expenses 25 per cent across a range of countries.[33]

Insofar as addressing economic inequality in the healthcare sector can be linked with a commitment to universal access, distinctions in competition reforms can be drawn between how a 'core' of universal access is defined, as distinct from supplementary or complementary healthcare services, regardless of whether the system is taxation-funded (such as the English NHS) or based on insurance (such as the Netherlands).[34] Thus in the Netherlands, elements of competition might be considered to focus primarily around the 'core' of the basic insurance package, while in England, competition reforms were located within the 'core' of NHS service delivery.[35]

What emerges from this overview that scoping is vital: it is important to be clear about where competition may be beneficial in addressing healthcare access and affordability (so should be encouraged), and where it would prove detrimental. At an extreme, this approach explains why emergency or specialist services may be considered to fall outside the scope of competition reforms, but routine treatments such as cataract surgery, may not. An interesting example of how tensions can play out between healthcare access and affordability on the one hand, and competition reforms on the other is seen with dental services, because of the potential for significant disparities in access to, and affordability of, dental care as this is not always included within universal health coverage.[36] In the Netherlands, ongoing concerns about dental care costs have led to repeated calls[37] for more

[31] World Health Organisation Fact Sheet, Universal Health Coverage, 1 April 2021. www.who.int/news-room/fact-sheets/detail/universal-health-coverage-(uhc) accessed 20 February 2022.

[32] OECD, Universal Health Coverage. www.oecd.org/els/health-systems/universal-health-coverage.htm accessed 20 February 2022.

[33] OECD (n 3).

[34] Odudu (n 16) takes a different approach, distinguishing three funding sources: 'discretionary' ('by which individuals exercise autonomy on how to make provision to pay for any treatment or care that may be required'); 'compulsory' ('by which individuals are mandated to participate in a particular scheme … that will pay for treatment or care required'); and 'taxation', where payment may be made by the state. For the purposes of the present discussion, it is noted that 'compulsory' and 'taxation' dimensions of Odudu's matrix can be combined insofar as healthcare paid for out of general taxation is 'compulsory' and represents a notable majority of healthcare provision within taxation-funded systems.

[35] For further discussion in the context of the applicability of competition law, see Guy (n 7) 75–83.

[36] For a discussion, see TT Wang, MR Rathur and H Schmidt, 'Universal health coverage, oral health, and personal responsibility' (2020) 98 *WHO Bulletin* 719.

[37] For example, F Baltesen, 'Dokters van de Wereld wil tandartszorg in de basispakket' ('Doctors of the World want dental care to be added to basic health insurance') 19 August 2021. www.skipr.nl/nieuws/dokters-van-de-wereld-wil-tandartszorg-in-basispakket/ accessed 20 February 2022.

dental treatment to be brought within the scope of basic health insurance since experiments with liberalising prices for dental care in 2012 were found to generate higher costs.[38] This experience may suggest that the question of *whether* competition law *can/should* engage with economic inequality with regard to accessing dental treatment may have taken priority over considerations of *how* it could. In England, dentistry has seen 'private absorption' of (NHS) patients in response to limited availability of NHS services[39] over many years, leading in 2012 to the then competition authority recommending reform of the NHS dental contract alongside development of the private dentistry market.[40] This experience appears to indicate ambivalence about whether competition law (if understood as restricted to antitrust and state aid rules) can engage with economic inequality regarding access to dental treatment, while acknowledging that there may be a role for some degree of competition regulation.

The questions of *whether/how* competition law *can/should* engage with economic inequalities in a healthcare context are given a further dimension in national reforms as substantive and institutional aspects combine, inter alia around the intersection of competition law and (economic) regulation. This in turn can reflect challenging political and social questions about the appropriate dividing line between market and state.[41] As noted above, following a political decision to introduce competition reforms in healthcare, thus answering the *whether – can/should* questions, the focus is *how* competition law *can/should* engage, and which agencies oversee this (with a complex dynamic typically emerging between government, competition authority and sectoral regulator). Such a regulatory framework is intended to enable combination of expertise – of the healthcare sector (and, relatedly, questions of healthcare access and affordability) and of competition. The English experience is examined below, but the Dutch experience is also illustrative of this.

Following the competition reforms of 2006 in Dutch healthcare, broadly parallel competition regimes were in operation, with the Authority for Consumers and Markets (ACM) having competence to apply general EU and Dutch competition law (including antitrust rules and merger control), and the Dutch Healthcare Authority (NZa) applying sector-specific rules. With regard to addressing economic

[38] A-L Trescher, S Listl, O van der Gallien, ADVOCATE Consortium, F Gabel and O Kalmus, 'Once bitten, twice shy? Lessons learned from an experiment to liberalize price regulations for dental care' (2020) 21 *European Journal of Health Economics* 425.

[39] W Whittaker and S Birch, 'Provider incentives and access to dental care: Evaluating NHS reforms in England', (2012) 75 *Social Science & Medicine* 2515.

[40] Office of Fair Trading (OFT), Dentistry – An OFT Market Study, May 2012. OFT1414. docplayer.net/6194397-Dentistry-an-oft-market-study-may-2012-oft1414.html accessed 20 February 2022. Department of Health, 'Government response to the Office of Fair Trading Market Study into Dentistry', 24 August 2012. www.gov.uk/government/publications/government-response-to-the-office-of-fair-trading-market-study-into-dentistry (accessed 20 February 2022).

[41] N Dunne, *Competition Law and Economic Regulation – Making and Managing Markets* (Cambridge, Cambridge University Press, 2015) 149.

inequality, this might be seen primarily in connection with the NZa's competence, and its obligation to prioritise the 'general consumer interest' in its activities[42] – including advising on hospital mergers, or investigating cases of 'significant market power'.[43] While consumers and their interests have prompted questions of definition and framing within wider considerations of competition policy,[44] two particular aspects characterise the conceptualisation of the 'general consumer interest' in the healthcare context. First, the 'general consumer interest' serves as a proxy for the healthcare values of accessibility, affordability and quality[45] which then provide criteria for assessing effects of anticompetitive conduct, or mergers. Second, while the 'general consumer interest' ostensibly focuses on 'final consumers', there is also scope for distinguishing between individuals as both patients and policyholders which may create tensions.[46]

The coexistence of two regimes (between approximately 2006 and 2015, prior to transfer of some NZa competition powers to the ACM), and the particular focus on the 'general consumer interest' indicate responses to the questions of *how* competition law *can* engage with economic inequalities in the healthcare sector. This can be illustrated by the scope for trade-offs and tensions between the aforementioned healthcare values[47] where, for example, a merger may contribute to quality and reduce prices, but inhibit accessibility[48] – which may have implications for engaging with economic inequalities in healthcare. The scope for tension within the 'dual identity' of patients and insurance policyholders also indicates engagement with economic inequalities in the healthcare sector as illustrated by proposals to change access to healthcare providers according to different types of health insurance policy.[49] In addition, the question of *how* competition law *should*

[42] Wmg, Art 3(4).

[43] For further discussion, see Guy (n 7) 144–148.

[44] See, eg, A. Macculloch, 'The Consumer and Competition Law' in G Howells, I Ramsay and T Wilhelmsson (eds) *Handbook of Research on International Consumer Law*, 2nd edn (Cheltenham, Edward Elgar, 2018) ch 4, V Daskalova, 'Consumer Welfare in EU Competition Law: What is it (not) about?' (2015) 11(1) *Competition Law Review* 131, P Akman, 'Consumer' versus 'Customer': The Devil in the Detail' (2010) 37(2) *Journal of Law and Society*, 315, KJ Cseres, 'Controversies of the Consumer Welfare Standard' (2006) 3(2) *Competition Law Review* 121.

[45] Which also suggest a linking of governmental oversight of the public interests of affordability, accessibility and quality providing a framework for the NZa's focus on the 'general consumer interest'. For further discussion, and information about the definition of the values and their interaction, see NZa, 'Visiedocument: (In) het belang van de consument' ('Vision Document: (In) the general consumer interest') (Utrecht, NZa, 2007).

[46] W Sauter, 'Is the general consumer interest a source of legitimacy for healthcare regulation? An analysis of the Dutch experience' (2009) 2–3 *European Journal of Consumer Law* 419. M Canoy and W Sauter, 'Out of control? Hospital mergers in the Netherlands and the public interest' (2010) 31(9) *European Competition Law Review* 377. This can also be seen in the context of the English NHS, where individuals have a 'dual identity' as patients and taxpayers. For further discussion, see Guy (n 7) 149.

[47] Sauter (n 46).

[48] Interview with Chris Fonteijn (former CEO of the ACM) cited in ML Louisse and M Wiggers, ch 6 *'Toezicht'* ('Regulation') in M Wiggers and W Oostwouder, *Handboek compliance in de zorg* (Compliance in Healthcare Handbook) (Uitgeverij Paris, Zutphen, 2017) 134.

[49] Notably in proposals to amend Art 13 Dutch Health Insurance Act 2006 and the 'free choice of healthcare provider' (*vrije artsenkeuze*), and the political sensitivities which attached to this. See Guy (n 7) 28.

engage with economic inequalities in the healthcare sector has been revealed to encompass various complexities in the interaction between government and competition (with the sectoral regulator occupying a difficult place between the two). This was evidenced by the interactions regarding the assessment of Dutch hospital mergers, with the ACM being emphatic that its scope for intervention is limited: it can only intervene where competition law is breached, and this may be inconsistent with the Dutch government's ambitions for competition reforms.[50]

If both the *how – can/should* questions, and the *whether – can/should* questions can be identified at a national level, albeit with potential for varying sequencing, other considerations come into play at EU level. While it does not follow that the EU level requires Member States to engage with competition reforms, its influence is undoubtedly notable, and can include explicit effects, such as the enactment of Article 122 Dutch Health Insurance Act 2006 to ensure that Dutch competition law applies to private health insurers even though EU competition law may not.[51] The extent to which the overarching whether and how questions feature in the EU competition law framework is now considered.

III. The EU Competition Law Framework and Healthcare Access and Affordability

Connections between the EU competition law framework and economic inequality in the healthcare context can best be illustrated by breaking down the *whether/how – can/should* questions, since answers to these are not straightforward. Here again, it is moot which sequencing is most logical, since this appears determined by a range of factors. The ability of EU competition law to engage with economic inequality in the healthcare context is linked to both the overarching *whether* and *how* questions. In the present discussion these are distinguished to reflect questions of applicability of EU competition law (predominantly *whether*) and the position assuming applicability (*how*).

A. Whether EU Competition Law Can Engage with Economic Inequality in Healthcare

It is possible to discern a broad framework in which EU competition law is deemed applicable to healthcare providers, but not to healthcare purchasers[52]

[50] Guy (n 7) 13. ACM, Position Paper Autoriteit Consument en Markt Rondetafelgesprek 'Kwaliteit loont' ('ACM Position Paper on the 'Quality Pays' roundtable discussion') 17.04.2015.

[51] Further on this, see JW van de Gronden and E Szyszczak, 'Introducing competition principles into health care through EU law and policy: a case study of the Netherlands' (2014) 22 *Medical Law Review* 238.

[52] See, eg, van de Gronden and Rusu (n 22).

through cases explicitly concerned with healthcare such as *Pavlov*,[53] *Ambulanz Glöckner*,[54] *AOK Bundesverband*,[55] *FENIN*,[56] and reinforced recently by *Dôvera*.[57] This case law has followed the traditional approach to the functional definition of the trigger requirement of an 'undertaking' for competition law to apply, namely that there is an 'economic activity',[58] which consists in offering goods or services on a market.[59] While the latter criterion can explain the aforementioned distinction between healthcare *providers* and *purchasers*, the former requirement for an 'economic activity' has generated much comment. The emphasis has – logically – been on aspects such as whether the healthcare providers/insurers are engaged in profit-making activities, and whether the activity takes place within a system exclusively based on solidarity (as distinct from competition). While these suggest clear lines – either an activity is profit-making or not; a healthcare system is, or is not, exclusively based on solidarity – it is difficult to provide clear-cut answers when healthcare systems incorporate elements of both solidarity and competition within an overarching aim of addressing inequality via sustainability of the healthcare system. The contortions of both academic commentary and case decisions have generated assessments of whether there is enough competition in a healthcare system for competition law to apply, and what this means – with de facto, potential, and even hypothetical competition representing different thresholds.[60]

An alternative approach to establishing an 'undertaking' has been proposed which foregrounds public interest rather than questions of profit-making within economic activities.[61] This makes use of a three-prong test from *CEPPB*[62] with three cumulative (not alternative) elements, which can be illustrated as follows:

(i) the supply of the services or goods of these providers is mainly dependent on public funding;
(ii) the aim of this funding is the attainment of an objective of public interest; and
(iii) the activities concerned are closely related to this objective.

[53] Joined cases C-180/98 to C-184/98, *Pavel Pavlov and Others v Stichting Pensioenfonds Medische Specialisten*, ECLI:EU:C:2000:428.

[54] Case C-475/99, *Firma Ambulanz Glöckner v Landkreis Südwestpfalz*, ECLI:EU:C:2001:577.

[55] Joined cases C-264/01, C-306/01, C-354/01 and C-355/01, *AOK Bundesverband, Bundesverband der Betriebskrankenkassen (BKK) et al.v Ichthyol-Gesellschaft Cordes et al.*, ECLI:EU:C:2004:150.

[56] Case C-205/03 P, *Federación Española de Empresas de Tecnología Sanitaria (FENIN) v Commission of the European Communities*, ECLI:EU:C:2006:453.

[57] Joined Cases C-262/18 P and C-271/18 P *European Commission and Slovak Republic v Dôvera zdravotná poisťovňa, a.s.* ECLI:EU:C:2020:450.

[58] Case C-41/90, *Klaus Höfner and Fritz Elser v Macrotron GmbH*, ECLI:EU:C:1991:161.

[59] Case C-35/96, *Commission of the European Communities v Italy*, ECLI:EU:C:1998:303.

[60] See Nikolić (n 1), who links potential competition with *Ambulanz Glöckner*, and de facto competition with the *IRIS-H* state aid case. See also D Sinclair, '"Undertakings" in competition law at the public-private interface – an unhealthy situation' (2014) 35(4) *European Competition Law Review* 167.

[61] JW van de Gronden, 'Services of general interest and the concept of undertaking: does EU competition law apply?' (2018) 41 *World Competition* 197. JW van de Gronden and M Guy, 'The role of EU competition law in health care and the 'undertaking' concept' (2021) 16 *Health Economics, Policy and Law* 76.

[62] Case C-74/16 *Congregación de Escuelas Pías Provincia Betania*, 27 June 2017, ECLI:EU:C:2017:496.

In a healthcare context, this test can be used to distinguish differing activities of healthcare providers, notably between the provision of 'regular' medical services (which would be subject to competition law) and 'specialist' medical services which cannot be provided effectively within the market (thus would not be subject to competition law).[63] The logic of the test is thus not to displace the option of designating activities as SGEI, but, recognising that this mechanism offers only a partial exemption, to provide further scope for a range of activities to be exempted from the reach of competition law. The Dutch case *Gendia v Ministry of Health, Wellbeing and Sport*,[64] which saw the provision of Non-Invasive Prenatal Tests and counselling at subsidised rates by Dutch university hospitals classified as SGEI, has been discussed in light of the *CEPPB* test with the implication that these services may fall outside the scope of EU competition law.[65] Maternity services provide an important aspect of healthcare provision which would benefit from particular treatment within competition law as these are typically linked more to emergency services (which may be more likely to fall outside the scope of competition law) than to elective services (which may be more likely to fall within the scope of competition law).

Both the standard, functional 'economic activity' test from *Höfner*, and the 'public interest'-focused test from *CEPPB* offer useful insights into how different healthcare services can fall within or outside of the EU competition law framework. However, addressing inequalities and healthcare access and affordability may suggest that further nuances of healthcare provision need to be clarified, perhaps necessitating a fundamental rethink of the logic which suggests that competition and solidarity are more distant than being 'two sides of the same coin'.[66] This is particularly evident with regard to private providers delivering public healthcare services, given the tension which arises between the logic suggesting that such providers are indeed subject to competition law,[67] and the grey area arising from the 'implicit' finding of the CJEU in *FENIN* that provision of public healthcare services was not an economic activity.[68]

The idea that the ultimate purpose of an activity is what determines whether or not competition law applies as articulated in *FENIN* has attracted much criticism. However, it highlights an important consideration for developing how competition law can address questions of inequality, healthcare access and affordability. This is evident when it is recalled that standard medical procedures, such as cataract

[63] Van de Gronden and Guy (n 61).

[64] Case No 200.225.476/01, Gerechtshof Den Haag, 11 December 2018, ECLI:NL:GHDHA:2018:3331.

[65] Van de Gronden and Guy (n 61).

[66] S Belhaj and JW van de Gronden, 'Some room for competition does not make a sickness fund an undertaking. Is EC competition law applicable to the health care sector? (Joined cases C-264/01, C-306/01, C-453/01 and C-355/01 *AOK*)' (2004) 25(11) *European Competition Law Review* 682.

[67] Nikolić (n 1) relies on *Pavlov* and *Ambulanz Glöckner* to reach this conclusion.

[68] Nikolić (n 1).

operations, can be provided effectively by the market, but are done so in different ways for different groups of patients.[69] Where there is competition between private providers to deliver public healthcare services, this may require the delineation of a separate market, something which is long-standing in CMA assessments in England (where consideration of the interaction between the NHS and private healthcare is standard). However, the scope for this has also been identified with regard to the EU level by analogy with the possibility identified for competitive provision of public/universal service obligations,[70] and even in connection with merger assessment in the US.[71]

B. Whether EU Competition Law Should Engage with Economic Inequality in Healthcare

As Member States have started to experiment with marketisation reforms and expanded roles for the private sector within their healthcare systems, questions have been raised about the applicability of EU competition law, and challenges of anticompetitive conduct brought by private providers. This has generated much discussion about the extent of EU involvement in healthcare, and concerns about inconsistent approaches taken by the European Commission and the Court of Justice of the European Union (CJEU).[72]

While EU-level commitment to tackling health inequality is not in doubt,[73] a seamless connection with EU competition policy is difficult to discern. Nevertheless, links may be drawn via EU fiscal policy, with competition reforms being viewed as a means to support financial sustainability of healthcare systems following the 2008–2009 economic crisis.[74]

[69] For example, with a greater choice of lens being available to patients who can afford to pay, and a more basic service provided to patients accessing public healthcare.

[70] W Sauter, *Public Services in EU Law* (Cambridge, Cambridge University Press, 2015) 233–234.

[71] With the identification of vulnerable, high-risk consumers as a separate relevant market. T Stavroulaki, 'Mergers that Harm our health' (2022) 19(10) *Berkeley Business Law Journal* 89.

[72] For recent examples, see Nikolić (n 1) and AJB Morton, 'European Health Care Systems and the Emerging Influence of European Union Competition Policy', (2021) 46(3) *Journal of Health Politics, Policy and Law* 467.

[73] Council Conclusions on Common values and principles in European Union Health Systems, Official Journal of the European Union (2006/C 146/01), 1.

[74] For example, exhortations to remove restrictions on competition in medical services were included in structural reforms linked with the Economic Adjustment Programme for Ireland. For a discussion, see DGECFIN, 'The Economic Adjustment Programme for Ireland', *Occasional Papers* 76, February 2011, 66. ec.europa.eu/economy_finance/publications/occasional_paper/2011/pdf/ocp76_en.pdf, accessed 20 February 2022. In 2015, France received a Country-Specific Recommendation (CSR) in the context of the European Semester annual economic policy assessment exhorting the removal of restrictions on access to, and exercise of, regulated professions, in particular as regards the health professions. eur-lex.europa.eu/legal-content/EN/TXT/PDF/?uri=CELEX:32015H0818(15)&from=EN CSR 4. Although not formulated as a CSR, these concerns had been articulated in 2012 as well. /eur-lex.europa.eu/legal-content/EN/TXT/PDF/?uri=CELEX:52012DC0313&from=EN, para 15.

At least part of the answer to *whether* EU competition law *should* engage with economic inequality in connection with healthcare appears to lie in the respective EU-level and national competences regarding healthcare system organisation. While Article 168(7) TFEU is described as a 'subsidiarity clause' for healthcare,[75] the rules governing applicability of EU competition law suggest that this is a porous barrier,[76] and one which sets out a 'delicate and sophisticated balance' with regard to competition cases.[77]

This would seem to be reinforced by the Member State competences both regarding health policy and healthcare system organisation,[78] and the designation of SGEI.[79] It should be noted that the combination of these two competences is critical here: while the former can offer scope for differing degrees of experimentation with marketisation reforms,[80] consensus appears to grow around the view that a decision to engage with marketisation reforms may indeed be a national one, but that such a decision has consequences, namely triggering applicability of EU competition law.[81]

While the SGEI mechanism is considered to provide a serviceable exception for Member States wishing to experiment with competition reforms,[82] it provides only a partial exception,[83] and has also been considered cumbersome to the point that countries may prefer to try and exempt their healthcare systems completely from the reach of EU competition law by scaling back their marketisation reforms.[84]

C. How EU Competition Law Can Engage with Economic Inequality in Healthcare

How EU competition law *can* engage with questions of inequality may thus be considered perhaps to take place primarily in a negative sense, insofar as it is

[75] Hancher and Sauter (n 30).

[76] A Andreangeli, 'Healthcare Services, the EU Single Market and Beyond: Meeting Local Needs in an Open Economy – How Much Market or How Little Market?' (2016) 43(2) *Legal Issues of Economic Integration* 145.

[77] JW van de Gronden and E Szyszczak, 'Conclusions: Constructing a 'Solid' Multi-Layered Health Care Edifice' in JW van de Gronden, E Szyszczak, U Neergaard and M Krajewski (eds), *Health Care and EU Law* (The Hague, TMC Asser Press, 2011) 481.

[78] Treaty on the Functioning of the European Union, Art 168(7).

[79] Consolidated Version of the Treaty on European Union – Protocol (No 26) on Services of General Interest. Official Journal 115, 09/05/2008, 0308–0308.

[80] For example, the differing approaches taken in England and Scotland while the UK was an EU Member State. Andreangeli (n 76).

[81] T Prosser, 'EU competition law and public services' in E Mossialos, G Permanand, R Baeten and TK Hervey (eds), *Health Systems Governance in Europe: The Role of European Union Law and Policy* (Cambridge, Cambridge University Press, 2010). Nikolić (n 1).

[82] O Odudu, 'Are State-owned healthcare providers undertakings subject to competition law?' (2011) 32(5) *European Competition Law Review* 231.

[83] van de Gronden and Guy (n 61).

[84] Nikolić (n 1).

the (partial) exceptions of Services of General Interest and SGEI which explicitly recognise solidarity and equality aims. Where these values may be more or less explicitly considered is in assessment of the SGEI exception. For example, in *Ambulanz Glöckner*, emergency ambulance services were considered to be designated SGEI by virtue of requirements under German law for the provision of public ambulance services. Perhaps unsurprisingly, such values have also featured in state aid cases, with subsidies to public hospitals in Belgium and Italy being approved by, respectively, the Commission[85] and the General Court.[86] The possibility of protecting values of affordability and accessibility alongside a competition-based system was also considered with regard to the Dutch Risk Equalisation Scheme being permitted.[87]

Although it is typically the SGEI exception – and not, for example, recourse to Article 101(3) TFEU – which has been considered most serviceable in a social (thus healthcare) context,[88] the aforementioned temporary relaxation frameworks introduced in response to COVID-19 have relied predominantly on the narrower exceptions of Article 107(3) TFEU.[89]

The State Aid Temporary Framework was introduced on 19 March 2020, has been updated six times, and is expected to be in operation in different forms during 2022 and at least into 2023.[90] The health-specific guidance relates to going beyond the exceptions permitting aid to facilitate development of certain economic activities or areas,[91] or remedying a 'serious disturbance' in a Member State economy.[92] Both the guidance and subsequent cases include a focus on 'crisis' response,[93] for example, facilitating COVID-19-relevant research and development,[94]

[85] SA.19864 (NN54/2009 – 2014/C) Public financing of Brussels public IRIS hospitals. This positive decision in 2016 involved a re-assessment by the Commission following a lengthy unfolding of the case, with the original complaints being lodged in 2005 and the Commission's 2009 decision being annulled by the General Court in 2012.

[86] Case T-223/18 *Casa Regina Apostolorum della Pia Società delle Figlie di San Paolo v European Commission* ECLI:EU:T:2021:315. This case is currently (as at October 2021) subject to further appeal to the CJEU, and follows approval by the Commission in SA.39913 (2017/NN) Alleged compensation of public hospitals in Lazio.

[87] SA.18426 (N541/2004) Retention of financial reserves by Dutch Health Insurance Funds. For discussion, see Hancher and Sauter (n 30) 274–5.

[88] T Prosser, *The Limits of Competition Law* (Oxford, Oxford University Press, 2005) 27.

[89] M Guy, 'Can COVID-19 change the EU competition law framework in health?', Opinion Paper No 25, September 2020, *Observatoire Social Européen*, Brussels.

[90] ec.europa.eu/competition-policy/state-aid/coronavirus/temporary-framework_en accessed 20 February 2022.

[91] TFEU, Art 107(3)(c).

[92] TFEU, Art 107(3)(b).

[93] With regard to the temporary relaxation framework for the antitrust rules, a primary focus is the need recognised for greater cooperation to ensure supply and adequate distribution of essential scarce products, including medicines and medical equipment used to test and treat COVID-19 patients or necessary to mitigate and possibly overcome the outbreak. However, the Commission recognised that cooperation in the health sector might need to go even further to overcome critical supply shortages, such as coordinating reorganisation of production to allow producers to satisfy demand for urgently-needed medicines across Member States. European Commission (n23), paras 4 and 14.

[94] European Commission (n 24), section 3.6.

producing COVID-19-relevant products,[95] and approving state aid for time-bounded UK and Italian schemes, respectively, to distribute free medical grade personal protective equipment (PPE) across various healthcare providers,[96] and to produce and supply medical equipment such as ventilators, masks and goggles.[97] While these examples may have only a tenuous link with seemingly specific questions of addressing economic inequality in healthcare (but are undoubtedly part of wider considerations), cases decided under the State Aid Temporary Framework also indicate considerations of healthcare access. For example, in the Czech Republic, restrictions on the operations of providers of curative rehabilitation spa treatment meant that this could only be provided if it is at least partially reimbursed from public health insurance.[98] The effect of this is that spas could accept patients from hospitals.[99] The Covid-Spas subsidy programme was initially extended from 1 January 2021 to 30 June 2021, but was extended to 31 December 2021 due to further disruptions in the latter part of 2020.[100] The Commission's decision not to raise objections to this subsidy[101] is based on Article 107(3)(b) TFEU, and is couched in terms of supporting employment, but would appear to have benefits for some access to health treatments.

A further example was seen with the Netherlands, with the Commission permitting[102] temporary payments of direct grants by the Dutch Ministry of Health, Wellbeing and Sport to cover costs for the purchase, leasing, licensing and implementation of e-health applications to support providers of general practitioner care, district nursing, mental health care and social support services. This was in operation between April and December 2020. The need for this subsidy has arisen from increased demand for 'virtual' access to healthcare provision among groups most affected by the social distancing rules imposed by the Dutch Government (such as the elderly, at-risk groups and mentally ill patients).[103]

Outside the realm of different exception mechanisms, where EU competition law has been deemed applicable with regard to healthcare providers, the question

[95] Including medicinal products (such as vaccines), medical devices and equipment, disinfectants and data collection/processing tools. European Commission (n 24), Section 3.8.

[96] Case SA.58477.

[97] Case SA.56786.

[98] Resolution of the Government of the Czech Republic of 30 October 2020, No 116. www.vlada.cz/assets/media-centrum/aktualne/23_R_retail-sales-and-the-sale_1108_30102020.pdf accessed 20 February 2022.

[99] www.vlada.cz/en/media-centrum/aktualne/measures-adopted-by-the-czech-government-against-coronavirus-180545/ accessed 20 February 2022.

[100] ibid. Case SA.61912 ec.europa.eu/competition/elojade/isef/case_details.cfm?proc_code=3_SA_61912 (accessed 20 February 2022) which extended Case SA.58018 ec.europa.eu/competition/elojade/isef/case_details.cfm?proc_code=3_SA_58018 accessed 20 February 2022.

[101] Case SA.58018 and Case SA.61912.

[102] Case SA.57897 ec.europa.eu/competition/state_aid/cases1/202030/287111_2174861_86_2.pdf accessed 20 February 2022. This decision extends an initial application under Case SA.56915 ec.europa.eu/competition/state_aid/cases1/202015/285387_2146214_33_2.pdf accessed 20 February 2022.

[103] ibid, page 3.

of *how* it *can* engage with questions of healthcare access and affordability remain. Certainly it has been noted that EU competition cases concerning the healthcare sector have not taken account of the effects on patients deemed to be the 'end users' or 'ultimate consumers' of healthcare.[104] If EU competition law is to (explicitly) engage with questions of economic inequality in the healthcare sector, effects of competition law decisions on patients should be incorporated, particularly where these may prove disadvantageous to patients from lower socio-economic groups, in light of the governing principles of universal coverage underpinning healthcare systems. While the flexibility of EU competition law (and particularly Article 101 TFEU) to accommodate healthcare values,[105] and specifically equity,[106] have been discussed, these are open questions, with answers likely to be very much context-dependent, both on a specific allegation of anticompetitive conduct and the healthcare system in question.

D. How EU Competition Law Should Engage with Economic Inequality in Healthcare

The foregoing may suggest an ambivalence regarding EU competition law's engagement with questions of economic inequality in the healthcare sector. However, the apparent willingness to support use of the SGEI exception would seem to suggest less that the EU level is dismissive of questions of access and affordability in healthcare, and more that it regards this as a matter for national decision.

Given the parameters outlined above regarding the applicability of EU competition law between the 'undertaking' concept and the SGEI mechanism, calls for further EU-level clarification of the SGEI mechanism in the healthcare context continue to be welcome.[107]

Where competition law is deemed applicable, then the scope for considering concerns about equity should be developed, for example to include considerations of how particular conduct (and subsequent decisions) may affect patients, and particularly those in lower socio-economic groups,[108] although defining such groups in a cohesive way across 27 Member States may prove a particular challenge.

[104] Sauter (n 12).

[105] JW van de Gronden, 'The Treaty Provisions on Competition and Health Care' in JW van de Gronden, E Szyszczak, U Neergaard and M Krajewski (eds), *Health Care and EU Law* (The Hague, TMC Asser Press, 2011) 265–94.

[106] Stavroulaki (n 11).

[107] Van de Gronden and Szyszczak (n 51); Guy (n 7).

[108] In an approach analogous to the distinction drawn between NHS and private patients in the UK by the CMA. A need to identify 'vulnerable, high-risk consumers' as a separate relevant market has also been identified in the US context – Stavroulaki (n 71).

IV. Experiences from England: Competition in Healthcare

In contrast to the EU level, it might be anticipated that the *whether/how-can/should* questions regarding competition law and economic inequalities in healthcare may be subject to a different kind of sequencing at a national level, given that healthcare system organisation is a matter for Member State competence. As suggested in section I, the decision to engage with competition reforms in healthcare is a political one, which might indicate – perhaps counterintuitively – that the question of *whether* competition law *should* engage with economic inequalities in healthcare not only predominates, but also is largely answered. The focus therefore falls on the questions of *how* competition law *can* and *should* engage with economic inequalities in the healthcare sector as a way to respond to the remaining *whether/can* question, even if this may be seen as a more logical starting point.

To illustrate these considerations, it is useful to consider the experience of making use of competition law in competition reforms in English healthcare. The distinction is important because while competition reforms started under the Conservative Government of the late 1980s and continued to develop under New Labour (1997–2010),[109] the explicit recourse to primary and secondary legislation (as distinct from policy) is much more recent. It is possible to speak of a defined period between the Health and Social Care Act 2012 (HSCA 2012)[110] and the current progress of the Health and Care Bill in the UK Parliament, which removes the HSCA 2012 competition provisions, and is expected to be enacted by April 2022.[111]

This time-bounded experiment suggests that it is possible to answer the (political) question of *whether* competition law *should* engage with economic inequalities in the healthcare sector both in the affirmative and the negative. This provides a framework for examining the *whether/can* question, as well as the *how – can/should* questions. Before unpacking the four questions, however, it is useful to bear in mind some considerations about the nature of English healthcare.

The structure of the healthcare system – as encompassing both the NHS and private healthcare – across the UK, but in England in particular, given the significant development of the private healthcare market,[112] offers significant potential to generate and exacerbate health inequalities. The capacity for providers to operate in the private healthcare market, the NHS, or both, and for patients to move between the two, indicate the scope for a broad sense of competition between

[109] For further discussion, see Guy (n 7) ch 1.

[110] Introduced by the Liberal Democrat-Conservative Government (2010–2015).

[111] NHS England and NHS Improvement, 'Integrating Care – Next Steps to building strong and effective integrated care systems across England', November 2020. 2.

[112] CMA, 'Private Healthcare Market Investigation', Final Report, 2 April 2014. CMA25. 2.11, 2.25, 2.36, 2.73.

the two.[113] This has led to the CMA regarding the two as separate markets which nevertheless can impact each other in cases of merger assessment and antitrust cases.[114]

The dynamic between the NHS and private healthcare market is further complicated by the NHS effectively fulfilling three functions: acting as the majority healthcare provider (in the public healthcare system), operating in the private healthcare market (via private patient units), and fulfilling the function of 'provider of last resort' relative to the private healthcare market, as evidenced by unplanned transfers of private patients to NHS hospitals.[115]

This complex coexistence of the NHS and private healthcare nevertheless provided a basis for successive competition reforms in the NHS.[116] These revolved around the expansion of private sector delivery of NHS services underpinned by patient choice policies which hinted at the scope for economic inequality and questions of healthcare access and affordability:

> The overriding principle is clear. We should give poorer patients … the same range of choice [i.e. of private provider] the rich have always enjoyed.[117]

In order to engage with the question of how competition law can relate to economic inequality/healthcare access and affordability, it is useful to recall that competition reforms in English healthcare have been defined by reference to two parameters: the separation of purchasing and providing functions, and the interaction between the NHS and the private healthcare sector. This has made it possible to speak of 'four categories'[118] described in Figure 9.1, in which categories one and two represent the NHS and categories three and four the private healthcare sector. In essence, the applicability of UK competition law and oversight by the competition authority has not been in question with regard to categories three and four, but has proved controversial in connection with category two in particular.[119]

[113] For a discussion, see M Guy, 'Between 'going private' and 'NHS privatisation': patient choice, competition reforms and the relationship between the NHS and private healthcare in England' (2019) 39 *Legal Studies* 479.

[114] See, eg, CE/9784-13, Private Ophthalmology: investigation into anti-competitive information exchange and pricing agreements. Infringement decision. 20.08.2015.

[115] In addition, this has served as a criterion for private patients in assessing private hospitals. CMA, Press Release, 'Better information for private patients moves closer', 1 December 2014.

[116] Broadly three phases: the Enthoven-inspired NHS internal market (1989–1997); New Labour choice and competition reforms (approx. 2000–2010) and the HSCA 2012 and 'opening up public services' reforms of the Conservative/Liberal Democrat coalition Government (2010–2015). For discussion, see Guy (n 7) ch 1.

[117] T Blair 'We must not waste this precious period of power', speech given at South Camden Community College, London, 23 January 2003, cited in Z Cooper Competition in Hospital Services, OECD Working Party No 2 on Competition and Regulation (DAF/COMP/WP2(2012)2, 2012).

[118] Guy (n 7) 40, and developed from the relationships as set out in Office of Fair Trading (OFT), *Private Healthcare Market Study*, OFT1396, 13, and O Odudu, 'Competition Law and the National Health Service', *Competition Bulletin: Competition Law Views from Blackstone Chambers*, 8 October 2012.

[119] With regard to category 1, Odudu has suggested that where the purchaser and the provider are the same legal entity there is no transaction to which competition law can be applied.

Figure 9.1 The four categories of English healthcare

1.	2.	3.	4.
Public Purchaser	Public Purchaser	Private Purchaser	Private Purchaser
and	and	and	and
Public Provider	Private Provider	Public Provider	Private Provider

A. Whether Competition Law Should Engage with Economic Inequality in Healthcare

The question of whether competition law should concern itself with economic inequality in the English healthcare context via engagement with the NHS, has proven contested over the course of successive competition reforms (from the late 1980s to approximately 2015). The contentions might be understood as comprising both substantive and institutional concerns, encompassing the ongoing criticism that the general UK competition regime designed to regulate private sector activity would be insufficient for the NHS;[120] concerns that expanding private sector delivery of NHS services would trigger both applicability and application of EU competition law; and concerns that the competition authority would have control over NHS activity.

What emerged from this was an 'NHS-specific' competition regime, initially policy-based under New Labour, with the NHS Principles and Rules of Competition and Cooperation (NHS PRCC), overseen by the NHS Cooperation and Competition Panel, a regulator located within the then Department of Health. These arrangements have been interpreted as meaning that NHS activity was 'exempt by fiat' from the general competition law frameworks and competition authority oversight,[121] and considered, variously, to comprise the principles of competition law[122] and an 'alternative source' of competition law.[123]

The NHS PRCC have further been viewed as a means of demonstrating compliance with EU competition law while avoiding recourse to law.[124] This might also be seen as consistent with the view that competition law engages with questions of economic inequality in healthcare fundamentally via exceptions. The difference emerges in the starting point of the perspective insofar as 'shielding' the NHS from

[120] D Dawson, 'Regulating competition in the NHS. The Department of Health guide on mergers and anti-competitive behaviour', *University of York Centre for Health Economics Discussion Paper* 131, March 1995. Odudu (n 16) notes that this criticism persists.

[121] M Gaynor and R Town, 'Competition in Health Care Markets' in M Pauly et al. (ed), *Handbook of Health Economics*, Part 2 (Oxford, Elsevier, 2012) 559.

[122] Odudu (n 82).

[123] Odudu (n 118).

[124] N Timmins, *The Five Giants – A Biography of the Welfare State*, 3rd edn (London, William Collins, 2017) 643.

the reach of competition law implies that competition law is likely to be either neutral or detrimental to questions of economic inequality in healthcare.

Perhaps unsurprisingly, the question of whether competition law should engage with the NHS met with resistance during the passage of the HSCA 2012, with a three-month pause being called to address concerns. Although the HSCA 2012 was eventually enacted, thus still indicating an affirmative political decision for competition law to engage with the NHS, the acceptance of this was much more qualified. What emerged from ongoing criticism and controversy included effective enshrinement of the NHS PRCC in legislation as the National Health Service (Procurement, Patient Choice and Competition) Regulations (No 2) 2013, and a scaling-back of the role envisaged for the CMA. Indeed, the changes introduced prior and subsequent to the HSCA 2012 can be seen as capable of uniting both those opposed to, and in favour of, competition reforms in healthcare.[125]

B. How Competition Law Can/Should Engage with Economic Inequality in Healthcare

The HSCA 2012 reforms demonstrate that *how* competition law *can* engage with economic inequality in the healthcare context is by the coexistence of general, and sector-specific regimes, and by recourse to modifications of general frameworks. This can be illustrated by two examples, which also show that the *how – can/should* questions can be conflated.

First, section 64(2) HSCA 2012 enshrined the concept of 'anticompetitive behaviour'[126] to reflect the terminology of primarily the prohibition on anticompetitive agreements, and form the basis of prohibitions imposed on purchasers (NHS commissioners)[127] and (NHS and private) providers delivering services for the NHS.[128] Furthermore, one of NHS Improvement's general duties as a competition regulator was to '... exercise its functions with a view to preventing anti-competitive behaviour in the provision of health care services for the purposes of the NHS which is against the interests of people who use such services'.[129] Indeed this might be read as a clear attempt to suggest *how* competition law *should* engage with questions of economic inequalities in the healthcare sector.

[125] Guy (n 7) 57–58, 222.

[126] HSCA 2012, s 64(2), which provides: 'Anti-competitive behaviour' means behaviour which would (or would be likely to) prevent, restrict or distort competition and a reference to preventing anti-competitive behaviour includes a reference to eliminating or reducing the effects (or potential effects) of the behaviour.

[127] Regulation 10 of the National Health Service (Procurement, Patient Choice and Competition) Regulations (No 2) 2013, SI 2013/500, prohibits 'anticompetitive conduct.'

[128] Within the 'Competition Oversight' aspect of the Choice and Competition condition of the NHS Provider Licence.

[129] HSCA 2012, s 62(3).

The existence of section 64(2) HSCA indicated the development of an 'NHS-specific' competition regime *within* the 'core' of solidarity,[130] where applicability of EU competition law may be contested, or at least extremely politically sensitive. The total lack of recourse to either section 64(2) HSCA 2012 specifically, or to the aforementioned prohibitions regarding NHS purchasing or providing activity might suggest that merely replicating the terminology of general competition law is not sufficient, and more thought needs to be given to how to conceptualise competitive harms within the context of a public healthcare system intended to engage with economic inequality in healthcare.

Second, section 79 HSCA 2012 provides for a modified version of general UK merger control[131] to apply to certain types of NHS hospital mergers. How this can indicate engagement with economic inequality in healthcare can be seen by the role afforded to NHS Improvement under section 79(5) HSCA 2012, to identify 'relevant customer benefits' to a merger, thereby obviating the need for a Phase II investigation, or to offset any substantial lessening of competition which may be generated. This was subsequently reconceptualised as 'relevant patient benefits', and extended to cover aspects of NHS policy, such as the move towards a '7 day NHS',[132] or the wider NHS policy move towards integrated care systems,[133] in contrast to the narrower 'relevant customer benefits' exception of UK general merger control.[134] However, it is important to note that this requirement to identify 'relevant patient benefits' only applied to certain NHS hospital mergers, and not all mergers with potential implications for NHS patients, thus a merger between two private providers delivering NHS services, would only be assessed under general UK merger control.[135]

If the conceptualisation of 'relevant patient benefits' demonstrates *how* competition law *can* engage with NHS policy, then the approach taken by the CMA in such merger cases indicates *how* competition law *should*, and a conflation of the two questions. The 2017 Manchester Hospitals merger was notable for the CMA's explicit recognition that competition played a limited role in the NHS and was not the basic organising principle for the provision of NHS services.[136] Although

[130] In contrast to the competition reforms in Dutch healthcare, which developed *around* a core of solidarity. For further discussion, see Guy (n 7) ch 2.

[131] Enterprise Act 2002, Pt 4.

[132] In a Phase II decision by the CMA, A report on the anticipated merger of Ashford and St Peter's Hospitals NHS Foundation Trust and Royal Surrey County Hospital NHS Foundation Trust, 16 September 2015.

[133] See from the 2017 Manchester Hospitals merger onwards until the final merger assessed under this framework – CMA, ME/6875-19 – Anticipated merger between The Royal Bournemouth and Christchurch Hospitals NHS Foundation Trust and Poole Hospital NHS Foundation Trust Decision on relevant merger situation and substantial lessening of competition. 27 April 2020.

[134] EA 02, s 30(1)(a), which defines 'relevant customer benefits' in terms of reductions in price or improvements in quality.

[135] CMA, A report on the completed acquisition by Cygnet Health Care Ltd and Universal Health Services, Inc. of the Cambian Adult Services Division of Cambian Group plc, 16.10.2017. See further, Guy (n 7) ch 4.

[136] CMA, Central Manchester University Hospitals/University Hospital of South Manchester Merger Inquiry, Final Report, 1 August 2017.

NHS hospital mergers continued to be assessed by the CMA up until April 2020,[137] the changing focus of wider NHS policy – from competition to integration – and recognition of this in merger cases, prompted questions of whether NHS merger assessment had become effectively a 'rubber stamping' exercise in the absence of recourse to substantive exceptions.[138] This would appear to suggest a conflation of the *how – whether-should* questions.

C. Whether Competition Law (Actually) Can Engage with Economic Inequality in Healthcare

The foregoing reflections on the English experience suggest that answering the question of whether competition law (actually) can engage with economic inequality in healthcare via the proxy of supporting NHS reforms is not straightforward. With the current Health and Care Bill revocation of the HSCA 2012 competition provisions, it might be considered that it cannot.

However, policy documentation preceding the Health and Care Bill indicated an important distinction between competition in the sense of the HSCA 2012 provisions, and the application of competition law by the CMA to tackle excessive pricing abuses by pharmaceutical companies vis-à-vis the NHS.[139] This may indicate that the question to be asked is not at a very wide and general level of *whether*, but a more focused *where* competition law can engage with economic inequality in the healthcare sector, which may relate as much to specific healthcare services as to particular demographic groups.

Given the political sensitivities which have surrounded competition reforms in the NHS, it might further be considered that a further factor shaping the *whether-can* question is relative perceptions of flexibility at the levels of policy and law.[140] The NHS PRCC was largely enshrined by the subsequent National Health Service (Procurement, Patient Choice and Competition) Regulations (No 2) with the HSCA 2012 reforms, but lost an important aspect which may have facilitated a focus of competition on economic inequalities, namely acknowledging the nature of the complex interactions between NHS commissioners and NHS patients (with the additional identity of being taxpayers),[141] thus underpinning a system better equipped to address economic inequalities and questions of healthcare access and affordability. This led to the NHS PRCC being described – persuasively – as a

[137] See n 127 above.
[138] Guy (n 7) 227.
[139] NHS England, The NHS Long Term Plan, January 2019, para 7.14, page 113.
[140] See further on this, ACL Davies, 'This Time, It's For Real' (2013) 76(3) *Modern Law Review* 564, and M Guy, 'Demarketisation, Deregulation, Dejuridification? Removing competition from the English NHS with the Health and Care Bill' (2021) Lancaster University Law School Working Paper, 1 September 2021. papers.ssrn.com/sol3/papers.cfm?abstract_id=3915776 accessed 20 February 2022.
[141] Guy (n 7) 49.

'new style' of competition law for quasi-markets,[142] which did not transfer to the HSCA 2012 reforms which sought to align the NHS with more standard markets. The scope for general competition law to make assessments based on nuanced dual identities might be considered less than the ability for policy to do this.

Independent of the Health and Care Bill reforms, there has been a relaxation of the anticompetitive agreements prohibition in response to COVID-19 to enable closer cooperation between the NHS and private healthcare sector.[143] While this was introduced primarily as an initial crisis response, there have been a variety of agreements notified which extend into wider continuity responses, including cooperation to address lengthening NHS waiting lists. This may add further weight to a negative response to the question of whether competition law *can* (and *should*) engage with economic inequality in healthcare.

V. Conclusion

This chapter started from the premise that although few explicit links between tackling economic inequality in healthcare and competition law have been drawn, these may nevertheless be inferred from competition reforms being used as a mechanism to address ongoing issues regarding the sustainability of healthcare systems in the face of rising healthcare costs. From this starting-point, it quickly becomes apparent that while a matrix of *whether – can/should* and *how – can/should* questions provides a useful framework for analysing competition reforms and the application of competition law, other questions and considerations emerge when examination of the EU and national levels is juxtaposed. This has given rise to at least three main insights.

First, that the overarching *whether* and *how* questions can be difficult to sequence, and (may) be too easily intertwined. For example, it may appear that *how/whether-can* is a logical starting-point, but this can be displaced by considerations of *should*. This can be seen at EU level with regard to the Member State competence regarding healthcare (Article 168(7) TFEU) and the determinative role Member States play in identifying SGEI. At a national level, *whether-should* may prove the leading question, with considerations of *whether-can* and *how – can/should* being secondary.

Second, that a related question of *where* competition law *can/should* engage with economic inequality in healthcare assumes importance. This might be seen as an answer to the overarching *whether* question, or can form a separate, more focused question. The experience of excessive pricing in the pharmaceutical

[142] I Lianos, 'Toward a Bureaucracy-Centred Theory of the Interaction between Competition Law and State Activities' in TK Cheng, I Lianos, and DD Sokol (eds), *Competition and the State* (Stanford, Stanford University Press, 2014).

[143] Competition Act 1998 (Health Services for Patients in England) (Coronavirus) (Public Policy Exclusion) Order 2020, SI 2020/368.

sector provides a clear instance of *where* a specific sector may benefit from using competition law. *Where* therefore suggests a more disaggregated approach which, by identifying specific treatments as a starting point, may move the analysis onto *how* competition law *can/should* engage with economic inequalities in terms of substantive assessments, rather than at the level of *whether* competition law applies. Thus, a question may be *whether/how* competition law assessments *can/should* accommodate economic inequalities with regard to basic dental treatment.

Third, that the EU and national levels demonstrate two different approaches – a case-by-case approach (EU level) and a macro approach of wider-ranging competition reforms (national level). This also has implications for the overarching *how* and *whether* questions.

Finally, there are a range of wider considerations which can affect responses to the overarching *whether* and *how* questions, beyond more standard considerations about competition law. These include interaction between EU and national levels, the use of legislation rather than policy, and the relationship between government, the competition authority and sectoral regulator.

10

Foregrounding Distributive Justice in European Labour Antitrust

PASCAL McDOUGALL*

I. Introduction

This book addresses a longstanding debate about the relationship between efficiency – the maximisation of a group's aggregate economic well-being regardless of who in the group is well off – and distributive justice.[1] This 'efficiency-equity' conflict or 'trade-off' has taken on a particular significance for labour lawyers, whose discipline is built around the use of a redistributive policy tool, labour unions bargaining to increase wages, considered quintessentially inefficient by many economists. Unions have indeed long been described and modelled as labour monopolists or cartels wastefully depressing employment and output as they raise wages (this is the so-called 'monopoly union' model).[2]

This notion that collective bargaining is inefficient is one of the factors that has led to an intellectual and political clash between labour law and antitrust, a term that will refer here to both the contemporary legal regimes inspired by the American Sherman Act and the older criminal and civil rules against 'restraint of trade'.[3] That clash, once it became sufficiently acute and indeed violent as to

* For comments on earlier drafts of this chapter, I thank Jan Broulík, Kati Cseres, Christine Desan, Duncan Kennedy, Nastazja Potocka-Sionek, and Dina Waked, as well as the participants of a workshop organised by the European University Institute's EU Law and Human Rights working groups in November 2020.

[1] J Rawls, *A Theory of Justice* (Cambridge, MA, Harvard University Press, 1971) 60–61; A Okun, *Equality and Efficiency: The Big Tradeoff* (Washington, DC, Brookings Institution Press, 1975) 75–76; E Anderson, 'What is the Point of Equality?' (1999) 109 *Ethics* 287, 292–94; L Kaplow and S Shavell, *Fairness Versus Welfare* (Cambridge, MA, Harvard University Press, 2002) 28–32, 120–124; A Sen, *The Idea of Justice* (Cambridge, MA, Harvard University Press, 2008) 296. Some much older controversies in political philosophy could also be seen to revolve around a tension between maximisation and distribution. See, eg, TW Smith, 'Aristotle on the Conditions for and Limits of the Common Good' (1999) 93 *The American Political Science Review* 625, 632–33.

[2] See below section II.

[3] See G Auzero, D Baugard and E Dockès, *Droit du travail*, 31st edn (Paris, Dalloz, 2017) 1666; H Hovenkamp, 'Labor Conspiracies in American Law, 1880–1930' (1988) 66 *Texas Law Review* 919.

provoke concern among policymakers and statesmen,[4] has ultimately produced, at various points in the first half of the twentieth century depending on the country involved, a settlement whereby labour unions were given at least partial antitrust immunity. In legal doctrinal terms, that settlement was and is called the antitrust 'labour exemption'.[5] In Europe, the truce was reached within each country and much later reproduced in EU competition law.[6]

This chapter makes a proposal as to how European competition law should treat distributive concerns (and therefore inequality) in labour markets. The focus here is entirely on the labour exemption and the rules as to what kind of collective bargaining activity is authorised, although the approach developed here most definitely has implications for other domains of competition law to be explored in future work. This chapter criticises the way in which the labour exemption has been delineated and applied in European competition law.

In the EU, the labour exemption – which renders some labour union activity legal under competition law – has been couched in terms of 'solidarity' and 'social protection', concepts seen as antithetical to economic analysis and efficiency. This justification of the labour exemption is emphatically not framed in distributive terms. Rather, it is based on organicist ideas like that of a 'social dialogue' between corporate entities and is applied without regard to who wins or loses from any given form of collective bargaining.[7] Moreover, the labour exemption has been held to apply only to employees and not to independent contractors, ie workers who are not tightly or not at all 'controlled' by an employer (paradigmatic examples include individual agricultural and craft producers, as well as 'gig economy' workers).[8] The collective bargaining activities of independent contractors remain subject to antitrust scepticism and scrutiny in the name of efficiency.

[4] K Tenfelde, 'Conflict and Organization in the Early History of the German Trade Union Movement' in WJ Mommsen and H-G Husung (eds), *The Development of Trade Unionism in Great Britain and Germany, 1880–1914* (London, Routledge, 1985) 201, 203–04; AA White, 'Workers Disarmed: The Campaign Against Mass Picketing and the Dilemma of Liberal Labor Rights' (2014) 49 *Harvard Civil Rights – Civil Liberties Law Review* 59, 68–74.

[5] G Monti, 'Collective Labour Agreements and EU Competition Law: Five Reconfigurations' (2021) 17 *European Competition Journal* 1, 2; DJ Gifford, 'Redefining the Antitrust Labor Exemption' (1988) 72 *Minnesota Law Review* 1379.

[6] See Auzero, Baugard and Dockès (n 3) 1666; Tenfelde (n 4) 203–04. On the development of the European Union's labour exemption in the late 1990s, see below section III.

[7] See below section III.A.

[8] See below section III.B. On some of the social, economic, and cultural complexities relevant to debates about which legal rules should govern the work of independent contractors, see S Paul, 'The Enduring Ambiguities of Antitrust Liability for Worker Collective Action' (2016) 47 *Loyola University Chicago Law Journal* 101; V Dubal, 'The Drive to Precarity: A Political History of Work, Regulation, and Labor Advocacy in San Francisco's Taxi & Uber Economies' (2017) 38 *Berkeley Journal of Employment and Labor Law* 73; TJ Scrase, 'Precarious Production: Globalisation and Artisan Labour in the Third World' (2003) 24 *Third World Quarterly* 449; KJ Cseres, '"Acceptable" Cartels at the Crossroads of EU Competition Law and the Common Agricultural Policy: A Legal Inquiry into the Political, Economic, and Social Dimensions of (Strengthening Farmers') Bargaining Power' (2020) 65 *The Antitrust Bulletin* 401.

This bifurcation – non-economic solidarity for employees and economic efficiency for independent contractors – can be found in other jurisdictions[9] but is particularly strong in Europe. This European doctrinal configuration is described in section III, after section II's presentation of the conventional analysis of labour unions as inefficient.

This chapter proposes that we give distributive justice a central, perhaps even exclusive role in labour antitrust, including when dealing with independent contractors, but that we operationalise distributive justice using economic analysis. That is, this chapter resists both the efficiency-based rejection of collective bargaining for independent contractors and the solidarity-based rejection of economic analysis for employees. Instead, it proposes that we conceptualise and assess the effects of labour unionism in distributive terms, using analyses of the impact of collective bargaining on prices and quantities of factors and goods. In relying on this inquiry for institutional design, the main and perhaps even the only question we should be asking is whether any given policy tool or type of collective bargaining allows us to reach better distributive outcomes.

This chapter's argument for replacing both efficiency and organicist solidarity with distribution proceeds in three steps. The first step, presented in section IV.A, relies on old but curiously marginalised models of collective bargaining. These are models of 'price-quantity' collective bargaining, whereby labour unions bargain with firms over both wages (the price of labour) and employment (the quantity of labour hired). This enables wage increases that do not reduce employment or output, as a price-quantity bargaining union forces employers to accept bargains along a vertical 'contract curve' rather than the labour demand curve.[10] The contract curve is a locus of many equally efficient outcomes. Each point along the contract curve entails a different distribution of income but no employment or output reduction.

To the extent price-quantity collective bargaining can be expected to occur, efficiency becomes irrelevant, because all possible outcomes are efficient within the narrow meaning usually ascribed to that term. The only remaining question is how income should be distributed, making inequality the only concern of competition law. One implication of this line of analysis is that, if output and employment are indeed reduced by a union engaging in collective bargaining, it must be because the union has failed to bargain on both wages and employment. We should therefore see the conventional inefficient 'monopoly union' outcome as

[9] See the recent appraisal of US law on this point by EK Kim, 'Labor's Antitrust Problem: A Case for Worker Welfare' (2020) 130 *Yale Law Journal* 428, 451–60.

[10] In recent work, I propose that we make these models central to the economic analysis of labour law: P McDougall, 'The Institutionalist Law and Economics of Labor Union Renewal' 44 *Berkeley Journal of Employment and Labor Law* (forthcoming, 2022); P McDougall, 'European Cross-Sectoral Collective Bargaining as Post-Crisis Social Policy' 29 *Indiana Journal of Global Legal Studies* (forthcoming, 2022).

a failure of *policy*, insofar as existing laws and institutions fail to allow for redistribution that does not lower output and employment.

The second step of the argument, presented in section IV.B, has to do with how to conceptualise output and employment reductions that do occur if and when price-quantity collective bargaining fails to obtain and the union can only raise wages while leaving employers free to lower output. Contrary to what is suggested by the conventional monopoly analysis of unions presented in section II, we should conceptualise this policy failure not mainly as an inefficient output loss that fails to maximise the size of the pie, but rather as potentially *distributively* counterproductive. In the view proposed here, output and employment reductions are undesirable to the extent that they harm the intended beneficiaries of the income redistribution (eg workers in the unionised sector who lose their job), and not because of the lost output per se. This view is based on the postulate that aggregate output or GDP is much more directly determined by dynamic factors, like capital accumulation spurred by monetary policy and productive innovation spurred by industrial policy, than it is by static output-maximisation.[11] The claim that the static effects of labour unions are of relatively little importance for the overall level of output reinforces the case for focusing on the distributive effects of labour union activity.

The third step of the argument is presented in section V. Having repositioned any output and employment reductions that do occur as policy failures of a distributive instead of an efficiency kind, section V argues that competition law and policy should focus on finding ways to minimise or eliminate these distributive drawbacks. It summarily presents a few policy tools to that end, drawing on past work and existing scholarship. These tools are (A) work sharing within the union sector, (B) cross-sectoral collective bargaining, (C) job creation through macroeconomic stimulus operating alongside collective bargaining, and (D) fiscal spending as a redistributive instrument replacing collective bargaining. Though section V mentions a few examples of EU institutional developments relevant to each of these mechanisms, its goal is not to present an exhaustive policy analysis on any specific topic. Rather, its goal is to exemplify the general approach proposed here: maximising the distributive benefits and minimising the distributive costs of any given legal intervention so that a more normatively desirable outcome is reached. The conclusion ends by addressing the question of which institution should perform this inquiry, and specifically whether courts should do so or defer to other law-making institutions, an important question in an EU context marked by a thorough judicialisation of labour market regulation issues in recent decades.

[11] This marginalisation of static efficiency in favour of dynamic factors builds on various strands of influential economic thought familiar to competition lawyers. For example, the importance of 'productive' as opposed to 'static' efficiency has long been a theme of antitrust analysis that has led some to relativise the static harms of market concentration. See below section IV.B.

I want to stress that this chapter does not propose a theory of what distribution of income and other social goods is just. Rather, it proposes an analytical framework or approach one can use once one has decided that the prevailing distribution is at least somewhat unjust – and potentially curable by (poorer) workers or producers bargaining collectively for higher wages or incomes.[12] This deferral of normative inquiry is a very established move within economics,[13] and one that we may well find attractive from a left-wing perspective.[14] Indeed, despite its normative agnosticism, this approach highlights distributive interests that are obscured by efficiency analysis as well as by organicist notions of solidarity. This analytical foregrounding strikes me as quite congenial to tackling inequality, an issue this book usefully contributes to bringing back to the core of a discipline that has long marginalised it.

II. The Monopoly Analysis of Collective Bargaining

This section presents the briefest sketch of the conventional economic analysis of labour unions as inefficient monopolies. This analysis is a central, if not the main ground for cartels of working people to be suspect under competition law and in need of an 'exemption' to be shielded from illegality, as will be outlined at some length in section III.[15] This analysis is best understood using the graph in Figure 10.1:

[12] If one judges the prevailing distribution of income and other social goods to be perfectly just, then there is no need to do much according to the approach proposed here. Since many find the status quo distributively unjust, as the very existence of this book demonstrates, I feel justified in presenting an argument about *how* to go about addressing distributive injustice without touching on the question of *whether* the prevailing distribution is anywhere normatively acceptable.

[13] See, eg, L Robbins, *An Essay on the Nature and Significance of Economic Science*, 2nd edn (London, Macmillan, 1935) 150.

[14] The kind of leftism I espouse largely rests on the existentialist idea that prevailing notions of right and desert fail to satisfactorily determine who should have what in society, and therefore that the normative desirability of any given distribution is 'political' in the deep sense of not being determinable by correct legal or philosophical or social-scientific inquiry. In this view, egalitarianism better accounts for our inability to know what others or we ourselves 'deserve'. For elaboration see P McDougall, 'Capabilities, Utility, or Primary Goods? On Finding a Conceptual Framework for (International) Labour Law' in B Langille (ed), *The Capabilities Approach to Labour Law* (Oxford, Oxford University Press, 2019) 180.

[15] Competition law rationales based on 'rights' or 'fairness', ie deontological principles thought to have value independently of the normative desirability of the *consequences* of any given legal rule adopted in pursuit of them, are intentionally kept out of this chapter. This choice is based on the legal realist critique of the concepts of rights and fairness as too indeterminate to settle the question of how bargaining power should be distributed (see below n 96). This chapter's focus also reflects the centrality of efficiency in motivating scepticism of collective bargaining within competition law, as distinct from other legal fields like EU internal market law. For more on rights-based opposition to labour unionism in other fields of EU law, see McDougall, 'European Cross-Sectoral Collective Bargaining' (n 10).

Figure 10.1 Labour Market, Price-Only Bargaining

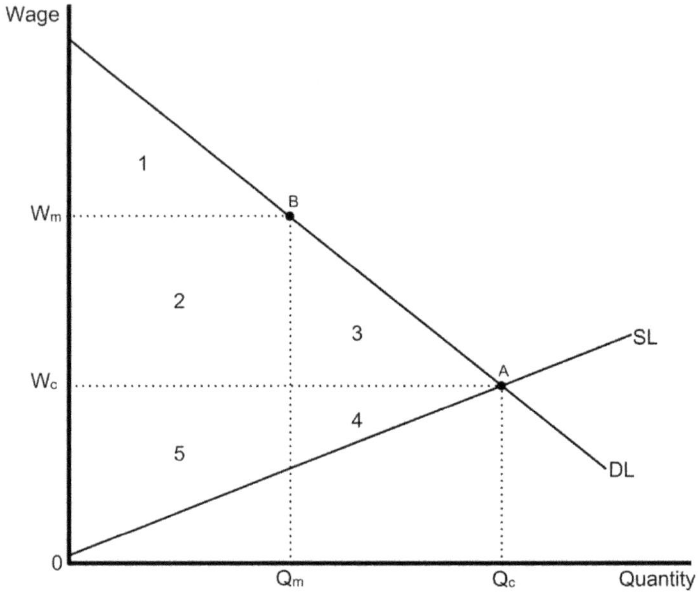

This graph represents a labour market, comprising several competing workers selling labour to several competing employers who make the same product. The usual analysis of unions as inefficient monopolies starts at point A, where the supply of labour (SL) intersects the demand for labour (DL). This competitive outcome leads to a Q_c level of employment at a wage of W_c. The labour union then comes in and bargains to raise the wage of all workers in the labour market, up to W_m. Employers react by moving to point B along their labour demand curve DL, decreasing the quantity of labour hired to Q_m. Workers appropriate a surplus of area 2 but cause a 'deadweight loss' of areas 3 and 4 as they reduce employment.[16] Area 1 remains with the employers. Deadweight loss like that of areas 3 and 4 represents a net waste of well-being or welfare, as mutually beneficial transactions between Q_c and Q_m are eliminated.[17] Point B is therefore inefficient.[18]

The 'surplus' under the labour demand curve and above the W_c wage line can come from consumers or suppliers of other factors of production, including those

[16] See A Rees, 'The Effects of Unions on Resource Allocation' (1963) 6 *Journal of Law and Economics* 69, 70; H Varian, *Intermediate Microeconomics: A Modern Approach*, 7th edn (New York, WW Norton and Company, 2006) 432; G Borjas, *Labor Economics*, 2nd edn (London, Irwin McGraw-Hill, 2000) 403.

[17] See NG Mankiw, *Principles of Microeconomics*, 5th edn (Boston, Cengage Learning, 2008) 326; R Posner, *Antitrust Law*, 2nd edn (Chicago, University of Chicago Press, 2001) 13.

[18] Point A is a Pareto optimum, a point at which nobody can be made better off without someone else being made worse off. A move away from a Pareto optimum like that to point B is said to be inefficient because it eliminates mutually advantageous transactions. See JL Coleman, 'Efficiency, Utility, and Wealth Maximization' (1980) 8 *Hofstra Law Review* 509, 513–14.

we might identify as 'employers' (eg managers) or 'owners' (eg financial capital providers). The precise proportion in which each group ends up being the source of union wage gains depends on how inelastic (how steep) product demand and factor supply curves are in the markets related to Figure 10.1's labour market.[19] The employment quantity reduction in Figure 10.1, from Q_c down to Q_m, amounts to a contraction of output, which in turn affects consumers (who see prices rise when output falls) and other factors of production (the demand for which is reduced when output falls).

The normative desirability of any given wage gain will no doubt sometimes depend on exactly who is disfavoured by it, and I have made detailed proposals elsewhere to shift more of the burden of any wage gain onto more privileged actors like capital and managers instead of consumers.[20] That said, for the purposes of the rudimentary efficiency analysis sketched here, these ramifications of the labour market analysis of Figure 10.1 are of secondary importance; what matters is that areas 3 and 4 represent net loss caused by the transfer of area 2.

Figure 10.1 also suffices to shed light on one of the *distributive* aspects that will be emphasised in sections IV and V below: when collective bargaining takes the 'monopoly' form of Figure 10.1, it is likely to harm some of its intended beneficiaries (the workers between Q_c and Q_m) by depriving them of their job. What is more, any such job losses will lower the wages of workers outside the unionised sector. This is because the unemployed workers will move to other sectors and depress wages there as they cause an increase – a rightward shift – of the labour supply curve against an unchanged downward-sloping labour demand curve, leading to higher employment and a lower wage.[21]

This basic supply and demand analysis has been criticised by generations of progressive scholars, who can be categorised according to whether they use the concept of 'market failures' or whether they argue that even perfect markets are shaped by legal rules and institutions, of which labour unions are just one example among many.[22] One market failure often relied on is employer market power or

[19] There is much work to do to relate these conventional analyses of distributive outcomes based on supply and demand elasticities to the scholarship, cited below n 22 and 95–96, showing that legal institutions are important determinants of the distribution of income. My own approach, elaborated in detail elsewhere, is to make supply and demand elasticities a function of the *coverage* of the bargaining-power-creating legal rules described below n 96 and to make the ultimate distribution of the surplus – that which is made available when supply and demand are rendered inelastic – a function of the precise *configuration* of these rules. See McDougall, 'The Institutionalist Law and Economics of Labor Union Renewal' (n 10).

[20] See, eg, McDougall, 'European Cross-Sectoral Collective Bargaining' (n 10).

[21] See Borjas (n 16) 403; L Kahn, 'The Effect of Unions on the Earnings of Nonunion Workers' (1978) 31 *Industrial and Labor Relations Review* 205, 216; D Neumark and M Wachter, 'Union Effects on Nonunion Wages: Evidence from Panel Data on Industries and Cities' (1995) 49 *Industrial and Labor Relations Review* 20, 35.

[22] For examples of the latter strategy, see K Klare, 'Workplace Democracy and Market Reconstruction: An Agenda for Legal Reform' (1988) 38 *Catholic University Law Review* 1, 17; S Paul, 'Antitrust as Allocator of Coordination Rights' (2020) 67 *UCLA Law Review* 378. For market failure-oriented analyses see below nn 23–25.

monopsony, which leads to sub-competitive wages that lower employment quantity along the labour supply curve, away from equilibrium.[23] Monopsony models show that, contrary to the Figure 10.1 analysis, a labour union obtaining higher wages will increase output and employment, up along the labour supply curve.[24]

My own approach is to accept that a supply and demand graph like Figure 10.1 can bear some resemblance to the 'real world' *if* we incorporate factors like market failures and legal institutions within it. In particular, while market failures like employer monopsony can allow for wage gains with no employment reduction, a graph like Figure 10.1 can be taken to represent what happens once a labour union has fully 'countervailed' monopsony power, ie has raised wages along the labour supply curve all the way up to the supply and demand equilibrium that would obtain in the absence of employer market power.[25] It is therefore more likely that a union obtaining *large* wage increases would lead to the outcome of Figure 10.1, because these increases might go beyond that which expands employment by countering monopsony power.

The last point to be made about Figure 10.1 as part of this thumbnail sketch is that it is best understood as the result of sectoral (as opposed to single-firm) bargaining, in a closed (as opposed to open) economy setting. Indeed, a union facing a single employer among many would have little if any room for wage increases; the single employer would face a very elastic product demand seeing as the other – by hypothesis non-union – employers would not be subject to the wage increases and would outcompete the union employer.[26] Sectoral bargaining, which for the purposes of basic economic analysis simply means enabling a union to cover all the firms producing the same good using the same kind of labour, can take many forms. This includes the iconic European regimes of administrative extension to an entire sector of collective agreements signed by only some employers,[27] as well as the American twentieth-century practice of 'pattern

[23] B Kaufman, 'Labor Law and Employment Regulation: Neoclassical and Institutional Perspectives' in KG Dau-Schmidt, SD Harris and O Lobel (eds), *Labor and Employment Law and Economics* (Cheltenham, Elgar, 2009) 3, 29–35; JE Stiglitz, 'Equilibrium Wage Distribution' (1985) 95 *Economic Journal* 595, 605.

[24] ibid. Another market failure often said to render union wage gains employment-neutral is the 'voice face' effect, whereby unions increase productivity by improving information sharing in the firm and insuring workers against expropriation of their investments in firm-specific skills. See generally R Freeman and J Medoff, *What Do Unions Do?* (New York, Basic Books, 1984). Rather than a move along the labour supply curve, this efficient effect of unions is best represented as an expansion of labour demand (a rightward movement of the entire DL schedule in Figure 10.1).

[25] See D Mitchell and C Erickson, 'De-Unionization and Macro Performance: What Freeman and Medoff Didn't Do' in JT Bennett and B Kaufman (eds), *What Do Unions Do?: A Twenty-Year Perspective* (London, Routledge, 2007) 369, 385. Similarly, Figure 10.1 can be seen to apply once all 'voice face' productivity effects (see ibid) have accrued and DL is at its furthest possible location to the right.

[26] RG Ehrenberg and RS Smith, *Modern Labor Economics: Theory and Public Policy*, 11th edn (London, Prentice Hall, 2012) 98.

[27] See, eg, J Kirchner, PR Kremp and M Magotsch (eds), *Key Aspects of German Employment and Labour Law*, 2nd edn (Berlin, Springer, 2010) 194.

bargaining', whereby negotiation is coordinated by different firm-level unions.[28] Of course, if a sector is not competitive but monopolistic, a single firm-level union will be 'sectoral' for our purposes here.

Similarly, if the good produced by the unionised firm(s) is tradable, ie sold in competition with firms abroad not subject to national labour laws and unions, the analysis of Figure 10.1 is not likely to be relevant, as the firms in the 'sector' are not all covered. The labour unions will render the unionised firms less competitive (assuming the wage gains need to come from higher product prices), which will provoke job losses taken up by firms abroad rather than inefficient output and employment reductions. This kind of open-economy unionism lies beyond the scope of this chapter.[29] In any given country or region, there are sectors that are subject to foreign competition ('tradable' sectors) and sectors that are not, for instance because the goods or services must be produced where they are consumed ('non-tradable' sectors). The analysis of this chapter can therefore be taken to apply to non-tradable sectors, including the service sector, where we find many low-wage workers who should arguably be at the centre of any concern about inequality.

III. The Current Approach to the EU Labour Exemption

The efficiency analysis presented in section II underlies competition law's longstanding hostility to labour unionism[30] and prompted the creation of a labour exemption as part of a political and legal truce. This section describes the way in which the labour exemption is structured in the European Union. It looks at the two groups subject to EU labour antitrust: employees (who benefit from the labour exemption) and independent contractors, called 'self-employed persons' in EU law (who do not). This chapter criticises the approach taken by EU institutions as to both these groups; neither is subject to the kind of distributive economic analysis called for here, ie an analysis of the likely effects on various individuals of any given collective bargaining scheme.

This chapter is not concerned with the outcome of any court case per se but with the *approach* taken and the analysis conducted. For reasons given in sections IV and V, I favour a broad use of collective bargaining as a redistributive

[28] RC Marshall and A Merlo, 'Pattern Bargaining' (2004) 45 *International Economic Review* 239, 239.

[29] See P McDougall, 'Global Value Chains, Labor Rights, and the Nature of Transnational Law' (forthcoming, 2022) *American Journal of Comparative Law*; P McDougall, 'The Place of Labor Rights in the European Union's Environmental Policies' (2021) 22 *German Law Journal* 1.

[30] Recall that the terms 'antitrust' and 'competition law' are used here in a broad sense that includes modern criminal and civil prohibitions on 'restraints of trade'. The hostility mentioned in the text accompanying this note has a long history that is not emphasised in this section's description of contemporary European case law. That said, the rules applicable to independent contractors, ie to those who lie outside the scope of the labour exemption, can be seen to be a remnant of this hostility.

tool, albeit one that we should be careful to configure in the most distributively desirable way. Exactly what kinds of collective bargaining are desirable in any given situation will depend on the institutional and socio-economic context.

Finally, as the conclusion of this chapter emphasises, it is an altogether distinct and important question *which* institution (eg judicial or legislative ones) should make decisions as to who benefits from the labour exemption using the analytical approach proposed here. In short, the criticism offered below, and the following presentation of the EU labour exemption, focus on the analysis conducted and the justification offered, not on specific decisions made by any given actor.

A. 'Solidarity' for Employees

Article 101 of the Treaty on the Functioning of the European Union, the most directly relevant competition law rule, prohibits 'agreements between undertakings' and 'concerted practices' that 'have as their object or effect the prevention, restriction or distortion of competition within the internal market'.[31] The Court of Justice of the European Union (CJEU) concluded in the *Becu* case[32] that employees' concerted practices and agreements are generally exempted from competition law because employees, unlike independent contractors, are not 'undertakings', the kind of actor targeted by EU competition law.[33] The Court added that employees do not become 'undertakings' for the purposes of competition law just because they are 'linked … by a relationship of association' with one another.[34]

After rendering *Becu*, the CJEU had to rule on the legality of *sectoral* collective agreements under competition law in a series of cases starting with *Albany International BV*.[35] The exclusion of employees from the definition of the term 'undertaking' did not settle the issue of the conformity of sectoral collective bargaining regimes with EU competition law in part because the *Albany* case involved a challenge to sectoral collective agreements that made affiliation to a pension fund mandatory for the entire sector, excluding outside pension providers.[36] There was at least arguably a restriction of competition beyond the mere agreement between employees on the terms of their competition with one another.

That said, the deeper reason why the definition of the term 'undertaking' was not dispositive of the legality of sectoral collective bargaining is arguably the one

[31] Treaty on the Functioning of the European Union, [2012] OJ C326, Art 101 (hereinafter TFEU).

[32] Case C-22/98 *Jean Claude Becu* ECLI:EU:C:1999:419, [1999] ECR I-5665.

[33] C Townley, 'The Concept of "Undertaking": The Boundaries of the Corporation – A Discussion of Agency, Employees and Subsidiaries' in G Amato and C-D Ehlermann (eds), *EC Competition Law: A Critical Assessment* (Oxford, Hart Publishing, 2007) 3, 4–6.

[34] *Becu* (n 32) para 28.

[35] Case C-67/96 *Albany International BV v Stichting Bedrijfsfonds Textielindustrie* ECLI:EU:C:1999:430, [1999] ECR I-5751. The collective agreements at issue in *Becu* may well have been sectoral, or even national, but this played no role in the Court's reasons. See *Becu* (n 32) para 5.

[36] *Albany* (n 35) para 48.

pointed out by Advocate General Jacobs in his *Albany* opinion.[37] AG Jacobs noted that 'every collective agreement between management and labour contains an implied agreement between undertakings on the employers' side',[38] ie an agreement 'to negotiate jointly and to be bound by the result of the bargaining'.[39] This is perfectly in line with the conventional analysis – rehearsed above in Figure 10.1 – of the 'monopoly' effect of unions that capture an entire sector and achieve wage gains by constraining employers to restrict output. In this conventional analysis, achieving wage gains in a competitive industry indeed requires that unions restrict competition between employers on labour costs and obtain parallel output reductions from all employers in the sector.

AG Jacobs went on to propose that the competition law exemption for labour unions be limited to collective agreements that deal with 'core subjects of collective bargaining such as wages and working conditions and which d[o] not directly affect third parties or markets', where third parties include 'clients, suppliers, competing employers, or consumers'.[40] AG Jacobs also thought the labour exemption should be denied to agreements which 'apparently deal with core subjects of collective bargaining such as working time but which merely function as cover for a serious restriction of competition between employers on their product markets'.[41]

As we are about to see, AG Jacobs' proposals were not adopted by the CJEU in *Albany*. They are nevertheless worth citing to show there existed well-articulated efficiency-based arguments that would render many kinds of collective bargaining illegal but were kept at bay. AG Fennelly, in the subsequent *van der Woude* case[42] reassessing the legality of collective bargaining under EU competition law, adopted an approach similar to that of AG Jacobs. After noting that in *Albany* the CJEU had declined to adopt AG Jacobs' 'third party' limitation to the labour exemption, AG Fennelly nevertheless proposed a proportionality test whereby '[t]hose allegedly harmed by … anti-competitive restrictions … may always challenge them on the basis that the agreement does not pursue a genuine social objective because the restrictions resulting from it, or from its application, go beyond what is required by the pursuit of its objective'.[43]

In both *Albany* and *van der Woude*, the CJEU rejected the Advocates General's proposed restrictions and opted for more categorical antitrust exemptions for labour union activity and collective agreements. In *Albany*, the Court adopted a

[37] Case C-67/96 *Albany International BV v Stichting Bedrijfsfonds Textielindustrie* ECLI:EU:C:1999:28, [1999] ECR I-5774, Opinion of AG Jacobs.

[38] ibid para 244.

[39] ibid para 73.

[40] ibid para 193.

[41] ibid para 192.

[42] Case C-222/98 *Hendrik van der Woude v Stichting Breatrixoord* ECLI:EU:C:2000:475, [2000] ECR I-7111, para 13.

[43] Case C-222/98 *Hendrik van der Woude v Stichting Breatrixoord* ECLI:EU:C:2000:226, [2000] ECR I-7113, Opinion of AG Fennelly, para 32.

'nature and purpose' test whereby a collective agreement is exempted from antitrust if its nature and purpose 'justify' it.[44] The Court held that the sectoral collective agreements before it should be exempted from EU competition law because their nature was that of being the outcome of negotiations between organisations of employees and employers and their purpose was that of 'improving one of [the employees'] working conditions, namely their remuneration'.[45] This is of course true of any labour union wage gain.

In stating that the nature part of the exemption criterion was satisfied, the *Albany* Court emphasised that the sectoral collective agreements at issue were of the same nature as agreements concluded under EU social dialogue, a corporatist legislative procedure involving pan-European employer and worker associations.[46] It also emphasised that the EU treaties create 'not only a "system ensuring that competition in the internal market is not distorted" but also "a policy in the social sphere"'.[47] It described that social policy as aiming for 'improved living and working conditions, proper social protection, dialogue between management and labour, the development of human resources with a view to lasting high employment and the combatting of exclusion'.[48]

The *van der Woude* Court essentially confirmed the *Albany* holding, in a context where the impact of the collective agreements on third parties – in that case health insurers that were not retained to provide the health insurance contracted for by the sectoral labour union – was emphasised even more than in *Albany*.[49] In both cases, therefore, the CJEU refrained from adopting a proportionality test or qualified exemption to parse out which union agreements and activities should be legal as proposed by the Advocates General, holding instead that agreements and activities that have the right nature and purpose 'fall outside the scope' of competition law completely.[50] In 2010, another Advocate General criticised the *Albany* reasoning as 'cursory' and proposed the adoption of AG Fennelly's *van der Woude* balancing test.[51] The CJEU again declined to adopt this test and confirmed that the *Albany* 'nature and purpose' doctrine still governs, going on to resolve the case based on internal market instead of competition law.[52]

Though the CJEU did not use the term 'solidarity' in establishing the labour exemption, and despite the fact that this term is used in EU competition law in a

[44] *Albany* (n 35) para 60.

[45] ibid para 63.

[46] ibid para 62. On social dialogue, see R Dukes and C Cannon, 'The Role of Social Partners' in A Bogg, C Costello and ACL Davies (eds), *Research Handbook on EU Labour Law* (Cheltenham, Edward Elgar, 2016) 89, 91.

[47] *Albany* (n 35) para 54.

[48] ibid para 57.

[49] See *van der Woude* (n 42) para 13. The holding was confirmed again in Case C-437/09 *AG2R Prévoyance v Beaudout Père et Fils SARL* ECLI:EU:C:2011:112, [2011] ECR I-973, paras 33–35.

[50] *Albany* (n 35) para 60; *van der Woude* (n 42) para 22.

[51] Case C-271/08 *European Commission v Federal Republic of Germany* ECLI:EU:C:2010:183, [2010] ECR I-07091, Opinion of AG Trstenjak, paras 60–61.

[52] Case C-271/08 *European Commission v Federal Republic of Germany* ECLI:EU:C:2010:426, [2010] ECR I-01885, paras 47–48.

more technical sense to designate certain kinds of social insurance mechanisms,[53] I think that term captures the CJEU's approach to the labour exemption well.[54] Solidarity refers to the fact that the collectivist or 'social' nature of labour unionism is held to trump the economic considerations that usually drive antitrust analysis. The CJEU refuses to consider in any way who among workers, consumers, and suppliers of other factors of production wins or loses, as proposed by the Advocates General in *Albany* and *van der Woude.* These distributive costs and benefits are the subject matter of both efficiency and distributive analysis. By refusing to consider them, the CJEU rejects both modes of analysis in favour of a categorical exemption based on collectivist slogans.[55]

Several commentators have also noted that the reasoning in *Albany* and the other labour exemption cases is unsatisfactory because it does not as much as acknowledge the potential economic effects of collective bargaining which the Advocates General stressed in each of the cases.[56] EU labour lawyers, for their part, have often applauded the Court's unwillingness to engage with the economics of collective bargaining.[57] The Court's casting out of economics in fact mirrors various rationales elaborated by labour lawyers to justify the labour exemption, including fundamental labour rights and freedoms,[58] 'social justice',[59]

[53] See *Albany* (n 35) para 75.

[54] See the following analyses using the term solidarity to describe the Court's approach: F Cengiz, 'The Conflict Between Market Competition and Worker Solidarity: Moving From Consumer to a Citizen Welfare Standard in Competition Law' (2021) 41 *Legal Studies* 73, 81; A Gerbrandy, 'Solving a Sustainability-Deficit in European Competition Law' (2017) 40 *World Competition* 539, 557.

[55] As is well known, the CJEU took an entirely different approach in internal market law, where the effect of labour laws and unions on free trade is assessed as part of a proportionality analysis. See D Ashiagbor, 'Collective Labour Rights and the European Social Model' (2009) 3 *Journal of Law and Ethics of Human Rights* 222, 227–35.

[56] S Evju, 'Collective Agreements and Competition Law: The Albany Puzzle and van der Woude' (2000) 17 *International Journal of Comparative Labour Law and Industrial Relations* 165, 174; G Monti, *EC Competition Law* (Cambridge, Cambridge University Press, 2007) 98; C Townley, *Article 81 EC and Public Policy* (Oxford, Hart Publishing, 2009) 61–62; R van den Bergh and PD Camesasca, 'The Court of Justice Exempts Collective Labour Agreements from the Wrath of Antitrust' (2000) 25 *European Law Review* 492, 501–08.

[57] J Kenner, *EU Employment Law: From Rome to Amsterdam and Beyond* (Oxford, Hart Publishing, 2003) 19–21; B Bercusson, *European Labour Law*, 2nd edn (Cambridge, Cambridge University Press, 2009) 294.

[58] M Freedland and N Countouris, 'Some Reflections on the "Personal Scope" of Collective Labour Law' (2017) 46 *Industrial Law Journal* 52, 64; V De Stefano, 'The Rise of the "Just-in-Time Workforce": On-Demand Work, Crowdwork, and Labor Protection in the "Gig Economy"' (2016) 37 *Comparative Labor Law and Policy Journal* 471, 500; S Garben, 'Online Platform Work at European Level' (2019) 3 *Geneva Global Policy Brief* 1, 4; S Robin-Olivier, 'Les normes sociales internationales et européennes et le développement du droit par les juges en Europe' (2016) 3 *Droit Social* 219, 227.

[59] M Biasi, 'We Will All Laugh at Gilded Butterflies. The Shadow of Antitrust Law on the Collective Negotiation of Fair Fees for Self-Employed Workers' (2018) 9 *European Labour Law Journal* 354, 372; S Sciarra, 'How Social Will Social Europe Be in the 2020s?' (2020) 21 *German Law Journal* 85, 85; H Collins, 'Fat Cats, Production Networks, and the Right to Fair Pay' (2022) 85 *Modern Law Review* 1, 16–24.

non-domination,[60] fighting 'social dumping',[61] and redressing unequal bargaining power in labour markets.[62] Concepts like these may be useful insofar as they merely express the normative desirability of a more equal distribution of income and power. However, it seems more productive for egalitarian-minded scholars to fully engage with economics and the prediction of the likely effects of collective bargaining than to ignore them. The concepts just mentioned often function to pre-empt rather than foster this kind of analysis.

B. Efficiency for Independent Contractors

As we have seen, the EU labour exemption is conditioned on not involving 'undertakings' on the worker side;[63] it therefore does not extend to independent contractors or 'self-employed persons'. As soon as independent contractors do engage in anything that looks like collective bargaining as to the price they charge, this practice is likely to be held illegal because it 'distort[s] the formation of prices in the markets in question'.[64] This is unmistakably efficiency language. Redeeming efficiencies of a collective bargaining scheme by independent contractors may factor into its legality, for instance if the scheme provides 'a significant counterweight to the contractual power of large producers and make[s] way for more effective competition'[65] or if it concerns only a marginal part of the business and/or allows for 'economies of scale' in contracting.[66]

Collective bargaining on price is therefore prima facie prohibited and redeemable based on efficiency considerations where independent contractors are concerned. This treatment of agreements among independent contractors to fix

[60] A Bogg and C Estlund, 'Freedom of Association and the Right to Contest: Getting Back to Basics' in A Bogg and T Novitz (eds), *Voices at Work: Continuity and Change in the Common Law World* (Oxford, Oxford University Press, 2014) 141; B Rogers, 'Employment Rights in the Platform Economy: Getting Back to Basics' (2016) 10 *Harvard Law and Policy Review* 479, 500–03.

[61] I Lianos, N Countouris and V De Stefano, 'Re-Thinking the Competition Law/Labour Law Interaction: Promoting a Fairer Labour Market' (2019) 10 *European Labour Law Journal* 291, 318–20; J Prassl, *Humans as a Service, The Promise and Perils of Work in the Gig Economy* (Oxford, Oxford University Press, 2018) 10; G Davidov, 'Non-Waivability in Labour Law' (2020) 40 *Oxford Journal of Legal Studies* 482, 495, 503.

[62] D Schiek and A Gideon, 'Outsmarting the Gig-Economy Through Collective Bargaining – EU Competition Law as a Barrier to Smart Cities?' (2018) 32 *International Review Law, Computers and Technology* 275, 283; R Dukes and W Streeck, 'Labour Constitutions and Occupational Communities: Social Norms and Legal Norms at Work' (2020) 47 *Journal of Law and Society* 612, 630–33; M Weiss, 'Re-Inventing Labour Law?' in B Langille and G Davidov (eds), *The Idea of Labor Law* (Cambridge, Cambridge University Press, 2011) 43, 48–49.

[63] See above n 32–33 and accompanying text.

[64] Case T-217/03 *FNCBV v Commission* ECLI:EU:T:2006:391, [2006] ECR II-4987, para 85. See similarly Case 45/85 *Verband der Sachversicherer e.V. v Commission* ECLI:EU:C:1987:34, [1987] ECR 405, para 42.

[65] Case C-250/92 *Gottrup-Klim v Dansk Landbrugs Growareselskab AmbA* ECLI:EU:C:1994:413, [1994] ECR I-5671, para 32.

[66] Case C-184/98 *Pavlov E.A.* ECLI:EU:C:2000:428, [2000] ECR I-6451, paras 93–95.

prices is an instance of the phenomenon, documented by several competition lawyers, whereby the EU authorities rely on notions of efficiency enacted through conclusory legal language rather than elaborate economic analysis.[67]

But who exactly is an 'independent contractor' rather than an employee? The answer: someone who controls their own work to a sufficient extent that they can be thought to be their own boss, according to strikingly similar legal doctrines in many different jurisdictions.[68] The CJEU's most recent pronouncement on this issue in the context of 'gig economy' work suggests trouble for the project of redistributing income through collective bargaining. In the *Yodel Delivery* case, the CJEU strongly suggested that a delivery worker like so many in the contemporary economy should not be considered an employee because he had considerable leeway to choose his schedules and which tasks to accept.[69]

Denying the antitrust exemption to certain workers on the ground that they are independent contractors (and defining independent contractor broadly as in *Yodel Delivery*) has dramatic consequences even for workers who are *not* considered independent contractors.[70] Indeed, the CJEU has held in *FNV Kunsten* that even those workers who are employees cannot bargain to apply their own rates of pay to independent contractors who will undercut them and do their jobs, unless the independent contractors are 'falsely' independent and are in reality employees.[71]

The draft guidelines published by the European Commission in December 2021 to authorise collective bargaining by certain 'solo self-employed persons'[72] seem likely to nuance but not overhaul the prevailing approach. The guidelines deal with those independent contractors who cannot be classified as falsely self-employed, ie as employees.[73] The main independent contractors who can benefit from this

[67] Monti (n 56) 48–49; K Stylianou and M Iacovides, 'The Goals of EU Competition Law: A Comprehensive Empirical Investigation' (report commissioned by the Swedish Competition Authority, 2021) www.konkurrensverket.se/globalassets/dokument/kunskap-och-forskning/forskningsprojekt/19-0407_the-goals-of-eu-competition-law.pdf. Evidence that the legality of collective bargaining under EU law is assessed in light of its bearing on efficiency can be found in the fact that in each of the labour exemption cases, the Advocates General dealt extensively with efficiency. For yet more suggestive evidence that efficiency often intervenes in EU labour antitrust, see O Odudu, 'The Distributional Consequences of Antitrust' in P Marsden (ed), *Handbook of Research in Trans-Atlantic Antitrust* (Cheltenham, Edward Elgar, 2006) 605, 607–08.

[68] See generally G Davidov and B Langille (eds), *Boundaries and Frontiers of Labour Law: Goals and Means in the Regulation of Work* (Oxford, Hart Publishing, 2006).

[69] Case C-692/19 *B. v Yodel Delivery Network Ltd.* ECLI:EU:C:2020:288, paras 35–43. On various possible interpretations of the EU concept of false self-employment, see T Gyulavari, 'Collective Rights of Platform Workers: The Role of EU Law' (2020) 27 *Maastricht Journal of European and Comparative Law* 406, 419–22.

[70] The reader may have noticed that I use the term 'worker' to encompass both employees and independent contractors. EU competition law, by contrast, equates 'worker' with 'employee', thereby depriving us of a term to encompass both kinds of actors.

[71] Case C-413/13 *FNV Kunsten Informatie en Media v. Staat der Nederlanden* ECLI:EU:C:2014:2411, paras 27–31.

[72] European Commission, 'Guidelines on the Application of EU Competition Law to Collective Agreements Regarding the Working Conditions of Solo Self-Employed Persons' COM (2021) 8838 final, 9 December 2021.

[73] ibid 3.

newly expanded labour exemption are those who are 'in a situation comparable to that of' employees.[74]

The Commission enumerates three such groups of independent contractors: (1) those who are 'economically dependent' on a counterparty to whom they 'provide their services exclusively or predominantly' while forming an 'integral part' of the counterparty's business; (2) those who perform the same or similar tasks 'side by side' with employees under a sufficient degree of control by their contractual counterparty; and (3) those whose tasks are 'organised' by a 'digital labour platform'.[75] The draft guidelines also propose to extend the labour exemption to a fourth category of 'solo self-employed persons' who are *not* in a situation comparable to that of employees in one of the three senses just mentioned but who are in a 'weak bargaining position' vis-à-vis the buyer of their services, as evidenced by the size of that buyer's business.[76]

The Commission's proposal can be interpreted as expanding the scope of the doctrine of false self-employment, using criteria that are mostly not very different from the notion of 'control' used in legal definitions of employment.[77] This interpretation is very much in line with the Commission's initial June 2020 statement of intent in elaborating these guidelines. The Commission had remarked that the distinction between employees and self-employed workers has 'become blurred' and that 'many individuals have no other choice than to accept a contract as self-employed'.[78] Its mention of the need to 'clarify' and 'define the scope of the self-employed who need to participate in collective bargaining' evoked the maintenance of a distinction that will make collective bargaining illegal for some independent contractors,[79] which is what we see in the December 2021 draft guidelines.[80]

The Commission's most recent intervention therefore essentially maintains the bifurcation of EU labour antitrust: a broad prohibition of collective bargaining

[74] ibid 8.

[75] ibid 7–11.

[76] ibid 13.

[77] The fourth category mentioned in the draft guidelines, that of self-employed persons who are not in a situation comparable to that of employees but are nevertheless in a weak bargaining position due to their contractual partner's size, is the only category that does not rely on a criterion akin to control of the work by the buyer of the services. Recall from note 65 and accompanying text above that countervailing employer market power is one efficiency that can put in question the presumptive illegality of collective bargaining by independent contractors.

[78] European Commission, 'The European Commission Launches a Process to Address the Issue of Collective Bargaining for the Self-Employed' (30 June 2020) ec.europa.eu/commission/presscorner/detail/en/ip_20_1237.

[79] ibid.

[80] The December 2021 guidelines also reproduce an ambiguity that had been submitted to but not resolved by the CJEU: the Commission states that it does not intend to exempt collective agreements that fix the price paid by consumers as distinct from the wage of the workers involved. European Commission (n 72) 5. As AG Jacobs' *Albany* opinion had suggested, many wage-raising collective agreements are likely to raise consumer prices, making this distinction quite hollow. See above n 38–39 and accompanying text.

for independent contractors in the name of efficiency and a blanket authorisation of collective bargaining for employees in the name of solidarity understood in non-economic terms. The reasoning that led to this outcome is problematic as an intellectual or analytical matter, as argued below. But the outcome is also problematic from a practical and normative point of view. Indeed, many workers who are arguably worthy of redistribution simply cannot be considered (even 'disguised') employees. This is true of many small agricultural and craft producers in the lower-income countries of the European East and South.[81] The prevailing approach makes it hard to use collective bargaining to redistribute income towards those workers. Maintaining a distinction between independent contractors and employees, and prohibiting collective bargaining for the former, is therefore likely to have normatively undesirable effects, in addition to being analytically problematic for the reasons given in the remaining sections of this chapter.

IV. Rethinking the Legal Economics of Collective Bargaining and Growth

This section proposes some basic analytical tools to rethink the efficiency/solidarity bifurcation described in section III. Section IV.A has to do with the economics of collective bargaining proper and summarises work showing that, under certain ideal conditions, collective bargaining need not decrease employment and output, making efficiency irrelevant in determining its proper scope when the ideal conditions obtain. Section IV.B has to do with the economics of growth and the determination of a country or region's aggregate income. It argues that any output reductions that *are* caused by labour unions operating under non-ideal conditions are likely to be insignificant given that other sources of economic growth are probably much more important than static efficiency in determining a country's GDP. This supports the argument that output reductions, if they happen and the output-neutral kind of collective bargaining described in section IV.A fails to materialise, should not be of concern *as output reductions*. Rather, they raise a distributive issue: the job losses and non-union wage reductions they might bring about harm some of the workers, the very people who are by hypothesis worthy of distributive concern.

A. Displacing Monopoly Unionism as the Default Model

There has long been a strand of labour economics that acknowledges the possibility of simultaneous price and quantity bargaining along a 'contract curve'

[81] On the legality of collective bargaining by agricultural producers in the EU, see Cseres (n 8) 405–06.

(not the demand curve), allowing the parties to choose among many equally efficient outcomes that distribute the surplus between them without negatively affecting production.[82] This kind of contracting has been called the 'price-quantity type of monopolistic trading' by Wassily Leontief,[83] 'efficient bargaining' by Ian McDonald and Robert Solow,[84] and 'all or none' bargaining by Milton Friedman.[85]

The important feature of this kind of bargaining, as the terms 'price-quantity' indicate, is that the union bargains on both wages and labour quantity (employment) at once. This is by contrast to the traditional 'monopoly' union of Figure 10.1, which raises wages and leaves employers free to lower employment to Q_m in response. Price-quantity bargaining, whereby the union raises wages but insists that employers maintain a higher employment level than in Figure 10.1, can lead to many different labour market outcomes, the simplest of which is captured by Figure 10.2:

Figure 10.2 Labour Market, Price-Quantity Bargaining

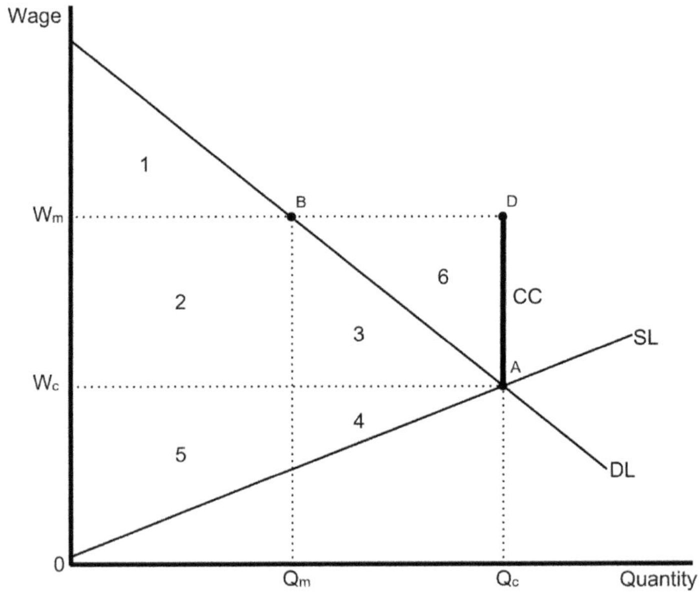

[82] W Leontief, 'The Pure Theory of the Guaranteed Annual Wage Contract' (1946) 54 *Journal of Political Economy* 76, 78; I McDonald and R Solow, 'Wage Bargaining and Employment' (1981) 71 *American Economic Review* 896, 900.

[83] Leontief (82) 79.

[84] McDonald and Solow (n 82) 904.

[85] M Friedman, *Price Theory: A Provisional Text* (New Brunswick, NJ, Transaction Publishers, 1962) 15.

Figure 10.2 is similar to Figure 10.1, with the same non-union outcome A and monopoly union outcome B.[86] The added element is the vertical bold line CC, the contract curve. At all points along that curve, the union can obtain higher wages with no employment reduction. At the outermost point D, the union will have secured a wage bill of W_m times Q_c, which is equal to the sum of the maximum wage employers would be willing to pay for each of the labour units bought by employers absent unions. The visual proof of this is that triangle 6 is identical to triangle 1, so that the surface 2-3-6, acquired by the union bargaining to point D, is identical to the surface 1-2-3. The distribution of the surplus at point D is the same as if the union could engage in 'perfect price discrimination',[87] ie as if the union could charge a different wage for every labour unit all along the labour demand curve so as to pluck away the surface 1-2-3 from employers.

As we move to points below D on the curve CC, the union cedes to employers part of areas 2-3-6, all the way down to point A where the union has lost all the surplus under the labour demand curve (but above the competitive W_c wage line). Point D thus represents the maximum surplus the union can appropriate, assuming it has total bargaining power. Other intermediary outcomes between A and D are possible.

Like Figure 10.1, Figure 10.2 represents an entire labour market (and therefore an industry or sector) composed of many employers on the buying side and distributed along the industry labour demand curve. The outcome of Figure 10.2 can be achieved only through sectoral bargaining, just as was true of the simple 'monopoly' outcome of Figure 10.1. Indeed, if a union covering a single employer among many tried to reach the Figure 10.2 outcome, it would be outcompeted on product and factor markets by the other firms in the industry.[88] For point D to be sustainable as a single industry price and quantity, it must be the case that each buyer is at a point like D on its *individual* labour demand curve (on a graph that would be identical to Figure 10.2 except for the fact that the demand curve is that of a single firm).[89] The sum of all the firms' price-quantity packages needs to be Figure 10.2's point D.

As long as each firm is at a point like D in relation to its own labour demand curve, there is no need to have further price (ie wage) discrimination *in the labour market*. In particular, the union does not need to engage in 'perfect' wage discrimination (charge a different wage for each labour unit sold in the industry). As just noted, at point D, the total wage bill extracted from all the firms is the same *as if* the union could engage in perfect wage discrimination. But if a single firm buys

[86] 'Monopoly union' refers here to inefficient, price-only collective bargaining, as distinct from efficient, price-quantity collective bargaining.

[87] H Varian, 'Price Discrimination' in R Schmalensee and R Willig (eds), *Handbook of Industrial Organization* (Amsterdam, North Holland, 1989) 587, 601.

[88] See Ehrenberg and Smith (n 26) 69.

[89] ibid.

many units of labour, as is always the case, each firm can be charged a single wage and forced to spread the cost of a bargain like point D over all the units of labour it buys. Labour costs at both the firm and industry level are thus at the highest level at which they can be without inducing some employers to forego production.

Of course, a firm will not go to point D in relation to its individual labour demand curve on its own, ie if the union fixes only wages and lets the firm choose quantity.[90] The union needs to offer each firm a predetermined package of Q_c units at W_m per unit, hence the occasional description of this kind of bargaining as 'all or none'.[91] If the union succeeds in doing this for each firm, the industry outcome will be one like Figure 10.2's point D.

The firms' ability to hand over the surplus area under their labour demand curve will be contingent on their ability to secure that surplus from the actors to which it belongs. Whose surplus figures under the labour demand curve depends on the four 'laws of derived demand';[92] essentially, the determinative factor is the capacity of consumers and other factors of production (for instance capital and management) to access other products and industries not subject to the union-caused price increase or income decrease. This capacity in turn depends on institutional design: a union with broader (eg cross-sectoral) coverage can reduce consumers and capital/management's outside options, making more of their surplus potentially available.[93] That said, it is one thing for a class of actors' surplus to be potentially available and quite another for the firms to in fact be able to capture it. And it could well be that price discrimination is required for the firms to appropriate surplus to hand over to the union.

Taking the case of consumers, we can visualise this by considering that the firms in the unionised sector will have a graph like Figure 10.2 in the product market, on which they are the suppliers. In that market, output must be left intact while the price of the consumer good is raised in such a way as to appropriate an amount of surplus just like Figure 10.2's areas 2-3-6. It is very likely, however, that the consumers in a product market graph like Figure 10.2 each buy one – or not many more than one – unit of the good. If that is the case, the firms have to charge a different price for different units of the good, ie engage in price discrimination. They cannot rely on the method described above for the labour market, whereby each buyer (in the labour market this meant each firm or employer) is forced to spread the price increase over the many units it buys. Here, again taking Figure 10.2 to be a product market for just a moment, the potential consumers of the units between Q_m and Q_c will not buy those units at the price of W_m. The union

[90] By choosing point B instead of point D, the firm recuperates the equivalent of triangle 6 in surplus while also causing the loss of triangles 3 and 4. The gain of triangle 6 makes point B preferable to point D for the firm.

[91] Eg, Friedman (n 85) 15.

[92] See JR Hicks, *The Theory of Wages*, 2nd edn (New York, A.M. Kelley, 1966) 241–47; A Marshall, *Principles of Economics*, 8th edn (London, Macmillan, 1923) 518–38.

[93] McDougall, 'The Institutionalist Law and Economics of Labor Union Renewal' (n 10). See below section V.B.

therefore needs to force the firms to price discriminate among consumers. I leave for another time the question of whether price discrimination is always necessary on capital or management markets; suffice it to say here that it may well often be.[94]

Price-quantity collective bargaining thus turns out to require price discrimination by firms in product, and perhaps other-factor, markets.[95] If we assume perfect information, price discrimination will be perfect in all markets, and bargaining over the joint surplus can proceed with no reduction in output or employment. The outcome, ie where we end up between points A and D in the labour market of Figure 10.2, will depend on legal rules, in particular labour law rules on permissible pressure tactics,[96] as well as the other factors – such as sociological and psychological ones – that condition bargaining outcomes.

For Figure 10.2 not to be the default picture of how labour unions work, we would have to be in the presence of market failures and imperfect information so strong that no kind of price discrimination, even the less demanding second and third-degree kinds,[97] is possible on product and input markets. While information is never perfect, there is a bulky competition law literature on price discrimination,[98] including work that describes the far-reaching possibilities for differential pricing unlocked by digital technologies.[99] This work also happens to show that price-quantity collective bargaining is possible in many labour markets.[100]

[94] ibid.

[95] Price discrimination is therefore a more theoretically and practically important phenomenon than many antitrust analyses let on. Indeed, price discrimination, when contract, labour, and corporate laws are configured to make economic surplus available to the price-discriminating actor, allows for zero-sum distributive transfers under conditions of large numbers and economic heterogeneity. That is, price discrimination should be treated not as a curiosity or special case but rather as the way to enact a basic and fundamental social process: distributive struggle over the joint surplus of production. This chapter's emphasis on price discrimination dovetails with recent work centring Ricardian rent, the very kind of surplus transferred through price discrimination, in institutionalist legal economics. See D Kennedy, 'Law Distributes I: Ricardo Marx CLS' unpublished manuscript (2021); BH Fried, *The Progressive Assault on Laissez Faire: Robert Hale and the First Law and Economics Movement* (Cambridge, MA, Harvard University Press, 1998) 116–59; R Woodcock, 'The Antitrust Case for Consumer Primacy in Corporate Governance' (2020) 10 *UC Irvine Law Review* 1395, 1402–03.

[96] This is meant as an incorporation by reference of an entire scholarly tradition that describes the distribution of income as a function of the bargaining power conferred by any given configuration of the legal rules used by market actors. See R Hale, 'Coercion and Distribution in a Supposedly Non-Coercive State' (1923) 38 *Political Science Quarterly* 470, 478; J Commons, *The Distribution of Wealth* (first published 1983, New York, A.M. Kelley, 1965) 111.

[97] For introductory analyses of these kinds of price discrimination, see Varian (n 16) 448–59; W Nicholson and C Snyder, *Intermediate Microeconomics and Its Applications*, 11th edn (Mason, OH, South-Western Cengage Learning, 2010) 545–46.

[98] See, eg, LA Stole, 'Price Discrimination and Competition' in M Armstrong and RH Porter (eds), *Handbook of Industrial Organization* (London, Elsevier, 2007) 2223, 2226; JC Cooper, L Froeb, DP O'Brien and S Tschantz, 'Does Price Discrimination Intensify Competition? Implications For Antitrust' (2005) 72 *Antitrust Law Journal* 327.

[99] RA Woodcock, 'Big Data, Price Discrimination, and Antitrust' (2017) 68 *Hastings Law Journal* 1371, 1386–91; O Bar-Gill, 'Algorithmic Price Discrimination When Demand Is a Function of Both Preferences and (Mis)perceptions' (2019) 86 *University of Chicago Law Review* 217, 218–19.

[100] The foregoing is essentially a theoretical argument about what we should take to be the normal or paradigmatic way in which collective bargaining operates. It does raise the empirical question of

Imperfect information may also plague the labour market bargaining of Figure 10.2, as distinct from the firms' capturing of consumer and other-factor surplus. That is, even firms that can and do engage in price discrimination on product and capital/management markets may be able to prevent price-quantity bargaining by exploiting the union's inability to know what the shapes of the contract and labour demand curves are under constantly changing market conditions. I have written elsewhere about mechanisms labour unions can use to cure such defects, including the use of legal prohibitions on lay-offs not motivated by 'genuine' economic reasons to force firms to disclose the market conditions they face.[101] Incidentally, these lay-off restrictions have faced strict scrutiny by the CJEU under the EU internal market rules that protect the property rights of foreign investors.[102] Removing these judge-made obstacles to the use of lay-off restrictions to facilitate price-quantity collective bargaining may be a promising avenue to improve the performance of labour law regimes in the EU.

The important theoretical implication of the foregoing is that output or employment reductions like those of Figure 10.1 must be seen to be the product of market failures – like imperfect information – impeding price-quantity bargaining. For the state not to remedy such market failures is in turn a policy failure. Figure 10.1 should therefore be dethroned as the default or ideal representation of collective bargaining in favour of Figure 10.2 and its many efficient collective bargaining outcomes.

In order to fully achieve that theoretical transformation, we will need to bring the model of price-quantity collective bargaining developed by the likes of Leontief, Solow, and McDonald out of its marginal status even within labour economics[103] and into conversation with the core of welfare economics, not to mention institutionalist thought about the role of legal rules in shaping economic outcomes. This is in itself a pressing scholarly agenda, one I can only gesture towards here. But since price-quantity collective bargaining is relatively well researched theoretically if not widely known, providing only this primer here seems sufficient.

The takeaway of this section should be that, on the level of theory and under ideal conditions, we should not presume that labour unionism involves an efficiency/equity trade-off of the kind modelled in Figure 10.1. In the price-quantity bargaining scenario, which may not be so rare given the widespread availability of price discrimination to firms, the only normative question raised by collective bargaining is distributive: who deserves how much?

whether unions do in fact bargain over price and quantity. However, my suspicion is that, particularly in the Anglo-American world, actually existing unions have often been too weak to reach the kind of sectoral price-quantity bargaining outcomes modelled here, making empirical studies of what those unions do of limited interest.

[101] See McDougall, 'The Institutionalist Law and Economics of Labor Union Renewal' (n 10).

[102] See Case C-201/15 *AGET Iraklis* ECLI:EU:C:2016:972, paras 9–11.

[103] One reason for this marginalisation appears to be the mistaken notion that price-quantity collective bargaining can only happen if the labour market is imperfectly competitive on the employer side. For a refutation of this notion, see McDougall, 'The Institutionalist Law and Economics of Labor Union Renewal' (n 10).

B. Reconceptualising Monopoly Unionism as a Distributive Drawback

Let us now set aside the first-best kind of collective bargaining of Figure 10.2 and reintroduce the employment and output reductions of Figure 10.1. This section argues that these reductions should be conceptualised as concerns about distribution, not efficiency or maximisation. The problem with output-reducing unionism is not that it diminishes output or total welfare but that it may well harm some workers to benefit others, as described in section II. This conclusion is based on the postulate that the level of output in a society is a function of many other factors besides the presence or absence of monopolies that raise prices without controlling the quantity bought by their contractual partners. These other sources of output increases (ie of economic growth) can plausibly be thought to make the elimination of monopolisation a negligible source of output gains. Therefore, even in lower-income countries that could not be thought to have 'enough' output to meet everyone's needs in an environmentally sustainable way, it could be argued that output can and should be raised first and foremost by means other than the elimination of (otherwise distributively desirable) monopolies.

The first source of growth to mention is the increase in productivity enabled by organisational and industrial structures that make possible better production techniques. This is the phenomenon schematised in Oliver Williamson's famous article illustrating how mergers and industrial concentration, even if they lead to deadweight loss and consumer harm, might create more wealth than they destroy, by lowering costs of production.[104] These cost reductions have most often been described as stemming from 'economies of scale' in anything from transportation, operation, and marketing to coordinated management and R&D.[105]

The important point for our purposes here is that this kind of cost reduction is distinct from static efficiency and is in fact often in tension with it, in the sense that it can sometimes arguably only be reached if we allow industrial structures that are statically inefficient. 'Productive efficiency' is a name often given to this non-static kind of efficiency.[106] This established antitrust literature should be read alongside more recent work on industrial structures outside the Anglo-American world that are said to have led to productivity increases as well as technological progress, increasing output and competitiveness in tradable industries.[107]

[104] O Williamson, 'Economies as an Antitrust Defense: The Welfare Trade-Offs' (1968) 58 *American Economic Review* 18, 21.

[105] See A Fisher and RH Lande, 'Efficiency Considerations in Merger Enforcement' (1983) 71 *California Law Review* 1582, 1559–60; DA Crane, 'Rethinking Merger Efficiencies' (2011) 110 *Michigan Law Review* 347, 355.

[106] E Elhauge and D Geradin, *Global Competition Law and Economics*, 2d edn (Oxford, Hart Publishing, 2011) 1244.

[107] See, eg, A Amsden, *The Rise of the Rest: Challenges to the West from Late-Industrializing Economies* (Oxford, Oxford University Press, 2001) 273–77; D Waked, 'Antitrust Goals in Developing Countries: Policy Alternatives and Normative Choices' (2015) 38 *Seattle University Law Review* 945; P Hall and

The second source of growth to mention is monetary and fiscal stimulus by the state. Making these policies a source of output gains requires us to set aside the postulate of 'money neutrality', ie the idea that – in the 'long run' – the expansion of the money supply only causes inflation and does not increase output or employment.[108] In the neutrality view, investment is financed by saving out of current consumption and output, which is a real variable not affected by its monetary denomination.[109] Against this idea, many economists have proposed theories as to why expanding the money supply, eg enabling more bank lending by central bank policies like open-market operations and discount-window lending[110] or direct government lending, might spur investment and output growth that would otherwise not occur. These reasons are sometimes said to have to do with market failures like imperfect information on credit markets that lower the quantity of available capital[111] or infant industry-like phenomena that make output-enhancing investments impossible to finance through existing ('private') banking structures.[112]

Scholars in the Keynesian and post-Keynesian tradition have developed an even more thorough refutation of monetary neutrality, arguing that money supply expansions always affect long-run output in addition to prices, so that money is never neutral, even in the absence of market failures of the kind just mentioned.[113]

D Soskice, 'An Introduction to Varieties of Capitalism' in P Hall and D Soskice (eds), *Varieties of Capitalism: The Institutional Foundations of Comparative Advantage* (Oxford, Oxford University Press, 2004) 1, 22–27.

[108] See the intellectual history retraced by RE Lucas Jr, 'Nobel Lecture: Monetary Neutrality' (1996) 104 *Journal of Political Economy* 661, 668–72. The argument that monetary expansion is neutral in the long run supposes that the higher prices brought about by monetary expansion only increase output against fixed factor prices (wages), by lowering real production costs. As factor prices become changeable and go up, output gains are cancelled. See A Abel, B Bernanke and D Croushore, *Macroeconomics*, 7th edn (Boston, Addison-Wesley, 2011) 313–17. As for the effect of fiscal policy, it is thought to be that deficit spending stimulates demand for money against a money supply assumed to be unchanged, which bids up the 'price' of money, ie the interest rate. Interest rate increases caused by added economic activity eliminate ('crowd out') other pre-existing output, such that the composition but not the level of economic activity increases. See OJ Blanchard, 'Crowding Out' in SN Durlauf and LE Blume (eds), *The New Palgrave Dictionary of Economics* (New York, Palgrave Macmillan, 2008) 327, 329.

[109] D Romer, *Advanced Macroeconomics* (New York, McGraw-Hill, 2006) 20; NG Mankiw, *Macroeconomics*, 9th edn (New York, Worth Publishers, 2016) 417.

[110] For a standard textbook account of these policies see P Krugman and R Wells, *Economics*, 2nd edn (New York, Worth Publishers, 2009) 813–15.

[111] JE Stiglitz, 'The Role of the State in Financial Markets' (1993) 7 *World Bank Economic Review* 19, 30; B Bernanke and M Gertler, 'Inside the Black Box: The Credit Channel of Monetary Policy Transmission' (1995) 9 *Journal of Economic Perspectives* 27, 34.

[112] B Armendariz de Aghion, 'Development Banking' (1999) 58 *Journal of Development Economics* 83, 84; E Levy Yeyati, A Micco and U Panizza, 'Should the Government Be in the Banking Business? The Role of State-Owned and Development Banks' (2004) RES Working Paper 4379, Inter-American Development Bank Research Department, 1, 9.

[113] See, eg, P Davidson, 'Keynes's Finance Motive' (1965) 17 *Oxford Economic Papers* 47, 61; M Lavoie, 'The Endogenous Flow of Credit and the Post Keynesian Theory of Money' (1984) 18:3 *Journal of Economic Issues* 771, 779–80; B Moore, 'The Demise of the Keynesian Multiplier: A Reply to Cottrell'

The Keynesian and post-Keynesian argument should be taken to be that expansion of the money supply *can* lead to lastingly lower real interest rates, thereby durably lowering the cost of capital.[114] This spurs private investment and consumption. It also enables ('monetised') fiscal stimulus that creates new economic activity instead of merely displacing pre-existing output and demand.[115] Some historical work supports this view of growth as always at least enabled, if not driven, by expansions of the money supply through public channels.[116]

There are many other factors that go into explaining why and how countries or regions grow their national or regional incomes. This section merely points to two broad sets of policy tools, productivity-enhancing industrial organisation and investment-enhancing monetary policy, that could be and have been argued to be universally important ones. As it happens, EU institutions have been said to place undue restraints on the policy autonomy of lower-income Member States as to these two sets of policy levers.[117] A fuller policy analysis would do well to map these constraints on potential sources of output and employment gains in the EU. The more theoretical point of this section is that, to the extent labour unionism leads to output reductions, these reductions should not be big concerns, because there are always other more important possible sources of output increases. Rather, the concern with unionism of the Figure 10.1 variety, if any, should be that it has the potential to harm some of the intended beneficiaries of the income redistribution in the ways described in section II.

(1994) 17 *Journal of Post Keynesian Economics* 121, 127–28; R Hockett and S Omarova, 'Public Actors in Private Markets: Toward a Developmental Finance State' (2015) 93 *Washington University Law Review* 103, 154.

[114] I take these Keynesian and post-Keynesian scholars to be foregrounding what Bernanke and Gertler call the 'cost of capital' channel of monetary policy. See Bernanke and Gertler (n 111) 27.

[115] This passage frames the choice between fiscal deficits financed by borrowing – emitting bonds in exchange for specie or central bank reserves – and 'printing money' in the same way as A Lerner, 'Functional Finance and the Federal Debt' (1943) 10 *Social Research* 38, 48. But the analysis here is equally compatible with the view that governments in fact always 'monetise' their spending at the outset when they emit checks which the recipient's bank can give back to the central bank in exchange for central bank reserves. In this latter view, governments can decide to tax and/or emit bonds which the central bank can sell in open-market operations, but these actions come after the initial spending by checks cashed in exchange for central bank reserves. Budget deficits are therefore always 'accommodated' or monetised to start with. See LR Wray, *Modern Money Theory: A Primer on Macroeconomics for Sovereign Monetary Systems*, 2nd edn (London, Palgrave Macmillan, 2015) 90–101; S Bell, 'The Role of the State and the Hierarchy of Money' (2001) 25 *Cambridge Journal of Economics* 149, 149–50.

[116] See R Rajan and L Zingales, 'Financial Dependence and Growth' (1998) 88 *American Economic Review* 559, 562; C Desan, 'The Power of Paradigms in Histories of Economic Development' (*Just Money Blog*, 12 March 2020) justmoney.org/c-desan-the-power-of-paradigms-in-histories-of-economic-development/.

[117] On industrial and monetary policy, see respectively D Kukovec, 'Economic Law, Inequality, and Hidden Hierarchies on the EU Internal Market' (2016) 38 *Michigan Journal of International Law* 1; D Gabor and C Ban, 'Banking on Bonds: The New Links Between States and Markets' (2016) 54 *Journal of Common Market Studies* 617.

V. Mechanisms to Limit Distributive Backfiring in a 'Second-Best' World

Section IV has established that, under certain ideal conditions of the kind commonly postulated in stylised economic models, collective bargaining does not reduce employment or total economic well-being, and that when collective bargaining does have that effect it raises concerns related to distribution, not efficiency or output-maximisation. Recall that the distributive concerns in question are that some union workers lose their jobs and therefore lower wages in other industries. We might also be preoccupied with the consumers who see the price of their product rise as output is reduced. This section provides some basic descriptions of policy tools that can be used to eliminate or limit the distributive losses caused by labour unionism when the price-quantity outcomes of section IV.A are unattainable. The goal of this section is to exemplify the kind of distributive analysis competition policy-makers should engage in to select the most desirable policy tools.

A. Work Sharing by Output-Decreasing Unions

The first mechanism we might envisage to lessen the distributive losses caused by imperfect collective bargaining of the Figure 10.1 variety is work sharing, ie the redistribution of units of labour (eg hours) more evenly across the union workers.[118] The idea would be to spread the quantity reductions of Figure 10.1 ($Q_c - Q_m$ units) among all the workers who were employed when Q_c units were bought. If we combined work sharing with the kind of collective bargaining leading to point B in Figure 10.1, no one would lose their job, and everyone would work less for a higher total pay. The worker side of Figure 10.1's labour market would suffer no loss, as it would receive a net gain of area 2 minus area 4. Workers outside the unionised industry would also suffer no loss because there would be no increase of labour supply into their industry.[119] To be sure, consumers would still

[118] JC Messenger and N Ghosheh (eds), *Work Sharing During the Great Recession* (Cheltenham, Edward Elgar Publishing, 2013); M Skuterud, 'Identifying the Potential of Work-Sharing as a Job-Creation Strategy' (2007) 25 *Journal of Labor Economics* 265; R Hart and T Sharot, 'The Short-Run Demand for Workers and Hours: A Recursive Model' (1978) 45 *Review of Economic Studies* 299, 301.

[119] We could imagine a scenario in which the union workers decide to use their free time to work part-time elsewhere, thereby increasing labour supply and lowering wages there. Such a scenario is however very unlikely. Wages in non-union sectors are by hypothesis no higher than W_c, otherwise workers would have gone to the other sectors before unionisation of Figure 10.1. Q_c is the maximum quantity of labour workers in Figure 10.1 will provide at W_c. When wages rise to W_m, work-sharing workers are better off because they have *both* more income and more leisure. One would have to value leisure *very* little, and income *very* much, to want to provide more labour at the lower wage W_c after having been made better off on both the leisure and the income front.

be hurt by the output reductions, and so workers could be affected in their capacity as consumers. But if the harm is spread among many consumers including some who are not workers, work sharing will allow us to significantly lessen the distributive drawbacks of output-reducing unionism for workers.

Work sharing can take many different forms that may or may not succeed in decreasing the number of workers who are completely unemployed following a wage increase. It is probably not enough to put a cap on extreme lengths of working days and weeks as done by the EU Working Time Directive[120] and typical contemporary working hour laws. The work sharing scheme needs to reduce the actual working time of the bulk of the workforce in the union sector of Figure 10.1, not only those who work exceptionally long periods. Another consideration, not fully captured by a basic static analysis like the one presented here, is the degree of flexibility as to when and how hours per worker are to be reduced; are the reductions concentrated on certain days, available at any time chosen by the employer, or delayed until the end of workers' careers as with early retirement schemes?[121] The quantity reductions need to correspond to the actual needs (ie the labour demand) of each firm at each relevant moment for the basic analysis of the previous paragraph to be applicable.

The need to allow for reductions of the quantity of labour supplied by *all* workers in a way that is flexible and tailored points to firm-level worker organisations as better vehicles to administer work sharing than either legislatures enacting working hour laws or sectoral unions (recall that the union obtaining the wage increase here is by hypothesis sectoral, ie not necessarily locally embedded in each firm). There are costs to work sharing that arguably cannot be eliminated even with local, firm-level actors offering all the flexibility employers need as to when and how labour quantity per worker is reduced.[122] These costs will, other things being equal, reduce labour demand and employment. Local worker organisations are nevertheless probably always in a better position to minimise the costs of work sharing and assess when work sharing *can* on net reduce the employment impact of a wage gain. The creation and promotion of German-style works councils[123] that have a say over lay-offs and working time, which was the original but quickly

[120] Directive 2003/88/EC of the European Parliament and of the Council of 4 November 2003 concerning certain aspects of the organisation of working time, [2003] OJ L299/9.

[121] J Hunt, 'Has Work-Sharing Worked in Germany?' (1999) 114 *The Quarterly Journal of Economics* 117, 118.

[122] Some of these costs might stem from imperfect substitutability of hours provided by different people due to 'fit' and fixed costs of learning about firm-specific requirements and tasks. See R Freeman, 'Work-Sharing to Full Employment: Serious Option or Populist Fallacy?' in R Freeman and P Gottschalk (eds), *Generating Jobs: How to Increase Demand for Less-Skilled Workers* (New York, Russell Sage Foundation, 1998) 195, 201–02.

[123] As is well known, works councils are firm-level, non-union worker organisations that are given rights to contest lay-offs and restructurings in regimes like that of German 'codetermination'. See Kirchner, Kremp and Magotsch (n 27) 13–17. Works councils most often also oversee work sharing schemes in German firms. See Hunt (n 121) 118.

defeated intent behind the creation of European Works Councils by the EU institutions in 1994,[124] could be an interesting avenue to promote a more extensive use of work sharing alongside union wage gains in the EU.

B. Cross-Sectoral Collective Bargaining

Cross-sectoral collective bargaining refers to modes of bargaining that cover many sectors. The simplest form we can imagine this taking is that of national or 'peak-level' collective agreements of the kind used in many continental western European countries.[125] These national collective agreements harmonise working conditions across sectors on specific topics, with sectoral and firm-level collective agreements complementing and sometimes derogating from the national agreements.[126] As with sectoral bargaining of the kind discussed in sections II and IV.A, cross-sectoral coverage can be attained without creating a new level of bargaining, merely by coordinating the various local – here meaning sectoral – collective agreements so that they result in a 'pattern' whereby one sectoral settlement is followed in other sectors.[127]

According to an analysis I have developed in recent work,[128] cross-sectoral collective bargaining can be expected to improve the outcome of collective bargaining in distributive terms when some factors of production other than labour are mobile between the sectors and the suppliers of those factors are richer than workers. It is plausible that providers of financial capital and managers are always mobile cross-sectorally, as most firms need these inputs in more or less the same form. The fact that capital and management can easily be hired in another industry makes it difficult for a merely sectoral union to appropriate their income. As a result, sectoral unions can be expected to obtain much of their gains at the expense of consumers by raising price instead of reducing capital or manager income.

[124] The creation of European Works Councils (EWCs) by an EU Directive in 1994 was originally intended by some to amount to the establishment, at the pan-European level, of bodies akin to the works councils so central to German codetermination. However, EWCs turned out to be essentially deprived of any power to influence firm decisions on employment. See J Waddington, *European Works Councils and Industrial Relations: A Transnational Industrial Relations Institution in the Making* (London, Routledge, 2011) 2; W Streeck, 'Neither European nor Works Councils: A Reply to Paul Knutsen' (1997) 18 *Economic and Industrial Democracy* 325, 328–30.

[125] See Organisation for Economic Co-operation and Development, *OECD Employment Outlook* (Paris, OECD, 2017) 153.

[126] SK Andersen, JE Dølvik and CL Ibsen, *Nordic Labour Market Models in Open Markets* (Brussels, ETUI, 2014) 29–38; U Rehfeldt and C Vincent, 'The Decentralisation of Collective Bargaining in France: An Escalating Process' in S Leonardi and R Pedersini (eds), *Multi-employer Bargaining Under Pressure: Decentralisation Trends in Five European Countries* (Brussels, ETUI, 2018) 151, 153–64.

[127] See P Du Caju, E Gautier, D Momferatou and M Ward-Warmedinger, 'Institutional Features of Wage Bargaining in 23 European Countries, the US and Japan' (2008) *European Central Bank Working Paper Series No 974*, www.ecb.europa.eu/pub/pdf/scpwps/ecbwp974.pdf, 23–24.

[128] McDougall, 'European Cross-Sectoral Collective Bargaining' (n 10).

If we can coordinate collective bargaining cross-sectorally in (many of) the non-tradable sectors that have been the focus of this chapter, we can reach any given wage gain with less of an employment reduction because each wage gain now comes with a larger capital/manager income reduction than under merely sectoral bargaining. As I explain and model in recent work,[129] the supply of capital and management services is made less elastic by broader union coverage, which by the laws of derived demand makes labour demand less elastic. In Figure 10.1 above, DL will be steeper, and the wage W_m will be attainable at a higher employment level, somewhere between Q_m and Q_c.[130] Higher employment and output for any given wage gain will also mean that consumer prices are raised less, making consumers better off than under merely sectoral bargaining. Cross-sectoral bargaining can thus make both workers and consumers better off at the expense of mobile factors of production like capital and management.[131]

In the EU, expanding the use of cross-sectoral collective bargaining would cut against a strong tendency, reinforced by the EU institutions during the debt crises of the 2010s, of urging Member States to decentralise collective bargaining down to the level of each firm to increase 'competition'.[132] That said, the EU also has a long history of purporting, at least in words if not in deeds, to promote collective bargaining at the European level, which by definition encompasses many non-tradable good sectors.[133] As recently as in late 2019, the European Parliament called for a 'coordinated EU initiative' to 'strengthen opportunities for collective bargaining', including for 'platform workers', so as to fight 'in-work poverty' and reach a more 'compressed wage structure'.[134] In 2015, the European Commission held a high-level conference to launch a 'new start for social dialogue'[135] referring to the legislative procedure and collective bargaining forum involving unions

[129] ibid.

[130] The union coverage needs to be considerable, enough to reduce the flight options of capital and managers, for this result to be reached. For that reason, minimum wage laws cannot bring about the outcome described here if not that many sectors in the economy pay sub-minimum wages.

[131] It has long been noted that labour unions may be able to appropriate some monopoly rents that would otherwise go to capital and management. For a recent discussion of this point in an antitrust context, see DA Crane, 'Antitrust and Wealth Inequality' (2016) 101 *Cornell Law Review* 1171, 1192–93. The phenomenon described in this section is a little different: it involves the appropriation of capital and management's inframarginal rents rather than the transfer of the monopoly rents captured from consumers, although the means used to appropriate those inframarginal rents is the coordinated monopolisation of the labour markets of various sectors. See McDougall, 'European Cross-Sectoral Collective Bargaining' (n 10).

[132] See A Koukiadaki, 'The Legacy of the Economic Crisis for Labour Law in Europe' in A Bogg, C Costello and ACL Davies (eds), *Research Handbook on EU Labour Law* (Cheltenham, Elgar, 2016) 64, 79.

[133] See European Commission, Directorate-General for Employment, Social Affairs and Inclusion, 'Employee Involvement – Transnational Company Agreements' ec.europa.eu/social/main.jsp?catId=707&langId=en&intPageId=214.

[134] European Parliament, Resolution of 10 October 2019 on Employment and Social Policies of the Euro Area, 2019/2111(INI), paras 16, 27, 30, recital x.

[135] T Müller, Z Rasnaca and K Vandaele, 'Wages and Collective Bargaining: Time to Deliver on the European Pillar of Social Rights' in European Trade Union Institute (ed), *Benchmarking Working Europe 2019* (Brussels: ETUI, 2019) 47, 62.

and employers across the EU mentioned earlier in this chapter.[136] Cross-sectoral collective bargaining is therefore to a certain extent on the political agenda in Europe, at both the national and EU levels.

C. Job Creation through Macroeconomic Stimulus

Section IV.B has mentioned a tradition of economic theory that argues that fiscal and monetary policy can always expand output and employment. Scholars in this tradition reject the idea that we are ever at 'full employment' in the sense that expansions of the money supply, ie policies by the central bank that lead to increased commercial bank lending or 'monetised' fiscal spending, cannot augment output. Monetary expansion does raise output and therefore employment, in more or less 'inflationary' ways depending on institutional configuration. This raises the possibility of responding to unemployment like that of Figure 10.1 with stimulus to create jobs.

As an alternative to indiscriminate expansionary monetary policy or broad fiscal spending, Hyman Minsky, a central figure in the post-Keynesian tradition, proposed long ago that the state enact a 'job guarantee' policy, ie that it intervene directly to create jobs in response to increases in unemployment.[137] Minsky argued that this policy would be a less inflationary and unstable way to eliminate unemployment than monetary and fiscal stimulus of the traditional kind.[138] Others in the post-Keynesian tradition have elaborated on Minsky's proposal since.[139] We could imagine using job guarantee programmes to alleviate unemployment of the Figure 10.1 variety. In fact, job guarantee programmes are particularly relevant to a chapter on EU competition law such as this one because they were considered in several EU Member States as policy responses to the coronavirus-induced economic crises.[140]

It is not entirely clear to me that fiscal and monetary stimulus, or a job guarantee for that matter, can eliminate any and all job losses that would stem from a large-scale reliance on price-only collective bargaining as an income redistribution instrument. One would have to work out how inflationary any given job guarantee or fiscal/monetary stimulus is likely to be and determine how that policy is likely

[136] See above n 46.

[137] H Minsky, 'Effects of Shifts of Aggregate Demand upon Income Distribution' (1968) 50 *American Journal of Agricultural Economics* 328, 338; H Minsky, *Stabilizing an Unstable Economy* (New York, McGraw-Hill, 2008) 343–49.

[138] ibid.

[139] PR Tcherneva, *The Case for a Job Guarantee* (Cambridge, Polity Press, 2020); LR Wray, 'The Job Guarantee, Full Employment and Human Rights' in U Mattei and J Haskell (eds), *Research Handbook on Political Economy and Law* (Cheltenham, Edward Elgar Publishing, 2015) 205.

[140] See, eg, G Argitis and N Koratzanis, 'A European Job Guarantee to Foster Wellbeing' (*Social Europe*, 7 January 2021) socialeurope.eu/a-european-job-guarantee-to-foster-wellbeing.

to interact with the wage gains of labour unions.[141] Minsky himself thought that labour union wage gains are an important source of inflation, ie of price increases unaccompanied by any change in output.[142] By contrast, the analysis of Figure 10.1 above depicted union wage gains not as inflationary but as employment- and output-reducing, so that the real wages of the union workers do in fact increase.

If union wage gains are inflationary, coupling them with stimulus might simply make them more inflationary. And even if the union wage gains do not themselves cause inflation, the systematic use of fiscal and monetary stimulus to counter job reductions of the Figure 10.1 variety may cause inflation rather than lasting employment gains, depending on the specific institutional configuration of the stimulus.[143] The Minskyan tradition and recent policy discussions on the job guarantee are not obviously useful for the specific distributive question posed in this section, because they contemplate employment-creation that is not systematically coupled with union wage-raising.

I do not mean to reject out of hand the possibility that macroeconomic stimulus play a role in alleviating job losses like those of Figure 10.1, and I do find it plausible that a job guarantee scheme would be a much better tool in this regard than more indiscriminate monetary and fiscal stimulus. I only mean to exemplify, in a very preliminary way, the kind of analysis we should engage in to identify the likely distributive effects of different policy mixes. In fact, this discussion gives me an occasion to emphasise the importance of coupling the kind of static distributive analysis that occupies the bulk of this chapter with *dynamic* analysis like that of macroeconomics generally and Keynesian and post-Keynesian scholarship more specifically.

In static analysis, many economic and social factors are held constant in order to examine the likely impact of a specific institutional change. Graphs like Figures 10.1 and 10.2, for example, are drawn holding constant preferences, technology, aggregate demand, and the supply of financial capital. Varying any one of these factors will shift supply and demand curves in Figures 10.1 and 10.2, making it necessary to assess static effects *alongside* dynamic changes. Uniting dynamic and static distributive analysis is a pressing area for future work, one that does not fit neatly in introductory samples like the ones provided here.[144] Suffice it to say,

[141] Indeed, to the extent a stimulus policy is inflationary, it does not increase employment. The belief that monetary and fiscal stimulus is never *merely* inflationary as it is in theories of long-run monetary neutrality need not imply that there cannot be sizeable inflationary effects to a given stimulus.

[142] H Minsky, 'The Strategy of Economic Policy and Income Distribution' (1973) 409 *Annals of the American Academy of Political and Social Science* 92, 98; Minsky, *Stabilizing an Unstable Economy* (n 137) 348–49.

[143] This is the analysis of the causal relationship between labour unions and inflation adopted by people as diverse as Milton Friedman and Gøsta Esping-Andersen. See M Friedman, 'Some Comments on the Significance of Labor Unions for Economic Policy' in D McCord Wright (ed), *The Impact of the Union* (New York, Harcourt, Brace and Company, 1951) 204, 227–28; G Esping-Andersen, *The Three Worlds of Welfare Capitalism* (Cambridge, Blackwell, 1990) 163, 189.

[144] The two following pieces strike me as useful advances on that front: N Tankus and L Herrine, 'Competition Law as Collective Bargaining Law' in S Paul, S McCrystal and E McGaughey (eds), *The Cambridge Handbook of Labor in Competition Law* (Cambridge, Cambridge University Press, 2022) 72;

then, that macroeconomic stimulus should be kept in mind as a possible complement to redistributive collective bargaining, to be further analysed using static *and* dynamic distributive analysis.[145]

D. Fiscal Spending Instead of Collective Bargaining

The three policy tools described so far in section V are meant to accompany price-only collective bargaining and compensate for its effects. However, we could well imagine other policies that would replace collective bargaining as the tool used to redistribute income. Indeed, this is often what the analysis of the inefficiency of collective bargaining does; it compares not so much points A and B in Figure 10.1 – ie redistribution through collective bargaining and no redistribution at all – but instead assesses different means to redistribute. And the claim is often made that any given distributive gain can be achieved more efficiently through tax and transfer than by cartelising markets.[146] This is said to be particularly true of lump-sum taxes, ie taxes that can be levied in such a way that no payer has the possibility of changing the amount of the tax by altering their course of action.[147] There is also the argument that even a distortionary income tax might be more efficient than raising the price of the goods produced by low-wage workers because the income tax avoids the 'double distortion' caused by differential commodity price increases.[148]

Some arguments in favour of the use of fiscal measures to redistribute income are compelling and merit consideration. The arguments I find compelling, however, are not those relating to the superior efficiency of lump-sum or income taxation. As is well known, lump-sum taxes are never a viable redistributive tool, and the

D Kennedy, 'Legal Economics of U.S. Low Income Housing Markets in Light of "Informality" Analysis' (2002) 4 *Journal of Law in Society* 71. For a somewhat dated but useful introduction to the problem of merging dynamic and static analysis, see ER Weintraub, 'The Microfoundations of Macroeconomics: A Critical Survey' (1977) 15 *Journal of Economic Literature* 1.

[145] The reader may well have noticed that another dynamic effect of labour unionism is not examined here: that of stimulating aggregate (and therefore labour) demand by transferring income to actors with a higher marginal propensity to consume, ie union workers. See the following recent attempt at modelling this: B Kaufman, 'Richard Lester's Institutional-Industrial Relations Model of Labor Markets and the Near-Zero Minimum Wage Employment Effect: The Model Card and Krueger Ignored but Shouldn't Have' (2020) 54 *Journal of Economic Issues* 1002, 1021–26. If the wage increases are not disproportionately spent on buying the product made by the workers in question, the exclusion of aggregate demand effects from the analysis may well be sound. In the context of a large unionisation drive leading to wage increases in many sectors employing low-wage workers, the aggregate demand impact of the wage increases might become more of a factor to consider.

[146] Eg, R Epstein, 'A Common Law for Labor Relations: A Critique of the New Deal Labor Legislation' (1983) 92 *Yale Law Journal* 1357, 1362; see also, ch 8 in this volume.

[147] A Mas-Collel, M Whinston and J Green, *Microeconomic Theory* (Oxford, Oxford University Press, 1995) 547.

[148] A Atkinson and JE Stiglitz, 'The Design of Tax Structure: Direct versus Indirect Taxation' (1976) 6 *Journal of Public Economics* 55, 68; L Kaplow and S Shavell, 'Why the Legal System Is Less Efficient than the Income Tax in Redistributing Income' (1994) 23 *Journal of Legal Studies* 667, 669.

double distortion argument does not hold in sectors that produce goods that are consumed in combination with leisure.[149] Moreover, cross-sectoral collective bargaining of the kind mentioned in section V.B might in fact be less welfare-reducing than the income tax because it targets goods (factors) that are in inelastic demand (supply), a central theorem of efficient taxation.[150] In addition to arguably being as potentially distortive of economic activity as unions, tax-and-transfer could be less efficiently administered than a labour union with local knowledge of the firm and the industry. Not to mention that associational activity has some organisational, psychological, and social benefits beyond just wage gains, however central those may be.[151]

The arguments about the superiority of fiscal measures I do find plausible revolve not so much around static efficiency as they do around the *distributive* impact of fiscal spending to establish, say, a universal basic income.[152] In particular, it is attractive that fiscal spending could allow the poorer, redistribution-worthy workers to bear none of the cost of their income gains, eliminating even employment losses made smaller by the other mechanisms described in section V. This could be achieved by making sure the fiscal spending is not 'paid for' with taxes on low-wage workers or their industries. Most economists now agree that fiscal spending is not necessarily 'paid for' with taxes, at the very least in an environment in which the interest rate on government debt is lower than the economy's growth rate.[153] Some would even argue that many states in fact control their own government debt interest rate through their monetary policy and can reduce the cost of their public debt by 'monetising' it,[154] though changes to the EU's monetary structure would be required for lower-income Member States to gain more of this kind of sovereign prerogative.[155]

Government spending organised in this way could plausibly be set up so that no low-wage worker bear any of the cost of the spending. This is a distributive, not an efficiency benefit; the advantages of fiscal measures have to do with the fact that they are not financed by output reductions within the low-wage workers' own industries. That said, there are other benefits of collective bargaining to be weighed against these, including the organisational, psychological, and social

[149] See McDougall, 'European Cross-Sectoral Collective Bargaining' (n 10).

[150] ibid.

[151] On these points see MH Gottesman, 'Whither Goest Labor Law: Law and Economics in the Workplace' (1991) 100 *Yale Law Journal* 2767, 2793.

[152] The arguments developed here have quite a bit in common with those of Cynthia Estlund in 'What Should We Do After Work? Automation and Employment Law' (2018) 128 *Yale Law Journal* 254.

[153] See, eg, O Blanchard, 'Public Debt and Low Interest Rates' (2019) 109 *American Economic Review* 1197.

[154] Lerner (n 115) 48; LR Wray, 'When Are Interest Rates Exogenous?' in M Setterfield (ed), *Complexity, Endogenous Money and Macroeconomic Theory: Essays in Honour of Basil J. Moore* (Cheltenham, Edward Elgar, 2006) 271, 274; R Hockett and S Omarova, 'The Finance Franchise' (2017) 102 *Cornell Law Review* 1143, 1167–75; K Pistor, 'From Territorial to Monetary Sovereignty' (2017) 18 *Theoretical Inquiries Law* 491, 493.

[155] See Pistor (n 154); Gabor and Ban (n 117).

ones just mentioned.[156] We must also keep in mind that, to the extent collective bargaining raises employment by compensating for workplace market failures[157] or can otherwise be organised to cause minimal job losses, there is no reason to replace it with fiscal measures. The comparative distributive advantages of fiscal spending arise only if and when union wage gains start to eliminate jobs (and lower non-union wages) as in Figure 10.1.

VI. Conclusion

This chapter has proposed a critique of the approach to the antitrust labour exemption adopted by the Court of Justice of the European Union and the European Commission. It has argued that a blanket exemption of unionised employees from antitrust based on the idea that 'solidarity' precludes the kind of economic analysis applied to other kinds of cartels is not a very productive way to approach the issue. Collective bargaining should also be subjected to economic analysis, albeit of a distributive rather than efficiency-oriented kind. This distributive approach is warranted because the main concern of static efficiency analysis, that of maximising output by reaching equilibrium prices that enable mutually beneficial transactions on the basis of exogenous tastes, technology, and aggregate demand, is not among the central factors that determine a country's GDP or level of output. As long argued by scholars working in various theoretical traditions, static equilibrium pricing plays a much less important role in generating output than productivity-increasing industrial organisation and stimulative monetary and fiscal policy.

In the analysis proposed and sampled here, the merits of collective bargaining should instead be assessed in distributive terms: does any given kind of collective bargaining harm some of the people it is intended to help, and are there ways to make it more effective in bringing about just distributive outcomes? This approach invites an economic analysis that is ignored by the CJEU in its labour antitrust case law insofar as it applies to employees. This approach also, conversely, casts doubt on the CJEU's presumptive prohibition of collective bargaining for independent contractors, including gig economy workers who have flexible and decentralised working conditions. This chapter's analysis of collective bargaining as in principle capable of leading to no employment reduction, and as amenable to being improved when it does lead to employment reductions, suggests that collective bargaining should play an important role in income redistribution policies, even for independent contractors like gig economy, agricultural, and craft workers. Even though I have refrained from definitively taking a position on the normative desirability of any second-best redistributive scheme like those of section V, I have provided reasons to think that collective bargaining is sometimes, perhaps often,

[156] See above n 151 and accompanying text.
[157] See above nn 23–25 and accompanying text.

a good redistribution tool, albeit one that we should always strive to configure in the best way possible.

The notion that collective bargaining has potential distributive drawbacks that must be assessed and minimised need not entail that a court like the CJEU is the best actor to perform this analysis, or even that the Court should have a say at all in what kinds of collective bargaining are lawful. I have criticised the CJEU's *approach* of refusing to engage in economic reasoning in its labour exemption cases, but it could well be that we do not want the CJEU to itself enter this terrain.[158] The CJEU's case law on the employee side could then be understood as an admission of institutional incompetence, of deference to other actors and institutions on labour matters. However, if this kind of abstention is institutionally warranted, it should be extended to the other side of the worker spectrum, that of independent contractors.

And if not the Court, *someone* should take interest in the kind of distributive economics this chapter has proposed, building on the work of generations of pioneering labour economists and antitrust scholars. Unfortunately, many of my fellow labour lawyers have tended to adopt the CJEU's approach of shunning economic analysis,[159] doing some damage to public discourse and reflection around the place of collective bargaining in redistributive policy-making. If we indeed need a non-judicial paradigm of labour antitrust in the EU, it should be one that is grounded in earnest distributive economics. This analytical disposition is no substitute for normative decision, political judgment, and willingness to take risks under uncertainty. It is however a crucial complement to these traits, and it constitutes, like them, a political virtue.

[158] It is an old tendency among progressives in the Anglo-American world to argue for judicial abstention ('deference') in matters of market regulation. See, eg, L Brandeis, 'The Living Law' (1916) 10 *Illinois Law Review* 461, 463–64. For a sophisticated contemporary example of this approach in EU labour law, see S Garben, 'Balancing Fundamental Social and Economic Rights in the EU: In Search of a Better Method' in B Vanhercke, D Ghailani, S Spasova and Philippe Pochet (eds), *Social Policy in the European Union 1999–2019: The Long and Winding Road* (Brussels, ETUI, 2020) 57.

[159] See above nn 57–62 and accompanying text.

BIBLIOGRAPHY

Acemoglu, D and Robinson, JA, *The Narrow Corridor* (London, Viking-Penguin, 2019).

Adams, W, 'Antitrust and a Free Economy' (1977) 46 *Antitrust Law Journal* 794.

Ahamat H, Rahman, NS and Mohamed, AMH, 'Competition Law and Affirmative Action in Malaysia: Complementarity or Conflict?' (2015) 23 *Pertanika Journal of Social Sciences and Humanities* 13.

Ahlborn, C, Evans, DS and Padilla, AJ, 'Competition Policy in the New Economy: Is European Competition Law up to the Challenge?' (2001) 5 *European Competition Law Review* 156.

—— 'The Antitrust Economics of Tying: A Farewell to Per se Illegality' (2004) 49 *The Antitrust Bulletin* 287.

Akman, P, '"Consumer" versus "Customer": The Devil in the Detail' (2010) 37 *Journal of Law and Society* 315.

—— *The Concept of Abuse in EU Competition Law: Law and Economic Approaches* (Oxford, Hart Publishing, 2012).

—— 'The Role of "Freedom" in EU Competition Law' (2014) 34 *Legal Studies* 183.

Albertyn, C, 'Contested Substantive Equality in the South African Sonstitution: Beyond Social Inclusion Towards Systemic Justice' (2018) 34 *South African Journal on Human Rights* 441.

Alexander, JC, 'Critical Reflection on 'Reflexive Modernization' (1996) 13 *Theory, Culture and Society* 133.

Amsden, A, *The Rise of the Rest: Challenges to the West from Late-Industrializing Economies* (Oxford, Oxford University Press, 2001).

Anderson, E, 'What is the Point of Equality?' (1999) 109 *Ethics* 287.

—— 'Liberty, Equality and Private Government' in M Matheson (ed), *The Tanner Lectures on Human Values*, vol 35 (Cambridge, Cambridge University Press, 2016) 63–122.

Andersen, SK, Dølvik, JE and Ibsen, CL, *Nordic Labour Market Models in Open Markets* (Brussels, ETUI, 2014).

Andreangeli, A, 'Healthcare Services, the EU Single Market and Beyond: Meeting Local Needs in an Open Economy – How Much Market or How Little Market?' (2016) 43 *Legal Issues of Economic Integration* 145.

Andrew, A, Bernanke, B and Croushore, D, *Macroeconomics*, 7th edn (Boston, Addison-Wesley, 2011).

Aristoteles, *Ethica Nikomachea* (I Bywater ed, Oxford, Oxford University Press, 1962).

Armendariz de Aghion, B, 'Development Banking' (1999) 58 *Journal of Development Economics* 83.

Arrow, KJ and Debreu, G, 'Existence of an Equilibrium for a Competitive Economy' (1954) 22 *Econometrica* 265.

Arrow, KJ, 'General Economic Equilibrium: Purpose, Analytic Techniques, Collective Choice' (1974) 64 *The American Economic Review* 253.

—— 'Vertical Integration and Communication' (1975) 9 *Bell Journal of Economics* 173.

Ashenfelter, O, Hosken, D and Weinberg, M, 'Did Robert Bork Understate the Competitive Impact of Mergers? Evidence from Consummated Mergers' (2014) 57 *The Journal of Law and Economics* 67.

Ashiagbor, D, 'Collective Labour Rights and the European Social Model' (2009) 3 *Journal of Law and Ethics of Human Rights* 222.

Atkinson, A, *Inequality: What Can be Done?* (Massachusetts, HUP, 2015).

Atkinson, A and Stiglitz, JE, 'The Design of Tax Structure: Direct versus Indirect Taxation' (1976) 6 *Journal of Public Economics* 55.

Auer, D, Manne, GA and Bowman, S, 'Should ASEAN Antitrust Laws Emulate European Competition Policy?' (2021) *The Singapore Economic Review* 1.

Auer, M, *Der privatrechtliche Diskurs der Moderne* (Tübingen, Mohr Siebeck, 2014).
Autor, D et al, 'The Fall of the Labor Share and the Rise of Superstar Firms' (2017) 135 *The Quarterly Journal of Economics* 645.
Auzero, G, Baugard, D and Dockès, E, *Droit du travail*, 31st edn (Paris, Dalloz, 2017).
Aydin, U and Büthe, T, 'Competition Law & Policy in Developing Countries: Explaining Variations in Outcomes; Exploring Possibilities and Limits' (2016) 79 *Law and Contemporary Problems* 1.
Azar, J, Marinescu, I and Steinbaum, M, 'Measuring Labor Market Power Two Ways' (2019) 109 *AEA Papers and Proceedings* 317.
Baker, JB, 'Economics and Politics: Perspectives on the Goals and Future of Antitrust' (2013) 81 *Fordham Law Review* 2175.
Baker, JB and Salop, SC, 'Antitrust, Competition Policy, and Inequality' (2015) 104 *Georgetown Law Journal Online* 1.
Baker, JB, *The Antitrust Paradigm: Restoring a Competitive Economy* (Cambridge, MA, Harvard University Press, 2019).
Bambra, C, Riordan, R, Ford, J, Matthews, F, 'The COVID-19 Pandemic and Health Inequalities' (2020) 74 *BMJ Journal of Epidemiology and Community Health* 964.
Banerjee, AV and Duflo, E, *Good Economics for Hard Times* (New York, PublicAffairs, 2019).
Bar-Gill, O, 'Algorithmic Price Discrimination When Demand Is a Function of Both Preferences and (Mis)perceptions' (2019) 86 *University of Chicago Law Review* 217.
Barnes, DW, 'Nonefficiency Goals in the Antitrust Law of Mergers' (1989) 30 *William and Mary Law Review* 787.
—— 'Antitrust, the Rule of Reason, and Democracy: A Letter from Justice William O. Douglas' (1999) 14 *Review of Industrial Organization* 2.
Barth, E et al, 'It's Where You Work: Increases in the Dispersion of Earnings across Establishments and Individuals in the United States' (2016) 34 *Journal of Labor Economics* 67.
Baschenhof, P, 'The Digital Markets Act (DMA): A Procompetitive Recalibration of Data Relations?' (2022) 101 *University of Illinois Journal of Law Technology and Policy*.
Beck, U, *Risk Society: Towards a New Modernity* (M Ritter tr, New York, Sage, 1992).
—— 'The Reinvention of Politics: Towards a Theory of Reflexive Modernization' in U Beck, A Giddens and S Lash (eds), *Reflexive Modernization: Politics, Tradition and Aesthetics in the Modern Social Order* (Cambridge, Polity Press, 1994) 1–55.
Beck, U and Bonß, W, *Die Modernisierung der Moderne* (Frankfurt am Main, Suhrkamp, 2001).
Beck, U, Bonß, W and Lau, C, 'The Theory of Reflexive Modernization: Problematic, Hypotheses and Research Programme' (2003) 20 *Theory, Culture and Society* 1.
Beck, U, Giddens, A and Lash, S (eds), *Reflexive Modernization: Politics, Tradition and Aesthetics in the Modern Social Order* (Cambridge, Polity Press, 1994).
Behrens, P, 'The Ordoliberal Concept of "Abuse" of a Dominant Position and Its Impact on Article 102 TFEU' in F Di Porto and R Podszun (eds), *Abusive Practices in Competition Law* (Cheltenham, Edward Elgar, 2018).
Belhaj, S and van de Gronden, JW, 'Some Room for Competition Does Not Make a Sickness Fund an Undertaking. Is EC Competition Law Applicable to the Health Care Sector? (Joined cases C-264/01, C-306/01, C-453/01 and C-355/01 *AOK*)' (2004) 25 *European Competition Law Review* 682.
Bell, S, 'The Role of the State and the Hierarchy of Money' (2001) 25 *Cambridge Journal of Economics* 149.
Bercusson, B, *European Labour Law*, 2nd edn (Cambridge, Cambridge University Press, 2009).
Bergh, R van den and Camesasca, PD, 'The Court of Justice Exempts Collective Labour Agreements from the Wrath of Antitrust' (2000) 25 *European Law Review* 492.
Bergh, R van den, *Comparative Competition Law and Economics* (Cheltenham, Edward Elgar, 2017).
Berlin, I, 'Two Concepts of Liberty' in H Hardy (ed), *Liberty: Incorporating Four Essays on Liberty* (Oxford, Oxford University Press, 2002) 166–217.
Bernanke, B and Gertler, M, 'Inside the Black Box: The Credit Channel of Monetary Policy Transmission' (1995) 9 *Journal of Economic Perspectives* 27.

Berry, S, Gaynor, M and Morton, FS, 'Do Increasing Markups Matter? Lessons from Empirical Industrial Organization' (2019) 33 *Journal of Economic Perspectives* 44.
Besen, SM and Farrell, J, 'Choosing How to Compete: Strategies and Tactics in Standardization' (1994) 8 *Journal of Economic Perspectives* 2.
Besley, T, Fontana, N and Limodio, N, 'Antitrust Policies and Profitability in Nontradable Sectors' (2021) 3 *American Economic Review: Insights* 251.
Beyleveld, AD, *Taking a Common Concern Approach to Economic Inequality: Implications for (Cooperative) Sovereignty over Corporate Taxation* (Leiden, Brill, 2022).
Bhattacharjea, A, 'Who Needs Antitrust?: Or, Is Developing-Country Antitrust Different? A Historical-Comparative Analysis' in DD Sokol et al (eds), *Competition Law and Development* (Stanford, Stanford University Press 2013) 52–65.
Bholat, D, 'How Would Adam Smith Fix the Financial Crisis?' (2009) 52 *Challenge* 60.
Biasi, M, 'We Will All Laugh at Gilded Butterflies. The Shadow of Antitrust Law on the Collective Negotiation of Fair Fees for Self-Employed Workers' (2018) 9 *European Labour Law Journal* 354.
Bishop, S and Walker, M, *The Economics of EC Competition Law: Concepts, Application and Measurement*, 3rd edn (London, Sweet & Maxwell, 2010).
Blanchard, OJ, 'Crowding Out' in SN Durlauf and LE Blume (eds), *The New Palgrave Dictionary of Economics* (New York, Palgrave Macmillan, 2008) 327.
—— 'Public Debt and Low Interest Rates' (2019) 109 *American Economic Review* 1197.
Blumkin, T and Margalioth, Y, 'On the Limits of Redistributive Taxation: Establishing a Case for Equity-Informed Legal Rules' (2005) 25 *Virginia Tax Review* 1.
Bogg, A and Estlund, C, 'Freedom of Association and the Right to Contest: Getting Back to Basics' in A Bogg and Ta Novitz (eds), *Voices at Work: Continuity and Change in the Common Law World* (Oxford, Oxford University Press, 2014) 141.
Borjas, G, *Labor Economics*, 2nd edn (London, Irwin McGraw-Hill, 2000).
Bork, RH, 'Legislative Intent and the Policy of the Sherman Act' (1966) 9 *The Journal of Law and Economics* 7.
—— 'The Goals of Antitrust Policy' (1967) 57 *The American Economic Review* 242.
—— *The Antitrust Paradox: A Policy at War with Itself* (New York, Basic Books, 1978).
—— 'The Role of the Courts in Applying Economics' (1985) 54 *Antitrust Law Journal* 21.
—— *The Antitrust Paradox: A Policy at War with Itself*, 2nd edn (New York, The Free Press, 1993).
Bork, RH and Bowman, WS Jr, 'The Crisis in Antitrust' (1965) 65 *Columbia Law Journal* 363.
Boucoyannis, D, 'The Equalizing Hand: Why Adam Smith Thought the Market Should Produce Wealth Without Steep Inequality' (2013) 11 *Perspectives on Politics* 1051.
Bourguignon, F, 'The Poverty-Growth-Inequality Triangle?' in Research Department, Agence Française de Développement (ed), *Poverty, Inequality and Growth: Proceedings of the AFD-EUDN Conference, 2003* (Paris, Maggelan, 2004) 85–98.
Böhm, F, 'Das Problem der Privaten Macht' (1928) 3 *Die Justiz* 324.
—— 'Privatrechtsgesellschaft und Marktwirtschaft' (1966) 17 *Jahrbuch für die Ordnung von Wirtschaft und Gesellschaft* 75.
—— 'Freiheit und Ordnung in der Marktwirtschaft' (1971) 22 *Jahrbuch für die Ordnung von Wirtschaft und Gesellschaft* 11.
—— *Freiheit und Ordnung in der Marktwirtschaft* (first published 1971, Baden-Baden, Nomos, 1980).
—— 'Rule of Law in a Market Economy' in A Peacock and H Willgerodt (eds), *Germany's Social Market Economy: Origins and Evolution* (London, MacMillan, 1989) 46–67.
—— 'Freiheit und Ordnung in der Marktwirtschaft' in N Goldschmidt (ed), *Grundtexte zur Freiburger Tradition der Ordnungsökonomik* (first published 1971, Tübingen, Mohr Siebeck, 2008) 299–312.
—— *Wettbewerb und Monopolkampf: Eine Untersuchung zur Frage des wirtschaftlichen Kampfrechts und zur Frage der rechtlichen Struktur der geltenden Wirtschaftsordnung* (first published 1933, Baden-Baden, Nomos, 2010).
—— 'Democracy and Economic Power in Cartel and Monopoly in Modern Law' in DA Crane and H Hovenkamp (eds), *The Making of Competition Policy: Legal and Economic Sources* (first published 1961, New York, Oxford University Press, 2013) 264–81.

Bradford, A and Chilton, AS, 'Competition Law around the World from 1889 to 2010: The Competition Law Index' (2018) 14 *Journal of Competition Law and Economics* 393.
Bradford, A, Chilton, AS and Lancieri, FM, 'The Chicago School's Limited Influence on International Antitrust' (2020) 87 *The University of Chicago Law Review* 297.
Brandeis, LD, *Other People's Money: And How The Bankers Use It* (New York, Frederick A. Stokes Company, 1914).
—— 'The Living Law' (1916) 10 *Illinois Law Review* 461.
—— 'Shall We Abandon the Policy of Competition?' in DA Crane and H Hovenkamp (eds), *The Making of Competition Policy: Legal and Economic Sources* (first published in 1934 in The Curse of Bigness, New York, Oxford University Press, 2013) 185–89.
Brennan, TJ, 'Should Antitrust Go Beyond "Antitrust"?' (2018) 63 *The Antitrust Bulletin* 49.
Brietzke, PH, 'The Constitutionalization of Antitrust: Jefferson, Madison, Hamilton, and Thomas C. Arthur' (1987) 22 *Valparaiso University Law Review* 275.
Brisimi, V, *The Interface between Competition and the Internal Market: Market Separation under Article 102 TFEU* (Oxford, Hart Publishing, 2014).
Brodley, JF, 'Limiting Conglomerate Mergers: The Need for Legislation' (1979) 40 *Ohio State Law Journal* 867.
—— 'The Economic Goals of Antitrust: Efficiency, Consumer Welfare, and Technological Progress' (1987) 62 *New York University Law Review* 1020.
Broulík, J, 'Preventing Anticompetitive Conduct Directly and Indirectly: Accuracy Versus Predictability' (2019) 64 *The Antitrust Bulletin* 115.
Brozen, Y, 'The Concentration-Collusion Doctrine' (1977) 46 *Yale Law Journal* 826.
Bruner, J, *The Process of Education* (Cambridge, MA, Harvard University Press, 1960).
Brusick, P and Evenett, SJ, 'Should Developing Countries Worry about Abuse of Dominant Power' (2008) 2 *Wisconsin Law Review* 269.
Budzinski, O and Beigi, MHA, 'Generating instead of Protecting Competition' in MS Gal et al (eds), *The Economic Characteristics of Developing Jurisdictions: Their Implications for Competition Law* (Cheltenham, Edward Elgar, 2015) 223–247.
Buthelezi, T, Mtani, T and Mncube, L, 'The Extent of Market Concentration in South Africa's Product Markets' (2019) 7 *Journal of Antitrust Enforcement* 352.
Buttigieg, E, *Competition Law: Safeguarding the Consumer Interest: A Comparative Analysis of US Antitrust Law and EC Competition Law* (The Netherlands, Wolters Kluwer, 2009).
Buxbaum, HL, 'German Legal Culture and the Globalization of Competition Law: A Historical Perspective on the Expansion of Private Antitrust Enforcement' (2005) 23 *Berkley Journal of International Law* 474.
Calcagno, C and Walker, M, 'Excessive Pricing: Towards Clarity and Economic Coherence' (2010) 6 *Journal of Competition Law and Economics* 891.
Canoy, M and Sauter, W, 'Out of Control? Hospital Mergers in the Netherlands and the Public Interest' (2010) 31 *European Competition Law Review* 377.
Card, D, 'The Effect of Unions on the Structure of Wages: A Longitudinal Analysis' (1996) 64 *Econometrica: Journal of the Econometric Society* 957.
Cassidy, J, *How Markets Fail: The Logic of Economic Calamities* (New York, Farrar, Straus and Giraux, 2009).
Causa, O, De Serres, A and Ruiz, N, 'Can Pro-Growth Policies Lift All Boats? An Analysis Based on Household Disposable Income' (2015) *OECD Journal: Economic Studies* 227.
Cengiz, F, 'The Conflict Between Market Competition and Worker Solidarity: Moving From Consumer to a Citizen Welfare Standard in Competition Law' (2021) 41 *Legal Studies* 73.
Chabane, N, Roberts, S and Goldstein, A, 'The Changing Face and Strategies of Big Business in South Africa: More Than a Decade of Political Democracy' (2006) 15 *Industrial and Corporate Change* 549.
Chancel, L and Piketty, T, 'Indian Income Inequality, 1922–2015: From British Raj to Billionaire Raj?' (2019) 65 *Review of Income and Wealth* S33.
Chang, H-J, *Kicking Away the Ladder: Development Strategy in Historical Perspective* (London, Anthem Press, 2003).

Chang, KS, 'Reflexive Modernization' in KS Chang, CF Epstein, P Kivisto and W Outhwaite (eds), *The Wiley-Blackwell Encyclopedia of Social Theory* (Hoboken, John Wiley and Sons, 2017).

Cheng, TK, 'Convergence and Its Discontents: A Reconsideration of the Merits of Convergence of Global Competition Law' (2012) 12 *Chicago Journal of International Law* 433.

—— *Competition Law in Developing Countries* (Oxford, Oxford University Press, 2020).

Chu, YW, 'The Asian Developmental State: Ideas and Debates' in YW Chu (ed), *The Asian Developmental State: Reexaminations and New Departures* (London, Palgrave Macmillan, 2016) 1–25.

Ciani, A et al, *Making It Big: Why Developing Countries Need More Large Firms* (Washington DC, World Bank Group, 2020).

Cicero, MT, *De Officis* (AP Peabody tr, Boston, Little, Brown, and Co., 1887).

—— *On the Commonwealth and On the Laws* (Cambridge, Cambridge University Press, 1999).

Coady, D and Dizioli, A, 'Income Inequality and Education Revisited: Persistence, Endogeneity and Heterogeneity' (2018) 50 *Applied Economics* 2747.

Coase, RH, 'The Problem of Social Cost' (1960) 3 *Journal of Law and Economics* 1.

Coibion, O et al, 'Innocent Bystanders? Monetary Policy and Inequality' (2017) 88 *Journal of Monetary Economics* 70.

Coke, E, *Institutes of the Laws of England* (1628).

Cole, M, 'Ordoliberalism and Its Influence on EU Tying Law' (2015) 36 *European Competition Law Review* 255.

Coleman, JL, 'Efficiency, Utility, and Wealth Maximization' (1980) 8 *Hofstra Law Review* 509.

Collins, H, 'Fat Cats, Production Networks, and the Right to Fair Pay' (2022) 85 *Modern Law Review* 1.

Comanor, WS and Smiley, RH, 'Monopoly and the Distribution of Wealth' (1975) 89 *The Quarterly Journal of Economics* 177.

Commons, J, *The Distribution of Wealth* (first published 1893, New York, A.M. Kelley, 1965).

Constant, B, *Political Writings* (Cambridge, Cambridge University Press, 1988).

Cookson, R, Dusheiko, M, Hardman, G and Martin, S, 'Competition and Inequality: Evidence from the English National Health Service 1991–2001' (2010) 20 *Journal of Public Administration Research and Theory* 181.

Cookson, R, Laudicella, M, Li Donni, P and Dusheiko, M, 'Effects of the Blair/Brown Health Reforms on Socioeconomic Equity in Health Care' (2012) 17(Suppl1) *Journal of Health Services Research and Policy* 55.

Cookson, R, Laudicella, M, Li Donni, P, 'Does Hospital Competition Harm Equity? Evidence from the English National Health Service' (2013) 32 *Journal of Health Economics* 410.

Cooper, JC, Froeb, L, O'Brien, DP and Tschantz, S, 'Does Price Discrimination Intensify Competition? Implications For Antitrust' (2005) 72 *Antitrust Law Journal* 327.

Cooter, R and Ulen, T, *Law and Economics*, 6th edn (New York, Pearson, 2014).

Crane, DA, 'Rethinking Merger Efficiencies' (2011) 110 *Michigan Law Review* 347.

—— 'The Tempting of Antitrust: Robert Bork and the Goals of Antitrust Policy' (2014) 9 *Antitrust Law Journal* 835.

—— 'Antitrust and Wealth Inequality' (2016) 101 *Cornell Law Review* 1171.

—— 'How Much Brandeis Do the Neo-Brandeisians Want' (2019) 64 *The Antitrust Bulletin* 531.

Creedy, J and Dixon, R, 'The Relative Burden of Monopoly on Households with Different Incomes' (1998) 65 *Economica* 285.

Creedy, J and Dixon, R, 'The Distributional Effects of Monopoly' (1999) 38 *Australian Economic Papers* 223.

Cseres, KJ, 'Controversies of the Consumer Welfare Standard' (2006) 3 *Competition Law Review* 121.

Dabbah, MM, *International and Comparative Competition Law* (Cambridge, Cambridge University Press, 2012).

Danieli, D, 'Excessive Pricing in the Pharmaceutical Industry: Adding Another String to the Bow of EU Competition Law' (2021) 16 *Health Economics, Policy and Law* 64.

Daskalova, VI, 'Consumer Welfare in EU Competition Law: What Is It (Not) About?' (2015) 11 *The Competition Law Review* 133.

Davidov, G, 'Non-Waivability in Labour Law' (2020) 40 *Oxford Journal of Legal Studies* 482.
Davidov, G and Langille, B (eds), *Boundaries and Frontiers of Labour Law: Goals and Means in the Regulation of Work* (Oxford, Hart Publishing, 2006).
Davidson, P, 'Keynes's Finance Motive' (1965) 17 *Oxford Economic Papers* 47.
Davies, ACL, 'This Time, It's For Real' (2013) 76 *Modern Law Review* 564.
Davies, G, 'The Consumer, the Citizen, and the Human Being' in D Leczykiewicz and S Weatherill (eds), *The Images of the Consumer in EU Law* (Oxford, Hart Publishing, 2016).
De Geest, G, *Rents: How Marketing Causes Inequality* (New York, Beccaria Books, 2018).
De Loecker, J, Eeckhout, J and Unger, G, 'The Rise of Market Power and the Macroeconomic Implications' (2020) 135 *The Quarterly Journal of Economics* 561.
De Stefano, V, 'The Rise of the "Just-in-Time Workforce": On-Demand Work, Crowdwork, and Labor Protection in the "Gig Economy"' (2016) 37 *Comparative Labor Law and Policy Journal* 471.
Decker, R et al, 'Declining Business Dynamism: What We Know and the Way Forward' (2016) 106 *American Economic Review* 203.
Delis, MD, Hasan, I and Kazakis, P, 'Bank Regulations and Income Inequality: Empirical Evidence' (2014) 18 *Review of Finance* 1811.
Demsetz, H, 'Two Systems of Belief About Monopoly' in HJ Goldschmid, HM Mann, JF Weston (eds), *Industrial Concentration: The New Learning* (Boston, Little Brown, 1974) 164–83.
Deutscher, E, *Of Masters, Slaves, Behemoths and Bees: The Rise and Fall of the Link Between Competition, Competition Law and Democracy* (Florence, European University Institute, 2020).
Deutscher, E and Makris, S, 'Exploring the Ordoliberal Paradigm: The Competition-Democracy Nexus' (2016) 11 *Competition Law Review* 181.
Di Porto, F and Podszun, R (eds), *Abusive Practices in Competition Law* (Cheltenham, Edward Elgar, 2018).
Dierx, A et al, 'Distributional Macroeconomic Effects of the European Union Competition Policy: A General Equilibrium Analysis' in M Martinez Licetti et al (eds), *A Step Ahead: Competition Policy for Shared Prosperity and Inclusive Growth* (Washington, DC, World Bank Group, 2017) 155–85.
Director, A and Levi, EH, 'Law and the Future: Trade Regulation' (1956) 51 *Northwestern University Law Review* 281.
Doepke, M and Schneider, M, 'Inflation and the Redistribution of Nominal Wealth' (2006) 114 *Journal of Political Economy* 1069.
Dorsey, E et al, 'Consumer Welfare & the Rule of Law: The Case against the New Populist Antitrust Movement' (2020) 47 *Pepperdine Law Review* 861.
Dowdle, MW, 'On the Public-Law Character of Competition Law: A Lesson from Asian Capitalism' (2015) 38 *Fordham International Law Journal* 301.
Drexl, J, Bakhoum, M, Fox, EM, Gal, MS and Gerber, DJ (eds), *Competition Policy and Regional Integration in Developing Countries* (Cheltenham, Edward Elgar 2012).
Dubal, V, 'The Drive to Precarity: A Political History of Work, Regulation, and Labor Advocacy in San Francisco's Taxi & Uber Economies' (2017) 38 *Berkeley Journal of Employment and Labor Law* 73.
Dukes, R and Cannon, C, 'The Role of Social Partners' in A Bogg, C Costello and ACL Davies (eds), *Research Handbook on EU Labour Law* (Cheltenham, Edward Elgar, 2016) 89.
Dukes, R and Streeck, W, 'Labour Constitutions and Occupational Communities: Social Norms and Legal Norms at Work' (2020) 47 *Journal of Law and Society* 612.
Dunne, N, *Competition Law and Economic Regulation – Making and Managing Markets* (Cambridge, Cambridge University Press, 2015).
—— 'Regulating Prices in the European Union' (2018) 37 *Yearbook of European Law* 344.
Easterbrook, FH, 'The Limits of Antitrust' (1984) 63 *Texas Law Review* 1.
Economides, N, 'Public Policy in Network Industries' in P Buccirossi (ed), *Handbook of Antitrust Economics* (Boston, The MIT Press, 2008) 469–518.
Edwards, CD, 'Conglomerate Bigness as a Source of Power' in GJ Stigler (ed), *Business Concentration and Price Policy* (NBER, Princeton, Princeton University Press, 1955) 331–59.
Ehlermann, CD and Atanasiu, I (eds), *European Competition Law Annual 2003: What is an Abuse of a Dominant Position?* (Oxford, Hart Publishing, 2006).

Ehlermann, CD and Marquis, M (eds), *European Competition Law Annual 2007: A Reformed Approach to Article 82 EC* (Oxford, Hart Publishing, 2008).
Ehrenberg, RG and Smith, RS, *Modern Labor Economics: Theory and Public Policy*, 11th edn (London, Prentice Hall, 2012).
Elhauge, E, 'Horizontal Shareholding' (2016) 129 *Harvard Law Review* 1267.
Elhauge, E and Geradin, D, *Global Competition Law and Economics*, 2nd edn (Oxford, Hart Publishing, 2011).
Elzinga, K, 'The Goals of Antitrust: Other than Competition and Efficiency, What Else Counts?' (1977) 125 *University of Pennsylvania Law Review* 1191.
Ennis, SF, Gonzaga, P and Pike, C, 'Inequality: A Hidden Cost of Market Power' (2019) 35 *Oxford Review of Economic Policy* 518.
Ennis, SF and Kim, Y, 'Market Power and Wealth Distribution' in M Martinez Licetti et al (eds), *A Step Ahead: Competition Policy for Shared Prosperity and Inclusive Growth* (Washington, DC, World Bank Group, 2017) 133–53.
Epstein, R, 'A Common Law for Labor Relations: A Critique of the New Deal Labor Legislation' (1983) 92 *Yale Law Journal* 1357.
Ergas H, 'Should Developed Countries Require Developing Countries to Adopt Competition Law? Lessons from the Economic Literature' (2009) 5 *European Competition Journal* 347.
Erhard, L, *Prosperity Through Competition* (New York, Frederick Praeger, 1958).
Erjavec, E and Kovac, M, 'Public Law, Higher Education and the Ex-ante Removal of the Causes of Inequality' (2018) 1 *Sorbonne Student Law Review* 230.
Esping-Andersen, G, *The Three Worlds of Welfare Capitalism* (Cambridge, Blackwell, 1990).
Estlund, C, 'What Should We Do After Work? Automation and Employment Law' (2018) 128 *Yale Law Journal* 254.
Etro, F and Kokkoris, I, 'Toward an Economic Approach to Article 102 TFEU' in F Etro and I Kokkoris (eds), *Competition Law and the Enforcement of Article 82* (Oxford, Oxford University Press, 2010).
Eucken, W, *Grundsätze der Wirtschaftspolitik* (Tübingen, Mohr Siebeck, 2004).
Evans, D, 'Why Different Jurisdictions Do Not (and Should Not) Adopt the Same Antitrust Rules' (2009) 10 *Chicago Journal of International Law* 161.
Evans, D and Padilla, J, 'Excessive Prices: Using Economics to Define Administrable Legal Rules' (2005) 1 *Journal of Competition Law and Economics* 97.
Evenett, SJ, 'Competition Law and the Economic Characteristics of Developing Countries' in MS Gal et al (eds), *The Economic Characteristics of Developing Jurisdictions: Their Implications for Competition Law* (Cheltenham, Edward Elgar, 2015) 15–30.
Evju, S, 'Collective Agreements and Competition Law: The Albany Puzzle and van der Woude' (2000) 17 *International Journal of Comparative Labour Law and Industrial Relations* 165.
Eyal, Z and Teichman, D, *Behavioural Law and Economics* (Oxford, Oxford University Press, 2020).
Ezrachi, A (ed), *Article 82: Reflections on Its Recent Evolution* (Oxford, Hart Publishing, 2009).
—— *EU Competition Law: An Analytical Guide to the Leading Cases*, 5th edn (Oxford, Hart Publishing, 2016).
—— 'Sponge' (2017) 5 *Journal of Antitrust Enforcement* 49.
Ezrachi, A and Gilo, D, 'Are Excessive Prices Really Self-Correcting?' (2009) 5 *Journal of Competition Law and Economics* 249.
Farber, HS et al, 'Unions and Inequality over the Twentieth Century: New Evidence from Survey Data' (2021) 136 *The Quarterly Journal of Economics* 1325.
Farrell, J and Saloner, G, 'Installed Base and Compatibility: Innovation, Product Preannouncements and Predation' (1986) 76 *American Economics Review* 940.
Faull, J and Nikpay, A, *The EC Law of Competition*, 2nd edn (Oxford, Oxford University Press, 2007).
Fedderke, JW, 'Growth and Inequality: The South African Case in International Context – The Central Role of the Labor Market' (2019) 3 *Journal of Development Perspectives* 191.
Ferro, B, 'Poverty and Recognition in Hegel's Philosophy of Right' in G Schweiger (ed), *Poverty, Inequality and the Critical Theory of Recognition* (Switzerland, Springer, 2020) 59–80.

Fine, B and Rustomjee, Z, *The Political Economy of South Africa: From Minerals–Energy Complex to Industrialisation* (Johannesburg, Wits University Press, 1996).

Fisher, A and Lande, RH, 'Efficiency Considerations in Merger Enforcement' (1983) 71 *California Law Review* 1582.

Fleischacker, S, 'Adam Smith on Equality' in CJ Berry, MP Paganelli and C Smith (eds), *The Oxford Handbook of Adam Smith* (Oxford, Oxford University Press, 2013) 485–500.

Forrester, I, 'Where Law Meets Competition: Is Wouters Like a Cassis de Dijon or a Platypus' in CD Ehlermann and I Atanasiu (eds), *European Competition Law Annual 2004: The Relationship Between Competition Law and the (Liberal) Professions* (Oxford, Hart Publishing, 2006).

Foucault, M, *The Order of Things: An Archaeology of the Human Sciences* (New York, Pantheon Books, 1970).

Fox, EM, 'Antitrust, Mergers, and the Supreme Court: The Politics of Section 7 of the Clayton Act' (1975) 26 *Mercer Law Review* 389.

—— 'The Modernization of Antitrust: A New Equilibrium' (1981) 66 *Cornell Law Review* 1140.

—— 'The Battle for the Soul of Antitrust' (1987) 75 *California Law Review* 3.

—— 'What is Harm to Competition? Exclusionary Practices and Anticompetitive Effect' (2002) 70 *Antitrust Law Journal* 371.

—— 'Economic Development, Poverty, and Antitrust: The Other Path' (2007) 13 *Southwestern Journal of Law and Trade in the Americas* 211.

—— 'The Efficiency Paradox' in R Pitofsky (ed), *How the Chicago School Overshot the Mark: The Effect of Conservative Economic Analysis on U.S. Antitrust* (Oxford, Oxford University Press, 2008).

—— 'Competition, Development and Regional Integration: In Search of a Competition Law Fit for Developing Countries' in J Drexl, M Bakhoum, EM Fox, MS Gal and DJ Gerber (eds), *Competition Policy and Regional Integration in Developing Countries* (Cheltenham, Edward Elgar, 2012) 273–90.

—— 'Monopolization and Abuse of Dominance: Why Europe is Different' (2014) 59 *The Antitrust Bulletin* 129.

—— 'Competition Policy at the Intersection of Equity and Efficiency: The Developed and Developing World' in D Gerard and I Lianos (eds), *Reconciling Efficiency and Equity: A Global Challenge for Competition Policy* (Cambridge, Cambridge University Press, 2019).

Fox, EM and Bakhoum, M, *Making Markets Work for Africa: Markets, Development and Competition Law In Sub-Saharan Africa* (Oxford, Oxford University Press, 2019).

Fox, EM and Healey, D, 'When the State Harms Competition – The Role for Competition Law' (2014) 79 *Antitrust Law Journal* 769.

Fox, EM and Sullivan, LA, 'Antitrust-Retrospective and Prospective: Where Are We Coming From? Where Are We Going?' (1987) 62 *New York University Law Review* 936.

Freedland, M and Countouris, N, 'Some Reflections on the "Personal Scope" of Collective Labour Law' (2017) 46 *Industrial Law Journal* 52.

Freeman, R, 'Work-Sharing to Full Employment: Serious Option or Populist Fallacy?' in R Freeman and P Gottschalk (eds), *Generating Jobs: How to Increase Demand for Less-Skilled Workers* (New York, Russell Sage Foundation, 1998) 195.

Freeman, R and Medoff, J, *What Do Unions Do?* (New York, Basic Books, 1984).

Fried, BH, *The Progressive Assault on Laissez Faire: Robert Hale and the First Law and Economics Movement* (Cambridge, MA, Harvard University Press, 1998).

Friedman, M, 'Some Comments on the Significance of Labor Unions for Economic Policy' in D McCord Wright (ed), *The Impact of the Union* (New York, Harcourt, Brace and Company, 1951) 204.

—— *Price Theory: A Provisional Text* (New Brunswick, NJ, Transaction Publishers, 1962).

Fumagalli, C, Motta, M and Calcagno, C, *Exclusionary Practices: The Economics of Monopolisation and Abuse of Dominance* (Cambridge, Cambridge University Press, 2018).

Furceri, D, Loungani, P and Zdzienicka, A, 'The Effects of Monetary Policy Shocks on Inequality' (2018) 85 *Journal of International Money and Finance* 168.

Furman, J and Orszag, P, 'A Firm-Level Perspective on the Role of Rents in the Rise in Inequality' in M Guzman (ed), *Toward a Just Society: Joseph Stiglitz and Twenty-First Century Economics* (New York, Columbia University Press, 2018) 19–47.

Furse, M, 'Competition Law in Vietnam: A Critique' (2010) 33 *World Competition* 163.

Gabor, D and Ban, C, 'Banking on Bonds: The New Links Between States and Markets' (2016) 54 *Journal of Common Market Studies* 617.

Gal, MS, *Competition Policy for Small Market Economies* (Cambridge, MA, Harvard University Press, 2003).

—— 'Monopoly Pricing as an Antitrust Offense in the U.S. and the EC: Two Systems of Belief about Monopoly?' (2004) 49 *The Antitrust Bulletin* 343.

—— 'The Social Contract at the Basis of Competition Law: Should We Recalibrate Competition Law to Limit Inequality?' in D Gerard and I Lianos (eds), *Reconciling Efficiency and Equity: A Global Challenge for Competition Policy* (Cambridge, Cambridge University Press, 2019) 88–108.

Gal, MS and Bakhoum, M, 'Introduction' in MS Gal et al (eds), *The Economic Characteristics of Developing Jurisdictions: Their Implications for Competition Law* (Cheltenham, Edward Elgar, 2015) 1–14.

Gal, MS, Bakhoum, M, Drexl, J, Fox, EM and Gerber, DJ (eds), *The Economic Characteristics of Developing Jurisdictions: Their Implications for Competition Law* (Cheltenham, Edward Elgar, 2015).

Gal, MS and Fox, EM, 'Drafting Competition Law for Developing Jurisdictions: Learning from Experience' in MS Gal et al (eds), *The Economic Characteristics of Developing Jurisdictions: Their Implications for Competition Law* (Cheltenham, Edward Elgar, 2015) 296–356.

Galbraith, K, *A History of Economics: The Past as the Present* (London, Penguin Books, 1991).

Galle, BD, 'Is Local Consumer Protection Law a Better Redistributive Mechanism than the Tax System?' (2010) 65 *New York University Annual Survey of American Law* 525.

Galor, O and Moav, O, 'From Physical to Human Capital Accumulation: Inequality and the Process of Development' (2004) 71 *Review of Economic Studies* 1001.

Gans, J et al, 'Inequality and Market Concentration, When Shareholding is More Skewed Than Consumption' (2019) 35 *Oxford Review of Economic Policy* 550.

Garben, S, 'Online Platform Work at European Level' (2019) 3 *Geneva Global Policy Brief* 1.

—— 'Balancing Fundamental Social and Economic Rights in the EU: In Search of a Better Method' in B Vanhercke, D Ghailani, S Spasova and P Pochet (eds), *Social Policy in the European Union 1999–2019: The Long and Winding Road* (Brussels, ETUI, 2020) 57.

Gaynor, M and Town, R, 'Competition in Health Care Markets' in M Pauly et al (eds), *Handbook of Health Economics*, vol 2 (Oxford, Elsevier, 2012).

Gerard, D and Lianos I, 'Introduction' in D Gerard and I Lianos (eds), *Reconciling Efficiency and Equity: A Global Challenge for Competition Policy* (Cambridge, Cambridge University Press, 2019) 1–16.

—— *Reconciling Efficiency and Equity: A Global Challenge for Competition Law?* (Cambridge, Cambridge University Press, 2019).

Gerber, DJ, 'Law and the Abuse of Economic Power in Europe' (1988) 62 *Tulane Law Review* 57.

—— 'Constitutionalizing the Economy: German Neo-Liberalism, Competition Law and the "New" Europe' (1994) 42 *American Journal of Comparative Law* 25.

—— *Law and Competition in Twentieth Century Europe: Protecting Prometheus* (Oxford, Oxford University Press, 2001).

—— 'Economic Development and Global Competition Law Convergence' in DD Sokol et al (eds), *Competition Law and Development* (Stanford, Stanford University Press, 2013) 13–34.

—— 'Adapting the Role of Economics in Competition Law: A Developing Country Dilemma' in MS Gal et al (eds), *The Economic Characteristics of Developing Jurisdictions: Their Implications for Competition Law* (Cheltenham, Edward Elgar, 2015) 248–64.

Gerbrandy, A, 'Solving a Sustainability-Deficit in European Competition Law' (2017) 40 *World Competition* 539.

Giddens, A, 'Living in a Post-Traditional Society' in U Beck, A Giddens and S Lash (eds), *Reflexive Modernization: Politics, Tradition and Aesthetics in the Modern Social Order* (Cambridge, Polity Press, 1994) 56–109.

Gifford, DJ, 'Redefining the Antitrust Labor Exemption' (1988) 72 *Minnesota Law Review* 1379.

Gillespie, J, 'Localized Global Competition Law in Vietnam: A Bottom-up Perspective' (2015) 64 *The International and Comparative Law Quarterly* 935.

Giocoli, N, 'Competition versus Property Rights: American Antitrust Law, the Freiburg School, and the Early Years of European Competition Policy' (2009) 5 *Journal of Competition Law and Economics* 747.

Goldfine, AD and Vorrasi, KM, 'The Fall of the Kodak Aftermarket Doctrine: Dying a Slow Death in the Lower Courts' (2004) 72 *Antitrust Law Journal* 209.

Goldman, EF, *Rendezvous With Destiny: A History of Modern American Reform* (New York, Knopf, 1952).

Gormsen, LL, *A Principled Approach to Abuse of Dominance in European Competition Law* (Cambridge, Cambridge University Press, 2010).

Gottesman, MH, 'Whither Goest Labor Law: Law and Economics in the Workplace' (1991) 100 *Yale Law Journal* 2767.

Greaney, T and Odudu, O, 'Introduction to Antitrust and the Provision of Healthcare in the United States and the European Union – Common Challenges' in D Orentlicher and TK Hervey (eds), *The Oxford Handbook of Comparative Health Law* (Oxford, Oxford University Press, 2021).

Gronden, JW van de, 'The Treaty Provisions on Competition and Health Care' in JW van de Gronden, E Szyszczak, U Neergaard and M Krajewski (eds), *Health Care and EU Law* (The Hague, TMC Asser Press, 2011).

Gronden, JW van de, 'Services of General Interest and the Concept of Undertaking: Does EU Competition Law Apply?' (2018) 41 *World Competition* 197.

Gronden, JW van de and Guy, M, 'The Role of EU Competition Law in Health Care and the 'Undertaking' Concept' (2021) 16 *Health Economics, Policy and Law* 76.

Gronden, JW van de and Rusu, CS, 'EU Competition Law and Policy and Health Systems' in TK Hervey, CA Young and LE Bishop (eds), *Research Handbook on EU Health Law and Policy* (Cheltenham, Edward Elgar, 2017).

Gronden, JW van de and Szyszczak, E, 'Conclusions: Constructing a 'Solid' Multi-Layered Health Care Edifice' in JW van de Gronden, E Szyszczak, U Neergaard and M Krajewski (eds), *Health Care and EU Law* (The Hague, TMC Asser Press, 2011).

Gronden, JW van de and Szyszczak, E, 'Introducing Competition Principles into Health Care through EU Law and Policy: A Case Study of the Netherlands' (2014) 22 *Medical Law Review* 238.

Guy, M, *Competition Policy in Healthcare: Frontiers in Insurance-Based and Taxation-Funded Systems* (Cambridge, Intersentia, 2019).

—— 'Between 'Going Private' and 'NHS Privatisation': Patient Choice, Competition Reforms and the Relationship Between the NHS and Private Healthcare in England' (2019) 39 *Legal Studies* 479.

Gyselen, L, 'Vertical Restraints in the Distribution Process: Strength and Weakness of the Free-Rider Rationale under EEC Competition Law' (1984) 21 *Common Market Law Review* 647.

Gyulavari, T, 'Collective Rights of Platform Workers: The Role of EU Law' (2020) 27 *Maastricht Journal of European and Comparative Law* 406.

Habermas, J, *The Philosophical Discourse of Modernity: Twelve Lectures* (F Lawrence tr, New Jersey, Wiley, 1990).

Hale, R, 'Coercion and Distribution in a Supposedly Non-Coercive State' (1923) 38 *Political Science Quarterly* 470.

Haley, JO, 'Competition Law for the Asia-Pacific Economic Cooperation Community: Designing Shoes for Many Sizes' (2002) 1 *Washington University Global Studies Law Review* 1.

Hall, P and Soskice, D, 'An Introduction to Varieties of Capitalism' in P Hall and D Soskice (eds), *Varieties of Capitalism: The Institutional Foundations of Comparative Advantage* (Oxford, Oxford University Press, 2004) 1.

Han, M and Pyun, JH, 'Markups and Income Inequality: Causal Links, 1975–2011' (2021) 49 *Journal of Comparative Economics* 290.

Hancher, L and Sauter, W, *EU Competition and Internal Market Law in the Health Care Sector* (Oxford, Oxford University Press, 2012).

Hart, R and Sharot, T, 'The Short-Run Demand for Workers and Hours: A Recursive Model' (1978) 45 *Review of Economic Studies* 299.

Hausman, J and Leibtag, E, 'Consumer Benefits from Increased Competition in Shopping Outlets: Measuring the Effect of Wal-Mart' (2007) 22 *Journal of Applied Econometrics* 1157.

Hayek, FA, *The Fatal Conceit*, vol 1 (WW Bartley ed, London, Routledge, 1988).

—— *The Constitution of Liberty* (first published 1960, Chicago, University of Chicago Press, 2011).

Hegel, GWF, *Grundlinien der Natur des Rechts* (first published 1821, E Moldenhauer and KM Michel eds, Frankfurt am Main, Suhrkamp, 1986).

—— *Outlines of the Philosophy of Right* (first published 1821, TM Knox tr, S Houlgate ed, Oxford, Oxford University Press, 2008).

Heyer, K, 'A World of Uncertainty: Economics and the Globalization of Antitrust' (2005) 72 *Antitrust Law Journal* 375.

Hicks, JR, *The Theory of Wages*, 2nd edn (New York, A.M. Kelley, 1966).

Hill, S, *Europe's Promise: Why the European Way is the Best Hope in an Insecure Age* (California, University of California Press, 2010).

Hoa, NT, 'How Large is Vietnam's Informal Economy?' (2019) 39 *Economic Affairs* 81.

Hockett, R and Omarova, S, 'Public Actors in Private Markets: Toward a Developmental Finance State' (2015) 93 *Washington University Law Review* 103.

—— 'The Finance Franchise' (2017) 102 *Cornell Law Review* 1143.

Hofstadter, R, 'What Happened to the Antitrust Movement' in DA Crane and H Hovenkamp (eds), *The Making of Competition Policy: Legal and Economic Sources* (New York, Oxford University Press, 2013) 223–51.

Holmes, S, 'Climate Change, Sustainability, and Competition Law' (2020) 8 *Journal of Antitrust Enforcement* 354.

Horkheimer, M and Adorno, T, *Dialectic of Enlightenment* (first published 1944, E Jephcott tr, GS Noerr ed, Stanford, Stanford University Press, 2002).

Hou, L, 'Excessive Prices within EU Competition Law' (2011) 7 *European Competition Journal* 47.

Hovenkamp, H, 'Labor Conspiracies in American Law, 1880–1930' (1988) 66 *Texas Law Review* 919.

Howard, MP, 'Exclusive Dealing' (1982) 25 *Journal of Law and Economics* 1.

Hsu, S-L, 'The Rise and Rise of The One Percent: Considering Legal Causes of Wealth Inequality' (2015) 64 *Emory Law Journal Online* 2043.

—— 'Antitrust and Inequality: The Problem of Super-Firms' (2018) 63 *The Antitrust Bulletin* 104.

Hunt, J, 'Has Work-Sharing Worked in Germany?' (1999) 114 *The Quarterly Journal of Economics* 117.

Hylton, KN and Deng, F, 'Antitrust around the World: An Empirical Analysis of the Scope of Competition Laws and Their Effects' (2007) 74 *Antitrust Law Journal* 27.

Jacobides, MG and Lianos, I 'Ecosystems and competition law in theory and practice' (2021) 30/3 *Industrial and Corporate Change* 1199.

Jauch, S and Watzka, S, 'Financial Development and Income Inequality: A Panel Data Approach' (2016) 51 *Empirical Economics* 291.

Jebsen, P and Stevens, R, 'Assumptions, Goals and Dominant Undertakings: The Regulation of Competition under Article 86 of the European Union' (1996) 64 *Antitrust Law Journal* 443.

Jolls, C, 'Behavioural Economic Analysis of Redistributive Legal Rules' (1998) 51 *Vanderbilt Law Review* 1653.

Jones, A and Sufrin, B, *EC Competition Law: Text, Cases and Materials*, 4th edn (Oxford, Oxford University Press, 2010).

—— *EU Competition Law: Text, Cases, and Materials*, 6th edn (Oxford, Oxford University Press, 2016).

Jost, TS, Dawson, D and Den Exter, A, 'The Role of Competition in Health Care: A Western European Perspective' (2006) 31 *Journal of Health Politics, Policy and Law* 687.

Kallaugher, J and Sher, B, 'Rebates Revisited: Anti-Competitive Effects and Exclusionary Abuse Under Article 82' (2004) 25 *European Competition Law Review* 263.

Kaplow, L, 'On the Choice of Welfare Standards in Competition Law' in D Zimmer (ed), *The Goals of Competition Law* (Cheltenham, Edward Elgar, 2012) 7–25.

Kaplow, L and Shavell, S, 'Why the Legal System Is Less Efficient than the Income Tax in Redistributing Income' (1994) 23 *Journal of Legal Studies* 667.

—— 'Should Legal Rules Favour the Poor? Clarifying the Role of Legal Rules and the Income Tax in Redistributing Income' (2000) 29 *Journal of Legal Studies* 821.

—— *Fairness Versus Welfare* (Cambridge, MA, Harvard University Press, 2002).

Katz, ML and Shapiro, C, 'Technology Adoption in the Presence of Network Externalities' (1986) 94 *Journal of Political Economics* 822.

—— 'Systems Competition and Network Effects' (1994) 8 *Journal of Economic Perspectives* 93.

Kaufman, B, 'Labor Law and Employment Regulation: Neoclassical and Institutional Perspectives' in KG Dau-Schmidt, SD Harris and O Lobel (eds), *Labor and Employment Law and Economics* (Cheltenham, Edward Elgar, 2009) 3.

—— 'Richard Lester's Institutional-Industrial Relations Model of Labor Markets and the Near-Zero Minimum Wage Employment Effect: The Model Card and Krueger Ignored but Shouldn't Have' (2020) 54 *Journal of Economic Issues* 1002.

Kaysen, C and Turner, DF, *Antitrust Policy: An Economic and Legal Analysis* (Cambridge, MA, Harvard University Press, 1959).

Kee, HL and Hoekman, B, 'Imports, Entry and Competition Law as Market Disciplines' (2007) 51 *European Economic Review* 831.

Kemp, K, 'Concealed Data Practices and Competition Law: Why Privacy Matters' (2020) 16 *European Competition Journal* 628.

Kennedy, D, 'Legal Economics of U.S. Low Income Housing Markets in Light of "Informality" Analysis' (2002) 4 *Journal of Law in Society* 71.

Kenner, J, *EU Employment Law: From Rome to Amsterdam and Beyond* (Oxford, Hart Publishing, 2003).

Kerber, W and Hartig, S, 'The Rise and Fall of the German Miracle' (1999) 13 *Critical Review* 337.

Khan, LM, 'Amazon's Antitrust Paradox' (2017) 126 *Yale Law Review Journal* 564.

Khan, L and Vaheesan, S, 'Market Power and Inequality: The Antitrust Counterrevolution and Its Discontents' (2017) 11 *Harvard Law and Policy Review* 235.

Kim, EK, 'Labor's Antitrust Problem: A Case for Worker Welfare' (2020) 130 *Yale Law Journal* 428.

Kingston, S, 'Integrating Environmental Protection and EU Competition Law: Why Competition Isn't Special' (2010) 16 *European Law Journal* 780.

Kirchner, J, Kremp, PR and Magotsch, M (eds), *Key Aspects of German Employment and Labour Law*, 2nd edn (Berlin, Springer, 2010).

Kirkwood, JB and Lande, RH, 'The Chicago School's Foundation Is Flawed: Antitrust Protects Consumers, Not Efficiency' in R Pitofsky (ed), *How the Chicago School Overshot the Mark: The Effect of Conservative Economic Analysis on U.S. Antitrust* (Oxford, Oxford University Press, 2008) 89–97.

Klaaren, J, 'Laying the Table: The Role of Business in Establishing Competition Law and Policy in South Africa' (2018) 33 *International Review of Applied Economics* 119.

Klare, K, 'Workplace Democracy and Market Reconstruction: An Agenda for Legal Reform' (1988) 38 *Catholic University Law Review* 1.

Knight, C, 'Theories of Distributive Justice and Post-Apartheid South Africa' (2014) 41 *South African Journal of Political Studies* 23.

Kotler, P and Keller, KL, *Marketing Management* (New York, Pearson Prentice Hall, 2012).

Koukiadaki, A, 'The Legacy of the Economic Crisis for Labour Law in Europe' in A Bogg, C Costello and ACL Davies (eds), *Research Handbook on EU Labour Law* (Cheltenham, Edward Elgar, 2016) 64.

Krueger, AB and Ashenfelter, O, 'Theory and Evidence on Employer Collusion in the Franchise Sector' [2021] *Journal of Human Resources* 1019.

Krugman, P and Wells, R, *Economics*, 2nd edn (New York, Worth Publishers, 2009).

Kukovec, D, 'Economic Law, Inequality, and Hidden Hierarchies on the EU Internal Market' (2016) 38 *Michigan Journal of International Law* 1.

Kwoka, JE Jr, *Mergers, Merger Control, and Remedies: A Retrospective Analysis of U.S. Policy* (Cambridge, MA, MIT Press, 2015).

Lande, RH, 'Wealth Transfers as the Original and Primary Concern of Antitrust: The Efficiency Interpretation Challenged' (1982) 34 *Hastings Law Journal* 65.

—— 'Chicago's False Foundation: Wealth Transfers (Not Just Efficiency) Should Guide Antitrust' (1989) 58 *Antitrust Law Journal* 2.

—— 'A Traditional and Textualist Analysis of the Goals of Antitrust: Efficiency, Preventing Theft from Consumers, and Consumer Choice' (2013) 81 *Fordham Law Review* 2349.

Langa, P, 'Transformative Constitutionalism' (2006) 17 *Stellenbosch Law Review* 351.

Larouche, P and De Streel, A, 'The European Digital Markets Act: A Revolution Grounded on Traditions' (2022) 12 *Journal of European Competition Law and Practice* 542.

Latour, B, *We Have Never Been Modern* (Boston, Harvard University Press, 1993).

Lavoie, M, 'The Endogenous Flow of Credit and the Post Keynesian Theory of Money' (1984) 18 *Journal of Economic Issues* 771.

Leigh, A and Triggs, A, 'Markets, Monopolies and Moguls: The Relationship between Inequality and Competition' (2016) 49 *Australian Economic Review* 389.

Leitzel, J, *Concepts in Law and Economics: A Guide for the Curious* (Oxford, Oxford University Press, 2015).

Leontief, W, 'The Pure Theory of the Guaranteed Annual Wage Contract' (1946) 54 *Journal of Political Economy* 76.

Lerner, A, 'Functional Finance and the Federal Debt' (1943) 10 *Social Research* 38.

Lewis, D, *Enforcing Competition Rules in South Africa: Thieves at the Dinner Table* (Cheltenham, Edward Elgar, 2013).

Lianos, I, 'Competition Law in the European Union after the Treaty of Lisbon' in D Ashiagbor, N Countouris and I Lianos (eds), *The European Union after the Treaty of Lisbon* (Cambridge, Cambridge University Press, 2012).

—— 'Toward a Bureaucracy-Centred Theory of the Interaction between Competition Law and State Activities' in TK Cheng, I Lianos and DD Sokol (eds), *Competition and the State* (Stanford, Stanford University Press, 2014).

—— 'The Poverty of Competition Law: The Short Story' in D Gerard and I Lianos (eds), *Reconciling Efficiency and Equity: A Global Challenge for Competition Policy* (Cambridge, Cambridge University Press, 2019).

—— 'Competition Law as a Form of Societal Regulation' (2020) 65 *The Antitrust Bulletin* 3.

Lianos, I et al, 'Is There a Tension Between Development Economics and Competition?' in DD Sokol et al (eds), *Competition Law and Development* (Stanford, Stanford University Press, 2013) 35–51.

Lianos, I, Countouris, N and Stefano, V, 'Re-Thinking the Competition Law/Labour Law Interaction: Promoting a Fairer Labour Market' (2019) 10 *European Labour Law Journal* 291.

Liebowitz, SJ and Margolis, SE, 'Are Network Externalities a New Source of Market Failure?' (1995) 17 *Research in Law and Economics* 1.

Lilburne, J 'Postscript to The Freeman's Freedom Vindicated. 16 June 1646' in A Sharp (ed), *The English Levellers* (Cambridge, Cambridge University Press, 2004) 31–32.

—— 'England's New Chains Discovered. 26 February 1649' in A Sharp (ed), *The English Levellers* (Cambridge, Cambridge University Press, 2004) 140–57.

Lilburne, J et al, 'The Petition of 11 September 1648' in A Sharp (ed), *The English Levellers* (Cambridge, Cambridge University Press, 2004) 131–39.

Lind, R and Muyset, P, 'Innovation and Competition Policy: Challenges for the New Millennium' (2003) 87 *European Competition Law Review* 91.
Lucas, RE Jr, 'Nobel Lecture: Monetary Neutrality' (1996) 104 *Journal of Political Economy* 661.
Luhmann, N, *Die Gesellschaft der Gesellschaft*, vol 2 (Frankfurt am Main, Suhrkamp, 1998).
Lusty, G and King, S, 'Article 101(3)', in D Bailey and LE John (eds), *Bellamy & Child: European Union Law of Competition*, 8th edn (Oxford, Oxford University Press 2018) 205–256.
Luu, LH, 'Vietnam', in K Groshinski and C Davies (eds), *Competition Law in Asia Pacific: A Practical Guide* (Alphen aan den Rijn, Kluwer Law International, 2015) 715–66.
—— 'Vietnam's Competition Law Adoption: From Passive to Active' in S Van Uytsel et al (eds), *Research Handbook on Asian Competition Law* (Cheltenham, Edward Elgar, 2020) 134–50.
Ma, TC, 'Antitrust and Democracy: Perspectives from Efficiency and Equity' (2016) 12 *Journal of Competition Law and Economics* 233.
Macculloch, A, 'The Consumer and Competition Law' in G Howells, I. Ramsay and T Wilhelmsson (eds), *Handbook of Research on International Consumer Law*, 2nd edn (Cheltenham, Edward Elgar, 2018).
Maher, I, 'The Institutional Structure of Competition Law' in MW Dowdle et al (eds), *Asian Capitalism and the Regulation of Competition: Towards a Regulatory Geography of Global Competition Law* (Cambridge, Cambridge University Press, 2013) 55–78.
Maier-Rigaud, F, 'On the Normative Foundations of Competition Law – Efficiency, Political Freedom and the Freedom to Compete' in D Zimmer (ed), *The Goals of Competition Law* (Cheltenham, Edward Elgar, 2012) 132–168.
Makgetla, NS, 'The Structural Dimensions of Inequality in South Africa: The Systemic Underpinnings of Inequality in South Africa' in M Nassen Smith (ed), *Confronting Inequality: The South African Crisis* (Johannesburg, Jacana Media, 2018).
Makris, S, 'Openness and Integrity in Antitrust' (2021) 17 *Journal of Competition Law and Economics* 1.
Mankiw, NG, *Principles of Microeconomics*, 5th edn (Boston, Cengage Learning, 2008).
—— *Macroeconomics*, 9th edn (New York, Worth Publishers, 2016).
Marktanner, M, 'Addressing the Marketing Problem of the Social Market Economy' in C Glossner and D Gregosz (eds), *60 Years of Social Market Economy: Formation, Development and Perspectives of a Peacemaking Formula* (Sankt Augustin, Konrad-Adenauer-Stiftung, 2010).
Marshall, A, *Principles of Economics*, 8th edn (London, Macmillan, 1923).
Marshall, RC and Merlo, A, 'Pattern Bargaining' (2004) 45 *International Economic Review* 239.
Mas-Colell, A, Whinston, MD and Green, JR, *Microeconomic Theory* (Oxford, Oxford University Press, 1995).
Maughan, CW and McGuinness, L, 'Towards an Economic Theory of the Corporation' (2001) 1 *Journal of Corporate Law Studies* 141.
McCartney, G, Popham, F, McMaster, R, Cumbers, A, 'Defining Health and Health Inequalities', (2019) 172 *Public Health* 22.
McDonald, I and Solow, R, 'Wage Bargaining and Employment' (1981) 71 *American Economic Review* 896.
McDonnell, B, 'The Economists' New Arguments' (2003) 88 *Minnesota Law Review* 86.
McDougall, P, 'Capabilities, Utility, or Primary Goods? On Finding a Conceptual Framework for (International) Labour Law' in B Langille (ed), *The Capabilities Approach to Labour Law* (Oxford, Oxford University Press, 2019) 180.
—— 'The Place of Labor Rights in the European Union's Environmental Policies' (2021) 22 *German Law Journal* 1.
—— 'European Cross-Sectoral Collective Bargaining as Post-Crisis Social Policy' (forthcoming 2022) 29 *Indiana Journal of Global Legal Studies.*
—— 'Global Value Chains, Labor Rights, and the Nature of Transnational Law' (forthcoming 2022) *American Journal of Comparative Law.*
Melamed, AD and Petit, N, 'The Misguided Assault on the Consumer Welfare Standard in the Age of Platform Markets' (2019) 54 *Review of Industrial Organisation* 741.

Messenger, JC and Ghosheh, N (eds), *Work Sharing During the Great Recession* (Cheltenham, Edward Elgar, 2013).

Mestmäcker, EJ, 'Competition Policy and Antitrust: Some Comparative Observations' (1980) 136 *Zeitschrift für die Gesamte Staatswissenschaft* 387.

—— 'The Role of Competition in a Liberal Society' in P Koslowski (ed), *The Social Market Economy, Theory and Ethics of the Economic Order* (Heidelberg, Springer, 1998) 329–50.

—— *Wirtschaft und Verfassung in der Europäischen Union* (Baden-Baden, Nomos, 2003).

Miksch, L, *Wettbewerb als Aufgabe: Grundsätze einer Wettbewerbsordnung* (Godersberg, Verlag Helmut Küpper, 1947).

Milanović, B, *Capitalism, Alone: The Future of the System That Rules the World* (Cambridge, MA, Harvard University Press, 2019).

Minsky, H, 'Effects of Shifts of Aggregate Demand upon Income Distribution' (1968) 50 *American Journal of Agricultural Economics* 328.

—— 'The Strategy of Economic Policy and Income Distribution' (1973) 409 *Annals of the American Academy of Political and Social Science* 92.

—— *Stabilizing an Unstable Economy* (New York, McGraw-Hill, 2008).

Mishel, L and Eisenbrey, R, 'How to Raise Wages: Policies That Work and Policies That Don't' (2015) 45 *Stetson Law Review* 43.

Mitchell, S, 'The View from the Shop – Antitrust and the Decline of America's Independent Businesses' (2016) 61 *The Antitrust Bulletin* 498.

Mitchell, DJB and Erickson, C, 'De-Unionization and Macro Performance: What Freeman and Medoff Didn't Do' in JT Bennett and B Kaufman (eds), *What Do Unions Do?: A Twenty-Year Perspective* (London, Routledge, 2007) 369.

Montesquieu, C-L de Secondat, *De l'esprit des lois* (first published 1748, Paris, Garnier-Flammarion, 1979).

Monti, G, 'Article 81 EC and Public Policy' (2002) 39 *Common Market Law Review* 1057.

—— *EC Competition Law* (Cambridge, Cambridge University Press, 2007).

—— 'Collective Labour Agreements and EU Competition Law: Five Reconfigurations' (2021) 17 *European Competition Journal* 1.

Moore, B, 'The Demise of the Keynesian Multiplier: A Reply to Cottrell' (1994) 17 *Journal of Post Keynesian Economics* 121.

More, T, *The Utopia: In Latin From the Edition of March 1518, and In English From The First Edition of Ralph Robynson's Translation in 1551 with Additional Translations, Introduction and Notes by J.H. Lupton* (first published 1516, Oxford, Clarendon Press, 1895).

—— *Utopia: Translated, Edited and Introduced by Dominic Baker-Smith* (first published 1516, London, Penguin Classics, 2012).

Morton, AJB, 'European Health Care Systems and the Emerging Influence of European Union Competition Policy', (2021) 46 *Journal of Health Politics, Policy and Law* 467.

Moseneke, D, 'The Fourth Bram Fischer Memorial Lecture: Transformative Adjudication' (2002) 18 *South African Journal on Human Rights* 309.

Motta, M and de Streel, A, 'Exploitative and Exclusionary Excessive Prices in EU Law' in CD Ehlermann and I Atanasiu (eds), *European Competition Law Annual 2003: What is an Abuse of a Dominant Position?* (Oxford, Hart Publishing, 2006).

Motta, M, *Competition Policy: Theory and Practice* (Cambridge, Cambridge University Press, 2009).

Muller, E, 'Democracy, Economics Development, and Income Inequality' (1988) 53 *American Sociological Review* 50.

Mussa, M 'Adam Smith and the Political Economy of a Modern Financial Crisis' (2009) 44 *Business Economics* 3.

Müller, T, Rasnaca, Z and Vandaele, K, 'Wages and Collective Bargaining: Time to Deliver on the European Pillar of Social Rights' in European Trade Union Institute (ed), *Benchmarking Working Europe 2019* (Brussels: ETUI, 2019) 47.

Müller-Armack, A, *Wirtschaftslenkung und Marktwirtschaft* (Kastell, 1946).

—— 'The Social Market Economy as an Economic and Social Order' (1978) 36 *Review of Social Economy* 325.

Naidu, S, Posner, EA and Weyl, G, 'Antitrust Remedies for Labor Market Power' (2018) 132 *Harvard Law Review* 536.

Neumann, F, *Behemoth: The Structure and Practice of National Socialism* (New York, Oxford University Press, 1942).

Ngcobo, S, 'South Africa's Transformative Constitution: Towards an Appropriate Doctrine of Separation of Powers' (2011) 22 *Stellenbosch Law Review* 37.

Nguyen, TT, 'Competition Law in Vietnam, A Paper or Young Tiger?' (2012) 57 *The Antitrust Bulletin* 409.

Nicholson, MW, 'An Antitrust Law Index for Empirical Analysis of International Competition Policy' (2008) 4 *Journal of Competition Law and Economics* 1009.

Nicholson, W and Snyder, C, *Intermediate Microeconomics and Its Applications*, 11th edn (Mason, OH, South-Western Cengage Learning, 2010).

Nihoul, P, 'Freedom of Choice: The Emergence of a Powerful Concept in European Competition Law' (2012) 3 *Concurrences Review* 55.

Nikolić, B, 'Applicability of European Union Competition Law to Health Care Providers: The Dividing Line between Economic and Noneconomic Activities' (2021) 46 *Journal of Health Politics, Policy and Law* 49.

Novokmet, F, Piketty, T and Zucman, G, 'From Soviets to Oligarchs: Inequality and Property in Russia 1905–2016' (2018) 16 *Journal of Economic Inequality* 189.

Nowag, J, *Environmental Integration in Competition and Free-Movement Laws* (Oxford, Oxford University Press, 2016).

O'Donoghue, R and Padilla, J, *The Law and Economics of Article 102 TFEU*, 3rd edn (Oxford, Hart Publishing, 2020).

Odudu, O, 'The Distributional Consequences of Antitrust' in P Marsden (ed), *Handbook of Research in Trans-Atlantic Antitrust* (Cheltenham, Edward Elgar, 2006) 605.

—— 'Are State-Owned Healthcare Providers Undertakings Subject to Competition Law?' (2011) 32 *European Competition Law Review* 231.

—— 'Health Care Services and EU Competition Law' in D Orentlicher and TK Hervey (eds), *The Oxford Handbook of Comparative Health Law* (Oxford, Oxford University Press, 2021).

Offe, C, 'The European Model of "Social" Capitalism: Can It Survive European Integration?' (2003) 11 *Journal of Political Philosophy* 437.

Ohnesorge, JKM, 'Developing Development Theory: Law and Development Orthodoxies and the Northeast Asian Experience' (2007) 28 *University of Pennsylvania Journal of International Law* 219.

Okun, AM, *Equality and Efficiency: The Big Tradeoff* (Washington, DC, Brookings Institution Press, 1975).

Oliver, H, 'German Neoliberalism' (1960) 74 *The Quarterly Journal of Economics* 117.

O'Loughlin, R, 'EC Competition Rules and Free Movement Rules: An Examination of the Parallels and their Furtherance by the ECJ Wouters Decision' (2003) 24 *European Competition Law Review* 62.

O'Reilly, T, 'Principles of Efficient Tax Law: Apocrypha' (2008) 27 *Virginia Tax Review* 583.

Orhun, AY and Palazzolo, M, 'Frugality Is Hard to Afford' (2019) 56 *Journal of Marketing Research* 1.

Ostry, JD, Loungani, P and Berg, A, *Confronting Inequality: How Societies Can Choose Inclusive Growth* (New York, Columbia University Press, 2019).

Overton, R, 'An Arrow Against all Tyrants. 12 October 1646' in A Sharp (ed), *The English Levellers* (Cambridge, Cambridge University Press, 2004) 54–72.

Overton, R and Walwyn, W, 'A Remonstrance of Many Thousand Citizens. 7 July 1646' in A Sharp (ed), *The English Levellers* (Cambridge, Cambridge University Press, 2004) 33–53.

Oxenham, J, Currie, M-J and Stargard, A, 'Changing South Africa's Competition Law Regime: A Populist Departure from International Best Practices' (2019) 10 *Journal of European Competition Law and Practice* 232.

Pace, LF and Seidel, K, 'The Drafting and the Role of Regulation 17: A Hard-Fought Compromise' in KK Patel and H Schweitzer (eds), *The Historical Foundations of EU Competition Law* (Oxford, Oxford University Press, 2013) 54–88.

Padilla, AJ and Ahlborn, C, 'From Fairness to Welfare: Implications for the Assessment of Unilateral Conduct under EC Competition Law' in C-D Ehlermann and M Marquis (eds), *European Competition Law Annual 2007: A Reformed Approach to Article 82 EC* (Oxford, Hart Publishing, 2008) 55–101.

Page, HW and Lopatka, JE, 'Network Externalities' in G De Geest and B Bouckaert (eds), *Encyclopaedia of Law and Economics* (Cheltenham, Edward Elgar, 2000) 952–80.

Park, JW, 'The Utopian Economics of Sir Thomas More' (1971) 30 *The American Journal of Economics and Sociology* 275.

Parret, L, 'The Multiple Personalities of EU Competition Law: Time for a Comprehensive Debate on Its Objectives' in D Zimmer (ed), *The Goals of Competition Law* (Cheltenham, Edward Elgar, 2012).

Paul, S, 'The Enduring Ambiguities of Antitrust Liability for Worker Collective Action' (2016) 47 *Loyola University Chicago Law Journal* 101.

—— 'Antitrust as Allocator of Coordination Rights' (2020) 67 *UCLA Law Review* 378.

Peltzman, S, 'Industrial Concentration under the Rule of Reason' (2014) 57 *The Journal of Law and Economics* 101.

Peritz, RJ, 'A Counter-History of Antitrust Law' (1990) 39 *Duke Law Journal* 263.

Peterson, N, 'Antitrust Law and the Promotion of Democracy and Economic Growth' (2013) 9 *Journal of Competition Law and Economics* 593.

Petit, N, *Big Tech and the Digital Economy: The Moligopoly Scenario* (Oxford, Oxford University Press, 2020).

Pettit, P, 'Freedom as Antipower' (1996) 106 *Ethics* 576.

—— *Republicanism: A Theory of Freedom and Government* (Oxford, Oxford University Press, 1997).

—— *On The People's Terms: A Republican Theory and Model of Democracy* (Cambridge, Cambridge University Press, 2012).

Pham, A, 'The Development of Competition Law in Vietnam in the Face of Economic Reforms and Global Integration' (2006) 26 *Northwestern Journal of International Law and Business* 547.

Philippon, T, *The Great Reversal: How America Gave up on Free Markets* (Cambridge, MA, Harvard University Press, 2019).

Pickett, K and Wilkinson, R, *The Spirit Level: Why Equality is Better for Everyone* (London, Penguin, 2009).

Piketty, T, *Capital in the Twenty-First Century* (Cambridge, MA, Harvard University Press, 2014).

—— 'About Capital in the Twenty-First Century' (2015) 105 *American Economic Review* 48.

—— *Capital and Ideology* (Boston, Harvard University Press, 2020).

Piketty, T, Yang, L and Zucman, G, 'Capital Accumulation, Private Property, and Rising Inequality in China, 1978–2015' (2019) 109 *American Economic Review* 2469.

Pistor, K, 'A Legal Theory of Finance' (2013) 41 *Journal of Comparative Economics* 315.

—— 'From Territorial to Monetary Sovereignty' (2017) 18 *Theoretical Inquiries Law* 491.

—— *The Code of Capital: How the Law Created Wealth and Inequality* (Princeton, Princeton University Press, 2019).

Pitofsky, R, 'The Political Content of Antitrust' (1979) 127 *University of Pennsylvania Law Review* 1051.

Polanyi, M, *The Logic of Liberty* (London, Routledge, 1951).

Polus, A, Kopiński, D and Tycholiz, W, 'Reproduction and Convertibility: Examining Wealth Inequalities in South Africa' (2020) 42 *Third World Quarterly* 292.

Posner, RA, 'The Chicago School of Antitrust Analysis' (1979) 127 *University of Pennsylvania Law Review* 925.

—— *Antitrust Law*, 2nd edn (Chicago, University of Chicago Press, 2001).

—— *Economic Analysis of Law*, 8th edn (New York, Wolters Kluwer, 2011).

Prassl, J, *Humans as a Service: The Promise and Perils of Work in the Gig Economy* (Oxford, Oxford University Press, 2018).

Prosser, T, *The Limits of Competition Law: Markets and Public Services* (Oxford, Oxford University Press, 2005).
—— 'EU Competition Law and Public Services' in E Mossialos et al (eds), *Health Systems Governance in Europe: The Role of European Union Law and Policy* (Cambridge, Cambridge University Press, 2010).
Rajan, R and Zingales, L, 'Financial Dependence and Growth' (1998) 88 *American Economic Review* 559.
Rawls, J, *A Theory of Justice* (Cambridge, MA, Harvard University Press, 1971).
—— *A Theory of Justice* (Oxford, Oxford University Press, 1999).
—— *Justice as Fairness: A Restatement* (Cambridge, MA, Harvard University Press, 2001).
Rees, A, 'The Effects of Unions on Resource Allocation' (1963) 6 *Journal of Law and Economics* 69.
Rehfeldt, U and Vincent, C, 'The Decentralisation of Collective Bargaining in France: An Escalating Process' in S Leonardi and R Pedersini (eds), *Multi-employer Bargaining Under Pressure: Decentralisation Trends in Five European Countries* (Brussels, ETUI, 2018) 151.
Richman, BD, 'Contracts and Cartels, Reconciling Competition and Development Policy' in DD Sokol et al (eds), *Competition Law and Development* (Stanford, Stanford University Press, 2013) 155–66.
Rieter, H and Schmolz, M, 'The Ideas of German Ordoliberalism 1938–1945: Pointing the Way to a New Economic Order' (1993) 1 *European Journal of the History of Economic Thought* 87.
Riley, A, 'The EU Reform Treaty and the Competition Protocol: Undermining EC Competition Law' (2007) 28 *European Competition Law Review* 703.
Ritzer, G, *Classical Sociological Theory*, 8th edn (New York, McGraw-Hill, 2000).
Robbins, L, *An Essay on the Nature and Significance of Economic Science*, 2nd edn (London, Macmillan, 1935).
Robin-Olivier, S, 'Les normes sociales internationales et européennes et le développement du droit par les juges en Europe' (2016) 3 *Droit Social* 219.
Roe, M, 'Rents and Their Corporate Consequences' (2001) 53 *Stanford Law Review* 1463.
Rogers, B, 'Employment Rights in the Platform Economy: Getting Back to Basics' (2016) 10 *Harvard Law and Policy Review* 479.
Romer, D, *Advanced Macroeconomics* (New York, McGraw-Hill, 2006).
Roosevelt, T, 'The Trusts, the People, and the Square Deal' in DA Crane and H Hovenkamp (eds), *The Making of Competition Policy: Legal and Economic Sources* (New York, Oxford University Press, 2013) 107–17.
Rosanvallon, P, *Le libéralisme économique: Histoire de l'Idée de marché* (Paris, Seuil, 1989).
Roser, M and Cuaresma, JC, 'Why Is Income Inequality Increasing in the Developed World?' (2016) 62 *Review of Income and Wealth* 1.
Rothschild, E, 'Adam Smith and Conservative Economics' (1992) 45 *The Economic History Review* 74.
Rousseau, J-J, *Du contrat social* (first published 1767, Paris, Flammarion, 2001).
Rousseva, E, *Rethinking Exclusionary Abuses in EU Competition Law* (Oxford, Hart Publishing, 2010).
Rowe, F, The Decline of Antitrust and the Delusion of Models: The Faustian Pact of Law and Economics' (1984) 72 *Georgetown Law Journal* 1511.
Rubinfeld, D, 'Antitrust Enforcement in Dynamic Network Industries' (1998) 43 *The Antitrust Bulletin* 859.
Saez, E and Zucman, G, 'The Rise of Income and Wealth Inequality in America: Evidence from Distributional Macroeconomic Accounts' (2020) *34 Journal of Economic Perspectives* 3.
Samkalden, I and Druker, I, 'Legal Problems Relating to Article 86 of the Rome Treaty' (1966) 3 *Common Market Law Review* 158.
Samuelson, W and Zeckhouser, R, 'Status Quo Bias and Decision Making' (1988) 1 *Journal of Risk and Uncertainty* 7.
Sandel, MJ, *The Tyranny of Merit: What's Become of the Common Good?* (London, Penguin Books, 2020).
Sauter, W, 'Is the General Consumer Interest a Source of Legitimacy for Healthcare Regulation? An Analysis of the Dutch Experience' (2009) 2-3 *European Journal of Consumer Law* 419.

—— 'The Impact of EU Competition Law on National Healthcare Systems,' (2013) 38 *European Law Review* 457.

Sauter, W, *Public Services in EU Law* (Cambridge, Cambridge University Press, 2015).

Scanlon, TM, *Why Does Inequality Matter?* (Oxford, Oxford University Press, 2018).

Schäfer, HB and Ott, C, *The Economic Analysis of Civil Law* (Cheltenham, Edward Elgar, 2004).

Scherer, FM, *Industrial Market Structure and Economic Performance,* 2nd edn (Boston, Houghton Mifflin, 1980).

—— 'Antitrust, Efficiency, and Progress' (1987) 62 *New York University Law Review* 998.

Schiek, D and Gideon, A, 'Outsmarting the Gig-Economy Through Collective Bargaining – EU Competition Law as a Barrier to Smart Cities?' (2018) 32 *International Review Law, Computers and Technology* 275.

Schwartz, LB, 'Institutional Size and Individual Liberty: Authoritarian Aspects of Bigness' (1960) 55 *Northwestern University Law Review* 4.

—— 'Justice and Other Non-Economic Goals of Antitrust' (1979) 127 *University of Pennsylvania Law Review* 1076.

—— 'On the Uses of Economics: A Review of the Antitrust Treatises' (1979) 128 *University of Pennsylvania Law Review* 244.

Schweitzer, H, 'The History, Interpretation and Underlying Principles of Section 2 Sherman Act and Article 82 EC' in CD Ehlermann and M Marquis (eds), *European Competition Law Annual 2007: A Reformed Approach to Article 82 EC* (Oxford, Hart Publishing, 2008).

—— 'The Art to Make Gatekeeper Positions Contestable and the Challenge to Know What is Fair: A Discussion of the Digital Markets Act Proposal' (2021) *Zeitschrift für Europäisches Privatrecht* 1.

Schweitzer, M, 'Disentangling Status Quo and Omission Effects: An Experimental Analysis' (1994) 58 *Organizational Behaviour and Human Decision Processes* 457.

Schumpeter, J, *Capitalism, Socialism and Democracy* (first published 1943, Routledge, Taylor & Francis e-Library, 2003).

Scrase, TJ, 'Precarious Production: Globalisation and Artisan Labour in the Third World' (2003) 24 *Third World Quarterly* 449.

Seekings, J and Nattrass, N, *Class, Race, and Inequality in South Africa* (New Haven, Yale University Press, 2005).

Sen, A, *On Ethics and Economics* (Oxford, B. Blackwell, 1987).

—— *The Idea of Justice* (Cambridge, MA, Harvard University Press, 2008).

Sierra, JLB, *Exclusive Rights and State Monopolies under EC Law: Article 86 (former Article 90) of the EC Treaty* (A Read tr, Oxford, Oxford University Press, 1999).

Sinclair, D, "Undertakings' in Competition Law at the Public-Private Interface – An Unhealthy Situation' (2014) 35 *European Competition Law Review* 167.

Shapiro, C, 'Exclusivity in Network Industries' (1999) 8 *George Mason Law Review* 1.

—— 'Antitrust in a Time of Populism' (2018) 61 *International Journal of Industrial Organization* 714.

Shapiro, C and McClennen, EF, 'Law and Economics from a Philosophical Perspective' in P Newman (ed), *The New Palgrave Dictionary on Economics and the Law,* vol 2 (London, MacMillan, 1998) 460–65.

Shavell, S, 'A Note on Efficiency vs Distributional Equity in Legal Rulemaking: Should Distributional Equity Matter Given Optimal Income Taxation?' (1981) 71 *American Economic Review Papers and Proceedings* 414.

Skinner, Q, *Liberty before Liberalism* (Cambridge, Cambridge University Press, 1998).

—— 'A Third Concept of Liberty: Isaiah Berlin Lecture' in The British Academy (ed), *Proceedings of the British Academy: 2001 Lectures*, vol 117 (Oxford, Oxford University Press, 2002) 237–68.

Skuterud, M, 'Identifying the Potential of Work-Sharing as a Job-Creation Strategy' (2007) 25 *Journal of Labor Economics* 265.

Smith, A, *An Inquiry Into the Nature and Causes of the Wealth of Nations,* vol 1 (first published 1776, WB Todd ed, Oxford, Oxford University Press, 1976).

Smith, A, *The Theory of Moral Sentiments* (first published 1759, New York, Penguin, 2009).

Smith, TW, 'Aristotle on the Conditions for and Limits of the Common Good' (1999) 93 *The American Political Science Review* 625.
Sokol, DD, 'Tensions between Antitrust and Industrial Policy' (2015) 22 *George Mason Law Review* 1247.
—— 'Antitrust, Industrial Policy, and Economic Populism' in D Gerard and I Lianos (eds), *Reconciling Efficiency and Equity: A Global Challenge for Competition Policy* (Cambridge, Cambridge University Press, 2019) 281–90.
Sokol, DD et al, 'Introduction' in DD Sokol et al (eds), *Competition Law and Development* (Stanford, Stanford University Press, 2013) 1–11.
Sokol, DD, Cheng, TK and Lianos, I (eds), *Competition Law and Development* (Stanford, Stanford University Press, 2013).
Sokol, DD and Stephan, A, 'Prioritizing Cartel Enforcement in Developing World Competition Agencies' in DD Sokol et al (eds), *Competition Law and Development* (Stanford, Stanford University Press, 2013) 137–154.
Solt, F, 'Standardizing the World Income Inequality Database' (2009) 90 *Social Science Quarterly* 231.
Song, J et al, 'Firming Up Inequality' (2019) 134 *The Quarterly Journal of Economics* 1.
Standing, G, *The Corruption of Capitalism: Why Rentiers Thrive and Work Does Not Pay* (London, Biteback, 2016).
Starr, E, Prescott, JJ and Bishara, N, 'Noncompetes in the US Labor Force' (2021) 64 *Journal of Law and Economics* 53.
Stavroulaki, T, 'Connecting the Dots: Quality, Antitrust and Medicine' (2019) 31 *Loyola Consumer Law Review* 175.
—— 'Mergers that Harm Our Health' (forthcoming 2022) *Berkeley Business Law Journal.*
Steuart, J, *An Inquiry into the Principles of Political Oeconomy: Being An Essay on the Science of Domestic Policy in Free Nations* (London, A. Millar and T. Cadell, 1768).
Stiglitz, JE, 'Equilibrium Wage Distribution' (1985) 95 *Economic Journal* 595.
—— 'The Role of the State in Financial Markets' (1993) 7 *World Bank Economic Review* 19.
—— 'Lessons from the Global Financial Crisis of 2008' (2010) 23 *Seoul Journal of Economics* 321.
—— *The Price of Inequality: How Today's Divided Society Endangers Our Future* (New York, WW Norton, 2012).
—— *The Price of Inequality: How Today's Divided Society Endangers our Future* (New York, W. W. Norton & Company, 2013).
—— 'Towards a Broader View of Competition Policy' in T Bonakele, E Fox and L Mncube (eds), *Competition Policy for the New Era: Insights from the BRIC Countries* (Oxford, Oxford University Press, 2017) 4–21.
—— *People, Power, and Profits: Progressive Capitalism for an Age of Discontent* (London, Allen Lane, 2019).
Stole, LA, 'Price Discrimination and Competition' in M Armstrong and RH Porter (eds), *Handbook of Industrial Organization* (London, Elsevier, 2007) 2223.
Streeck, W, 'Neither European nor Works Councils: A Reply to Paul Knutsen' (1997) 18 *Economic and Industrial Democracy* 325.
Stucke, ME, 'Reconsidering Antitrust's Goals' (2012) 53 *Boston College Law Review* 551.
Sullivan, LA, 'Antitrust, Microeconomics, and Politics: Reflections on Some Recent Relationships' (1980) 68 *California Law Review* 1.
Talbot, C, 'Ordoliberalism and Balancing Competition Goals in the Development of the European Union' (2016) 61 *The Antitrust Bulletin* 264.
Tankus, N and Herrine, L, 'Competition Law as Collective Bargaining Law' in S Paul, S McCrystal and E McGaughey (eds), *Labour in Competition Law* (Cambridge, Cambridge University Press, forthcoming 2022).
Taylor, L and Ömer, O, *Macroeconomic Inequality from Reagan to Trump: Market Power, Wage Repression, Asset Price Inflation, and Industrial Decline* (Cambridge, Cambridge University Press, 2020).

Tcherneva, PR, *The Case for a Job Guarantee* (Cambridge, Polity Press, 2020).
Teachout, Z and Khan, LM, 'Market Structure and Political Law: A Taxonomy of Power' (2016) 9 *Duke Journal of Constitutional Law and Public Policy* 37.
Teece, D and Coleman, M, 'The Meaning of Monopoly: Antitrust Analysis in High-Technology Industries' (1998) 43 *The Antitrust Bulletin* 801.
Temple, LJ, *European Community Antitrust Law: Innovation Markets and High Technology Industries* (New York, Fordham, 1996).
Tenfelde, K, 'Conflict and Organization in the Early History of the German Trade Union Movement' in WJ Mommsen and H-G Husung (eds), *The Development of Trade Unionism in Great Britain and Germany, 1880–1914* (London, Routledge, 1985) 201.
Thorelli, HB, *The Federal Antitrust Policy: Origination Of An American Tradition* (Baltimore, The John Hopkins Press, 1955).
Timmins, N, *The Five Giants: A Biography of the Welfare State*, 3rd edn (London, William Collins, 2017).
Tinbergen, J, *On the Theory of Economic Policy* (Amsterdam, North-Holland, 1952).
Townley, C, 'The Concept of "Undertaking": The Boundaries of the Corporation – A Discussion of Agency, Employees and Subsidiaries' in G Amato and C-D Ehlermann (eds), *EC Competition Law: A Critical Assessment* (Oxford, Hart Publishing, 2007) 3.
—— *Article 81 EC and Public Policy* (Oxford, Hart Publishing, 2009).
Trescher, A-L, Listl, S, van der Gallien, O, ADVOCATE Consortium, Gabel, F and Kalmus, O, 'Once Bitten, Twice Shy? Lessons Learned from an Experiment to Liberalize Price Regulations for Dental Care' (2020) 21 *European Journal of Health Economics* 425.
Tritter, J, Koivusalo, M, Ollila, E and Dorfman, P, *Globalisation, Markets and Health Policy: Redrawing the Patient as Consumer* (Abingdon, Routledge, 2010).
Tversky, A and Kahneman, D, 'Prospect Theory: An Analysis of Decision under Risk' (1979) 47 *Econometrica* 263.
Urzúa, CM, 'Distributive and Regional Effects of Monopoly Power' (2013) 22 *Economía Mexicana Nueva Época* 279.
Valletti, TM and Zenger, H, 'Increasing Market Power and Merger Control' (2019) 5 *Competition Law and Policy* Debate 26.
Van Arnum, BM and Naples, MI, 'Financialization and Income Inequality in the United States, 1967–2010' (2013) 72 *American Journal of Economics and Sociology* 1158.
Van Hook, J, *Rebuilding Germany: The Creation of the Social Market Economy, 1945–1957* (Cambridge, Cambridge University Press, 2004).
Varian, H, 'Price Discrimination' in R Schmalensee and R Willig (eds), *Handbook of Industrial Organization* (Amsterdam, North Holland, 1989) 587.
—— *Intermediate Microeconomics: A Modern Approach*, 7th edn (New York, WW Norton and Company, 2006).
Vatiero, M, 'The Ordoliberal Notion of Market Power: An Institutionalist Reassessment' (2010) 6 *European Competition Journal* 689.
—— 'Dominant Market Position and Ordoliberalism' (2015) 62 *International Review of Economics* 291.
Veldman, A and De Vries, S, 'Regulation and Enforcement of Economic Freedoms and Social Rights: A Thorny Distribution of Sovereignty' in T van den Brink et al (eds), *Sovereignty in the Shared Legal Order of the EU* (Cambridge, Intersentia, 2015).
Veljanovski, C, 'EC Antitrust in the New Economy: Is the European Commission's View of the Network Economy Right?' (2001) 22 *European Competition Law Review* 115.
Vielle, P, 'How the Horizontal Social Clause can be Made to Work: The Lessons of Gender Mainstreaming' in N Bruun, K Lörcher and I Schömann (eds), *The Lisbon Treaty and Social Europe* (Oxford, Hart Publishing, 2012).
Vijver, T van der, 'Article 102 TFEU: How to Claim the Application of Objective Justifications in the Case of *prima facie* Dominance Abuses?' (2013) 4 *Journal of European Competition Law and Practice* 121.

Viscusi, KW, Harrington, JE and Vernon, JM, *Economics of Regulation and Antitrust*, 4th edn (Cambridge, The MIT Press, 2005).
Vita, MG and Wellford, CP 'Regulating the Electromagnetic Environment: Alternative Approaches to Policy' in JR Fleming and HA Gemery (eds), *Science, Technology, and the Environment: Multidisciplinary Perspectives* (New York, University of Akron Press, 1994) 238–54.
Voigt, S, 'The Effects of Competition Policy on Development – Cross-Country Evidence Using Four New Indicators' (2009) 45 *Journal of Development Studies* 1225.
Waddington, J, *European Works Councils and Industrial Relations: A Transnational Industrial Relations Institution in the Making* (London, Routledge, 2011).
Waked, DI, 'Antitrust Goals in Developing Countries: Policy Alternatives and Normative Choices' (2015) 38 *Seattle University Law Review* 945.
—— 'Antitrust as Public Interest Law: Redistribution, Equity, and Social Justice' (2020) 65 *The Antitrust Bulletin* 87.
Walwyn, W, 'Gold Tried in the Fire. 4 June 1647' in A Sharp (ed), *The English Levellers* (Cambridge, Cambridge University Press, 2004) 73–91.
Wang, TT, Rathur, MR and Schmidt, H, 'Universal health coverage, oral health, and personal responsibility' (2020) 98 *WHO Bulletin* 719.
Weatherill, S, *EU Consumer Law and Policy*, 2nd edn (Cheltenham, Edward Elgar, 2013).
—— *The Internal Market as a Legal Concept* (Oxford, Oxford University Press, 2017).
Weche, JP and Wambach, A, 'The Fall and Rise of Market Power in Europe' (2021) 241 *Jahrbücher für Nationalökonomie und Statistik* 555.
Weintraub, ER, 'The Microfoundations of Macroeconomics: A Critical Survey' (1977) 15 *Journal of Economic Literature* 1.
Weiss, M, 'Re-Inventing Labour Law?' in B Langille and G Davidov (eds), *The Idea of Labour Law* (Cambridge, Cambridge University Press, 2011) 43.
Werden, GJ, 'Concentration and Rising Market Power: Fears and Facts', in P Akman, O Brook and K Stylianou (eds), *Research Handbook on Abuse of Dominance and Monopolization* (Cheltenham, Edward Elgar, forthcoming 2022).
Werden, GJ and Froeb, LM, 'Don't Panic: A Guide to Claims of Increasing Concentration' (2018) 33 *Antitrust* 74.
Wessel, D, 'Is Lack of Competition Strangling the U.S. Economy?' (2018) *Harvard Business Review* 106.
Whish, R and Bailey, D, *Competition Law*, 8th edn (Oxford, Oxford University Press, 2015).
—— *Competition Law*, 9th edn (Oxford, Oxford University Press, 2018).
—— *Competition Law*, 10th edn (Oxford, Oxford University Press, 2021).
White, AA, 'Workers Disarmed: The Campaign Against Mass Picketing and the Dilemma of Liberal Labor Rights' (2014) 49 *Harvard Civil Rights – Civil Liberties Law Review* 59.
White, L, *The Clash of Economic Ideas* (Cambridge, Cambridge University Press, 2012).
Whittaker, W and Birch, S, 'Provider Incentives and Access to Dental Care: Evaluating NHS Reforms in England' (2012) 75 *Social Science and Medicine* 2515.
Wiggers, M and Oostwouder, W, *Handboek compliance in de zorg* (Zutphen, Uitgeverij Paris, 2017).
Williams, M, *Competition Policy and Law in China, Hong Kong and Taiwan* (Cambridge, Cambridge University Press, 2005).
Williamson, O, 'Economies as an Antitrust Defense: The Welfare Trade-Offs' (1968) 58 *American Economic Review* 18.
Wils, W, 'The Judgment of the EU General Court in *Intel* and the So-Called "More Economic Approach" to Abuse of Dominance' (2014) 37 *World Competition* 405.
Wilson, W, *The New Freedom* (Leipzig, Tauchnitz, 1913).
—— 'The Tariff and the Trusts' in DA Crane and H Hovenkamp (eds), *The Making of Competition Policy: Legal and Economic Sources* (New York, Oxford University Press, 2013) 119–24.
Witt, A, *The More Economic Approach to EU Antitrust Law* (Oxford, Hart Publishing, 2016).
Wittman, D, *Economic Foundations of Law and Organization* (Cambridge, Cambridge University Press, 2006).

Wolf, M, *Why Globalization Works* (New Haven, Yale University Press, 2004).
Woodcock, R, 'Big Data, Price Discrimination, and Antitrust' (2017) 68 *Hastings Law Journal* 1371.
—— 'The Antitrust Case for Consumer Primacy in Corporate Governance' (2020) 10 *UC Irvine Law Review* 1395.
Wray, LR, 'When Are Interest Rates Exogenous?' in M Setterfield (ed), *Complexity, Endogenous Money and Macroeconomic Theory: Essays in Honour of Basil J. Moore* (Cheltenham, Edward Elgar, 2006) 271.
—— 'The Job Guarantee, Full Employment and Human Rights' in U Mattei and J Haskell (eds), *Research Handbook on Political Economy and Law* (Cheltenham, Edward Elgar, 2015) 205.
—— *Modern Money Theory: A Primer on Macroeconomics for Sovereign Monetary Systems*, 2nd edn (London, Palgrave Macmillan, 2015).
Wright, JD et al, 'Requiem for a Paradox: The Dubious Rise and Inevitable Fall of Hipster Antitrust' (2018) 51 *Arizona State Law Journal* 293.
Wu, T, *The Curse of Bigness: Antitrust in the New Gilded Age* (New York, Columbia Global Reports, 2018).
Zingales, L, 'Towards a Political Theory of the Firm' (2017) 31 *Journal of Economic Perspectives* 113.
Zuboff, S, *The Age of Surveillance Capitalism: The Fight for a Human Future at the New Frontier of Power* (London, Profile Books, 2019).
Zucman, G, 'Global Wealth Inequality' (2019) 11 *Annual Review of Economics* 109.
Zweig, K, *The Origins of the German Social Market Economy: The Leading Ideas and their Intellectual Roots* (London, Adam Smith Institute, 1980).

INDEX

www.ingramcontent.com/pod-product-compliance
Ingram Content Group UK Ltd.
Pitfield, Milton Keynes, MK11 3LW, UK
UKHW020906190926
475560UK00010B/297

9 781509 959235